P9-APE-179

Sixth Edition

EDUCATIONAL ADMINISTRATION

Theory, Research, and Practice

Wayne K. Hoy
The Ohio State University

Cecil G. Miskel
The University of Michigan

Boston Burr Ridge, IL Dubuque, IA Madison, WI New York San Francisco St. Louis
Bangkok Bogotá Caracas Lisbon London Madrid
Mexico City Milan New Delhi Seoul Singapore Sydney Taipei Toronto

0018062

McGraw-Hill Higher Education
A Division of The ***McGraw-Hill*** *Companies*

EDUCATIONAL ADMINISTRATION: THEORY, RESEARCH, AND PRACTICE
SIXTH EDITION

Published by McGraw-Hill, an imprint of The McGraw-Hill Companies, Inc., 1221 Avenue of the Americas, New York, NY 10020. Copyright © 2001, 1996, 1991, 1987, 1982, 1978 by The McGraw-Hill Companies, Inc. All rights reserved. No part of this publication may be reproduced or distributed in any form or by any means, or stored in a database or retrieval system, without the prior written consent of The McGraw-Hill Companies, Inc., including, but not limited to, in any network or other electronic storage or transmission, or broadcast for distance learning.

Some ancillaries, including electronic and print components, may not be available to customers outside the United States.

This book is printed on acid-free paper.

1 2 3 4 5 6 7 8 9 0 QPF/QPF 0 9 8 7 6 5 4 3 2 1 0

ISBN 0–07–232289–6

Vice president and editor-in-chief: *Thalia Dorwick*
Editorial director: *Jane E. Vaicunas*
Sponsoring editor: *Beth Kaufman*
Developmental editor: *Teresa Wise*
Marketing manager: *Daniel M. Loch*
Project manager: *Christine Walker*
Senior media developer: *James Fehr*
Production supervisor: *Laura Fuller*
Coordinator of freelance design: *Michelle D. Whitaker*
Freelance cover designer: *Diane Beasley*
Cover image: *©Bob Krist, Tony Stone Images*
Compositor: *Carlisle Communication, Ltd.*
Typeface: *10/12 Palatino*
Printer: *Quebecor Printing Book Group/Fairfield, PA*

Library of Congress Cataloging-in-Publication Data

Hoy, Wayne K.
Educational administration : theory, research, and practice / Wayne K. Hoy, Cecil G. Miskel — 6th ed.
p. cm.
Includes bibliographical references and index.
ISBN 0–07–232289–6
1. School management and organization—United States. I. Miskel, Cecil G. II. Title.

LB2805 .H715 2001
371.2'00973—dc21 00–032903
CIP

www.mhhe.com

In Memory of

Donald J. Willower
Scholar, Colleague, and Friend

Wayne Calvin Hoy
Scholar, Administrator, and Father

Their Legacies Live On

Dedicated to

Anita
Simply the Best

—Wayne

Dedicated to Sue—
My True Love and Best Friend

And to Mac
My Writing Supervisor from Atop the Monitor

—Cecil

About the Authors

Wayne K. Hoy received his B.S. from Lock Haven State College in 1959 and his D.Ed. from The Pennsylvania State University in 1965. After teaching at Oklahoma State University for several years, he moved to Rutgers University in 1968, where he was a distinguished professor, department chair, and Associate Dean for Academic Affairs. In 1994, he was selected as the Novice G. Fawcett Chair in Educational Administration at The Ohio State University. His primary professional interests are theory and research in administration, the sociology of organizations, and the social psychology of administration.

In 1973, he received the Lindback Foundation Award for Distinguished Teaching from Rutgers University; in 1987, he was given the Alumni Award for Professional Research from the Rutgers University Graduate School of Education; in 1991, he received the Excellence in Education Award from The Pennsylvania State University; in 1992, he was given the Meritorious Research Award from the Eastern Educational Research Association; and in 1996, he was made an Alumni Fellow of The Pennsylvania State University. He is past secretary-treasurer of the National Conference of Professors of Educational Administration (NCPEA) and is past president of the University Council for Educational Administration (UCEA).

Professor Hoy is coauthor with D. J. Willower and T. L. Eidell of *The School and Pupil Control Ideology* (1967); with Patrick Forsyth, *Effective Supervision: Theory into Practice* (1986); with C. J. Tarter and R. Kottkamp, *Open Schools-Healthy Schools: Measuring Organizational Climate* (1991); with C. J. Tarter, *Administrators Solving the Problems of Practice* (1995) and *The Road to Open and Healthy Schools* (1997); and with D. Sabo, *Quality Middle Schools* (1998). He is also on the editorial boards of the *Educational Administration Quarterly, Journal of Educational Administration, McGill Journal of Education, Journal of School Leadership,* and the *Journal of Research and Development in Education.*

Cecil G. Miskel is a professor of educational administration and policy at the University of Michigan. From 1988 to 1998, he was the dean of the School of Education at Michigan. He also served the University of Utah as a professor and chairperson of the Department of Educational Administration from 1982 to 1983 and professor and dean of the Graduate School of Education from 1983 to 1988. He also spent 12 years at the University of Kansas, where he held positions as assistant, associate, and full professor of educational administration as well as associate dean for research administration and associate vice chancellor for research, graduate studies, and public service. His public school experience includes being a science teacher and principal in the secondary schools of Oklahoma.

Professor Miskel holds an undergraduate degree in science education from the University of Oklahoma, and M.S and Ed.D. degrees from Oklahoma State University. He teaches graduate classes and guides scholarly inquiry in school organization, administration, and policy. His current research program deals with reading policy. He served as editor of the *Educational Administration Quarterly* for the 1987 and 1988 volumes and has been a member of its editorial board for nine years.

Professor Miskel received the William Davis Award for the most outstanding article published in Volumes 16 and 19 of the *Educational Administration Quarterly.* In addition to being a coauthor of the six editions of *Education Administration: Theory, Research, and Practice,* Professor Miskel has published widely in a variety of scholarly journals.

PREFACE

We continue the sixth edition in the tradition of the first five—with the strongly held belief that a substantive body of knowledge about educational organizations is available but is often neglected by both professors and practitioners in educational administration. We believe that administrative practice can become more systematic, reflective, and effective when guided by sound theory and relevant research. An open-social systems model of schools provides the overarching theoretical framework that organizes and relates this theory and research for educational administrators.

Our approach is a pragmatic one, selecting the theories and research that are most useful in solving the problems of practice and discarding those that are not. At the heart of our social-systems model are four critical elements of organizational life—structure, individuals, culture, and politics. These elements interact in the context of teaching and learning; indeed, we have extended our open social-systems model of the school by using the teaching-learning process to situate school behavior. To that end, a new chapter on teaching and learning has been added to the text (Chapter 2, "The Technical Core: Learning and Teaching"). The environment provides a set of opportunities and constraints for the schools; the outcomes of the school are examined in terms of effectiveness and quality. Four key administrative processes—deciding, motivating, communicating, and leading—remain central to effective administration. We incorporate new theories and contemporary research into our analyses of the critical elements and processes of teaching, learning, and administering. Because the basic aim of educational administrators is to solve real problems, we provide an authentic case at the conclusion of each chapter to challenge students to apply relevant theories and research to solve contemporary problems of practice in schools.

Our colleagues and students continue to be important sources of ideas and criticism. We would like to thank Janet Alleman, Michigan State University; Terry Astuto, New York University; James Bliss, Rutgers University; Mike Boone, Southwest Texas State Univesity; Lyn Bradshaw, East Carolina University; Denise Brennan, University of the Pacific; Michael DiPaola, William and Mary University; Angela Eilers, University of Illinois, Urbana–Champaign; Patrick Forsyth, Oklahoma State University; Jeffrey Geist, Ohio State University; Roger Goddard, University of Michigan; Pamela Harquait, Tennessee State University; Rita King, California Polytechnic State University; MaryAlice Obermiller, University of Houston; Edward A. Poole, Aurora University; Brian Rowan, University of Michigan; Gail Schneider, University of Wisconsin–Milwaukee; James Sinden, Ohio State University; Page Smith, Ohio State University; Christoperh Sumami, Ohio State University; Scott Sweetland, Ohio State University; C. J. Tarter, St. Johns University; Megan Tschannen-Moran, Ohio State University; Cynthia Uline, Ohio State University; Brad Woods, Ohio State University; and Anita Woolfolk Hoy, Ohio State University.

Finally, we owe a special thanks to all our students who have helped enrich the explanations and ground the theories with their experiences.

Wayne K. Hoy
Cecil G. Miskel

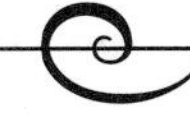

CONTENTS IN BRIEF

0018062

CONTENTS

CHAPTER 8 *Effectiveness and Quality of Schools* 287

CHAPTER 9 *Decision Making in Schools* 316

CHAPTER 1

THE SCHOOL AS A SOCIAL SYSTEM

Although we set out primarily to study reality, it does not follow that we do not wish to improve it; we should judge our researches to have no worth at all if they were to have only a speculative interest. If we separate carefully the theoretical from the practical problems, it is not to the neglect of the latter; but, on the contrary, to be in a better position to solve them.

Emile Durkheim
The Division of Labor in Society

PREVIEW

1. Organizational theory is a set of interrelated concepts, definitions, and generalizations that systematically describes and explains patterns of regularities in organizational life.
2. The functions of theory are to explain, to guide research, to generate new knowledge, and to guide practice.
3. Theory informs practice in three important ways: it forms a frame of reference; it provides a general model for analysis; and it guides reflective decision making.
4. The evolution of organizational thought and theory can be viewed using three competing systems perspectives: rational, natural, and open.
5. A rational-systems perspective views organizations as formal instruments designed to achieve organizational goals; structure is the most important feature.
6. A natural-systems perspective views organizations as typical socials groups intent on surviving: people are the most important aspect.
7. An open-systems perspective has the potential to combine rational and natural elements in the same framework and provide a more complete perspective.
8. Schools are open social systems with four important elements or subsystems: the structural, the individual, the cultural, and the political. Organizational behavior is a function of the interaction of these elements in the context of teaching and learning.
9. The teaching-learning process is the technical core of the school social system; it is a complex

process that can be usefully viewed from three perspectives—the behavioral, cognitive, and constructivist.

10. The environment is also a critical aspect of organizational life; it not only provides resources for the system but also provides additional constraints and opportunities.
11. We posit a congruence postulate: Other things being equal, the greater the degree of congruence among the elements of the system, the more effective the system.
12. Our open-systems model of schools provides a conceptual basis for organizational analysis and administrative problem solving.

The systematic study of educational administration is as new as the modern school; the one-room schoolhouse of rural America did not need specialized administrators. Research on administration and development of theories of organization and administration are relatively recent phenomena. Before exploring conceptual perspectives of educational administration, however, we need a basic understanding of the nature and meaning of organizational theory. Consequently, we begin the chapter by defining theory and science, delineating the major components of theory, and discussing the interrelationships among theory, research, and practice.

THEORY

Much of the skepticism about theory is based on the assumption that educational administration is incapable of becoming a science. This is a skepticism that has plagued all social sciences. Theory in the natural sciences, on the other hand, has attained respectability not only because it necessarily involves precise description, but also because it describes ideal phenomena that "work" in practical applications.

Most people think that scientists deal with facts whereas philosophers delve into theory. Indeed, to many individuals, including educational administrators, facts and theories are antonyms; that is, facts are real and their meanings self-evident, and theories are speculations or dreams. Theory in educational administration, however, has the same role as theory in physics, chemistry, biology, or psychology—that is, it provides general explanations and guides research.

Theory and Science

The purpose of all science is to understand the world in which we live and work. Scientists describe what they see, discover regularities, and formulate theories (Babbie, 1990). Organizational science attempts to describe and explain regularities in the behavior of individuals and groups within organizations. Organizational scientists seek basic principles that provide a general understanding of the structure and dynamics of organizational life, a relatively recent goal in educational administration (Roberts, Hulin, and Rousseau, 1978).

Some researchers view science as a static, interconnected set of principles that explains the universe in which we live. We view **science** as a dynamic process of developing, through experimentation and observation, an interconnected set of propositions that in turn produces further experimentation and observation (Conant, 1951). In this view the basic aim of science is to find general explanations, called *theories.* Thoughtful individuals trying to understand how things work create theories; however, no theory is ever taken as final because a better one may be devised at any time. Indeed, one of the basic strengths of science is that it is self-critical and self-corrective (Willower, 1994, 1996). The norms of science and theory are oriented toward open-mindedness, public communication of results, and impersonal criteria of assessment (Zucker, 1987).

As the ultimate aim of science, theory has acquired a variety of definitions. Donald J. Willower (1975) provides a parsimonious definition: theory is "a body of interrelated, consistent generalizations that serves to explain" (p. 78). We suggest a more comprehensive definition of theory in educational administration based on the work of Fred N. Kerlinger (1986). **Theory** *is a set of interrelated concepts, assumptions, and generalizations that systematically describes and explains regularities in behavior in educational organizations.* This definition suggests three things:

- Theory logically comprises concepts, assumptions, and generalizations.
- The major function of theory is to describe, explain, and predict regularities in behavior.
- Theory is heuristic; that is, it stimulates and guides the further development of knowledge.

Theories are by nature general and abstract; they are not strictly true or false but rather useful or not. Theories are useful to the extent that they generate accurate predictions about events and help us understand and influence behavior. Albert Einstein, one of the greatest theorists of all times, and Leopold Infeld (Einstein and Infeld, 1938) capture the essence of theorizing in the following quotation:

> In our endeavor to understand reality we are somewhat like a man trying to understand the mechanism of a closed watch. He sees the face and the moving hands, even hears its ticking, but he has no way of opening the case. If he is ingenious he may form some picture of a mechanism, which could be responsible for all the things he observes, but he may never be quite sure his picture is the only one, which could explain his observations. He will never be able to compare his picture with the real mechanism, and he cannot even imagine the possibility of the meaning of such a comparison. (p. 31).

Theory and Reality

Reality exists, but our knowledge of it always remains elusive and uncertain. It should not be surprising that different individuals often draw different conclusions from the same perceptual experiences because they hold different theories that affect their interpretation of events (Carey and Smith, 1993).

Our knowledge consists of our theories. The form of the theory, however, is less important than the degree to which it generates useful understanding. Ultimately, research and theory are judged by their utility (Griffiths, 1988).

The use of theory in organizational analysis seems indispensable to reflective practice. The beginning student of educational administration may ask, "Do these theories and models really exist?" Our position is the same as Mintzberg's (1989). The models, theories, and configurations used to describe organizations in this book are mere words and pictures on pages, not reality itself. Actual organizations are much more complex than any of these representations; in fact, our conceptual frameworks are simplifications of organizations that underscore some features and neglect others. Hence, they distort reality. The problem is that in many areas we cannot get by without theoretical guidance (implicit, if not explicit theories), much as a traveler cannot effectively navigate unknown territory without a map.

Our choice is not usually between reality and theory but rather between alternative theories. Mintzberg (1989) captures the dilemma nicely:

> No one carries reality around in his or her head, no head is that big. Instead we carry around impressions of reality, which amount to implicit theories. Sometimes these are supplemented with explicit frameworks for identifying the concepts and interrelating them—in other words, with formal theories, built on systematic investigation known as research, or at least on systematic consideration of experience. In fact, some phenomena cannot be comprehended without such formal aid—how is one to develop an implicit theory of nuclear fission, for example? (p. 259).

We all use theories to guide our actions. Some are implicit and others are explicit; in fact, many of our personal implicit theories are formal ones that have been internalized. To paraphrase John Maynard Keynes, practical administrators who believe themselves to be exempt from any theoretical influences are usually the slaves of some defunct theory. Good theories and models exist, and if we do our job well in this book, they will exist where all useful knowledge must exist—in our minds. Reality is not in our heads, but we begin to understand it in the course acting, adjusting, and refining our theories and models (Selznick, 1992; Hoy, 1996).

Components of Theory

The nature of theory can be better understood by looking at the meanings of each of the components of theory—concepts, assumptions, and generalizations—and how they are related to one another.

Concepts

A **concept** is a term that has been given an abstract, generalized meaning. Examples of concepts in administration are standardization, leadership, motivation, culture, power, authority, and formal and informal organization. Scientists invent concepts that help them study and analyze a given phenomenon systematically. In other words, they invent a language to describe behavior in the real world. Two important advantages are derived from defining theoretical concepts (Reynolds, 1971). First, we can agree on the meaning of such terms. Second, their abstractness ensures generality.

Although concepts are by definition abstract, different levels of abstraction are used (Willower, 1963). Examples of terms arranged along a concrete to abstract continuum are Jefferson Elementary School, school, service organization, organization, social system, and system. Each succeeding term is more general and abstract. Generally speaking, terms that are specific to a particular time or place are concrete and are less useful in developing theories. Most concepts, generalizations, and theories discussed in this book are in the middle range—that is, they are somewhat limited in scope rather than all-embracing. They are not attempts to summarize all we know about organizations; rather, they explain some of the consistencies found in organizations, particularly schools.

A concept can be defined in at least two ways. First, a **constitutive definition** defines a concept in terms of other words or concepts. For instance, we might define permissiveness as the degree to which a teacher employs a relaxed mode of pupil control—that is, permissiveness is defined in terms of "relaxedness." Although this kind of definition often provides one with a better understanding of the term, it is inadequate from a scientific point of view. The researcher must be able to define the concept in measurable terms.

A set of operations or behaviors that has been used to measure a concept is its **operational definition.** For example, an operational definition of permissiveness might be the number of hall passes a teacher issues per day. This definition is limited, clear, and concise. The concept is the specific set of operations measured. IQ is the standard operational definition of intelligence, and leadership can be operationalized using Bass's Multi-Factor Leadership Questionnaire (Bass, 1985a). Operationalism mandates that the procedures involved in the relation between the observer and the measures for observing be explicitly stated so that they can be duplicated by any other equally trained researcher (Dubin, 1969).

A concept that has an operational definition is often referred to as a variable. In fact, many researchers and scientists loosely use the terms *concept* and *variable* interchangeably. Technically, however, a **variable** is a property of a concept to which numerical values are assigned. The number can represent a category (e.g., gender: male or female), the magnitude of the property (e.g., age in years), or the presence or absence of the property (e.g., participation: yes or no). Variables are thus properties that take on values.

Assumptions and Generalizations

An assumption is a statement that is taken for granted or accepted as true. Assumptions, accepted without proof, are not necessarily self-evident. Consider the following two assumptions concerning teaching:

1. There is no one best way to teach.
2. Different ways of teaching are not equally effective.

The first assumption challenges the conventional idea that there are universal principles for effective teaching, regardless of time or place. The second assumption challenges the notion that complexity and diversity in teaching make it futile to seek guiding principles. We add two additional assumptions, which begin to situate the process of teaching:

3. The best way to teach depends on the subject being taught and what students already know.
4. The best way to teach depends on the student's learning style.

A **generalization** is a statement that indicates the mutual relationship of two or more concepts. In other words, a generalization links concepts in a meaningful fashion. Many kinds of generalizations are found in theoretical formulations: (1) **assumptions** are generalizations if they specify the relationship among two or more concepts; (2) **hypotheses** are generalizations with limited empirical support (see below); (3) **principles** are generalizations with substantial empirical support. Depending on the level of empirical support, the same generalization, at different stages of theory and research development, can be a hypothesis or a principle.

Theory and Research

Research is inextricably related to theory; therefore, many of the misconceptions and ambiguities surrounding theory are reflected in the interpretation of the meaning and purpose of research. Kerlinger (1986: 10) provides a formal definition: "Scientific research is systematic, controlled, empirical, and critical investigation of hypothetical propositions about the presumed relations among natural phenomena." This definition suggests that research is guided by hypotheses that are empirically checked against observations about reality in a systematic and controlled way. Results of such tests are then open to critical analyses by others.

Haphazard observations followed by the conclusion that the facts speak for themselves do not qualify as scientific research; in fact, such unrefined empiricism can distort reality and does not lead to the systematic development of knowledge. Well-conceived surveys and ethnographic studies for the express purpose of developing hypotheses are at times useful starting points in terms of hypothesis and theory development. Ultimately, however, knowledge in any discipline is expanded by research that is guided by hypotheses that are derived from theory. In brief, facts from research are not as important as the general patterns and explanations that they provide.

Hypotheses

A **hypothesis** is a conjectural statement that indicates a relationship between at least two variables. The following two examples illustrate this point.

- The stronger the collective teacher efficacy of a school, the higher the level of mathematics achievement in the school.
- The greater the external pressure from the community on their schools, the higher the level of academic achievement.

Several observations can be made about these hypotheses. First, each hypothesis specifies the relationship between at least two variables. Second, each clearly and concisely describes that relationship. Third, the variables of each hypothesis are such that each could be empirically tested. For example, the first expresses the relationship between two variables—collective teacher efficacy and mathematics achievement. Schools that have high collective efficacy are predicted to have higher student achievement levels in mathematics. Such hypotheses bridge the gaps between theory and research and provide a means to test theory against observed reality; in fact, they are developed from theory. For example, the first hypothesis can be derived from efficacy theory discussed in Chapter 4. The second hypothesis can be derived from the conceptual perspectives on organizational climate provided in Chapter 5.

The hypothesis is the researcher's bias. If it is deduced from a theory, the investigator expects that it will be supported by data. Hypothesis testing is essential to the development of knowledge in any field of study. Support of the hypothesis in empirical research demonstrates the usefulness of the theory as an explanation. The fact that knowledge depends in part upon unsupported theories and assumptions should not cause discouragement. The goal of organizational researchers is to test our assumptions and theories, refining explanations and reformulating the theories as more data are gathered and analyzed.

The basic form of knowledge in all disciplines is similar; it consists of concepts, generalizations, and theories, each dependent on the one preceding it (Willower, 1963). Figure 1.1 summarizes the basic components of theory that are necessary to the development of knowledge. It shows that concepts are eventually linked together into generalizations that in turn form a logically consistent set of propositions providing a general explanation of a phenomenon (a theory). The theory is empirically checked by the development and testing of hypotheses deduced from the theory. The results of the research provide

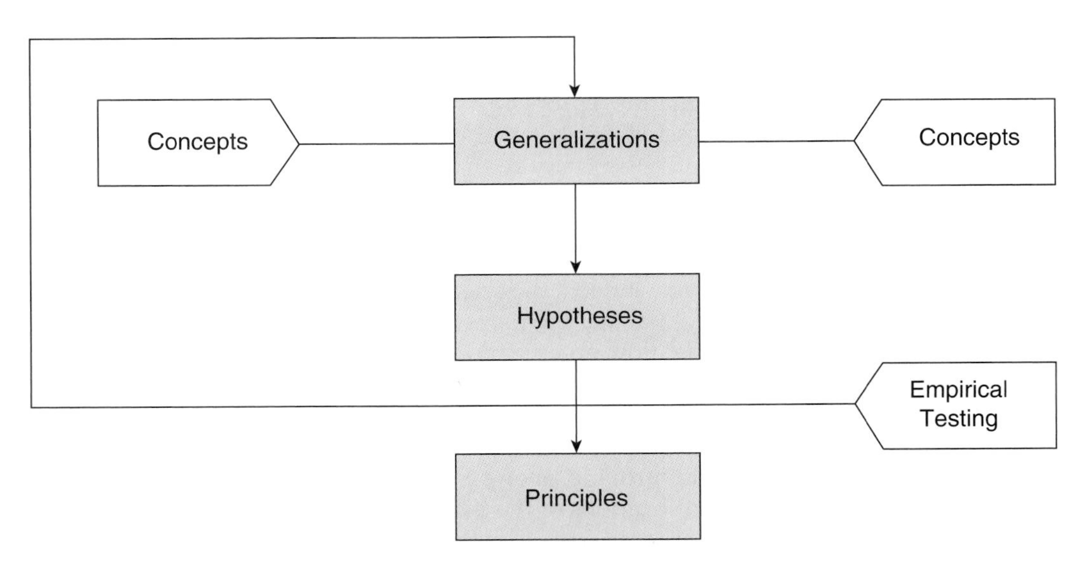

FIGURE 1.1 *Theoretical System*

the data for accepting, rejecting, reformulating, or refining and clarifying the basic generalizations of the theory. Over time, with continued empirical support and evidence, the generalizations develop into principles that explain the phenomenon. In the case of organizational theory, principles are developed to explain the structure and dynamics of organizations and the role of the individual in organizations. Theory is both the beginning and the end of scientific research. On the one hand, it serves as the basis for generating hypotheses that describe and predict observable behavior. On the other hand, the ultimate objective of all scientific endeavors is to develop a body of substantive theory, that is, to provide reliable general explanations. Good theories help us understand and solve all kinds of problems from the ordinary to the complex.

Theory and Practice

Theory is directly related to practice in at least three ways. First, theory forms a frame of reference for the practitioner. Second, the process of theorizing provides a general mode of analysis of practical events. And third, theory guides decision making.

Theory gives practitioners the analytic tools and a frame of reference needed to sharpen and focus their analysis of the problems they face (Dewey, 1933). Administrators so armed can develop alternative solutions to pragmatic problems. It is wrong, however, to think that any social science theory can supply definitive programs and immediate solutions. Theory does not directly generate immediate applications to practical problems. As William James (1983) noted, what is needed is an intermediary inventive mind to make the application, by using its own originality and creativity. There is no substitute for reflective thinking.

Administrators themselves maintain that the most important qualification for their jobs is the ability to use concepts. It is a mistake, however, to assume that the ability to label aspects of a problem by using theoretical constructs from sociology or psychology automatically provides a solution to a problem. Designating a problem as one of role conflict, goal displacement, or cognitive processing, for instance, does not in itself solve the problem; it may, however, organize the issues so that a reasonable plan of action can emerge.

The theory-practice relationship goes beyond using the concepts of theorists to label the important aspects of a problem. The scientific approach provides a way of thinking about events, *a mode of analysis,* for both theorists and practitioners alike. Indeed, the scientific approach is the very embodiment of rational inquiry, whether the focus is theoretical analysis and development, a research investigation, organizational decision making, or problem solving at the personal level. A good general description of this approach is found in John Dewey's (1933) analysis, *How We Think.* The process involves identifying a problem, conceptualizing it, proposing generalizations in the form of hypotheses that provide answers to the problems, deducing the consequences and implications of the hypotheses, and testing the hypotheses.

Some differences do exist in the specific ways that theorists, researchers, and practitioners implement and use the scientific approach, but the differences are a matter of degree of rigor and level of abstraction rather than approach. Theorists operate on a higher level of abstraction and generality than researchers, who test hypotheses. Practitioners, in turn, operate on an even lower level of abstraction than researchers because they are primarily concerned with specific problems and events in their organizations.

Similarly, theorists and researchers typically use the scientific approach more rigorously than practitioners, and for good reason. Theorists usually preface their propositions with the phrase "other things being equal," and researchers attempt to control all other variables except those under study. In contrast, practitioners function in a world where other things typically are not equal and all variables are not controllable. Practitioners are constrained by their positions, responsibilities, authority, and the immediacy of their problems. Although they do not abandon a reflective approach, practitioners are forced to be more flexible in applying the scientific method. For example, educational administrators are probably less concerned than theorists or researchers with generalizability—that is, the extent to which their solutions work for other administrators in other districts. Nonetheless, the approach of theorists, researchers, and thoughtful practitioners is basically the same; it is a systematic and reflective one.

One final relationship between theory and practice needs to be mentioned—theory guides administrative decision making. We can define administration as both the art and the science of applying knowledge to administrative and organizational problems. Arthur Blumberg (1984, 1989) calls it a craft. Such definitions imply that administrators have access to knowledge needed for making decisions. Without theory, however, there is virtually no basis for knowledge because the meaningful research that provides information presupposes a theory. Unfortunately, theory and research in educational administration continue to make only modest gains at best. Nonetheless, reflective administrators are more likely to be guided by theories, as imperfect as they are, than by impulse or the biases of dubious beliefs. Erroneous beliefs and bias will never disappear, but they can be held in check by mental habits that promote sound reasoning (Gilovich, 1991). Theories are no substitute for thought, but they are guides for administrative decision making and problem solving.

Administrative theory does influence practice. Over the last 90 years, the evolution of organizational thought and theory can be described in a number of ways. We view the history of organizational thought through a series of systems lenses.

A Systems Perspective

The system concept has a rich history in the physical as well as the social sciences. Both Alfred N. Whitehead (1925) and George C. Homans (1950) have observed that the idea of an organized whole, or system, occurring in an environment is fundamental and essential to science.

A significant development in the analysis of organizational behavior is the distinction between open and closed systems. Early system analyses of the school (Getzels and Guba, 1957) viewed organizations as closed systems—that is, sealed off from the outside world. Explanations were given in terms of the internal workings of the organization with little or no attention to external constraints in the environment. Today, however, few contemporary organizational theorists accept the premise that organizations can be understood in isolation of events occurring externally; in fact, Marshall Meyer (1978: 18) argues, "the issue of open versus closed systems is closed, on the side of openness."

Although contemporary organizational thought is anchored in modern social science, three competing systems perspectives have emerged and continue each with its share of advocates. W. Richard Scott (1987, 1992, 1998) calls them the rational-systems, natural-systems, and open-systems perspectives. These three popular views of organizations are relatively distinct, yet they are partly overlapping, partly complementary, as well as partly conflicting; and each has its antecedents in earlier organizational thought. Drawing heavily from Scott's (1992, 1998) work, each will be discussed in some detail.

Rational System: A Machine Model

The **rational-systems perspective** views organizations as formal instruments designed to achieve specific organizational goals. Rationality is the extent to which a set of actions is organized and implemented to achieve predetermined goals with maximum efficiency (Scott, 1992). The rational approach has its early roots in the classical organizational thought of the scientific managers.

Scientific Management: The Beginning

Frederick Taylor, the father of the **scientific management** movement, sought ways to use people effectively in industrial organizations. Taylor's background and experience as laborer, clerk, machinist, supervisor, chief drafter, and finally, chief engineer reinforced his belief that individuals could be programmed to be efficient machines. The key to the scientific management approach is the machine metaphor.

Taylor and his associates thought that workers, motivated by economics and limited by physiology, needed constant direction. In 1911 Taylor (1947) formalized his ideas in *Scientific Management.* A sampling of his ideas reveals the flavor of his managerial theory. Taylor and his followers—the human engineers—focused on physical production, and their **time and motion studies** sought workers' physical limits and described the fastest method for performing a given task (Barnes, 1949: 556–67). They believed that by systematically studying a work task and timing how long it took to perform various tasks they could determine the most efficient way to complete the task. Although Taylor's work had a narrow physiological focus and ignored psychological and sociological variables, he demonstrated that many jobs could be performed more efficiently. He also helped the unskilled worker by improving productivity enough to raise the pay of unskilled nearly to that of skilled labor (Drucker, 1968).

Whereas Taylor's human engineers worked from the individual worker upward, the administrative managers worked from the managing director downward. Henri Fayol, like Taylor, took a scientific approach to administration. Fayol was a French mining engineer and successful executive who later taught administration. According to Fayol (Urwick, 1937: 119), administrative behavior consists of five functions—planning, organizing, commanding, coordinating, and controlling. Luther Gulick (1937) later amplified these functions in answer to the question, "What is the work of the chief executive?" He responded, "POSDCoRB," an acronym for his seven administrative procedures: planning, organizing, staffing, directing, coordinating, reporting, and budgeting.

To the administrative managers, **division of labor** was a basic principle of organization. Accordingly, the more a task could be broken down into its components, the more specialized and, therefore, the more effective the worker would be in performing the task. To complement the division of labor, tasks were grouped into jobs, and these jobs were then integrated into departments. Although the criteria for division could pose conflicting demands, division of labor and the departmentalization it entailed were necessary aspects of management.

Span of control, or the number of workers supervised directly, was a second principle. In subdividing from the top downward, each work unit had to be supervised and coordinated with other units, and the span of control considered to be most effective was 5 to 10 subordinates. This rule of thumb is still widely used in building administrative organizations. A single executive, with power and authority flowing uniformly from the top to the bottom, heads the pyramid-shaped structures stemming from this second principle.

A third operating tenet of the administrative manager was the **principle of homogeneity** of positions. According to Gulick (1937), a single department could be formed of positions grouped in any of four different ways: major purpose, major process, clientele, or location.

- *Major purpose* joined those who shared a common goal.
- *Major process* combined those with a similar skill or technology.
- *Clientele* or material grouped those who dealt with similar clients or materials.
- Organization based on *location* or geographic area brought together those who worked together regardless of function.

Organizing departments in these four ways presents obvious problems. For example, should a school health activity be placed in a department of education or of health? How one answers the question will alter the nature of the service. Homogenizing departments in one of the four ways does not homogenize them in all ways. "The question is not which criterion to use for grouping," James D. Thompson (1967: 57) has observed, "but rather in which priority are the several criteria to be exercised?"

Both the human engineers and the scientific managers emphasized formal or bureaucratic organization. They were concerned with the division of labor, the allocation of power, and the specifications for each position; they conspicuously neglected individual idiosyncrasies and the social dynamics of people at work. This perspective, aptly termed a "machine model," implies that an organization can be constructed according to a blueprint, as one would build a bridge or an engine (Worthy, 1950).

As detailed by Roald Campbell and his colleagues (1987), developments in educational administration parallel those in the broad field of administration. Similar to Taylor's scientific managers, although lacking the rigor of the human engineers, early students of educational administration such as Franklin Bobbit (1913) looked at organizational behavior from the vantage point of job analyses. They observed administrators at work, specifying the component tasks to be performed, determining more effective ways to perform each task, and suggesting an organization to maximize efficiency. Raymond E. Callahan's (1962) analysis of schools and of the "cult of efficiency," concentrating on the period from 1910 through 1930, clearly indicates the influence of the scientific managers in the literature on schools.

It would be incorrect, however, to view Taylor's scientific management as a passing fad; in fact, Kanigel (1997) argues that Taylorism has been absorbed into the living tissue of modern organization as well as into American life itself. Taylor's obsession with time, order, productivity, and efficiency translates today into our fascination with electronic organizers, mobile phones, voice mail, and beepers, all to keep us productive and efficient. Today, Taylorism may be intellectually out of fashion, but few deny its lasting impact on American society. For better and worse, Taylorism lives on.

Contemporary Rational Systems: A Structural View

For those who have a rational-systems perspective, behavior in organizations is seen as purposeful, disciplined, and rational. The concerns and concepts of rational-systems theorists are conveyed by such terms as "efficiency," "optimization," "rationality," and "design." Furthermore, emphasis is placed upon the limitations of individual decision makers in the context of organizations; hence, the notions of opportunities, constraints, formal authority, rules and regulations, compliance, and coordination represent key elements of rationality. Contemporary rational-systems theorists stress goal specificity and formalization because these elements make important contributions to the rationality and efficiency of organizations (Scott, 1998).

Goals are the desired ends that guide organizational behavior. Specific goals direct decision making, influence the formal structure, specify the tasks, guide the allocation of resources, and govern design decisions. Ambiguous goals hinder rationality because without clear goals, ordering alternatives and making rational choices are not possible; hence, even when the general organizational goals are vague (as they often are in education), the actual daily operations are guided by specific objectives. Educators may argue endlessly about the merits of progressive and traditional education, but within each school considerable agreement develops around issues such as graduation requirements, discipline policies, and school regulations.

Formalization, or the level of rules and job codification, is another feature that makes organizations rational; formalization produces standardization and regulation of work performance. Rules are developed that precisely and explicitly govern behavior; jobs are carefully defined in terms of acceptable behaviors; role relations are defined independently of personal attributes of incumbents; and sometimes the work flow itself is clearly specified. Formalization is the organization's means to make behavior predictable by standardizing and regulating it. As Simon (1947: 100) cogently states, "Organizations and institutions permit stable expectations to be formed by each member of the group as to the behavior of the other members under specific conditions. Such stable expectations are an essential precondition to a rational consideration of the consequences of action in a social group."

Formalization also contributes to the rational functioning of the organization in a number of other important ways (Scott, 1992). It makes visible the structure of the organizational relationships; thus, managers to improve performance can modify formal structures. Management by objectives (MBO), planning, programming, and budgeting systems (PPBS), strategic planning, and performance evaluation and review techniques (PERT) are examples of technical tools used by managers to facilitate rational decision making. Formal structure also promotes discipline and decision making based on facts rather than emotional ties and feelings; in fact, formalization reduces to some extent both positive and negative feelings that members have toward each other. As Merton (1957: 100) observes, "Formality facilitates the interaction of the occupants of offices despite their (possibly hostile) private attitudes toward one another." Moreover, formalization renders the organization less dependent on particular individuals. The replacement of individuals is routinized so that appropriately trained individuals can be replaced with minimal disturbance. Even leadership and innovation needs are addressed by formalization. As Seldon Wolin (1960: 383) notes, "Organization, by simplifying and routinizing procedures, eliminates the need for surpassing talent. It is predicated on average human beings."

For those committed to attaining organizational goals, rationality, formalization and efficiency are the hallmarks of that quest. How can a structure be created to get the job done efficiently? That is the driving question for rational-systems theorists. We summarize the rational-systems model with the following set of concepts and propositions:

1. *Goals:* Organizations exist primarily to accomplish their goals.
2. *Division of labor:* Subdividing any operation into its basic components to ensure workers' performance can attain efficiency.
3. *Specialization:* Specialization produces higher levels of expertise and performance.
4. *Standardization:* Breaking tasks into component parts allows for routinized performance.
5. *Formalization:* Standard operating procedures can be codified in a system of rules and regulations.
6. *Hierarchy:* To coordinate and control the organization, decision making is centralized in a hierarchy of authority, with responsibility flowing from top to bottom and providing unity of command.

7. *Span of control:* Control and coordination are possible only if each superior at any level has a limited number of subordinates to supervise; scientific managers argued for a narrow span of control (limited from 5 to 10 subordinates).
8. *Exception principle:* Subordinates handle all routine matters, but superiors must deal with all exceptional situations that are not covered by the existing rules.
9. *Coordination:* Administrative control is essential for effective organizational functioning.
10. *Formal organization:* Organizations can be designed and structured to be efficient and effective; the official blueprint of the organization is critical.

Perhaps the greatest shortcoming of machine theory is its rigid conception of organization. As James G. March and Herbert Simon (1958) have observed, the structure and functioning of an organization may be greatly affected both by events outside the organization and by events imperfectly coordinated within it, and neither of these occurrences can be fixed in advance. Contemporary critics also note the undue emphasis on parts rather than the whole. Senge and his colleagues (Kofman and Senge, 1993; Senge, 1990), for example, argue that restricting attention to the parts of an organization and believing that optimizing each part amounts to maximizing the whole is shortsighted because it neglects the primacy of the whole, forces artificial distinctions, and denies the systemic functioning of organizations.

Natural System: An Organic Model

The **natural-systems perspective** provides another view of organization that stands in contrast to the rational-systems perspective. The natural-systems perspective had its early roots in the human relations' approach of the 1930s; it developed in large part as a reaction to the scientific managers and perceived inadequacies of the rational-systems model.

Human Relations: The Beginning

Mary Parker Follett was a pioneer in the human relations movement. She wrote a series of brilliant papers dealing with the human side of administration and argued that the fundamental problem in all organizations was developing and maintaining dynamic and harmonious relationships. In addition, Follett (1924: 300) thought that conflict was "not necessarily a wasteful outbreak of incompatibilities, but normal process by which socially valuable differences register themselves for enrichment of all concerned." Despite Follett's work, the development of the human relations approach is usually traced to studies done in the Hawthorne plant of the Western Electric Company in Chicago. These studies are basic to the literature describing informal groups, and the study of informal groups is basic to an analysis of schools.

The **Hawthorne studies** (see Roethlisberger and Dickson, 1939) began with three experiments conducted to study the relation of quality and quantity of illumination to efficiency in industry. The first illumination experiment was made in three departments. The level of illumination intensity in each department was increased at stated intervals. The results were puzzling. Increased production rates did not correspond with increased lighting, nor did production decline with reduced illumination.

In a second experiment, a test group in which illumination intensities were varied was compared to a control group with illumination held constant. Both groups showed increases in production rates that were not only substantial but also nearly identical.

Finally, in a third experiment, when the lighting for the test group was decreased and that for the control group held constant, the efficiency of both groups increased. Furthermore, the production rates increased in the test group until the light became so poor that the workers complained they could no longer see what they were doing.

The results were neither as simple nor as clear-cut as the experimenters had originally anticipated. Two conclusions seemed justified: employee output was not primarily related to lighting conditions; and too many variables had not been controlled in the experiments. The startling nature of the findings stimulated more research.

Two Harvard professors—Elton Mayo, an industrial psychologist, and Fritz Roethlisberger, a social psychologist—were retained to continue studying the relationship between physical conditions of work and productivity. The company suspected that psychological as well as physiological factors were involved. From 1927 through 1932 the two researchers conducted a series of experiments that have since become research classics in the social sciences—the Hawthorne studies. One generalization became clear almost immediately. The workers' behavior did not conform to the official job specifications. An informal organization emerged that affected performance. **Informal organization** is an unofficial social structure that emerges within the organization that has informal leaders as well as informal norms, values, sentiments, and communication patterns.

The researchers found that informal patterns of interactions developed as soon as the men were put together to work on tasks. Friendships formed and well-defined groups emerged. These informal cliques were evident in interaction patterns both on and off the job. For example, one clique, rather than another, engaged in certain games during off-hours. Even more important than the different interaction patterns were the informal norms that emerged to govern behavior and unify the group. Too much work, and one was a rate buster. Too little work constituted the equally serious, informal offense of chiseling. A no-squealing norm also emerged; no group member should say anything that might injure a fellow member. Other norms included not acting officiously or self-assertively; one was expected to be a "regular guy" and not to be noisy and anxious for attention and leadership.

The work group enforced respect for informal norms through ostracism, sarcasm, and invective to pressure deviant members. One mechanism to enlist compliance was binging—a quick, stiff punch on the upper arm. The bing was not physically damaging, nor was it meant to be; it was a symbolic gesture of group displeasure.

Much activity in the group countered formal role prescriptions. Workers did not stick to their jobs as prescribed but frequently traded jobs, had informal contests, and helped each other. The group also restricted production. Group norms defined a fair day's work below management's expectations, although not so far below so as to be unacceptable. Most work was done in the morning. Faster workers simply slowed their pace earlier or reported less work than they had accomplished to save production for slow days. The informal production levels were consistently maintained, even though higher production was possible. Because the group was on a piece rate, higher output would have meant higher wages. Thus, behavior was a function of group norms, not economic incentives. The experiments at the Hawthorne plant were the first to question many of the basic assumptions made by human engineers and scientific managers, but others soon followed and reinforced the importance of the informal organization.

Although these findings date from the 1930s, they remain important. The human relations approach, however, is not without its detractors. Amitai Etzioni (1964) suggests that the human relations approach grossly oversimplifies the complexities of organizational life by glossing over the realities of work. Organizations have conflicting values and interests as well as shared ones; they are a source of alienation as well as human satisfaction. Worker dissatisfaction is just as likely to be symptomatic of real underlying conflicts of interests as indicative of a lack of understanding of the situation. Put simply, organizations are often not one big "happy family." Contemporary critics of the human relations movement (Clark et al., 1994; Scott, 1998) also argue that the concern for workers was not authentic, but rather management used it as a tool or strategy to manipulate subordinates. Nevertheless, one conclusion is clear: the human relations approach tempered the scientific managers' concentration on organizational structure with an emphasis on employee motivation and satisfaction and group morale.

The impact of the Hawthorne studies on schools was evident in writing and exhortation on democratic administration. The ill-defined watchword of the period was "democratic"—democratic administration, democratic supervision, democratic decision making, and democratic teaching. As Roald Campbell (1971) noted, this emphasis on human relations and democratic practices often meant a series of prescriptions as to how conditions ought to be and how persons in an organization ought to behave. Supposed "principles of administration" abounded, but they were usually no more than the observations of successful administrators or the democratic ideologies of college professors. In the 1940s and early 1950s, educational administration, as a democratic approach, was long on rhetoric and woefully short on research and practice (Campbell, 1971).

Contemporary Natural Systems: A Human Resources View

While rational-systems proponents conceive of organizations as structural arrangements deliberately devised to achieve specific goals, natural-systems advocates view organizations as primarily social groups trying to adapt and survive in their particular situation. Natural-systems analysts generally agree that goal specificity and formalization are characteristics of organizations, but they argue that other attributes are of much greater significance; in fact, some maintain that formal goals and structures have little to do with what is actually happening in organizations (Scott, 1998; also see Etzioni, 1975; Perrow, 1978).

The natural-systems view focuses on similarities among social groups. Thus, organizations, like all social groups, are driven primarily by the basic goal of survival—not by specifically devised goals of particular institutions. Gouldner (1959: 405) captures the essence of the natural-systems approach when he states, "The organization, according to this model, strives to survive and to maintain its equilibrium, and this striving may persist even after its explicitly held goals have been successfully attained. This strain toward survival may even on occasion lead to the neglect or distortion of the organization's goals." Survival, then, is the overriding goal. Formal organizations are viewed not primarily as means for achieving specific ends but as vehicles for individuals to satisfy their human needs. People are valuable human resources for the organization.

Just as the natural-systems analysts generally disregard goals as important attributes of organizations, they also view as unimportant the formal structures constructed to achieve goals. Although they acknowledge that formal structures do exist, they argue that behavior in organizations is regulated primarily by informal structures that emerge to transform the formal system. Thus, a natural-systems perspective emphasizes the informal organization rather than the formal, people rather than structure, and human needs rather than organizational demands. Individuals in organizations are never simply hired hands but bring along with them their heads and hearts. They enter the organization with their own needs, beliefs, values, and motivations. They interact with others and generate informal norms, status structures, power relations, communication networks, and working arrangements (Scott, 1992).

In sum, goals and structure do not make organizations distinctive; in fact, formal features of organization are overshadowed by more generic attributes such as the desire for the system to survive, characteristics of the individuals, and informal relationships. Whereas the rational-systems perspective stresses the importance of structure over individuals, the natural-systems approach emphasizes individuals over structure. In the stark terms of Warren G. Bennis (1959), the rational-systems focus is on "structure without people," whereas the clear reversal of priorities in the natural-systems model produces an orientation of "people without organization."

We summarize the natural-systems model with the following set of concepts and propositions:

1. *Survival:* Organizations are more than instruments to achieve goals; they are primarily social groups attempting to adapt and survive in their particular situation.
2. *Individuals:* People are more important than the structure.
3. *Needs:* Individual needs are the primary motivators of organizational performance; organizations are mechanisms for fulfilling human needs.

4. *Specialization:* Extreme specialization produces boredom, frustration, and reduces efficiency.
5. *Formalization:* Extreme formalization produces rigidity and fixation on the rules; individuals are active human beings, not passive cogs in a machine.
6. *Informal norms:* Unofficial expectations and operating procedures are often more important in performance than formal expectations.
7. *Hierarchy:* Top-down administration is dysfunctional because it neglects the talents of the rank and file; participative management is more effective.
8. *Span of control:* A narrow span of control is not a prerequisite to effective supervision; in fact, it can be dysfunctional because it encourages autocratic supervision.
9. *Communication:* The informal network of communication is more efficient and open than the formal.
10. *Informal organization:* Informal structures are more important than formal ones just as informal leaders are often more important than formal leaders; workers use the informal organization to protect themselves against arbitrary management decisions by responding as members of an informal work group not simply as individuals.

Open System: An Integraton

The **open-systems perspective** was a reaction to the unrealistic assumption that organizational behavior could be isolated from external forces. Competition, resources, and political pressures from the environment affect the internal workings of organizations. The open-systems model views organizations as not only influenced by environments, but also dependent on them. At a general level, organizations are easily pictured as open systems. Organizations take inputs from the environment, transform them, and produce outputs (see Figure 1.2). For example, schools are social systems that take resources such as labor, students, and money from the environment and subject these inputs to an educational transformation process to produce literate and educated students and graduates.

Because the rational-system approach, particularly the scientific managers, ignored the impact of individual needs and social relations and because the natural-systems, especially the human relations proponents, discounted formal structure, both of these systems perspectives are limited and incomplete. Clearly both the formal and informal as well as structure and people are critical to understanding organizations. An open-systems perspective supplies such a vantage point.

Chester I. Barnard (1938) was one of the first to consider both views in his analysis of organizational life in *Functions of the Executive.* The product of Barnard's years as president of Bell Telephone Company of New Jersey, this book offers a comprehensive theory of cooperative behavior in formal organizations. Barnard provided the original definitions of formal and informal organizations and cogently demonstrated the inevitable interaction between

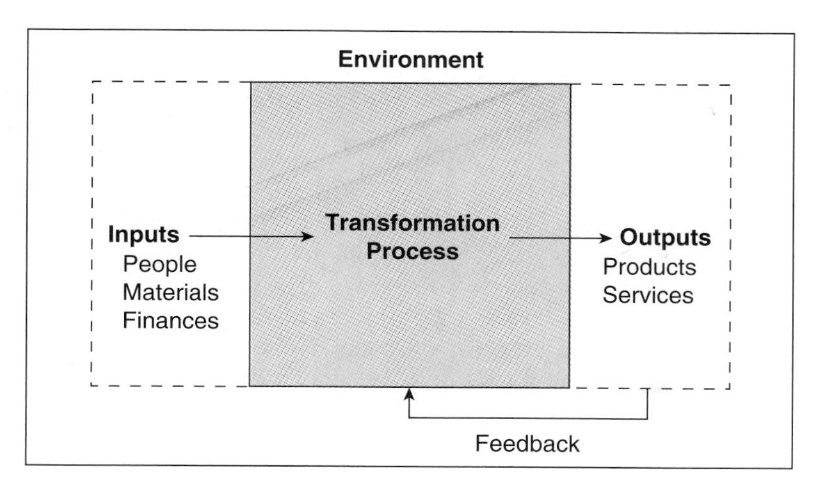

FIGURE 1.2 *Open System with Feedback Loop*

them. Barnard (1940) himself summarized the contributions of his work in terms of structural and dynamic concepts. The structural concepts he considered important were the individual, the cooperative system, the formal organization, the complex formal organization, and the informal organization. His important dynamic concepts were free will, cooperation, communication, authority, the decision process, and dynamic equilibrium.

Herbert Simon (1947), in *Administrative Behavior,* extended Barnard's work and used the concept of organizational equilibrium as a focal point for a formal theory of work motivation. The organization was seen as an exchange system in which inducements are exchanged for work. Employees remain in the organization as long as they perceive the inducements as larger than their work contributions.

The organization, although providing the framework, information, and values for rational decisions, is limited in its ability to collect and process information, search for alternatives, and predict consequences. Therefore, questions are resolved through satisficing rather than through optimizing. In Simon's view, no best solution exists to any given problem, but some solutions are more satisfactory than others (see Chapter 9).

Another important theoretical formulation of organizations (see Chapter 3) evolved from the writings of Max Weber (1947). Although many of Weber's views are consistent with those espoused by the scientific managers, Weber's discussions of bureaucracy and authority have provided present-day theorists with a starting point in their conceptions of organizations as social systems that interact with and are dependent upon their environments. It remained to Talcott Parsons (1960), however, to stress the importance of the environment on the organization and anticipate a conception of the organization as an open system—a social system dependent on and influenced by its environment.

The open-systems model has the potential to provide a synthesis by combining the rational and natural perspectives. Organizations are complex and dynamic. They have formal structures to achieve specified goals, but are composed of people who have their own idiosyncratic needs, interests, and beliefs that often conflict with organizational expectations. Thus, organizations have planned and unplanned features, rational and irrational characteristics, and formal and informal structures. In some organizations rational concerns dominate the relationships and natural, social relationships predominate in others. In all organizations, however, both rational and natural elements coexist within a system that is open to its environment.

Some scholars argue that contemporary organizations are either open, natural systems or open, rational systems, which are adaptations to different kinds of environments (Lawrence and Lorsch, 1967). Our view is that schools are open systems confronted with both rational and natural constraints that change as the environmental forces change; to neglect either the rational or the natural elements is shortsighted. Open-systems theory is our general framework for exploring the conceptual foundations of educational administration in this text. Although many theories are discussed in our analyses, the open-systems perspective is the overarching framework that underscores four internal subsystems that interact to influence organizational behavior: the structural, cultural, individual, and political systems.

Key Properties Of Open Systems

An open system is concerned with both structure and process; it is a dynamic system with both stability and flexibility, with both tight and loose structural relationships. The organization as an arrangement of roles and relationships is not static. To survive, the organization must adapt and to adapt, it must change. The interdependence of the organization and its environment is critical. Instead of neglecting the environment, as the rational-systems perspective does, or seeing it as hostile, as is the case with the natural-systems perspective, "the open-systems model stresses the reciprocal ties that bind and interrelate the organization with those elements that surround and penetrate it. Indeed, the environment is even seen to be the source of order itself" (Scott, 1987: 91).

There is some agreement about the key properties and processes that characterize most social systems. We begin by presenting, defining, and discussing nine central concepts. An open system is a set of interacting elements that acquires *inputs* from the outside, transforms them, and produces outputs for the environment. People, raw materials, information, and money are the typical inputs for organizations. In the *transformational process,* these inputs are changed into something of value called *outputs,* which are then exported back into the environment. Outputs are usually products and services, but they may also include employee satisfaction and other by-products of the transformation process. Classrooms, books, computers, instructional materials, teachers, and students are critical inputs for schools. Ideally, students are transformed by the school system into educated graduates, who then contribute to the broader environment, or society. These three elements of an open system are illustrated in Figure 1.2.

The system's capacity for feedback facilitates the repetitive and cyclic pattern of "input-transformation-output." *Feedback* is information about the system that enables it to correct itself. Formal communication structures—PTA and various advisory councils—and informal political contacts are established inside and outside the school building to provide feedback to the school. Unlike mechanical systems, however, social systems do not always use the information to change. The superintendent of a school system who receives information about falling SAT scores and increased difficulties of graduates to get jobs and enter the colleges of their choice can use this information to identify factors within the system that are contributing to the problem and take corrective action. Yet not all superintendents choose to act. Hence, although feedback provides self-correcting opportunities, the potential is not always realized.

Systems have *boundaries*—that is, they are differentiated from their environments. The boundaries are less clear for open than for closed systems, but they do exist. Are parents part of the school system? It depends. In some schools they are considered part of the schools and in others they are not. Regardless of whether parents are considered to be inside the boundaries, schools expend substantial energy in boundary-spanning activities such as parent-teacher meetings, community service projects, and adult education programs.

The *environment* is anything outside the boundaries of the system that either affects the attributes of the internal components or is changed by the social system itself (see Chapter 7 for a detailed consideration of external environment). For a specific school, district policies, central administrators, other school buildings, and the community are important features of the school's environment. Although organizational environment is typically understood to refer to conditions external to the organization, the clear separation of the organization from its environment is virtually impossible when applied to open systems such as schools. In practice, however, some administrators attempt to control the openness of the school. For example, only appropriate clientele are allowed into the school building, people from the street are locked out, and visitors are required to sign in at the principal's office.

The process by which a group of regulators acts to maintain a steady state among the system components is called *homeostasis.* A biological analogy illustrates the concept: when an organism moves from a warm environment to a cold one, homeostatic mechanisms trigger reactions to maintain body temperature. Similarly, in a school building, crucial elements and activities are protected so that overall stability is maintained. Systems that survive tend to move toward a steady state—equilibrium. This steady state, however, is not static. Energy from and to the environment is continuously imported and exported. Although forces that seek to maintain the system counter any force that threatens to disrupt the system, systems do exhibit a growth dynamic. Events that throw the system out of balance are addressed by actions that are calculated to move the system toward a new state of balance, or equilibrium. As administrators are well aware, disruptive stresses upset this equilibrium and create temporary periods of disequilibrium. A community group may demand that a course such as sex education be deleted. This causes disequilibrium, but the system either changes itself or neutralizes the disruptive forces impinging on it; that is, it restores equilibrium.

The tendency for any system to run down—to cease to exist—is called *entropy.* Open systems can overcome entropy by importing energy from their environment. Organizations, for example, seek to maintain a favorable position with respect to their environments by adapting to changing environmental demands. Pressure from a state department of education for new programs typically results in accommodation to those demands, albeit with more taxes and resources for the system.

The principle of *equifinality* suggests that systems can reach the same end from different initial positions and through different paths. Thus, no one best way exists to organize and, likewise, there is no one best way to reach the same end. For instance, schools may select a variety of means (e.g., discovery learning, independent projects, interactive technologies) to achieve improvements in critical thinking skills of students.

Social-Systems Model: Basic Assumptions

The notion of a social system is a general one. It can be applied to social organizations that are carefully and deliberately planned or to those that emerge spontaneously. The school is a system of social interaction; it is an organized whole comprising interacting personalities bound together in an organic relationship (Waller, 1932). As a social system, the school is characterized by an interdependence of parts, a clearly defined population, differentiation from its environment, a complex network of social relationships, and its own unique culture. As with all formal organizations, analysis of the school as a social system calls attention to both the planned and unplanned—the formal and informal—aspects of organizational life.

Thus far in our discussion of systems we have made several implicit assumptions. Let us now make these and others explicit as we examine the school as a social system. We have gleaned these assumptions from the literature, but the primary sources are Jacob W. Getzels and Egon G. Guba (1957); Jacob W. Getzels, James Lipham, and Ronald F. Campbell (1968); Charles E. Bidwell (1965), and W. Richard Scott (1992; 1998).

- Social systems are open systems. Schools are affected by the values of the community, by politics, and by history. In brief, community and societal forces affect them.
- Social systems are peopled. People act on the basis of their needs as well as their roles and statuses. In schools, people perform the roles of administrator, teacher, student, custodian, and so forth.
- Social systems consist of interdependent parts, characteristics, and activities that contribute to and receive from the whole. When one part is affected, a ripple goes through the social system. For example, when the principal is confronted by parental demands for new courses, not only is the principal affected directly but also are the teachers and students.

- Social systems are goal oriented. Indeed they often have multiple goals. In a school, student learning and control are just two of many goals. The central goal of any school system is the preparation of its students for adult roles.
- Social systems are structural. Different components are needed to perform specific functions and allocate resources. School systems are to some degree bureaucratic; they have division of labor (e.g., math and science teachers), specialization (e.g., teachers, guidance counselors, and administrators), and hierarchy (superintendent, principals, assistant principals, and teachers).
- Social systems are normative. Formal rules and regulations as well as informal norms prescribe appropriate behavior. Expectations are well known by all participants.
- Social systems are sanction bearing. The norms for behavior are enforced with reward and punishment. Formal mechanisms include expulsion, suspension, termination, tenure, and promotion. Informal sanctions include the use of sarcasm, ostracism, and ridicule.
- Social systems are political; power relations inevitably enter into social relations.
- Social systems have distinctive cultures, that is, a dominant set of shared values.
- Social systems are conceptual and relative. The social systems construct is a general one that applies to social organizations regardless of size. For one purpose, a classroom can be considered a social system. For other purposes, the school or school district may be taken as a social system.
- All formal organizations are social systems. But all social systems are not formal organizations.

These assumptions suggest that a school consists of a number of important elements or subsystems that affect organizational behavior.

Key Elements of the School Social System

All social systems have some activities and functions that are accomplished in a fairly stable fashion. For example, if we conceive of society itself as a social system, then the routine and imperative functions of educating, protecting, and governing are performed by educational, legal, and governmental institutions. Regardless of the nature of the social system, patterns of behavior become regular and routine.

When the accomplishment of an objective requires collective effort, individuals often set up organizations specifically designed to coordinate the activities and to furnish incentives for others to join them in this purpose. Such an organization—explicitly established to achieve certain goals—is a **formal organization.** Our concern is with the school social system as a formal organization.

Figure 1.3 pictures the major elements, or subsystems, of a social system. Behavior in formal organizations is influenced not only by structural and individual elements but also by cultural and political elements. *Structure* is defined in terms of formal bureaucratic expectations, which are designed and organized to fulfill the goals of the organization. The *individual* is viewed in terms of the needs, goals, beliefs, and cognitive understandings of work roles; the individual provides the energy and capacity to achieve the organization's goals. *Culture* is the shared work orientations of participants; it gives the organization special identity. *Politics* is the system of informal power relations that emerge to resist other systems of control. Further, all the elements and interactions within the system are constrained by important forces from both the *technical core* and the *environment;* the system is open. Finally, formal organizations as social systems must solve the basic problems of adaptation, goal achievement, integration, and latency if they are to survive and prosper.[1]

The model of formal organization that we are proposing takes all of these factors into consideration. We begin by examining internal elements of the system and then discuss the impact of the environment and technical core (teaching-learning process) on the school and its outcomes.

Structure

Bureaucratic expectations are formal demands and obligations set by the organization; they are the key building blocks of organizational structure. **Bureaucratic roles** are defined by sets of expectations, which are combined into positions and offices in the organization. In schools, the positions of principal, teacher, and student are critical ones and each is defined in terms of a

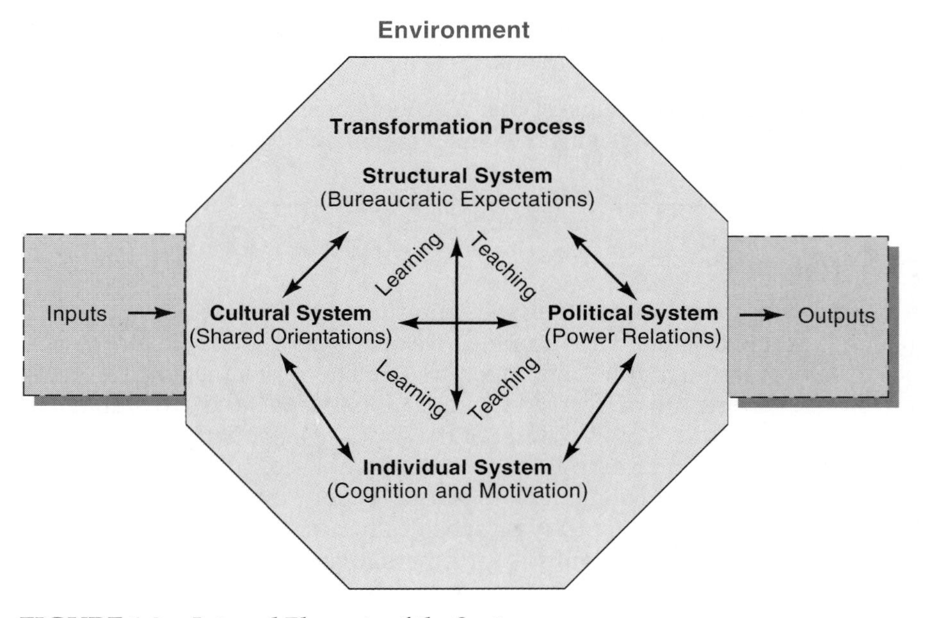

FIGURE 1.3 ***Internal Elements of the System***

set of expectations. The bureaucratic expectations specify the appropriate behavior for a specific role or position. A teacher, for instance, has the obligation to plan learning experiences for students and has the duty to engage students in a pedagogically effective manner. Bureaucratic roles and expectations are the official blueprints for action, the organizational givens of the office.

Some formal expectations are critical and mandatory; others are more flexible. Many roles are not precisely prescribed; that is, the expectations associated with most positions are wide ranging. This range of freedom makes it feasible for teachers with quite different personalities to perform the same roles without undue tension or conflict (Parsons and Shils, 1951). Roles derive their meaning from other roles in the system and in this sense are complementary. For example, it is difficult, if not impossible, to define either the role of student or that of teacher in a school without specifying the relationship of teacher to student. Likewise, the role of principal is dependent on its relationship to the roles of teacher and student.

From a vast array of vague and contradictory expectations, formal organizations select a few general bureaucratic expectations that are reasonably consistent with the organization's goals. These expectations often are formalized, codified, and adopted as official rules and regulations of the organization; they may delineate such things as arrival times, building assignments, and job descriptions. Specialization—the expectation that employee behavior will be guided by expertise—complements the rules and regulations. Thus, a teacher is expected to behave in appropriate ways based on the school's rules and the expertise demanded by the instructional job.

Put simply, formal organizations such as schools have structures composed of bureaucratic expectations and roles, a hierarchy of offices and positions, rules and regulations, and specialization. Bureaucratic expectations define organizational roles; roles are combined into positions and offices; and positions and offices are arranged into a formal hierarchy of authority according to their relative power and status. Rules and regulations are provided to guide decision making and enhance organizational rationality, and labor is divided as individuals specialize in tasks. Some structures facilitate the operation of the organization and others hinder, and undoubtedly, behavior in an organization is determined in part by the structural arrangement of the school.

Individual

The fact that a social unit has been formally established does not mean that all activities and interactions of its members conform strictly to structural requirements—the official blueprint. Regardless of official positions and elaborate bureaucratic expectations, members have their own individual needs, beliefs, and cognitive understandings of their jobs.

Just as not all expectations are relevant for the analysis of organizational behavior, not all individual needs are relevant to organizational performance. What are those facets of the individual that are most instrumental in determining an individual's organizational behavior? We postulate several important cognitive aspects of the individual: needs, goals, beliefs, and cognition.

Work motivation constitutes the single most relevant set of needs for employees in formal organizations. We will elaborate extensively later, but for now work needs are defined as basic forces that motivate work behavior.

Cognition is the individual's use of mental representations to understand the job in terms of perception, knowledge, and expected behavior. Workers seek to create meaningful, coherent representations of their work regardless of its complexity. They learn what their job is about by monitoring and checking their own behavior. Their needs, personal beliefs, goals, and previous experiences become the bases for constructing organizational reality and interpreting their work. Their motivation and cognition are influenced by such factors as beliefs about personal control and competence, individual goals, personal expectations for failure and success, and work motives. In brief, the salient aspects of the individual system are personal needs, beliefs, goals, and cognitive orientations to work.

Although we have examined the influence of structural *(S)* and individual *(I)* elements separately, behavior is a function *(f)* of the interaction of bureaucratic role expectations and the relevant work orientations of the organizational member $[B = f(S \leftrightarrow I)]$. For example, the evaluation of the teaching staff is affected by district policy as well as by the principal's own needs. The rules and regulations state that the principal is expected to evaluate each teacher at given intervals with a specified evaluation instrument. The principal acts as a result of this policy. Each principal's behavior differs in the evaluation meetings, perhaps because of individual cognition and motivational needs. One building administrator who has a great personal desire for social acceptance from the teachers may treat these sessions as an opportunity for friendly socializing rather than for evaluating. But another principal, lacking such a need for social acceptance, may follow the book and remain analytical in the evaluation. The two principals are affected by both elements, but the first is more influenced by individual needs and the second by bureaucratic role expectations.

The ratio of bureaucratic expectations to individual work needs, which at least partly determines behavior, will vary with the specific type of organization, the specific job, and the specific person involved. Figure 1.4 presents pictorially the general nature of this interaction. Vertical line *A* represents a hypothetical situation in which the proportion of behavior controlled by the bureaucratic structure is relatively large; line *B* (at the right) represents the situation in which behavior is primarily controlled by individual needs.

Military organizations commonly are considered to be represented by line *A*—more bureaucratic control—whereas research and development organizations are better represented by line *B*. Most schools probably fall between these two extremes. Free, open-concept, or Montessori schools would be close to line *B*. Church-related schools are typically thought to be closer to line *A*. Where do administrators and students fall in this regard? Individuals differ; some tend toward line *B*—free spirits—and some toward line *A*—bureaucrats. In our example of the two principals in evaluation sessions, the first with a high need for social acceptance would be near line *B* and the second closer to line *A*.

0018062

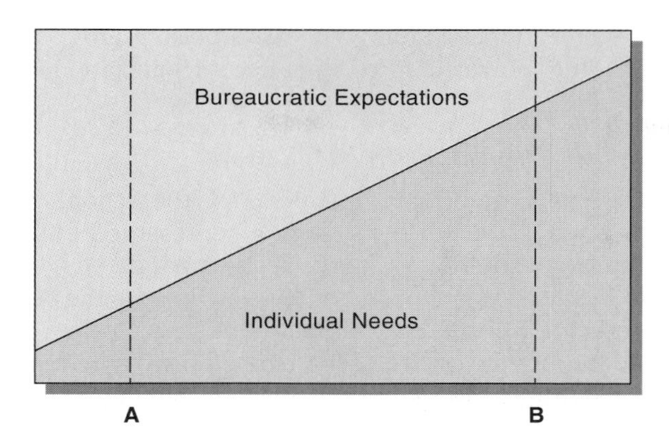

FIGURE 1.4 *Interaction of Bureaucratic and Individual Elements Affecting Behavior*

Culture

There is a dynamic relationship between bureaucratic role demands and individual work needs as people are brought together in the workplace. Organizations develop their own distinctive cultures. As organizational members interact, shared values, norms, beliefs, and ways of thinking emerge. These shared orientations form the culture of the organization. Culture distinguishes one organization from another and provides members with a sense of organizational identity (Hellriegel, Slocum, and Woodman, 1992; Daft, 1994). In a school, shared beliefs and informal norms among teachers have a significant impact on behavior. Culture provides members with a commitment to beliefs and values that go beyond themselves; individuals belong to a group that is larger than themselves. When the culture is strong, so is their identification with the group and the influence of the group.

Culture represents the unwritten, feeling part of the organization (Daft, 1994). Communication of feelings is easy among peers, especially friends. Shared orientations help maintain cohesiveness and feelings of personal integrity, self-respect, and belonging. Because many interactions in organizations are informal, they are personal and not dominated by authority. They furnish opportunities for the individual to maintain his or her personality against the attempts of the bureaucratic organization to submerge, if not destroy, it (Barnard, 1938). Members receive important rewards from the group and group norms are significant in guiding their behavior. For example, accepted informal procedures, not formal rules, may develop among the teachers for disciplining students; in fact, the custodial informal norms for controlling students become the criteria for judging "effective" teaching in many schools. Good control is equated with good teaching.

Behavior in formal organizations is influenced not only by structural and individual elements but also by emergent values and shared orientations of the

work group. Organizational culture, with its important group norms, values, and beliefs, is another powerful force that affects organizational behavior.

Politics

Structure represents the formal dimension of the school social system, whereas the personal aspect of the system is represented in the individual. Culture is the collective dimension of the system that blends the formal with the personal to create a system of shared beliefs. But it is the political dimension that spawns the informal power relations that emerge often to resist other systems of legitimate control. Members who work within the confines of the structure, culture, and individual systems usually contribute directly to the needs of the organization at large. Structure provides formal authority; culture generates informal authority; and the individual brings the authority of expertise to the organization. Politics, in contrast, is typically informal, often clandestine, and frequently illegitimate. It is illegitimate because it is behavior usually designed to benefit the individual or group at the expense of the organization. Consequently, most politics is divisive and conflictual, pitting individuals and groups against each other and against the organization at large (Mintzberg, 1983a).

Politics, however, is an inevitable part of organizational life. There are always those who want to seize power for their own personal ends. In its extreme, one can conceive of an organization "as a mass of competing power groups, each seeking to influence policy in terms of its own interest, or, in terms of its own distorted image of the [organization's] interest" (Strauss, 1964: 164).Power relations get played out in a variety of ways: political tactics and games, bargaining, and conflict resolution. Members are invariably forced to play the power game of politics. Allison (1971: 168) puts it succinctly, "Power . . . is an elusive blend . . . of bargaining advantages, skill, and will in using bargaining advantages. . . ." Although politics is informal, divisive, and typically illegitimate, there is little doubt that it is an important force influencing organizational behavior.

To understand organizational life one must look at both formal and informal as well as legitimate and illegitimate forms of power. Hence, structure, individual, culture, and politics are critical elements of the social systems; these elements can become individual frames or lenses to view organizational behavior, but remember behavior is a function of the *interaction* of these elements.

Environment

As a general definition, environment is everything that is outside the organization. But unlike physical systems, social systems are open; hence, the boundaries are much more ambiguous and the environment more intrusive. There is no doubt that environment is critical to the organizational functioning of schools. It is the system's source of energy. It provides resources, values, technology, demands, and history—all of which place constraints and opportunities on organizational action.

Which features of the environment are most salient for constraining behavior in schools? There is no quick or simple answer. Both broad and specific environmental factors influence the structure and activities of schools. Larger social, legal, economic, political, demographic, and technological trends have a potentially powerful impact on schools, but the effects of such general environmental forces are by no means clear. In contrast, interested constituencies and stakeholders, such as parents, taxpayers, unions, regulatory agencies, colleges and universities, state legislatures, accrediting agencies, and educational associations, have more immediate and direct effects on schools. But again the results are not certain.

The degree of uncertainty, the degree of structure or organization, and the degree of scarcity in the environment condition the response of the school to environmental factors. School decision makers monitor the environment for information, and their perceptions determine to a large degree the future directions of the organization. Schools, like all organizations, attempt to reduce uncertainty and control their environments; therefore, administrators often resort to strategies to minimize external effects. Moreover, if the groups and organizations of the environment are highly organized, then the school is faced with a potent set of demands and constraints, and the result will likely be compliance. Finally, schools compete in an environment made up of various resource pools. If resources of a particular kind are scarce, then the internal structure and activities will develop in ways that will facilitate their acquisition.

In brief, schools are open systems that are affected by external forces. Although there is basic agreement on the importance of the environment, its complexity makes analysis difficult. Nonetheless, we need to consider what factors individually and in relation to others create the basic external demands, constraints, and opportunities to which schools respond. We will return to a detailed analysis of the environment in Chapter 7.

Outcomes

A school, then, can be thought of as a set of elements—individual, structural, cultural, and political. However, behavior in organizations is not simply a function of its elements and environmental forces; it is a function of the interaction of the elements. Thus, organizational behavior is the result of the dynamic relationship among its elements. More specifically, behavior is a function of the interaction of structure, individual, culture, and politics as constrained by environmental forces. To understand and predict the behavior in schools, it is useful to examine the six pairs of interactions among the elements in terms of their harmony. We posit a **congruence postulate:** other things being equal, the greater the degree of congruence among the elements of the system, the more effective the system.[2] For example, the more consistent the informal norms and the formal expectations, the more likely the organization will be to achieve its formal goals. Likewise, the better the fit between individual motivation and bureaucratic expectations, the more effective the performance. In Table 1.1, examples of critical questions concerning the congruence of each pair of key elements are outlined.

TABLE 1.1

Congruence between Pairs of Key Elements

Congruence Relationships	Crucial Questions
Individual ↔ Structural	To what extent do individual work needs enhance bureaucratic expectations?
Individual ↔ Culture	To what extent are shared orientations of organizational culture consistent with individual work needs?
Individual ↔ Politics	To what extent do power relations conflict with individual work needs?
Structural ↔ Cultural	To what extent do the bureaucratic expectations reinforce the shared orientations of the cultural system?
Structural ↔ Political	To what extent do the power relations undermine bureaucratic expectations?
Political ↔ Culture	To what extent do the power relations conflict with and undermine the shared orientations of the culture?

Performance outcomes are indicators of goal accomplishment. Performance outcomes include such indicators as achievement, job satisfaction, absenteeism, and overall performance quality. In any case, the critical aspects of behavior are defined by the outputs of the system. The model assumes that the effective achievement of these behavioral outcomes is a function of the degree of congruence among the system elements. Hence, organizational effectiveness is the degree to which actual outcomes are consistent with expected outcomes. The key elements, their interactions, the demands and constraints of the environment, and the behavioral outcomes are summarized in Figure 1.5.

Internal Feedback Loops

The social-systems model pictured in Figure 1.5 also has both internal and external feedback mechanisms. For example, the formal school structure and the informal groups both attempt to influence individual behavior (Abbott, 1965b). Feedback informs individuals how the bureaucratic structure and the informal organization view their behavior. Although the bureaucracy has formal mechanisms and the work group informal ones, both have internal feedback loops.

The formal school organization provides an official definition of the position, its rank in the hierarchy, and a set of expected behaviors that go with it. In fact, the bureaucratic structure has an established incentive pattern for ensuring appropriate behavior. If the school bureaucracy approves of an in-

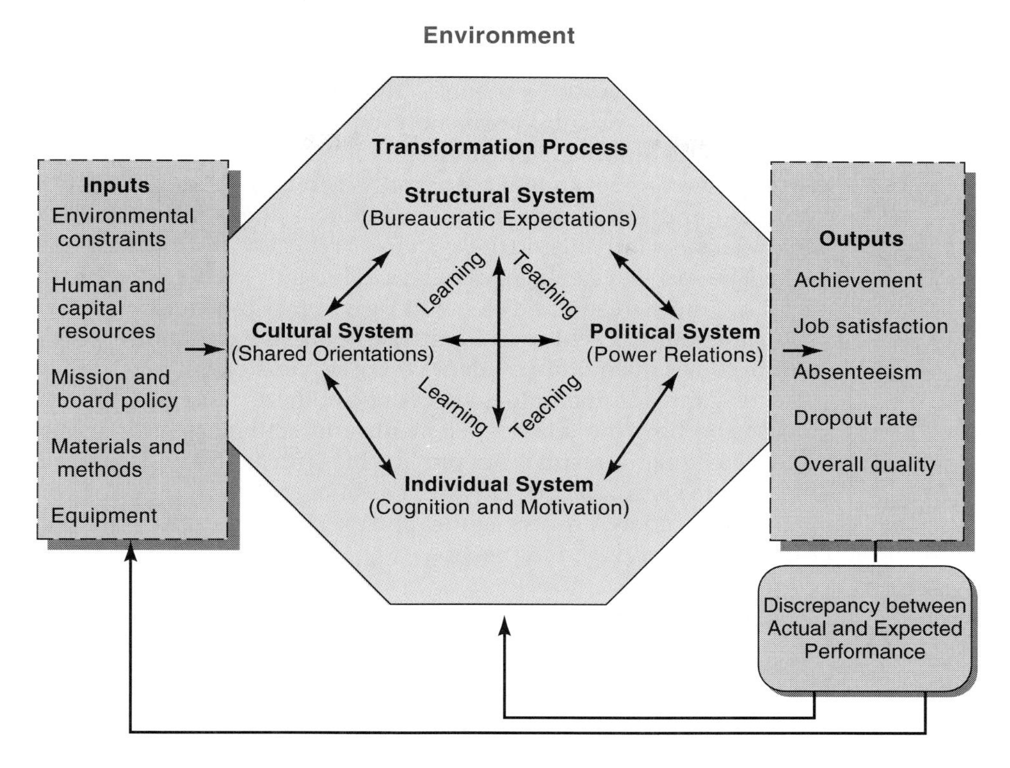

FIGURE 1.5 *Social System Model for Schools*

dividual's performance, positive rewards reinforce his or her behavior. If that person's behavior is evaluated as inferior, positive incentives are reduced and negative incentives are increased.

Informal groups similarly influence behavior. As our discussion of the Hawthorne studies explained, group norms control behavior. In the school building, norms exist within and among all informal peer groups. For example, teachers expect their peers to act appropriately to control students. If a teacher fails to maintain discipline in the classroom, the other teachers apply sanctions: sarcasm and ostracism in the teachers' lounge can have devastating effects on an individual.

External Feedback Loops

Behavior in schools also is monitored through external feedback loops. The culture of the community provides environmental constraints that directly influence bureaucratic expectations, group norms, and organizational goals that indirectly influence individual needs. In spite of attempts by a school to isolate itself, it remains open to community, state, and national forces. The introduction of AIDS education into the school curriculum, for example, rarely goes unnoticed by the public. In fact, organized community groups provide important inputs about what they consider the goals and outcomes of an acceptable AIDS education program.

Social behavior in a school is thus affected directly by at least four internal elements, or subsystems—structure, individual, culture, and politics. Moreover, as Figure 1.5 illustrates, internal and external feedback reinforce appropriate organizational behavior. When there is a discrepancy between expected and actual outcomes, the feedback loops inform individuals and groups inside and outside the system.

The social-systems model gives a dynamic view of the school, with the feedback mechanisms and elements providing the action components. Good, bad, and neutral events occur constantly, and the dynamic nature of the system becomes even more evident when we consider the ways that students, teachers, and administrators affect one another's behavior. Systems analysis focuses on how the totality—elements and activities—produces a given result. The dynamic result is not predictable with complete accuracy because of the infinite variations that can occur as bureaucracy, subgroups, and individuals modify goals, express values, and exert power through leadership, decision making, and communication.

The School as a Learning Organization

It should be abundantly clear by now that organizational life is complex because it is part of an intricate network of social relationships. The full meaning of any event can only be understood in the context of the system; that is, by contemplating the whole rather than isolated parts of the system. Such an approach has been termed "systems thinking" (Senge, 1990), and it fits well into viewing the school as a social system.

Schools are service organizations that are committed to teaching and learning. The ultimate goal of the school is student learning; in fact, its very existence is based on such activity. Schools more than any other kind of organization should be **learning organizations.** They should be places where participants continually expand their capacities to create and achieve, where novel patterns of thinking are encouraged, where collective aspirations are nurtured, where participants learn how to learn together, and where the organization expands its capacity for innovation and problem solving (Senge, 1990; Watkins and Marsick, 1993). A complementary definition of a learning organization is one in which the participants pursue common purposes with a collective commitment to routinely assessing the value of those purposes, modifying them when appropriate, and continually developing more effective and efficient ways to achieve those purposes (Leithwood and Louis, 1998).

Although the concept of learning organization has gained widespread notoriety since Senge's pioneering analysis of the art and practice of the learning organization (1990), the literature has been long on theoretical analysis and short on research evidence, a condition that led Weick and Westley (1996) to comment that "there appear to be more reviews of organizational learning than there is substance to review (p. 40)." Empirical research, however, is just beginning to emerge in schools (Ben-Peretz and Schonmann, 1998; Leithwood,

Jantzi, and Steinbach, 1998, and Louis and Kruse, 1998) that support the compelling theoretical rationale of schools as learning organizations.

If schools are to be effective learning organizations, they must find ways to create structures (Chapter 3) that continuously support teaching and learning and enhance organizational adaptation; develop organizational cultures and climates that are open, collaborative, and self-regulating (Chapter 5); attract individuals who are secure, efficacious and open to change (Chapter 4); and prevent vicious and illegitimate politics from displacing the legitimate activities of learning and teaching (Chapter 2). Transformational leadership (Chapter 11), open and continuous communication (Chapter 10), and shared decision making (Chapter 9) are mechanisms that should and can enhance organizational learning in schools. The challenge is to create schools that have the capacity to respond effectively not only to contemporary problems (Chapter 7), but also to new and emerging issues of school effectiveness (Chapter 8).

Emergent Nontraditional Perspectives

Thus far our treatment of organizational thought has been grounded in standard social science; in fact, much of the remainder of this book emphasizes mainline theory and research, which is anchored in the traditions and scientific methods of the social sciences. There are emerging, however, a number of critical alternative approaches to scrutinizing organizations. These perspectives, taken together, present an intellectual challenge to the established knowledge about organizational behavior, and they force discussion of important, but often ignored, organizational problems.

These emergent nontraditional perspectives question both the assumptions and the methods of science. More specifically, they often repudiate the claims of objectivity, causality, rationality, materialistic reality, and the universal rules of inquiry used by the scientific social sciences and substitute subjectivity, indeterminacy, irrationality, illusion, and personal interpretation. Confidence in emotion replaces impartial observation. Relativism is sought rather than objectivity. Fragmentation is preferred to unity, the unique to the regular (Rosenau, 1992). Moreover, as David Clark and his colleagues (1994) note, the alternative views have often been inspired by neo-Marxist approaches that maintain people are active agents in constructing their worlds; knowledge and power are inextricably related; and social structures conceal as much as they reveal.

These challenges and counterassertions supply a countervailing set of forces to traditional organizational science and theory.[3] The alternative views focus attention on important contemporary organization issues—the irrational, the unique, the repressed, the borderline, the rejected, the marginal, the silenced, the decentered, and the powerless. At appropriate points throughout the text, three alternative perspectives—post-modernism (Chapter 3), critical theory (Chapter 6), and feminist theory (Chapter 3)—are used to illustrate some of the challenges to mainline organizational theory. The three have much in common: they overlap in their assumptions; they question contemporary organizational thought; and, to be sure, they are all critical of scientific social analysis.

THEORY INTO PRACTICE

Analyze Your School by Doing the Following:

- Name each person in the school who has formal authority over teachers. What is the role of each? Their titles? How much formal authority do they have and give examples of how they exert it. Describe the division of labor and specialization in the school. Is there a narrow or broad span of control? How fixed or flexible is the curriculum? How much independence do teachers have to make their own decisions?
- Name each person in the organization who has informal power but does not have formal authority. Why does each person have such power? Where do they get their power? Describe the important informal norms that exist in your school. How do the informal and formal leaders get along? Give some examples of their cooperation. What group of teachers is the "in-group"? Does the group have a rival? How do the informal groups get along?
- How much conflict is there between those with formal authority and those with only informal authority? What is the conflict about? Give some examples.
- Which is more important in your school, the formal or the informal organization? Why? What area does each control? Where do you fit into the power relations in your school? What improvements would you try to make to the formal and informal relations in your school if you became the principal? Why?
- Who are the people in your school whose voices have been silenced and why? Are there marginal groups in the school who are not heard or are oppressed? Describe them and their plight. Why have they been silenced?
- Finally, analyze the leadership behavior of your principal. To what extent does she or he rely on the formal organization and informal organization to get things done? What is the balance between the two? Which is more important? From your view is the balance good or could it be improved? How?

Consider the Following Case

Rash Decision?

Imagine that you are the superintendent of the Indianola School District. The town of Indianola is a suburban community 10 miles south of a large midwestern city. The town of 30,000 people has become increasingly more professional and diverse as young professionals have moved into the community to complement the old-time community residents who are mostly blue- and white-collar workers. As you pick up the morning paper, you are startled to find the following account:

An Indianola eighth grader is spending seven days at home on suspension after being accused of assaulting a teacher with a weapon: poison ivy. After classmates reported her, Angela Kim, 14, admitted to her parents and school officials that she had rubbed the plant on the chair of her science teacher, Tom Jones, at Oak Street Middle School. Angela was upset at Jones; she accuses Jones of treating her differently from other students because she is Asian, said her mother, Angie Kim. The family is Korean.

Jones did not develop a rash, but middle school Principal Chris Smith said the district's policy defines a weapon as a gun, knife, dangerous object, or chemical. Principals can suspend students for up to seven days without consulting the central office, and that is precisely what he did last Thursday. "If you do something to hurt someone else and do it on purpose, it's wrong," the principal exclaimed.

THEORY INTO PRACTICE, (Continued)

Angela's father, Hop Kim, is meeting today with the principal to ask that the suspension be reconsidered. Mr. Kim said his daughter complained to him about Jones earlier in the school year. "She said he called her names and treated her differently than he did other kids," Mr. Kim said. "I told her she might have misunderstood him. I tried to blame it on her. I told her to respect her teachers and pay more attention in class and not pay so much attention to personal conflict." But, "Now I am not sure. Maybe the atmosphere of the school is poor. How could the principal suspend my daughter, who is an honor student and who has never been in trouble, without talking to her parents before taking such drastic action?"

Mr. Kim emphasized that he did not seek news media attention, noting that Fred Reiss, a friend of his, called *The News*. Reiss, an Indianola resident and attorney, said the school's punishment is excessive and he urged the Kims to fight the decision. He believes that the punishment is a reaction to incidents around the country, including the shooting deaths at Columbine High School in Colorado.

"This is not going to give any serious credibility to the issue of weapons possession in the schools," Reiss said. "Is someone going to be punished because they're carrying peanuts? Leaves? We need to have any punishment fit the offense."

Family members say Angela gathered the leaves, which were near the school, because the teacher and her classmates were harassing her; in fact, "the teacher was doing nothing to prevent other students from making fun of her. She is a very good kid," Mrs. Kim said. "She is a spelling bee champion in schools. She never made any trouble." She simply lashed out because she thought the teacher insulted her. The parents admit that what she did was wrong, but they say they are worried about her safety and emotional health because this issue has been blown out of proportion. "We moved to Indianola because we believed it would be a good place to raise our children and now we find that the school does not support people who are of a different race or color." Principal Smith admitted that Angela Kim was not a troublesome student, but he is adamant that the offense was serious and warrants a seven-day suspension. "We have zero tolerance for violence in this school," he exclaimed.

When pressed on the charges of teacher and student racism, the principal simply rejected the charges as "groundless fabrications." Angela will get her homework assignments and, according to district policy, will be allowed to make up 60 percent of her work for credit. For his part, Mr. Kim says things are out of control, and he blames the principal and teacher for not setting a good example. "This is America," he says, "everyone should be treated fairly and with respect."

- Should you, as superintendent, get involved?
- Do you need to touch base with the principal before the meeting or "keep your hands off"?
- What implications does this case have for the structure and procedures of the school? For district policy? For the culture of the school? For student-teacher relations?
- Consider the relationship between the news media and the school. Does the press treatment seem fair?
- Could racism be a problem?
- Can the school function as a learning organization, that is, learn from this incident? How?

Summary and Suggested Readings

Theory is not simply idealistic speculation, nor is it "common sense." Because facts do not speak for themselves, a framework is needed to give facts meaning. Organizational theory provides that framework and functions in the same way theory does in the natural sciences and in the other social sciences: it provides an explanatory system connecting otherwise unrelated information. In addition, theory gives direction to empirical research; it may generate new knowledge, and it serves as a rational guide to action as well. Theory is refined through research, and when theory, in the light of research findings, is applied to individual action, it is transformed into practice. Such application is neither simple nor mechanical; it involves an inventive and creative mind.

We trace the history of organizational theory and thought by using three systems perspectives: rational, natural, and open. First, a rational-systems perspective views organizations as formal instruments designed to achieve organizational goals; structure is the most important feature. A natural-systems perspectives views organizations as typical socials groups intent on surviving: people are the most important aspect. Finally, an open-systems perspective is used to combine rational and natural elements in the same framework and provide a more complete perspective.

Our social-systems model calls attention to rational and natural aspects of organizational life. Contemporary theory and research are used to elaborate the components of the model: organizational structure, the individual, climate and culture, politics, teaching and learning, environment, and effectiveness. In addition, key administrative processes are used to influence the interaction among these social system elements. Significant bodies of knowledge inform attempts to decide, communicate, and lead in school organizations. Each of the following chapters considers in substantial detail the major theoretical and research underpinnings of the social-systems model and its administrative processes. Our approach in this text is pragmatic, pluralistic, and empirical: we try to select the best theories (traditional and nontraditional), frameworks, and research that will help administrators understand and explain the complex nature of order and change in organizations.

All students should read two classic analyses of social systems: Getzels and Guba's (1957) treatment of the school as a social system and Katz and Kahn's (1966) pioneering development of open-systems theory. Senge's contemporary work, *The Fifth Discipline* (1990), is a popular and perceptive attempt to use systems thinking to build "learning organizations." Scott's (1992) comprehensive treatment of systems perspectives is difficult, but worth the effort. Finally, Thomas Greenfield and Peter Ribbins (1993) provide a critical analysis of organizational theory in general and social-systems theory in particular.

We recommend several other insightful discussions of the utility of organizational theory for practice and research (DiMaggio, 1995; Sutton and Staw, 1995; Weick, 1995, 1999). Calas and Smircich (1997) present an interesting set of readings on post-modern management theory. The evolution of organizational thought has been treated comprehensively by a number of other scholars (Burrell and Morgan, 1980; Gross and Etzioni, 1985; Scott, 1998;

Clark et al. 1994). Gareth Morgan (1986, 1997) provides a useful alternative and novel way of viewing organizations. He uses metaphors to develop images of organizations that represent important partial truths about them. Contemporary organizational theory, however, is not without its critics (Greenfield and Ribbins, 1993; English, 1994, 1998; Foster, 1986; Maxey, 1995). Finally, for two attempts to map the domain of knowledge in educational administration see Hoy, Astuto, and Forsyth (1994) and Donmoyer, Schurich, and Imber (1994). For a recent historical assessment of the impact of scientific management, read *The One Best Way* (Kanigel, 1997).

There are many journals containing research relevant to educational administration. Two journals in education that link administrative theory and research are the *Educational Administration Quarterly* and the *Journal of Educational Administration. Planning and Changing, The Journal of School Leadership,* and *The Canadian Administrator* are examples of research journals that focus on the application of research and theory to practice in educational administration. Finally, a great many administrative journals publish important papers from all areas of administration; they include such journals as the *Academy of Management Journal, Academy of Management Review, Administrative Science Quarterly, Journal of Management Inquiry, Organizational Behavior and Human Decision Processes, Organizational Science,* and *Personnel Psychology.*

How to Use This Book

Obviously, you will make the final judgment on how best to study this book. We suggest, however, that you seriously consider the following strategy. Each chapter begins with a short summary called the "Preview." You may have a tendency to skip over the preview to get right to the meat of the text. Don't. Take time to study the preview, which is deliberately short and terse. Research on information processing (Reder and Anderson, 1980; Anderson, 1990) suggests that memory for a text is facilitated by the initial study of the key points of the exposition. Hence, the previews are the most important points covered in the book. Each chapter also reinforces the preview with a concluding summary. Check yourself. Make sure that you have mastered the points in the preview and final summary. If you have not, there has been a serious shortcoming in learning. Of course, we hope you will learn more than the general ideas in the summary, but what you learn beyond that will depend on you—your purposes, your interest, and your perseverance.

John R. Anderson (1990), a cognitive psychologist interested in learning theory, elaborates the role of preview summaries in learning. Such summaries have three functions. First, they reflect the general structure of each chapter. If you have mastered the summary, you will know how the major themes and ideas of the chapter relate to each other. Second, preview summaries outline the most important new concepts and ideas. You fix in memory the key points and prepare yourself for how the text will relate, expand, and clarify the ideas. Third, the previews provide criteria against which you can test your mastery of the chapter.

Anderson suggests that to use these previews to greatest advantage, you make up a list of questions, based on the preview, to keep in mind as you read the text. When you finish the chapter, you should be able to answer the questions and elaborate on each issue. The question-generation process should guide your reading and encourage you to think more deeply about the text. The process also encourages you to do some spacing in your study. You might proceed by first studying the main points in the preview and developing your questions. Then skim the entire chapter. Next read each section carefully and then review that section. When you finish, review the whole chapter, making sure that you can answer your guiding questions and that you know the key concepts and ideas introduced in the text. Finally, test yourself to see how well you can apply the concepts and ideas as you grapple with the Theory into Practice exercises at the end of each chapter.

Notes

1. Our model is primarily a synthesis and extension of the work of Getzels and Guba (1957); Abbott (1965b); Leavitt, Dill, and Eyring (1973); Scott (1981, 1987, 1987b); Mintzberg, (1983a); Nadler and Tushman (1983, 1989); Lipham (1988).
2. Many theoretical formulations have proposed such an assumption. For example, see Getzels and Guba (1957); Etzioni (1975); and Nadler and Tushman (1989).
3. For two contrasting views of theory and research in educational administration, see Willower and Forsyth (1999) and Donmoyer (1999).

Key Concepts and Ideas

Assumption
Bureaucratic roles
Cognition
Concept
Congruence postulate
Constitutive definition
Division of labor
Formal organization
Formalization
Generalization
Goal
Hawthorne studies
Hypothesis
Informal organization
Learning organization
Natural-systems perspective
Open-systems perspective
Operational definition
Principle
Principle of homogeneity
Rational-systems perspective
Science
Scientific management
Span of control
Theory
Time and motion studies
Variable

CHAPTER 2

The Technical Core: Learning and Teaching[1]

Knowledge is not a copy of reality. To know an object, to know an event, is not simply to look at it and make a mental copy or image of it. To know an object is to act on it. To know is to modify, to transform the object, and to understand the process of this transformation, and as a consequence to understand the way the object is constructed.

Jean Paiget
Development and Learning

Preview

1. The technical core of all schools is teaching and learning.
2. Learning occurs when experience produces a stable change in someone's knowledge or behavior.
3. There are three general learning perspectives—behavioral, cognitive, and constructivist—each of which helps us understand learning and teaching.
4. Many students confuse negative reinforcement and punishment; reinforcement strengthens behavior, but punishment suppresses or weakens behavior.
5. Learning objectives, mastery learning, and direct instruction (often including review, presentation, guided practice, checks for understanding, and independent practice) are applications of behavioral learning approaches.
6. Cognitive explanations of learning highlight the importance of prior knowledge in focusing attention, making sense of new information, and supporting memory.
7. Information processing is a cognitive theory of memory that describes how information is taken in, processed, stored in long-term memory (in the forms of episodes, productions, images, and schemas), and retrieved.
8. Learning strategies and tactics such as underlining, highlighting, and graphing are applications of the cognitive approach.
9. Constructivist views explain learning in terms of the individual and social construction of knowledge. Knowledge is judged not so much by its accuracy as by its usefulness.
10. There are three varieties of constructivism—rational, dialectical, and radical.

11. Situated learning emphasizes the idea that learning is specific to the situation in which it is learned and difficult to transfer.
12. Features of constructivist applications include complex real-life tasks, social interaction, shared responsibility, multiple representations of content, and student-centered teaching.
13. Three promising applications of the constructivist approach are inquiry or problem-based learning, cognitive apprenticeships, and cooperative learning.

Talcott Parsons (1960) was the first to propose three distinct levels of structure in the organization—the technical, managerial, and institutional. The technical level or **technical core** is the system of organizational activity where the actual "product" of the organization is produced, and in schools is exemplified by the teaching and learning in the classroom. The managerial system, the next level up, is responsible for administering the internal affairs of the organizations and for mediating between the organization and the environment. Finally, at the top is the institutional level, whose function is to connect the organization to the environment, specifically to provide legitimacy for the organization in terms of the larger social context. In the case of schools, the board of education is the chief formal mechanism of the institutional level and its function is to legitimate school activities to the community at large. Parsons (1960) makes the point that there are qualitative breaks in the line-authority relations at each point where the levels come together. Although the managerial level is the primary focus of this book on administration, the other levels are also important because they provide critical points of articulation between the school and its student-clients and the school and its citizen-clients.

Just as the institutional level draws attention to the organizational constraints of the environment (see Chapter 7), the technical level underscores the significance of teaching and learning in administrative decision making. In the case of schools the technical function is the process of teaching and learning, the heart and soul of all educational organizations. We are remiss in the analysis of the school as a social system if we do not examine the technical core of the school—the teaching-learning process—because it shapes many of the administrative decisions that must be made (Rowan, 1998; Rowan, Raudenbush, and Cheong, 1993).

Learning: A Definition

When we hear the word learning, many of us think of ourselves in school studying for an exam or learning how to drive a car or learning a new song or mastering a new computer program. We learn subjects, skills, and appropriate behavior for a host of social situations. Learning is clearly not limited to school, yet in the final analysis that is what school is all about. What is learning? In a broad sense, **learning** *happens when experience produces a stable change in someone's knowledge or behavior.* The change may be intentional or not, but to qualify as learning the change must occur because of experience as the individual interacts with his or her environment. Changes simply due to maturation such as growing taller or getting bald are not instances of learning. Similarly, temporary changes due to illness, fatigue, or short-lived physical deprivations are not part of learning, but of course, people do learn how to cope with such problems.

Our definition of learning indicates that there is a change in the individual's knowledge or behavior. Although most experts on learning would agree with this general proposition, some would tend to emphasis behavior and others knowledge. Our position is that learning is a complex cognitive process and there is no one best explanation of learning. In fact, different theories of learning offer more or less useful explanations depending on what is to be explained. We emphasize three general theories of learning, each with a different focus:

- *Behavioral* theories of learning stress observable changes in behaviors, skills, and habits.
- *Cognitive* theories of learning underscore such internal mental activities as thinking, remembering, creating, and problem solving.
- *Constructivist* theories of learning are interested in how individuals make meaning of events and activities; hence, learning is seen as the construction of knowledge.

The application of each of these theoretical perspectives has different implications for teaching. Thus our discussion of learning will also provide an analysis of teaching.

A Behavioral Perspective On Learning

The modern behavioral approach to learning emerged from the scholarship of Skinner and his followers, who emphasized the importance of antecedents and consequences in changing behavior. The focus of this perspective is clearly on behavior. Learning is defined as a change in behavior brought about by experience with virtually no concern for the mental or internal processes of thinking. Behavior is simply what a person does in a given situation. Think of a behavior as sandwiched between two sets of environmental influences: its antecedents, which precede it, and its consequences, which follow it (Skinner, 1950). This relationship is shown simply as antecedent–behavior–consequence, or A–B–C. As behavior happens, a given consequence transforms into an antecedent for the next ABC sequence. Behavior, then, is altered by changes in antecedents, consequences, or both. Early behavioral work focused on outcomes or consequences.

Consequences

In the behavioral view of learning, consequences of behavior to a great extent determine whether that behavior will be repeated. In particular, the kind and timing of the consequence either will strengthen or weaken the propensity of an individual to repeat behavior. There are two kinds of consequences—those that reinforce behavior and those that punish and weaken behavior.

Reinforcement

The common meaning of reinforcement is reward, but in learning theory reinforcement has a specific connotation. A reinforcer is a consequence that strengthens the behavior that it follows; thus by definition, reinforcement increases the frequency or duration of a given behavior. The following diagram shows the process:

Research demonstrates that food is almost certain to be a strong reinforcer for a hungry animal, but does it work the same way for people? As one would expect, things are more complicated for people. We don't know why an event acts as a reinforcer for an individual; in fact, there are many competing theories that explain why reinforcement works with people. For example, some psychologists believe that reinforcers satisfy needs. Others argue that reinforcers diminish tensions or stimulate a part of the brain (Rachlin, 1991). The extent to which consequences are reinforcing likely depends on the person's perception of the event and the meaning it holds for the individual. For example, students who are routinely sent to the principal's office for misbehaving in class may be getting reinforcement for such behavior. There is probably *something* about this consequence (getting sent to the office) that is reinforcing for them, even if it doesn't seem desirable to their teachers. Perhaps the behavior provides needed attention or produces status among fellow students. Behaviorists would argue that repeated misbehavior is being reinforced in some way for that student.

Let's examine reinforcement more closely. There are two types—positive and negative reinforcement. **Positive reinforcement** occurs when a behavior produces a new stimulus or motivating force. For example, wearing a cool jacket may produce praise and many compliments for the student. Likewise "tripping and falling down" in class may result in laughter. Of course, if this "clumsy role" is played out repeatedly to the laughter and cheers of classmates, teachers are apt to explain the behavior as simply a way "to get attention." This explanation is a behavioral one; teachers are applying the principle of positive reinforcement to explain the behavior by assuming that the attention is a positive reinforcer for the student. Notice that the behavior is reinforced for the student in spite of the fact that it is not positive from the teacher's perspective. Positive reinforcement of inappropriate behavior is a potential problem for all teachers because often teachers unintentionally reinforce misbehavior of students. In brief, when a consequence strengthens a behavior by providing the *addition* of a stimulus, positive reinforcement has occurred.

In contrast, **negative reinforcement** occurs when the consequence that reinforces or strengthens behavior is obtained by eliminating (*subtracting*) a stimulus. When a particular action leads to stopping or avoiding a negative or aversive situation, that behavior is likely to be repeated because the individual has learned how to avoid something negative or uncomfortable. For example, car manufacturers have equipped their cars with seat belts attached to buzzers. Put the key in the ignition and an irritating buzz erupts, which stops as soon as you attach your seat belt. Thus you are likely to repeat the action of "buckling up" (the behavior is reinforced) because it removes the irritation (eliminates a negative stimulus). In other words, a behavior is reinforced or strengthened by removing a negative or aversive stimulus. Consider the parent who is continually complaining about a teacher and insisting the student's teacher be changed. To eliminate the constant complaining you as the principal change the student's teacher. You have eliminated the aversive situation with the parent, and if there are no further negative consequences, you are likely to repeat your behavior to quell other parents' similar complaints. Eliminating a negative stimulus (in this case a nagging parent) has reinforced your behavior. The "negative" in negative reinforcement does not necessarily mean that the behavior being reinforced is bad, but rather negative implies something is being subtracted from the situation that reinforces behavior. Think of positive and negative as associated with numbers—positive reinforcement *adds* something following behavior that reinforces behavior whereas negative reinforcement *subtracts* something following behavior that strengthens that behavior.

Punishment

Negative reinforcement is commonly confused with punishment. If you know the difference, you know more than most people. Reinforcement, whether positive or negative, always involves a strengthening of the behavior. **Punishment** involves weakening or suppressing behavior; that is, behavior followed by punishment is less likely to be repeated in similar situations in the future. Remember, however, that it is the effect of decreasing behavior that defines the consequence as punishment. Different people have different perceptions of what is punishing. Suspension from school is a punishment for some students but not for others. The punishment process is noted simply as follows:

	CONSEQUENCE	EFFECT
Behavior ⟶	Punishment ⟶	Weakened or Decreased Behavior

Like reinforcement, there are two kinds of punishment defined in behavioral theory—Type I and Type II. Neither label is very informative so we call Type I **direct punishment** because it occurs when the appearance of the stimulus following the behavior suppresses or weakens the behavior; something is added to suppress behavior. When teachers assign detention, extra work, and lower grades to punish students, they are assigning direct punishment. The second kind of punishment (Type II) is **removal punishment** because a stimulus is removed to punish. For example, when parents or teachers remove privileges from a student they are engaging in removal punishment;

they are removing something that is desired. Thus direct punishment *adds* something to slow or stop behavior and removal punishment *subtracts or deletes* something to decrease or weaken behavior. The interaction of the processes of reinforcement and punishment is summarized in Figure 2.1.

Antecedents

Antecedents are the events preceding behavior. They provide information about which **b**ehaviors will lead to positive **c**onsequences and which to negative ones (**A**→B→C). Perceptive people learn to discriminate among situations; that is, they learn to read the antecedent. When should a principal request more resources to purchase new curriculum materials, after a budget defeat or after a positive story in the local newspaper about your school? The antecedent cue of the principal standing in the hall helps students discriminate the probable consequences of "running in the hall" or perhaps even "sneaking a smoke" in the boys lavatory. People react to such antecedent cues without fully thinking about the process and how their behavior is influenced. Nevertheless, antecedents in the form of cues can be deliberately used.

Cueing is providing an antecedent stimulus just prior to a particular behavior. It is especially useful in preparing for a behavior that must occur at a specific time but is easily forgotten. Cueing furnishes information about which behaviors will be reinforced or punished in a particular situation. A police car sitting under an overpass or simply along the highway provides an instantaneous cue about the consequences of speeding.

Teachers and principals often correct students after the fact. For example, they exclaim, "I cannot believe that you. . . ." The problem is, of course,

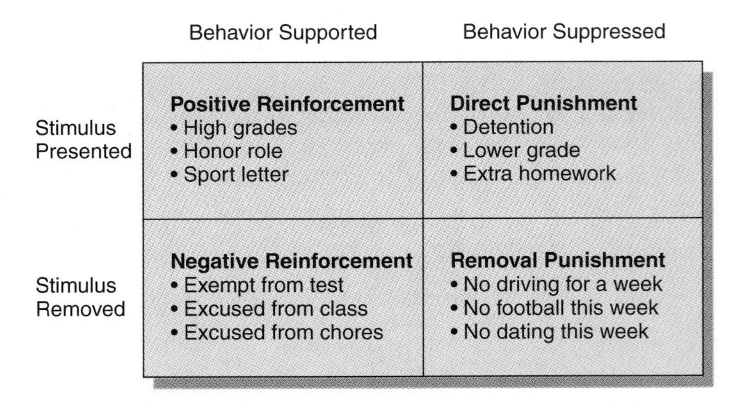

Reinforcement and punishment are often confused.

Remember:
Reinforcement always encourages or strengthens behavior.
Punishment suppresses or weakens behavior.

FIGURE 2.1 *Kinds of Reinforcement and Punishment*

that the misbehavior has already occurred. The student has only a few choices—to promise not to do it again or to try harder or the more aggressive response, "Leave me alone." None of these reactions is particularly useful, but providing a nonjudgmental cue can help avoid a negative confrontation with the student. For example, for teachers and principals, simply attending an athletic function makes it more unlikely that students will demonstrate poor sportsmanship. Moreover, when students perform appropriately after such a cue, teachers can reinforce student behavior without resorting to punishment.

Prompting is providing an additional cue following the first cue. Sometimes people need extra help in responding appropriately to a cue. Becker and his colleagues (1975) propose two principles for using cues and prompts:

- Make sure the environmental stimulus that you want to become a cue occurs right before your prompt, so students will learn to respond to the cue, not rely only on the prompt.
- Fade the prompt as soon as possible; don't make students dependent on it.

An example of prompting is providing students with a checklist or a "to do list" when they work in pairs as part of peer tutoring. As students learn the procedures, the checklist gradually is withdrawn. When the students have learned the procedures, no written or oral prompts are necessary. They have learned how to react appropriately to the cue of working in pairs; they have learned how to work in peer tutoring. Teachers should continue to monitor the process, praise good work, and correct mistakes. The teacher's role is now one of coaching students to improve their tutoring skills.

Teaching Applications of the Behavioral Approach

Experienced and expert teachers make good use of behavioral theory. They apply with care and skill the basic principles of reinforcement and punishment in their teaching and classroom management. Before we provide examples of the contributions of behavioral theory to teaching and learning, we summarize some of the guiding principles:

- Give clear and systematic praise, but only if deserved.
- Recognize genuine accomplishments.
- Set standards for praise based on individual abilities and limitations.
- Attribute the student's success to effort and ability to build confidence.
- Recognize positive behavior in ways that students value.
- Give plenty of reinforcement when students tackle new materials or skills.
- Set clear and specific goals so you know what to reinforce.

- Use cues to help establish new behaviors
- Use a variety of reinforcers and let students choose among them.
- Try to structure the situation to use negative reinforcement rather than punishment.
- Adapt the punishment to fit the misbehavior (Woolfolk, 1998).

Learning objectives, mastery learning, and direct instruction are specific examples of the application of behavioral theory to classroom teaching. Such approaches are especially useful when the goal is to learn new behaviors or explicit information and when the learning is sequential or factual.

Learning Objectives

There are many different approaches to writing objectives; however, all assume that the first step is to decide what changes should take place in the student—what is the goal of teaching. An **instructional objective** is a clear and unambiguous description of the teacher's educational aims for students.

Robert Mager has developed perhaps the most influential system for writing behavioral objectives. His idea is that objectives should describe what students will be doing to demonstrate their achievement and how a teacher will know when students are successful (Mager, 1975). According to Mager, a good objective has three parts:

(a) The objective describes the intended student behavior—what must the student do?
(b) The objective lists the conditions under which the behavior will occur—how will this behavior be recognized or tested?
(c) The objective gives the criteria for acceptable performance on the behavior—how well has the student done?

Mager argues that students often teach themselves if they are given such well-stated objectives.

Are objectives useful? They can be, but only under certain conditions. First, objectives are more successful in promoting learning with such loosely structured activities as lectures, films, and research projects. With structured materials such as programmed instruction, objectives seem less useful (Tobias and Duchastel, 1974). Second, if the significance of information is unclear from the learning materials and activities themselves, instructional objectives focus students' attention and thus increase achievement (Duchastel, 1979). When the task, however, is simply getting the gist of a passage or transferring information to a new situation, objectives are less effective. In these situations, it is better to use questions that focus on meaning and to insert the questions right before the passage to be read (Hamilton, 1985).

Today most school districts still require teachers to complete lesson plans that include learning objectives. Good learning objectives, where the objectives and steps are clearly mapped, can be beneficial and enhance learning. Objectives are not only used in classrooms with students; administrators have used them with varying degrees of success. Management by objectives and goal setting (Locke and Latham, 1990) are organizational attempts to use behavioral theory to improve performance. We discuss both in Chapter 4.

When both the objectives and means to achieve them are clear, how might students also go about learning? The mastery learning approach is consistent with behavioral principles.

Mastery Learning

Mastery learning is based on the assumption that given enough time and the proper instruction, most students can master any learning objective (Bloom, 1968; Guskey and Gates, 1986). To use the mastery approach, a teacher must break down what is to be learned into small units of study. Each unit involves mastering several specific objectives. "Mastery" usually means a score of 80 to 90 percent on some kind of assessment. The teacher informs students of the objectives and the criteria of success for each. Students who do not reach the minimum level of mastery or who reach this minimum but want to improve their performance (thus raising their grades) can repeat the unit. When they think they are ready, they take another form of the unit test. The challenge in mastery learning is to provide appropriate help for students who don't achieve success the first time.

Mastery learning is most useful when the focus of instruction is on key concepts or skills that serve as a foundation for subsequent learning. In mathematics, for example, some students will fall farther and farther behind if they move on to more complex procedures before they master elementary ones. If they don't understand fractions, by the time they reach division of fractions, they will be lost. Mastery learning has been successful when students get the extra time and support—especially through corrective instruction outside class or inside class from peer tutors or cooperative learning group members (Kulik, Kulik, and Bangert-Drowns, 1990; Shuell, 1996).

In practice, mastery learning has not erased achievement differences among students, as some proponents have hoped. Left to work at their own pace, some students will learn much more and leave a unit with much better understanding than others. Some will work much harder to take advantage of the learning opportunities, but others will be frustrated instead of encouraged by the chance to recycle (Grabe and Latta, 1981). There are other behavioral approaches more teacher-centered than mastery learning. Direct instruction is one such approach; it works best when the objectives and the paths to success are clear.

Direct Instruction

The direct instruction procedures described in this section fit a specific set of circumstances because they have evolved from a common strand of inquiry. Researchers have elaborated on direct instruction models by comparing teachers whose students learned more than expected with teachers whose students performed at an expected or average level. The researchers focused on existing teaching practices in American classrooms. Effectiveness was usually defined as average improvement in standardized test scores for a whole class or school. Thus the results hold for large groups, but not necessarily for every student in the group. For example, even when the average achievement of a group improves, the achievement of some individuals may decline (Brophy and Good, 1986; Good, 1996; Shuell, 1996).

The direct instruction models described below apply best to the teaching of **basic skills**—clearly structured knowledge and essential skills, such as science facts, mathematics computations, reading vocabulary, and grammar rules (Rosenshine and Stevens, 1986). These skills involve tasks that can be taught step-by-step and tested by standardized tests. One caveat: the teaching approaches described below are not necessarily appropriate for helping students to write creatively, solve complex problems, or mature emotionally.

Psychologists have identified a direct teaching approach consistent with behavioral theory that helps improve student learning. Barak Rosenshine calls this approach **direct instruction** (1979) or explicit teaching (1988), whereas Tom Good (1983) uses the term active teaching for a similar approach. Weinert and Helmke (1995) describe direct instruction as follows:

> (a) The teachers' classroom management is especially effective and the rate of student interruptive behaviors is very low; (b) the teacher maintains a strong academic focus and uses available instructional time intensively to initiate and facilitate students' learning activities; (c) the teacher insures that as many students as possible achieve good learning progress by carefully choosing appropriate tasks, clearly presenting subject-matter information and solution strategies, continuously diagnosing each student's learning progress and learning difficulties, and providing effective help through remedial instruction. (p. 138)

How do teachers transform these admonitions into actions?

Rosenshine's Six Teaching Functions

Rosenshine and his colleagues (Rosenshine, 1988; Rosenshine and Stevens, 1986) have underscored six teaching functions based on the research on effective instruction. They provide a framework for teaching basic skills:

1. *Review and check the previous day's work.* Reteach if necessary.
2. *Present new material.* Teach in small steps, with many examples and nonexamples.
3. *Provide guided practice.* Question students, give practice problems, and listen for misconceptions. Reteach if necessary. Continue guided practice until students answer about 80 percent of the questions correctly.
4. *Give feedback and correctives based on student answers.* Reteach if necessary.
5. *Provide independent practice.* Let students apply the new learning on their own, either in seatwork, cooperative groups, or homework. The success rate during independent practice should be about 95 percent. This means that students must be well prepared for the work by the presentation and guided practice and that assignments must not be

too difficult. The poin[illegible] is for the students to practice until the skills become overlearned [illegible]nd automatic—until the students are confident.

6. *Review weekly and m*[illegible]*thly.* Consolidate learning and include some review items as h[illegible]ework. Test often and reteach material missed on the tests.

These six fun[illegible]s are not steps to be blindly followed, but they are all elements of effe[illegible]nstruction. For example, feedback, review, or reteaching should occ[illegible]enever necessary and should match the abilities of the students. Th[illegible] a number of models of direct instruction, but most share the elemen[illegible]nted above. Hunter's Mastery Teaching approach (1982) and Goo[illegible]ws and Ebmeier's Missouri Math (1983) are other examples of dire[illegible]tion.

[illegible] *of Direct Instruction*

[illegible]e that direct instruction is limited to lower-level objectives, based [illegible]nal teaching methods, ignores innovative models, and discourages independent thought and action. Some critics go so far as to claim [illegible]ect instruction is based on the *wrong* theory of learning. Teachers [illegible] material into small segments, present each segment clearly, and rein[illegible] or correct mistakes, thus *transmitting* accurate understandings from [illegible]her to student. According to these critics, the student is seen as an "empty [illegible]ssel" waiting to be filled with knowledge rather than an active constructor of knowledge (Anderson, 1989a; Berg and Clough, 1991).

But there is ample evidence that direct instruction can help students learn actively, not passively. Particularly for younger and less experienced learners, student learning without teacher direction and instruction can lead to systematic deficits in the students' knowledge. Without guidance the understandings that students construct are sometimes incomplete and misleading (Weinert and Helmke, 1995). Deep understanding and fluid performance—whether in dance or mathematical problem solving or reading—require models of expert performance and extensive practice with feedback (Anderson, Reder, and Simon, 1995). Guided and independent practices with constructive feedback are keys to the direct instruction model. When specific skills and behaviors need to be learned, a teaching approach consistent with behavioral learning theory makes a lot of sense.

A Cognitive Perspective on Learning

The cognitive perspective traces its beginning roots back to the ancient Greek philosophers, who discussed the nature of knowledge, the value of reason, and the contents of the mind (Hernshaw, 1987); however, cognitive science was dormant as behaviorism flourished in the early and middle 1900s. By the end of the Second World War, however, cognitive research emerged as the computer revolution and breakthroughs in understanding language developed. Evidence accumulated that people do more than simply respond to reinforcement and punishment. For example, individuals plan their responses, use systems to help them remember, and organize their materials in meaningful and unique ways (Miller, Galanter, and Pribram, 1960; Shuell, 1986). With the growing realization that learning is an active mental process, educational psychologists became intrigued with how people think, learn concepts, and solve problems (e.g., Ausubel, 1963; Bruner, Goodnow, and Austin, 1956).

Interest in concept learning and problem solving soo[illegible] way to the puzzle of how knowledge was represented and recalled. R[illegible]ering and forgetting were major topics of study in cognitive psycholo[illegible] 1970s and 80s. The information-processing model of memory domin[illegible] research in cognitive science. Today, there are other models of memory in[illegible] to information processing, and many cognitive theorists have a rene[illegible] interest in learning, thinking, and problem solving.

Knowledge and Learning

Current cognitive approaches suggest that one of the most important elements in the learning process is what the individual brings to the learning situation. What we already know determines in large part what we will pay attention to, perceive, learn, remember, and forget (Alexander, 1996; Greeno, Collins, and Resnick, 1996; Resnick, 1981; Shuell, 1986). Pat Alexander (1996) explains that what we already know—our existing knowledge base—"is a scaffold that supports the construction of all future learning" (p. 31). Thus knowledge is both a means and an end, more than the product of previous learning; it also guides new learning.

Recht and Leslie (1988) show the significance of knowledge in understanding and remembering new information. In their study, they identified junior high school students who were either very good or very poor readers, and tested them on their knowledge of baseball. Knowledge of baseball was not related to reading ability. Next, they identified four groups of students: good readers/high baseball knowledge, good readers/low baseball knowledge, poor readers/high baseball knowledge, and poor readers/low baseball knowledge. All the students read a passage describing a baseball game and were tested in a number of ways to see if they understood and remembered what they had read.

The results demonstrated the power of knowledge as a scaffold for new learning. Poor readers who knew baseball remembered more than good readers with little baseball knowledge and almost as much as good readers who knew baseball. Poor readers who knew little about baseball remembered the least of what they had read. A good basis of knowledge can be more important than good learning strategies in understanding and remembering—but extensive knowledge plus good strategy is even better.

In the cognitive perspective, "knowledge emphasizes understanding of concepts and theories in different subject matter domains and general cognitive abilities, such as reasoning, planning, solving problems, and comprehending language" (Greeno, Collins, and Resnick, 1996, p. 16). Thus there are different kinds of knowledge—general and domain-specific:

- **General knowledge** applies to a variety of situations. For example, general knowledge about how to read or use a word processor is useful in many situations.
- **Domain-specific knowledge** relates to a particular task or subject. For example, knowing there are nine innings in a game is specific to the domain of baseball.

Another way of categorizing knowledge is as declarative, procedural, or conditional (Paris and Cunningham, 1996; Paris, Lipson, and Wixson, 1983).

Another common way to categorize knowledge is as:

- **Declarative knowledge** is "knowledge that can be declared, usually in words, through lectures, books, writing, verbal exchange, Braille, sign language, mathematical notation, and so on" (Farnaham-Diggory, 1994: 468).
- **Procedural knowledge** is "knowing how" to do something such as divide fractions or overhaul an air conditioner—procedural knowledge is demonstrated.
- **Conditional knowledge** is "knowing when and why" to apply declarative and procedural knowledge.

Declarative knowledge is "knowing that" something is the case. The range of declarative knowledge is broad. You can know very specific facts (the average brain has over one hundred billion neurons), or generalities (some trees lose their leaves in autumn), or personal preferences (I hate peas), or personal events (what happened on my first date), or rules (to add fractions, convert each fraction so they have the same denominator and then add the numerators and maintain the common denominator). Small units of declarative knowledge are often organized into larger units; for example, principles of reinforcement and punishment can be organized into a theory of behavioral learning (Gagné, Yekovich, and Yekovich, 1993).

Repeating the rule to add fractions shows declarative knowledge—the student can state the rule, but to show procedural knowledge, the student must demonstrate the knowledge. When faced with fractions to add, the student must perform the procedures correctly. Students or teachers demonstrate procedural knowledge when they solve an equation or correctly translate a French passage.

Conditional knowledge is "knowing when and why" to apply your declarative and procedural knowledge. In many kinds of math problems, it takes conditional knowledge to know *when* to apply one formula rather than another, for example, when to compute area and when to get the volume. It takes conditional knowledge to know when to read a text carefully and when to skim. Conditional knowledge is a stumbling block because it requires correct use of both facts and procedures. Often students know the facts and can do the procedures, but don't apply them at the appropriate time. Table 2.1

TABLE 2.1

Six Kinds of Knowledge and Examples

	General Knowledge	Domain-Specific Knowledge
Declarative	Hours the bank is open. Highway safety rules.	Lines from Shakespeare's "Hamlet." Definition of educational leadership.
Procedural	How to use a computer. How to drive a car.	How to solve a quadratic equation. How to progam in C++.
Conditional	When to abandon one approach and try another. When to skim and when to read carefully.	When to use the formula for volume. When to run to the net in tennis.

summarizes and combines our two systems for describing knowledge. To use knowledge, you must remember it. But how do people remember? What do we know about memory?

Information-Processing Model

The information-processing model is one cognitive perspective of the structure and processes of memory. The model is based on the analogy between the mind and the computer; it includes three storage systems: the sensory memory, working (also called short-term) memory, and long-term memory.

- **Sensory memory** is a holding system that maintains stimuli briefly so that perceptual analysis can occur (Bruning, Schraw, and Ronning, 1995).
- **Working memory,** or short-term memory, holds from five to nine bits of information at a time for up to about 20 seconds, which is long enough for processing to occur. Information is encoded and perceptions determine what will be held in working memory.
- **Long-term memory** stores huge amounts of information for long periods of time. Information may be coded verbally or visually or both.

In long-term memory, some information is stored and interrelated in terms of images and schemas—data structures that allow us to represent large amounts of complex information, make inferences, and understand new information.

Information is retrieved from long-term memory by activation; that is, one memory activates other related information. Think about how one memory triggers another as you think about something. Remembering is recon-

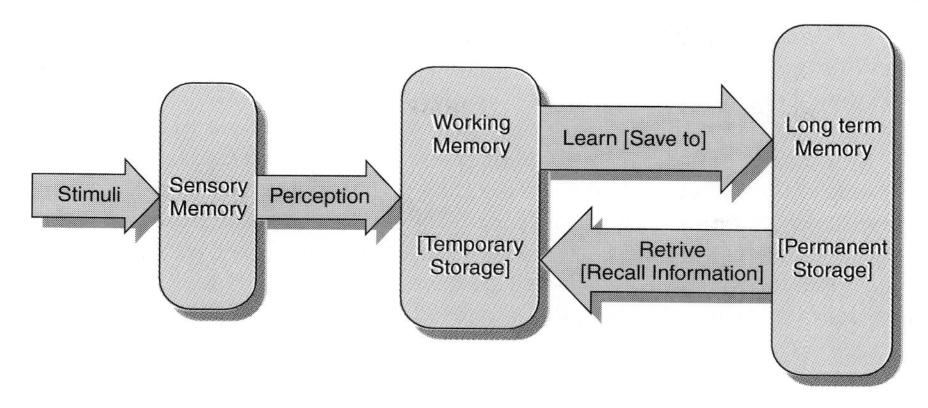

FIGURE 2.2 *Information Processing System*

structing, which leads to accurate, partly accurate, or inaccurate recall. Accurate retrieval depends in part on how the information was learned to begin with. Figure 2.2 is a pictorial summary of an information-processing system. Let's look at this system in more depth.

Sensory Memory

Sensory memory is the initial system that briefly holds stimuli so that perceptional analysis can occur. The meaning we give to the basic information received through our senses is called **perception.** Meaning is constructed from both objective reality and our existing knowledge. For example, consider the symbol I. If asked what the letter is, you would say "I." If asked what the number is, you would say one. The actual mark remains the same; the perception of it—its meaning—changes with the context and your expectation to recognize either a number or a letter. To a child without the knowledge to perceive a number or a letter, the mark is probably meaningless (Smith, 1975). To recognize patterns rapidly as well as to note specific features, we use existing knowledge about the situation to make meaning.

If all variations in color, movement, sound, smell, temperature, and so on had to be perceived simultaneously, life would be impossible. Thus, we pay attention to some stimuli and ignore others; we select from all the possibilities what we will process. But attention is a limited resource because we can pay attention to only one demanding task at time (Anderson, 1995). For example, when you first learned to drive a car, especially if it were a stick shift, there probably was a time when you couldn't both listen to the radio and drive. After practice, however, you could listen to and enjoy it and drive without difficulty, but you might turn off the radio when traffic is heavy. Many processes that initially require attention and concentration become automatic with practice. Automaticity, however, is a matter of degree—we are not completely automatic but rather more or less automatic in our performances depending on how much practice we have had (Anderson, 1995). When full attention is critical, we must block out other stimuli.

Attention is the first step in learning. Students cannot process what they don't recognize or perceive. Many factors in the classroom influence student attention. Dramatic displays or actions can draw attention at the beginning of a lesson. A teacher might begin a science lesson on air pressure by pumping the air out of a gallon can until it collapses. Bright colors, underlining, highlighting of written or spoken words, calling on students at random, surprising students, asking puzzling questions, posing challenging dilemmas, changing tasks and teaching methods, as well as changes in voice level, lighting, or pacing can all help get the attention of students. But gaining student attention is only half the battle—keeping them focused and on task is also critical.

Working Memory

Once a stimulus has been registered and transformed into patterns of images or sounds, the information in sensory memory is available for further processing. Working memory is where this new information is held briefly and combined with knowledge from long-term memory. Working memory is sometimes called short-term memory, but as information models have shifted from emphasis storage to processing, the term "working memory" has replaced "short-term memory." Working memory in some ways resembles the screen of a computer—its content is activated information—what you are thinking about at the moment, your consciousness.

Capacity and Contents

Working memory capacity is limited. In experimental situations, the capacity of working memory is only about five to nine separate new items (chunks of meaningful information) at once (Miller, 1956). For example, when you get a phone number from information, you can usually remember it long enough to dial the number. Get two new phone numbers (14 digits) and most of us are in trouble. We simply cannot recall this much *new* information because we cannot hold it in working memory. In everyday activity we hold more than nine bits of information at once. While you are dialing that seven-digit phone number you just looked up, you are have other things "on your mind"—in your memory—such as who you are calling and why. You don't have to pay attention to these things because they are not new knowledge; in fact, some of the processes, like dialing, have become automatic. But imagine that you are in a foreign country and are trying to use an unfamiliar telephone system, you may have trouble remembering the phone number because you were trying to figure out the phone system at the same time.

Some theorists argue that working memory is limited not by the number of bits of information it can store, but rather by the amount of information we can rehearse (repeat to ourselves) in about 1.5 seconds (Baddeley, 1986). The seven-digit telephone number fits this limitation. Recent theories, however, suggest that there are actually two working memory systems—one for language-based information and another for nonverbal, spatial, visual information (Baddeley, 1986; Jurden, 1995). One thing is clear: the duration of information is short in working memory, about 5 to 20 seconds. You may think that a memory system with a 20-second time limit is not useful. Think again. Without this short-term memory, you would have already forgotten what you read in the first part of this sentence before you came to these last few words. Understanding sentences would be difficult to say the least.

Retaining Information in Working Memory

Working memory is fragile. It must be kept activated or the information will be lost. To keep information activated in working memory for longer than 20 seconds, most people need to engage in specific remembering strategies. Rehearsal is one option.

There are two types of **rehearsal** (Craik and Lockhart, 1972) strategies—maintenance and elaborative rehearsal. Maintenance rehearsal is repeating the information in your mind. As long as you repeat the information, it can be maintained in working memory. Such rehearsal is useful for retaining something, like a phone number that you plan to use and then forget. Elaborative rehearsal is associating the information you are trying to remember with something you already know—information from long-term memory. For example, if you meet a parent whose name is the same as your assistant principal's, you don't have to repeat the name to keep it in memory, you just have to make the correct association. Elaborative rehearsal not only improves working memory, but it helps move information from short-term to long-term memory.

A strategy of **chunking** can be used to overcome the limited capacity of working memory. The number of bits of information, not the size of each bit, is the limitation for working memory. You can retain more information if you can group or chunk individual bits of information into meaningful units. For example, if you have to remember the six digits 1, 5, 1, 8, 2, and 0, it is easier to put them together into three chunks of two digits each (15, 18, 20) or two chunks (151, 820). If you can make these changes, then there are only two or three chunks of information to hold at one time rather than six.

Long-Term Memory

Working memory holds the information that is temporarily activated, such as a telephone number you have been given to dial. Long-term memory holds the information that you have learned, for example, telephone numbers you already know.

Capacity and Duration of Long-Term Memory

Information enters working memory very quickly, but to store it in long-term memory (remember it) requires some effort. Whereas the capacity of working memory is limited, the capacity of long-term memory is virtually unlimited. Most of us never approach our capacity of long-term memory, and once information is securely stored in long-term memory, it can remain there indefinitely. Theoretically, although we should be able to remember as much as we want for as long as we want, the challenge is recall, that is, finding the right information when we want it. Access to information requires time and effort because we have to search the vast amount of information in long-term memory, and the less information is used, the harder it is to find.

Contents of Long-Term Memory

Most cognitive theorists distinguish among three kinds of long-term memory: episodic, procedural, and semantic. Memory about information associated with a particular place and time, especially personal memories about the events of your own life, is called *episodic memory.* Episodic memory keeps things ordered; it is where details of a conversation as well as jokes, gossip, or plots from films are stored. Memory for how to do things is called *procedural memory.* It may take a while to learn a procedure—such as how to do a school budget, hit a golf ball, or conduct a school board meeting—but once learned, this knowledge is remembered for a long time. Procedural memories are represented as conditional statements such as, if A occurs, then do B. For example, "If I want to lower resistance to an innovation, involve participants in making decisions," or "To improve student achievement, focus on the academic task." People can't necessarily state all their conditional rules, but they act on them nonetheless. The more practiced the procedure, the more automatic the action (Anderson, 1995). *Semantic memory* is memory for meaning; it is the memory of general concepts, principles, and their associations. Two important ways that semantic memories are stored are images and schemas. Let's examine each.

Images are representations based on visual perceptions—on the structure or appearance of the information (Anderson, 1995). As we form images, we try to remember or recreate the physical characteristics and spatial structure of information. For example, when asked how many windows are in a given school, most people call up an image of the school "in their mind's eye" and count the number of windows (Mendell, 1971). Images are useful in making many practical decisions such as how a desk might look in your office or how to drive to the next school. Images may also be helpful in abstract reasoning. Physicists, such as Feynman and Einstein, report creating images to reason about complex new problems (Gagné, Yekovich, and Yekovich, 1993; Feynman, 1985).

Schemas (sometimes called schemata) are abstract knowledge structures that organize large amounts of information. A schema is a pattern or guide for understanding an event, a concept, or a skill. My simplified schema for reinforcement is summarized in Figure 2.3; it is a partial representation of knowledge about reinforcement; it tells you what features are typical of a category, what to expect. A schema is a pattern, specifying the "standard" relationships in an object or situation. The pattern has "slots" that are filled with specific information as we apply the schema in a particular situation. Schemas are individual. For example, a teacher and a principal may have very different schemas about shared decision making—who makes what

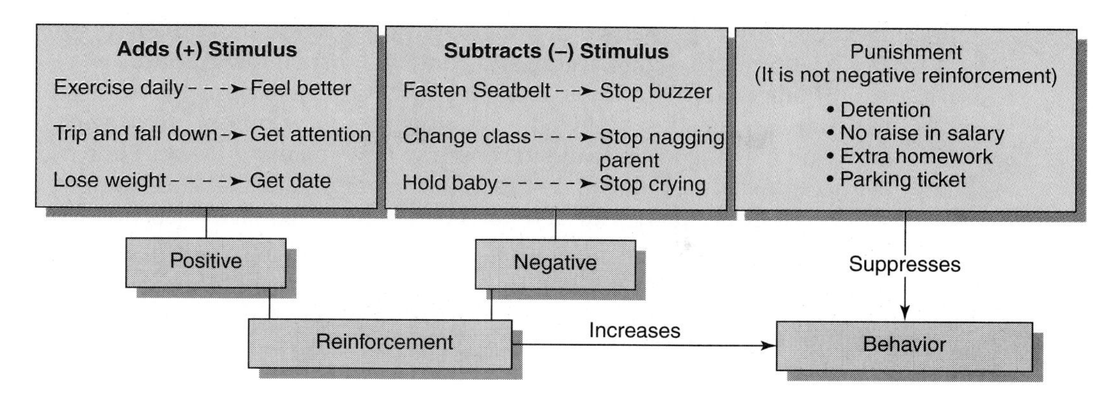

FIGURE 2.3 *Simple Schema for Reinforcement*

school decisions and when, where, and how. In Chapter 9, we have produced an idealized schema for participation in decision making (Figure 9.5); it specifies, when to involve teachers, how to involve them for each situation, the structure of the process, and the various roles of the principal depending on the situation.

Another type of schema is a "story grammar" or "story structure," which helps people understand and remember stories (Gagné, Yekovich, and Yekovich, 1993; Rumelhart and Ortony, 1977). A story grammar is something like the following: vandalism discovered (mystery), search for clues, eyewitness is found, confrontation of guilty student by eyewitness account, student confesses—mystery is solved! In other words, a story grammar is a general structure that could fit many specific stories. To understand a story, we select an appropriate schema. We use this framework to decide what is important, which details and what information we need to remember. The schema is a proposed explanation about what should occur in the story. It guides us in understanding the text by highlighting the specific information we expect to find to make sense of the story. If we activate our "vandalism mystery schema" we are alert for clues or an eyewitness (Resnick, 1981). Without a good schema, trying to understand a novel, textbook, or a even a lecture is an arduous process, akin to trying to find your way in unfamiliar place without a map. A schema representing the typical sequence of events in an everyday life, such as eating at a restaurant, is called a script, and children as young as 3 have basic scripts for the familiar events in their lives (Nelson, 1996).

Storing and Retrieving Information in Long-Term Memory

How do people "save" information permanently, that is, create semantic, episodic, or procedural memories? How can we make the most effective use of our virtually unlimited capacity to learn and remember? Your initial learning—the way you process it at the outset—seems to affect its recall. If you integrate new material with information already stored in long-term memory as you construct an understanding, you are more likely to remember. Elaboration, organization, and context aid such integration.

Elaboration is adding meaning to new information by connecting it with already existing knowledge. In other words, we apply our schemas and draw on existing knowledge to construct new meaning as we refine our existing knowledge. Often elaboration occurs automatically. For example, new information about a prior experience of a teacher activates our existing knowledge about that teacher and provides a better and more complete understanding of the teacher.

Information that is elaborated when first learned is easier to recall because it is a form of rehearsal that keeps the material activated in working memory long enough to improve the likelihood of permanent storage in long-term memory. Moreover, elaboration builds extra links to existing knowledge. The more one chunk of information is associated with others, the more routes there are to follow to get to the original chunk. Put simply, you have several "handles" or retrieval cues to recognize or "pick up" the information you might be seeking (Schunk, 1996a). The more individuals elaborate new ideas, the more they "make them their own," and the better their understanding memory for the knowledge. We try to help students elaborate by asking them to put information into their own words and creating examples. Of course, if students elaborate new information by making incorrect connections and developing misguided explanations, unfortunately these misconceptions will be stored and remembered too.

Organization also improves learning. Well-organized material is easier to learn and remember than unorganized bits and pieces, especially when the information is complex. Putting concepts in a structure helps you learn and remember both general definitions and specific examples. Structure serves as a guide back to the information when you need it. For example, knowing the basic dimensions of power helps us remember the key aspects of power relationships as well as specific examples of each.

Context is another element of processing that influences learning. The physical and emotional aspects of context—places, how we feel on a particular day, who is with us—are learned along with other information. When you try to remember the information, it helps if the current context is similar to the original one. So studying for a test under "testlike" conditions may result in improved performance. Of course, you can't always go back to the same place you learned something but if you can picture the setting, the time of day, and your companions, you can often prod your memory.

Craik and Lockhart (1972) suggest that the length of time information is remembered is determined by how the information is analyzed and integrated with other information; the more completely information is processed, the better our chances of remembering it. For example, if you are asked to sort pictures of dogs based on the color of their coats, you might not remember many of the pictures later, but if asked to determine how likely each dog is to chase you as you jog, you are likely to remember more of the pictures because you will pay attention to details in the pictures, relate features of the dogs to characteristics associated with danger, and so on.

Retrieving Information from Long-Term Memory

When we need information from long-term memory, we search for it. Sometimes the search is conscious, as when you see a familiar face and search for the name, and other times it is automatic, as when you dial a telephone. Think of long-term memory as a huge shed full of tools and supplies ready to be used when needed. Because the shed (long-term memory) is so large and full, it is often difficult to find what you need. The workbench (working memory) is small, but everything is ready for immediate use. But the workbench can get cluttered and supplies (chunks of information) can be lost, fall off, or get covered as one bit of information interferes with another (Gagné, 1985).

Even though the long-term memory network is huge, only a small area can be activated at a given time—the information you are currently using in working memory. Information is retrieved in this network by the spread of activation. When we are thinking about a particular concept, other related knowledge often is activated as well, and the activation spreads through the network (Anderson, 1993; Gagné, Yekovich, and Yekovich, 1993). For example, if you think, "I need to give Susan a makeup exam today," related ideas such as, "I need to change some questions on the test," and "I need to warm up the car before I leave for school," come to mind. As activation spreads from the "makeup" to "warming the car," the original thought disappears from working memory because of the limited space.

In long-term memory the information is still available, even though you are not thinking about it. If spreading activation does not "find" the needed information, then we might still be able to reconstruct it by using logic, cues, and other knowledge to fill in the missing parts. Unfortunately, sometimes-reconstructed recollections are incorrect. For example, in 1932, F. C. Bartlett conducted a series of famous studies on remembering stories. He read a complex, unfamiliar Native American tale to students at England's Cambridge University. After various lengths of time, he asked students to recall the story. The recalled stories were generally shorter and were reconstructed into the concepts and language of their culture. For example, many students remembered the story of a seal hunt as a "fishing trip," which was more consistent with their experience and schemas.

Forgetting and Long-Term Memory

Information lost from working memory truly disappears; you cannot bring it back. But lost information in long-term memory sometimes can be found with the right cues. Until recently many psychologists believed that nothing was ever lost from long-term memory. Recent research, however, casts doubts on this belief (Schwartz and Reisberg, 1991). Apparently, information can be lost from long-term memory through two processes: time decay and interference. For example, consider this interesting research finding. Memory for Spanish-English vocabulary decreases for about three years after a person's last course in Spanish, then stays level for about 25 years, then drops again for the next 25 years. Neural connections, like muscles, may grow weak without use (Anderson, 1995). In addition, newer memories may interfere, replace, or obscure older memories, and older memories may interfere with memory for new material.

Nevertheless, long-term memory is remarkable. After a comprehensive analysis of the research, Semb and Ellis (1994) concluded that, "contrary to popular belief, students retain much of the knowledge taught in the classroom" (p. 279). Teaching strategies that encourage student engagement and lead to higher levels of initial learning (such as frequent reviews and tests, elaborated feedback, high standards, mastery learning, and active involvement in learning projects) are associated with longer retention.

Metacognition, Regulation, and Individual Differences

Why do some people learn and remember more than others? For those who hold an information-processing view, part of the answer lies in how the information is processed. We have already discussed maintenance rehearsal, elaborative rehearsal, organization, and elaboration. These processes are sometimes called **metacognitive skills,** because the processes can be intentionally used to regulate cognition.

Metacognition and Regulation

Metacognition is an individual's awareness of his or her own cognitive processing and how it works (Meichenbaum, Burland, Gruson, and Cameron, 1985). Individuals use their own knowledge to monitor and regulate their cognitive processes, that is their reasoning, comprehension, problem solving, learning, and so on. Because people differ in their metacognitive knowledge and skills, they also differ in how efficiently they learn (Brown, Branford, Ferrara, and Campione, 1983; Morris, 1990).

Planning, monitoring, and evaluation are three crucial cognitive skills (Brown, 1987; Nelson, 1996). Planning is deciding how much time to give to a task, what strategies to use, how to begin, what to gather, what order to follow, what to skim, what to focus on, and so on. Monitoring is the awareness of how I'm doing. Is this making sense? Am I trying to go too fast? Do I have it yet? Evaluation is making judgments about the outcomes of thinking and learning. Should I change strategies? Get help? Give up for now? Is this report (proposal, budget, formula, model, action plan, supervisory report, etc.) finished or does it need more work? Many planning, monitoring, and evaluation processes are not conscious, especially among adults and experts. They become automatic; in fact, experts often have difficulty explaining their own processing (Schraw and Moshman, 1995).

Individual Differences in Metacognition

Some differences in metacognitive abilities are due to development. As children grow older they are more able to exercise control and use strategies. They know when they have understood instructions (Markman, 1977, 1979) or have studied long enough to remember a set of items (Flavell, Friedrichs, and Hoyt, 1970). Older children automatically use more efficient techniques for memorizing information than younger children. Metacognitive skills begin to develop around ages 5 to 7 and improve throughout school, but most children go through a transitional period when they can apply a particular strategy if reminded but not on their own (Flavell, 1985; Flavell, Greene, and Flavell, 1995; Garner, 1990).

Not all differences in metacognitive abilities can be explained by age or maturation. Some individual differences are caused by biology or by different learning experiences. Students vary greatly in their ability to attend to information in their environment; in fact, many students diagnosed as learning disabled actually have attention disorders (Hallahan and Kauffman, 1997). Attention is also influenced by such individual and cultural differences as learning abilities and preferences, cognitive styles, and cultural background. For example, students who are field dependent have difficulty perceiving elements in a pattern and tend to focus on the whole. Although there is great variability even among students of the same developmental level, many of these differences do not appear to be related to intellectual abilities; in fact, superior metacognitive skills can compensate for lower levels of ability (Swanson, 1990). Fortunately, metacognitive skills can be taught; thus they are an important basis of teaching.

Teaching Applications Of The Cognitive Approach

Just as experienced and expert teachers make good use of behavioral theory, they also incorporate sound cognitive approaches in their teaching. Before we provide examples of the contributions of cognitive theory to teaching and learning, we summarize some of the guiding principles:

- Perception and attention are flexible, but limited.
- Make sure that you have the student's attention.
- Perception and attention are guided by previous knowledge.
- Help students focus on the most important information.
- Help students make connections between new information and what they already know.
- Resources and data limitations restrain learning.
- Help students organize information in meaningful chunks.
- Provide students with opportunities to use both verbal stories and visual images.
- Provide review and repetition of information.
- Present information in an organized and clear fashion.
- Focus on meaning, not memorization.
- Make sure that students have the needed declarative knowledge to understand new information.
- Students should learn to manage their resources, know their own cognitive skills, use them deliberately, monitor comprehension—that is, become self-regulated. (Bruning, Schraw, and Ronning, 1995; Woolfolk, 1998).

Some of the most important applications of cognitive theories are teaching students how to learn and remember by using learning tactics and strategies. Learning strategies are general plans for accomplishing learning goals, an overall plan of attack, whereas tactics are more specific techniques that make up the plan (Derry, 1989). For example, if you are reading this chapter, your overall strategy for learning the material might include the tactics of using mnemonics to remember key terms, skimming the chapter to identify the organization, and then writing sample answers to possible essay questions. Let's examine some useful strategies—underlining, highlighting, note taking, visual mappings, and mnemonics—in more detail.

Underlining or Highlighting

If you are like most people, you underline or highlight key phrases in textbooks. Are the words turning yellow or pink at this very moment? Do you outline or take notes? Underlining and highlighting are probably two of the most commonly used strategies among graduate students. Few students, however, know the best ways to underline or highlight, so it is not surprising that many use ineffective strategies. How many times have you looked down to see virtually the entire page highlighted?

Most students underline or highlight much too much. Less is often better and selectivity is crucial. In studies that limit how much students can underline (e.g., to only one sentence per paragraph) learning has improved (Snowman, 1984). In addition to being selective, it helps if you actively transform the information into your own words as you underline or take notes. Don't rely on the words of the book. Think of connections between what you are reading and other things you know. Draw diagrams and pictures to illustrate relationships. Diagrams help you find the missing gaps as well as synthesize what you are trying to learn. Finally, look for organization in the material and use the patterns to guide your underlining (Irwin, 1991; Kiewra, 1988).

Taking Notes

As you sit in class, taking notes, frenetically trying to keep up with your professor, you may wonder if any of it matters. The answer is yes because taking notes has at least two important functions. First, note taking focuses attention and helps encode information so it has a better chance of making it into long-term memory. When you record the key ideas in your own words—translate, connect, elaborate and organize—it helps you process deeply. Even if students don't review their notes before a test, just taking notes appears to aid learning. Like many things, note taking is a skill that requires practice. Students, for example, must be careful that taking notes does not detract from listening and making sense of the presentation. (Kiewra, 1989; Van Metter, Yokoi, and Pressley, 1994). Second, notes provide a "permanent" record that permits students to return and review. Students who use their notes to study tend to perform better on tests, especially if they take notes that capture key ideas, concepts, and relationships (Kiewra, 1985, 1989).

Research (Van Metter, Yokoi, and Pressley, 1994) demonstrates that understanding is best when students use note taking to underscore important ideas. As a course progresses, skillful students match notes to their anticipated use. In addition, they make modifications in strategies after tests or assignments, use personal codes to flag difficult material, fill in gaps by consulting other sources (including classmates), and record information verbatim only when required. In general, successful students are strategic about taking and using notes.

Visual Tools

Effective use of underlining and note taking requires an understanding of the structure and organization of the material to be learned. Visual mapping strategies are useful in this regard. Creating graphic organizers such as concept maps, diagrams, or charts is more effective than simply outlining the text (Robinson and Kiewra, 1995). For example, Armbruster and Anderson (1981) taught students specific techniques for diagramming relationships among ideas presented in a text and found that they improved learning. Mapping relationships by noting causal connections, making comparisons and contrasts, and providing examples improves recall. For instance, it is helpful when students compare one another's "maps" and discuss the differences. Other useful techniques are Venn diagrams, which show how ideas or concepts overlap, and tree diagrams, which demonstrate how ideas branch from each other. Tree diagrams are especially useful, for example, in developing decision-making strategies (see Chapter 9).

Mnemonics

Mnemonics are systematic procedures for improving memory. Many mnemonic strategies use imagery (Levin, 1985; McCormick and Levin, 1987). For example, to remember a grocery list, you might visualize each item in an especially memorable place in your house—perhaps a bunch of bananas hanging from a kitchen plant, a quart of milk on top of the refrigerator, a turkey on top of the stove, and so forth. These places are the pegs that help you remember. So every time you have a list to remember, use the same peg (places) but substitute the objects of the new list.

Acronyms help individuals remember information for long periods of time. An acronym is a form of abbreviation—a word formed from the first letter of each word or a phrase, such as AASA, the American Association of School Administrators. POSDCoRB (Planning, Organizing, Staffing, Directing, Coordinating, Reporting, and Budgeting) is an acronym to recall the seven functions of administration. Another method forms phrases or sentences out of the first letter of each word or item in a list. For example, the question, "How do I cause regularity?" is a good prompt to remember the fundamental features of bureaucracy—*H*ierarchy, *D*ivision of labor, *I*mpersonality, *C*areer orientation, and *R*ules and regulations. Another approach is to incorporate all the items to be memorized into a jingle with rhymes, like "i before e except after c" to help spell certain words.

The mnemonic system that has been most extensively applied in teaching is the keyword method. A person trying to remember a foreign word, for example, might first choose an English word, preferably a concrete noun that sounds like the foreign word or a part of it. The second step is to associate the meaning of the foreign word with the English word through an image or sentence. Hence, the Spanish word carta (meaning "letter") sounds like the English word "cart." Cart becomes the keyword: then imagine a shopping cart filled with letters on its way to the post office, or make up a sentence such as "The cart full of letters tipped over" (Pressley, Levin, and Delaney, 1982).

Teaching strategies based on cognitive views of learning, particularly information processing, highlight the importance of attention, organization, rehearsal (practice), and elaboration in learning and provide ways to give students more control over their own learning by developing and improving their own metacognitive learning strategies. The focus is on what is happening "inside the head" of the learner.

A Constructivist Approach To Learning

Cognitive theories such as information processing, conceive of the human mind as a symbol-processing system, which converts sensory information into symbol structures (e.g., images, schemas), then processes those symbol structures so knowledge can be stored in memory and retrieved when needed. Learning is modification of the internal symbol structures. The outside world is a source of information, but the important learning happens "inside the head" of the individual (Schunk, 1996a). Constructivist perspectives challenge such views of learning.

Constructivist theories are grounded in the educational philosophy of John Dewey and the research of Piaget, Vygotsky, and the Gestalt psychologists Bartlett and Bruner, to mention just a few intellectual pioneers. There is no one constructivist theory of learning, but there are constructivist approaches in science and mathematics education, in educational psychology and anthropology, and in computer-based education. Some constructivist views emphasize the shared and social construction of knowledge; others see social forces as less important (Cognition and Technology Group at Vanderbilt, 1991; Driscoll, 1999; Perkins, 1991; Wittrock, 1992).

Types of Constructivism

Today, many educators use the term "constructivism" and not always in the same way. In general, constructivism assumes that people create and construct knowledge rather than internalize it from the external environment, but there are a variety of different approaches to constructivism. We have adapted Moshman's (1982, 1997)) categories to help organize three different approaches, which we call rational, radical, and dialectical constructivism.

Rational Constructivism

Rational constructivism emphasizes the ways individuals reconstruct external reality. They build accurate mental representations using schemas and condition-action rules. Thus learning is building accurate mental structures that reflect "the way things really are" in the external world. Many aspects of information processing are consistent with this view of constructivism; in fact, some scholars treat this brand of constructivism as part of a cognitive perspective, for example, a cognitive/rational view (Greeno, Collins, and Resnick, 1996). This view of constructivism recognizes the superiority of some understandings over others; consequently, direct teaching, feedback, and explanation are seen as appropriate ways to affect learning. Knowledge is acquired by transforming, organizing, and reorganizing previous knowledge.

Piaget's theory is the most typical of this form of constructivism. He proposes a universal sequence of developmental stages, each involving forms of cognition more sophisticated and functional than those at the previous stage (Miller, 1993). Piaget's special concern was with logic and necessary knowledge such as understanding that the set or class must have at least as many members as any of its subsets (Smith, 1993). For example, we cannot determine whether there are more girls or boys in a given school without empirical evidence about their relative numbers, but we can be sure that there are at least as many humans in any school as there are girls, without any empirical evidence. Knowledge about the relation of classes to their subclasses, Piaget argued, is not dependent on knowledge about a particular environment and cannot be learned from those environments. On the contrary, such knowledge is about the essentials inherent in our classification behaviors and is constructed via coordination of and reflection on these behaviors. In brief, rational constructivism sees construction as a rational process generating increasingly warranted outcomes (Moshman, 1997).

Radical Constructivism

Radical constructivism maintains that knowledge is *not* a mirror of the external world in spite of the fact that experience affects thinking and thinking influences knowledge. Knowledge is constructed largely by interpersonal interactions and the constraints of culture and ideology. There is no basis for evaluating or interpreting any belief as any better or any worse than any other. Radical constructivists argue that information processing is trivial constructivism because it does not take the idea of knowledge construction far enough (Derry, 1992; Garrison, 1995).

Radical constructivism has become popular in recent years with the rise of post-modern thought and critique in American education; in fact, it has been called a species of post-modernism (Moshman, 1997). This situation is particularly troubling for those who are concerned about development and education. How can knowledge be meaningfully constructed as a developmental process unless there is some progress in understanding or reasoning? How can efforts to get students to construct knowledge be justified unless there is some reason to believe that the constructed knowledge is an improvement in their understanding (Moshman, 1997)? We agree with those scholars and researchers (Chandler, 1997; Moshman, 1997; Phillips, 1997) who are critical of this perspective. After all, if all ideas and beliefs are equally good, then why bother—we might just as well let students believe whatever they want to believe.

Dialectical Constructivism

Dialectical constructivism is the middle ground, suggesting that knowledge grows through the interactions of internal (cognitive) and external (environmental and social) factors. On the one hand, dialectical constructivism shares little with the radical view except the perspective that knowledge is constructed and that social factors influence those constructions. On the other hand, it departs from a purely rational view because it rejects the Piagetian notion that construction of knowledge must proceed through a rational process to a particular endpoint. Rather, dialectical constructivism is a process in which rationality is intrinsic to the processes of reflection and coordination, not in successive approximations of a particular endpoint. Therefore, it is possible to produce multiple constructions of knowledge, but some constructions are better than others and not all constructions are equally defensible. Knowledge reflects the outside world as filtered through and influenced by culture, language, beliefs, and interactions with others.

Vygotsky's theory as a description of cognitive development through the appropriation, internalization, and use of cultural tools such as language is a good example of dialectical constructivism (Bruning, Schraw, and Ronning, 1995). Vygotsky argues that knowledge is socially constructed, that is, that knowledge is built upon what participants contribute and construct together. Thus, development may proceed differently in different cultural contexts; in other words, learning is situated. This does not mean that all constructions are equally defensible, but it does open the possibility of multiple constructions of reality, with different explanations working differently in different situations. Vygotsky acknowledges the possibility of universals without insisting either that universal knowledge is necessarily more fundamental than context-specific aspects of cognition or that universal sequences are the only true developmental changes. Dialectical constructivism is a pluralist and rational perspective that avoids the extreme relativism of radical constructivists without committing itself to the universalism that has been associated with rational constructivism (Moshman, 1997).

Knowledge: Accuracy Versus Usefulness

Most constructivists believe the world is knowable; there is an external reality "out there," and an individual can learn to understand it. The understanding may be more or less accurate—knowledge constructions may be filled with misconceptions about how the world operates. For example, young children sometimes construct a subtraction procedure that says, "Subtract the smaller number from the larger number, no matter which number in a problem is on top." Rational and dialectical constructivists are concerned with accurate representations of reality.

Radical constructivists, on the other hand, do not assume that the world is knowable. They maintain that all knowledge is constructed and based upon not only prior knowledge but also the cultural and social context. They argue that what is true in one time and place—such as the "fact" before Columbus's time that the earth was flat—becomes false in another time and place. These constructivists are not concerned with accurate, "true" representations of the world, but only with useful constructions. Individual ideas may be useful within a specific community of practice, such as fifteenth-century navigation, but useless outside that community. New knowledge is determined in part by how well the new idea fits with current accepted practice. Over time, the current practice may be questioned and even overthrown, but until such major shifts occur, current practice will shape what is considered useful.

The idea of a community of practice brings us to another, related view of learning, one that is increasingly influential in teaching—situated learning.

Situated Learning

Information processing as well as such rational constructivist perspectives as Piaget's focus on the individual as an information processor, trying to explain how individuals make sense of the world. Thus cognitive psychologists study individual and developmental differences, but often ignore the social situation in which learning occurs. In contrast, psychologists who emphasize the social construction of knowledge and situated learning affirm Vygotsky's notion that learning is inherently social and embedded in a particular cultural setting. Learning in the real world is more like an apprenticeship than learning in the classroom. Apprentices, with the support of an expert guide and model, assume more and more responsibility until they are able to perform effectively and independently. They move from participation on the edges of the community to participation in the center. For those who take a situated view, authentic learning is important, that is, ensuring that learning corresponds to actual real-world experiences—in factories, around the dinner table, in high school halls, in street gangs, in the business office, and on the playground.

Situated learning is sometimes described as "enculturation" or adopting the norms, behaviors, skills, beliefs, language, and attitudes of a particular community. The particular community varies; it might be mathematicians or gang members or students in an eighth grade class or Republicans—any group that has particular ways of thinking and doing. The practices of the community—the ways of interacting and getting things done, as well as the tools the community has created—constitute the knowledge of that community. Learning means becoming more able to participate in those practices and use of those particular tools (Derry, 1992; Garrison, 1995; Greeno, Collins, and Resnick, 1996; Palincsar, 1998).

At the most fundamental level, "situated learning . . . emphasizes the idea that much of what is learned is specific to the situation in which it is learned" (Anderson, Reder, and Simon, 1995: 5). Thus, some constructivists would argue, learning to do calculations in school may help students do more school calculations, but may not help them balance a checkbook, because the skills can be applied only in the context in which they were learned, namely school (Lave, 1988; Lave and Wenger, 1991). One implication is that students should learn skills and knowledge in meaningful contexts, with connections to the "real-life" situations in which the knowledge and skill will be useful. There is evidence that some learning is tied to the situation in which it was learned, but also some learning can be applied across contexts that were not part of the initial learning situation. For example, people use their ability to read and calculate to do their income tax, even though income tax forms were not part of their high school curriculum (Anderson, Reder, and Simon, 1995).

Much of the work within constructivist perspectives has focused on teaching. Many of the new standards for teaching, such as the National Council of Teachers of Mathematics' Curriculum and Evaluation Standards for School Mathematics and the American Association for the Advancement of Science's Benchmarks for Science Literacy are based on constructivist assumptions and methods. Many of the efforts to reform and restructure schools are attempts to apply constructivist perspectives on teaching and learning to the curriculum and organization of entire schools.

Teaching Applications of Constructivist Approaches

Expert teachers use good constructivist theories as well as sound behavioral and cognitive theories. Before we provide examples of the contributions of constructivist approaches to teaching and learning, we summarize some of the guiding principles:

- Develop multiple strategies for acquiring and assessing information.
- Frame tasks using processes such as classifying, analyzing, predicting and creating.
- Organize instruction to facilitate knowledge construction.
- Use raw data and primary sources as well as manipulative, interactive, and physical materials.
- Create a thinking and problem-solving environment.
- Encourage student dialogue both with the teacher and with each other.
- Use coaching and scaffolding to build student understanding.
- Encourage and support student initiative and autonomy.
- Make openness and tolerance basic rules for classroom interaction.
- Alter teaching strategies to keep students' ideas and responses driving forces in the class.
- Make student discovery a primary mission of teaching. (Bruning, Schraw, and Ronning, 1995; Brooks and Brooks, 1993)

"Although there are several versions of the constructivist theories, most scholars agree that constructivist approaches dramatically change in the focus of teaching by putting the students' own efforts to understand at the center of educational enterprise" (Prawat, 1992: 357). Let's examine more closely some of the fundamental dimensions of most constructivist teaching.

Constructivists believe that students should not be given basic skills drills, and simple or artificial problems, but instead they should be challenged with complex situations and "fuzzy" problems, the kind they will find in the world outside the classroom. Such problems should be embedded in **authentic tasks** and activities, the kinds of situations that students will face as they apply what they are learning to real-world problems (Brown, 1990; Needles and Knapp, 1994).

Many constructivists share Vygotsky's belief that higher mental processes elaborate through social interaction; hence, collaboration in learning is crucial. The Language Development and Hypermedia Group suggests that a major goal of teaching is to develop students' abilities to establish and defend their own positions while respecting the positions of others, a goal that requires exchange—students must talk with each other.

When students encounter only one representation of content—one model, one analogy, or one way to understand complex content—they often oversimplify and try to apply that one approach to every situation. Richard Spiro and his colleagues (1991) recommend that revisiting the same material, at different times, in different contexts, for different purposes, and from different conceptual perspectives is a key to mastering advanced knowledge. The idea is not entirely new. Years ago Jerome Bruner (1966) described the advantages of a spiral curriculum, which introduces the fundamental structure of all subjects—the "big ideas"—early in the school years and then revisits the subjects in more and more complex forms over time.

The assumptions we make, our beliefs, and experiences shape what we come to "know." Different assumptions and experiences lead to different conclusions. Constructivists stress the importance of understanding how knowledge is constructed so that students will be aware of the influences that shape their thinking. Then they are able to select, elaborate, and defend positions in a self-critical way while respecting the views of others.

Three examples of constructivist approaches to teaching, which are consistent with these guiding principles, are inquiry and problem-based learning, cognitive apprenticeships, and cooperative learning.

Inquiry and Problem-Based Learning

John Dewey first described his basic **inquiry learning** process in 1910. Although there have been many adaptations of his strategy, the form usually includes the following elements (Pasch et al., 1991): The teacher presents a puzzling event, question, or problem and the students:

- Formulate hypotheses to explain the problem.
- Collect data to test the hypotheses.

- Draw conclusions.
- Reflect on the original problem and thinking processes needed to solve it.

Sometimes, teachers pose a problem and students ask simple questions to gather data and test hypotheses and the teacher monitors students' thinking and guides the process. Consider the following example that Pasch and her colleagues offer (Pasch et al., 1991):

1. After clarifying ground rules of questioning, the teacher blows softly across the top of an 8½ by-11-inch sheet of paper, and the paper rises. She challenges students to figure out why it rises.
2. Students ask questions to gather more information and to isolate relevant variables. The teacher answers only "yes" or "no." Students ask if temperature is important (no). They ask if the paper is special (no). Does air pressure have anything to do it? (yes). Further questions.
3. Students develop and test causal relationships. In this case, they ask if the movement of air across on top causes the paper to rise (yes). They ask if the fast movement of the air produces less pressure on the top (yes). Then they test their ideas with other materials—for example, thin plastic.
4. Students form a generalization (hypotheses): "If the air on the top moves faster than the air on the bottom of a surface, then the air pressure on top is lessened, and the object rises." Later lessons expand students' understanding of principles and physical laws through further experiments.
5. The teacher leads students in a discussion of their analyses and thinking processes. What were the key variables? How did you determine the cause-and-effect relations?

The inquiry approach has much in common with guided discovery learning. Both require extensive preparation, organization, and monitoring to ensure that students are engaged and challenged (Pasch et al., 1991).

Computer and video technologies can support inquiry and problem-based learning. For example, the Cognition and Technology Group at Vanderbilt University (CTGV 1990, 1993) developed a videodisc-based learning environment for the fifth and sixth graders. The series, *The Adventures of Jasper Woodbury,* challenges students with complex situations that require problem finding, goal setting (including subgoals), and the application of concepts from mathematics, science, history, and literature to solve problems. The situations are complex and lifelike and can be solved using data embedded in the stories. In one adventure, Jasper sets out in a small motorboat and heads to Cedar Creek to inspect an old cruiser he is considering buying. Along the way he has to check maps, use his marine radio, monitor fuel, deal with repair problems, and eventually buy the cruiser. After the purchase, he must determine whether enough fuel and time remain to sail his purchase home before sundown.

The Vanderbilt group calls its problem-based approach, anchored instruction. Their anchor is the rich, authentic, and challenging situation, which provides a reason for setting goals, planning, and using mathematical tools. The aim is to develop useful and flexible knowledge. Initial research suggests that students as young as fourth grade and as old as high school can work with the adventures (CTGV, 1990). Students work in groups to solve the problems, and even group members with limited skills can contribute because they can notice key information in the videotape or sometimes suggest creative ways to approach the situation.

Cognitive Apprenticeships

Apprenticeships are an effective form of education. By working with a master and sometimes other apprentices, neophytes have learned many skills, trades, and crafts. Why are they effective? Apprenticeships are rich in information because the experts with extensive knowledge guide, model, demonstrate, and correct, as well as provide a personal bond that is motivating. The performances required of the learner are real, important, and grow more complex as the learner becomes more competent (Collins, Brown, and Holum, 1991).

Collins and his colleagues (1989) argue that knowledge and skills learned in school often are irrelevant to the world beyond school. To address this problem, schools sometimes adopt many of the features of apprenticeship, but rather than learning to sculpt or lay bricks, apprenticeships in schools focus on cognitive objectives such as reading comprehension or mathematical problem solving or application of professional skills in internships. Most cognitive apprenticeship models share six features:

- Students observe an expert (usually the teacher) model the task.
- Students get support through coaching or tutoring—including hints, feedback, models, and reminders.
- Conceptual scaffolding—outlines, explanations, notes, definitions, formulas, procedures, etc.—is provided and then gradually reduced as the student becomes more competent and proficient.
- Students continually articulate knowledge—putting their understanding into their own words.
- Students reflect on their progress and compare their problem solving both to an expert's performance and to their own earlier performances.
- Students explore new ways to apply what they are learning—ways they have not practiced at the master's side.

Cooperative Learning

Collaboration and cooperative learning have a long history in American education. In the early 1900s, John Dewey criticized the use of competition in education and urged educators to structure schools as democratic learning communities, and his ideas gained acceptance in the early 1900s; however, cooperation fell from favor in the 1940s and 1950s, as the popularity of competition increased. In the 1960s, there was another swing—back to individualized and cooperative learning structures, stimulated in part by concern for civil rights and interracial relations (Webb and Palincsar, 1996).

Today, evolving constructivist views of learning fuels interest in collaboration and cooperative learning. Two key characteristics of constructivist teaching are complex, real-life learning environments and social interaction. As educators turn to learning in real contexts, "there is a heightened interest in situations where elaboration, interpretation, explanation, and argumentation are integral to the activity of the group and where learning is supported by other individuals" (Webb and Palincsar, 1996: 844). Let's examine a few of the popular cooperative learning techniques.

Jigsaw

One format for cooperative learning, Jigsaw, emphasizes high interdependence. Each group member is given part of the material to be learned by the whole group and becomes an "expert" on that piece. Students teach each other, so they depend on each other and everyone's contribution is important. A more recent version, Jigsaw II, adds expert meetings in which students who have the same material consult to make sure they understand their assigned part and then plan how teach the information to their group. After the expert meeting, students return to their groups and bring their expertise to the learning sessions. Finally, students take an individual test on all the material and earn points for their learning team score. Teams work either for rewards or simply for recognition (Slavin, 1995).

Scripted Cooperation

Donald Dansereau and his colleagues have developed a method for learning in pairs called scripted cooperation. Students work cooperatively on some task—reading a selection of text, solving math problems, or editing writing drafts. For example, in reading, both partners read a passage. Then one student gives an oral summary and other comments on the summary, noting omissions or errors. Next the partners collaborate to refine and improve the information—create associations, images, mnemonics, ties to previous work, examples, analogies, and so on. The partners switch the reading and commentary roles for the next passage and continue to take turns until they finish the assignment (Dansereau, 1985; O'Donnell and O'Kelly, 1994).

There are many other forms of cooperative learning. Kagan (1994) and Slavin (1995) have written extensively on cooperative learning and developed and refined a variety of formats. Regardless of the format, the key to learning in groups is the quality of the discourse among the students. Talk that is interpretive—that analyzes and discusses explanations, evidence, reasons, and alternatives—is more useful than talk that is only descriptive. Teachers play an important role in cooperative learning; they are important guides. Effective teachers seed the discussion with ideas and alternatives that push and prod student thinking (Palincsar, 1998). See Table 2.2 for a summary of learning perspectives discussed in this chapter.

TABLE 2.2

Four Learning Perspectives

	Behavioral	*Cognitive*	*Rational Contructivist*	*Dialectical Constructivist*
	Skinner	**Anderson**	**Piaget**	**Vygotsky**
Knowledge	A fixed body of knowledge to acquire	Fixed body of knowledge to acquire	Changing body of knowledge, individually constructed in the social world—but some understandings clearly superior to others	Socially constructed knowledge; knowledge reflects the outside world as filtered through and influenced by culture, language, beliefs, and interactions with others
Learning	Acquisition of facts, skill, concepts.	Acquisition of facts, skill, concepts, and strategies	Active construction and reconstruction of prior knowledge	Collaborative construction of socially defined knowledge and values
	Occurs through explanation, demonstration, and guided practice	Occurs through the effective application of strategies	Occurs through multiple opportunities to connect with what is already known	Occurs through socially constructed opportunities
Teaching	Transmission—telling	Transmission—guiding toward more accurate and complete information	Challenging and guiding students toward a more complete understanding	Teacher and student coconstructing knowledge
Role of Teacher	Supervisor—correct wrong answers	Guide—model effective strategies and correct misconceptions	Guide and facilitator—listen to student's ideas and thinking and guide	Guide, facilitator, and partner—listen to socially constructed knowledge and help coconstruct knowledge
Role of Classmates	Not essential	Not essential, but can facilitate information processing	Not essential, but can stimulate questions and raise questions	Part of the process of knowledge construction
Role of Student	Receiver of information; active in practice	Processor of information; strategy user	Active constructor of knowledge; Active thinker and interpreter	Active coconstructor of knowledge; active social participant
Example of Teaching Approaches	Learning objectives; direct instruction	Visual tools—graphs and charts; mnemonic strategies	Conceptual change teaching; pure discovery learning	Cognitive apprenticeship; reciprocal teaching

THEORY INTO PRACTICE

Cooperative Learning: Sound Practice or Social Experiment?

This is your second year as principal of Jackson Middle School. The first year was a major adjustment for you because you went directly from being teacher to principal, and most of your energy was focused on keeping the school running smoothly, but this year is different. This year you have a plan to begin to improve the achievement of weak students in Jackson. You have started in a modest way by getting three sixth grade teachers to volunteer to use cooperative learning in their classes. The teachers took a two-course sequence in cooperative learning at the university last summer and now they are well into the second month of the innovation—enjoying the challenge and believing they are making a difference.

You are more than a little upset because you just got a call from Dr. Anita Rodriquez, your superintendent. Dr. Rodriquez has always been very supportive; in fact, it was she who talked you into moving into the principalship. But the phone conversation was troubling. The superintendent reported that she and several of the board members were getting calls from parents about the "cooperative learning experiment," as the parents put it. The superintendent remained supportive, but she concluded her phone conversation with you by saying that she just wanted you to know that there was opposition to your new cooperative learning experiment and that you should be prepared for some trouble.

Indeed you had personally experienced a number of parental complaints about the cooperative learning program that you had dismissed as the growing pains of the new program. For example, one parent complained that the cooperative learning was "just another passing educational fad" and that she wanted her children to learn the basics. She had attended parochial school as a child and was proud of her no-nonsense education. She concluded that, " learning is not fun and play—it is serious business and hard work." You tried to assure her that her son would learn and perhaps come to enjoy the process of learning, but she left still seemingly unconvinced of the merits of cooperative learning. It was also true that another parent expressed some alarm that the school was "experimenting" with her daughter. In that case, after reviewing some of the facts and purposes of the cooperative leaning program, you thought you were successful in defusing the issue because the parent left feeling much better about school and her daughter. As you reflect further on your interactions, you realize that perhaps there is more resistance than you originally thought—obviously the superintendent and the board are getting complaints. You are committed to the program and want to support the three teachers who volunteered and are moving forward with the innovation.

You decide to talk directly with the teachers about reactions from the parents. An after-school meeting with the three teachers for the purpose of gauging community resistance and assessing the progress of the program yield some surprises. Your teachers have been handling many more negative complaints than you are aware of, yet they are enthusiastic and committed to the program. They believe that they have turned the corner because most of the students are truly enjoying the teamwork, and student performance, especially of the slower students, is definitely improving. What are the parental criticisms of the program?

- The program slows down my child; she is smart and doesn't need help.
- I don't like you experimenting with my kids.
- Competition, not cooperation, is what makes this country great. In the business world, it is dog eat dog.
- My child is going to get lower grades because she is being dragged down by others in her group.
- The kids don't work hard; they play and it is a waste of time.
- My son does all the work for his group and it is not fair.

THEORY INTO PRACTICE, (Continued)

- I spend all my spare time driving my daughter around to work on group projects with classmates.
- My son does fine on his own; he doesn't like group work.
- Kids in the group are mean to my son; they don't include him; he hates school.

You all agree that too many parents are misinformed about cooperative learning and need to be educated not only about the basic principles under girding the new program but also about other learning strategies that are occurring in the classroom. To that end you agree, with the help of your cooperative-learning teachers, to prepare a short speech for the next PTA. The talk will review the new cooperative learning program, address each of the listed criticisms of the program, and use learning and teaching principles from the behavioral, cognitive, and constructivist perspectives to bolster the teaching and learning program of the school. The aim is to educate and allay parent anxiety.

You are that middle school principal so it is up to you to prepare the speech. Do it.

SUMMARY

The teaching-learning function is the technical core of the school. Although theorists disagree about definitions of learning, most concede that learning occurs when experience causes a change in a person's knowledge or behavior. There is no one best way to teach and no one best explanation of learning. Different theories of learning offer better or worse explanations depending on what is to be explained. Three perspectives on learning—behavioral, cognitive, and constructivist—are especially useful for teachers and educational administrators.

Behavioral views of learning emphasize the role of external events—antecedents and consequences—in changing observable behaviors. Consequences that increase behaviors are called reinforcers, whereas punishment suppresses or decreases behaviors. The use of learning objectives is an application of behavioral approach in teaching. Learning objectives specify the outcomes of learning so that the final goals or student behaviors are clear. When objectives are clear, students and teachers are more likely to reach them. Mastery leaning is another behavioral approach. The teacher breaks down what is to be learned into small units of study such that each unit involves mastering specific objectives. Direct instruction is consistent with behavioral principles and is appropriate for teaching explicit information to groups or the whole class. One framework for direct instruction includes reviewing yesterday's work, presenting new material, giving guided practice, giving feedback and corrections, providing independent practice (or homework), and reviewing weekly and monthly.

Cognitive views of learning focus on the human mind's active attempts to make sense of the world. Knowledge is a central force in cognitive perspectives. The individual's prior knowledge affects what he or she will pay attention to, recognize, understand, remember, and forget. Knowledge can be general or domain-specific and declarative, procedural, or conditional, but to be useful, knowledge must be remembered. One influential cognitive theory is information processing. The model describes how information moves from sensory memory (which holds a wealth of sensations and images very briefly) to working memory (where the information is elaborated and connected to existing knowledge) to long-term memory (where the information can be held for a long time, depending on how well it was learned in the first place and how interconnected it is to other information). People vary in how well they learn and remember based in part on their metacognitive knowledge—their abilities to plan, monitor, and regulate their own thinking. There are many teaching applications of cognitive views including highlighting, mnemonics, imagery, and other learning strategies to help organize and elaborate material.

Constructivist perspectives on learning and teaching, which are increasingly influential today, are grounded in the research of Piaget, Brunner, Dewey, and Vygotsky. The essence of the constructivist approach is that it places the students' own efforts at the center of the educational process. In general, constructivism assumes that people create and construct knowledge rather than internalize it from the external environment, but there are a variety of approaches—three of which are rational, radical, and dialectical. Rational constructivism emphasizes the way individuals construct external reality by using mental representations such as schemas. Radical constructivism rejects the notion that knowledge mirrors the external world and maintains that knowledge is constructed largely by interpersonal interactions and the constraints of culture and ideology. Dialectical constructivism is the middle ground, suggesting that knowledge grows through the interactions of internal (cognitive) and external (environmental, cultural, and social) factors. Constructivists believe that students should not be given stripped-down, simplified problems, and basic skills drills, but instead should deal with complex situations and "fuzzy," ill-structured problems. The use of inquiry learning is one important application of constructivism. Here teachers pose a problem and students ask questions to gather data, formulate hypotheses and test them as the teacher monitors students' thinking and guides the process. The cognitive apprenticeship is another constructivist application. Experts with extensive knowledge guide, model, demonstrate, and correct, as well as provide personal motivation in the performance of real-life tasks. Finally, cooperative learning provides yet another constructivist application in which students work cooperatively in groups to solve complex real-life problems.

Note

1. Wayne K. Hoy and Anita Woolfolk Hoy wrote this chapter jointly.

Key Concepts and Ideas

- Authentic tasks
- Basic skills
- Chunking
- Conditional knowledge
- Cueing
- Declarative knowledge
- Dialectical constructivism
- Direct and removal punishment
- Direct instruction
- Domain-specific knowledge
- General knowledge
- Inquiry learning
- Instructional objective
- Learning
- Long-term memory
- Mastery learning
- Metacognition
- Metacognitive skills
- Perception
- Positive and negative reinforcement
- Procedural knowledge
- Prompting
- Punishment
- Radical constructivism
- Rational constructivism
- Rehearsal
- Sensory memory
- Situated learning
- Technical core
- Working memory

CHAPTER 3

STRUCTURE IN SCHOOLS

Every organized human activity—from the making of pots to the placing of a man on the moon—gives rise to two fundamental and opposing requirements: the division of labor into various tasks to be performed, and the coordination of these tasks to accomplish the activity. The structure of the organization can be defined simply as the sum total of the ways in which it divides its labor into distinct tasks and then achieves coordination among them.

Henry Mintzberg
The Structuring of Organizations

PREVIEW

1. Five key organizational features define the classic Weberian bureaucracy: division of labor, impersonal orientation, hierarchy of authority, rules and regulations, and career orientation.
2. The Weberian model is criticized because of its dysfunctional consequences, neglect of the informal organization, internal inconsistencies, gender bias, oppressive features, and organizational pathologies.
3. Rules have both positive and negative consequences for organizational participants; administrators must consider both.
4. Enabling and coercive bureaucracies are two contrasting types of structure, one productive and the other not.
5. Bureaucratic and professional dimensions of organization combine to define four structural arrangements for schools: Weberian, authoritarian, professional, and chaotic.
6. There is no one best way to organize. Building effective structures demands matching the structure with its goals, environment, technology, people, and strategy.
7. Designing an effective organizational structure also involves balancing a host of countervailing forces created by the basic organizational dilemma of needing both order and freedom.
8. Organizations monitor and control work by mutual adjustment, direct supervision, standardization of work, standardization of outputs, and standardization of skills.
9. The key elements of structure are the strategic apex, middle line,

operating core, support staff, and technostructure.

10. School structures vary widely. Some are simple structures; others are machine bureaucracies; a few are professional bureaucracies; most are hybrids, but for some, structure is irrelevant—they are politicized.
11. Structural elements can be tightly and loosely coupled; both arrangements have positive and negative consequences and both exist in schools.
12. A fundamental source of conflict for professionals working in organizations comes from the systems of social control used by bureaucracies and the professions.
13. Organizations accommodate to this conflict by establishing loose structures, developing dual authority structures, or engaging in socialization.

The structural element of the school as social system is found in its formal organization. Max Weber's (1947) classic analysis of bureaucracy is a good beginning point for our discussion of the organizational structure in schools because it is the theoretical basis of most contemporary treatments (e.g., Blau and Scott, 1962; Hall, 1962; 1991; Perrow, 1986; Bolman and Deal, 1997; Scott, 1998).

Weberian Model of Bureaucracy

Almost all modern organizations, including schools, have the characteristics enumerated by Weber: a division of labor and specialization, an impersonal orientation, a hierarchy of authority, rules and regulations, and a career orientation.

Division of Labor and Specialization

According to Weber, **division of labor** and **specialization** mean "the regular activities required for the purposes of the bureaucratically governed structure are distributed in a fixed way as official duties" (Gerth and Mills, 1946: 196). Because the tasks in most organizations are too complex to be performed by a single individual, division of labor among positions improves efficiency. In schools, for example, division of labor is primarily for instructional purposes. Within that division, subspecialties are based on level—elementary and secondary—and subject—math, science, and so forth.

Efficiency increases because division of labor produces specialization, which in turn leads to employees who become knowledgeable and expert at performing their prescribed duties. Such division enables the organization to employ personnel on the basis of technical qualifications. Hence, division of labor and specialization produce more expertise in school personnel.

Impersonal Orientation

Weber (1947: 331) argued that the working atmosphere of a bureaucracy should provide an **impersonal orientation,** "the dominance of a spirit of formalistic impersonality, 'sine ira et studio,' without hatred or passion, and hence without affection or enthusiasm." The bureaucratic employee is expected to make decisions based on facts, not feelings. Impersonality on the part of administrators and teachers assures equality of treatment and facilitates rationality.

Hierarchy of Authority

Offices are arranged vertically in bureaucracies; that is, "each lower office is under the control and supervision of a higher one" (Weber, 1947: 330), which produces a **hierarchy of authority.** This bureaucratic trait is made manifest in the organizational chart, with the superintendent at the top and assistants, directors, principals, teachers, and students at successively lower levels.

Hierarchy is perhaps the most pervasive characteristic in modern organizations. Almost without exception, large organizations develop a well-established system of superordination and subordination, which attempts to guarantee the disciplined compliance to directives from superiors that is necessary for implementing the various tasks and functions of an organization.

Rules and Regulations

Weber (1947: 330) asserts that every bureaucracy has a system of **rules and regulations,** a "consistent system of abstract rules which have normally been intentionally established. Furthermore, administration of law is held to consist in the application of these rules to particular cases." The system of rules covers the rights and duties inherent in each position and helps coordinate activities in the hierarchy. It also provides continuity of operations when there are changes in personnel. Rules and regulations thus ensure uniformity and stability of employee action.

Career Orientation

Because employment in a bureaucratic organization is based on technical qualifications, employees think of their work as a career. Whenever there is such a **career orientation,** Weber (1947: 334) maintains, "there is a system of promotion according to seniority, achievement, or both. Promotion is dependent on the judgment of superiors." To foster loyalty to the organization, individuals with special skills must be protected from arbitrary dismissal or denial of promotion. Employees are protected in the sense that superiors are encouraged to make dispassionate decisions. Bureaucracies also institutionalize protection through such deeds.

Efficiency

To Weber (1947: 337), bureaucracy maximizes rational decision making and administrative efficiency: "Experience tends to universally show that the purely bureaucratic type of administrative organization . . . is, from a purely technical point of view, capable of attaining the highest degree of efficiency." Division of labor and specialization produce experts, and experts with an impersonal orientation make technically correct, rational decisions based on the facts. Once rational decisions have been made, the hierarchy of authority ensures disciplined compliance to directives and, along with rules and regulations, a well-coordinated system of implementation and uniformity and stability in the operation of the organization. Finally, a career orientation provides the incentive for employees to be loyal to the organization and to produce extra effort. These characteristics function to maximize administrative efficiency because committed experts make rational decisions that are executed and coordinated in a disciplined way.

Ideal Type

Although Weber's conception of bureaucracy is an **ideal type** that may or may not be found in the real world, it does highlight or emphasize basic tendencies of actual organizations. Hence, as an ideal type, it is quite useful for analytic purposes. As Alvin Gouldner (1950) explains, the ideal type may serve as a guide to help us determine how a formal organization is bureaucratized. Some organizations will be more bureaucratically structured than others. A given organization can be more bureaucratized on one characteristic and less on another. The model, as a conceptual scheme, raises important questions about organizing different kinds of formal bureaucracies. For example, under what conditions are the dimensions of bureaucracy related in order to maximize efficiency? Under what conditions does such an arrangement hinder efficiency?

Criticisms of the Weberian Bureaucratic Model

The Weberian model of bureaucracy has been attacked on a number of fronts. First, Weber is criticized for not being attentive to the dysfunctional features of his formulation. Second, the model has been criticized for its neglect of the informal organization. Third, Weber does not deal with the potential internal contradictions among the elements in the model. Finally, feminists denounce the model as gender biased. We turn to an analysis of each of these criticisms.

Functions and Dysfunctions of the Model

Weber's model of bureaucracy is functional in that application of the principles can promote efficiency and goal attainment. There is, however, the possibility of dysfunctional, or negative consequences—a possibility to which Weber pays limited attention. Let us consider each of the above bureaucratic characteristics or principles in terms of both possible functions and dysfunctions.

Although division of labor and specialization can produce expertise, they also can produce boredom. The literature is replete with instances where such boredom leads to lower levels of productivity or to a search on the part of employees for ways to make their work life more interesting, for example, the Hawthorne Studies discussed in Chapter 1. Indeed, many highly bureaucratized organizations that have experienced the negative consequences of extreme division of labor are enlarging employee responsibility to alleviate boredom.

Impersonality may improve rationally in decision making, but it also may produce a rather sterile atmosphere in which people interact as "nonpersons," resulting in low morale. Low morale, in turn, frequently impairs organizational efficiency.

Hierarchy of authority does enhance coordination, but frequently at the expense of communication. Two of the major dysfunctions of hierarchy are distortion and blockage in communication. Every level in the hierarchy produces a potential communication block because subordinates are reluctant to communicate anything that might make them look bad in the eyes of their superiors; in fact, there is probably a tendency to communicate only those things that make them look good or those things that they think their superiors want to hear (Blau and Scott, 1962).

Rules and regulations, on the one hand, do provide for continuity, coordination, stability, and uniformity. On the other hand, they often produce organizational rigidity and goal displacement. Employees may become so rule oriented that they forget that the rules and regulations are means to achieve goals, not *ends* in themselves. Disciplined compliance with the hierarchy, and particularly with the regulations, frequently produces rigidity and an inability to adjust. Such formalism may be exaggerated until conformity interferes with goal achievement. In such a case, the infamous characteristic of bureaucratic red tape is vividly apparent (Merton, 1957).

Career orientation is healthy insofar as it produces a sense of employee loyalty and motivates employees to maximize effort. Promotion, however, is based on seniority and achievement, which are not necessarily compatible. For example, rapid promotion of high achievers often produces discontent among the loyal, hard-working, senior employees who are not as creative.

The potential dysfunctional consequences of each bureaucratic characteristic are not adequately addressed in Weber's ideal type. Merton, for example, was one of the first to argue that structural arrangements established to maintain reliability and efficiency—rules, disciplined compliance, a graded career, impersonal decision making—can "also lead to an over-concern with strict adherence to regulations which induces timidity, conservatism, and technicism" (1957: 199). Table 3.1 summarizes some of the dysfunctions as well as the functions of the Weberian model. The question now becomes: Under what conditions does each characteristic lead to functional but not dysfunctional consequences? Whatever the answer to this question, the model remains quite useful as both an analytical tool and a guide to scientific research.

Functions and Dysfunctions of Rules

To illustrate the analytic and research usefulness of the model, we focus on Gouldner's (1954) discussion of organizational rules. Almost without excep-

TABLE 3.1

Functions and Dysfunctions of the Weberian Model

Bureaucratic Characteristic	Dysfunction	Function
Division of labor	Boredom	Expertise
Impersonal orientation	Lack of morale	Rationality
Hierarchy of authority	Communication blocks	Disciplined compliance and coordination
Rules and regulations	Rigidity and goal displacement	Continuity and uniformity
Career orientation	Conflict between achievement and seniority	Incentive

tion, large, formal organizations have systems of rules and regulations that guide organizational behavior. For example, most school districts have elaborate policy manuals. Rules are so universally present because they serve important functions.

Organizational rules have an explication function—that is, they explain in rather concise and explicit terms the specific obligations of subordinates. Rules make it unnecessary to repeat a routine order; moreover, they are less ambiguous and more carefully thought out than the hasty verbal command. Rules act as a system of communication to direct role performance.

A second function of rules is to screen—that is, to act as a buffer between the administrator and his or her subordinates. Rules carry a sense of egalitarianism because they can be applied equally to everyone. An administrator's denial of a request from a subordinate can be on the grounds that the rules apply to everyone, superior and subordinate alike, and cannot be broken. Subordinate anger is therefore redirected to the impersonal rules and regulations. As Gouldner (1954) explains, rules impersonally support a claim to authority without forcing the leader to legitimize personal superiority; conversely, they permit a subordinate to accept directives without betraying his or her sense of being any person's equal.

Organizational rules may also legitimize punishment. When subordinates are given explicit prior warning about what behavior will provoke sanctions and about the nature of those sanctions, punishment is legitimate. As Gouldner (1954) indicates, there is a deep-rooted feeling in our culture that punishment is permissible only when the offender knows in advance that certain behaviors are forbidden; ex post facto judgments are not permissible. In effect, rules not only legitimize but also impersonalize the administration of punishment.

Rules also serve a bargaining, or "leeway," function. Using formal rules as a bargaining tool, superiors can secure informal cooperation from subordinates. By *not* enforcing certain rules and regulations, one's sphere of authority can be expanded through the development of goodwill among subordinates. Rules are serviceable because they create something that can be given up as well as given use.

For each functional consequence of rules discussed thus far, a corresponding dysfunctional outcome results. Rules reinforce and preserve apathy by explicating the minimum level of acceptable behavior. Some employees remain apathetic because they know how little is required for them to remain secure. When apathy is fused with hostility, the scene is set for "organizational sabotage," which occurs when conforming to the letter of the rule violates the express purpose of the rule (Gouldner, 1954).

Although rules screen the superior from subordinates, that protection may become dysfunctional. **Goal displacement** develops; the means, in this case rules, become ends in themselves. By using rules to make important decisions, administrators may focus attention on the importance of a rule orientation, often at the expense of more important goals.

Another dysfunctional consequence that emerges from the screening and punishment functions of rules is legalism. When rules and punishments are pervasive, subordinates can adopt an extremely legalistic stance. In effect, they become "Philadelphia lawyers," willing and potentially able to win their case on a technicality. In its extreme form, employees may use legalism as an excuse for inactivity in any area not covered by a rule. When an individual is asked why he or she is not performing a reasonable task, the pat answer is "no rule says I have to." To say the least, such extreme legalism creates an unhealthy climate in schools.

The leeway function of rules—not enforcing them in exchange for informal cooperation—involves the ever-present danger of being too lenient. The classic example of this kind of permissiveness is seen in the indulgency pattern described in Gouldner's study of a factory in which few, if any, rules were enforced; although superior-subordinate relations were friendly, productivity suffered. The functions and dysfunctions of rules are summarized in Table 3.2.

School administrators who are aware can avoid the dysfunctional consequences of rules, but the path is not easy. For example, by taking advantage of the screening function of bureaucratic rules, administrators can gain and maintain some control over organizational activities. They anticipate that general and impersonal rules will be "good" because they provide direction without creating status distinctions. Control is thus maintained by using bureaucratic rules. Use of bureaucratic rules, however, may produce unanticipated consequences. Because bureaucratic rules provide knowledge about minimum acceptable standards (explication function), an unanticipated consequence may be that minimums become maximums (apathy-preserving and goal-displacement dysfunctions), and the difference between actual behavior and expected behavior for goal achievement becomes visible and unacceptable, thereby prompting close supervision. In brief, because the equilibrium originally sought by instituting the bureaucratic rules is upset, the demand for more control is created.

TABLE 3.2

The Double-Edged Nature of Bureaucratic Rules

Functions		**Dysfunctions**
Explication	←→	Apathy reinforcement
Screening	←→	Goal displacement
Punishment-legitimizing	←→	Legalism
Leeway	←→	Indulgency

Thus, although rules are used to mitigate some tensions, they may create others. As a matter of fact, rules may actually perpetuate the tensions that they were meant to dispel. For example, close supervision can produce high visibility of power relations and a high degree of interpersonal tension; yet the use of rules to reduce tension may unintentionally perpetuate the need for additional close supervision; hence, the cycle begins again. The major problems of low motivation and minimal role performance simply are not solved by more rules.[1]

Educational administrators must learn how to anticipate and avoid the negative consequences of bureaucratic rules. They must ask: How can the functional consequences of rules be maximized and the dysfunctional consequences minimized? Gouldner's (1954) research provides some guidelines. He maintains that rules having a punishment-centered pattern are most likely to evoke negative consequences. *Either workers or administrators initiate punishment-centered rules,* but not jointly, to coerce the other group to comply; and they result in punishment of one group by the other when the rules are violated, producing tension and conflict.

On the other hand, **representative rules** are initiated and supported by *both* workers and administrators. Although such rules are enforced by the administration and obeyed by subordinates, they result in efforts to educate because rule violations are interpreted as a lack of information. Representative rules are least likely to evoke dysfunctional consequences because they have been jointly initiated, are generally supported by the parties concerned, and they empower subordinates. Therefore, representative rules, as contrasted with **punishment-centered rules**, are more likely to have the desired functional consequences without many of the unintended dysfunctional consequences.

Neglect of the Informal Organization

The Weberian model of organization also has been criticized for its omission of the informal structure. **Informal organization** is a system of interpersonal relations that forms spontaneously within all formal organizations. It is a system that is not included in the organizational chart or official blueprint. It is the natural ordering and structuring that evolves from the needs of participants as they interact in their workplace. It contains structural, normative, and behavioral dimensions; that is, it includes informal structure, informal norms, and informal patterns of leadership (Scott, 1992). Teachers, administrators, and students within schools inevitably generate their own informal systems of status and power networks, communication, and working arrangements and structures.

The Development of Informal Organization

As people interact in organizations, networks of informal relations emerge that have important effects on behavior. Official as well as unofficial roles, norms, values, and leaders all shape individual behavior. Informal relations comprise patterns of such social interactions as communicating, cooperating, and competing. When individuals find themselves together in formal organizations, informal interaction inevitably occurs. People talk to each other about personal and social issues. As a consequence, some individuals are liked, others disliked. Typically, people seek continued interactions with those they like and avoid interactions with those they dislike. These informal social exchanges produce differences in social relations among group members and, importantly, define the informal status structure of the group.

A member's status in the group, therefore, depends upon the frequency, duration, and character of interaction patterns with others, and the extent to which others respect the individual in the group. Consequently, some group members are actively sought out, whereas others are avoided; some are admired, others are not; some are leaders, others are followers; and most are integrated as members of a group, although a few are isolated.

The informal interactions produce subgroups; cliques develop within the group structure, some of which have more status, power, and significance than others. Clique membership provides status in the larger group through the prestige of the subgroup. In brief, the differential patterns of interactions among individuals and groups, and the status structure characterized by them, define the social structure of the informal organization.

In addition to the social structure, a normative orientation emerges that serves as a guide for behavior. As individuals engage in social interaction, common conceptions of desirable and acceptable behavior occur. Common values arise to define ideal states of affairs, and social norms develop that prescribe what individuals should do under different situations and the consequences of deviations from those expectations. Norms contain two important features: a general agreement about appropriate behavior and mechanisms to enforce expectations. The distinction between norms and values is sometimes a fuzzy one, but generally values define the ends of human behavior, and social norms provide the legitimate and explicit means for pursuing those ends (Blau and Scott, 1962). Finally, and in addition to the general values and norms which are shared and expected to integrate the group, sets of expectations are differentiated according to the role or status position of the individual in the group. The role of "task master" is quite different from the role of "group comedian"; the role of leader is quite different from the role of follower. In brief, the main components of informal organization are the social structure and normative orientation of the group.

A Hypothetical Illustration in Schools

Imagine the situation of a new school, where the superintendent hires a new principal who in turn hires an entire new staff of teachers, none of whom know each other. At the beginning of the year, we simply have a collection of individuals bound together by the formal requirements of the school and their jobs. The professional staff, however, will quickly become more than the sum of the individuals composing it. Behavior will not only be determined by the formal expectations of the school but also by the informal organization that spontaneously emerges as the participants interact.

As school begins, faculty and staff begin to work together, attend meetings, eat together, socialize in the faculty lounge, and plan school activities. Teacher relations will, in part, be determined by the physical features of the school, such as a faculty lounge, a faculty lunch room, the library, and the arrangement of the classrooms; the technical aspects of the job—for example, department structure, team teaching, and extracurricular responsibilities; and social factors such as the leadership styles of the superintendent and principals. The initial relations of teachers in a school can be examined in terms of formal activities and interactions. Teachers have a need to keep their jobs, and a formal system has been established to achieve school objectives. This formal organization comprises a hierarchy of authority, division of labor, formal rules and regulations, impersonality, and a formal communication structure, developed and implemented to achieve school goals.

A number of consequences follow from the establishment of the initial, formal relations. New sentiments develop that are different from the work-motivated ones that brought teachers together in the first place. The new sentiments are ones of liking and disliking other teachers and groups within the school. Some of the teachers will become well liked and respected; their colleagues will frequently ask them for advice and seek them out. Such sentiments and behavior serve as the basis for an informal ranking of individuals and groups. Moreover, new informal activities will develop, some of which are a direct reaction to the formal organization. For example, the inability of faculty to influence policy through the formal structure may result in informal activities, conversations, and initiatives. New patterns of interaction will elaborate themselves in the school—for example, association in cliques, informal webs of communication, discipline networks centering on informal leadership, and a status structure among groups of teachers. Some informal groups will become more prestigious and powerful than others.

In addition to the informal social structure that develops, a system of informal shared values and beliefs will emerge—the normative orientation. The faculty will define ideal and appropriate behavior. Their ideal, for example, may be a school characterized by hard work, mastery of the basics, an academic orientation, and positive student-teacher relations. To this end, norms emerge to guide teacher behavior: few hall passes will be issued; substantial and meaningful homework assignments will be made; orderly and industrious classrooms will be maintained; and extra help for students will be readily available. If teachers violate these norms, they lose the respect of their colleagues, and social sanctions will be applied. They may find themselves disparaged and isolated by their colleagues. Teachers will also assume specific informal roles; an unofficial teacher spokesperson may serve as a powerful liaison with the principal; another teacher may provide a strong critical voice of school policy in faculty meetings; still another teacher may organize social activities for the faculty; and there may be the teacher who always offers comic relief, especially when events are tense.

The informal organization, then, arises from the formal organization and then reacts to it. The development of group norms, the division into cliques, and the ranking of individuals and subgroups are conditioned directly by the formal structure and indirectly by the school environment. Hence, we can begin with the formal system of the school and argue that the informal is continually emerging from the formal and continually influencing the formal. The formal and informal systems go together; after all, there is only one organization. Yet the distinction is useful because it calls attention to the dynamic nature of organizational life in schools and to the continuous processes of elaboration, differentiation, and feedback in schools. The dynamic character of the informal organization as well as its interplay with the formal organization is summarized in Figure 3.1.

The impact of the informal on the formal organization can be constructive or destructive. For example, the Hawthorne Studies (see Chapter 1) showed that the informal organization restricted production. Evidence also exists, however, that the informal organization can be a constructive force in efficient operation of bureaucratic organizations as well as a mechanism for change. In Chester Barnard's (1938) classic theoretic analysis of organizations, he argued that informal organizations have at least three crucial func-

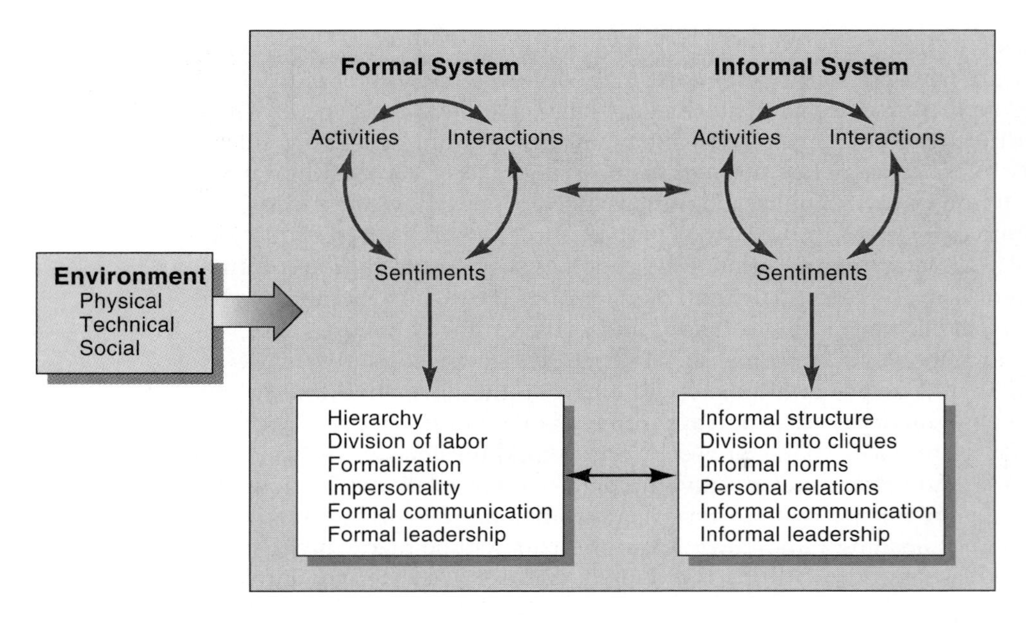

FIGURE 3.1 *Elements of the Formal and Informal Organization*

tions: as effective vehicles of communication, as a means of developing cohesion, and as devices for protecting the integrity of the individual.

Formal communications systems in organizations such as schools are typically insufficient and are inevitably supplemented by informal ones; in fact, informal communication systems, so-called grapevines, exist in all organizations regardless of how elaborate the formal communications system (Iannaconne, 1962; Hoy and Forsyth, 1986; Robbins, 1991) and are used constructively in effective organizations (Peters and Waterman, 1982). The informal structure provides a channel for circumventing formally prescribed rules and procedures. Many pressing problems emerge for which efficient solutions or communications are not possible within the formal framework; hence, the informal structure assumes added importance. Official communications must be routed through the "chain of command," which often is a long-drawn-out process. Frequently, circumventing the official communication channel through the grapevine appears to be precisely what is necessary for solving crucial problems (Page, 1946; Peters and Waterman, 1982). The knowledgeable and flexible administrator uses the grapevine, thus avoiding the bureaucratic frustration of those who only play it by the book. As a communication vehicle, the grapevine often provides efficient machinery. Indeed, generally speaking, the informal organization is an important device for implementing many important organizational objectives.

Informal organization also can promote cohesion. Patterns of social relationships usually emphasize friendliness, cooperation, and preservation of the group. Informal groups emerge spontaneously and are built on shared interests and friendships. They arise from such simple events as common classroom areas, liking certain colleagues, shared lunch hours, car pools, same planning periods, and other fortuitous activities. Such situations and the accompanying social relationships can provide the social cement that binds faculty by promoting an atmosphere of cordiality and friendliness that is potent enough to cause members to feel that they belong to the group; cohesion and solidarity are the by-products of informal groups (Boyan, 1951; Robbins, 1991).

The informal organization functions to maintain a sense of personal integrity, self-respect, and independence for individuals (Barnard, 1938). Unlike the formal, hierarchy, impersonality, and formal authority do not dominate the informal. Rather, the informal is an outgrowth of the individual and personal needs of members. It is a means by which teachers can maintain their individual personalities in spite of organizational demands that invariably attempt to depersonalize individuals (Hoy and Forsyth, 1986).

The informal organization exists. It is not an enemy to be eliminated or suppressed; on the contrary, it can be a useful vehicle for improving efficiency. It is irrational to administer a formal organization, such as a school, according to the purely technical criteria of rationality and formality because that ignores the nonrational aspects of informal organization (Blau, 1956). From a theoretical perspective, our position is that administrative practice is enhanced by using both the formal (rational) and the informal (nonrational) components of schools.

Dual Structure of the Bureaucratic Model

Another frequent criticism of the Weberian model is the internal contradictions among certain bureaucratic principles of organization. According to Weber, all characteristics of his ideal type are logically consistent and interact for maximum organizational efficiency; however, both theoretical and empirical analyses indicate that things are not so smooth and integrated in the real world of organizational functioning.

Talcott Parsons (1947) and Gouldner (1954) question whether the guiding principle of bureaucracy is authority based on technical competence and knowledge or authority based on legal powers and discipline. Weber (1947: 339) maintains that "bureaucratic administration means fundamentally the exercise of control on the basis of knowledge." On the other hand, he writes, "The content of discipline is the consistently rationalized, methodically trained and exact execution of the received order, in which all personal criticism is unconditionally suspended and the actor is unswervingly and exclusively set for carrying out the command" (Gerth and Mills, 1946: 196). Hence, Weber is proposing the central importance of discipline as well as expertise. Is bureaucratic administration based primarily on expertise, or is it based on disciplined compliance with directives? Unless one assumes that there will be no conflict between authority based on "technical competence and expertise" and that based on "incumbency in a hierarchical position," the seed of contradiction and conflict rests within these two authority bases that are integral to the Weberian model. In fact, Gouldner (1954) and Constas (1958) suggest that Weber may have been implicitly describing not one but two types of bureaucracy, a conclusion supported by a number of empirical studies (Stinchcombe, 1959; Udy, 1959).

Similarly, Blau and Scott's (1962) analysis of the dual nature of the Weberian model also led them to conclude that Weber failed to distinguish bureaucratic from professional principles. They similarly maintain that bureaucratic discipline and professional expertise are alternative methods for coping with uncertainty. Discipline reduces the scope of uncertainty, whereas expertise provides the knowledge to handle uncertainty. The crux of the problem seems to be that professionals are often employees of bureaucratic organizations; hence, these alternative modes of rationality are frequently mixed, producing strain and conflict. A typical example is the school principal. Does his or her authority reside in the bureaucratic office or in professional expertise? Obviously, a mixture is present and seems to result in some degree of strife.

A Feminist Critique of Bureaucracy

Feminists are often critical of bureaucratic organizations in fundamental ways that go far beyond the common accusation that qualified women in modern organizations do not receive equal treatment or compensation (Scott, 1992, 1998). Joanne Martin (1990b; Martin and Knopoff, 1999), for example, argues that in spite of Weber's analysis of the central features of bureaucracy being gender neutral and universal in his description of administration based on expertise, women are disadvantaged. The emphasis on full-time commitment and extensive training as qualifications for job holding hinders women who routinely confront the conflicting demands of job and family responsibilities. Women often lack equal access to training programs and discussions of bureaucracy frequently overlook the interdependence of job and family responsibilities, treating work as public and masculine and family as private and feminine (Bose, Feldberg, and Sokoloff, 1987; Martin, 1990a). Hence, bureaucracies are gender biased not only in their *application* of appointment and promotion criteria but also in their *selection* of the criteria (Scott, 1992).

Feminists also argue that bureaucratic structures perpetuate systems of male domination. Ferguson (1984), for one, argues that bureaucracy with its patent emphasis on authority, rules, regulations, and rationality, recreates paternalistic domination. Bureaucratic structures give priority to masculine virtues and values. Scott (1992: 325) explains, "The principles by which organizations are structured—inequality, hierarchy, impersonality—devalue alternative modes of organizing that are alleged to be more characteristic of women's values: equalitarian and personalized associations." In the same vein, Ferguson (1984) argues that bureaucratic control invades social life by "feminizing" participants—that is, by making them nonassertive and dependent; in fact, women are bound to supportive roles by structures that see feminine characteristics as subordinate and masculine ones as dominant. Male characteristics of independence, rationality, and competitiveness are dominant instrumental features of bureaucracy, whereas the more feminine features of dependence, emotionality, and cooperation are subordinate properties of organizations. The hallmarks of achievement—competition and independence—are quite different from the nurturant expressive behaviors of the feminine style (Gilligan, 1982; Ferguson, 1984). In fact, the feminine side is often repressed and devalued by bureaucracies creating an oppression of women. Bureaucracies are not caring institutions, but reproducers of patriarchy and reinforcers of patterns of domination (Clark et al., 1994).

Feminist critics also challenge the bureaucratic notion that superior domination though hierarchical patterns of authority is essential to achievement of important goals; in fact, they argue that hierarchy is typically restrictive of the growth of the group and individual members (Denhardt and Perkins, 1976). Moreover, the usual defense of the hierarchical division of labor as a structural device to develop expertise and improve efficiency is seen largely as a guise to conceal the control function of hierarchy. Invariably all workers, but especially women, are isolated, alienated, and depersonalized as communications are mystified and the dominance of bureaucratic control is disguised. Radical feminists make it clear that they are committed to an **antibureaucratic structure:**

- Groups are decentralized.
- Personal, face-to-face relations are substituted for impersonal rules and regulations.
- Relationships are egalitarian not hierarchical.
- Skills and information are to be shared, not hoarded. (Ferguson, 1984)

Hirschhorn's Post-Modern Critique[2]

Larry Hirschhorn (1997) argues that America is in a post-industrial revolution, which calls for post-modern organizations to replace traditional bureaucracies. Organizations are confronted by the computer revolution with new communication technologies, the information highway, greater interdependency, and an information explosion. These changes mean that organizations need more information, more insight for sound decision making, more decentralized structures, more openness, more participation and collaboration, and more individual responsibility.

Hirschhorn is critical of bureaucracy on a number of levels. First, centralization of authority is dysfunctional because upward identification is no longer sufficient in contemporary organizations. The wider technological, economic, and social changes that superiors face make it virtually impossible for them to project the certainty, confidence, and power they once could; thus, their subordinates become quickly disappointed and disillusioned in their superiors' failure to live up to their leadership responsibilities.

Second, modern organizations depersonalize individuals by placing them in hierarchical roles and reducing their exercise of autonomy and power. The modern enterprise offers employees a psychological deal with the devil: in exchange for predictability and protection from arbitrary actions, they are forced to withdraw the "psychological presence" from their work (Hirschhorn, 1997).

Third, modern organizations abdicate by substituting rules and procedures for judgments and relationships. Bureaucracy depersonalizes decision making so that individuals at various levels can be secure in just following the rules. In doing so, however, they lose a sense of personal accountability for their decisions. Thus, they feel less responsible for unpredictable negative consequences for the decisions; after all, they did their part—they followed the rules and procedures. Because authority is vested in rules and not relationships, unity of command and rules drive out spontaneity and responsibility.

Fourth, division of labor produces expertise, but complexity and change also cause interdependence. Older individuals who worked hard to gain their expertise and skills resent younger employees who dismiss their knowledge as obsolete, just as younger workers resent older people who block their mobility and ignore their ideas. Fragmented and separated relationships produce resentment in an organizational context that requires expertise but also collaboration, cooperation, and flexibility.

Finally, career security has its own hidden costs. The price that many people had to pay to "make it" in the bureaucracy and climb the ladder of success was to conform closely to the organization's code of behavior. Don't rock the boat, dress appropriately, show proper deference, participate in staged meetings, avoid dissent, just go along, and be loyal. The exchange was clear. The organization would protect individuals from the market, but only if they surrendered substantial individuality. As we move to a post-industrial society, however, contemporary organizations are shedding their paternalism. They do longer protect workers from the market. Secure careers are no longer assured, and even in schools, there is talk of abolishing tenure.

So what is the nature of the Hirschhorn's post-modern organization? The image of many centers of powers replaces the image of centralized authority. Organizational power is "deconstructed," that is, it is replaced by a network of personal authority rather than staying concentrated at the organizational center. Yet, there is a paradox of sorts. Decentralization brings more autonomy in decision making but increases the need for cooperation and interdependence.

The post-modern organization is highlighted by individuals who use doubt as a basis for learning and expose themselves to the feelings that others stimulate. Doubt is not masked but rather openly acknowledged. The individual is open, but to be open is to be vulnerable to others. People learn from mistakes. But the nagging question is " If I think my idea is a good one but others don't, will they think I am stupid or courageous for "stepping out of the box?" An important property of post-modern organizations is a culture of being open to others, which means that leaders, followers, and peers trust each other enough to make themselves vulnerable to each other.

In post-modern organizations personal authority is the key to successful relationships. Individuals must learn to rely more on internalized images of themselves rather than depend on the organization. When individuals rely on personal rather than organizational authority, they bring more of themselves—their skills, knowledge, feelings, and values—to the task. This means that individuals have to work harder psychologically, learn to assume the viewpoints of others, and risk greater embarrassment as they make more mistakes in the wake of creative problem solving.

Relationships are personalized in post-modern organizations. This means relaxing rigid definitions of roles and giving individuals freedom to negotiate their own roles and to express their talents in creative ways. Leaders must learn how to personalize their own roles in ways that help followers personalize their roles. Leaders must behave openly and authentically so that everyone knows what matters to them and why. Being open makes the leader more transparent and vulnerable but also more trustworthy. The temptation of most leaders is to retreat behind a shield of authority in an attempt to depersonalize relationships, but the key is personalization, not depersonalization of relationships.

Although organizations cannot rid themselves completely of hierarchy, the post-modern organization infuses structure with passion and enlivens it with delegation and participation. Leaders delegate leadership and authority, but they do not relinquish responsibility. This means leaders never abandon their subordinates to the power of rules and regulations or hide behind the mask of authority. On the contrary, they work together with subordinates across recognized authority boundaries with each retaining his or her distinctive role and all engaged in collective problem solving.

The paradox of the post-modern organization is that it is both a "transmission belt for fragmentation and disruption and a crucible for the development of a psychological sense of community" (Hirschhorn, 1997: 118). To deal successfully with the paradox, participants in post-modern organizations must create a culture of openness in which they learn how to relate deeply with others, develop personal authority, and create self-fulfilling conditions in the workplace. In brief, the key properties of Hirschhorn's (1997) post-modern organization are:

- Decentralization of authority
- A culture of openness
- Personal authority
- Personalization of relationships
- Flexibility of roles
- Delegation of authority
- Infusion of structure with passion and participation

Other Bureaucratic Pathologies[3]

Organizational theorists have noted still other pathologies of bureaucratic structures. Scott (1998), for example, argues as we do, that there is close correspondence between the very best and worst features of organizational structures. In some instances, as we have seen, similar processes with slight variations produce both an organization's strengths and its weaknesses. For example, representative rules empower workers, whereas punishment-centered rules subordinate and alienate them. Scott (1998) also suggests four bureaucratic pathologies—alienation, overconformity, unresponsiveness, and relentlessness—each of which merits attention because of its pervasiveness and negative consequences for participants.

Alienation

Alienation remains a persistent problem in society in general and in organizations in particular. Much time and effort have been expended on the impact of organizations on personal characteristics and behavior of their participants. Perhaps Marx, more than any theorist, underscored the alienation of the worker. To Marx, workers were alienated from the product of their labor as well as from the process of production, and consequently, they were alienated from each other in the work setting (Marx, 1963). Enter capitalism and it is not only work that alienates but also exploitation of workers by the misuse of power (Scott, 1998). Such power, and hence exploitation, is institutionalized in the formal organizations of a capitalistic society.

Rigid bureaucratic structures alienate workers (Aiken and Hage, 1968; Kakabadse, 1986), produce dissatisfaction (Arches, 1991), stifle innovation (Bennis, 1966; Bailyn, 1985), foster mistreatment of clients (Mintzberg, 1979), increase absenteeism, promote strikes, and even produce sabotage of the operation of the organization (Rousseau, 1978; Gouldner, 1954). Moreover, individuals in self-directed jobs are less authoritarian, less self-deprecatory, less fatalistic, less conforming, and more self-confident and more responsible to standards of morality (Spenner, 1988). There is no question that one can find in the research and theoretical literature evidence to support the contention that bureaucratic organizations are a source of alienation and estrangement to their participants. But this view of bureaucratic alienation is only half the story because one can also find contradictory evidence, a point to which we will return later. In the meantime, consider Hirschhorn's conclusion that in a well-functioning bureaucracy ". . . the leader absorbs the primary risks of managing the enterprise and then delegates authority and accountability to others to accomplish the more limited but still complicated and important tasks. The leader in his or her role represents the organization as a whole and integrates the actions of its various divisions" (Hirschhorn, 1997: 66).

Overconformity

We have already seen that bureaucratic structures tend to produce overconformity in following rules. The very elements, which produce efficiency, in general produce inefficiency in specific instances (Merton, 1957). Rules, discipline, and a graded career can lead to a strict adherence to bureaucratic procedures, which promotes overconformity and technicism. For example, goal displacement, the tendency for means to become ends-in-themselves, is prevalent in bureaucratic organizations (Selznick, 1949; Gouldner, 1954; Dalton, 1959). In schools, often teachers become so enamored with maintaining good discipline that they forget that order is only a means to ensure successful teaching and learning, and discipline and order become ends-in-themselves rather than merely means to the broader goal of learning. In addition, teachers who want to get ahead and become administrators are also more likely to focus on the letter of the law, that is, conform rigidly to the administrative rules to show allegiance and demonstrate loyalty to their principals.

The most unsettling findings on conformity are found in Milgram's classic experimental studies (Milgram, 1963, 1974). In order to determine whether individuals would conform to and obey commands from a relatively powerless stranger, Milgram designed a series of ingenious experiments. Participants in the study were told that they were taking part in a study of the influence of punishment on learning. Their role was to deliver electric shock to a male learner (actually an accomplice of the researcher) each time he gave an incorrect answer. Intensity of the shocks increased throughout the experiment from 15 to 450 volts. Both the teacher and the student were actors, and of course, no shock was administered. The only real shock was a mild pulse from the third button used to convince participants that the equipment was real. You might expect that most respondents would not obey orders to administer the shock. Wrong. In fact, about 65 percent were fully compliant even through the full 450-volt shock. Of course, many participants expressed concern and questioned the commands, but most yielded to the order even as the victim pounded against the wall as if to protest the pain.

The results were quite consistent over a wide variety of subjects from Yale undergraduates to professionals to blue-collar workers. Authority was a strong factor in forcing people to conform. As we examine the experiment in detail, we see that it has many of the features of bureaucracy—unitary authority, rules, disciplined compliance, implicit agreement to follow orders of superiors. Thus, the results are consistent with others that demonstrate the power of authority in forcing compliance and conformity. Milgram explains that people feel responsible to the authority directing them but do not feel responsible for the content of the actions being ordered. He concludes, "Morality does not disappear—it acquires a radically different focus: the subordinate person feels shame or pride depending on how adequately he has performed the actions called for by authority" (1973: 77).

Unresponsiveness

All organizations must supply benefits to their external publics—customers, clients, or citizens—if they are to continue to survive (Scott, 1998). In service organizations, like schools, there is a special concern that the school be responsiveness to demands from the community. After all, the public and students are prime beneficiaries of their services.

Weber, himself, warned of the potential trouble that would accompany the growth of bureaucracy—not inefficiency and mismanagement—but rather efficiency and reliability would pose the threat. With the growth of bureaucracy was the likelihood of the expansion of power in public officials. Weber (1947) warned:

> Under normal conditions, the power position of a fully developed bureaucracy is always overpowering. The "political master" finds himself in the position of the "dilettante" who stands opposite the "expert," facing the trained official who stands within the management of administration. (pp. 232–33)

The public seeks to keep the school responsive by its lay board of education, but the average citizen often feels unable to deal with an unresponsive formal organization and its formidable hierarchy. Moreover, the superintendent and influential board members often form an administrative oligarchy to control organizational activities. Although power is expected to reside in the general public, it is the administrative officials and key board members who have the power, and they are likely to respond first to matters that guarantee their continued control and influence, often at the expense of the public at large. Michel's (1949) called this general tendency of associations to move toward increasing centralization of control and the desire of leaders to retain and extend their power the "iron rule of oligarchy." Such tendencies make bureaucracies unresponsive to their publics and are a continuous problem for schools and professional associations.

Relentlessness

Another concern of organizations functioning in relation to their publics is the relentlessness of organizational behavior. Scott (1998) argues that this relentlessness is not a malfunction of the organization but a pathology of "normal" organizational activities.

James Coleman's (1974) analysis is instructive. Coleman distinguishes between the persons, like you and me, and corporate actors—organizations. Organizations are composed of roles and positions, not persons. From the perspective of the person, organizations are agents for attaining desired goals, but from the perspective of the corporate actor, individuals are agents hired to achieve the goals of the collective actor (Scott, 1998). Coleman (1974) elaborates as follows: It is the corporate actors, the organizations that obtain their power from persons and use that power for corporate ends, which are the primary actors in the social structure of contemporary society. What are the practical consequences of this arrangement? It produces a peculiar bias in the direction of social and economic activities. Among the broad range of interests that individuals hold, those interests that have been successfully collected to create corporate actors are the ones that dominate society. Moreover, nonorganized interests of individuals are simply ignored or neglected in a society dominated by organizations.

Furthermore, organizational members, including administrators, are constrained by both organizational goals and roles. Administrators are expected to act as agents of the organization, and organizations are often relentless in the pursuit of their narrow goals. For example, the Pentagon is expected to strengthen our defenses and they do so without much regard for the long-term consequences of the national economy or the survival of the human race. The point is that organizations are focused and specialized; they rigorously pursue their goals, often without regard to the consequences for other organizations and individuals, and without regard for their long-term outcomes or concern for other values. We need to be concerned about the "organizational imperative" that "whatever is good for man can only be achieved through modern organizations" and "therefore all behavior must enhance the health of such modern organizations" (Hart and Scott, 1975: 261). It is the specialization, focus, and impersonality of bureaucratic organizations that make them relentless in the pursuit of narrow goals, which often have negative consequences for other segments of society.

Twenty years ago Coleman (1974) argued that persons are losing power to organizations at a rapid rate, which gives rise to a situation of widespread powerlessness among individuals. Because the outcome of events is only partly determined by the desires and interests of individuals, society functions less than fully in the interests of the individuals who comprise it. Scott (1998), in a recent work, concludes that this stripping of power from the worker is the ultimate form of alienation; power lost by one person may not be gained by another but is absorbed by a corporate actor and used to pursue its specialized goals.

In brief, organizations, especially bureaucratic ones, often suffer from the pathologies of alienation, overconformity, relentlessness, and unresponsiveness. These are not conditions that are either inevitable or irreversible; in fact, the remainder of this chapter will continue to suggest strategies and structures to ameliorate these difficulties.

Two Types of Bureaucracy

Bureaucracies can alienate individual participants, but that is only half the story because research also suggests they can improve worker satisfaction (Michaels, Cron, Dubinsky, and Joachimsthaler, 1988), increase innovation (Damanpour, 1991; Craig, 1995), reduce role conflict (Senatra, 1980), and reduce feelings of alienation (Jackson and Schuler, 1985). Indeed, organizational research depicts two conflicting views of the human outcomes of bureaucracy.

The negative side suggests that bureaucracy alienates, fosters dissatisfaction, stifles creativity, and demotivates employees, whereas the positive view maintains that it provides needed guidance, clarifies responsibility, reduces role stress, and helps individuals feel and be more effective (Adler and Borys, 1996). How can we reconcile these two views?

Paul Adler and Bryan Borys (1996) offer a possible solution as they interpret formalization as an organizational technology and identify two types of formalization—enabling and coercive. In the Weberian sense, formalization is the extent of written rules, regulations, procedures, and instructions. The notion of enabling and coercive formalization is not unlike Gouldner's (1954) representative and punishment-centered rules, but Adler and Borys (1996) provide a much deeper theoretical analysis of how the features, design, and implementation of two types of formalization influence work practices.

Let's begin with definitions of the two types of formalization. **Enabling formalization** is a set of procedures that help employees deal more effectively with inevitable problems. Rules and procedures do not have to be designed to make the work foolproof; in fact, they cannot be. Rather what is needed is a flexible set of guidelines or best practices that enable one to deal more effectively with the surprises that occur. For example, a rule not to act until data can be accumulated provides the stimulus for problem solving and is enabling rather than restraining. On the other hand, an automatic detention for talking back to a teacher is punishing and does enable the student to make improvements. **Coercive formalization** is a set of procedures that punishes and attempts to force reluctant subordinates to comply. Rules and procedures become substitutes for commitment rather than complements to it. Instead of giving committed employees access to accumulated organizational learning and best-practice guidelines, coercive procedures are designed to force compliance and extract recalcitrant effort.

The contrasting features of the two types of formalization are stark. Enabling procedures call for two-way communication, viewing problems as learning opportunities, cooperation, supporting differences, openness, trust, delighting in the unexpected, and ease in correcting mistakes. Coercive procedures typically are characterized by one-way communication (top-down), viewing problems as constraints, forced consensus, suspicion of differences, watchful mistrust, fear of the unexpected, and punishment for mistakes.

Formulating enabling and coercive procedures are also quite different. The process of developing enabling strategies is one of participation and cooperation, for example, teachers and principals working together to find ways that solve problems in a mutually satisfying way. Trust is the heart of the enterprise and improvement is the goal. In contrast, the formulation of coercive procedures is typically unilateral, top-down with the view of controlling subordinates; for example, principals are intent on watching and controlling teachers. Superiors simply don't trust subordinates; consequently, suspicion, control, and punishment imbue the process. Research in schools (Hoy and Sweetland, 2000) is beginning to show that enabling and coercive bureaucracies exist in schools, and not surprisingly, enabling formalization does enhance the administration of schools.

In sum, good and bad procedures as experienced by employees have different features, develop through different design processes, and are implemented in different organizational contexts (see Table 3.3). Furthermore, this conceptual refinement of formalization provides a potential explanation for the conflicting findings regarding the impact of bureaucracy on participants—namely, it is the kind and not the degree of formalization that explains the negative effects of bureaucracy. Enabling procedures produce positive outcomes; coercive ones yield negative outcomes. In other words, enabling bureaucracies are functional: coercive ones are dysfunctional.[4]

Formal Structure in Schools

Schools are formal organizations with many of the same characteristics as bureaucratic organizations. Max Abbott (1965a: 45), for example, using the characteristics of the Weberian model developed earlier in this chapter, has concluded: "The school organization as we know it today . . . can accurately be described as a highly developed bureaucracy. As such, it exhibits many of the characteristics and employs many of the strategies of the military, industrial,

TABLE 3.3

Two Types of Formalization: Enabling and Coercive

	Enabling Formalization	**Coercive Formalization**
Features	Two-way communication	One-way, top-down communication
	Problems are learning opportunities	Problems are constraints
	Mutual solution	Forced consensus
	Supports differences	Suspicious of differences
	Openness	Watchful mistrust
	Delight in the unexpected	Fear of the unexpected
	Ease in correcting mistakes	Punishment for mistakes
Design Process	Participative decision making	Unilateral decision making
	Focus on problem solving	Focus on authority
Context for Implementation	**Flexible context with:**	**Rigid context with:**
	• Employee security	• Employee insecurity
	• Professional (self-regulated workers)	• Not self-regulated workers
	• Cohesive work groups	• Conflict within the work groups
	• Little management-labor conflict	• Management-labor conflict
	• Disturbing organizational needs	• Indifference
	• Employee voice	• No employee voice
	• Employee skill	• Limited employee skill
	• Process control	• Little process control

and governmental agencies with which it might be compared." The bureaucratic model is the one that many school administrators adopt, and this may explain why the model can be used to analyze behavior in schools (Abbott, 1965a; Miles, 1965; Firestone and Herriott, 1981; Abbott and Caracheo, 1988; Corwin and Borman, 1988).

A basic assumption of bureaucracies is that every subordinate has less technical expertise than his or her superior. This assumption certainly does not apply in schools, nor does it apply in other professional organizations. On the contrary, professionals often have more competence and technical expertise than the administrators who occupy a higher level in the organization. Consequently, to find strain and tension in schools between teachers and administrators should not be surprising.

Rather than thinking of schools as bureaucratic or nonbureaucratic, a more useful approach is to examine the degree of bureaucratization with respect to the important components of the Weberian model. Such an approach differentiates types of organizational structures and also provides a tool to test empirically the extent to which the theoretical components of the model are consistent. Richard H. Hall (1962, 1987, 1991), Lee Bolman and Terrence Deal (1991, 1997), and Henry Mintzberg (1979, 1989) are among the theorists and researchers who have systematically examined structure.

Hall on Bureaucratic Structure

One of the earliest systematic attempts to measure bureaucratization is Hall's (1962) development of an organizational inventory to measure six central characteristics of bureaucratic structure: (1) hierarchy of authority, (2) specialization, (3) rules for incumbents (i.e., those assuming an organizational role), (4) procedure specifications, (5) impersonality, and (6) technical competence. D. A. MacKay (1964) subsequently adapted and modified the organizational inventory in his study of the bureaucratization of schools. He measured bureaucratic patterns in schools using the school organizational inventory (SOI), a questionnaire that operationalizes the same six dimensions of structure.

The interrelationships of these bureaucratic characteristics of schools also have been explored empirically (Kolesar, 1967; Isherwood and Hoy, 1973; Abbott and Caracheo, 1988). Studies indicate that there are two relatively distinct patterns of rational organization rather than one completely integrated bureaucratic pattern. Hierarchy of authority, rules for incumbents, procedural specifications, and impersonality tend to vary together, and specialization and technical competence similarly vary together; however, the two groups are found to be independent of or inversely related to each other.

Organizational Types

In the school, as in other kinds of organizations, the components of Weber's ideal type do not necessarily form an inherently connected set of variables; instead, there are likely to be distinct types of rational organization. These results are summarized in Table 3.4.

TABLE 3.4

Two Types of Rational Organization in the School Setting

Organizational Characteristics	Organizational Patterns
Hierarchy of authority Rules for incumbents Procedural specifications Impersonality	Bureaucratic
Technical compe tence Specialization	Professional

In Table 3.4 we have labeled the first set of characteristics "bureaucratic" and the second set "professional." The distinction once again calls attention both to the potential conflict between authority based on technical competence and expertise and that based on holding an office in a hierarchy and to the potential incompatibility between professionalization and bureaucratization. To lump together the bureaucratic and professional patterns in a single model of bureaucracy seems to obscure important differences among schools. Indeed, separating two patterns of rational organization and administration makes it possible to explore combinations of the two patterns. For example, if each pattern is dichotomized, as shown in Figure 3.2, then four types of organizations are possible.

A Weberian school structure is one in which professionalization and bureaucratization are complementary; both are high. This pattern is similar to the ideal type described by Weber; hence we call it a **Weberian structure.**

An **authoritarian structure** emphasizes bureaucratic authority at the expense of professional consideration. Authority is based on position and hierarchy. Disciplined compliance to the rules, regulations, and directives is the basic principle of operation. Power is concentrated and flows from top to bottom. Rules and procedures are impersonally applied. The superior

		Professional Pattern	
		High	Low
Bureaucratic Pattern	High	Weberian	Authoritarian
	Low	Professional	Chaotic

FIGURE 3.2 *Typology of School Organizational Structure*

always has the last say. Furthermore, promotions to administrative positions typically go to those who have been loyal to the organization and to their superiors. In many respects, this authoritarian structure is similar to the one Gouldner (1954) described as a punishment-centered bureaucracy.

A **professional structure** is one in which substantial decision making is delegated to the professional staff. Members of the staff are viewed as professionals who have the expertise and competence to make important organizational decisions. Rules and procedures serve as guides rather than as strict formats to be applied uniformly. Special cases are likely to be the rule rather than the exception. Teachers have much power in the organizational decision-making process. In brief, decisions are made by those who have the knowledge and expertise to make them. We refer to this type of school structure as professional.

Finally, a **chaotic structure** has a low degree of bureaucratization and professionalization, therefore confusion and conflict typify day-to-day operations. Inconsistency, contradiction, and ineffectiveness are likely to pervade the chaotic structure. Invariably, strong pressures will arise to move toward one of the other structural types.

This typology presents four potential school structures that are quite different and probably have different consequences for teachers and students alike. Henry Kolesar (1967), for example, found that a sense of student powerlessness was significantly higher in authoritarian than in professional school structures. Geoffrey Isherwood and Wayne K. Hoy (1973) uncovered the same finding for teachers in the two types of schools. Overall, the sense of powerlessness among teachers was much greater in authoritarian than in professional structures. But organizationally and socially oriented teachers (those who identify themselves with the values and goals of the organization and of family and friends, respectively) had less of a sense of powerlessness in the authoritarian structure than professionally oriented teachers. Apparently, individual work orientation mediates the relationship between organizational structure and alienation. Teachers with an organizational orientation may not be alienated by authoritarian structures and procedures and indeed may be quite content. Gerald H. Moeller and W. W. Charters' (1966) finding that teachers in highly bureaucratic systems had more sense of power than those in less bureaucratic systems lends support to this speculation.

It is also true that the type of school organizational structure may influence student achievement. Research (MacKay, 1964; B. Anderson, 1971; MacKinnon and Brown, 1994) suggests the possibility that highly bureaucratic structures may have negative effects on student achievement and innovation. Finally, the evidence continues to mount that specialization (professional pattern) and centralization (bureaucratic pattern) are mildly, but negatively related (Hage, 1980; Corwin and Herriott, 1988; Hall, 1991).[5]

Changing School Structures

The classification of school structures into these four structural types seems useful; in fact, the typology can serve as a basis for a theory of school development. Chaotic structures are ineffective and candidates for swift action. Boards of education will be under great pressure from both within and without to bring order to the existing chaos. The typical response is to get "new leadership." The new leadership invariably turns to starkly bureaucratic and authoritarian procedures to gain order. That is, it seems likely that chaotic structures will move to authoritarian ones.

Authoritarian structures are mechanistic. Power and authority rest almost exclusively in a tightly coupled organizational structure; administrators engage in unilateral decision making and teachers are expected to comply with their directives without question. Relations are typically formal, impersonal, and vertical. A single set of clear, formal goals buttressed by bureaucratic authority guide organizational behavior. Instruction is coordinated by administrative enforcement of schedules, rules, and procedures. Expected conflict is moderate—lower than that found in chaotic structures, but higher than that found in Weberian and professional structures. School effectiveness is predicted to be moderate, provided the environment is supportive, stable, and simple.

The next logical step in an evolutionary development of school structure is toward a Weberian configuration. Here the forces of centralization and specialization are balanced. The bureaucratic attributes of hierarchy, rules, procedures, and impersonality complement the technical competence and specialization of teachers. Administrators and teachers share in decision making, with both groups focused on common interests and with both committed to a single set of shared goals. Conflict between teachers and administrators is limited, yet the couplings between organizational parts are moderately tight. In brief, there is an integration of formal and informal properties. School effectiveness is predicted to be high, and such a structure should function most effectively in a simple and stable environment.

Most individuals prefer order to chaos; hence, movement from a chaotic structure to an authoritarian one is relatively straightforward. The challenge, however, of moving an authoritarian school structure to a Weberian one is much more difficult. Our own experience and research (Isherwood and Hoy, 1973; Firestone and Herriott, 1982; Hoy, Blazovsky, and Newland, 1983; Abbott and Carecheo, 1988) suggest that many schools remain basically authoritarian; they do not readily evolve into Weberian structures. Nonetheless, we expect to see pressures for movement toward Weberian and professional structures as the reform in education presses for teacher empowerment (Casner-Lotto, 1988; Maeroff, 1988; Sickler, 1988; Goldring and Chen, 1992), school-based management (Sirotnik and Clark, 1988; Malen, Ogawa, and Kranz, 1990; Malen and Ogawa, 1992), decentralization (Brown, 1990; Hill and Bonan, 1991; Bimber, 1993), and a general restructuring of schools (Cohen, 1987; Elmore, 1988; David, Purkey, and White, 1989; Clune and White, 1990).

As the occupation of teaching becomes more fully professionalized, a few school structures may evolve from Weberian to professional structures. The professional structure is loose, fluid, and informal. Teacher professionals control decision making; indeed, teacher groups are the dominant source of power. Administrators are subordinate to teachers in the sense that their primary role is to serve teachers and facilitate the teaching-learning process. The burden for integrating the activities of the school rests with the teacher professionals. Professional structures are complex organizations with a highly professional staff, multiple sets of goals, high teacher autonomy, and horizontal rather than vertical relations. Ultimately, the effectiveness of such organizations depends almost exclusively on the expertise, commitment, and service of the teachers. Professional organizations have the potential for high effectiveness in a stable and complex environment.

We have proposed a model of school development in which schools move progressively from chaotic to authoritarian to Weberian to professional structures. There is nothing inevitable about the evolution; in fact, we suspect it will be difficult for schools to become professional structures or even Weberian structures in the near future. Moreover, it is likely that many school structures will slip back to chaos as the environment becomes turbulent. Remember also that the four types of structures are ideal types; most schools are variations on these four themes. Nonetheless, the framework should be useful to administrators and students of school organizations as they analyze and attempt to change their own school structures and empower teachers. In Table 3.5 we have summarized the characteristics of each of these school structures and predicted some likely outcomes.

Mintzberg on Structure

Henry Mintzberg (1979, 1980, 1981, 1983a, 1983b, 1989) provides another, more comprehensive conceptual framework for examining organizational structure. He describes structure simply as the ways in which an organization divides its labor into tasks and then achieves coordination among them. Five basic **coordinating mechanisms** are the fundamental means organizations use to monitor and control work: mutual adjustment, direct supervision, standardization of work processes, standardization of outputs, and standardization of worker skills. These mechanisms glue the organization together.

Coordinating Mechanisms

Mutual adjustment is coordination through the simple process of informal communication. Workers coordinate their efforts by informal discussion and adjustment. Mutual adjustment is direct and basic; it is necessary not only in the simplest organization, but also in the most complicated.

Direct supervision is coordination through personal command. One individual has the responsibility for monitoring and controlling the work of others. As the size of an organization increases, the more likely it is that mutual adjustment will become less effective and direct supervision more necessary. As work activities become more and more complicated, however, neither mutual adjustment nor direct supervision is sufficient. Hence, the work is standardized; coordination of parts is achieved by incorporating them in a carefully planned program for the work. There are three basic ways to obtain standardization in organizations: standardize the work processes, the outputs, or the skills.

TABLE 3.5

Types of School Structures and Their Properties

Organizational Property	Chaotic Structure	Authoritarian Structure	Weberian Structure	Professional Structure
Integrating principle	None	Formal goals and bureaucratic authority	Bureaucratic authority and professional authority	Professional authority
Goals	Irrelevant	A single set of clear, formal goals	A single set of clear, shared goals	Multiple sets of goals
Dominant source of power	Political	Bureaucratic	Bureaucratic and professional	Professional
Decision-making process	Nonrational and individualistic	Top-down and rational	Shared and rational problem solving	Horizontal-rational and incremental
Coordination of instruction	None	Administrative enforcement of rules and schedule	Professional standardization of instruction	Standardization of training
Expected level of conflict	High	Moderate	Limited	Low
Coupling	Loose	Tight	Moderately tight	Loose
Predicted effectiveness	Low	Moderate	High	High
Expected environment	Dynamic and hostile	Simple and stable	Simple and stable	Complex and stable

Standardization of work is achieved by specifying or programming the contents of the work. The written directions to develop a lesson plan are an example. The process of developing the plan is described carefully in step-by-step directions.

Standardization of output is attained by specifying the results of the work; the fundamental dimensions of the product or of the performance are enumerated. Taxicab drivers, for example, are not usually given a route; they are merely told the destination. Similarly, teachers may simply be told that the student should be able to perform at a basic level in a given area; the means to achieve that level may be left to the teacher. The outcomes of the work are described carefully and employees are expected to achieve the standard.

Standardization of skills is a coordination mechanism that provides indirect control of work. Here specifying the kind of training required to do the work standardizes skills and knowledge. Training supplies workers with patterns of work to be performed as well as the bases of coordination. Mintzberg observes that when an anesthesiologist and a surgeon meet in the operating room, typically little communication occurs; by virtue of their respective training, each knows precisely what to expect. Their standardized skills provide most of the coordination.

Key Parts

Although most organizations of any size use all five means of coordination, each organization specializes in one, a fact that has important consequences for the basic structure of the organization. Mintzberg also identifies five key parts of the organization (see Figure 3.3). These are the significant aspects of the structure, each with a critical function to perform.

The **operating core** comprises those who perform the basic work—activities directly related to the production of products and services. The core is the heart of the organization; it produces the essential output. In schools, teachers are the operating core and teaching and learning are the outcomes.

The administrative component of the organization has three parts. First, the **strategic apex** consists of the top administrators (superintendent and assistants) who are charged with the responsibility of ensuring that the organization effectively serves its mission. Those administrators who connect the apex with the operating core through the formal authority structure, constitute the **middle line.** In school systems, principals are the middle managers. Any organization that relies primarily on direct supervision for control and coordination is bound to have a large middle line. The **technostructure** is the administrative component charged with the responsibility of planning. It is composed of analysts who standardize the work of others and apply their an-

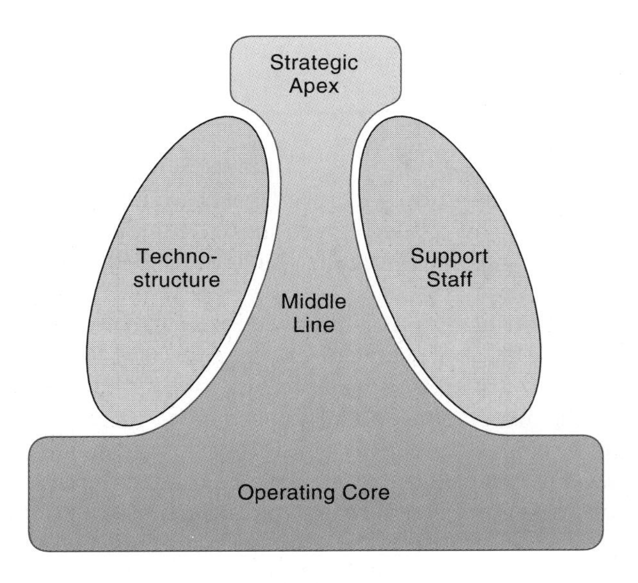

FIGURE 3.3 ***The Five Basic Parts of Organizations***

Source: Henry Mintzberg, *The Structuring of Organizations* (Englewood Cliffs, NJ: Prentice Hall, 1979), p. 20.

alytic techniques to help the organization adapt to its environment. These analysts design, plan, and train, but they do not directly manage. Curriculum coordinators and instructional supervisors are often members of the school technostructure; their role is to help teachers design and plan instruction and to provide in-service opportunities for professional growth and development.

Finally, a fifth component—the **support staff**—is composed of specialized units that exist to provide support for the organization outside the operating workflow. In schools, for example, we find a building and grounds department, a maintenance department, a cafeteria, and a payroll department. None of these units is part of the operating core, but each exists to provide indirect support for the school.

These five key parts of the organization and the five coordination mechanisms that hold them together serve as the basis for five configurations.

- *Simple structure:* The strategic apex is the key part and direct supervision is the central coordinating device.
- *Machine bureaucracy:* The technostructure is the key part and standardization of work processes is the central coordinating device.
- *Professional bureaucracy:* The operating core is the key part and standardization of skills is the central coordinating device.
- *Divisionalized form:* The middle line is the key part and standardization of outputs is the central coordinating device.
- *Adhocracy:* The support staff is the key part and mutual adjustment is the central coordinating device.[6]

Our discussion will focus on the forms most likely to be found in schools.

Mintzberg's Perspective Applied to Schools

The configurations that Mintzberg describes are abstract ideals, yet these simplifications of more complex structures do come to life in the analysis of schools. Schools experience the basic forces that underlay these configurations: the pull to centralize by top management, the pull to formalize by the technostructure, and the pull to professionalize by teachers.[7] Where one pull dominates, then the school will likely be organized close to one of Mintzberg's ideal configurations; that is, the pull to formalize moves the organization toward machine bureaucracy; the pull to centralize yields to simple structure; and the pull to professionalize leads to professional bureaucracy (see Figure 3.4). One pull, however, does not always dominate and the basic processes may have to coexist in balance. Highly professional teachers may have their efforts tightly directed by a dynamic administrator as in a simple professional bureaucracy. Although such an arrangement may work well over the short run, it leads to conflict between the administration and teachers. We turn to structural configurations expected in most schools.

Simple Structure An organization that is coordinated by a high degree of direct supervision, that has a small strategic apex with virtually no middle line, and that is highly centralized is a **simple structure.** In such an organization

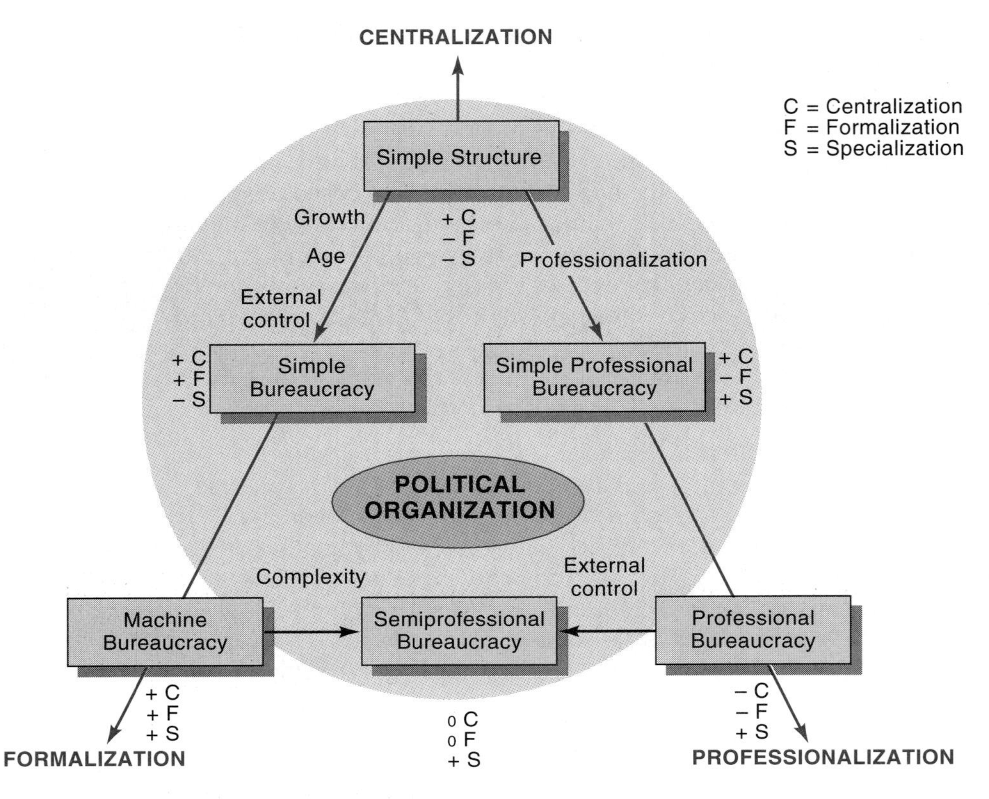

FIGURE 3.4 *Configurations of School Structure*

there is little elaboration—little technostructure, little support staff, little division of labor and specialization, and a small administrative hierarchy.

Because power over important decisions tends to be centralized in the hands of the top administrator, the strategic apex is the key part of the organization. Standardization in a simple structure is unnecessary because things are worked out as they arise; there are loose, informal working relations among participants. Thus, communication flows informally, but most of it is between the top administrator and everyone else. The name tells it all—the structure is simple.

New organizations usually begin simply and elaborate their administrative structures as they grow. Many small organizations, however, retain a simple structure. Informal communications remain effective and a one-person strategic apex attends to coordination. There are variants of the simple structure. For example, the *autocratic organization* is a simple structure where the top administrator hoards power and rules by fiat; and the *charismatic organization* is a variant where the leader has the same power not because it is hoarded but because the followers lavish it upon the leader. The major strength of the simple structure is its flexibility; only one person must act.

The simple structure is of interest because many schools, particularly small elementary school districts, have such a structure. Autocratic and sometimes charismatic principals who rule with an iron hand administer them. Although some teachers enjoy working in a small, intimate school, where its charismatic principal leads the way, others perceive the simple structure as highly restrictive and autocratic. Such structures are highly dependent upon the expertise, imagination, and energy of the chief executive. As the executive goes, so goes the organization. These are highly centralized structures with the top administrator making all major decisions and formal authority flows in one direction—top-down. Schools with simple structures face especially difficult problems in executive succession and as growth renders direct supervision inadequate. A simple structure can be relatively enduring or only a phase in the development and maturing of an organization. Mintzberg (1979, 1989) defines organizational structures that rely on any form of standardization for coordination as bureaucratic. Of the common school configurations derived from Mintzberg's formulation, the simple structure is the only one that is nonbureaucratic; its structure is organic.

Machine Bureaucracy An organization that is fine-tuned and standardized to run as an integrated, regulated machine is called a **machine bureaucracy.** The work processes in this kind of structure are routine and standard. Indeed, standardization of work is the prime coordinating mechanism and the technostructure is the key part of the structure because it contains the analysts who do the standardizing. In these organizations, a high degree of centralization is supported by considerable formalization: rules and regulations permeate the structure; formal communication *predominates* at all levels; and decision making follows the hierarchical chain of authority.

This is the Weberian structure of bureaucracy—standardized responsibilities, technical qualifications, formal communication channels, rules and regulations, and hierarchy of authority. It is a structure geared for precision, speed, clarity, continuity, unity, subordination, and efficiency. Machine bureaucracy is obsessed with control; a control mentality develops from top to bottom. As Mintzberg (1979: 321) cogently notes, "The problem in the Machine Bureaucracy is not to develop an open atmosphere where people can talk the conflicts out, but to enforce a closed, tightly controlled one where the work can get done despite them."

Considerable power rests with the administrators of the strategic apex; in fact, the only others to share much power with the top administrators are the analysts of the technostructure because their role is standardizing the work processes of the organization. Machine structures work best when the work is routine—that is, when an integrated set of simple, repetitive, tasks must be performed precisely and consistently by people (Mintzberg, 1979).

A few schools or school districts are machine bureaucracies; they are usually large districts where an elaborate technostructure attempts to standardize the work or in states with elaborate statewide technostructures. Behavior is formalized by an extensive set of rules, procedures, and job descriptions. Moreover, power tends to be highly centralized in the apex of the structure; authority flows downward. Although many schools have the trappings, most are not machine bureaucracies in the pure sense because typically they lack an elaborate administrative structure, a large middle line, and an elaborate technostructure. In fact, the structure of many public schools is a cross between the simple structure and the machine bureaucracy—what Mintzberg calls a simple bureaucracy.

Professional Bureaucracy Bureaucratic structure can be defined in terms of "the extent to which behavior is predetermined or predictable, in effect, standardized" (Mintzberg, 1979: 86). Thus, organizations can be bureaucratic without being centralized. A **professional bureaucracy** is a structure that permits both decentralization and standardization at the same time. These organizations use standardization of skills as the prime coordinating mechanism; the operating core is the key organizational part; and professionalization is the crucial process. All such structures rely on the skills and knowledge of their operating professionals to function effectively.

The professional bureaucracy receives its coordination indirectly by relying on the standardization of skills that professionals have acquired in their training; hence, it is not surprising to find relationships in these organizations to be much more loosely coupled than in machine or simple bureaucracies. Professionals are hired and given considerable control over their own work. Many professionals work relatively independently of their colleagues, but closely with their clients. For example, teacher autonomy seems undeniable in some schools. Teachers work alone in their classrooms, are relatively unobserved by colleagues and superiors, and possess broad discretionary authority over their students (Bidwell, 1965). This structural looseness of the school supports a professional basis of organization; however, the demand for uniformity in product, the need for movement of students from grade to grade and school to school in an orderly process, and the long period over which students are schooled require a standardization of activities and hence, a bureaucratic basis of school organization (Mintzberg, 1979).

The administrative structure of the professional bureaucracy is relatively flat. It does not need an elaborate hierarchy to control and coordinate or a technostructure to design work standards. Professionals control themselves and, in a sense, develop their own work standards. The standards of the professional bureaucracy originate largely from outside its structure, in self-governing associations to which the professionals belong. These associations set general standards that are taught by the universities and are used by all organizations of the profession. As we have noted before, two sources generate organizational authority. Machine and simple bureaucracies rely on the authority of the position or office, and professional bureaucracies are built on the authority of knowledge and expertise.

Professional bureaucracy is decentralized; a great deal of power rests with the professionals in the operating core. The work is too complex to be supervised directly by managers or standardized by analysts; hence, professionals have a great deal to say about what they do and how they do it. Professionals have close working relations with clients and loose ones with colleagues. It makes more sense to think in terms of a personal strategy for each professional rather than an integrated organizational strategy. Some schools have the characteristics of the professional bureaucracy—a skilled operating core, standardized work skills, professional norms and autonomy, professional associations, structural looseness, and a flat administrative structure. Such schools are staffed by highly competent and well-trained teachers who control their own work and who seek collective control over decisions that affect them.

We have suggested that some small elementary schools are simple structures; they are centralized, but informal structures. The chief administrator provides strong (often autocratic) direction in an informal atmosphere unfettered with rules and regulations. A few schools are machine bureaucracies; they are usually found in large districts where an elaborate technostructure attempts to standardize the work or in states with elaborate statewide technostructures. Behavior is formalized by an extensive set of rules, procedures, and job descriptions. Moreover, power tends to be highly centralized in the apex of the structure; authority flows downward. A few schools are also professional bureaucracies. They are staffed by highly competent and well-trained teachers who control their own work. The structure is decentralized and democratic among the professionals. Although some schools fit into one of these three configurations, most schools are hybrid variants of the three "ideal types" that have been described.

Simple Bureaucracy The **simple bureaucracy** has the basic characteristics of both a simple structure and a machine bureaucracy: it is highly centralized and highly bureaucratic, but it has a relatively flat administrative structure. Nonetheless, control remains a major obsession; hence such organizations are confronted by most of the dysfunctional characteristics of bureaucracy already discussed in our analysis of the Weberian model. As long as control, accountability, standardized educational outcomes, and inexpensive services are demanded by society for schools, simple bureaucratic structures will be a common configuration for schools.

Although there is high centralization and formalization in simple bureaucracies, there is limited specialization. Firestone and Herriott (1981, 1982) refer to such school structures as rational bureaucracies, and their research suggests that a large number of elementary schools, perhaps most, are simple bureaucracies in which a single set of agreed-upon goals guides internal behavior. The power and authority of the principal is dominant. Instruction and curriculum are standardized and teachers are supervised directly by the principal. Teachers' activities are for the most part controlled by the principal and coordinated by an elaborate system of fixed rules, standard procedures, and administrative schedules.

Simple Professional Bureaucracy Another hybrid variant, the **simple professional bureaucracy,** is more common in secondary than elementary schools. This variant is a combination of the simple structure and the professional bureaucracy. Centralization is high, but so is specialization. Here highly trained teacher-professionals practicing standard teaching skills often take the lead from a strong principal. The formal authority of the principal, however, is complemented by the professional authority of teachers; in fact, principals maintain their effective use of power only as long as the teachers perceive that their interests and the interests of their students are being effectively served. Teachers and administrator share goals, and the goodwill and cooperation of teachers are essential, as the principal provides strong direction and leadership. In this configuration the school is like a symphony orchestra; it is staffed with skilled teachers who teach a standardized curriculum under the watchful eye of a strong professional and sometimes dictatorial principal. The principal is the person with recognized ability to guide the professional enterprise.

Semiprofessional Bureaucracy Another hybrid of organizational structure sometimes found in schools is a blend of machine and professional bureaucracy. The structure of a **semiprofessional bureaucracy** is not as centralized or formalized as the machine bureaucracy nor is it as loose as the professional bureaucracy. Although some aspects of the curriculum and instruction are standardized, teacher professionals go about the business of teaching in a reasonably autonomous fashion. Within broad constraints, teachers have the freedom to set their own instructional goals, and although principals have substantial authority in these structures, it is shared with teachers. Delegation and shared decision making are not uncommon. The complexity of learning and teaching and the demands of the school public for accountability are countervailing forces that promote this configuration. This structure promotes professionalism within a context of moderate structure and is sometimes the configuration found in secondary schools staffed with a highly competent faculty and administrators who are committed to the professional development of their school.

Political Organization The **political organization** has to do with power, not structure. Politics is usually overlaid on all conventional organizations, but at times it becomes so powerful that it creates its own configuration. In effect, it captures the organization and becomes its dominating process. In such situations, power is exercised in illegitimate ways. There is no primary method of coordination, no single dominant part of the organization, no clear form of decentralization; everything depends on informal power and politics, marshaled to win individual issues (Mintzberg, 1989).

When power becomes so pervasive that it dominates, coordination as well as the formal structure become irrelevant; in fact, politics acts to the detriment of coordination by producing disorder. Negotiation, coalition formation, and political games are the keys to understanding life in such structures. Indeed, political activity is a substitute for the legitimate systems of influence found in conventional configurations. Power and politics will be discussed in detail in Chapter 6.

Conflict is usually high in the political organization; thus, there is pressure for negotiation and alliance formation. The political organization, however, is a dysfunctional configuration for schools because it hinders learning and teaching. Too much energy and activity are diverted to game playing, negotiations, and political machinations. Teaching and learning become secondary considerations. Schools are politicized from time to time and occasionally develop into political organizations, but such structures in schools are usually short-lived because of their ineffectiveness.

Of these seven structural configurations, our own long-term predilection for schools is for the professional model, but the evidence (Firestone and Herriott, 1981, 1982; Hoy, Blazovsky, and Newland, 1983) suggests that most schools are not professional organizations. Moreover, it is unlikely that schools will move dramatically to the configuration that Mintzberg calls a professional bureaucracy; however, movement toward simply semi-professional or professional bureaucracies not only seems possible but highly desirable, especially if schools and teaching are to become more fully professional.

A number of elements in the situation influence the particular configuration of schools. For instance, the age and size of a school are likely to influence its structure. As schools age and grow, informal relations and direct supervision are likely to be replaced by formalization and bureaucratic control. When the technical system is defined as complex (i.e., teaching viewed as a complex process requiring individualization and multiple and changing strategies), then a highly professional workforce is needed and decentralization of decision making is required. When, on the other hand, the technical system is defined as routine (i.e., teaching is viewed as a routine process of providing standard and simple minimum skills), then the technical system can be regulated through bureaucratic procedures. Moreover, the more organizations are controlled externally, the more centralized and bureaucratic they tend to become. Mintzberg argues that the two most effective means to control an organization from the outside are to hold its most powerful decision maker responsible and to impose specific standards, usually in the form of rules and regulations.

As school districts are increasingly faced with demands for accountability, minimum basic skills, tests for graduation, and myriad other performance targets from state departments of education, the pulls are for more formalization, more centralization, less professionalization, and a more well-developed state technostructure to regulate and control schools. On the other hand, school reformers continue to lament the negative impact of bureaucratic control and call for redesigning school structures to make them more hospitable to competent and skilled teachers (Darling-Hammond, 1985; Darling-Hammond and Wise, 1985; McNeil, 1986, 1988a, 1988b; Elmore, 1988; Wise, 1988; Prestine, 1991); here the pull is away from formalization and toward more decentralization and increased professionalization.

Loose Coupling Perspective

A body of theory and research challenges some of the notions of the school as a bureaucratic structure. Investigators are questioning rationalistic assumptions about the relationship of structure and process to organizational goals. Terrence E. Deal and Lynn E. Celotti (1980) argue that the formal organization and the administration of the school do not significantly affect methods of classroom instruction. In similar fashion, James G. March and Johan P. Olsen (1976) refer to educational organizations as "organized anarchies." Karl E. Weick (1976) and Howard E. Aldrich (1979) propose that elements or subsystems in organizations are often tied together loosely and argue that educational institutions are good examples of loosely coupled systems. Finally, John Meyer and associates (Meyer and Rowan, 1977, 1978; Rowan, 1982; Meyer and Scott, 1983) propose an institutional explanation to describe loose coupling in schools as they assert that bureaucratic structure and instruction are disconnected (see Chapter 7). In brief, schools are seen as organizations with ambiguous goals, unclear technologies, fluid participation, uncoordinated activities, loosely connected structural elements, and structures that have little effect on outcomes. Analyses such as these are of the **loose coupling perspective** and are useful additions to standard bureaucratic theory.

More than three decades ago Charles Bidwell (1965) analyzed structural looseness in school organizations. He noted that in order to deal with the problem of variability in student abilities on a day-to-day basis, teachers need to have freedom to make professional judgments. Professional autonomy seems undeniable in schools. Teachers work alone in their classrooms, are relatively unobserved by colleagues and administrators, and possess broad discretionary authority over their students. The result is a structural looseness *within* the school. Similarly, structural looseness exists *among* the school units in the system. Administrators and teachers of each school enjoy broad discretionary powers with respect to curriculum, teaching methods, and teacher selection. For example, even though the system recruits teachers, they typically are not assigned to a particular school without the principal's approval.

The structural looseness of the school supports a professional basis of organization; however, the demand for uniformity in product, the need for movement of students from grade to grade and school to school in an orderly process, and the long period of time over which students are schooled require a routinization of activities and, hence, a bureaucratic basis of school organization. Bidwell (1965), therefore, depicts the school as a distinctive combination of bureaucracy and structural looseness.

Loose coupling theorists (Weick, 1976; Aldrich, 1979) and institutional theorists (Meyer, 1978; Meyer and Rowan, 1977, 1978; Rowan, 1982) focus on the disconnectedness of behavior and outcomes in organizations. Weick (1976) develops probably the most thorough analysis of the concept of loose coupling. By **loose coupling,** he conveys "the image that coupled events are responsive, but that each event also preserves its own identity and some evidence of its physical or logical separateness" (Weick, 1976: 5). Loose coupling connotes weak or infrequent ties between elements that are minimally interdependent; hence, the phrase is invoked to refer to a variety of situations.

Most organizations are concerned with who does the work and how well it is performed. Weick (1976) suggests that in schools there is loose control over how well the work is done. Inspection of the instructional activities is infrequent, and even when evaluation of teaching does occur, it is usually perfunctory. Under these conditions, tight organizational controls over who does the work—through such activities as hiring, certifying, and scheduling—are exerted.

Meyer and Rowan (1977, 1978) expand Weick's thesis. They claim that educators typically "decouple" their organizational structure from instructional activities and outcomes and resort to a **logic of confidence.** Their argument is that schools are basically personnel-certifying agencies of society. Standardized curricula and certified teachers produce standardized types of graduates, who are then given their appropriate place in the economic and stratification system on the basis of their certified educational backgrounds. Ritual classifications such as elementary teacher, English teacher, principal, fourth grader, or college prep student provide the basis for tightly structured educational organizations. Schools gain community support and legitimacy by conforming to the legal and normative standards of the wider society. Much less control is exerted over teaching activities because close supervision and rigorous evaluation might uncover basic flaws in the instructional program and produce uncertainties. It is much easier to demonstrate conformity to abstract ritual classifications than to evaluate the effectiveness of the teaching-learning process. Therefore, schools decouple their ritual structure from instructional activities and buttress the decoupling by embracing an assumption of good faith (Okeafor and Teddlie, 1989). The community has confidence in members of the board of education, who in turn have confidence in the teachers. These multiple exchanges of confidences are supported by an abiding faith in the process by which school officials have been certified as professionals.

Empirical evidence to support the existence, extent, and patterns of loose couplings in schools is mixed. On the one hand, a number of studies depict the school as a highly centralized and formalized organization; in fact, one of the most salient features of secondary schools in New Jersey is the apparent rigid hierarchy of authority (Hoy, Newland, and Blazovsky, 1977; Hoy, Blazovsky, and Newland, 1980, 1983). High school teachers maintain that they must ask permission and get approval before they do "almost anything"; even small matters have to be referred to a superior for a final answer (Hoy, Newland, and Blazovsky, 1977).

On the other hand, the picture of schools presented by Meyer and Rowan (1978), and others (Abramowitz and Tenenbaum, 1978; Deal and Celotti, 1980; Meyer, 1978) is quite different. These investigators paint schools as loosely coupled systems where instructional work is basically removed from the control of the organizational structure. Perhaps when teachers claim that they must ask permission and get approval before they do almost anything they are excluding instructional activity. Although it seems hard to believe that teachers make such a distinction, professional discretion of teachers may be so broad and their autonomy so great concerning classroom instruction that questions of supervision are considered by teachers only within a framework of routine school and classroom management practices.

Several studies on the images of school organizations by William Firestone and his colleagues (Firestone and Herriott, 1981, 1982; Firestone and Wilson, 1985; Herriott and Firestone, 1984) specifically examine contrasting school structures. Their work suggests that schools can be grouped into two clusters: rational bureaucracy and anarchy, or loosely coupled systems. Elementary schools were much more likely to be rational bureaucracies characterized by goal consensus, hierarchy of authority, centralization, formalization, and limited teacher autonomy. Secondary schools, in contrast, were more loosely coupled systems with more teacher autonomy but with little goal consensus and much less centralization.

The crude distinction between bureaucracy and loosely coupled systems can be misleading (Corwin and Borman, 1988) and counterproductive. Most elementary schools are more tightly structured than secondary schools, but it is a matter of degree. Routine tasks and functions are bureaucratically organized in secondary schools. In fact, a comparative analysis of public secondary schools and social welfare agencies by Hoy and his colleagues (Hoy, Blazovsky, and Newland, 1983) found schools to be dramatically more formalized and centralized than the welfare agencies. Not one welfare agency had as much hierarchical control or rule enforcement as the *least* centralized or least formalized high school. Finally, in a comprehensive review of the loose coupling literature, R. M. Ingersoll (1993: 108) concludes, "that the loose coupling perspective has offered an incomplete and faulty view of the organization of schools."

Are public schools, then, rigid bureaucracies that need to be loosened or organizational anarchies that need to be tightened? Our analysis leads us to the conclusion that there are probably at least two basic organizational domains: a bureaucratic one consisting of the institutional and managerial functions of mediating between the school and community, implementing the law, administering internal affairs, procuring and allocating necessary resources, and mediating between students and teachers; and a professional one involved with the actual technical processes of teaching and learning.[8] The bureaucratic domain is typically a tightly linked and cohesive structure, at times too rigid, preventing adaptation and producing alienation among teachers. The professional sphere is much more loosely structured; teachers have broad discretion to make professional judgments about the teaching-learning process; at times, too much independence produces conflict, confusion, and coordination problems—reducing productivity and hindering efficiency.[9] Schools are affected by their environments; they are open systems. As forces in society change, pressures to tighten and loosen organization linkages also vary. Clearly, administrators need to know the organization and be aware of and sensitive to the negative consequences of *both* tight and loose coupling. In general, the public school is a distinctive combination of bureaucratic and professional elements, a theme which we will now explore in more detail.

Professional and Bureaucratic Conflict

Professionals and semiprofessionals employed in formal organizations bring into focus a basic conflict between professional values and bureaucratic expectations. Although many similarities exist between professional and bureaucratic principles, the potential for conflict remains because differences do exist. The major similarities and differences are summarized in Table 3.6.

Both bureaucrats and professionals are expected to have technical expertise in specialized areas, to maintain an objective perspective, and to act

TABLE 3.6

Basic Characteristics of Professional and Bureaucratic Orientations: Similarities and Differences

Professional Orientation	Bureaucratic Orientation
Technical expertise	Technical expertise
Objective perspective	Objective perspective
Impersonal and impartial approach	Impersonal and impartial approach
Service to clients	Service to clients
Major Sources of Conflict	
Colleague-oriented reference group	Hierarchical orientation
Autonomy in decision making	Disciplined compliance
Self-imposed standards of control	Subordinated to the organization

impersonally and impartially. Professionals, however, are expected to act in the best interests of their clients, whereas bureaucrats are expected to act in the best interests of the organization. This apparent conflict between the interests of clients and the organization poses a problem for many formal organizations, but for service organizations such as schools, social work agencies, and hospitals it may not be a major dilemma. Unlike business concerns, the prime beneficiary of service organizations is the client. For service organizations, then, the prime objective of both the bureaucrat and the professional is the same—service to clients.

A fundamental source of **professional-bureaucratic conflict** does emerge from the system of social control used by bureaucracies and the professions. Professionals attempt to control work decisions. They have been taught to internalize a code of ethics that guides their activities, and colleagues support this code of behavior. Professionals are basically responsible to their profession, and at times their colleagues may censure them. On the other hand, control in bureaucratic organizations is not in the hands of the colleague group; discipline stems from one major line of authority. As Blau and Scott (1962: 63) explain, "Performance is controlled by directives received from one's superiors rather than by self-imposed standards and peer-group surveillance, as is the case among professionals."

Considerable variation exists, however, among various professional groups and in the scope of their professional domains. For example, elementary and secondary schoolteachers may have a relatively narrow scope, whereas physicians and scientists typically have broad authority (Scott, 1981). The ultimate basis for a professional act is professional knowledge; however, the ultimate justification of a bureaucratic act is its consistency with the organizational rules and regulations and approval by a superior. Therein lies the major source of conflict between the organization and the profession—conflict between "professional expertise and autonomy" and "bureaucratic discipline and control."

Nevertheless, Scott (1981, 1987b, 1992) argues that, although some conflict exists between professional and bureaucratic principles, the two arrangements are not incompatible in all respects. Both represent alternative paths to the rationalization of a field of action—and at a general level, the two orientations are compatible. But the interaction between bureaucrats and professionals can be strained. Teachers resent interference and directives from the administration and call for shared governance in schools. Of course, different ways are used to resolve the conflicts. In some organizations major structural changes have been made. In others, many professionals have developed orientations that are compatible with the demands of their bureaucratic organizations.

Professional and Bureaucratic Orientations in Schools

Whether or not teaching is a full-fledged profession is debatable. However, few would argue either that teachers are closer to the professional end of an occupational continuum than blue-collar and white-collar workers, or that they are further from the professional pole than physicians or lawyers. Nonetheless, the growth of theory and knowledge in teaching, the increased requirements for teacher education, teachers' sense of responsibility for student welfare, strong professional associations, and increased claims for teacher autonomy provide the basis for considering teaching a profession. Behind the drive to professionalize teaching is the desire for increased status and more control over work—in order to gain not only more responsibility but also more authority or power. For many years, teachers believed that they had professional obligations, such as staying after school to help students with their work; now they are demanding professional rights as well, such as selecting their own colleagues.

As we have already discussed, the characteristics of bureaucratic organizations are not totally compatible with a professional work group. Findings that many conflicts in schools derive from more general conflict between bureaucratic and professional principles should not be surprising. For example, Ronald G. Corwin (1965) studied teacher conflict in schools and found that almost half the conflict incidents involved teachers in opposition to administrators. The higher the level of professional orientation, the greater the number of conflicts. Similarly, DiPaola and Hoy (1994) in a study of teachers found that professional orientation was related to teacher militancy.

Few teachers escape the oral or written exhortations on "professionalism." Some administrators use the term "professionalism" as a cry to rally support for the school or for a given decision. For example, a decision to initiate a merit salary program in one school subsequently resulted in a confidential note to all teachers notifying them of their salaries plus the following addendum: "Salary is a confidential and personal matter. It is your professional obligation not to discuss your salary with other teachers." A safe prediction is that many educational administrators have a conception of a "professional" teacher as one who is loyal to the administration and the organization—that is, one who has a bureaucratic orientation.

Given the bureaucratization of schools and the growing professionalization of teachers, continued conflict seems likely. In teaching, the immediate issues of conflict revolve around the amount of control teachers should have over the selection of textbooks, teaching procedures and methods, and curriculum reform and development; however, the underlying issue is neither peculiar to teaching nor to school organizations. The conflict is between professional expertise and autonomy and bureaucratic discipline and control.

As long as the basic bureaucratic structure of the school tends to be authoritarian, teacher authority will continue to be a major source of tension. If the organizational structure of the school becomes more professional, then the chances for ameliorating the conflict and tension will be greatly improved. In fact, a dual orientation (local-cosmopolitan) of teachers might be the rule rather than the exception. In professional organizational structures, teachers might increasingly have high commitments both to the organization and to the profession. Some research supports the notion that bureaucratic orientation and professional attitudes of teachers need not be in conflict if schools increase the professional autonomy of teachers (Marjoribanks, 1977; DiPaola and Hoy, 1994).

Several other studies of teacher orientations are relevant. Edward Kuhlman and Wayne K. Hoy (1974) studied the bureaucratic socialization of new schoolteachers. They were interested in the extent to which the professional and bureaucratic orientations of beginning teachers were changed as a result of initial socialization attempts by the school organization. They theorized that a dual-role orientation might emerge among new teachers as they were socialized. New teachers, however, did not become both more professional and more bureaucratic in orientation during the first year of teaching. On the contrary, secondary teachers became significantly more bureaucratic and less professional during the first year. The orientations of beginning elementary teachers remained relatively constant, although as a group they were significantly more bureaucratic than secondary teachers. The hypothesis was not supported that a dual orientation would evolve during the initial experience of teaching and would enhance the effectiveness of both the professional and the organization. Furthermore, Harold Wilensky's (1964) contention regarding an interpenetration of bureaucratic and professional cultures in many organizations was not supported by the findings in secondary schools.

The forces of bureaucratic socialization in a majority of secondary schools seem strong. Most schools begin almost immediately to mold neophytes into roles devised to maintain stability, to encourage subordination, and to promote loyalty to the organization; in fact, the socialization process begins with the student-teaching experience. Student teachers, as a result of their practice teaching experience, appear to become significantly more bureaucratic in orientation (Hoy and Rees, 1977). Similar socialization forces and outcomes have been reported for other aspiring professions, especially for social work (Enoch, 1989).

In sum, research portrays the school as a service organization staffed predominantly with professionals and semiprofessionals. The structure of the school organization is basically bureaucratic, with authoritarian trappings. Teachers as a group are becoming somewhat more professional and more militant; yet the bureaucratic structure, especially at the secondary level, seems quite effective at socializing new members to the appropriate bureaucratic stance, often at the expense of professional considerations. Hence, the school milieu comprises a number of countervailing forces. One hopes that administrators and teachers alike will strive to make school organizations more professional and less authoritarian. In such organizations a dual orientation seems likely to become increasingly prevalent, with teachers who are highly committed to both the profession and the school.[10]

THEORY INTO PRACTICE

Problems at West High

You have been appointed the new principal at West High School. The school has 1,150 students, 85 teachers, an assistant principal, 4 secretaries, and 2 guidance counselors. West High is one of two high schools in a mid-sized school system on the East Coast. The school district is average in terms of support for education, falling about at the 48th percentile on statewide per pupil expenditures. You had been a high school teacher and assistant principal in a district 75 miles to the north. When the opportunity presented itself, you applied, were hired, and are eager to do well in your first job as principal of your own school. The job is a promotion and a significant step up in salary. Moreover, it is conveniently located at the site of the state university, where you are completing your doctoral study—albeit at a slower pace for a while.

Your predecessor at West High was a very popular principal who retired after 30 years on the job. Most of the veteran faculty members liked his unobtrusive style; in fact, his style might more aptly be described as indulgent. He permitted teachers to do just about anything they wanted as long as it caused no problems in the community and, for the most part, the community was apathetic. Occasionally an angry citizen would call asking why one of the teachers was at the bank or in the coffee shop when school was in session. Good "Old Bob," as his teachers fondly called him, always covered for them. "They were on school business." Old Bob had been around so long that many of the parents of the community had been students at the high school when he was a beginning principal, and his nickname then was "Mellow Bob." Although he had been a fixture at West High, few saw him as a leader, but most were satisfied. Why rock the boat was the common refrain when talk turned to change. Old Bob just sailed along blissfully in his role as high school principal. He had an assistant principal, Pete Marshall, who ran interference for him if he needed it and a loyal faculty who knew a good deal when they experienced it.

But things were changing. Statewide testing was revealing inadequacies in the instructional program. Students were getting into more trouble both in and out of school. Indeed, students were getting out of control—class cutting, fights, absenteeism, and dropouts were on the rise. Parents were beginning to request that their kids be sent to East High, the other high school in the district. Students of East High did better academically, socially, and the school was cleaner and had a more orderly environment. The administration at East High was directive and sometimes harsh with both students and faculty; but many parents wanted the strong discipline of East High rather than the laid-back approach at West High. As long as there were no crises, however, Old Bob was happy and so were most of his teachers.

Two years ago the school district had hired a new superintendent, Rebecca Goldberg, and the winds of change had been blowing ever since. Rebecca and Old Bob became antagonists almost immediately. Rebecca had a vision for the district, one of better schools, higher statewide test scores, more parental involvement, new curricular programs, and fewer dropouts. Well, two years of interference were more than Old Bob could take. At the early age of 62, he retired and said farewell to his friends. He steadfastly refused to "buckle under" to the new superintendent. Old Bob's teachers were loyal, and they were shocked and a little anxious when he decided to call it a career and re-

THEORY INTO PRACTICE, (Continued)

tire. After all, he was very teacher-friendly. He opposed bureaucratic rules and regulations because they constrained the activities of his professional faculty. He rewarded his loyal teachers with a hands-off policy. He never threw his position or title around—he was just "one of the boys," a saying that irritated some of the younger women teachers. Yet none said or did anything to offend Old Bob because he was benign. Any time they did need a favor, they could count on him. He had had a great relationship with the previous superintendent; they had been friends for 20 years and it had been about that long that Old Bob had engaged in a pattern of indulgency and benign neglect with his teachers. No one remembered the time when a new teacher did not get tenure; in fact, the way you got hired at West High was to know someone who knew Old Bob. Bob hired and the appointment was always approved by the superintendent and board—that was until two years ago. The new superintendent had different ideas; the board had hired Rebecca Goldberg with the goal of changing and improving the district. Some say Old Bob was just forced out; whatever the dynamics, Old Bob is gone and he left behind a faculty that he had handpicked.

Pete Marshall, Bob's 10-year assistant, had been personally groomed by Old Bob to take over the reins—so it was a bombshell when the school board decided to go outside to hire a successor. The board selected you because of your vision of a school with high academic standards, but one that was nurturing as well as rigorous. The Board of Education wanted you as principal because they liked your progressive ideas and energy and both the board and superintendent had given you a mandate for change. You arrived at West High just a month before school opened and now you have been on the job for nearly two months. You really believe that you can turn things around, but it is not going to be as easy as you originally thought. You have inherited a loyal faculty; unfortunately they are loyal to Old Bob and his assistant principal. It seems that you are being opposed on every issue. There are virtually no operating procedures in this school; teachers do what they want to do and the result is near chaos. When you question a teacher on anything, the response is always the same—"That's the way we always did it." When you suggest that perhaps a change could improve things, the common response is "That's not the way Old Bob did it."

Pete, your assistant principal, is distant and not particularly helpful: in fact, you get the idea that he is working to undermine you. Just last week you passed his office and overheard him remarking to a parent on the phone that you where never around and it made things difficult. You are trying to be supportive of Pete and work with him because you know he is disappointed that he did not get the job. Perhaps you should have taken up the superintendent on the offer to transfer Pete Marshall to East High. You have enough problems with teachers and students without having to watch your back with your assistant. This is a close-knit school and unfortunately, you are an outsider. The board and superintendent expect results and change, but you are getting blocked everywhere you turn. The faculty resents the professional development meetings you have scheduled as part of an upcoming in-service. The faculty resists any attempt to change. You cannot count on your assistant for support; you just don't trust him. Even your secretary (Old Bob's secretary) cannot be depended upon. She too is always idealizing Old Bob. You are sick and tired of hearing about how great Old Bob was; you know that was not the case. You suspect the degree of talk about your predecessor is simply and index of resistance to your leadership. You are frustrated and feel the need to make some drastic changes. The school year is only a month old, but you must do something. You are in charge. You have the support of the board and superintendent right now. You must act, but you need help and you need a plan. Today is the beginning of change at West High, you vow, as you pick up the phone to schedule an appointment with the superintendent. You figure you have a little time to sketch a plan of action, and you believe the superintendent is sympathetic to your plight.

THEORY INTO PRACTICE, (Continued)

- Should you ask that Pete Marshall be transferred?
- How can you get a supportive secretary?
- How can you use the authority of your office for change?
- Is it time for some unilateral changes in your school? Top-down changes?
- Is it time to institute a system of rules, regulations, and procedures? How?
- Do you need a series of strategic replacements?
- Is it time for a dramatic restructuring?
- Is democracy in this situation an unrealistic dream?

These are just some of the questions you must answer before you propose a plan for change to the superintendent. You are the principal; you have the support of your superiors but not your subordinates; your superiors expect improvement; the school needs change; and you need a plan.

SUMMARY AND SUGGESTED READINGS

Virtually all organizations have the distinctive characteristics of bureaucracy—division of labor, specialization, impersonality, hierarchy of authority, rules and regulations, and career orientation—described by Max Weber in his theory of bureaucracy. Weber's model has been criticized because it pays insufficient attention to possible dysfunctional consequences of each component, neglects the significance of the informal organization, ignores the conflict between disciplined compliance and expertise, is gender biased, and has some inherent pathologies. Furthermore, the basic structure of the bureaucracy is challenged by post-modernists as inappropriate and oppressive. Nevertheless, the Weberian perspective provides a strong conceptual basis for examining school structures because most schools have many of the features of bureaucracy.

Two contemporary views of organizational structure are examined. First, Hall's approach is used to develop four types of school organizational structures—Weberian, authoritarian, professional, and chaotic—that are quite different and seem to have different consequences for students and teachers. This typology is then used to outline a theory of structural development in schools. A second, more comprehensive analysis of the structure of organizations is provided by Mintzberg. He describes structure simply as the ways in which an organization divides its labor into tasks and achieves coordination among them. His framework when applied to schools yields a number of contemporary configurations of school structure as well as a political model of schools. The framework provides a basis for synthesizing much of the literature on school structure.

A loose coupling perspective offers a useful addition to bureaucratic and structural theories. The framework challenges many of the assumptions of bureaucratic theory and depicts the school as a distinctive combination of bureaucracy and structural looseness, one in which the institutional structure is decoupled from instructional activities. The natural tendency for bureaucratic and professional elements in school to conflict provides both the school structure and the individual teacher with a challenge to accommodate and change.

We recommend that all students read March and Simon's classic analysis, *Organizations* (1958, 1993). This book is about hierarchical structures and rational decision making. The introduction to the second edition is an intriguing reflection on the world of organizations during the past 35 years by two of the most distinguished organizational theorists of this century. For those students enthralled with the construct of bureaucracy, start with Weber (1947). Mintzberg supplies a readable and extensive contemporary treatment of organizational structure in *Mintzberg on Management* (1989) and Bolman and Deal (1997) provide yet another contemporary analysis of organizational structure. No one who is a student of organization should miss Ferguson's *The Feminist Case Against Bureaucracy* (1984). Those interested in an intriguing post-modern analysis should read Hirschhorn's *Reworking Authority: Leading and Following in the Post-Modern Organization* (1997). Finally, the research on Catholic schools (Coleman, 1990; Bryk, Lee, and Holland, 1993) is beginning to provide some strong evidence of how organizational structures influence a school's ability to achieve its goals.

Notes

1. The intended and unintended results of using rules to gain control has been described as Gouldner's model, and it is discussed in more detail in March and Simon (1993).
2. Radical post-modernists would likely reject Hirschhorn's (1997) post-modern critique as not radical enough. Hirschhorn not only deconstructs bureaucracy but has some guidelines for "reconstructing" post-modern organization, a contribution usually eschewed by radical post-modernists.
3. This section on pathologies draws heavily from Scott (1998).
4. Adler and Borys (1996) provide a much more detailed and refined analysis of these two types of bureaucracies.
5. The Aston studies done by D. S. Pugh and his associates (1968, 1969, 1976) at the University of Aston in Birmingham, England, is a comprehensive set of studies of bureaucracy using interview inventories to assess the structure of work organizations rather than questionnaires. The technique has been used by Canadian researchers (Newberry, 1971; Kelsey, 1973; Holdaway et al., 1975; Sackney, 1976) at the University of Alberta and by U.S. researchers (Sousa and Hoy, 1981; Guidette, 1982; Haymond, 1982) at Rutgers University to study educational organizations. Regardless of research strategy, the results of the study of bureaucratic structures in schools are quite consistent.
6. To these five original configurations, Mintzberg (1989) recently has added two additional ones—the missionary organization and the political organization. Sometimes either ideology or politics becomes so pervasive that it overrides the standard configurations and creates its own configuration. If the organization's ideology (culture) becomes so strong that its entire structure is built around it, Mintzberg labels the

configuration a missionary organization. If the politics becomes so strong that it captures the organization, the configuration is labeled a political organization. But typically, politics (Chapter 6) and ideology (Chapter 5) are components of the standard forms; they are overlays on the five conventional configurations.

7. Mintzberg (1979) also identifies the pull to Balkanize by managers of the middle line and the pull to collaborate by the support staff, which are less pronounced in schools and found predominately in divisional structures and adhocracies.
8. Parsons (1967) details the institutional, managerial, and technical functions in schools.
9. For an insightful discussion of the separate zones of control of principals and teachers, see Lortie (1969).
10. Carlson (1962) provides an intriguing research analysis of local-cosmopolitan orientations for superintendents as they affect administrator behavior, and Hoy and Aho (1973) and Ganz and Hoy (1977) do the same thing for secondary and elementary principals, respectively. See Gouldner (1958) for the classic study of local-cosmopolitan orientations.

Key Concepts and Ideas

Antibureaucratic structure
Authoritarian structure
Career orientation
Chaotic structure
Coercive formalization
Coordinating mechanisms
Direct supervision
Division of labor
Enabling formalization
Goal displacement
Hierarchy of authority
Ideal type
Impersonal orientation
Informal organization
Logic of confidence
Loose coupling
Loose coupling perspective
Machine bureaucracy
Middle line
Mutual adjustment
Operating core
Political organization
Professional bureaucracy
Professional-bureaucratic conflict
Professional structure
Punishment-centered rules
Representative rules
Rules and regulations
Semiprofessional bureaucracy
Simple bureaucracy
Simple professional bureaucracy
Simple structure
Specialization
Standardization of output
Standardization of skills
Standardization of work
Strategic apex
Support staff
Technostructure
Weberian structure

CHAPTER 4

INDIVIDUALS IN SCHOOLS

Among the mechanisms of agency, none is more central or pervasive than beliefs of personal efficacy. Unless people believe they can produce desired effects by their actions, they have little incentive to act.

Albert Bandura
Self-Efficacy: The Exercise of Control

PREVIEW

1. Individuals in schools are motivated by their needs, goals, and beliefs.
2. Maslow's hierarchy of needs theory postulates five basic categories of needs arranged in a hierarchy of prepotency: physiological, safety, belongingness, esteem, and self-actualization needs.
3. Herzberg's hygiene-motivator theory postulates two distinct sets of needs leading to satisfaction and dissatisfaction.
4. Achievement and autonomy needs are also strong motivating forces for many individuals.
5. Goal-setting theory suggests that when specific, realistic, and challenging goals are accepted by an individual, motivation will be strong, especially if feedback about progress is forthcoming.
6. Attribution theory explains that motivation will be strong when causes of outcomes are perceived to be internal, amenable to change, and controllable.
7. Equity theory maintains that individuals will work hard when they believe that they have been treated fairly—that is, that they have received appropriate rewards, that allocations of rewards are fair, and that they have been treated with respect.
8. Expectancy theory suggests that individuals will work hard if that extra effort will improve their performance, good performance will be noticed and rewarded, and they value the rewards.
9. Self-efficacy contributes to motivation by determining what goals individuals set for themselves, how much effort they expend, how long they persevere in the face of difficulties, and their resilience to failures.
10. Intrinsic and extrinsic motivation are two different strategies for motivating individuals.
11. Merit pay and management by objectives are two applications of extrinsic motivation used to motivate teachers.

12. The job-characteristics model provides a good illustration of the use of intrinsic motivation in job design.
13. Career ladders for teachers is a good example of a motivational application that combines both intrinsic and extrinsic strategies.

When administrators analyze their organizations, sometimes they focus on structure to the detriment of the individual. But organizations exist to serve human needs as much as to attain organizational goals. To neglect either the structural or individual element of the school social system is shortsighted and incomplete. As we saw earlier (see Chapter 1), students, teachers, and administrators bring with them needs and develop their own personal orientations and cognitive understanding of their roles. What facets of the individual are most instrumental in determining work and other behaviors in schools? What characteristics of the individual motivate behavior in school? Responses to such questions can be framed in many ways because individuals are so complex and because insights regarding human behavior are rooted in many perspectives and disciplines. We believe that a powerful way to gain insights about students, teachers, and administrators as individuals in the school social system is to examine their needs, goals, beliefs, and motivations.

Needs

Although people occupy roles and positions in schools, they are not merely actors devoid of unique needs; in fact, human needs and motivations are key elements in determining how individuals behave in organizations. Individuals working in organizations are always concerned about fulfilling their needs in the course of doing their jobs. Parents are concerned about the needs of their children, politicians are attuned to the needs of their constituencies, teachers try to meet the needs of their students, and most principals are sensitive to the needs of their teachers. There is little doubt that individual needs are important in organizations. People have different personal needs that shape their behavior. As far as possible, most individuals try to personalize their roles in an organization; that is, stamp their own brand of behavior on expected roles, behavior that is consistent with their needs. One reason why people who occupy the same roles behave so differently is that each has his or her own style. Teachers have different styles and so do students and administrators.

Despite the fact that needs are so commonplace in our analyses and conversations, formal definition of the concept is not as easy as it might appear at first blush. Some theorists, in fact, argue that the term is too vague and difficult to observe (Bolman and Deal, 1997). Nevertheless, people clearly have needs, for example, the needs for air, food, and sleep are certain and clear. Other human needs, for friendships, social interactions, and esteem, are more debatable. Such social needs, it is argued, are shaped so much by environment, socialization, and culture that they don't add much to an explanation of behavior.

Edwin A. Locke (1991) observes that needs are used loosely in everyday conversation, but in their biological context, needs are requirements for an organism's survival and well-being. More formally, **needs** are internal states of disequilibrium that cause individuals to pursue certain courses of action in order to regain internal equilibrium (Steers and Porter, 1991). Or as Christopher Hodgkinson (1991: 94) states, "The idea behind need is that of a discrepancy or undesirable imbalance in a state of affairs. Needs imply tension and disequilibrium and provide a dynamic for rectifying action." Consequently, the ultimate objective of goal-directed action is need fulfillment or the reduction of disequilibrium. The concept of need explains at a most basic level why living organisms behave and is the standard to judge whether a specific action is healthy or not. Locke (1991) provides the following observations about the nature and operation of needs:

- Needs do not account for individual differences because people have the same basic needs, for example, everyone needs food, water, self-esteem.
- Needs operate cyclically and are never permanently satisfied.
- Needs exist even if the individual is not aware of them (e.g., need for certain nutrients).
- Needs can lead to many different actions (e.g., individuals attempt many things to be accepted by peers).
- A particular behavior can stem from more than one need (e.g., earning money can link into many different needs).
- Needs confront people with a requirement for action in difficult situations, if they choose to live.

Hierarchy of Needs

The humanistic psychologist Abraham Maslow (1970) developed a fascinating theory of human needs; in fact, his need hierarchy model has become one of the most widely discussed and influential perspectives of human motivation. The model was derived primarily from Maslow's experience as a clinical psychologist and not from systematic research (Campbell and Pritchard, 1976; Steers and Porter, 1983). His theory posits a **need hierarchy**—a basic innate or inborn set of human needs arranged in a hierarchical order (Kanfer, 1990).

Five basic categories of needs, arranged in hierarchical levels (identified and described in Figure 4.1) constitute the foundation of Maslow's (1970) model:

- At the first level of the hierarchy are *physiological needs,* which consist of such fundamental biological functions as hunger and thirst.
- *Safety and security needs,* the second level, derive from the desire for a peaceful, smoothly running, stable society.
- On the third level, *belonging, love, and social needs* are extremely important in modern society. Maslow contends that maladjustment stems from frustration of these needs. He believes that some

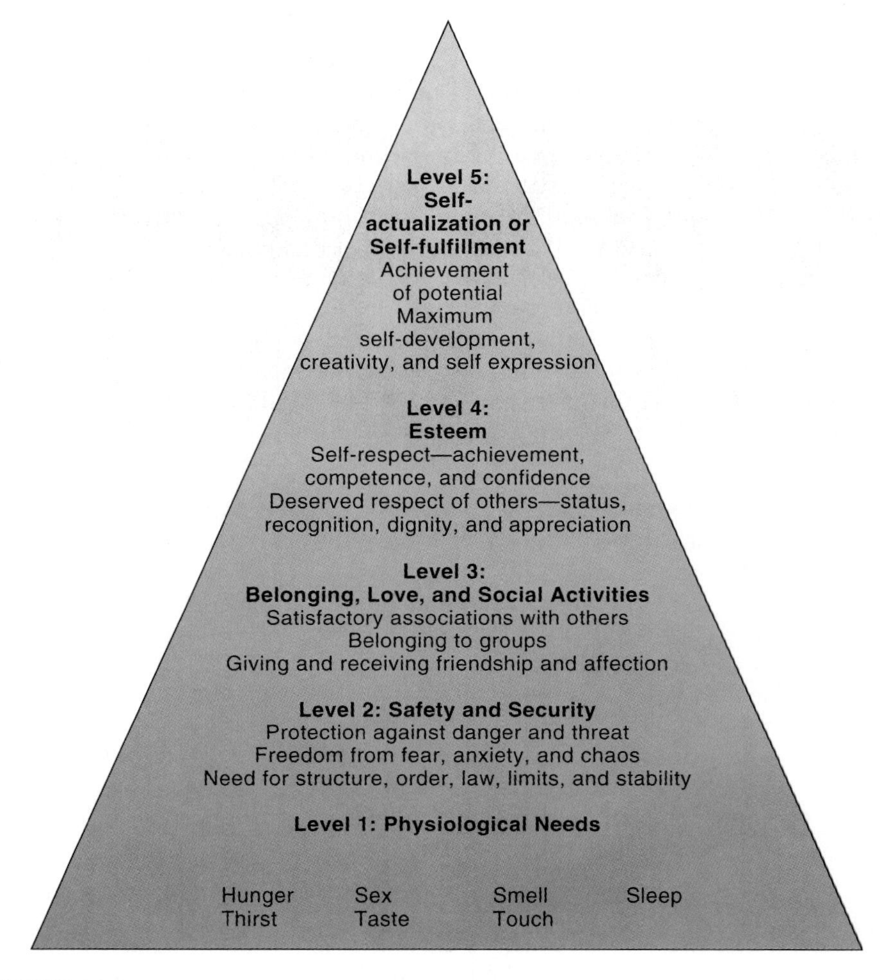

FIGURE 4.1 *Maslow's Need Hierarchy Theory*

proportion of youth rebellion, for example, is motivated by the profound need to belong to a group.

- *Esteem needs,* at the fourth level, reflect the desire to be highly regarded by others. Achievement, competence, status, and recognition satisfy esteem needs.
- Finally, Maslow maintains that discontent and restlessness develop unless individuals do what they are best suited to do—that is, unless they meet their need for *self-actualization,* the fifth level. The meaning of self-actualization is a subject of much discussion. A succinct and simple definition of **self-actualization** is that it is the need to be what an individual wants to be, to achieve fulfillment of life goals, and to realize the potential of his or her personality (Campbell and Pritchard, 1976). Maslow viewed self-actualization

> as a process, not an end state. Individuals are continually in the process of becoming more and more of what they are uniquely capable of becoming (Cherrington, 1991).

Maslow's needs are related to one another and are arranged in a hierarchy of prepotency, or urgency for survival, of the individual. The more prepotent a need is, the more it precedes other needs in human consciousness and demands to be satisfied. This observation leads to the fundamental postulate of Maslow's theory: *higher-level needs become activated as lower-level needs become satisfied.* Thus, Maslow suggests that a person lives by bread alone—when there is no bread. But when there is plenty of bread, other and higher needs emerge. They, in turn, dominate the person and, as they become satisfied, are displaced by new needs. The sequence—increased satisfaction, decreased importance, increased importance of next higher need level—repeats itself until the highest level of the hierarchy is reached. Therefore, individual behavior is motivated by an attempt to satisfy the need that is most important at that time (Lawler, 1973).

The successive emergence of higher needs is limited because lower-level needs are never completely satisfied; moreover, if an individual cannot satisfy needs at a given level for any period of time, those needs again become potent motivators. A completely satisfied need is not an effective motivator. Hence, the concept of gratification is as important as that of deprivation. Maslow reasons that gratification releases the person from the domination of one need, allowing for the emergence of a higher-level need. Conversely, if a lower-order need is left unsatisfied, it reemerges and dominates behavior.

A common misconception about Maslow's theory is that one need must be entirely satisfied before the next level of needs emerges. Maslow asserts that normal individuals are usually only partially satisfied in all their basic needs. A more realistic description of the need structure is that the percentage of satisfaction decreases as one goes up the hierarchy of prepotency. Maslow argues that for the majority of people, needs at the first three levels are regularly satisfied and no longer have much motivational effect; however, satisfaction of esteem and self-actualization needs is rarely complete. The higher-level needs continually motivate. In other words, most behavior is motivated by needs from more than one level of the hierarchy and new need states do not emerge in a crisp, all or nothing lockstep fashion (Pinder, 1984).

Several observations about work in educational organizations can be made using Maslow's theory. First, although physiological needs seem reasonably well met for educators, some students are deprived of even the most basic needs and therefore present a potent motivational problem. Moreover, the needs for safety and security, the second hierarchical level, certainly can become motivating factors for school employees and students alike. Violence to and from school and within the school has increasingly become a way of life for many students. It is difficult to concentrate on studying or teaching when you are frightened. Administrative actions that arouse uncertainty with respect to continued employment, or discrimination, can affect every individual from custodian to superintendent. Furthermore, Maslow theorizes that broader aspects of the attempt to seek safety and security are seen in the preference many people have for familiar rather than unfamiliar things, for the known rather than the unknown. In schools, those people who have high safety needs may resist change and desire job security, injury-compensation plans, and retirement programs to satisfy those needs.

The need to belong causes an individual to seek relationships with co-workers, peers, superiors, and subordinates. For educators, friendship ties, informal work groups, professional memberships, and school memberships satisfy this need. The need for esteem and status, the fourth hierarchical level, causes an educator to seek control, autonomy, respect from and for others, and professional competence. Finally, the need for self-actualization motivates educators to be the best people they are capable of being. This need is less frequently apparent than others, however, because many individuals are still concerned with lower-level needs. Nevertheless, Maslow (1965) clearly advocates that organizations such as schools should provide the highest level of need satisfaction that is possible because self-actualizing students, teachers, and administrators are the best performers.

Maslow's need hierarchy theory, then, is based on three fundamental postulates (Cherrington, 1991):

- Individual needs are universal and arranged in a hierarchy.
- Unfilled needs lead individuals to focus exclusively on those needs.
- Lower-level needs must be largely satisfied before higher-level needs can be felt and pursued.

One of the reasons that Maslow's theory is so popular is because it is intuitively appealing, but research designed to test it has yielded mixed results (Baron, 1998). There is no clear evidence showing that human needs are classified into five distinct categories, or that these categories are structured in any special hierarchy. In fact, the findings of a number of studies do not support the fundamental assumption of a hierarchy of prepotency; other studies have found modest support (Miner, 1980; Steers and Porter, 1983; Landy and Becker, 1987; Cherrington, 1991). Of three studies published since 1980, one strongly challenges the theory (Rauschenberger, Schmitt, and Hunter, 1980); and two show only modest support (Betz, 1984; Lefkowitz, Somers, and Weinberg, 1984).

In educational settings, an early study by Frances M. Trusty and Thomas J. Sergiovanni (1966) reports that the largest deficiencies for professional educators were satisfying esteem and self-actualization needs. In a more recent investigation, Mary Beth G. Anderson and Edward F. Iwanicki's (1984) findings are supportive of Trusty and Sergiovanni. However, the later study indicated a relatively large increase in the deficiency for security needs. Trusty and Sergiovanni also found that administrators, when compared to teachers, have fewer esteem need deficiencies and more self-actualization need deficiencies. The authors conclude that teachers' lack of self-esteem represents the largest source of need deficiency for them. Similarly, a study by Grace B. Chisolm and her colleagues (1980) shows that administrators exhibit fewer need deficiencies than teachers on all five subscales—security, social, esteem, autonomy, and self-actualization.

In brief, this appealing analysis of human needs should be viewed as an intriguing but unverified perspective for examining and explaining behavior.

Needs and Worker Satisfaction

Frederick Herzberg and his colleagues (Herzberg, Mausner, and Snyderman, 1959) developed a theory of motivation and job satisfaction based on the findings from their now famous study of engineers and accountants. The results led them to conclude that factors leading to positive job attitudes (motivators) do so because of their potential to satisfy the individual's need for self-actualization, or in Herzberg's terms, promote psychological growth. Conversely, a separate set of factors, hygiene factors, is related to physiological, safety, and social needs. Maslow focuses on general human needs of the psychological person, while Herzberg (1982) concentrates on the psychological person in terms of how the job affects basic needs.

The theory, which has been called motivation-hygiene theory, two-factor theory, dual-factor theory, and simply Herzberg's theory, has been widely accepted by administrators and policy makers. Herzberg and his colleagues found that positive events were dominated by references to achievement, recognition (for achievement), the work itself (challenging), responsibility, and advancement (promotion). Negative events were dominated by references to interpersonal relations with superiors and peers, technical supervision, company policy and administration, working conditions, salary, and personal life. They concluded that the presence of certain factors in the job act to increase an individual's job satisfaction, but absence of these same factors does not necessarily produce job dissatisfaction. The theory has several basic assumptions:

- There are two separate sets of factors in explaining work satisfaction and dissatisfaction.
- Motivators tend to produce satisfaction; and hygiene factors tend to produce dissatisfaction.
- Work satisfaction and dissatisfaction are not opposites, but rather separate and distinct dimensions.

Hence, motivation-hygiene theory postulates that the gratification of certain needs, called **motivators** (i.e., achievement, recognition, work itself, responsibility, and advancement), increases satisfaction, but when the motivators are not gratified, only minimal dissatisfaction results. On the other hand, when factors called **hygienes** (i.e., interpersonal relations, supervision, policy and administration, working conditions, salary, and personal life) are not gratified, negative attitudes are created, producing job dissatisfaction. Gratification of hygienes leads only to minimal job satisfaction. For example, being restricted in your ability to copy exams on the school's copy machine is likely to cause dissatisfaction, but the availability of such service is unlikely to promote high job satisfaction. Job satisfaction is more likely to come from autonomy, responsibility, and the challenge of the job itself. In brief, motivators tend to produce job satisfaction, whereas hygiene factors tend to produce job dissatisfaction. Why the name hygienes for factors that produce dissatisfaction and are relatively unimportant in promoting satisfaction? It's a medical metaphor: Although hygiene is very important in preventing serious infection, hygiene alone typically does not produce a cure just as hygiene factors alone cannot produce high levels of satisfaction.

Miner (1980) observes that the five-motivator factors are both conceptually and empirically related. When these elements are present in work, the individual's basic needs of personal growth and self-actualization will be satisfied; positive feelings and improved performance will also result. The hygiene factors, when provided appropriately, can serve to remove dissatisfaction and improve performance up to a point. But hygiene elements do not produce as positive feelings or as high performance levels as are potentially possible.

Although Herzberg's theory became quite controversial, it has had a major impact on the field of work motivation and job design. Steers and Porter (1991) argue that Herzberg deserves a great deal of credit. By calling attention to the need for improved understanding of the role played by motivation in work organizations, he filled a void in the late 1950s. His approach is systematic and his language understandable. He advanced a theory that is simple to grasp, based on empirical data, and offers specific action recommendations to administrators. Pinder (1984) offers an even stronger defense for the model. He argues that substantial evidence exists that Herzberg's ideas concerning the design of jobs have considerable validity and practical utility.

In brief, administrators should be aware of both sets of factors as they attempt to design and enrich teaching jobs to make them inherently challenging and interesting as well as to eliminate those aspects of the job that are most likely to produce dissatisfaction. Both hygiene and motivator factors are important but for different reasons. See Table 4.1.

TABLE 4.1

Herzberg's Motivation-Hygiene Theory

Hygienes	Motivators
• Interpersonal relations (with subordinates)	• Achievement
• Interpersonal relations (with peers)	• Recognition
• Supervision (technical)	• Work itself
• Policy and administration	• Responsibility
• Working conditions	• Advancement
• Personal life	
↓	↓
Dissatisfaction	Satisfaction

Need for Achievement

David C. McClelland's (1961, 1965, 1985) **achievement motivation theory** is commonly called need achievement or *n*-achievement theory.[1] The need to accomplish hard tasks, to overcome difficulties and obstructions, and to excel is the need for achievement. Individuals who strive for excellence in any field for the sake of achievement, not some other rewards, are considered to have a high need for achievement. In contrast to Maslow's fixed hierarchy and innate needs, McClelland's framework asserts that motives are learned; they become arranged in a hierarchy of potential for influencing behavior; and they vary from person to person. As people develop, they learn to associate positive and negative feelings with certain things that happen to and around them. Accordingly, the achievement value is learned when opportunities for competing with standards of excellence become associated with positive outcomes (Pinder, 1984). For an individual, achievement is directed toward the top of the motive hierarchy and it takes only minimal achievement cues to activate the expectation of pleasure. Thus, the likelihood of achievement striving is increased. Under such circumstances weaker motives will probably give way to the achievement and assume a distinct secondary role in influencing behavior (Miner, 1980).

McClelland (1961, 1985) hypothesized that individuals who are high in achievement motivation have three key characteristics:

- First, they have a *strong desire to assume personal responsibility* for performing a task or solving a problem. Consequently, they tend to work alone rather than with others. If the job requires others, they tend to choose co-workers on the basis of their competence rather than their friendship. Individuals with high achievement needs prefer situations that allow them to take personal responsibility and get personal credit for the outcomes (Miner, 1980). For example, persons with high achievement motivation compared those with low motives are more attracted to reward for performance systems (Turban and Keon, 1993).
- Second, those with high achievement needs tend to *set moderately difficult goals* and take intermediate levels of risk. Where tasks are too hard, the chance of succeeding and probability of satisfaction are low. Easy tasks represent things that anyone can do, thus little satisfaction will be gained in accomplishing them. High achievers tend to calculate the risks and select situations in which they anticipate feeling slightly overextended by the challenges, but not too overextended (Miner, 1980).
- Third, people with high achievement needs have a *strong desire for performance feedback.* These individuals want to know how well they have done and are anxious to receive information about results, regardless of whether they have succeeded or failed (Cherrington, 1991). There is little opportunity for achievement satisfaction when a person cannot tell success from failure.

Individuals with high achievement needs are characterized by their single-minded absorption with task accomplishment (Cherrington, 1991). Consequently, the need for achievement is an important motive in schools because students, teachers, and administrators who have a single-minded preoccupation are often successful. McClelland concluded from his research that the achievement motivation is apparently learned at an early age and largely influenced by child-rearing practices and other influences of parents. Children who see that their actions have an impact on their success and who are taught how to recognize good performance are more likely to grow up with the desire to excel (Schunk, 1996a).

Other theorists, however, view achievement motivation as a set of conscious beliefs and values that are shaped by recent experiences with success and failure and by such factors in the immediate situation as the difficulty of the task and available incentives. Thus a teacher may have high motivation with her algebra class because she is doing well with the class but low motivation with her geometry class because the class is disinterested and struggling (Stipek, 1993).

Harnessing an existing need for achievement in teachers or students is one thing, but developing the achievement need in those without it is quite a different challenge. McClelland (1965) provides some evidence that training programs that focus on developing achievement needs can produce entrepreneurial behavior among adults where it previously did not exist; hence, one general strategy for changing motives is through education and training (Katzell and Thompson, 1990). Attempts to instill achievement motivation should likely be characterized by:

- Situations in which individuals can succeed.
- Emphasis on setting reasonable and achievable goals.
- Accepting personal responsibility for performance.
- Providing clear feedback on performance .

Achievement motivation can be strengthened in schools and other settings through training, with favorable consequences for future success. The need for achievement, rather than being satisfied with accomplishment, seems to grow as it is attained rather than diminish (Wood and Wood, 1999). One caveat: Most of McClelland's research evidence pertains to boys and men, so his theory is currently limited to males; in fact, attempts to generalize it to females have been less successful (Pinder, 1984).

Need for Autonomy

The need for autonomy or self-determination is the desire to have choice in what we do and how we do it. In other words, it is the desire to act independently, rather than to have external pressures and rewards determine our actions (Deci and Ryan, 1985; Deci, Vallerand, Pelletier, and Ryan, 1991). People seek to be in charge of their own behavior. In fact, Porter (1961) has argued that the need for independent thought and action, autonomy, is a basic need. People resist and struggle against pressure from external forces such as rules, regulations, orders, and deadlines imposed by others because it interferes with their need for autonomy. Sometimes help is even rejected so the person can remain in control (deCharms, 1976, 1983).

Richard deCharms (1976, 1983) used the metaphor of individuals as "origins" and "pawns" to capture the difference between people with self-determination and those with other-determination. Origins perceive of themselves as the origin or source of their intentions to act. Pawns see themselves in a game controlled by others and powerless to determine their actions. When people are pawns, play becomes work, leisure becomes obligation, and intrinsic motivation becomes extrinsic motivation (Lepper and Greene, 1978). For example, you may have had the experience as a principal of deciding to involve teachers in decision making only to have your motivation dampened by a superintendent who insists on a well-defined program of site-based management. Your chance to be an origin is spoiled by a hierarchical attempt to control you. You have little appetite for site-based management that has been dictated from above because your sense of self-determination has been stolen; indeed, teachers are likely to feel the same way about top-down efforts by principals (Woolfolk, 1998).

DeCharms work with students led him to conclude that students are too little controlled by their own intrinsic motivation and too powerless to control their own actions. They are too often pawns rather than origins. It seems likely that teachers and administrators will suffer the same, perhaps stronger, consequences when they find themselves as pawns rather then origins—they become passive and take little responsibility for their work. Individual autonomy can be developed by activities and programs that emphasize setting realistic goals, personal planning of goals, accepting personal responsibility for actions, and developing self-confidence (Woolfolk, 1998). Results of some studies show that when individuals feel more like origins than pawns, they have higher self-esteem, feel more competent, and perform at higher levels of accomplishment (deCharms, 1976; Ryan and Grolnick, 1986). Needs for autonomy and self-determination can be enhanced by encouraging individuals to make their own choices, plan their own courses of action, and accept responsibility for the consequences of their choices. It seems likely that as we grow, develop, and mature, the need for autonomy becomes increasingly more important.

The needs for achievement, autonomy, social relations, self-esteem, and self-actualization are some of the key needs that motivate teachers and administrators and influence their perceptions and intellectual understandings of their organizational roles. Another driving force in influencing individual behavior is goals.

GOALS

A **goal** is a future state that an individual is striving to attain. Suppose you are getting ready for a big exam. Do you tell yourself that you will not stop studying until you have read so many pages, memorized your notes completely, done so many problems, and completed several practice exams? If you are a serious student, the chances are that you have set a series of similar goals to get ready for that important event. Most people set concrete goals for themselves because goals help eliminate the discrepancy between "where you are" and "where you want to be." Goal setting works for me. One reason that I have been successful in writing this book is that I set realistic writing goals for myself. For example, I write at least one page a day. I stick to it and you are reading the result.

Goals are aims or outcomes that an individual would like to achieve. They define for the individual an acceptable level of performance or direction of action. In terms of individual motivation, goals are always within the person, although they are often constructed from contextual information (Ford, 1992). For example, teachers will commonly adopt goals shared by other teachers or developed by the school. Locke and Latham (1990) suggest two key dimensions to goals—their content and intensity.

Goal content is the object or result being sought and varies from specific to abstract. Examples of concrete or specific goal content include losing 10 pounds in the next two months, an A on the next test, a new curriculum, or an improved set of teaching skills. Examples of more abstract content might include high achievement or better self-esteem. Goal content varies for individuals not only in specificity, but also in time perspective (short term or long term), difficulty (easy or hard), and number (few or many).

Goal intensity is the effort required to form the goal, the importance a person assigns the goal, and the commitment to the goal. Commitment is the degree to which the individual considers it important, is determined to reach it, and keeps it in the face of setbacks and obstacles. Factors that enhance commitment are ones that convince people that achieving the goal is possible and important or appropriate (Latham and Locke, 1991). Commitment influences and regulates goal striving because important goals are more likely to be accepted, to elicit intense involvement, and to foster persistent actions (Miner, 1980). It is virtually axiomatic that if there is no commitment to goals, then they do not work (Locke, Latham, and Erez, 1988).

Goal-Setting Theory

Although the historical origins of goals as important aspects of motivation date to the early twentieth century, Edwin A. Locke and his associate Gary P. Latham (Locke, 1968; Locke and Latham, 1984, 1990) are generally recognized for the development contemporary goal-setting theory. Actually, **goal-setting theory** did not begin as a theory, but was one of those cases in which an interesting research triggered the search for an explanation and—hence, the significance of goal-setting theory (Baron, 1998). The research finding was simple, clear, and impressive. Let's examine the details of the serendipitous study that begged for theoretical explanation.

Latham and Baldes (1975) studied lumber camp crews who hauled logs to a nearby sawmill. Before the study began, the crews loaded the large lumber trucks to about 60 percent capacity, which was wasteful because mileage for the huge trucks was horrendous—gallons per mile, not miles per gallon.

To improve the situation, Latham and Baldes engaged the workers in a discussion of the problem. Together, they set a specific goal: to load all trucks to a 94 percent capacity before transporting the logs to the sawmill. What happened? The performance levels improved dramatically and the increased performance persisted; in fact, in a follow-up study seven years later, crews were still loading the trucks to near capacity because the goal had become accepted and was now a regular part of the job (Baron, 1998).

Why do goals often improve our performance? Locke and Latham (1990) propose that successful goal performance meet four conditions:

- First, goals must be *specific.*
- Second, goals must be *challenging.*
- Third, goals must be *attainable.*
- Finally, individuals must be *committed* to the goals.

Research findings (Mento, Locke, and Klein, 1992; Wright et al., 1994) have demonstrated that when these four conditions are met, goal setting is an effective way of increasing motivation and performance.

What explains why goal setting is so effective? The basic postulate of the theory is that the intention to achieve a goal is a primary motivating force for behavior. Goals direct both mental and physical actions of individuals. Locke and Latham (1990) use four goal mechanisms to explain the positive effect of goals on action. First, goals *increase attention* to the immediate task; that is, they affect choice by helping individuals focus. Second, goals *increase the effort expended* on activities; they help people take action on goal-relevant activities while ignoring others. Third, goals *increase persistence* because there is less temptation to quit once a goal has been clearly established. Once a person decides on a goal, these three mechanisms become relatively automatic. Finally, goal setting increases motivation and performance by encouraging the *development of specific task strategies,* that is, ways of performing the task. Task strategies are conscious and deliberate plans the individual develops to achieve the goals. So whereas attention, effort, and persistence are fairly automatic consequences of goal setting, developing task strategies are conscious, deliberative, and creative consequences.

Feedback is also important in making goal setting an effective motivating force. In order to be motivated, the individual needs an accurate sense of the discrepancy between "where one is" and "the desired state." Feedback helps individuals evaluate their progress. If they have fallen short, then they can exert more effort or even try another strategy. When the feedback highlights accomplishment, the tendency is for the individual's self-confidence, analytic thinking, and performance to improve (Bandura, 1993).

Support for Locke's ideas came from a series of well-controlled laboratory experiments. Most of these studies used college students who performed relatively simple tasks for short periods of time. Because the theory originally relied on evidence from sheltered and contrived situations, the theory's proponents next attempted to respond to the following question: Can a practice so deceptively simple as setting specific, difficult goals increase the performance of employees in natural organizational settings where experimental effects are absent and goal acceptance is not easily obtained? Yes, the evidence from field studies indicates that goal-setting theory is valid for improving employee behavior in organizations such as schools (Latham and Yukl, 1975; Locke and Latham, 1990).

In particular, three generalizations from goal theory continue to enjoy substantial research support (Locke and Latham, 1990). First, *difficult goals, if accepted, result in higher levels of performance than easy ones.* An explanation of the goal-difficulty effect is that hard goals lead to greater effort and persistence than do easy goals, assuming they are accepted. Similarly, hard goals make self-satisfaction contingent on a higher level of performance than do easy goals.

Second, *specific goals produce higher levels of performance than such vague goals as "do your best" or no goals at all.* General goals are inherently ambiguous and people give themselves the benefit of the doubt in evaluating their performance; they assume that they have met the "do your best" criterion. From the standpoint of goal-setting theory, however, a specific hard goal clarifies for the person what constitutes effective performance, and the person is no longer able to interpret a wide range of performance levels as indicative of excellent performance (Latham and Locke, 1991). A recent study of teaching aids for elementary school students (Audia, Kristof-Brown, Brown, and Locke, 1996) underscores the significance of quantitative rather than qualitative goals. Quantity goals (make five products in a specific time) but not quality goals (make products without any defects) increased participants tendencies to use task strategies that increased production. Again we see that specific goals work more effectively than general ones.

A third and controversial generalization deals with the source of goals, commitment, and performance. Goals can be set in three ways: individuals can choose their own goals, they can be set jointly, or others can assign them. Because of the contradictory research findings, Locke and Latham (1990) helped design an elaborate set of research projects to test the effects of participation in goal settings on commitment and performance. The results suggested that the motivational effects of assigned goals can be as powerful as jointly set goals in generating high goal commitment and subsequent performance. Likewise, self-set goals are not consistently more effective in bringing about goal commitment or an increase in performance than other methods of goal setting. *The key to effective motivation seems to be whether the goals are embraced by individuals regardless of their origin.* People are generally more likely to accept and embrace goals if they are realistic, reasonably difficult, and meaningful (Erez and Zidon, 1984).

In sum, goal-setting theory suggests that specific and challenging but attainable goals can and often do increase motivation because such goals lead to increased focus, effort, and persistence as well as the development of specific task strategies to accomplish the goal. Feedback about progress toward achieving goals reinforces attention, effort, and persistence, or provides information for refining and altering the strategy to make it more effective (see Figure 4.2). The evidence of the effectiveness of goal-setting theory is overwhelming (Locke and Latham, 1990; Baron, 1998). Next we turn to how beliefs motivate and influence behavior.

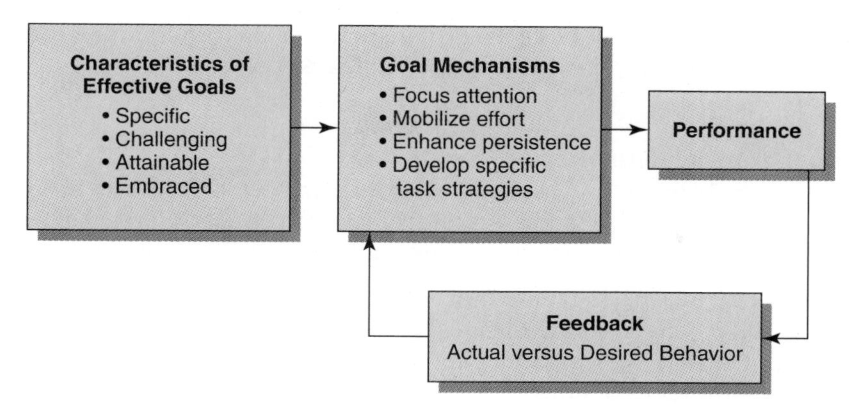

FIGURE 4.2 *Goal-Setting Theory*

BELIEFS

Individuals also act on their beliefs. **Beliefs** are general understandings or generalizations about the world; they are what individuals hold to be true. Beliefs are typically assertions of the existence of things such as intelligence or cause; they also often are associated with an ideal image that contrasts with the existing state; they are frequently associated with evaluations of what should be, for example, the fairness of school rules and regulations; and they are often linked to remembered episodes or events, for instance, the unfairness about school rules and regulations traced to an unfortunate episode in school (Nespor, 1987).

Beliefs play a pivotal role in motivating individuals to act. Individual beliefs about causality, fairness, intelligence, the consequences of our actions, and our ability to control our own destiny are a few of the pivotal beliefs that influence behavior. We turn to explanations of motivation that are anchored in beliefs.

Beliefs about Causality: Attribution Theory

As individuals see things happen to themselves and others, they ask why, and then make inferences or attributions about causes. For example, students ask: Why did I fail the final examination? Was it because of a lack of effort? Or am I not smart enough to understand the material? Based on such observations and questions, Bernard Weiner (1972, 1985, 1986, 1992, 1994a, 1994b) uses the notion of attribution to create a model of motivation. In essence, **attribution theory** deals with causal explanations that individuals make about past behaviors, especially in regard to achievement efforts and expectancies. Attribution theorists assume that individuals naturally search for understanding about why events happen, especially when the outcome is important or unexpected (Stipek, 1993). People attribute successes and failures to such factors as ability, luck, effort, mood, interest, and unfair procedures. When people make causal attributions, they are essentially seeking or creating beliefs about what happened and why. Once the explanation is created, individuals can often use it to better manage themselves and their environments.

Dimensions of Causality

Weiner (1985, 1986, 1992, 1994a, 1994b) argues that most of the causes to which individuals attribute their successes and failures can be characterized in terms of three **dimensions of causality**—locus, stability, and responsibility.

- *Locus* (internal versus external) defines the location of the cause. Ability and effort are the most common internal factors on the locus dimension. Task difficulty and luck are common external determinants of outcomes.
- *Stability* (stable versus unstable) designates causes as constant or varying over time. Ability is stable because an individual's aptitude for a task is thought to be relatively fixed, whereas effort is unstable because people can vary their labor from one situation to another.
- *Responsibility* (controllable versus uncontrollable) refers to personal responsibility, that is, whether the person can control the cause. Effort is controllable because individuals are thought to be responsible for how hard they try. In contrast, ability and luck are generally believed to be beyond personal control (Weiner, 1986; Kanfer, 1990; Graham, 1991).

Each of these three dimensions has important implications for motivation because they tend to generate emotional reactions to success and failure. For example, internal-external locus seems to be closely related to self-esteem. If success or failure is attributed to internal factors, then success typically produces pride, whereas failure diminishes self-esteem. The stability dimension is linked to emotions that implicate future expectations. For instance, stable causes for failure produce hopelessness, apathy, and resignation. The responsibility dimension is linked to a set of social emotions that includes guilt, shame, pity, and anger. We feel guilty when the causes of personal failure are due to factors under our control such as lack of effort and deciding not to take responsibility for action; we are proud if we succeed. Shame or anger is more likely if personal failures are due to uncontrollable factors such as ability or the difficulty of the task, whereas succeeding leads to feeling lucky or just grateful. Also, feeling in control of your own destiny seems related to choosing more difficult tasks, working harder, and persisting longer (Schunk, 1996a, Weiner, 1994a).

By attaching emotional reactions to the three attributional dimensions, outcomes may be perceived to have internal and unstable causes yet fall within an individual's responsibility and choice (Kanfer, 1990). For example, if new teachers perceive their failure to engage students in a class project as caused by a lack of preparation, then they will suffer low self-esteem and guilt for their poor performance. Their perception of the cause as being internal, unstable, and controllable—that is, within their power to change—enables them to be optimistic for future success. However, highly experienced teachers who have repeatedly failed to engage students in classroom projects are likely to attribute the cause of their failure to a lack of ability—that is, the cause is internal, stable, and uncontrollable. These teachers expect repeated failures, hopelessness, low self-esteem, and shame. They have low motivation to perform in the classroom. The reasons attributed to failure are varied and depend on combinations of the three dimensions.

Weiner (1994a) summarizes the sequence of motivation when failure is attributed to lack of ability a s follows:

Failure → Lack of Ability → Uncontrollable → Not Responsible → Embarrassment → Performance Declines

However, when failure is attributed to lack of effort, the sequence is as follows:

Failure → Lack of Effort → Controllable → Responsible → Guilt → Performance Declines

Some criticize attribution theory as no more than common sense (Graham, 1991). For example, we pity the handicapped but feel anger toward the lazy who are unwilling to work, or we expect to repeat our successes when we have high ability. Some might contend that such causal attributions are part of our shared ways of thinking about our social world and not scientific knowledge. Attribution theorists argue, however, that an important goal is to systematize what we know to be common sense and place it in a conceptual framework that accounts for a wide array of social phenomena. The research shows consistent support for the attribution mechanisms and effects of expectancy for future performance (Miner, 1980; Weiner, 1986, 1994a, 1994b; Kanfer, 1990).

The central ingredients of attribution theory can be summarized with a series of questions:

- The causal question: What are the causes of the outcome?
- The locus question: Is the cause internal (ability, effort) or external (task difficulty, luck)?
- The stability question: Are causes fixed or changing?
- The responsibility or controllability question: Can I control the causes?

Students, teachers, and administrators will be highly motivated when they know the causes of the outcomes; the causes are internal; the causes are amenable to change; and the causes are under their control.

Beliefs about Ability

Some of the most powerful attributions that affect motivation and behavior are beliefs about ability. If we examine those beliefs, we can begin to understand why people set inappropriate and unmotivating goals, why some teachers give up, and why students sometimes adopt self-defeating strategies.

Adults have two general views of ability—stable and incremental. A **stable view** (sometimes called an entity view) **of ability** assumes that ability is a stable and uncontrollable trait, that is, a characteristic of an individual that cannot be changed (Dweck and Bempechat, 1983). Accordingly, some people have more ability than others and the ability level is fixed. An **incremental view of ability,** on the other hand, assumes that ability is unstable and controllable—an expanding reservoir of knowledge and skills. Thus, people with an incremental view believe that by hard work, persistence, study, and practice knowledge can be increased and ability can be improved.

Young children hold almost an exclusively incremental view of ability (Nicholls and Miller, 1984). In the early grades in elementary school, for example, most students believe that effort is the same as intelligence. Smart people try hard and trying hard makes you smarter. So if you don't do well, you are not smart because you did not try hard enough. If you do well, you must be a smart, hard worker (Stipek, 1993). About the age of 12, however, students begin to differentiate between effort and ability. Students begin to realize that some people achieve without working hard and these are smart people. At this point, beliefs about ability begin to influence motivation (Anderman and Maehr, 1994).

People who hold a stable view of intelligence tend to set performance goals. They seek situations where they will look good and protect their self-esteem. They often continue to do what they can do well without expending too much effort or without risking failure because either working hard or failing suggests to them low ability. Moreover, to work hard and fail is a devastating blow to confidence and sense of ability. Such individuals would rather not try than fail; in fact, if you don't try, no one can accuse you of being dumb. When you fail, the reason is obvious—you just didn't prepare or try hard. So not trying or preparing becomes a strategy for protecting oneself from failure and looking dumb. We have all had experiences with students who are content with a C or just passing. Sometimes "just getting by" is a protective strategy for not looking bad. The student who tries for an A and gets a C risks feeling inadequate—so why try and risk humiliation when it is safe to just get by. Such strategies do protect one's self-esteem, but they do not enhance learning.

Individuals with an incremental view of intelligence, in contrast, tend to set learning goals and seek situations in which they can learn and progress because improvement means increasing their ability. To such people, children or adults, failure is not devastating; it merely suggests that more work is needed to improve. Ability is not threatened by failure; in fact, often failure is accepted as a challenge to work harder (Woolfolk, 1998). People with an incremental view of ability are most likely to set challenging, but realistic goals, and as we have seen, such goals are effective motivators.

In brief, one's beliefs about ability play an important role in motivation and performance in students, teachers, or administrators. Those individuals who believe that they can improve their ability are more likely to set leaning goals that are moderately difficult and challenging and are concerned with mastering the task at hand. On the contrary, those who hold a stable, fixed view of ability, are more likely to set performance goals that are either very easy or very difficult because they are concerned with self in the eyes of others; they want to look good and avoid anything that would threaten that image. Indeed they often equate high effort with low capabilities.

Beliefs about Fairness: Equity Theory

Students, teachers, and administrators, like most individuals in our society, are concerned about matters of basic fairness. We all know of teachers who barely do the minimum on their jobs. They often arrive late, give few tests, never volunteer for anything, leave promptly at the end of the school day, avoid all the meetings they can, and delegate their work to others. Imagine the chagrin of young, new teachers who work long hours, go the extra mile to help students after school, prepare hard for each class, and assist with extracurricular activities when they find that their malingering colleague is making twice the salary and doing half the work.

This basic unfairness in the workplace is what some theorists (Greenberg, 1993a; Tyler, 1994) call an inequity, and it brings us to yet another perspective on motivation called **equity theory,** which focuses on perceived fairness—individuals' beliefs about whether they are being treated fairly or not. The theory suggests that people care deeply about fairness in the workplace. How do individuals decide whether they are being treated unfairly? Equity theory suggests that the key mechanism for such decisions is social comparison; we compare ourselves and our own plight with others. In more technical terms, we compare our ratio of inputs (everything we contribute) to outputs (everything we receive) to the input/output ratio of others (Kulik and Ambrose, 1992). We don't choose just anyone for such comparisons, but rather we select those that are similar to us in various ways. In the example above, young teachers compare themselves with an older teacher. Two points seem worth making. Both young and old teachers were performing the same role, yet the older teacher had more seniority. The inequity would have been viewed as even greater if the teacher comparison had been among those with similar experience and age (see Figure 4.3). In the example above, some rationalization of the difference might occur because of the greater experience of the older teacher.

Equity theory explains that if the input/output ratios are about the same for those with whom we compare ourselves, then we view our treatment as fair. If, however, the ratios are not roughly equal, we believe that we have not been treated fairly and a sense of inequity develops. Inequities are annoying and we try to eliminate them. One of the potential consequences of feelings of inequity is reduced motivation. Baron (1998) explains that feelings of inequity interfere with work motivation and individuals attempt to reduce such feelings in three ways:

- They try to increase their outcomes—they seek increased benefits such as a raise or other reward.
- They try to leave—they quit and find another job.
- They reduce their inputs—they expend less effort on the job.

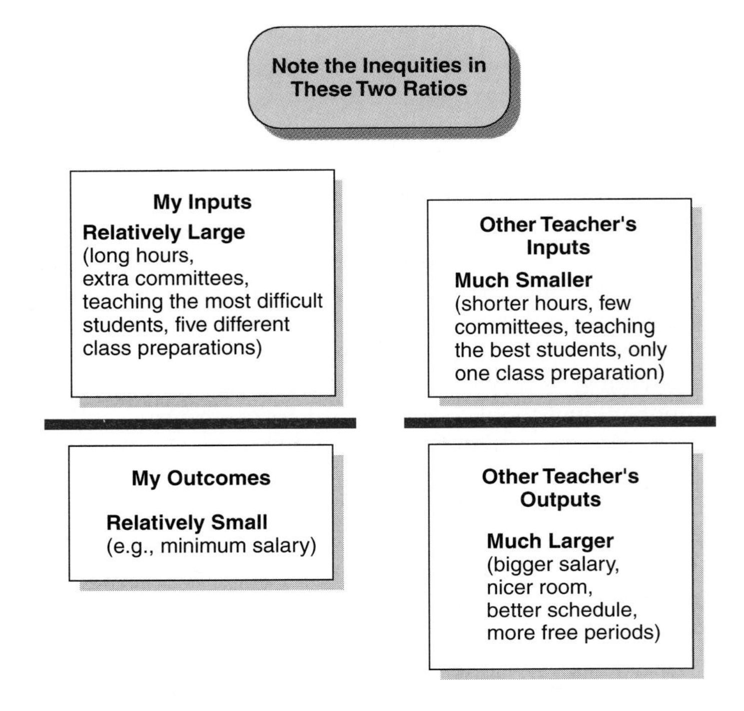

FIGURE 4.3 *Inequity Example*

The latter tactic seems quite common for individuals who conclude that they are being underrewarded, that is, are receiving less than they merit. They often reduce their efforts relative to those they believe are being treated fairly (Harder, 1992). Reduced performance is not the only demonstration of lowered motivation. For example, some workers attempt to balance things out by engaging in secret actions that yield extra benefits including theft (Greenberg and Scott, 1995; Greenberg, 1993b).

Three more issues should be noted about the theory. First, individual judgments about fairness are subjective; they are in the eye of the beholder. The individual does the comparing and makes the judgment about equity. Second, individuals are more sensitive to receiving less than they deserve rather than more (Greenberg, 1993a). It is easier to rationalize receipt of more rather than less than one deserves. Third, equity and justice are important motivating forces to many individuals. In brief, when students, teachers, or administrators conclude that they are being treated unfairly, their performance motivation often declines dramatically, and they may even plan to "even the score" by cheating or engaging in other questionable practices. Thus, there are important practical, as well as ethical, reasons for ensuring that fairness is the standard operating procedure in schools and other work organizations (Baron, 1998).

Beliefs about Outcomes: Expectancy Theory

One of the most reliable and valid explanations of what motivates people to work is expectancy theory. Although expectancy models have a long history in psychology, the approach was popularized and modified specifically for work settings during the 1960s by Victor Vroom (1964) and others (Graen, 1963; Galbraith and Cummings, 1967; Porter and Lawler, 1968). In fact, Vroom (1964) sparked an explosion of research with his formulation of expectancy theory. His model was developed to predict choices among jobs, tasks, and effort levels that yield the highest perceived benefits (Kanfer, 1990). During the late 1960s through the early 1980s, the prevalence of expectancy theory in the literature clearly indicates its centrality to the research on motivation in organizations. Although the frequency of publication has declined, its use has continued (Miller and Grush, 1988). Expectancy theory presents a complex view of individuals in organizations. The basic assumptions, concepts, and generalizations of expectancy theory, however, are easily identified and explained.

Expectancy theory rests on two fundamental premises. First, individuals make decisions about their own behavior in organizations using their abilities to think, reason, and anticipate future events. Motivation is a conscious and cognitive process. People subjectively evaluate the expected value on outcomes or personal payoffs resulting from their actions, and then they choose how to behave. Second, individual values and attitudes interact with environmental components, such as role expectations and school culture, to influence behavior. This second assumption is not unique to expectancy theory, and in fact, it was posed in Chapter 1 as a generalization from social systems theory.

Expectancy theory builds on these assumptions with three fundamental concepts—expectancy, instrumentality, and valence.

Expectancy is the extent to which an individual believes that hard work will lead to improved performance. The expectancy question is: If I work hard, will I be successful? For example, if teachers think that a high probability exists of improving student achievement by increasing their own efforts, then they have a high expectancy level. If students strongly believe that they can design and implement a project in science, then the students have high expectancy levels.

Instrumentality is the perceived probability that good performance will be noticed and rewarded. Instrumentality is high when individuals perceive a strong association between performance and being rewarded. The instrumentality question is: If I succeed, what will I receive in return? If teachers think that high student achievement in their classrooms is likely to result in public recognition of their teaching ability, then instrumentality is high. Similarly, if the students perceive that successfully designing and implementing a science project will increase their knowledge about science, then their instrumentalities are high.

Valence is the perceived value or attractiveness of a reward. The concept of valence is similar to the concept of values—that is, what people consider or believe beneficial to their welfare or important in its own right. It is the strength of a person's desire for a particular reward. The valence question is: How do I feel about the rewards of my efforts? Feelings of competence, autonomy, recognition, accomplishment, and creativity, for example, represent valued work outcomes for educators and produce high levels of satisfaction.

In general, motivation to behave in a certain way is greatest when the individual believes that:

- He or she has the ability to perform at the desired level (high expectancy).
- The behavior will lead to anticipated outcomes and rewards (high instrumentality).
- These outcomes have positive personal values (high valence).

When faced with choices about behavior, the individual goes through a process of considering three questions:

- The expectancy question: Can I perform the task if I work hard?
- The instrumentality question: If I perform at the desired level, what are the outcomes?
- The valence question: How do I like these outcomes?

The individual then decides to behave in the way that appears to have the best chance of producing the desired outcomes (Nadler and Lawler, 1977). In other words, individuals consider alternatives, weigh costs and benefits, and select courses of action of maximum utility (Landy and Becker, 1987).

The theory is summarized in Figure 4.4. Note that the strength of motivation is a function of the interaction of the expectancy, instrumentality, and valence. The interaction suggests that the motivation will not be strong if any of the three elements is near zero. For example, if I believe there is no possibility of improving my performance even if I work hard, then my motivation will be low regardless of how much I desire the outcome and its rewards. Similarly, even if I believe I can accomplish my goal through hard work, but I believe that either my performance will not be rewarded or that the rewards are insignificant, the strength of my motivation will remain low. Let's take a specific example. To motivate your teachers to commit to a new curricular program, you must first convince them that with extra effort the program can be implemented. Further, they have to believe that the consequences of the new program will be noticed and recognized and, finally, that the rewards are worthwhile—in this case that their students will do significantly better in their high school proficiency tests.

Several authors (Heneman and Schwab, 1972; Mitchell, 1974; Campbell and Pritchard, 1976) have systematically reviewed the research literature on expectancy motivation theory and their conclusions are similar. The force of motivation in an expectancy model is positively correlated with job satisfaction, effort, and performance in a variety of settings. Although the relationships between force of motivation and independent ratings of effort and performance have been significant statistically on a consistent basis, the associations have not been as strong as originally anticipated. In other words,

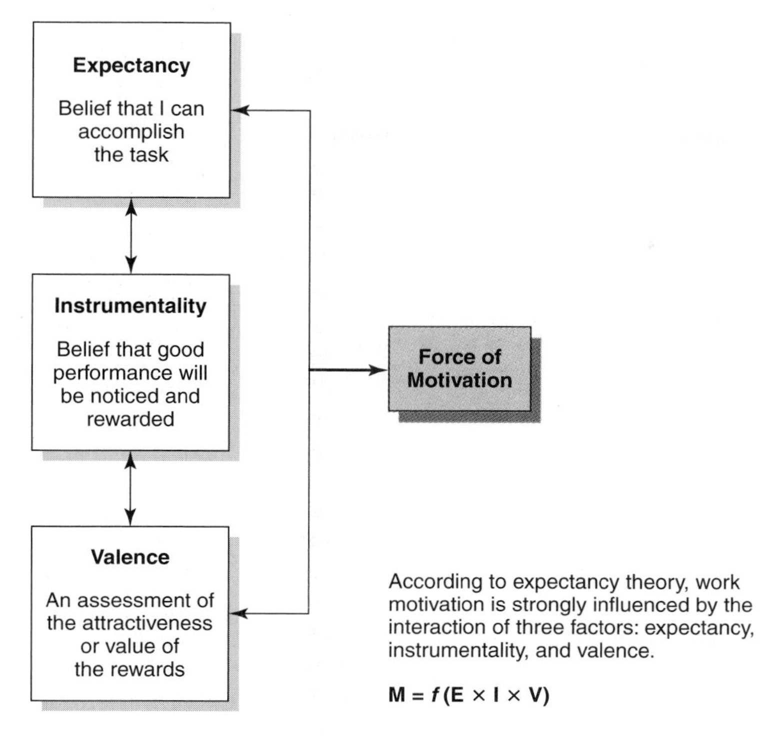

FIGURE 4.4 *Expectancy Theory*

expectancy motivation is an important factor in effort and performance, but other factors in the environment also are important contributors. In fact, stronger support for expectancy theory has been shown for predictions of job choice than for task effort or job performance (Kanfer, 1990). More recent studies also continue to confirm the theory (Tubbs, Boehne, and Dahl, 1993; Van Erde and Thierry, 1996).

Investigations conducted on educational organizations on the basis of expectancy theory show similar results. Richard T. Mowday (1978) found that school principals with higher expectancy motivation are more active in attempting to influence district decisions than those with low expectancy motivation. In a study examining the relationship between school structure and teacher motivation, H. Scott Herrick (1973) found strong negative correlations between expectancy motivational force and centralization and stratification. Thus, schools that were highly centralized and stratified were staffed with teachers having low forces of expectancy motivation.

In a study of secondary schools teachers, Cecil Miskel, JoAnn DeFrain, and Kay Wilcox (1980) related the force of motivation to job satisfaction and perceived job performance. The force of motivation was significantly related to job satisfaction and perceived performance for both groups. Similarly, Miskel and his colleagues David McDonald and Susan Bloom (1983) found that expectancy motivation of teachers was consistently related to teacher job satisfaction, student attitudes toward school, and perceived school effectiveness. Robert Kottkamp and John A. Mulhern (1987) found that expectancy is positively related to both the openness of school climate and humanism in pupil control ideology. Linda L. Graham (1980) found that expectancy theory predicted the satisfaction, participation in activities, and achievement of college students.

In sum, expectancy theory has generated a large number of investigations in educational as well as business settings. The results are generally supportive. Pinder (1984) concludes that there are grounds for optimism that the theory is a reasonably valid model of the causes of work behavior. The following conclusions are warranted from the literature:

- Expectancy theory is an excellent predictor of job satisfaction.
- Expectancy theory predicts performance but not as well as it predicts satisfaction.
- Expectancy theory demonstrates that people work hard when they think that working hard is likely to lead to desirable outcomes.

Beliefs about Capabilities: Self-Efficacy Theory

Among all the aspects of self-knowledge and self-regulation, personal efficacy is probably the most influential in everyday life. **Self-efficacy** is *a person's judgment about his or her capability to organize and execute a course of action that is required to attain a certain level of performance* (Bandura, 1986, 1991, 1997). In other words, it is an individual's overall judgment of his or her perceived capacity for performing a task. For example, the belief of a mathematics teacher that he or she can successfully teach calculus to a class of twelfth-grade students is an efficacy judgment. Similarly, principals with high self-efficacy might believe that they can have a positive effect on student achievement or they might increase the emphasis on academic learning in schools. Note that, in contrast to causal attributions where the focus is on the past, perceptions of self-efficacy represent future expectations of being able to attain certain levels of performance.

Self-efficacy beliefs contribute to motivation by determining the goals that individuals set for themselves, how much effort they expend, how long they persevere in the face of difficulties, and their resilience to failures (Wood and Bandura, 1989; Bandura, 1993). The stronger people believe in their capabilities, the greater and more persistent are their efforts. People tend to avoid tasks and situations that exceed their capacity; they seek activities they judge themselves capable of handling. The consequences of high self-efficacy—willingness to approach and persist on tasks, selection of task and situation, a focus on problem-solving strategies, reduced fear and anxiety, positive emotional experiences—affect achievement outcomes (Stipek, 1993). Hence, people who have the same skills but different levels of personal efficacy may perform at different levels because of the way they use, combine, and sequence their skills in a changing context (Gist and Mitchell, 1992).

Development of Self-Efficacy

Self-efficacy expectations develop from a variety of sources, including performance feedback, previous history, and social influence. However, self-efficacy is postulated to develop from four primary sources of experience—mastery experiences, modeling, verbal persuasion, and physiological arousal.

Mastery experience is the single most important source of self-efficacy. Performance successes and failures (i.e., actual experiences) in completing tasks have strong effects on self-efficacy. Recurrent successes raise efficacy perceptions; regular failures produce self-doubts and reduce self-efficacy, especially if failure occurs early in a task sequence and does not reflect a lack of effort or opposing external influences. Efficacy is facilitated as gradual accomplishments build skills, coping abilities, and exposure needed for task performance.

Modeling and vicarious experience affect self-perceptions of efficacy through two processes. First, it provides knowledge. Watching an expert complete a task conveys effective strategies for managing similar tasks in different situations. Second, people partly judge their capabilities using social comparisons. Seeing or visualizing people similar to oneself successfully perform a task can raise one's own beliefs about self-efficacy. By observing people modeling certain behaviors, individuals convince themselves that if others can do it, they can at least achieve some improvement in their own performance. Modeling experiences are most influential for individuals in situations in which they have limited personal experience with the task.

Verbal persuasion is widely used to try to talk people into believing that they have the capacity to achieve what they want to accomplish. Social persuasion alone has limited power to create lasting increases in self-efficacy, but it can contribute to successful performance if the heightened appraisal is within realistic bounds. To the extent that self-efficacy is boosted through verbal persuasion and people try hard to succeed, verbal persuasion can promote the development of skills and a sense of self-efficacy (Bandura, 1986; Gist, 1987; Wood and Bandura, 1989).

People also rely partly on information from their *physiological state* to judge their capability. Individuals make judgments about anticipated performance based on positive arousal such as excitement and enthusiasm and on negative factors such as fear, fatigue, stress, and anxiety. General physical condition, personality factors (Type A), and mood can all induce arousal (Gist, 1987). Hence, another way to modify beliefs of self-efficacy is for individuals to enhance their physical well-being and to reduce their stress (Wood and Bandura, 1989).

Gist and Mitchell (1992) propose that the relationships between the four types of experience and self-efficacy are mediated by analyses of the task situation and causal attributions. On the basis of experience, several situational factors might be considered. An analysis of the situation in terms of task requirements, human resources, and the school organization produces inferences about what it will take to perform successfully. In preparing to teach calculus to twelfth graders, for example, a teacher would determine the mathematical ability and motivational levels of the students; availability of instructional resources such as books, outside tutors, and computer support; and the environmental emphasis on student achievement. An analysis of causal attributions from previous experience in similar situations is likely to affect efficacy judgments. What produced earlier success? In the example of teaching calculus to twelfth graders, the actual experiences of the teacher in previous years, new modeling experiences, persuasion by the principal and colleagues, and his or her physical state will be filtered through the dimensions of locus, stability, and controllability. Gist and Mitchell believe that these analysis processes of the situation and attributions yield summary-level judgments that define self-efficacy.

In the general organization and management literature, empirical studies of self-efficacy have produced consistent results. Self-efficacy is associated with such work-related performance as productivity, coping with difficult tasks, career choice, learning and achievement, and adaptability to new technology (Gist and Mitchell, 1992). Similar results are evident in educational settings. Self-efficacy research in schools tends to focus on one of two areas or approaches. The first group of studies tests for the effects of student and teacher self-efficacy on various motivational and achievement indicators. The general finding is that self-efficacy is positively related to student achievement (Armor et al., 1976), course grades (Pintrich and Garcia, 1991), student motivation (Midgley, Feldlaufer, and Eccles, 1989), teacher adoption of innovations (Berman et al., 1977; Smylie, 1988), superintendents' rating of teachers' competence (Trentham, Silvern, and Brogdon, 1985), and classroom management strategies of teachers (Ashton and Webb, 1986). Moreover, experimental studies have consistently found that changing self-efficacy beliefs can lead to better use of cognitive strategies and higher levels of academic achievement for mathematics, reading, and writing tasks (Schunk, 1991).

To summarize, self-efficacy is an important motivational factor that influences a number of behavioral and performance outcomes. Self-efficacy is learned through a variety of experiences and is dynamic; it can change over time as new information and experiences are acquired. Issues that remain unresolved include the extent to which self-efficacy and performance can be raised and the overall elasticity of self-efficacy (Gist and Mitchell, 1992). Four, conclusions are warranted:

- Individuals who have stronger beliefs about their capabilities are more successful and persistent in their efforts.
- Individuals tend to avoid tasks and situations that exceed their capacity.
- Individuals seek activities they judge themselves capable of handling.
- Individuals develop self-efficacy through mastery experiences, modeling, persuasion, and physiological arousal.

Teacher Efficacy

Over the past 20 years, the construct of teacher efficacy has evolved from J. B. Rotter's (1966) locus of control theory and Albert Bandura's (1977, 1986, 1997) social cognitive theory. The meaning of teacher efficacy, however, has produced considerable debate and some confusion among scholars and researchers (Ashton, Olejnik, Crocker, and McAuliffe, 1982; Gibson and Dembo, 1984; Guskey, 1987; Guskey and Passaro, 1994; Pajares, 1996, 1997; Tschannen-Moran, Woolfolk Hoy, and Hoy, 1998).

Using the theoretical perspectives of Rotter (1966), researchers at the Rand Corporation studying the effectiveness of reading instruction first viewed teacher efficacy as the extent to which teachers believed that they could control the reinforcement of their actions. Teachers who believed that they could influence student achievement and motivation (internal locus) were more effective than those who thought the external forces could not be overcome. A second, more recent and useful conceptual strand of theory and research has evolved from the work of Bandura (1977). He defined teacher efficacy as a type of self-efficacy—the outcome of a cognitive process in which people construct beliefs about their capacity to perform well. These self-efficacy beliefs affect how much effort people expend, how long they will persist in the face of difficulties, their resilience in dealing with failures, and the stress they experience in coping with demanding situations (Bandura, 1997). The existence of the two separate but intertwined conceptual strands emerging from two theoretical perspectives has contributed some confusion about the nature of teacher efficacy; however, perceived self-efficacy is a much stronger predictor of behavior than locus of control (Bandura, 1997; Tschannen-Moran, Woolfolk Hoy, and Hoy, 1998).

A Model of Teacher Efficacy

In response to the conceptual confusion surrounding teacher efficacy and in keeping with the substantial body of research, Megan Tschannen-Moran, Anita Woolfolk Hoy, and Wayne K. Hoy (1998) developed an integrated model of teacher efficacy. **Teacher efficacy** is the *teacher's belief in his or her capability to organize and execute courses of action required to successfully accomplish a specific teaching task in a particular context.* Consistent with social cognitive theory (Bandura, 1986, 1997), the major influences on efficacy beliefs are the attributional analysis and interpretation of the four sources of information about efficacy—mastery experience, vicarious experience (modeling), verbal persuasion, and physiological arousal. All four of these sources are important in the interpretation and cognitive processing of information.

Teacher efficacy is context-specific; teachers do not feel equally efficacious for all teaching situations. Teachers feel efficacious for teaching particular subjects to certain students in specific settings, but often feel more or less efficacious under different circumstances. Even from one class period to another, teachers' levels of efficacy may change (Ross, Cousins, and Gadalla, 1996; Raudenbush, Rowen, and Cheong, 1992). Therefore, in making an efficacy judgment, consideration of the teaching task and its context are required as well as an assessment one's strengths and weaknesses *in relation to* the requirements of the task at hand.

In analyzing the *teaching task and its context,* the relative importance of factors that make teaching difficult or act as constraints are weighed against an assessment of the resources available that facilitate learning. In assessing *self-perceptions of teaching competence,* the teacher judges personal capabilities such as skills, knowledge, strategies, or personality traits balanced against personal weaknesses or liabilities in this particular teaching context. The interaction of these two components leads to judgments about self-efficacy for the teaching task at hand. The model is summarized in Figure 4.5.

One of the things that makes teacher efficacy so powerful is its cyclical nature. As noted in Figure 4.5, the proficiency of a performance creates a new mastery experience, which provides new information (feedback) that will be processed to shape future efficacy beliefs. Greater efficacy leads to greater effort and persistence, which leads to better performance, which in turn leads to greater efficacy. The reverse is also true. Lower efficacy leads to less effort and giving up easily, which leads to poor teaching outcomes, which then produce decreased efficacy. Thus, a teaching performance accomplished with a level of effort and persistence influenced by the performer's sense of efficacy, when completed, becomes a source of future efficacy beliefs. Over time this process stabilizes into a relatively enduring set of efficacy beliefs.

There are both theoretical and practical implications for the teacher-efficacy model. Both self-perception of teaching competence (including an assessment of internal resources and constraints) and beliefs about the task requirements in a particular teaching situation (including an assessment of resources and constraints external to the teacher) contribute to teacher efficacy and to the consequences that stem from efficacy beliefs. Once stabilized, beliefs about both the task of teaching and assessment of personal teaching competence are likely to remain unchanged unless "compelling evidence" intrudes and causes them to be reevaluated (Bandura, 1997). Consequently,

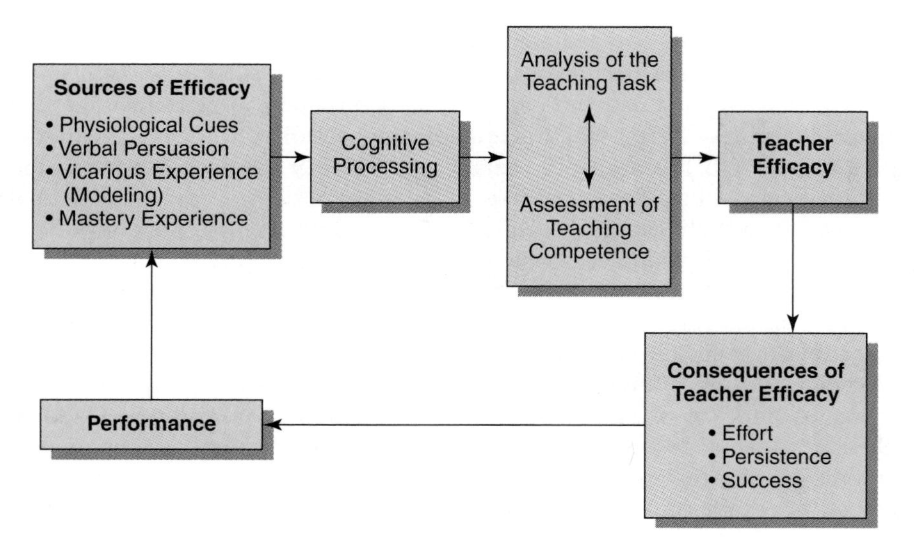

FIGURE 4.5 ***A Model of Teacher Efficacy***

Source: Adapted from Tschannen-Moran, Woolfolk Hoy, and Hoy, 1998.

helping teachers develop strong efficacy beliefs early in their careers will pay lasting dividends.

During the past two decades, researchers have consistently established strong connections between teacher efficacy and teacher behaviors that foster student achievement (Allinder, 1994; Ashton and Webb, 1986; Gibson and Dembo, 1984; Hoy and Woolfolk, 1990; Hoy and Woolfolk, 1993; Tschannen-Moran, Woolfolk Hoy, and Hoy, 1998; Woolfolk and Hoy, 1990; Woolfolk, Rosoff, and Hoy, 1990). Teaching success, effort, and persistence depend on the extent to which a teacher believes he or she has the capability to organize and execute teaching that will lead to successful learning in a specific situation. Thus, the key efficacy questions for teachers are:

- *Teaching Task Question:* How difficult is the teaching task at hand and can I do it?
- *Teaching Competence Question:* Given the task and situation, do I have the needed skills and knowledge?

Positive answers to these two questions reveal strong teacher efficacy.

A Model of Collective Teacher Efficacy

The shared beliefs of teachers and administrators influence the social milieu of schools. **Collective teacher efficacy** is the *shared perception of teachers in a school that the efforts of the faculty as a whole will have a positive effect on students.* According to Bandura (1993, 1997), collective teacher efficacy is an important school property. Just as individual teacher efficacy partially explains the effect of teachers on student achievement, from an organizational perspective, collective teacher efficacy helps explain the differential effect that schools have on student achievement. Bandura (1997) observes that because schools present teachers with a host of unique challenges involving such things as public accountability, shared responsibility for student outcomes, and minimal control over work environments, the task of developing high levels of collective teacher efficacy is difficult but possible.

At the collective level, efficacy beliefs are social perceptions, which are strengthened rather than depleted through their use. Thus, to the extent that collective teacher efficacy is positively associated with student achievement, there is strong reason to lead schools in a direction that will systematically develop teacher efficacy; such efforts may indeed be rewarded with continuous growth in not only collective teacher efficacy, but also student achievement.

Organizations, like individuals, learn (Cohen and Sproull, 1996); in fact, organizations use processes akin to learning in individuals (Cook & Yanon, 1996). Schools act purposefully in pursuit of their educational goals. For example, one school may be working to raise student achievement scores, whereas another works to increase the rate and quality of parental involvement. Organizational functioning depends on the knowledge, vicarious learning, self-reflection, and self-regulation of individual members. For example, a school that responds to declining achievement scores by implementing a curricular reform that was effective in a neighboring district is engaged in a self-regulatory process that is informed by the vicarious learning of its members. Such examples demonstrate the importance of vicarious learning and self-regulation at the organizational level, although we must recognize that it is through individuals that organizations act. As we have seen, the four primary sources of self-efficacy information are mastery experience, vicarious experience, social persuasion, and emotional arousal. Just as these sources are critical for individuals, they are also fundamental in the development of collective teaching efficacy.

Mastery experiences are important for organizations. Teachers as a group experience successes and failures. Successes build strong beliefs in a faculty's sense of collective efficacy; failures undermine it. If success, however, is frequent and too easy, failure is likely to produce discouragement. A resilient sense of collective efficacy requires experience in overcoming difficulties through persistent effort. Indeed, organizations learn by experience and thus are likely to succeed in attaining their goals (Huber, 1996; Levitt and March, 1996).

Direct experience is not the only source of information for teachers about their collective efficacy. Teachers also listen to stories about the accomplishment of their colleagues as well as success stories of other schools. Similarly, the effective schools research describes the characteristics of exemplary schools. So just as *vicarious experience and modeling* serve as effective sources of personal teacher efficacy, so too do they promote collective teacher efficacy. Organizations learn by observing other organizations (Huber, 1996).

Verbal persuasion is another means of strengthening a faculty's conviction that they have the capabilities to achieve what they seek. Teachers can be changed by talks, workshops, professional development activities, and feedback about achievement. In fact, the more cohesive the faculty, the more likely the group as a whole can be persuaded by sound argument. Verbal persuasion alone, however, is not likely to be a powerful change agent, but coupled with models of success and positive direct experience, it can influence the collective efficacy. Persuasion can promote extra effort and persistence, both of which can lead to the solution of problems.

Organizations have *affective states.* Just as individuals react to stress, so do organizations. Efficacious organizations tolerate pressure and crises and continue to function effectively; in fact, they learn how to adapt and cope with disruptive forces. Less efficacious organizations when confronted by such problems, react in dysfunctional ways, which often reinforce their basic dispositions of failure. They misinterpret stimuli—sometimes overreacting and other times underreacting or not reacting at all. The affective state of an organization has much to do with how challenges are interpreted by the organizations.

Although all four of these sources of information are pivotal in the creation of collective teacher efficacy, it is the processing and interpretation of the information that is critical. Consistent with the model of teacher efficacy described earlier, two key elements in the development of collective teaching efficacy are *analysis of the teaching task* and the *assessment of teaching competence.*

Teachers assess what will be required as they engage in teaching; we call this process the analysis of the teaching task. Such analysis occurs at two levels—the individual and the school. At the school level, the analysis produces inferences about the challenges of teaching in that school, that is, what it would take for the school to be successful. Considerations include the abilities and motivations of students, availability of instructional materials, community constraints, the quality of physical facilities of the school, as well as a general optimism about the capability of the school to deal with negative situations in the students' home as well as in the school. Teachers analyze the means needed to make the school successful, the barriers or limitations to be overcome, and the resources that are available.

Teachers analyze the teaching task in conjunction with their assessment of the teaching competency of the faculty; in fact, teachers make explicit judgments of the teaching competence of their colleagues in view of an analysis of the teaching task in their specific school. At the school level, the analysis of teaching competence leads to inferences about the faculty's teaching skills, methods, training, and expertise. Judgments of teaching competence might include faculty beliefs in the ability of all children in their school to succeed. Because the analyses of task and competence occur simultaneously, it is difficult to separate these two domains of collective teaching efficacy. They interact with each other as collective teacher efficacy emerges.

Research support for the model is limited to two studies. In his seminal study of collective teacher efficacy and student achievement, Bandura (1993) uncovered two important findings: (a) student achievement (aggregated to the school level) was significantly and positively related to collective efficacy, and (b) collective efficacy had a greater effect on student achievement than did student socioeconomic status (aggregated to the school level). Roger Goddard and colleagues (Goddard, Hoy, and Woolfolk Hoy, in press) also found strong support for the model and again confirmed the significance of collective teacher efficacy in facilitating high student achievement.

In sum, the major influences on collective teacher efficacy are assumed to be the analysis and interpretation of the four sources of information—mastery experience, vicarious experience, social persuasion, and emotional state. In these processes, the organization focuses its attention on two related domains: the teaching task and teaching competence. Both domains are assessed in terms of whether the organization has the capacities to succeed in teaching students. The interactions of these assessments lead to the shaping of collective teacher efficacy in a school. The consequences of high collective teacher efficacy will be the acceptance of challenging goals, strong organizational effort, and a persistence that leads to better performance. Of course, the opposite is also true. Lower collective efficacy leads to less effort, the propensity to give up, and a lower level of performance. The process and components of collective teacher efficacy are similar to those of teacher efficacy and are illustrated in Figure 4.6. As shown in the figure, the proficiency of performance provides feedback to the organization, which provides new information that will further shape the collective teacher efficacy of the school. Beliefs about both the task of teaching and the teaching competence, however, are likely to remain unchanged unless something dramatic occurs; hence, once established, the collective efficacy of a school is a relatively stable property that requires substantial effort to change.

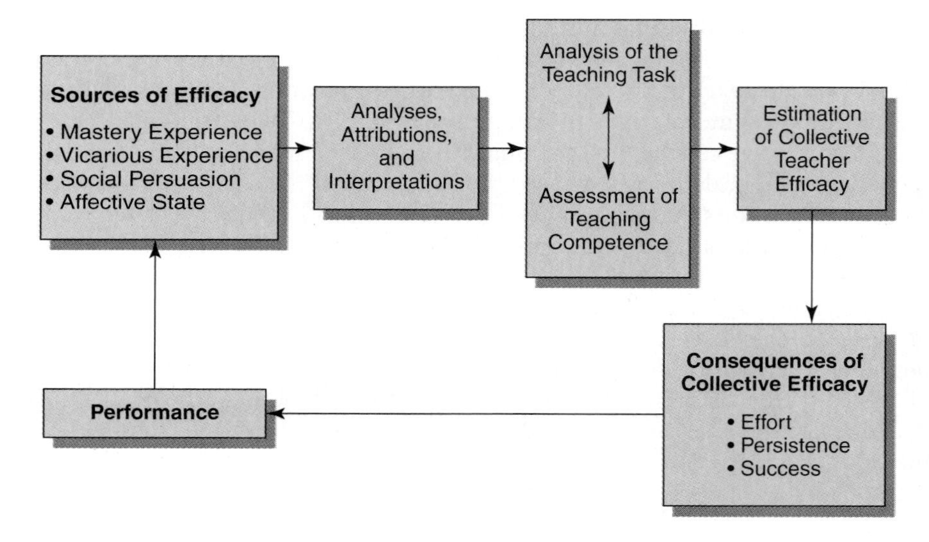

FIGURE 4.6 *A Model of Collective Efficacy*

Finally, for a summary of key motivating features of all the theories discussed thus far, see Table 4.2.

Intrinsic and Extrinsic Motivation

We have seen how needs, beliefs, and goals are important aspects of motivation. **Motivation** is generally defined as an internal state that stimulates, directs, and maintains behavior. Psychologists who study motivation have focused on five basic aspects: choices, initiation, intensity, persistence, and reaction (Graham and Weiner, 1996). We now turn to two important distinctions in examining theories of motivation—intrinsic and extrinsic. We all know what it feels like to be motivated—to energetically tackle a task. We also know how it feels to work hard even though the task is not all that intriguing. What energizes and directs our behavior? Some explanations argue that motivation is personal and internal and relies on needs, interests, curiosity, and enjoyment. Other explanations are linked to external and environmental factors such as incentives, rewards, pressure, punishment, and so on. We are concerned with **work motivation,** "a set of energetic forces that originate both within as well as beyond an individual's being, to initiate work-related behavior, and to determine its form, direction, intensity, and duration" (Pinder, 1984:8). The challenge for administrators is to develop motivated teachers who are actively engaged in teaching and learning, open to new ideas and approaches, and committed to students and who change over the lifetime of their teaching careers.

Motivation that comes from factors such as interest and curiosity is called **intrinsic motivation** (Woolfolk, 1998). Intrinsic motivation is the natu-

TABLE 4.2

Summary of How Needs, Goals, and Beliefs Motivate

Needs Theory

Suggest that people work hard when:

- Lower-order needs are met—physiological, safety, and belongingness needs.
- Higher-order needs present the challenge—esteem and self-actualization needs.

Motivation-Hygiene Theory

Suggests that:

- Unmet lower-level needs produce dissatisfaction with the job.
- Gratified higher-level needs produce job satisfaction.

Goal-Setting Theory

Suggests that people work hard when:

- They have realistic, specific, and challenging goals.
- They are committed to the goals.
- They receive feedback about progress toward the goals.

Attribution Theory

Suggests that people work hard when they believe that causes for success are:

- Internal—due to ability and effort.
- Not fixed—effort, for example, can be varied from one situation to another.
- Controllable—causes can be controlled by hard work, using proper strategy, etc.

Equity Theory

Suggests that people work hard when they have been fairly treated and:

- They have been given the rewards they deserve.
- The rewards have been allocated fairly.
- They have been treated with respect and courtesy.

Expectancy Theory

Suggests that people work hard when:

- They believe extra effort will improve performance.
- Good performance will be noticed and rewarded.
- The rewards are valued.

Self-Efficacy Theory

Suggests that people work hard when:

- They believe they have the capabilities to be successful.
- They believe that the task is not too difficult.
- They have had success at completing similar tasks.
- They have good models of success.

ral tendency to seek and accept challenges as we pursue personal interests and exercise capabilities (Deci and Ryan, 1985; Reeve, 1996). Punishment and rewards are not needed because *the activity itself is rewarding*. Simply put, intrinsic motivation is what stimulates us to do something when we don't have to do anything (Raffini, 1996). **Extrinsic motivation,** in contrast, is based on rewards and punishment. We act to earn a good grade or to get a merit increase or to get promoted or to avoid a grievance. We are not interested in the activity for its own sake, but rather for what the activity will bring us. Extrinsic motivation is a behavioral perspective on motivation because motivation and behavior are explained in terms of rewards and punishment. Extrinsic motivation stimulates us to act with incentives and disincentives.

The key difference between intrinsic and extrinsic motivation is the individual's reason for acting. Is the locus for action internal (intrinsic) or external (extrinsic)? If one freely chooses to act on the basis of personal preferences, the cause is internal and the motivation is intrinsic. The dichotomy between intrinsic and extrinsic is a bit too simple because many actions have traces of both kinds of motivation. For example, what starts out as extrinsic motivation, studying to get a good grade, may become intrinsic when curiosity takes over. Moreover, some individuals may choose to work hard on things that they don't particularly enjoy because they know that the activities are important in achieving a valued goal such as earning a superintendent's certificate. In the latter case, the person has internalized an external cause and the motivation is "in-between," that is, the person has freely chosen to respond to an external cause. Notwithstanding the blending of the two kinds of motivation in some cases (the dichotomy becomes a continuum), the distinction between intrinsic and extrinsic is useful and helps us understand the bases for motivation schemes in schools. Table 4.3 summarizes the variety of elements of motivation that seem critical if teachers and administrators are to be highly motivated in their work.

Next, we examine several examples of extrinsic motivational schemes used in schools, then an example of an intrinsic motivational application, and finally, an example of an application that combines both intrinsic and extrinsic strategies.

Application of Extrinsic Motivation: Merit Pay

The most controversial use of extrinsic rewards in schools is merit pay. In its pure form, **merit pay** is a compensation system in which pay is based on an individual's performance with at least a portion of a person's financial compensation being a performance bonus. High performers receive more money; low performers receive less money. The underlying principle is that some teachers or administrators earn more for doing the same work as others, only better (Firestone, 1991). As practiced in school settings, however, merit pay supplements the standard salary schedule and forms only a small part of an employee's salary (Hatry and Greiner, 1985; Hajnal and Dibski, 1993).

Since the early 1900s, numerous merit pay plans for educators have been instituted in the United States. The most recent flurry of activity was

TABLE 4.3

Summary of Key Elements in Opitimizing Work Motivation

	Optimum Characteristics of Work Motivation	Characteristics That Diminish Strong Work Motivation
Needs	Work satisfies high-level needs Specific	Work satisfies low-level needs General
Type of Goal	Realistic, challenging goals	Very difficult or very easy goals
Attributions	Successes and failures attributed to controllable effort and ability	Successes and failures attributed to uncontrollable causes
Achievement Motivation	Motivation by achievement	Motivation to avoid failure
Type of Involvement	Task-involved: Concerned with mastering the job	Ego-involved: Concerned with self in eyes of others
Beliefs about Equity	Fair and courteous treatment	Unfair and disrespectful treatment
Beliefs about Ability	Incremental view: Belief that ability can be improved with hard work and added knowledge and skills	Stable view: Belief that ability is stable, inherent trait
Self-Efficacy	High self- and collective efficacy	Low self- and collective efficacy
Source of Motivation	Intrinsic: The nature of the job itself is challenging, interesting, and enjoyable	Extrinsic: Environmental factors such as rewards, social pressures, and punishment

generated in the mid-1980s. Derek Bok (1993) suggests two reasons for this renewed interest. First was the familiar hope of using money to motivate teachers to work harder and increase productivity. Second was an unspoken suspicion that many educators were neither talented nor effective. The idea was to find a way to raise salaries in order to reward better teachers and attract able recruits without spending a lot on mediocre people.

Research and Evaluation

In their research, Mark A. Smylie and John C. Smart (1990) found teacher support for merit pay depends on its perceived effects on collegial relationships among teachers. Opposition is highest among teachers who believe that merit pay systems will increase competition and reduce cooperation among colleagues. Firestone (1991) made similar findings.

According to Betty Malen, Michael J. Murphy, and Ann W. Hart (1988), the criteria for receiving merit pay typically include being assessed as an excellent teacher (e.g., displaying prescribed teaching behaviors, increasing student test scores) and doing extra work for extra pay (e.g., serving as a mentor, leading extracurricular activities, conducting in-service workshops). Two common types of merit rewards are salary bonuses and increased status through public recognition of superior performance. They found that merit pay systems do not significantly alter either anticipated reward. As a salary benefit, merit pay is used to supplement, not supplant, the basic salary schedule. Even with a merit pay plan, the dominant portion of educator compensation is still the base salary determined by education and experience. Moreover, merit stipends are dispersed broadly to all or nearly all who apply. In such instances, merit pay becomes a general pay raise for all educators. In regard to status, procedural and peer pressures within schools combine to keep the recipients and rewards secret. In cases where public disclosure occurs, the benefit is offset by peer sanctions.

Although merit pay policies have been enacted, removed, revived, and retried for decades, few endure (Malen, Murphy, and Hart, 1988). Merit pay does not appear to be a viable approach to redistribute economic or status rewards in school settings. Even in the most favorable circumstances, true merit pay schemes are not likely to succeed (Astuto and Clark, 1985a; Johnson, 1986) and are not a promising way to strengthen incentives in schools (Bok, 1993). For the most part, teachers oppose merit pay because they tend to cause dissension, competition, and conflict among teachers (Firestone, 1991).

Another Extrinsic Application: Management by Objectives

Management by objectives (MBO) is another example of a management application that is based on extrinsic motivation. MBO was given prominence by Peter Drucker (1954) during the 1950s. Since its early popularization, a large variety of MBO or MBO-like programs have been implemented and have had widespread appeal in industrial organizations. As a major proponent of the technique, George S. Odiorne (1979) maintains that MBO has been used extensively in a variety of organizational settings, including many educational organizations.

Management by objectives is an administrative process that identifies and accomplishes organizational purposes by joining superiors and subordinates in the pursuit of mutually agreed goals that are specific, measurable, time bound, and joined to an action plan. Progress and goal attainment are assessed and monitored in appraisal sessions that focus on mutually determined standards of performance (McConkie, 1979). In educational settings, MBO is a system for motivating and integrating the efforts of school employees toward common objectives. The MBO process works by setting goals for the district as a whole and then cascading these goals down through each organizational level. As the goals cascade down the hierarchy, they become consistent across the hierarchical levels and more specific at each lower level. Assessment and monitoring occur at each level and the results are combined as they are passed up the hierarchy. Each level then helps attain goals at the next-highest level and ultimately for the entire school district. A typical scheme for designing and starting an MBO intervention in a school district would include the following five steps:

- Develop a set of overall educational goals for the school district.
- Establish goals for each job.
- Integrate the goals of the different positions so that every unit of the school district is working to accomplish the same overall goals.
- Establish plans for attaining the goals, methods for measuring the outcomes, and evaluation and feedback procedures.
- Implement the MBO program.

Although MBO has elements of participation, it is basically a top-down administrative approach, which attempts to motivate and integrate the efforts of school participants toward common goals that are set at the highest levels of the organization. Goals thus are initially external, but there is an attempt to get subordinates to internalize them. Rewards, however, are often linked to the accomplishment of goals. The extrinsic rewards vary from positive evaluations and promotions to bonuses and salary increase.

Research and Evaluation

During the 1980s extensive reviews of the MBO research literature were made by Jack N. Kondrasuk (1981), Stephen J. Carroll (1986), and R. C. Rogers and J. E. Hunter (1989). Even after reviewing 185 studies conducted in diverse settings, Kondrasuk (1981) concludes that rigorously designed research that tests the theoretical underpinnings of MBO programs remains somewhat limited. Nonetheless, approximately 90 percent of the studies reported positive outcomes for MBO. The support, however, was found to be inversely related to the power of the research design. In other words, as the sophistication of the research approach declined, the support for MBO increased. Case studies were very supportive; true experiments were at best partially supportive. Kondrasuk further concludes that he found some evidence, but not conclusive proof, for the effectiveness of MBO. The reviews by Carroll (1986) and Rogers and Hunter (1989) found similar results—MBO does have positive effects on performance. In brief, the research results on the effectiveness of MBO are generally supportive but not definitive.

Although the research evidence seems generally positive, the relative benefits may be marginal because of the costs and difficulties of introducing an MBO program in an educational setting. Until more research is available, administrators will have to make their own assessments about whether or not to experiment with formal goal-setting programs such as MBO. Before starting an MBO program, however, three of Kondrasuk's (1981) conclusions should be considered carefully:

- MBO is more likely to succeed in the private sector than in the public sector.
- MBO is more likely to succeed with administrative than with instructional staff.
- MBO is more likely to succeed in the short term than in the long term.

Table 4.4 concisely states the claims for and against the procedure.

TABLE 4.4

Conflicting Claims Regarding MBO

Claims by MBO Proponents	Counterclaims by MBO Critics
Enchances individual motivation to work by appealing to higher-order needs	Asserts that all individuals are ready to assume increased responsibility and self-discipline
Facilitates communication between superordinates and subordinates	Fails to allow lower-level employees full participation in setting objectives
Focuses on achieving organizational goals	Increases paperwork
Evaluates results, not personalities or politics	Emphasizes only quanitative evaluations of tangible results
Provides job improvement and personal growth	Generates extra work for administrators
Yields common understandings of organizational goals	Yields ambiguous and abstract goals in education

The needed congruence between getting individuals to strive toward specific, relatively difficult goals and accomplishing an overall organizational goal certainly is not an assured relationship (Miner, 1980). The basic idea of goals cascading down the school district level by level until an integrated group of goals emerge is problematic. Goal setting by individuals in schools with relatively ambiguous aims and loosely coupled organizational units can produce particularly diverse and marginally relevant sets of objectives.

Finally, politics and power struggles at the implementation stage can produce failures (Pinder, 1984). School districts typically are political and exhibit struggles among individuals and coalitions for power, influence, and resources. Failure to recognize and deal with the political factors at the time of implementation is bound to limit the success of an intervention. For example, MBO, properly practiced, calls for setting goals and sharing power and participation by the public, board of education, administrators, and teachers. This is a mix of issues and participants that will surely create political conflict.

As an overall assessment, MBO-type interventions now have strong theoretical and some research support, especially in the private sector. For educational organizations, implementing and maintaining long-term MBO programs will require large investments and their success seems problematic.

An Intrinsic Application: Job-Characteristics Model

The job-characteristics model (Hackman and Oldham, 1975, 1976, 1980) is a good illustration of the use of intrinsic motivation. The model suggests ways to design the job so that it is more meaningful and interesting—the classic aim of **job design.** Since the late 1970s, the dominant perspective on job design has been the **job-characteristics model** (Staw, 1984; Fox and Feldman, 1988). Ricky W. Griffin (1987) speculates that the reasons for its popularity are its provision of an academically sound model, a set of easily used measures, a package of practitioner-oriented implementation guidelines, and an initial body of empirical support.

The concepts and generalizations of the job-characteristics model are outlined in Figure 4.7. According to the model, the motivating potential of a job is a result of meaningfulness, autonomy, and feedback. The theory specifies that an employee will experience internal or intrinsic motivation when the job generates these three critical psychological states.

First, *feeling of meaningfulness* of the work is the degree to which the individual experiences the job as valuable and worthwhile. For work to be meaningful, three necessary characteristics are hypothesized: skill variety (work involves a number of activities using different skills and talents), task identity (job requires the completion of an entire segment of work), and task significance (job has a substantial impact on the lives of other people). Thus, meaningfulness is a function of skill variety, task identity, and task significance.

Second, *feeling of responsibility* for work outcomes is the degree to which the individual feels personally accountable for the results of the work he or she performs. Autonomy is postulated to be the primary job characteristic

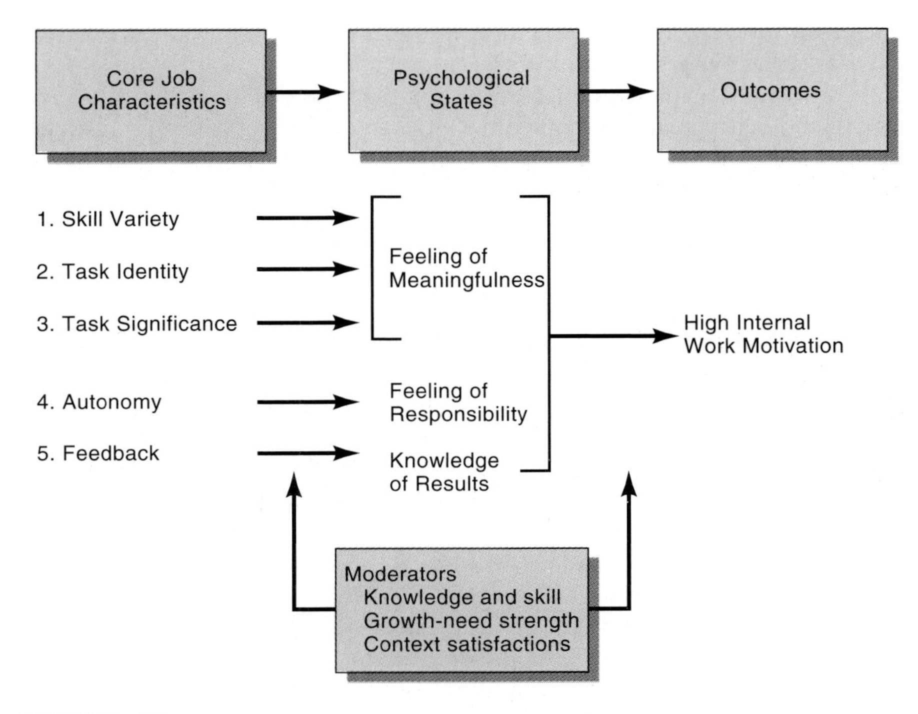

FIGURE 4.7 ***The Job-Characteristics Model***

Source: Adapted from J. Richard Hackman and Greg R. Oldham, *Work Redesign* (Reading, MA. Addison-Wesley, 1980), p. 83.

that creates a feeling of responsibility. Autonomy depends on the amount of freedom, independence, and discretion that an individual has to schedule the work and determine the procedures to be used. For educational settings, it is important to distinguish between autonomy and isolation (Hart, 1990b). Autonomy is control over time, decisions, important resources, and information necessary to accomplish the work. Isolation is aloneness and lack of interaction with peers.

Third, *knowledge of results* is the degree to which the individual knows and understands, on a continuous basis, how effectively he or she is performing the job. The focus is on feedback directly from the job—for example, when a teacher provides individual instruction to a student and observes the student's learning. In this case the knowledge of results comes from the work activities themselves and not from another person such as an administrator or colleague who collects data or assesses how well the job is being performed.

The three psychological states are internal to individuals and, therefore, not directly manipulable in designing work, but the five job characteristics are reasonably objective and can be changed in ways that foster the necessary internal states to produce work motivation. Jobs with high motivating potential create conditions that reinforce employees who have high performance levels (Hackman and Oldham, 1980). In other words, the characteristics of a job set the stage for the internal motivation or positive psychological states of individuals. Therefore, as the motivation of employees increases, the outcomes (intrinsic work motivation, growth satisfaction, job satisfaction, and work effectiveness) also increase.

However, for the relationships among the components (job characteristics, psychological states, and outcomes) to hold, three moderating conditions must be fulfilled (Hackman and Oldham, 1980; Gardner and Cummings, 1988). First, workers must possess sufficient knowledge and skills to perform the enriched jobs. Second, individuals must be satisfied with job-context factors such as compensation, job security, and relations with colleagues. Third, the employees must have strong needs for personal accomplishment, learning, and development—that is, growth-need strength. If high levels of the moderators are present, then the positive relationships among the components should be enhanced. The model is pictured in Figure 4.7.

Research and Evaluation

A major strength of the job-characteristics model is that the assessment of the core characteristics is relatively easy to accomplish. To measure the primary variables, Hackman and Oldham developed the job diagnostic survey (JDS) questionnaire (Hackman and Oldham, 1975, 1980), which has recently been revised (Cordery and Sevastos, 1993). The initial field research by Hackman and Oldham (1976) supports the major generalizations of the theory. Later investigations provide mixed support.[2] In a recent review of 31 well-designed studies, John Kelly (1992) also found limited support for the job-characteristics model. He concludes that although job redesign guided by the job-characteristics model appears to increase job satisfaction, no strong evidence was found that it motivates higher performance. Although Griffin (1991) tends to agree with this conclusion, his own research demonstrated a link between performance and job redesign using the job-characteristics model, but it took nearly four years for the performance increases to appear.

In the educational setting, a number of researchers have used many concepts of the model to assess the motivation potential of teaching positions.[3] In contrast, Larry Frase and his colleagues (Frase and Heck, 1992; Frase and Sorenson, 1992; Frase and Matheson, 1992) worked with a number of school districts to help redesign the jobs of educators based on the job-characteristics model. Their results generally support the model.

Hackman and Oldham (1980) acknowledge several shortcomings in their theory. Individual differences exist among people, and the best ways to define, measure, and include variations among individuals in the model remain open to question. Similarly, the links between job characteristics and psychological states are apparently not as strong as originally anticipated. Another problem is the lack of independence of the job characteristics. The model treats them as though they were independent or uncorrelated, but jobs that are high on one characteristic tend to be high on the others. The concept of feedback as used in the model is not adequately defined. Determining what is and is not job-based feedback is difficult. Finally, the relationships between objective properties of jobs and people's perceptions of those properties are not clear. The model does not consider the inevitable redefinition of the tasks that employees will make to draw more consistent relationships between their jobs and their needs, values, and attitudes.

Although recognizing its limitations, the job-characteristics model does provide measures and guidelines that can be used in diagnosing and implementing job redesign for professional employees (Miner, 1980; Oldham and Kulik, 1984). In this model, work redesign essentially involves improving the five-core characteristic of jobs, or increasing the overall motivating potential of a job. Six guidelines are typically given for directing job redesign efforts (Hackman and Suttle, 1977):

- Diagnose the work system to determine the need for systematic change in the core job characteristics.
- Focus the redesign on the work itself—that is, skill variety, task identity, task significance, autonomy, and feedback.
- Prepare contingency plans ahead of time for unanticipated problems and side effects.
- Monitor and evaluate the redesign efforts continuously to determine whether the anticipated changes are occurring or not.
- Confront the difficult problems as early in the project as possible.
- Design the change processes to fit the goals of the job-redesign program.

Hart (1990b) suggests that the job-characteristics model is a useful framework for examining teacher task, autonomy, and feedback structures in schools and their emerging influences on teacher motivation, attitudes, and performance. We agree. Overall, job redesign has high potential for producing positive results in educational organizations by making the job intrinsically rewarding, but given the difficulties in implementing the changes, success will not be easy.

An Integrated Approach: Career Ladders for Teachers

Career ladders is a good example of a motivational application that combines both extrinsic and intrinsic strategies. Career ladders became one of the most touted and widely mandated reforms of teaching and schools during the 1980s (Bacharach, Conley, and Shedd, 1986). In 1987, for example, approximately 40 states had or were developing career-ladder or other teacher-incentive programs (Hart, 1987). The extrinsic incentives for teachers built into career ladders include the formalization of rank and status, promotions, and increased pay. In other words, a system is created to motivate teachers by structuring career opportunities in ways so that teachers can gain more status, get promoted, and earn more money. On the intrinsic side is a plan to make the job increasingly more interesting and challenging as teachers develop and move up the career ladder and assume more responsibility.

Three reasons are generally offered as rationales for creating career-ladder programs. The first is based on the research finding that many of the best teachers leave their instructional careers after a brief foray in the classroom. Historically, about 50 percent of a teacher cohort will leave teaching during the first five to six years (Chapman and Hutcheson, 1982; Darling-Hammond, 1984; Mark and Anderson, 1985; Murnane, 1987). Moreover, a disproportionate percentage of those leaving teaching are the most academically talented (Vance and Schlechty, 1981, 1982). These data suggest that new teachers lack strong professional career orientations and that schools depend on new, transient college graduates to maintain the teaching force.

The second reason given for redesign is based on the observation that teaching in the elementary and secondary schools has a flat career path or is "unstaged" (Lortie, 1975). Teachers have limited opportunities for advancement in their instructional work. New and experienced teachers have the same role expectations. Teachers with motivations to advance or gain new responsibilities generally have two choices—they can remain frustrated in their self-contained classrooms or they can leave.

A third reason supporting the need for career ladders is that, although teaching is demanding work requiring creativity and versatility, it is repetitive. Despite the variety of classroom challenges and achievements, one year can look a lot like the next and there is little prospect to change the year-to-year pattern (Johnson, 1986). Hence, career-ladder programs were seen as ways to attract and retain highly talented individuals to education.

A **career-ladder program** redesigns jobs to provide individuals with prospects for promotion, formalizes status ranks for teachers, matches teacher abilities with job tasks, and distributes the responsibilities for school and faculty improvements to the professional staff (Murphy, 1985). In essence, the goal of career-ladder programs is to enrich work and enlarge teacher responsibilities (Johnson, 1986). **Job enrichment** is the enlargement of the job to include tasks at higher levels of skills and responsibility. Career ladders, like job-enrichment models, include promotions to higher ranks with the assumption of additional duties at each higher step—for example, mentoring and supervising new teachers, developing curriculum materials, and program evaluation. That is, the central conceptual features of career ladders are a differentiation of responsibilities among teachers and job enrichment (Bacharach, Conley, and Shedd, 1986).

By using job-enrichment strategies, career-ladder programs can address some of the concerns about teaching jobs. Such programs can provide teachers with opportunities and incentives to grow professionally, to develop new skills, to increase task variety and responsibility, to accept new challenges, and to promote collegiality. The innovation also increases teacher involvement in the professional aspects of schooling—that is, authority over the decision-making process for their clients. Career-ladder plans focus on recruitment, retention, and performance incentives to enhance the attractiveness of teaching. At its best, this approach to work redesign reflects the belief that intelligent and creative teachers can be attracted to teaching and that the overall quality of the teaching force can be improved by a staged career with differential staffing responsibilities and reward allocations.

A general characteristic of career-ladder plans that is based on a job-enrichment model is a hierarchical set of job categories, usually three or four, with different role expectations. A career-ladder program could include the following steps:

Status I: Beginning or novice teachers. These individuals assume the primary responsibility for teaching various student groups, receive modest levels of supervision and mentoring, and complete the probationary period of employment and certification.

Status II: Professional classroom teachers. They are autonomous teachers who are qualified to assume full responsibility for teaching the subjects and students in their areas of professional expertise.

Status III: A simple enlargement of the regular classroom teacher's job. The teacher would be encouraged to assume responsibility for special projects for extra compensation. For example, he or she might assume responsibility for designing an in-service workshop or create a new set of curriculum materials.

Status IV: The most advanced level, typically called teacher leader or master teacher. This is reserved for teachers who accept responsibilities beyond a single classroom (e.g., evaluate curriculum materials, supervise probationary teachers in their own schools and across the district, conduct research, develop and deliver in-service projects, and work as curriculum specialists). Usually these teachers continue to serve as classroom teachers, but with a reduced teaching load.

As a type of work redesign, career-ladder programs represent complex organizational interventions (Hart, 1995). For example, Hart and Murphy (1990) argue that restructuring requires explicit decisions about redesigning tasks, responsibilities, supervision, collegial and authority relationships, and compensation patterns. More specifically, as new organizational positions and levels of hierarchy are created, the actual content, processes, length of terms, and amount of special compensation of the new roles must be defined; existing role definitions of teachers, principals, and curriculum supervisors also require new formulations. Moreover, implementing a career-ladder program will likely create confusion, conflict, and extra work for everyone in the school system. Although the drawbacks are substantial, such work redesigns do have the potential to make greater use of professional expertise and provide teachers with motivating work and career experiences (Conley and Levinson, 1993).

Research and Evaluation

As is the case with most attempts to create and implement significant work-redesign programs, the research evidence for career-ladder programs is mixed. Malen, Murphy, and Hart (1988) probably conducted the most extensive series of empirical examinations of career-ladder programs. In a comprehensive analysis, they conclude that job expansion and job redesign in career-ladder programs can be successfully implemented. Although neither quick nor easy, they found that career-ladder interventions can be potent enough to improve teacher performance and retention. In a study of teachers with five years or less experience, Hart and Murphy (1990) found that the most talented ones held more favorable attitudes toward career-ladder programs than their less talented colleagues. In particular, the talented group showed relatively high interest in professionalism, power, and leadership. They also felt less constrained in their future career options and the prospect of new roles raised their expectations to high levels.

Hart (1987, 1990a) also reports on two studies of career-ladder programs. She found that teachers identified collegiality as important. Teachers participating in the program held more positive attitudes toward the interventions than nonparticipants and experienced teachers tend to be less involved and more critical than less experienced teachers. Hart also found that the norms, beliefs, and values common to the teaching occupation influenced the work redesign at both schools. Expectations of equality, cordiality, and privacy affect the way the teachers interpret career-ladder intervention. When these values are violated, support for the intervention declines and where the leaders were positive, the intervention was more successfully implemented.

William A. Firestone and his colleague Beth D. Bader (Firestone, 1991; Firestone and Bader, 1992) made an assessment of career-ladder programs in three school districts. Their findings indicate that job-enlargement programs can increase teacher motivation. Depending on the design and implementation processes, the outcomes varied substantially across the three districts. Their study and others (Rowan, 1990; Smylie, 1994) support the notion that professional changes such as job enlargement, teacher participation, and decentralization were more effective than the bureaucratic techniques of merit pay, top-down management, and a reliance on the organization to implement innovations.

Ebmeier and Hart (1992) report that teachers in schools with career-ladder programs exhibit more positive attitudes than do teachers in schools without such programs. Smylie and Smart (1990) found that teacher support for career-ladder programs is highest when they perceive that the redesign promotes professional learning and collegial relationships. Using a micropolitical perspective, Smylie and Brownlee-Conyers (1992) conclude that the principals and teacher leaders seek to reduce ambiguities and uncertainties, attempt to define their roles and relationships, and evoke strategies that influence the new roles. In contrast, Conley and Levinson (1993) found that participation in career-ladder programs is positively associated with satisfaction only for more experienced teachers. Finally, after a comprehensive review of the literature on incentive policies, Firestone and Pennell (1993) conclude that teachers prefer incentive programs with intrinsic incentives to those without, and career-ladder programs were preferred to merit programs.

Overall, the research findings indicate that career-ladder programs as examples of work redesign in schools are conceptualized and implemented with varying degrees of success. When designed and instituted appropriately, they can have positive effects on school programs, curricula, and instruction. Moreover, they can promote teacher and administrator satisfaction and motivation by making the work itself more interesting, increasing autonomy and responsibility, and raising expectations for psychological growth.

THEORY INTO PRACTICE

Motivational Challenge: The Superintendent Is Watching

You have just started as the new principal of Martin Luther King Elementary School. This is your first job as principal. After serving in a nearby elementary school, first as a teacher for five years and then as the assistant principal for one year, the opportunity opened for you to become the principal of your own school. Martin Luther King Elementary (K–4) is a relatively small school with only 15 teachers. The school is an urban one with a diverse student population—approximately 30 percent of the students are African American, 30 percent are Hispanic, 30 percent are white, and the remainder are of Asian descent. The school scores on statewide proficiency tests are slightly below average, falling at the forty-second percentile.

The first two months of school have passed quickly for everyone—especially for you as you spend most of the time getting to know your students and teachers and making sure that the school is running smoothly. You feel good about how things have gone thus far. There are always the routine problems with student discipline, complaining parents, teacher tensions, PTA initiatives, and bureaucratic directives, but you feel good about things on that front. Most would agree that your school was well administered.

But you have a nagging feeling about what is going on in the classrooms and how much progress students are making in the basic skill areas of reading, writing, and mathematics. Nothing specific leaps to mind except your final conversation with the superintendent, Dr. Rosa Young, the night you were hired. She was very direct in her message. On the one hand, she proclaimed confidence in your ability to improve student performance at Martin Luther King, but on the other hand, she was clear that you had two years to get up the proficiency test scores or else she would mandate new reading and math programs that she believed would make a difference. You embraced the challenge that evening and your words keep coming back. "No problem!"

THEORY INTO PRACTICE, (Continued)

you had exclaimed as you shook hands with Dr. Young. You were surprised a month later when she sent you a personal memo encouraging you to "make a difference." Moreover, she was offering you monetary support for professional development of teachers in your school. "No problem, make a difference," you keep thinking.

Now the reality of the challenge keeps flashing through your thoughts. "No problem, make a difference." It is time to move from maintaining the organization to initiating action that will have a positive impact on the teachers and students of your school. As you consider the teachers in your school, there are three groups. One group is composed of five teachers who are either second-year or third-year teachers plus two new teachers you helped select. All seven of these teachers are eager, enthusiastic and easy to work with. Five other teachers are good teachers, but they seem rather indifferent to any new ideas or innovative programs; they just do their jobs. Finally, like most schools, you have three teachers who are "Old Guard." These three account for 73 years of teaching experience, most of it in the same building stretching back to when the school was simply the Fourth Ward Elementary with a predominantly white population. The Old Guard is a negative group. No matter what comes up, they say, "It won't make any difference. We've been there and done that." The indifferent group usually just shrugs, whereas the new group tries to come up with some different ways of doing things.

At the last faculty meeting, you suggested that each grade level set goals to improve reading performance. Resistance had met your suggestion. "We tried that eight years ago and it made no difference," was the first response from the leader of the Old Guard, Sam Horton. What ensued for the next 30 minutes was general carping about the low ability and indifference of the students, lack of student and parent motivation, not enough time, not enough extra materials, not enough teaching aids, and on and on. The meeting was a fiasco. The Old Guard led the "do nothing" charge; the indifferents followed; and the new group said little and appeared to acquiesce. This was not what you had in mind, but you could see a pattern of apathy, indifference, and opposition to change emerging. The new group of seven is able and willing to move forward, but you are afraid that they will be influenced by the more experienced teachers into a mode of pessimistic rather than optimistic thinking.

You need a plan to motivate the teachers to do their best. The reading and mathematics instructional programs appear more than adequate. Each teacher has at least a part-time teaching aid. Class size is reasonable. Instructional materials are plentiful; teachers get what they need. All in all, the materials and curriculum are fine. What is lacking, in your judgment, is strong motivation on the part of some of your teachers. You decide that you have to encourage and protect the new teachers, stimulate the indifferents to commit to some new goals and procedures, and isolate the Old Guard while working one-on-one with each of them to improve the performance of their students. You have the resources that you need to engage in professional development with your teachers, that is, you have professional development days and money. What to do? Should you engage in different motivational strategies for each of the groups—new teachers, indifferents, and Old Guard? You consider the following options to motivate students and teachers at Martin Luther King Elementary School.

- Develop a strategy to enhance a high degree of collective efficacy among the new teachers and indifferents. What mastery experiences are needed and how will you get them for your teachers? What kinds of models or other vicarious experiences should your teachers have and where will they get them? What kind of activities will be useful to persuade teachers that they can improve the proficiency of their students? What kind of affective state is needed in your school to develop the collective efficacy that you need? How will you achieve that state?
- Develop a strategy to have your teachers set some realistic performance goals for their students. Make sure the goals are specific, challenging, and attainable. Also find ways to have teachers commit to the goals.

THEORY INTO PRACTICE, (Continued)

- Design a strategy to develop a high degree of teacher efficacy in selected teachers. How can you help develop in the teachers a belief that they have the capability to organize and execute the courses of action required to successfully improve the reading performance of their students? How can you make their task attainable? What kinds of skills and knowledge do they need?
- Develop a strategy to motivate the Old Guard teachers. What kind of motivation is mostly likely to work—intrinsic or extrinsic? What are you alternatives in each area? How much time should you invest in these teachers? Should you just forget about these teachers and focus all your energy on the others? But what about their students?

Suddenly a buzzing phone interrupts your thoughts, and your secretary informs you that Superintendent Young is on the line. You are surprised. Actually, it is not Dr. Young on the phone but her assistant who wants you to know that the superintendent's office is ready to do what it can to help you raise reading test scores for next year. The conversation that pursues is friendly and supportive, but there is an edge. The unspoken message is that if scores don't go up, the superintendent's office may well mandate changes. There is no question that you need a plan to motivate your teachers and their students to improve. You have just begun to consider what motivational strategies you will use. With whom should you consult? What motivation perspectives are most useful? What are your first steps? Your job is clear: ***Develop a plan and implementation strategy to motivate your teachers to improve the reading performance of their students.*** Just do it.

Summary and Suggested Readings

The individual is a key element of all social systems. Students, teachers, and administrators bring with them individual needs, goals, and beliefs and develop their own personal orientations and intellectual understanding of their roles. Just as structure helps shape behavior in schools so too do the needs, goals, and beliefs of individuals. Maslow describes a hierarchy of basic needs that motivate behavior ranging from biological to self-actualization needs, and Herzberg distinguishes between needs that produce worker satisfaction and those that cause dissatisfaction. The need for achievement and the need for autonomy are two other powerful motivating forces within individuals.

Individual goals and goal setting are also key ingredients of personal motivation, especially when the goals are embraced by the individual and are specific, challenging, and attainable. Similarly, beliefs are important motivational forces. Administrators, teachers, and students are likely to work hard if they believe that success is primarily due to their ability and effort, that causes of outcomes are under their control, that extra effort will improve performance, that good performance will be noticed and rewarded, that the rewards are valued, and that they have been treated fairly and with respect by their superiors. Moreover, effective performance is closely related to self-efficacy, the belief that one has the capability to organize and execute a course of action that is required to attain the desired level of performance.

Motivation that comes from the interest and challenge of the activity itself is intrinsic, whereas extrinsic motivation is based on rewards and punishment. Although both can motivate, intrinsic motivation is typically more effective. Merit pay and management by objectives are two attempts to build motivational systems on the basis of extrinsic rewards. The job-characteristics model is a good example of job design that is based on the application of intrinsic motivation. Finally, a career-ladder program for teachers is an attempt to wed intrinsic and extrinsic strategies of motivation into a plan to redesign and reform the school workplace.

A classic work on motivation is Maslow's (1970) *Motivation and Personality*. For a more contemporary analysis of theory and research on motivation, see Kanfer's (1990) thorough and integrative review and critique. The collection of readings by Steers and Porter (1991) is also instructive and provides a wide range of competing models. Finally, two books are must readings for all students of motivation: Locke and Latham's *A Theory of Goal Setting and Task Performance* (1990) and Bandura's treatise, *Self-Efficacy: The Exercise of Control* (1997). Locke and Latham provide the details of goal-setting theory as well as an extensive review of the literature. Bandura's book is a tour de force that summarizes two decades of research and theory on self-efficacy. Arguably, goal-setting theory and self-efficacy theory are the most important contemporary approaches to motivation. Check *The Journal of Applied Psychology* and the *Academy of Management Review,* which frequently publish articles on work motivation.

Notes

1. According to Campbell, Dunnette, Lawler, and Weick (1970), McClelland sought to refine and investigate a subset of motives from a longer list developed by H. A. Murray. Three motives received the most attention—need for achievement, need for power, and need for affiliation. Achievement motivation has received the most attention and was formalized into a theory of expectancy achievement motivation. For present purposes, we limit our discussion to the value portion of the theory.
2. Studies providing support include Oldham and Miller (1979); Orpen (1979); Bhagat and Chassie (1980); Kiggundu (1980); Johns, Xie, and Fang (1992). Investigations providing partial support include Evans, Kiggundu, and House (1979) and Griffeth (1985); ones showing little or no support include Arnold and House (1980); Adler, Skov, and Salvemini (1985); and Tiegs, Tetrick, and Fried (1992).
3. See, for example, Gorsuch (1977), Pastor and Erlandson (1982), Mennuti and Kottkamp (1986), and Barnabe and Burns (1994).

Key Concepts and Ideas

Achievement motivation theory
Attribution theory
Belief
Career-ladder program
Collective teacher efficacy
Dimensions of causality
Equity theory
Expectancy
Expectancy theory
Extrinsic motivation
Goal
Goal content
Goal intensity
Goal-setting theory
Hygienes
Incremental view of ability
Instrumentality
Intrinsic motivation
Job-characteristics model
Job design
Job enrichment
Management by objectives
Merit pay
Motivation
Motivators
Need hierarchy
Needs
Self-actualization
Self-efficacy
Stable view of ability
Teacher efficacy
Valence
Work motivation

CHAPTER 5

CULTURE AND CLIMATE IN SCHOOLS

The behavior of a group cannot be predicted solely from an understanding of the personality of each of its members. Various social processes intervene . . . the group develops a "mood," an "atmosphere." In the context of the organization, we talk about a "style," a "culture," a "character."

Henry Mintzberg
Power In and Around Organizations

PREVIEW

1. Organizational culture and organizational climate are two contemporary perspectives for examining the distinctive character of schools; they are partly competing, partly complementary.
2. Organizational culture is manifested in norms, shared values, and basic assumptions, each occurring at a different level of abstraction.
3. Strong organizational cultures can improve or hinder the effectiveness of an organization; different cultures are effective depending on environmental constraints.
4. School cultures can be interpreted by analyzing their symbols, artifacts, rites, ceremonies, icons, heroes, myths, rituals, and legends.
5. Often the most important thing about events in organizations is not what happened but what the events mean.
6. Organizational climate is a relatively enduring quality of a school that is manifested in teachers' collective perceptions of organizational behavior.
7. The climate of schools can be viewed from a variety of vantage points; three useful perspectives are the openness of behavior, the health of interpersonal relations, and the humanism of pupil-control ideologies.
8. Each of these climate perspectives can be reliably measured using the appropriate survey instrument.
9. The openness and health of a school are related to a number of important organizational outcomes including perceptions of school effectiveness and student achievement.

10. Humanism in pupil-control ideology is related to teacher efficacy as well as to such student outcomes as higher self-actualization, less alienation, and a better quality of school life.
11. There is no quick and simple way to change the culture or climate of schools, but long-term planning is more likely to produce change than will short-term fads.
12. Three complementary strategies for organizational change are a clinical view, a growth-centered approach, and a norm-changing plan.

Behavior in organizations is not simply a function of formal expectations and individual needs and motivation. The relationships among these elements are dynamic. Participants bring to the workplace a host of unique values, needs, goals, and beliefs. These individual characteristics mediate the rational aspects of organizational life. Moreover, a collective sense of identity emerges that transforms a simple aggregate of individuals into a distinctive workplace "personality" or culture.

This indigenous feel of the workplace has been analyzed and studied under a variety of labels, including "organizational character," "milieu," "atmosphere," "ideology," "climate," "culture," "emergent system," and "informal organization." Our analysis of the internal workplace environment will focus on two related concepts—organizational culture and organizational climate. Each of these notions suggests a natural, spontaneous, and human side to the organization; each suggests that the organizational whole is greater than the sum of its parts; and each attempts to uncover the shared meanings and unwritten rules that guide organizational behavior.[1]

Organizational Culture

Concern for the culture of the work group is not new. As we have seen, in the 1930s and 1940s, both Elton Mayo (1945) and Chester Barnard (1938) were stressing the importance of work-group norms, sentiments, values, and emergent interactions in the workplace as they described the nature and functions of informal organization. Philip Selznick (1957) extended the analysis of organizational life by viewing organizations as institutions rather than merely rational organizations. Institutions, according to Selznick (1957: 14), are "infused with value beyond the technical requirements at hand." This infusion of value produces a *distinctive identity* for the organization; it defines organizational character. Selznick (1957) continues:

> Whenever individuals become attached to an organization or a way of doing things as persons rather than technicians, the result is apprising of the device for its own sake. From the standpoint of the committed person, the organization is changed from an expendable tool into a valued source of personal satisfaction. Where institutionalization is well advanced, distinctive outlooks, habits, and other commitments are unified, coloring

> all aspects of organizational life and lending it a social integration that goes well beyond formal co-ordination and command. (p. 14)

Indeed, it is Selznick's formulation of organizations as institutions, each with distinctive competence and organizational character, that provides a basis for contemporary analyses of organizations as cultures (Peters and Waterman, 1982).

Organizational culture is an attempt to get at the feel, sense, atmosphere, character, or image of an organization. It encompasses many of the earlier notions of informal organization, norms, values, ideologies, and emergent systems. The popularity of the term "organizational culture" is in part a function of a number of popular books on successful business corporations that emerged in the 1980s (Peters and Waterman, 1982; Deal and Kennedy, 1982; Ouchi, 1981). The basic theme of all these analyses was that effective organizations have strong and distinctive corporate cultures and that a basic function of executive leadership is to shape the culture of the organization.

Definition of Organizational Culture

The notion of culture brings with it conceptual complexity and confusion. No intact definition for culture from anthropology exists; instead, we find numerous, diverse definitions. It should not be surprising, therefore, that there are many definitions of organizational culture. For example, William Ouchi (1981:41) defines organizational culture as "symbols, ceremonies, and myths that communicate the underlying values and beliefs of that organization to its employees." Jay Lorsch (1985:84), on the other hand, uses culture to mean "the beliefs top managers in a company share about how they should manage themselves and other employees and how they should conduct their business." Henry Mintzberg (1989:98) refers to culture as organization ideology, or "the traditions and beliefs of an organization that distinguish it from other organizations and infuse a certain life into the skeleton of its structure." Alan Wilkins and Kerry Patterson (1985:265) maintain that, "an organization's culture consists largely of what people believe about what works and what does not," while Joanne Martin (1985:95) argues that "culture is an expression of people's deepest needs, a means of endowing their experiences with meaning." Stephen Robbins (1998:595) defines organization culture as "a system of shared meaning held by members that distinguishes the organization from other organizations. Jerald Greenberg and Robert Baron (1997:471) describe organizational culture as "a cognitive framework consisting of attitudes, values, behavioral norms, and expectations shared by organizational members." Edgar Schein (1992, 1999), however, argues that the culture should be reserved for a "deeper level of basic assumptions, values, and beliefs" that become shared and taken for granted as the organization continues to be successful.

Organizational culture, then, is typically defined in terms of *shared orientations that hold the unit together and give it a distinctive identity.* But substantial disagreement arises about what is shared—norms, values, philosophies, perspectives, beliefs, expectations, attitudes, myths, or ceremonies. Another problem is determining the intensity of shared orientations of organizational members. Do organizations have a basic culture or many cultures? Moreover, there is disagreement on the extent to which organizational culture is conscious and overt or unconscious and covert.

Levels of Organizational Culture

One way to begin to untangle some of the problems of definition is to view culture at different levels. As illustrated in Figure 5.1, culture is manifested in norms, shared values, and basic assumptions, each occurring at different levels of depth and abstraction.

Culture as Shared Norms

A fairly concrete, some would say superficial, perspective on culture emerges when behavioral norms are used as the basic elements of culture (see Figure 5.1). **Norms** are usually unwritten and informal expectations that occur just below the surface of experience. Norms directly influence behavior. They are much more visible than either values or tacit assumptions; consequently, they provide a clear means for helping people understand the cultural aspects of organizational life. Moreover, if we are concerned with

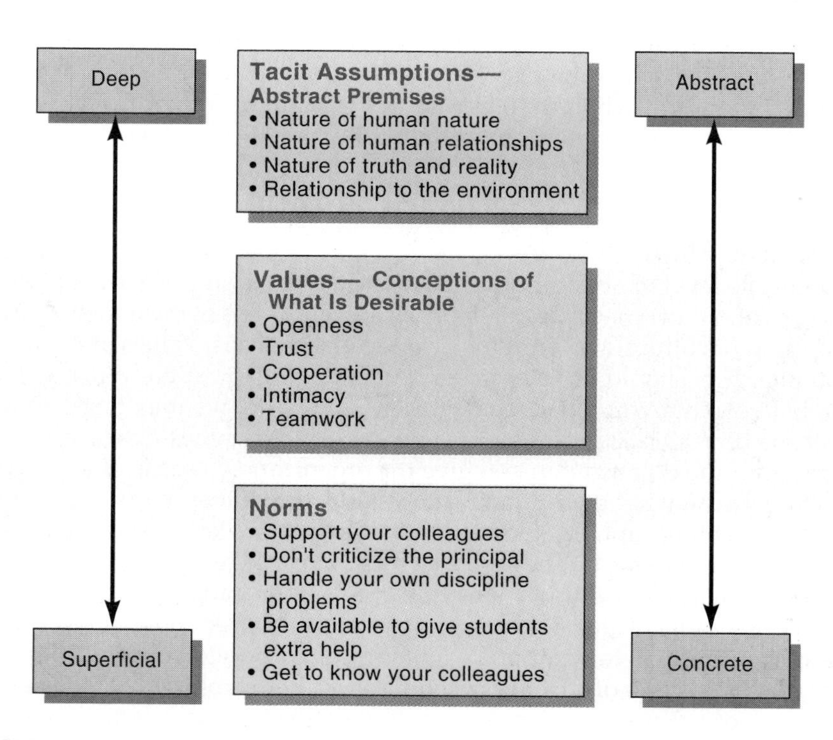

FIGURE 5.1 *Levels of Culture*

changing organizational behavior, then it is important to know and understand the norms of that culture. As Allen and Kraft (1982) cogently note:

> Norms are universal phenomena. They are necessary, tenacious, but also extremely malleable. Because they can change so quickly and easily, they present a tremendous opportunity to people interested in change. Any group, no matter its size, once it understands itself as a cultural entity, can plan its own norms, creating positive ones that will help it reach its goals and modifying or discarding the negative ones. (pp. 7–8)

Norms are also communicated to participants by stories and ceremonies that provide visible and potent examples of what the organization stands for. Sometimes stories about people are created to reinforce the basic norms of the organization. The principal who stood by the teacher despite overwhelming pressure from parents and superiors becomes a symbol of the cohesiveness and loyalty in a school's culture; it is a story that is retold many times to new teachers. Teachers quickly learn the norms, "don't tell tales out of school," "support your colleagues," and "support your principal." Norms determine the way people dress and talk; the way participants respond to authority, conflict, and pressure; and the way people balance self-interests with organizational interests. Examples of norms include the following: don't rock the boat; don't criticize fellow teachers to students or parents; all men wear neckties; handle your own discipline problems; don't let students out of class before the bell rings; and change the bulletin boards frequently. As noted in Chapter 1, norms are enforced by sanctions; people are rewarded and encouraged when they conform to norms and are confronted, ostracized, or punished when they violate the cultural norms of the group. In brief, the norms of the work group define a major slice of the culture of the organization.

Culture as Shared Values

At a middle level of abstraction, culture is defined as shared values. **Values** are conceptions of what is desirable. They are reflections of the underlying assumptions of culture, and lie at the next level of analysis. Values often define what members should do to be successful in the organization. When we ask people to explain why they behave the way they do, we may begin to discover the central values of the organization. Shared values define the basic character of the organization and give the organization a sense of identity. If members know what their organization stands for, if they know what standards they should uphold, they are more likely to make decisions that will support those standards. They are also more likely to feel part of the organization and that organizational life has important meaning.

William Ouchi's (1981) book on the success of Japanese corporations was one of the first contemporary analyses of corporate culture. Ouchi argued that the success of effective corporations in both Japan and America was a function of a distinctive corporate culture, one that was internally consistent and characterized by the shared values of intimacy, trust, cooperation, teamwork, and egalitarianism. Success of these organizations was not as much a matter of technology as it was of managing people. He labeled the American organizations with these values Theory Z cultures.

Theory Z organizations have a number of properties that promote this distinctive culture (see Table 5.1). Long-term employment opportunities create in employees a sense of security and commitment to the organization; participants become invested in the organization. The process of slower rates of promotion creates more opportunities to broaden experiences and diverse career paths as employees perform different functions and occupy different roles. This effectively produces company-specific skills and promotes career development. Participative and consensual decision making demands cooperation and teamwork, values that are openly communicated and reinforced. Individual responsibility for collective decision making demands an atmosphere of trust and mutual support. Finally, concern for the total person is a natural part of the working relationship, which tends to be informal and emphasizes the whole person and not just the individual's work role. This holistic perspective promotes a strong egalitarian atmosphere, a community of equals who work cooperatively on common goals rather than relying on the formal hierarchy. Thus Theory Z organizations are structured and operate to promote the basic values of intimacy, trust, cooperation, and egalitarianism. These **core values** of the culture are the dominant values that are accepted and shared by most of the organizational members; they influence virtually every aspect of organizational life.

Several other studies (Deal and Kennedy, 1982; Peters and Waterman, 1982) of successful corporations also suggest the pivotal importance of strong organizational cultures in fostering effectiveness. Deal and Kennedy (1982) suggest that successful organizations share some common cultural characteristics. They argue that such organizations have:

- A widely shared organizational philosophy.
- Concern for individuals that is more important than formal rules and policies.
- Rituals and ceremonies that build a common identity.
- A well-understood sense of the informal rules and exceptions.
- A belief that what employees do is important to others.

TABLE 5.1

Theory Z Organization and Culture

Organizational Characteristic		Core Value
1. Long-term employment	→	Organizational commitment
2. Slower promotion rates	→	Career orientation
3. Participative decision making	→	Cooperation and teamwork
4. Individiual responsibility for group decisions	→	Trust and group loyalty
5. Holistic orientation	→	Egalitarianism

Therefore, sharing information and ideas is encouraged.

Thomas J. Peters and Robert H. Waterman (1982: 15) found that excellent companies were brilliant on the basics: "Tools didn't substitute for thinking. Intellect didn't overpower wisdom. Analysis didn't impede action. Rather these companies worked hard to keep things simple in a complex world." Effective companies persisted and thrived because they had strong cultures. The shared values of those cultures included the following:

- *A bias for action:* Planning is not a substitute for action.
- *A client orientation:* Serve your customers.
- *An innovative orientation:* Respect autonomy and entrepreneurship.
- *A people orientation:* Productivity comes through people.
- *An achievement orientation:* High-quality products are essential.

In **strong cultures,** beliefs and values are held intensely, shared widely, and guide organizational behavior. It might be tempting to jump to the conclusion that a specific set of values defines excellence in organizations, but that would be unjustified. What promotes excellence yesterday does not necessarily promote it today or tomorrow (Aupperle, Acar, and Booth, 1986; Hitt and Ireland, 1987). In fact, a strong culture can be a liability in times of rapid change because the organization's culture may be so ingrained that it prevents adaptation to new constraints. Hanson (1991) observes that in many ways the link between culture and effectiveness is the same as that between structure and effectiveness. Both culture and structure can undermine outcomes by either stagnating or disrupting the system through rigidities, conflicts, and hidden agendas.

Culture as Tacit Assumptions

At its deepest level, culture is the collective manifestation of tacit assumptions. When members of an organization share a view of the world around them and their place in that world, culture exists. That is, a pattern of basic assumptions has been invented, discovered, or developed by the organization as it learned to cope with its problems of external adaptation and internal integration. This pattern has worked well enough to be considered valid and it is taught to new members as the correct way to perceive, think, and feel in relation to those problems. Because the assumptions have worked repeatedly, they have become so basic that they are taken for granted, tend to be nonconfrontable and nondebatable, and thus are highly resistant to change. From this perspective, the key to understanding organizational culture is to decipher the tacit assumptions shared by members and to discover how these assumptions fit together into a cultural pattern or paradigm.

Tacit assumptions are abstract premises about the nature of human relationships, human nature, truth, reality, and environment (Dyer, 1985). For example, is human nature basically good, evil, or neutral? How is truth ultimately determined—is it revealed or discovered? What are the assumed relationships among members of the group—primarily hierarchical, cooperative, or individualistic? When organizations develop consistent and articulate patterns of basic assumptions, they have strong cultures.

Consider two strong, but contrasting school cultures. The first school has a strong, distinctive culture based on the following assumptions as suggested by Schein (1985):

- Truth ultimately comes from teachers themselves.
- Teachers are responsible, motivated, and capable of governing themselves and making decisions in the best interests of their students.
- Truth is determined through debate, which often produces conflict and testing of ideas in an open forum.
- Teachers are a family; they accept, respect, and take care of each other.

These core assumptions give rise to such shared values as individualism, autonomy, openness, professionalism, and authority of knowledge.

In contrast, a second school is guided by the following assumptions.

- Truth ultimately comes from experienced teachers and administrators.
- Most teachers are committed and loyal to the school. (They are good "soldiers.")
- Relationships in the school are basically hierarchical.
- Yet, teachers respect and honor each other's autonomy in the classrooms.
- Teachers are family who take care of each other.

In this school the core assumptions produce such values as respect for authority, respect for territory, and conflict avoidance.

There is no simple way to uncover the basic patterns of assumptions that underlie what people value and do. Schein (1992, 1999) develops an elaborate set of procedures to decipher the culture of an organization. It is an approach that combines anthropological and clinical techniques and involves a series of encounters and joint explorations between the investigator and various motivated informants who live in the organization and embody its culture. Joint effort usually involves extensive data-gathering activities that explore the history of the organization, critical events, organizational structure, myths, legends, stories, and ceremonies. Schein (1992, 1999) eschews questionnaires as devices to identify tacit assumptions; at best, he argues, such instruments produce only some of the espoused values of group members. A few researchers (O'Reilly, Chatman, and Caldwell, 1991; Chatman and Jehn, 1994, Cameron and Quinn, 1999), however, have attempted to assess the shared values of culture using quantitative instruments.

Level of Analysis

The most penetrating definitions of culture emphasize the deepest level of human nature or at least refer to shared ideologies, beliefs, and values (Kilmann, Saxton, and Serpa, 1985). Theorists interested in understanding culture rather than managing it advocate such definitions. Organizational participants, however, have difficulty openly identifying their tacit assumptions or discussing their basic assumptions; in fact, they describe such exercises as merely academic. At the other extreme, those definitions of culture that focus on behavioral norms are more useful to consultants and practitioners who are interested in assessing and changing organizational cultures. According to Kilmann and his associates (1985), organizational members seem more willing and able to identify the prevailing norms of the culture and to discuss them with minimal levels of threat and discomfort. Although the more abstract approaches to defining culture initially seem to be more penetrating, in practice they are less useful; and although the more superficial approaches seem to ignore the more fundamental bases of culture, in practice they offer some specific ways to manage culture, albeit in a very narrow way. Clearly we have much to learn about culture. Therefore, at this point in the development of the concept of organizational culture it is valuable to view and study culture at *all* three levels—that is, in terms of shared norms, core values, and tacit underlying assumptions.

Functions of Culture

Although there may be no one best culture, strong cultures promote cohesiveness, loyalty, and commitment, which in turn reduce the propensity for members to leave the organization (Mowday, Porter, and Steers, 1982). Moreover, Robbins (1991) summarizes a number of important functions performed by the organization's culture:

- Culture has a boundary-defining function; it creates distinctions among organizations.
- Culture provides the organization with a sense of identity.
- Culture facilitates the development of commitment to the group.
- Culture enhances stability in the social system.
- Culture is the social glue that binds the organization together; it provides the appropriate standards for behavior.

Culture serves to guide and shape the attitudes and behavior of organizational members. It is important to remember, however, that a strong culture can be either functional or dysfunctional—that is, it can promote or impede effectiveness.

Types of Cultures

There are different types of organizational cultures. For example, Dan Denison's (1990) study of corporate culture and effectiveness suggests that effective organizations are ones in which there is a fit among strategy, environment, and culture. Other theorists have proposed other frameworks (Kets de Vries and Miller, 1986; Denison, 1996; Martin, 1992), but we prefer the Competing Values Framework developed by Cameron and Quinn (1999) because of its parsimony and consistency with well-know and well-accepted categorical schemes that organize the ways people think and process information, including their values and assumptions (e.g., Myers and Briggs, 1962; Mitroff and Kilmann, 1978).

Two general dimensions define the framework: (1) the extent of flexibility and discretion in the organization and (2) the degree to which organizations use internal or external criteria of effectiveness. Together these two dimensions form four types of organizations, each with indicators of what people value about an organization's performance. In effect, they represent competing values and assumptions of organization and define four major cultural types: hierarchy culture, market culture, clan culture, and the adhocracy culture (Cameron and Quinn, 1999).

The *hierarchy culture* is defined by emphases on stability, control, integration, and an internal focus. The goal of this kind of organization is to produce goods and services efficiently in the tradition of Weber's classic bureaucratic model (see Chapter 3). Efficiency, stability, predictability and harmony are core values. Leaders pride themselves on a smoothly and efficiently functioning organization.

The *market culture* is defined by emphases on stability, control, differentiation, and an external focus. The goal of this kind of organization is to respond quickly to changes in environment so as not to lose its competitive advantage. Competition, effectiveness, goal accomplishment, and winning are core values. Leadership is hard nosed and competitive, with leaders driving the organization toward its goals.

The *clan culture* is defined by emphases on flexibility, discretion, integration, and an internal focus. This type of organization is a team or family-like organization—a friendly place to work where concern for people is paramount. Cooperation, cohesion, participation, and loyalty are core values. Leadership is informal, friendly, and people oriented.

The *adhocracy culture* is defined by emphases on flexibility, discretion, differentiation, and an external focus. The goal of this kind of organization is to develop new and innovative products and services. Creativity, risk taking, change, and growth are core values. Leadership is visionary and innovative.

Each cultural type can be effective in the right circumstances. Cameron and Quinn (1999) provide a sophisticated method to measure and diagnose organizational culture using this framework. The four cultures are summarized in Figure 5.2.

Common Elements of Culture

At the core on any organizational culture is a set of shared values. A number of recent studies (O'Reilly, Chatman, and Caldwell, 1991; Chatman and Jehn, 1994) of business corporations suggest that there are seven primary elements that shape the culture of most organizations:

1. *Innovation:* the degree to which employees are expected to be creative and take risks.
2. *Stability:* the degree to which activities focus on the status quo rather than change.
3. *Attention to detail:* the degree to which there is concern for precision and detail.

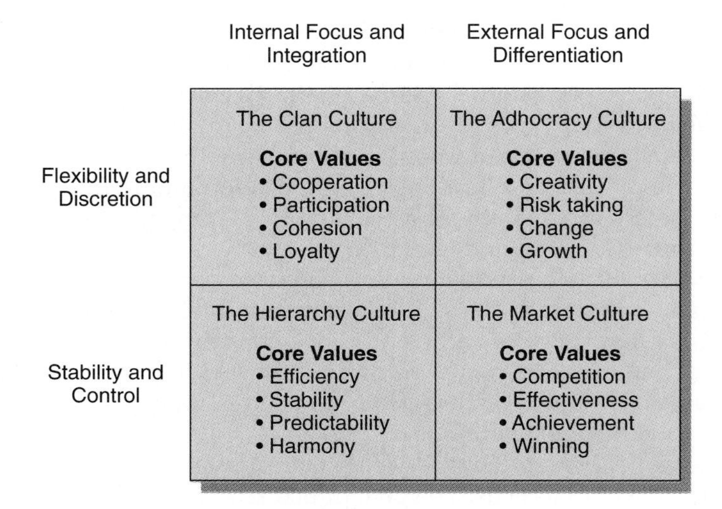

FIGURE 5.2 *Typology of Cultures*

4. *Outcome orientation:* the degree to which management emphasizes results.
5. *People orientation:* the degree to which management decisions are sensitive to individuals.
6. *Team orientation:* the degree of emphasis on collaboration and teamwork.
7. *Aggressiveness:* the degree to which employees are expected to be competitive rather than easygoing.

The culture of most organizations can be mapped by using these elements to describe the values that are dominant. Schein (1999), however, provides three cautions. First, cultures are deep, not superficial; thus if you assume that you can manipulate it, you are likely to fail. Second, culture is broad because it is formed by beliefs and assumptions about daily life in organizations; hence, deciphering culture is a major challenge that should be focused if it is to be successful. Third, culture is stable because it provides meaning and makes life predictable; consequently, changing it is difficult at best.

School Culture

Although organizational culture has become a fashionable construct for analysis in education, much of the recent discussion about school culture remains analytical, philosophical, and rhetorical rather than empirical (see Cusick, 1987). It is not difficult, for example, to use the research results on corporate cultures (Ouchi, 1981; Deal and Kennedy, 1982; Peters and Waterman, 1982) and the effective schools research (Brookover et al., 1978; Rutter et al., 1979; Clark, Lotto, and Astuto, 1984) to develop an ideal description of an effective school culture. For instance, Terrence Deal (1985) proposes that effective schools have strong cultures with the following characteristics:

1. Shared values and a consensus on "how we get things done around here."
2. The principal as a hero or heroine who embodies core values.
3. Distinctive rituals that embody widely shared beliefs.
4. Employees as situational heroes or heroines.
5. Rituals of acculturation and cultural renewal.
6. Significant rituals to celebrate and transform core values.
7. Balance between innovation and tradition and between autonomy and control.
8. Widespread participation in cultural rituals.

What are the core values that transform a school into an effective institution? Schools are for students; experiment with your teaching; teaching and learning are cooperative processes; stay close to your students; strive for academic excellence; demand high, but realistic performance; be open in behavior and communication; trust your colleagues; and be professional. Are these core values or empty slogans? If these beliefs are strongly shared and widely enacted, then these sloganlike themes can define a strong school culture. Unfortunately, there is little systematic research that directly examines the institutional cultures of effective schools.

Anthropological and sociological studies of school cultures are needed. The thick descriptions of qualitative studies are necessary to map the basic assumptions and common values of the cultures of schools. Educational researchers must consider the school as a whole and analyze how its practices, beliefs, and other cultural elements relate to the social structure as well as give meaning to social life. To understand culture one must be immersed in the complex clustering of symbols people use to give meaning to their world. In this vein, Geertz (1973) asserts:

> Believing with Max Weber that man is an animal suspended in webs of significance he himself has spun, I take culture to be those webs, and the analysis of it to be therefore not an experimental science in search of law but an interpretive one in search of meaning. It is explication I am after, construing social expressions on their surface enigmatical. (p. 5)

William Firestone and Bruce Wilson (1985) provide a useful framework for beginning to study the organizational cultures of schools. They suggest that the analysis of school culture can be addressed by studying its content, the expressions of culture, and primary communication patterns.

The symbols through which culture is expressed often help identify important cultural themes. Three symbol systems communicate the contents of a school's culture: stories, icons, and rituals.

- **Stories** are narratives that are based on true events, but they often combine truth and fiction.
- **Myths** are stories that communicate an unquestioned belief that cannot be demonstrated by the facts.
- **Legends** are stories that are retold and elaborated with fictional details.

For example, the principal, who stood by her teachers despite overwhelming pressure from parents and superiors, becomes a symbol of the cohesiveness and loyalty in the school's culture. It is a story that is retold many times to new teachers, one that takes on special meaning as it is interpreted and embellished. Stories are often about organizational heroes or heroines who epitomize the organization; they provide insight into the core values of the organization. Icons and rituals are also important.

- **Icons** are physical artifacts that are used to communicate culture (logos, mottoes, and trophies).
- **Rituals** are the routine ceremonies and rites that signal what is important in the organization.

Janice Beyer and Harrison Trice (1987) identify rites of passage, degradation, enhancement, and integration as examples of routine ceremonies used to develop and sustain organizational culture. Table 5.2 contains some school examples of these four rites and their likely consequences. Much of the culture of a school can be constructed from artifacts, rites, rituals, and ceremonies related to assemblies, faculty meetings, athletic contests, community activities, cafeteria, report cards, awards and trophies, lesson plans, and the general decor of the school.

An examination of the informal communication system is also important in the cultural analysis of a school. The communication system is a cultural network itself (Bantz, 1993; Mohan, 1993). As Deal and Kennedy (1982) have observed, storytellers, spies, priests, cabals, and whisperers form a hidden hierarchy of power within the school that communicates the basic values

TABLE 5.2

Examples of School Rites, Ceremonies, and Consequences

Type	Examples	Possible Consequences
Rites of Passage	Student teaching Tough class for neophytes Lunch duty Retirement	Facilitate transition to new role; socialization
Rites of Degradation	Negative evaluation Public rebuke	Reduce power; reaffirm appropriate behavior
Rites of Enhancement	Assembly recognition: Teacher of the year Debate team champions Football champions	Enhance power; reinforce appropriate behavior
Rites of Integration	Holiday party Coffee group Teacher's lounge	Encourage common experiences that bind the group together

of the organization. **Mythmakers** are storytellers who are so effective in informal communication that they create organizational myths. The identification of not only the myths, but also the process of their creation, are important to a full understanding of culture.

Studies of organizational culture often try to capture the essence of culture by using metaphors. For example, consider the use of the following metaphors to describe school cultures:

- *The academy:* The school is seen as a place where learning is dominant and the principal is a master teacher and learner.
- *The prison:* The school is a custodial institution for students in need of control and discipline and the principal is the warden.
- *The club:* The school is a social club where everyone has a good time and the principal is the social director.
- *The Community:* The school is a nurturing environment where people learn from and support each other and the principal is the community leader.
- *The factory:* The school is an assembly line producing finely tuned student-machines and the principal is the foreman.

Similarly, Deal and Wise (1983) use the metaphors of factories, jungles, and temples to describe schools with principals as CEOs, lion tamers, and gurus.

Research on School Culture

Good contemporary research on school culture is sparse, a conclusion confirmed by Firestone and Louis (1999) in their recent review of the literature on school culture. Although there have been numerous analyses of corporate cultures and extrapolations of those findings to public schools, few educational researchers have tested those findings directly in schools. There are several important theoretical and practical issues that must be addressed in the study of school culture. We have suggested that the conceptual frameworks developed by Firestone and Wilson (1985) and Deal (1985) are useful in the analysis of school cultures. Bates (1987), however, argues that such formulations treat organizational culture as synonymous with managerial culture and are much too narrow to capture the essence of culture. This observation leads to a more general issue of whether most schools have a culture or a variety of subcultures. To expect schools to bear unique and unitary cultures may be more hope than fact, but the issue is ultimately an empirical one.

Whether culture can or should be intentionally managed will be hotly contested. Much of the early literature on school cultures is directed toward change and school improvement and assumes that understanding culture is a prerequisite to making schools more effective (Deal, 1985; Metz, 1986; Rossman, Corbett, and Firestone, 1988; Deal and Peterson, 1990). The success of cultural change and its influence on effectiveness are worthy topics for inquiry. One argument suggests that the level and number of cultures in the organization influence the process of changing culture. A change of norms, for example, is more likely than a change in shared values or tacit assumptions.

Others contend that any change is difficult and fraught with ethical dilemmas. For example, Schein (1985) strongly argues that a large part of an organization's culture represents the ways its members have learned to cope with anxiety; therefore, attempts to change culture can be tantamount to asking people to surrender their social defenses. To Schein, the issue of cultural change becomes an ethical question. In a somewhat similar vein, Bates (1987) maintains that advocates of strong organizational cultures are conducting cultural analyses on behalf of managers. What is good for management is not necessarily good for the workers (Hoy, 1990).

Although frameworks for examining school culture in terms of the shared values, beliefs, and ideologies are available, the determination of culture at this level of analysis is not easy. The core values of a group or school may be easier to determine than the tacit assumptions, but the analysis remains difficult and time consuming. Anthropological studies of schools using ethnographic techniques and linguistic analysis are imperative if we are to begin to assess the culture of schools.

The analysis of schools in terms of culture calls attention to the symbolic nature of social interactions in schools (Bolman and Deal, 1997; Cunningham and Gresso, 1993). Often what is done or said is not nearly as important as its symbolic significance. Examining the culture of schools provides a less rational, more uncertain, and less linear view of organizational life than the standard perspectives on structure, rationality, and efficiency.

Lee Bolman and Terrence Deal (1997) refer to the culture perspective as the "symbolic frame" for viewing organizations. They argue that the frame is based on the following unconventional assumptions about the nature of organizations and behavior:

- What is most important about events in organizations is *not* what happened, but *what they mean.* Meaning is often more important than fact.
- Events and meanings, however, are often unclear because events have different meanings for different people. Individuals use different schemas to interpret their experiences. Meaning is elusive and sometimes not shared.
- Because events are typically ambiguous or uncertain, it is difficult to know what happened, why it happened, and what will happen next. Explanation is difficult.
- The greater the ambiguity and uncertainty in events, the more difficult it is to use rational approaches in organizational analysis. Rationality clearly has limits.
- Confronted with ambiguity and uncertainty, people create symbols and stories to resolve confusion and provide understanding. Stories create clarity.
- Thus, for many organizational events, their importance rests with what they express rather than what is produced; secular myths, rituals, ceremonies, and sagas give people the meanings they seek.

One conclusion from the literature on organizational culture is clear: much of what occurs in school organizations must be interpreted in the context of the school's culture.

ORGANIZATIONAL CLIMATE

Although the term "organizational culture" is currently in vogue, the concept of organizational climate has generated much more research and until recently was used by most organizational theorists to capture the general feel or atmosphere of schools. Unlike culture, from the beginning, organizational climate has been tied to the process of developing measuring instruments (Pace and Stern, 1958; Halpin and Croft, 1963, Denison, 1996; Hoy, 1997). Climate has its historical roots in the disciplines of social psychology and industrial psychology rather than in anthropology or sociology.

Definition of Organizational Climate

Climate was initially conceived as a general concept to express the enduring quality of organizational life. Renato Taguiri (1968:23) notes that "a particular configuration of enduring characteristics of the ecology, milieu, social system, and culture would constitute a climate, as much as a particular configuration of personal characteristics constitute a personality."

B. H. Gilmer (1966:57) defines organizational climate as "those characteristics that distinguish the organization from other organizations and that influence the behavior of people in the organizations." George Litwin and Robert Stringer (1968:1) introduce perception into their definition of climate—"a set of measurable properties of the work environment, based on the collective perceptions of the people who live and work in the environment and demonstrated to influence their behavior." Over the years, there has been some consensus on the basic properties of organizational climate. Marshall Poole (1985) summarizes the agreement as follows:

- Organizational climate is concerned with large units; it characterizes properties of an entire organization or major subunits.
- Organizational climate describes a unit of organization rather than evaluates it or indicates emotional reactions to it.
- Organizational climate arises from routine organizational practices that are important to the organization and its members.
- Organizational climate influences members' behaviors and attitudes.

School climate is a broad term that refers to teachers' perceptions of the general work environment of the school; the formal organization, informal organization, personalities of participants, and organizational leadership influence it. Put simply, the set of internal characteristics that distinguish one school from another and influence the behavior of each school's members is the **organizational climate** of the school. More specifically, **school climate** is a relatively enduring quality of the school environment that is experienced by participants, affects their behavior, and is based on their collective perceptions of behavior in schools. The definition of organizational climate as a set of internal characteristics is similar in some respects to early descriptions of personality. Indeed, the climate of a school may roughly be conceived as the personality of a school—that is, personality is to the individual as climate is to the organization.

Although the definitions of climate and culture are blurred and overlapping, one suggested difference is that culture consists of shared assumptions, values, or norms, whereas climate is defined by shared perceptions of behavior (Ashforth, 1985). To be sure, there is not a large conceptual step from shared assumptions (culture) to shared perceptions (climate), but the difference is real and may be meaningful.

Because the atmosphere of a school has a major impact on the organizational behavior, and because administrators can have a significant, positive influence on the development of the "personality" of the school, it is important to describe and analyze school climates. Climate can be conceived from a variety of vantage points (see Anderson, 1982; Miskel and Ogawa, 1988), but only three perspectives are described in this chapter. Each provides the student and practitioner of administration with a valuable set of conceptual capital and measurement tools to analyze, understand, map, and change the work environment of schools.

Teacher-Principal Behavior: Open to Closed

Probably the most well-known conceptualization and measurement of the organizational climate in schools is the pioneering study of elementary schools by Andrew W. Halpin and Don B. Croft (1962). They began mapping the organizational climate of schools when they observed that (1) schools differ markedly in their feel, (2) the concept of morale did not provide an index of this feel, (3) "ideal" principals who are assigned to schools where improvement is needed are immobilized by the faculty, and (4) the topic of organizational climate was generating interest.

The approach they used involved developing a descriptive questionnaire to identify important aspects of teacher-teacher and teacher-principal interactions. Nearly 1,000 items were composed, each of which was designed to answer the basic question: To what extent is this true of your school? From this original bank of items they developed a final set of 64 items called the Organizational Climate Description Questionnaire (OCDQ). The OCDQ is usually administered to the entire professional staff of each school, with each respondent asked to describe the extent to which each statement characterizes his or her school. The responses to each item are scaled along a four-point continuum: rarely occurs, sometimes occurs, often occurs, and very frequently occurs.

Halpin and Croft not only mapped climate profiles for each of the 71 elementary schools in their original sample but also identified, through factor analysis, six basic clusters of profiles—that is, six basic school climates that are arrayed along a rough continuum from open to closed climates.

Criticisms of the Original OCDQ

Although the OCDQ has been a widely used measure of school climate, it has a number of limitations. Paula Silver (1983) is critical of the conceptual underpinnings of the OCDQ; she argues that the framework lacks a clear underlying logic, is cumbersome, and lacks parsimony. For example, she notes that although Halpin and Croft define the hindrance subtest as one dimension of teacher behavior, the concept refers to administrative demands rather than interpersonal behavior of teachers. Other conceptual problems also arise. Halpin and Croft (1962) themselves question the adequacy of their concept of consideration by suspecting that two or more facets of considerate behavior have been confounded within a single measure. Moreover, the concept measured by the production-emphasis subtest seems mislabeled. The measure clearly taps close administration and autocratic behavior, with no emphasis on high production standards.

In a comprehensive empirical attempt to appraise the OCDQ, Andrew Hayes (1973) urged revision of the instrument. His analyses strongly suggested that many of the items on the OCDQ were no longer measuring what they were intended to measure, that some of the subtests were no longer valid (e.g., aloofness), that the reliabilities of some of the subtests were low, and that the instrument needed a major revision. More recent revisions of the OCDQ address many of the criticisms of the original instrument (see Hoy, Tarter, and Kottkamp, 1991; Hoy, Hoffman, Sabo, and Bliss, 1994; Hoy and Sabo, 1998); in fact, three new and simplified versions of the OCDQ were formulated for elementary, middle, and secondary schools—the OCDQ-RE, OCDQ-RM, and the OCDQ-RS.[2]

A Revised OCDQ for Elementary Schools

The revised climate instrument (OCDQ-RE) is a 42-item measure with six subtests that describe the behavior of elementary teachers and principals (Hoy and Clover, 1986; Hoy, Tarter, and Kottkamp, 1991). Three dimensions of principal behavior—supportive, directive, and restrictive—are identified. Genuine concern and support of teachers reflect supportive principal behavior. In contrast, directive principal behavior is starkly task oriented with little consideration for the personal needs of the teachers, and restrictive behavior produces impediments for teachers as they try to do their work. Likewise, three critical aspects of teacher behavior are identified—collegial, intimate, and disengaged. Collegial behavior is supportive and professional interaction among teacher colleagues, whereas intimate behavior involves close personal relations among teachers not only in but also outside school. On the other hand, disengaged behavior depicts a general sense of alienation and separation among teachers in a school. It is also interesting to note that the Australian version of the OCDQ for primary schools has only four dimensions, factors similar to the dimensions of supportive, directive, disengaged, and intimate (Thomas and Slater, 1972; Brady, 1985).

In the tradition of the original OCDQ, the six dimensions of organizational climate are measured by having teachers describe the interactions between and among teachers and the principal. The six dimensions of the OCDQ-RE are defined and sample items for each are provided in Table 5.3.

A factor analysis of the subtests of the OCDQ-RE revealed that the conceptualization and measure of climate rested on two underlying general factors. Disengaged, intimate, and collegial teacher behavior formed the first factor; restrictive, directive, and supportive behavior defined the second factor. Specifically, the first factor was characterized by teachers' interactions that are meaningful and tolerant (low disengagement); that are friendly, close, and supportive (high intimacy); and that are enthusiastic, accepting, and mutually respectful (high collegial relations). In general, this factor denotes an openness and functional flexibility in teacher relationships. Accordingly, it was labeled **openness in faculty relations** and an openness index can be created by combining the collegial, intimacy, and disengagement scores.

The second factor is defined by principal behavior that is characterized by the assignment of meaningless routines and burdensome duties to teachers (high restrictiveness); by rigid, close, and constant control over teachers (high directiveness); and by a lack of concern and openness for teachers and their ideas (low supportive). In general, the second factor depicts principal behavior along an open-to-closed continuum, with functional flexibility and openness at one pole and functional rigidity and closedness at the other; hence, the second general factor is the degree of **openness** (or closedness) **in principal behavior** and an openness index for principal behavior can be created by combining the supportiveness, restrictiveness, and directiveness scores.[3]

The conceptual underpinnings of the OCDQ-RE are consistent and clear. The instrument has two general factors—one a measure of openness of teacher interactions and the other a measure of openness (or closedness) of teacher-principal relations. Moreover, these two openness factors are independent. That is, it is quite possible to have open faculty interactions and closed principal ones or vice versa. Thus, theoretically, four contrasting types of school climate are possible. First, both factors can be open, producing congruence between the principal's and teachers' behavior. Second, both factors can be closed, producing a congruence of closedness. Moreover, there are two incongruent patterns. The principal's behavior can be open with the faculty, but teachers may be closed with each other; or the principal may be closed with teachers, whereas the teachers are open with each other (see Figure 5.3). Table 5.4 provides a summary of the patterns of four climate prototypes. Using this information, a behavioral picture of each climate can be sketched.

Open Climate

The distinctive features of the **open climate** are the cooperation and respect that exist within the faculty and between the faculty and principal. This combination suggests a climate in which the principal listens and is open to teacher suggestions, gives genuine and frequent praise, and respects the professional competence of the faculty (high supportiveness). Principals also give their teachers freedom to perform without close scrutiny (low directiveness)

TABLE 5.3

The Six Dimensions of the OCDQ-RE

	Description	Sample Items
	Principal's Behavior	
1. *Supportive Behavior*	Reflects a basic concern for teachers. The principal listens and is open to teacher suggestions. Praise is given genuinely and frequently, and criticism is handled constructively. Supportive principals respect the professional competence of their staffs and exhibit both a personal and a professional interest in each teacher.	The principal uses constructive criticism. The principal compliments teachers. The principal listens to and accepts teachers' suggestions.
2. *Directive Behavior*	Requires rigid, close supervision. Principals maintain close and constant control over all teacher and school activities, down to the smallest details.	The principal monitors everything teachers do. The principal rules with an iron fist. The principal checks lesson plans.
3. *Restrictive Behavior*	Hinders rather than facilitates teacher work. The principal burdens teachers with paperwork, committee requirements, routine duties, and other demands that interfere with their teaching responsibilities.	Teachers are burdened with busywork. Routine duties interfere with the job of teaching. Teachers have too many committee requirements.
	Teachers' Behavior	
4. *Collegial Behavior*	Supports open and professional interactions among teachers. Teachers are proud of their school, enjoy working with their colleagues, and are enthusiastic, accepting, and mutually respectful of the professional competence of their colleagues.	Teachers help and support each other. Teachers respect the professional competence of their colleagues. Teachers accomplish their work with vim, vigor, and pleasure.
5. *Intimate Behavior*	Reflects a cohesive and strong network of social support among the faculty. Teachers know each other well, are close personal friends, socialize together regularly, and provide strong support for each other.	Teachers socialize with each other. Teachers' closest friends are other faculty members at this school. Teachers have parties for each other.
6. *Disengaged Behavior*	Refers to a lack of meaning and focus to professional activities. Teachers are simply putting in time and are nonproductive in group efforts or team building; they have no common goal orientation. Their behavior is often negative and critical of their colleagues and the organization.	Faculty meetings are useless. There is a minority group of teachers who always oppose the majority. Teachers ramble when they talk at faculty meetings.

TABLE 5.4

Prototypic Profiles of Climate Types

Climate Dimension	Climate Type			
	Open	**Engaged**	**Disengaged**	**Closed**
Supportive	High	Low	High	Low
Directive	Low	High	Low	High
Restrictive	Low	High	Low	High
Collegial	High	High	Low	Low
Intimate	High	High	Low	Low
Disengaged	Low	Low	High	High

and provide facilitating leadership behavior devoid of bureaucratic trivia (low restrictiveness). Similarly, teacher behavior supports open and professional interactions (high collegial relations) among the faculty. Teachers know each other well and are close personal friends (high intimacy). They cooperate and are committed to their work (low disengagement). In brief, the behavior of both the principal and the faculty is open and authentic.

Engaged Climate

The **engaged climate** is marked, on the one hand, by ineffective attempts by the principal to control, and on the other, by high professional performance of the teachers. The principal is rigid and autocratic (high directiveness) and respects neither the professional competence nor the personal needs of the faculty (low supportiveness). Moreover, the principal hinders the teachers with burdensome activities and busywork (high restrictiveness). The teachers, however, ignore the principal's behavior and conduct themselves as professionals. They respect and support each other, are proud of their colleagues,

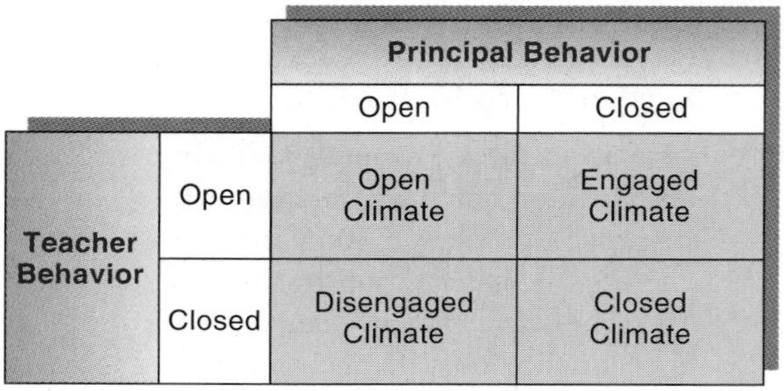

		Principal Behavior	
		Open	Closed
Teacher Behavior	Open	Open Climate	Engaged Climate
	Closed	Disengaged Climate	Closed Climate

FIGURE 5.3 *Typology of School Climates*

and enjoy their work (highly collegial). Moreover, the teachers not only respect each other's competence but they like each other as people (high intimacy), and they cooperate with each other as they engage in the task at hand (high engagement). In short, the teachers are productive professionals in spite of weak principal leadership; the faculty is cohesive, committed, supportive, and open.

Disengaged Climate

The **disengaged climate** stands in stark contrast to the engaged climate. The principal's behavior is open, concerned, and supportive. The principal listens and is open to teachers (high supportiveness), gives the faculty freedom to act on their professional knowledge (low directiveness), and relieves teachers of most of the burdens of paperwork and committee assignments (low restrictiveness). Nonetheless, the faculty is unwilling to accept the principal. At worst, the faculty actively works to immobilize and sabotage the principal's leadership attempts; at best, the faculty simply ignores the principal. Teachers not only do not like the principal, but also neither like nor respect each other as friends (low intimacy) or as professionals (low collegial relations). The faculty is simply disengaged from the task. In sum, although the principal is supportive, concerned, flexible, facilitating, and noncontrolling (i.e., open), the faculty is divisive, intolerant, and uncommitted (i.e., closed).

Closed Climate

The **closed climate** is virtually the antithesis of the open climate. The principal and teachers simply appear to go through the motions, with the principal stressing routine trivia and unnecessary busywork (high restrictiveness) and the teacher responding minimally and exhibiting little commitment (high disengagement). The principal's ineffective leadership is further seen as controlling and rigid (high directiveness) as well as unsympathetic, unconcerned, and unresponsive (low supportiveness). These misguided tactics are accompanied not only by frustration and apathy, but also by a general suspicion and lack of respect of teachers for each other as either friends or professionals (low intimacy and noncollegial relations). Closed climates have principals who are nonsupportive, inflexible, hindering, and controlling and a faculty that is divisive, intolerant, apathetic, and uncommitted.

OCDQ: Some Research Findings

The revised versions of the OCDQ for elementary, middle, and secondary schools are relatively recent developments. Nevertheless, a consistent body of research is beginning to emerge. We do know, for example, that the openness index from the original OCDQ is highly correlated with the new and refined subtests that measure openness. Moreover, openness in climate is positively related to open and authentic teacher and principal behavior (Hoy, Hoffman, Sabo, and Bliss, 1994). Thus, it is expected that results from earlier studies will be in large part replicated and refined with the new measures.

Those earlier OCDQ studies demonstrated that the openness of a school's climate was related to the emotional tone of the school in predictable ways. Schools with open climates have less sense of student alienation toward the school and its personnel than those with closed climates (Hartley and Hoy, 1972). As one might also suspect, studies that examine relationships between characteristics of the principal and the climate of the school often indicate that, in comparison to closed schools, open schools have stronger principals who are more confident, self-secure, cheerful, sociable, and resourceful (Anderson, 1964). Moreover, the teachers who work under principals in open schools express greater confidence in their own and the school's effectiveness (Andrews, 1965). Such principals have more loyal and satisfied teachers (Kanner, 1974).

More recent research (Tarter and Hoy, 1988; Reiss, 1994; Reiss and Hoy, 1998) with the new climate instruments also shows that open school climates are characterized by higher levels of loyalty and trust, faculty trust both in the principal and in colleagues, than closed climates. Principals in open schools also generate more organizational commitment to school—that is, identification and involvement in school—than those in closed climates (Tarter, Hoy, and Kottkamp, 1990). Further, openness of the climate is positively related to teacher participation in decision making (Barnes, 1994) as well as to ratings of school effectiveness (Hoy, Tarter, and Kottkamp, 1991) and, in middle schools, to student achievement in mathematics, reading, and writing as well as to overall effectiveness and quality (Hoy and Sabo, 1998).

In conclusion, the three versions of the OCDQ for elementary, middle, and secondary schools are useful devices for general charting of school climate in terms of teacher-teacher and teacher-principal relationships. The subtests of each instrument seem to be valid and reliable measures of important aspects of school climate; they can provide climate profiles that can be used for research, evaluation, in-service, or self-analysis. In addition, the openness indices provide means of examining schools along an open-closed continuum. Halpin and Croft suggest that openness might be a better criterion of a school's effectiveness than many that have entered the field of educational administration and masquerade as criteria. Openness is likely an important condition in fostering effective organizational change. Similarly, principals who want to improve instructional effectiveness are more likely to be successful if they first develop an open and trusting climate (Hoy and Forsyth, 1987). Although there is much argument about what constitutes school effectiveness (see Chapter 8), there is less doubt that the OCDQ measures provide a useful battery of scales for diagnostic as well as prescriptive purposes.

Organizational Dynamics: Healthy to Unhealthy

The **organizational health** of a school is another framework for conceptualizing the general atmosphere of a school (Hoy and Feldman, 1987; Hoy, Tarter, and Kottkamp, 1991; Hoy and Sabo, 1998). The idea of positive health in an organization is not new and calls attention to conditions that facilitate growth and development as well as to those that impede healthy organizational dynamics.

Matthew Miles (1969: 378) defines a healthy organization as one that "not only survives in its environment, but continues to cope adequately over the long haul, and continuously develops and extends its surviving and coping abilities." Implicit in this definition is the notion that healthy organizations deal successfully with disruptive outside forces while effectively directing their energies toward the major goals and objectives of the organization. Operations on a given day may be effective or ineffective, but the long-term prognosis is favorable in healthy organizations.

All social systems, if they are to grow and develop, must satisfy the four basic problems of adaptation, goal attainment, integration, and latency (Parsons, Bales, and Shils, 1953). In other words, organizations must successfully solve (1) the problem of acquiring sufficient resources and accommodating their environments, (2) the problem of setting and attaining goals, (3) the problem of maintaining solidarity within the system, and (4) the problem of creating and preserving the unique values of the system. Thus the organization must be concerned with the instrumental needs of adaptation and goal achievement as well as the expressive needs of social and normative integration; in fact, it is postulated that healthy organizations effectively meet both sets of needs. Talcott Parsons (1967) also suggests that formal organizations such as schools exhibit three distinct levels of responsibility and control over these needs—the technical, managerial, and institutional levels.

The technical level produces the product. In schools, the technical function is the teaching-learning process, and teachers are directly responsible. Educated students are the product of schools, and the entire technical subsystem revolves around the problems associated with effective learning and teaching.

The managerial level mediates and controls the internal efforts of the organization. The administrative process is the managerial function, a process that is qualitatively different from teaching. Principals are the prime administrative officers in schools. They must find ways to develop teacher loyalty and trust, motivate teacher effort, and coordinate the work. The administration controls and services the technical subsystem in two important ways: first, it mediates between the teachers and those receiving the services, students and parents; and second, it procures the necessary resources for effective teaching. Thus, teacher needs are a basic concern of the administration.

The institutional level connects the organization with its environment. It is important for schools to have legitimacy and backing in the community. Administrators and teachers need support to perform their respective functions in a harmonious fashion without undue pressure and interference from individuals and groups outside the school.

This Parsonian framework provides an integrative scheme for conceptualizing and measuring the organizational health of a school. Specifically, a **healthy organization** is one in which the technical, managerial, and institutional levels are in harmony. The organization is meeting both its instrumental and its expressive needs and is successfully coping with disruptive outside forces as it directs its energies toward its mission.

Organizational Health Inventory (OHI)

The organizational health of secondary schools is defined by seven specific interaction patterns in schools (Hoy and Feldman, 1987, 1999). These critical components meet both the instrumental and the expressive needs of the social system as well as represent the three levels of responsibility and control within the school.

The institutional level is examined in terms of the school's integrity. That is, institutional integrity is the school's ability to adapt to its environment and cope in ways that maintain the soundness of its educational programs. Schools with integrity are protected from unreasonable community and parental demands.

Four key aspects of the managerial level are considered—principal influence, consideration, initiating structure, and resource support. Influence is the ability of the principal to affect the decisions of superiors. Consideration is principal behavior that is open, friendly, and supportive, whereas initiating structure is behavior in which the principal clearly defines the work expectations, standards of performance, and procedures. Finally, resource support is the extent to which the principal provides teachers with all materials and supplies that are needed and requested.

Morale and academic emphasis are the two key elements of the technical level. Morale is the trust, enthusiasm, confidence, and sense of accomplishment that pervade the faculty. Academic emphasis, on the other hand, is the school's press for student achievement. These seven dimensions of organizational health are summarized by level of responsibility and functional need in Table 5.5. The Organizational Health Inventory, or OHI, is a 44-item descriptive questionnaire composed of seven subtests to measure each of the basic dimensions of organizational health. Like the OCDQ, the OHI is administered to the professional staff of the school. Teachers are asked to describe the extent to which each item characterizes their school along a four-point scale: rarely occurs, sometimes occurs, often occurs, and very frequently occurs. Sample items of the OHI, grouped by subtest, also are listed in Table 5.5.

Health profiles for three schools are graphed in Figure 5.4. School A represents a school with a relatively healthy climate; all dimensions of health are substantially above the mean. School C, in contrast, is below the mean in all aspects of health, and school B is a typical school—about average on all dimensions.

The subtests of the OHI are modestly correlated with each other; that is, if a school scores high on one subtest, there is some tendency to score higher on some of the other subtests. Furthermore, factor analysis of the subtests have demonstrated that one general factor, called school health, explains most of the variation among the subtests. The 78 secondary schools in the sample arrayed themselves along a continuum with a few schools having

TABLE 5.5

Dimensions of Organizational Health

	Description	Sample Items
	Institutional Level	
1. *Institutional Integrity*	Describes a school that has integrity in its education program. The school is not vulnerable to narrow, vested interests from community and parental demands. The school is able to cope successfully with destructive outside forces (instrumental need).	Teachers are protected from unreasonable community and parental demands. The school is vulnerable to outside pressures.* Select citizen groups are influential with the board.*
	Managerial Level	
2. *Principal Influence*	Refers to the principal's ability to affect the action of superiors. The influential principal is persuasive, works effectively with the superintendent, but simultaneously demonstrates independence in thought and action (instrumental need).	The principal gets what he or she asks for from superiors. The principal is able to work well with the superintendent. The principal is impeded by superiors.*
3. *Consideration*	Behavior by the principal that is friendly, supportive, open, and collegial (expressive need).	The principal is friendly and approachable. The principal puts suggestions made by the faculty into operation. The principal looks out for the personal welfare of faculty members.
4. *Initiating Structure*	Behavior by the principal that is task and achievement oriented. The principal makes his or her attitudes and expectations clear to the faculty and maintains definite standards of performance (instrumental need).	The principal lets faculty members know what is expected of them. The principal maintains definite standards of performance. The principal schedules the work to be done.
5. *Resource Support*	Refers to provisions at a school where adequate classroom supplies and instructional materials are available, and extra materials are easily obtained (instrumental need).	Extra materials are available when requested. Teachers are provided with adequate materials for their classrooms. Teachers have access to needed instructional materials.

(continued)

TABLE 5.5, (continued)

Dimensions of Organizational Health

	Description	Sample Items
	Technical Level	
6. *Morale*	Refers to a sense of trust, confidence, enthusiasm, and friendliness that is exhibited among teachers. Teachers feel good about each other and, at the same time, feel a sense of accomplishment from their jobs (expressive need).	Teachers in this school like each other. Teachers accomplish their jobs with enthusiasm. The morale of teachers is high.
7. *Academic Emphasis*	Refers to the school's press for achievement. High but achievable academic goals are set for students; the learning environment is orderly and serious; teachers believe in their students' ability to achieve; and students work hard and respect those who do well academically (instrumental need).	The school sets high standards for academic performance. Students respect others who get good grades. Students try hard to improve on previous work.

*Source is reversed.

profiles of very healthy organizations, a few with very unhealthy profiles, and most schools with somewhat mixed profiles in between the extremes. An index of health can be developed simply by combining the scores of the seven subtests; the higher the sum, the healthier the school dynamics (Hoy, Tartar, and Kottkamp, 1991; Hoy and Tarter, 1997b; Hoy and Feldman, 1999). It is possible to sketch the behavioral picture for each of the poles of the continuum—that is, the prototypes for very healthy and unhealthy school climates.

Healthy School Climate

The healthy school is protected from unreasonable community and parental pressures. The board successfully resists all narrow efforts of vested interest groups to influence policy. The principal of a healthy school provides dynamic leadership—leadership that is both task oriented and relations oriented. Such behavior is supportive of teachers and yet provides direction and maintains high standards of performance. Moreover, the principal has influence with his or her superiors as well as the ability to exercise independent thought and action. Teachers in a healthy school are committed to teaching and learning. They set high, but achievable goals for students; they maintain high standards of performance; and the learning environment is orderly and serious. Furthermore, students work hard on academic matters, are highly motivated, and respect other students who achieve academically. Classroom supplies and instructional materials are accessible. Finally, in a healthy school teachers like each other, trust each other, are enthusiastic about the work, and are proud of their school.

Unhealthy School Climate

The unhealthy school is vulnerable to destructive outside forces. Teachers and administrators are bombarded with unreasonable demands from parental and community groups. The school is buffeted by the whims of the public. The principal does not provide leadership: there is little direction, limited consideration and support for teachers, and virtually no influence with superiors. Morale of teachers is low. Teachers feel good neither about each other nor about their jobs. They act aloof, suspicious, and defensive. Finally, the press for academic excellence is limited. Everyone is simply "putting in time."

Health Inventories for Middle and Elementary Schools

Given the differences among elementary, middle, and high schools, it should not be surprising that there are different versions of the health inventory. The conceptual foundations are the same for all versions, but the items and dimensions used to measure school health are slightly different depending on the school level (Hoy, Tarter, and Kottkamp, 1991; Hoy and Sabo, 1998).

The Organizational Health Inventory for elementary schools (OHI-E) (Podgurski, 1990; Hoy, Tarter, and Kottkamp, 1991; Hoy and Tarter, 1997a) and for middle schools (OHI-RM) (Barnes, 1994; Hoy and Tarter, 1997b; Hoy and Sabo, 1998) have the same strong psychometric properties as the original OHI

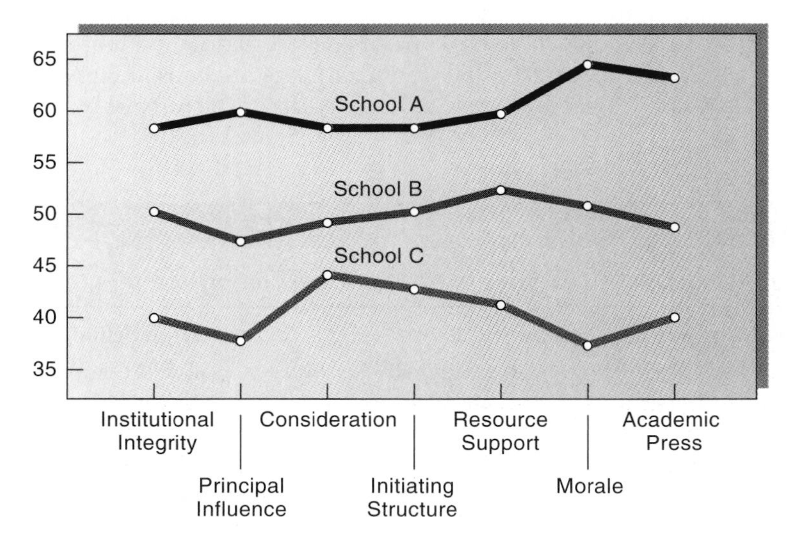

FIGURE 5.4 *Health Profiles of Three Schools*

for high schools. All the measures are reliable and have strong validity. In general, the differences in the measures are ones of differentiation of elements.

Compared to high schools, elementary schools have relatively simple structures. Consequently, as one moves from the elementary to the middle to the high school, the dimensions of climate become increasingly differentiated as structure becomes more complex. All three school levels are concerned with institutional integrity and with academic emphasis and teacher morale or affiliation, but the leadership of the principal becomes more differentiated as one moves from elementary to middle to high schools. At the elementary level there are only two dimensions of leadership, but these two divide into four by high school. Resource influence divides into principal influence and resource support as one moves from elementary to middle school, and collegial leadership behavior separates into initiation of structure and consideration as one moves from the middle to the high school (see Table 5.6). Thus, at the high school level, initiation of structure, consideration, principal influence, and resource support are all relatively separate dimensions of principal behavior.

In other words, elementary and middle school principals typically have more integrated leadership approaches. At the elementary level, principal influence and resource support are integrated into one role, and at the middle level, initiation of structure and consideration combine to form a unified collegial approach to leading teachers. The results suggest that, in general, the leadership of secondary schools is more complex and likely more difficult than that of elementary schools.

OHI: Some Research Findings

The OHI is a new instrument, and research using it is limited. Yet the OHI is a useful tool, with three versions—one each for elementary, middle, and high schools. The instruments measure key dimensions of organizational health of schools. Moreover, the conceptual underpinnings are consistent with many of the characteristics of effective schools. In addition, a study of high schools

TABLE 5.6

Comparison of the Elements of Health at School Levels

Elementary	Middle	High School
Institutional integrity	Institutional integrity	Institutional integrity
Collegial leadership	Collegial leadership	Initiating structure
		Consideration
Resource influence	Resource support	Resource support
	Principal influence	Principal influence
Teacher affiliation	Teacher affiliation	Morale
Academic emphasis	Academic emphasis	Academic emphasis

in Taiwan demonstrated stability in the factor structure of the OHI across cultures (Liao, 1994).

Research findings using the OHI are also encouraging. As one would expect, the healthier the organizational dynamics, the greater the degree of faculty trust in the principal, in colleagues, and in the organization itself (Tarter and Hoy, 1988; Hoy, Tarter, and Wiskowskie, 1992). Not surprisingly too, there is a correlation between the openness and the health of schools; healthy schools have high thrust, high esprit, and low disengagement (Hoy and Tarter, 1990). In brief, open schools tend to be healthy and healthy schools tend to be open. Health is also related to the organizational commitment of teachers to their schools; healthy schools have more committed teachers (Tarter, Hoy, and Bliss 1989; Tarter, Hoy, and Kottkamp 1990).

Research findings also show that organizational health is positively related to student performance; the healthier the school climate, the higher the achievement levels on math and reading achievement test scores of high school students (Hoy and Tarter, 1990); and the healthier the climate of middle schools, the higher the student achievement levels on standardized math, reading, and writing tests (Hoy and Hannum, 1997; Hoy, Hannum, and Tschannen-Moran, 1998; Hoy and Sabo, 1998; Goddard, Sweetland, and Hoy, 2000). A study of elementary teachers also demonstrated that a healthy school climate was conducive to the development of teacher efficacy, the belief that they could positively influence student learning (Hoy and Woolfolk, 1993). Our own research continues to demonstrate that school health is related to a host of other important school variables. For example, it is positively related to humanism, teacher participation in decision making, a strong school culture, and a variety of measures of school effectiveness. Finally, it seems likely that a school's health will be significantly related to less student alienation, lower dropout rates, and higher student commitment.

In conclusion, the health of a school can be reliably determined by use of the appropriate OHI instrument. Moreover, sound interpersonal dynamics in school life are not only important as ends in themselves but are predictive of school effectiveness, student achievement, organizational commitment, humanism in teacher attitudes, and faculty trust in colleagues and in the principal. Healthy schools are likely to have committed teachers who trust each other, who trust the principal, who hold high academic standards, who are open, and who have students who achieve at high levels. In such schools, the improvement of instruction and the continued professional development of teachers and administrators are achievable goals.

Pupil-Control Orientation: Custodial to Humanistic

Another way to conceptualize the social climate of the school is in terms of dominant control patterns that teachers and principals use to control students. Willard Waller (1932), in one of the first systematic studies of the school as a social system, called attention to the importance of pupil control with regard to both structural and normative aspects of the school culture. In fact, most studies that have focused on the school as a social system have described antagonistic student subcultures and attendant conflict and pupil problems (Gordon, 1957; Coleman, 1961; Willower and Jones, 1967). Donald J. Willower and Ronald G. Jones (1967) have described pupil control as the "dominant motif" within the school social system, the integrative theme that gives meaning to patterns of teacher-teacher and teacher-principal relations.

Control is a problem that all organizations face. Richard O. Carlson's (1964) analysis of the relationship of a client to a service organization indicates that public schools are the type of service organization in which control is likely to be the most acute problem. Public schools, along with prisons and public mental hospitals, are service organizations that have no choice in the selection of clients, and the clients must (in the legal sense) participate in the organization. These organizations are confronted with clients who may have little or no desire for the services of the organization, a factor that accentuates the problem of client control. As a strong cautionary note, there are important distinctions to be made when comparing public schools with prisons and public mental hospitals. For example, prisons and public mental hospitals are "total institutions" (Goffman, 1957); schools are not. Moreover, schools normally use much less intense coercive practices. The point is that although control is probably an essential ingredient of all group life it is especially important in service organizations in which clients are unselected and participation is mandatory.

Both empirical and conceptual considerations lead to the same conclusion: pupil control is a central aspect of school life. Given its saliency, the concept can be used to distinguish among school climates. The conceptualization of pupil control and research initiated by Donald J. Willower, Terry I. Eidell, and Hoy (1967) at the Pennsylvania State University provide the basis for such a perspective.[4] The Penn State researchers postulated a pupil-control continuum from custodial to humanistic. Prototypes of the two extremes are briefly summarized below.

The Custodial School Climate

The model for the **custodial prototype** is the traditional school, which provides a rigid and highly controlled setting in which maintenance of order is primary. Students are stereotyped in terms of their appearance, behavior, and parents' social status. Teachers who hold a custodial orientation conceive of the school as an autocratic organization with a rigid pupil-teacher status hierarchy. The flow of power and communication is unilateral and downward; students must accept the decisions of their teachers without question. Teachers do not attempt to understand student behavior but instead view misbehavior as a personal affront. They perceive students as irresponsible and undisciplined persons who must be controlled through punitive sanctions. Impersonality, cynicism, and watchful mistrust pervade the atmosphere of the custodial school.

The Humanistic School Climate

The model for the **humanistic prototype** is the school conceived of as an educational community in which students learn through cooperative interaction and experience. Learning and behavior are viewed in psychological and sociological terms. Self-discipline is substituted for strict teacher control. A humanistic orientation leads to a democratic atmosphere with two-way communication between pupils and teachers and increased self-determination. The term "humanistic orientation" is used in the sociopsychological sense suggested by Erich Fromm (1948); it stresses both the importance of the individual and the creation of an atmosphere that meets student needs.

The Pupil-Control Ideology (PCI) Form

In order to measure the pupil-control orientation of schools along the custodial-humanistic continuum, the Pupil-Control Ideology (PCI) form was developed by Willower, Eidell, and Hoy (1967: 47–48). The PCI is a 20-item scale with five response categories for each item, ranging from strongly agree to strongly disagree. A sample of specific items follows:

- It is desirable to require pupils to sit in assigned seats during assemblies.
- Directing sarcastic remarks toward a defiant pupil is a good disciplinary technique.
- Pupils should not be permitted to contradict the statements of a teacher in class.
- Too much pupil time is spent on guidance and activities and too little on academic preparation.

Reliability coefficients of the PCI instrument have been consistently high (Packard and Willower, 1972; Packard, 1988). Likewise, construct validity has been supported in numerous studies (Hoy, 1967, 1968; Willower, Eidell, and Hoy, 1967; Appleberry and Hoy, 1969; Hoy and Woolfolk, 1989). John Packard (1988) provides a critical discussion of the validity of the PCI. The pupil-control orientation can be measured by pooling the individual orientations of the professional staff of the school; this represents an estimate of the modal orientation of the school and provides an index of the degree of custodialism (or humanism) in pupil-control orientation of the school.

PCI: Some Research Findings

The PCI instrument does not provide the complex measure of either the OCDQ or the OHI. Yet the concept of pupil control and its measurement allows another view of the school climate, one that focuses on teacher-student relations rather than principal-teacher relations. Perhaps the PCI is a better measure of culture than climate because it deals directly with shared ideologies rather than shared perceptions of behavior. At any rate, the concept of pupil-control ideology has proved to be a powerful predictor of the tone or feeling of the school. Appleberry and Hoy (1969) and Hoy and Clover (1986) found that humanism in the pupil-control orientation of schools and the openness of the organizational climate of schools are strongly correlated.

Furthermore, in order to test the usefulness of the custodial-humanistic framework as an index of school tone or climate, Hoy and Appleberry (1970) used the OCDQ variables to compare the most humanistic schools and the most custodial schools in terms of their climate profiles. Schools with a custodial, pupil-control orientation had significantly greater disengagement, less esprit, more aloofness, and less thrust than those with a humanistic, pupil-control orientation. In other words, humanistic schools seem more likely than custodial schools to have the following:

- Teachers who work well together with respect to the teaching-learning task.
- Teachers who have high morale and are satisfied because of their sense of task accomplishment and fulfillment of social needs.
- Principals who deal with teachers in an informal, face-to-face situation rather than "go by the book."
- Principals who do not supervise closely but instead motivate through personal example.
- A climate marked by openness, acceptance, and authenticity.

Humanism in pupil-control orientation and openness of norms, although different elements of school climate, seem to be highly compatible.

The pupil-control orientation of a school is related to many important aspects of school life. Consider the general picture of the school's character that emerges from the following research findings:

- Custodial schools have more alienated students than humanistic schools; students suffer a greater sense of powerless and normlessness in custodial schools (Hoy, 1972).
- Humanistic schools provide healthy social climates for the development of mature self-images for the students: the more humanistic the pupil-control orientation of the school, the greater the chance that high school seniors were moving toward self-actualization (Diebert and Hoy, 1977).
- Students' perceptions of a humanistic school climate are positively related to their motivation, problem solving, and seriousness to learn (Lunenburg, 1983).
- A custodial climate is negatively related to students' perceptions of the quality of school life (Lunenburg and Schmidt, 1989).
- Pupil-control is also an important factor in the development of a sense of efficacy among prospective teachers (Woolfolk and Hoy, 1990).
- The more custodial the climate of the school the more student vandalism in the school, the more violent incidents, and the more suspensions (Finkelstein, 1998).

The evidence suggests a need for public schools that are less custodial, more humanistic, and more open in climate because such schools have less-alienated, more-satisfied, and more-productive students. Changes in the humanistic direction, however, are more easily described than made, and inevitably, they are slow in coming and often unsuccessful; nevertheless, the effort should be made.

Culture or Climate: A Comparison

We have developed two general perspectives—organizational culture and organizational climate—to describe the nature of the workplace. Both frameworks attempt to capture the intangible feel of organizational life. Individual schools may serve the same mission, but their traditions and organizational ideologies will invariably differ.

Culture is the fashionable term. Scholars of organizational culture most often use the qualitative and ethnographic techniques of anthropology and sociology to study the character of organizations. They are interested in "thick descriptions" that help students understand the symbols that are used to give meaning to the social world of organizations. They emphasize the organization as a whole, as a natural system, and how its practices, beliefs, and cultural elements function to maintain a social structure (Ouchi and Wilkins, 1985). Thus, the culture is defined in terms of symbolic systems, and its analysis becomes an abstract and interpretative one in search of meaning.

In some contrast, scholars of climate typically use quantitative techniques and multivariate analyses to identify patterns of perceived behavior in organizations. Climate researchers usually assume that organizations are rational instruments to accomplish purpose; hence, they search for critical patterns of behavior. The historical roots for the study of climate come chiefly from social and industrial psychology rather than anthropology or sociology. Survey techniques and multivariate statistics are used to map patterns of behavior that are significant in influencing organizational outcomes. Emphasis is placed on behavioral attributes of organizational life. The basic similarities and differences of the perspectives are summarized in Table 5.7.

It is premature to define culture as an aspect of climate (Anderson, 1982; Miskel and Ogawa, 1988) or to define climate as an outcome of culture (Ouchi and Wilkins, 1985; Schein, 1985: Moran and Volkwein, 1992). Moreover, confusion becomes chaos when the "school effectiveness" research masquerades as studies of climate or culture (Hoy, 1990). The distinction between the two frameworks is useful; it provides practitioners and students with competing conceptual schemes for understanding the dynamics of school life. The contrasting perspectives bring with them a natural tension, one that can breathe vitality and life into the study of schools.

Changing the Culture and Climate of Schools

We have little information on, let alone answers to, the complex problem of changing the school workplace. Two things are clear, however. There is no

TABLE 5.7

Contrasting Characteristics of Organizational Culture and Organizational Climate

	Organizational Culture	Organizational Climate
Discipline	Anthropology and sociology	Psychology and social psychology
Method	Ethnographic techniques Linguistic analysis	Survey research Multivariate statistics
Level of Abstraction	Abstract	More concrete
Shared Orientations	Assumptions and ideology	Perceptions of behavior

quick and simple way to change the culture or climate of schools. Long-term systemic effort is more likely to produce change than short-term fads.

Three general strategies for change are presented. Alan Brown (1965) has developed a clinical strategy as well as a growth-centered approach; and Ralph Kilmann (1984) has successfully implemented a procedure for changing the normative culture of organizations. The three strategies are not alternatives to each other; they can be used simultaneously and, indeed, all seem necessary for effective change. The clinical strategy focuses on the nature of the relationships among the school's subgroups; the growth-centered strategy is concerned with the nature of individual development within the school; and the normative procedure is used to change organizational norms. Each of these change strategies offers potential guidelines for the practicing administrator and will be reviewed briefly.

The Clinical Strategy

The manipulation of intergroup and interpersonal interactions can foster change. Such a **clinical strategy** for change can proceed through the following steps.

1. *Gaining knowledge of the organization:* The approach begins with a thorough knowledge of the dynamics of the school organization. Such knowledge, of course, comes through careful observation, analysis, and study. The perceptive principal may have acquired much of this knowledge through experience but, typically, a more systematic analysis is enlightening and valuable. As a prelude to such a study, he or she must understand the salient aspects of organizational life including the basic norms and values of the faculty. The conceptual perspectives provided by such measures as the OCDQ, OHI, and PCI can substantially aid this learning about the school organization.
2. *Diagnosis:* The second step in the process is diagnostic. Here again conceptual capital, from a variety of perspectives, can provide labels

for diagnosing potential trouble areas. Poor esprit, high disengagement, custodialism, distorted communication, unilateral decision making, weak motivation, and low academic expectations are examples of such conceptual labels. The extent to which these concepts are clearly defined in the mind of the practitioner and fit together in a broader perspective probably mediates the effectiveness of the diagnosis.

3. *Prognosis:* In the third step, the "clinician" judges the seriousness of the situation and develops a set of operational priorities to improve the situation.
4. *Prescription:* The appropriate course of action is often hidden. Suppose we decided that the school's atmosphere is too custodial in pupil-control orientation. How can the situation be remedied? We might replace a number of "custodial" teachers with younger "humanistic" teachers. Research suggests, however, that the pupil-control ideology of beginning teachers becomes significantly more custodial as they become socialized by the teacher subculture (Hoy, 1967, 1968, 1969; Hoy and Woolfolk, 1989), which in this case tends to equate tight control with good teaching. Merely replacing a number of custodial teachers without altering basic teacher norms about pupil control will probably have little or no impact. Altering basic teacher norms calls for a more sophisticated strategy (see below). A first step in such a strategy is to eliminate teacher and administrator ignorance about the PCI—that is, to erase the shared misperceptions of educators with respect to pupil-control ideology. Teachers generally think that principals are much more custodial in pupil-control ideology than they themselves are, and conversely, principals typically believe that teachers are more custodial in pupil-control orientation than they report themselves to be (Packard and Willower, 1972). These common misperceptions need to be swept away if a more humanistic perspective is to be achieved. In other words, developing prescriptions at first seems easy enough, but experience shows that solutions to various school problems are usually oversimplified and often irrelevant. If administrators are going to be successful in changing the school climate and culture, then they must change the norms and values of the teacher subculture as well as the basic, shared assumptions of the faculty and administration.
5. *Evaluation:* The last step in the clinical strategy is to evaluate the extent to which prescriptions have been implemented and are successful. Because planned change in social systems is often slow, continuous monitoring and evaluation are required.

The Growth-Centered Strategy

A **growth-centered strategy** simply involves the acceptance of a set of assumptions about the development of school personnel and the use of these assumptions as the basis for administrative decision making. The assumptions are the following:

1. *Change is a property of healthy school organizations.* The principal should see organizations, and hence organizational climate, in a constant state of flux.
2. *Change has direction.* Change can be positive or negative, progressive or regressive.
3. *Change should imply progress.* Change should provide movement of the organization toward its goals. Of course not all change represents progress; yet the principal's stance is progress oriented.
4. *Teachers have high potential for the development and implementation of change.* Principals are always ready to provide teachers with more freedom and responsibility in the operation of the school.

These basic assumptions, if acted upon, would allow for a growth policy, which in turn leads to increased opportunities for professional development. From this perspective, administrators would remove obstacles from the path of professional growth and not manipulate people. Finally, the approach should help facilitate a climate of mutual trust and respect among teachers and administrators.

The clinical and growth-centered approaches do not conflict in their assumptions, although they have different focuses—organizational and individual. The astute administrator draws on both strategies to change the climate of the school.

A Norm-Changing Strategy

Most organizational members can list the norms that operate in their work group and even suggest new norms that would be more effective for improving productivity or morale (Kilmann, Saxton, and Serpa, 1985). A number of ways can be used to surface actual norms, but participants are usually reluctant to specify norms *unless* they are confident that the information will not be used against them or the organization. Thus, anonymity and confidentiality of respondents are crucial in identifying the salient norms in an organization.

Kilmann and his associates (1985) have successfully used small groups in workshop settings to elicit norms. He suggests that with just a little prodding and a few illustrations to get the group started, members quickly begin to enumerate many norms; in fact, they revel in being able to articulate what beforehand was not formally stated and rarely discussed.

Prevailing norms map the "way things are" around the organization. Indeed, norm statements often begin with "around here." For example, "Around here, it is all right to admit mistakes, as long as you don't make them again." The key norms of an organization are usually related to such important areas as control, support, innovation, social relations, rewards, conflicts, and standards of excellence. To begin to identify the norms of a school, teachers might be asked to list their views of the school in terms of "around here" statements. For example, they are ask to complete the following statements:

1. At the end of a typical faculty meeting, everyone ________.
2. Around here, the real basis for reward ________.
3. Around here, control of students ________.
4. Around here, decisions are reached through ________.
5. Around here, risk taking ________.
6. Around here, differences in opinion are handled by ________.
7. Around here, achievement standards ________.
8. Around here, we handle problems by ________.

Unlike tacit assumptions, carefully constructed survey instruments often can reveal norms. The Kilmann-Saxton Culture-Gap Survey (Kilmann and Saxton, 1983), for example, has been used to determine not only the actual norms but also the desired norms of organizations. The instrument consists of 28 norm pairs in the areas of task support, task innovation, social relationships, and personal freedom. An example of a norm pair from the survey is the following: "(a) Share information only when it benefits your own work group, versus (b) share information to help the organization make better decisions." Members are asked to describe both the actual norms and the desired ones. The current normative culture is then determined as well as the gap between the desired and actual norms.

Kilmann (1984) recommends the following five-step procedure as a **norm-changing strategy:**

- *Surface norms.* Teachers, usually in a workshop setting, identify the norms that guide their attitudes and behaviors.
- *Articulate new directions.* Teachers discuss where the school is headed and identify new directions that are necessary for progress.
- *Establish new norms.* Teachers identify a set of new norms that they believe will lead to improvement and organizational success.
- *Identify culture gaps.* Examine the discrepancy between actual norms (step 1) and desired norms (step 3). This discrepancy is a culture gap; the larger the gap, the more probable that the existing norms are dysfunctional.
- *Close the culture gaps.* The act of listing new norms often results in many group members actually adopting the new and desired norms (Kilmann, 1984). But the teachers as a group must also agree that the desired norms will replace the old norms and that the changes will be monitored and enforced. Subsequent teacher meetings can then be used to reinforce the new norms and prevent regression to old norms and practices.

John Miner (1988) notes that this process is especially useful in identifying and changing negative aspects of an organization's culture. For example, negative norms surfaced in step 1 can be replaced by more desirable norms identified in step 3, as follows:

- *From:* Don't rock the boat; don't volunteer to do anything extra; don't share information; don't tell your colleagues or superiors what they don't want to hear.
- *To:* Experiment with new ideas; help others when they need help; communicate openly with your colleagues; persist in identifying problems.

Miner (1988) argues that this group approach to cultural change may be more useful for identifying dysfunctional aspects of the culture than for bringing about real change, and Schein (1985) charges that this process deals at best with the superficial aspects of culture. Nonetheless, Kilmann's five-step process seems a useful vehicle for helping groups of teachers get specific information about the nature of their workplace and for developing a plan for change. The process, together with the clinical and growth-centered approaches, provides teachers and administrators with specific techniques and procedures to change the character of the workplace.

THEORY INTO PRACTICE

What Is the Organizational Culture of Your School?

Sketch the organizational culture of your school by using the common elements of culture found in this chapter. That is, describe the extent to which your school is innovative, creative, attentive to detail, outcome oriented, people oriented, team oriented, and aggressive. Provide at least one example for each element that captures what your school culture is all about. Then do the following:

- Specify the core values of your school culture.
- What cultural type is your school? Clan, hierarchy, market, adhocracy, or other?
- Evaluate the culture in terms of strengths and weaknesses.
- How functional is the culture for student growth and achievement?
- How strong is the culture of your school?
- If you became the principal, what would you do to improve the culture?
- Describe your short- and long-term strategies for change.

Surprise at St. Clair Middle School

You have been principal at St. Clair Middle School for more than a year. St. Clair is one of three middle schools in East Hampton, a middle-class community of 30,000 people in the Midwest. Your middle school (5–8) has 20 teachers and just over 600 students. You believe that you have a good school with good faculty, but there is definitely room for improvement. Since your arrival at St. Clair, you have worked very hard to get to know the teachers. This is your first job as an administrator after teaching seven years as a middle school teacher in Aura, a community similar to East Hampton, but 100 miles to the west. You feel comfortable in your new role and believe that you have been accepted as the new leader at St. Clair.

You believe in collegial administration and share the decision making with teachers; after all, education in your view is a team effort that should involve students, teachers, administrators, and parents. "How am I doing?" you wonder. Things feel good, but are you deceiving yourself? You think not, but decide to get a more objective view of the workplace through the eyes of the teachers.

THEORY INTO PRACTICE, (Continued)

Your plan is to administer the Organizational Health Inventory (OHI) to your faculty at the next faculty meeting; the anonymous questionnaires should take only 10 minutes to complete and you can score them quickly. You also decide to complete the questionnaire yourself and then compare your perception of the school climate with those of the teachers.

Categories	Teachers' Perceptions	Your Perceptions
Institutional integrity	480 (slightly below average)	600 (high)
Collegial leadership	509 (average)	680 (very high)
Principal influence	520 (above average)	580 (high)
Resource support	600 (high)	720 (very high)
Teacher affiliation	600 (high)	660 (very high)
Academic emphasis	590 (high)	680 (very high)
Overall school health	549 (above average)	653 (very high)

You are right, the teachers seem glad to respond to the OHI; it takes only about 10 minutes, and not even a grumble from teachers. You are, however, quite surprised at the results. Indeed, surprised may be the wrong word, dismayed seems more appropriate. Clearly, your view of the school climate is much more optimistic than the teachers' perspective. The data provide a reality check.

- Do you have a problem here? If so, what is it?
- How should you share the data with your teachers? Or should you?
- Why the major discrepancies between your teachers' and your own perceptions on institutional integrity and collegial leadership?
- What should you do next?
- Should you use a growth-centered strategy? Clinical strategy?
- You need a plan, but what is it?

SUMMARY AND SUGGESTED READINGS

Two related and overlapping perspectives are used to analyze the character of the workplace. Organizational culture and organizational climate both go beyond the formal and individual aspects of organizational life. Each concept deals with the natural, spontaneous, and human side of the organization as attempts are made to uncover shared meanings and unwritten rules that influence behavior.

Organizational culture is the set of shared orientations that holds a unit together and gives it a distinctive identity. Although climate tends to focus on shared perceptions of behavior, culture is defined in terms of shared assumptions, values, and norms. These three levels of culture—shared assumptions, values, and norms—are explored as alternative ways of describing and analyzing the school cultures. The recent popularity of culture is an outgrowth of the business literature, which suggests that effective organizations have strong corporate cultures.

Organizational climate is a broad concept that denotes members' shared perceptions of tone or character of the workplace; it is a set of internal characteristics that distinguishes one school from another and influences the behavior of people in schools. Three important conceptualizations of school climate were considered. The climate of interaction among teachers can be described along an open-to-closed continuum, and can be measured by the appropriate organizational climate description questionnaire (OCDQ). Another conceptualization of climate examines the organizational health of schools—that is, the extent to which the school is meeting both its instrumental and its expressive needs while simultaneously coping with disruptive outside forces as it directs its energies toward its mission. The health of the school can be mapped using the appropriate Organizational Health Inventory (OHI); separate and reliable versions of the OHI exist for elementary, middle, and high schools. Finally, still another perspective views school climate in terms of a continuum of control over students, from humanistic to custodial, and are measured by the Pupil-Control Ideology (PCI) form.

The chapter concludes with three strategies that practitioners can use to change the nature of the school workplace. A clinical strategy deals with the nature of the relationships among the school's subgroups; a growth-centered strategy emphasizes the nature of individual development within the school; and a group procedure offers a strategy to change organizational norms.

Edgar Schein's (1992) book, *Organizational Culture and Leadership,* remains one of the most comprehensive analyses of organizational culture. For a diverse look at culture, a recent collection of readings, *Reframing Organizational Culture,* provides readers with exemplars of culture research as well as critiques, commentaries, and expositions (Frost et al., 1991). For those interested in corporate cultures, the early works of Peters and Waterman (1982) and Ouchi (1981) are worthwhile and provide a nice backdrop for Cameron and Quinn's (1999) *Diagnosing and Changing Organizational Culture.*

Students should begin their study of school climate with Andrew Halpin and Don Croft's (1963) pioneering study *The Organizational Climate of Schools.* Two more recent books, *Open Schools/Healthy Schools* (Hoy, Tarter, and Kottkamp, 1991) and *Quality Middle Schools* (Hoy and Sabo, 1998) summarize two decades of research on school climate. The two latter books give researchers six valid and reliable instruments to study school climate and provide practitioners with the tools to diagnose problems and analyze the climate of their schools. The instruments, norms, scoring instructions, interpretations of results as well as change strategies are all carefully illustrated. Finally, *The School and Pupil Control Ideology* (Willower, Eidell, and Hoy, 1967) is a seminal work on control in schools.

NOTES

1. Informal organization is another concept that describes the nature of the workplace in terms of the social structure and culture of the work group. You might find it useful to review the discussion of informal organization in Chapter 3.
2. The specifics for calculating the openness indices are found in Hoy, Tarter, and Kottkamp, 1991.
3. We discuss only the elementary version of the OCDQ in the text, but full descriptions of the other versions are available elsewhere. For the secondary school version, see Kottkamp, Mulhern, and Hoy, 1987; Hoy, Tarter, and Kottkamp, 1991; Hoy and Tarter, 1997b. For the middle school version, see Hoy, Hoffman, Sabo, and Bliss, 1994; Hoy and Tarter, 1997a; Hoy and Sabo, 1998.
4. Most of this large body of the research can be found in the Pupil Control Studies Archives, The Pennsylvania State University, Pattee Library, University Park, PA 16802.

KEY CONCEPTS AND IDEAS

Clinical strategy
Closed climate
Core values
Custodial prototype
Disengaged climate
Engaged climate
Growth-centered strategy
Healthy organization
Humanistic prototype
Icons
Legends
Mythmakers
Myths
Norm-changing strategy
Norms
Open climate
Openness in faculty relations
Openness in principal behavior
Organizational climate
Organizational culture
Organizational health
Rituals
School climate
Stories
Strong cultures
Tacit assumptions
Values

CHAPTER 6

POWER AND POLITICS IN SCHOOLS

Political realists see the world as it is: an arena of power politics moved primarily by perceived immediate self-interests, where morality is rhetorical rationale for expedient action and self-interest. It is a world not of angels but of angles, where men speak of moral principles but act on power principles.

Saul Alinsky
Rules for Radicals

Since my intention is to say something that will prove of practical use to the inquirer, I have thought it proper to represent things as they are in real truth, rather than as they are imagined.

Niccolo Machiavelli
The Prince

PREVIEW

1. Power is a broad construct that includes both legitimate and illegitimate methods of ensuring compliance.
2. Power can be classified not only as legitimate or illegitimate but also as formal or informal; hence, four basic kinds of organizational power exist: two forms of legitimate power—formal and informal authority—and two kinds of illegitimate power—coercive and political.
3. Legitimate power is more likely to promote commitment and compliance, whereas illegitimate power produces conflict and alienation.
4. Organizations are political arenas in which power and politics are central.
5. Coalitions of individuals and groups bargain to determine the distribution of power in organizations.
6. The external coalition can be dominated, divided, or passive, and affects the internal coalition.
7. Internal coalitions can be personalized, bureaucratic, ideologic, professional, or politicized, and they can affect the distribution of power.
8. Power often concerns itself with defining rather than discovering organizational reality.

9. Power and politics are realities of organizational life, and they often undermine rationality.
10. Although the means of politics are illegitimate, the ends need not be; politics can be cruel and destructive or considerate and constructive.
11. Ingratiating, networking, information management, impression management, coalition building, and scapegoating are common political tactics used by organizational members to gain advantage.
12. Political games are played to resist authority, to counter the resistance to authority, to build power bases, to defeat rivals, and to produce organizational change.
13. Conflict can be successfully managed by competing, collaborating, accommodating, compromising, or avoiding—depending on the situation.

All social organizations control their participants, but the problem of control is especially important in formal organizations, and the essence of organizational control is power. The classic definition of **power** is the ability to get others to do what you want them to do, or as Weber (1947: 152) defines it, "the probability that one actor within a social relationship will be in a position to carry out his own will despite resistance." Power for our purposes is a general and comprehensive term. It includes control that is starkly coercive as well as control that is based on nonthreatening persuasion and suggestion. Authority has a narrower scope than power. Weber (1947: 324) defines authority as "the probability that certain specific commands (or all commands) from a given source will be obeyed by a given group of persons." Weber is quick to indicate that authority does not include every mode of exercising power or influence over other persons. He suggests that a certain degree of voluntary compliance is associated with legitimate commands.

Organizations are created and controlled by legitimate authorities, who set goals, design structures, hire and manage employees, and monitor activities to ensure behavior is consistent with the goals and objectives of the organization. These official authorities control the legitimate power of the office or positions, but they are only one of many contenders for other forms of power in organizations (Bolman and Deal, 1997). We first examine legitimate forms of power and then turn to illegitimate ones.

Sources of Authority: Legitimate Power

Authority relationships are an integral part of life in schools. The basis of many student-teacher, teacher-administrator, or subordinate-superior relations is authority. Unfortunately, many individuals view authority and authoritarianism as synonymous. Because this is not the case, authority as a theoretical concept must be clearly defined.

Contrary to some popular beliefs, the exercise of authority in a school typically does not involve coercion. Herbert A. Simon (1957a: 126–27) proposed that **authority** is distinguished from other kinds of influence or power in that the subordinate "holds in abeyance his own critical faculties for choosing between alternatives and uses the formal criterion of the receipt of a command or signal as his basis of choice." Therefore, two criteria of authority in schools are crucial in superior-subordinate relationships: (1) voluntary compliance to legitimate commands; and (2) suspension of one's own criteria for decision making and acceptance of the organizational command.

Peter Blau and W. Richard Scott (1962) argue that a third criterion must be added to distinguish authority from other forms of social control. They maintain that a value orientation arises that defines the use of social control as legitimate, and this orientation arises only in a group context. Authority is legitimized by a value that is held in common by the group. Blau and Scott conclude that a basic characteristic of the authority relation is the subordinates' willingness to suspend their own criteria for making decisions and to comply with directives from the superior. This willingness results largely from social constraints exerted by norms of the social collectivity (teachers and students) and not primarily from the power the superior (administrator) brings to bear. Such social constraints are not typical of coercive power and other types of social influence. Authority relations in schools, then, have three primary characteristics: (1) a willingness of subordinates to comply; (2) a suspension of the subordinates' criteria for making a decision prior to a directive; and (3) a power relationship legitimized by the norms of a group.

Authority exists when a common set of beliefs (norms) in a school legitimizes the use of power as "right and proper." Weber (1947) distinguishes three types of authority—charismatic, traditional, and legal—according to the kind of legitimacy typically claimed by each.

Charismatic authority rests on devotion to an extraordinary individual who is leader by virtue of personal trust or exemplary qualities. Charismatic authority tends to be nonrational, affective, or emotional and rests heavily on the leader's personal qualities and characteristics. The authority of the charismatic leader results primarily from the leader's overwhelming personal appeal, and typically a common value orientation emerges within the group to produce an intense normative commitment to and identification with the person. Thus students may obey classroom directives because of a teacher's personal "mystique."

Traditional authority is anchored in an established belief in the sanctity of the status of those exercising authority in the past. Obedience is owed to the traditional sanctioned *position* of authority, and the person who occupies the position inherits the authority established by custom. In a school, for example, students may accept the authority of the position and the teacher because their parents and grandparents did so before them.

Legal authority is based on enacted laws that can be changed by formally correct procedures. Obedience is not owed to a person or position per se but to the *laws* that specify to whom and to what extent people owe compliance. Legal authority thus extends only within the scope of the authority vested in the office by law. In schools, obedience is owed to the impersonal principles that govern the operation of the organizations.

Other scholars and organizational theorists have extended these basic concepts of authority. Robert Peabody (1962) distinguishes the bases of formal authority—legitimacy and position—from the bases of functional authority—competence and personal or human relations skills, whereas Blau and Scott (1962) simply describe the authority relation as formal or informal dependent on the source of legitimacy for the power.

Formal authority is vested in the organization and is legally established in positions, rules, and regulations. In joining the organization, employees accept the authority relation because they agree, within certain limits, to accept the directives of their supervisors; the organization has the right to command and the employees have the duty to obey (March and Simon, 1958). The basis of formal authority, then, rests with the legally established agreement between the organization and the employees.

Functional authority has a variety of sources, including authority of competence and authority of person. Although Weber treats authority of competence as part of the legal-rational pattern of bureaucracies, competence is not always limited to position. Technical competence can provide the source for legitimate control and directives in a formal organization regardless of the specific position held. This fact poses a dilemma and conflict for professionals.

Informal authority is still another source of legitimate control stemming from personal behavior and attributes of individuals. Regardless of formal position, some organizational members develop norms of allegiance and support from their colleagues. These informal norms buttress and legitimize their power and provide informal authority.

Authority and Administrative Behavior in Schools

Authority is a basic feature of life in schools because it provides the basis for legitimate control of administrators, teachers, and students. A primary source of control is formal authority that is vested in the office or position and not in the particular person who performs the official role (Merton, 1957). When administrators, teachers, and students join a school organization, they accept the formal authority relation. They agree within certain limits to follow directives that officials issue for the school. In short, school members enter into contractual agreements in which they sell their promises to obey commands (Commons, 1924).

Formal authority, anchored and buttressed by formal sanctions, has a somewhat limited scope. The existence of what Chester Barnard (1938) refers to as a bureaucratic "zone of indifference"—in which subordinates, including administrator and teacher professionals, accept orders without question—may be satisfactory for eliciting certain minimum performance levels, but it seems likely that this does not lead to an efficient operation. Formal authority promotes minimal compliance with directives and discipline, but it does not encourage employees to exert effort, to accept responsibility, or to exercise initiative (Blau and Scott, 1962; Kotter, 1985). Therefore, a basic challenge facing all administrators, and one especially significant for first-level line supervisors such as school principals, is to find methods to extend their influence over their professional staff beyond the narrow limits of formal positional authority.

Hoy and Williams (1971) and Hoy and Rees (1974) have elaborated and empirically examined these ideas. They reasoned that many school administrators have the power and authority of their offices alone. In a sense, they are sterile bureaucrats, not leaders. Barnard (1938) suggests that only when the authority of leadership is combined with the authority of position will superiors be effective in inducing subordinates to comply with directives outside the bureaucratic zone of indifference. Indeed, the possession of both formal and informal authority distinguishes formal leaders from officers and informal leaders. Figure 6.1 illustrates these relationships.

How can school administrators broaden the bases of their authority and enhance their leadership position? The informal organization is an important source of authority that frequently remains untapped. Where legal contracts and position legitimize formal authority, the common values and sentiments that emerge in the work group legitimize informal authority. In particular, informal authority arises from the loyalty that the superior commands from group members (Blau and Scott, 1962). The significance of subordinate loyalty to superiors is clear. Administrators who command subordinate loyalty seem to have a distinct advantage in enlarging their authority base.

Although authoritarian principal behavior and teacher loyalty to principals are probably incompatible, one strategy some administrators use for extending the scope of formal authority over subordinates is domination (Blau and Scott, 1962). Authoritarian administrators, for example, attempt to increase control by resorting to formal sanctions or to threats of using those sanctions; however, their prolonged use probably tends to undermine their authority. Subordinates, particularly professionals, resent constant reminders of their dependence on the superior, especially in an egalitarian culture. Given a strategy of domination and close supervision, authoritarian administrators are *unlikely* to command loyalty and support from professionals easily. Blau (1955) neatly called this the *dilemma of bureaucratic authority.* The dilemma depends on the power of sanction, but it is weakened by frequent

		Formal Authority	
		Yes	No
Informal Authority	Yes	Formal Leader	Informal Leader
	No	Officer	Follower

FIGURE 6.1 ***Types of Authority Positions***

resort to sanctions. In fact, nonauthoritarian and supportive supervisors seem likely to engage in a contrasting strategy—one of leadership in which services and assistance are furnished to subordinates. Using formal authority to perform special favors, services, and support can create social obligations and build goodwill among subordinates. The result should be enhanced development of subordinate loyalty and informal authority.

The nature of supervision in schools should focus on helping, not directing, teachers to improve their teaching for a number of reasons. Teachers work in closed rooms and are not easily observed. Moreover, teachers frequently make strong claims for professional autonomy, and close supervision seems likely to be seen as an infringement on that autonomy. Finally, teachers attach great importance to authority on the basis of professional competence—much more so than similar professional groups such as social workers (Peabody, 1962). Therefore, it should not be surprising that consistently the research demonstrates that authoritarian principals in schools are not successful at generating trust and teacher loyalty, whereas supportive ones are highly successful (Hoy and Rees, 1974; Isaacson, 1983; Mullins, 1983; Hoffman, Sobo, Bliss, and Hoy, 1994; Reiss, 1994; Reiss and Hoy, 1998). Close, authoritarian control of teachers does not generate informal authority; supportive and helpful supervision does.

Emotional detachment and hierarchical independence are two other important characteristics of principal-teacher relationships. Emotional detachment is the ability of administrators to remain calm, cool, and collected in difficult situations; and hierarchical independence is the extent to which administrators demonstrate their autonomy from superiors as they interact with teachers. Principals stand in the middle—with the higher administration on one side and professional teaching faculty on the other. Their effectiveness depends on the support they receive from both, yet they are likely to be the objects of conflicting pressures from both groups. Consequently, emotional detachment from subordinates and independence from superiors are important in establishing social support from teachers for principals. Indeed, the research has demonstrated the significance of both, but especially emotional detachment, in generating teacher loyalty to principals (Hoy and Williams, 1971; Hoy and Rees, 1974; Isaacson, 1983; Mullins, 1983).

Similarly, hierarchical influence is another attribute of administrators who are likely to tap into the informal teacher groups for authority to lead. Administrators who are able and willing to exert their influences with their superiors on teachers' behalf are respected and valued by teachers, and they earn the confidence, support, and loyalty of their teachers (Isaacson, 1983; Mullins, 1983).

Finally, the authenticity of the principal in dealing with teachers is a critical factor in the administrative process, enabling principals to generate teacher loyalty and informal authority. Leader authenticity is a slippery concept. People glibly talk about genuine, real, and authentic behavior, yet clear definition is another matter. Based on the work of Henderson and Hoy (1983) and Hoy and Henderson (1983), principal authenticity is defined as the extent to which teachers describe their principals as accepting responsibility for their own actions, as being nonmanipulating, and as demonstrating a salience of self over role. In contrast, inauthentic principals are viewed as those who pass the buck, blame others and circumstances for not being successful, manipulate teachers, and hide behind their formal position. As one would expect, leader authenticity is strongly related to commanding trust and teacher loyalty (Hoffman, 1993).

The implications of these empirical studies seem clear. If educational administrators are to be successful in developing informal authority, then they need to behave in ways that foster teacher loyalty. In this regard, authoritarian behavior is doomed to failure. Instead, administrators need to be supportive, independent, and use their influence to help teachers. Furthermore, even in difficult situations, administrative behavior needs to be emotionally tempered, calm, and considerate. Perhaps most important, principals should be authentic in their behavior; they need to show a willingness to share in the blame, to be nonmanipulative of teachers, and to be unfettered by bureaucratic role demands (Blau and Scott, 1962; Hoffman, 1993; Reiss, 1994; Reiss and Hoy, 1998).

Sources of Power

Although authority implies legitimacy, not all power is legitimate. Individuals, groups, or organizations can use power. For example, a department or group can have power, which suggests that it has the ability to influence the behavior of other individuals or groups, perhaps in personnel or budgeting decisions. Likewise, an individual can have power, which indicates success in getting others to comply with directives or suggestions. Leaders have power; they get others to comply with their directives. As we have seen, whether a leader or not, most administrators have power simply because as representatives of the organization, they have the power of the organization. But administrators can derive power from personal as well as organizational sources; those who have power influence the behavior of others. One of the first attempts to analyze sources of power was the pioneering work of John R. P. French and Bertram H. Raven (1968). Their focus was on the bases of interpersonal power and led them to the identification of five kinds of power—reward, coercive, legitimate, referent, and expert. Their typology of interpersonal power has been extended to the organizational level.

Reward power is the administrator's ability to influence subordinates by rewarding their desirable behavior. The strength of this kind of power depends on the attractiveness of the rewards and the extent of certainty that a person can control the rewards. For example, the principal who controls the allocation of teaching assignments or developmental grants for teaching innovations, or who can release teachers from routine housekeeping duties, has reward power over teachers in that school. Teachers may comply with the principal's requests because they expect to be rewarded for compliance. It is important, however, that the rewards be linked to compliance and that the influence attempts are proper and ethical. Philip Cusick (1981) describes one principal's attempt to use reward power by administering the schedule, additional assignments, and unallocated resources. The principal controlled just the things that many teachers desired. The principal could award a department chairperson with a free period, a favorite class, a double lunch period, an honors section, or support for a new activity.

Coercive power is an administrator's ability to influence subordinates by punishing them for undesirable behavior. The strength of coercive power depends on the severity of the punishment and on the likelihood that the punishment cannot be avoided. Punishment can take many forms—official reprimands, undesirable work assignments, closer supervision, stricter enforcement of the rules and regulations, denial of salary increments, or termination. Punishment is not without its negative effects. An official reprimand to a teacher for consistently leaving school early may result in frequent absenteeism, refusing to provide extra help to students unless specified in the contract, and a general tendency to avoid all but the essential aspects of the job. Interestingly, the same relationship can be viewed as one of reward power in one situation but as coercive power in another. For example, if a teacher obeys a principal through fear of punishment, it is coercive power; but if another teacher obeys in anticipation of a future reward, it is reward power.

Legitimate power is the administrator's ability to influence the behavior of subordinates simply because of formal position. Subordinates acknowledge that the administrator has a right to issue directives and they have an obligation to comply. Every administrator is empowered by the organization to make decisions within a specific area of responsibility. This area of responsibility defines the activities over which the administrator has legitimate power. The further removed a directive is from the administrator's area of responsibility, the weaker his or her legitimate power. When directives from an administrator are accepted without question, they fall within the subordinate's "zone of indifference." Such an order lies within an area that was anticipated at the time the employee contracted with the organization and is seen by the employee as a legitimate obligation. For example, teachers expect to compute and turn in grades on time for each marking period. Outside the zone, however, legitimate power fades quickly. It is one thing for the principal to insist that grades be promptly computed and turned in to the office; it is quite another to order teachers to change a grade. The legitimacy of the first request is clear, but not so for the second; hence, compliance with the second request is questionable.

Referent power is an administrator's ability to influence behavior based on subordinates' liking and identification with the administrator. The individual with referent power is admired, respected, and serves as a model to be emulated. The source of referent power rests with the extraordinary personality and interpersonal skills of the individual. For example, young teachers may identify with the principal and seek to imitate the personal demeanor and perhaps the leadership style of the more experienced and well-liked principal. Not only individuals but also groups can have referent power. Members of a positive reference group can also provide a source of referent power. Referent power does not rest simply with the official power holders of an organization. Teachers as well as principals can have referent power; in fact, any highly attractive individual who develops respect, trust, and loyalty among colleagues is likely to develop such power.

Expert power is the administrator's ability to influence subordinates' behavior on the basis of specialized knowledge and skill. Subordinates are influenced because they believe that the information and expertise held by the administrator are relevant, are helpful, and are things they themselves do not have. Like referent power, expert power is a personal characteristic and does not depend on occupying a formal position of power. Expert power is, however, much narrower in scope than referent power. The useful knowledge defines the limits of expert power. New administrators are likely to have a time lag in the acquisition of expert power because it takes time for expertise to become known and accepted by subordinates. New principals must demonstrate that they know how to perform their administrative functions with skill before we willingly accept their attempts to implement new practices and procedures.

These five types of power can be grouped into two broad categories—organizational and personal. Reward, coercive, and legitimate power are bound to the organizational position. The higher the position, the greater the potential for power. In contrast, referent and expert power depend much more on the personal attributes of the administrator, such as personality, leadership style, knowledge, and interpersonal skill. In brief, some sources of power are more amenable to organizational control, whereas others are more dependent on personal characteristics.

Administrative Uses of Power

A large portion of any administrator's time is directed at "power-oriented" behavior—that is, "behavior directed primarily at developing or using relationships in which other people are to some degree willing to defer to one's wishes" (Kotter, 1978: 27). Administrators possess varying degrees and combinations of the types of power that have just been discussed. Moreover, the way administrators use one type of power can hinder or facilitate the effectiveness of other kinds.

Reward power is likely to produce positive feelings and facilitate the development of referent power, but coercive power has the opposite effect (Huber, 1981). Moreover, subordinates may view administrators who demonstrate expertise as having more legitimate power. In fact, expert power may be the most stable form of power. In one study, changes in the reward structure of an organization increased the perceived use of coercive power and reduced the perceived use of reward, legitimate, and referent power of the administrator, but expert power remained stable (Greene and Podsakoff, 1981).

Gary Yukl (1981) offers some guidelines to administrators for building and using each of the five kinds of power. The likely consequences of the uses of power are important considerations for administrators. Table 6.1 summa-

TABLE 6.1

Probable Subordinate Responses to Power

	Probable Subordinate Responses to Power		
Type of Power	**Commitment**	**Simple Compliance**	**Resistance**
Referent	XXX	XX	X
Expert	XXX	XX	X
Legitimate	XX	XXX	X
Reward	XX	XXX	X
Coercive	X	XX	XXX

XXX—Most likely.
XX—Less likely.
X—Least likely.

rizes the probable outcomes of each form of power in terms of commitment, simple compliance, or resistance. For example, the use of referent power is most likely to promote commitment, next most likely is to result in simple compliance, and least likely is to create resistance and develop alienation. Commitment is most likely with the use of referent and expert power; legitimate and reward power are most likely to promote a simple compliance; and coercive power will probably produce resistance and eventually alienation. Amitai Etzioni (1975) draws similar conclusions in his analysis of the consequences of using power in organizations.

Referent power depends on personal loyalty to the administrator that grows over a relatively long period of time. The development of loyalty to one's superior is a social exchange process, which is improved when administrators demonstrate concern, trust, and affection for their subordinates. Such acceptance and confidence promote goodwill and identification with superiors, which in turn create strong loyalty and commitment. Referent power is most effective if administrators select subordinates, who are most likely to identify with them, make frequent use of personal appeals, and set examples of appropriate role behavior—that is, lead by example.

Expertise itself is usually not enough to guarantee commitment of subordinates. Successful use of expert power requires that subordinates recognize the administrator's knowledge and perceive the exercise of that expertise to be useful. Thus, administrators must demonstrate their knowledge convincingly by maintaining credibility, keeping informed, acting decisively, recognizing subordinate concerns, and avoiding threats to the self-esteem of subordinates. In short, administrators must promote an image of expertise and then use their knowledge to demonstrate its utility.

Authority is exercised through legitimate power. Legitimate requests may be expressed as orders, commands, directives, or instructions. The outcome of the administrator's request may be committed compliance, simple compliance, resistance, or alienation depending on the nature and manner of the request. There is less likelihood of resistance and alienation if the administrator makes the request politely and clearly, explains the reasons for the request, is responsive to the concerns of subordinates, and routinely uses legitimate authority (Yukl, 1981, 1994).

The use of reward power is a common administrative tactic to achieve compliance with organizational rules or specific leader requests. The rewards may be either explicit or implicit, but it is important that they are contingent on compliance with administrative directives. Compliance is most likely when the request is feasible, the incentive is attractive, the administrator is a credible source of the reward, the request is proper and ethical, and the compliance to the request can be verified. There are some dangers in the use of rewards. Subordinates can perceive reward power as manipulative, a common cause of subordinate resistance and hostility. Moreover, the frequent use of reward power can define the administrative relationship in purely economic terms; thus, subordinate response becomes calculated on the basis of tangible benefits. When rewards are given to express an administrator's personal appreciation for a job well done, however, it can become a source of increased referent power. People who repeatedly provide incentives in an acceptable manner gradually become better liked by the recipients of the rewards (French and Raven, 1968).

Most effective administrators try to avoid the use of coercive power because it typically erodes the use of referent power and creates hostility, alienation, and aggression among subordinates. Absenteeism, sabotage, theft, job actions, and strikes are common responses to excessive coercion. The use of coercion is usually considered when the problem is one of discipline and is most appropriate when used to deter behavior detrimental to the organization—for example, stealing, sabotage, violation of rules, fighting, and direct disobedience to legitimate directives (Yukl, 1981, 1994). To be most effective, subordinates need to be informed about the rules and penalties for violations. Coercion is never without the potential to alienate; thus discipline must be administered promptly, consistently, and fairly. The administrator must maintain credibility, stay calm, avoid appearing hostile, and use measured and appropriate punishments. Three guides should be helpful to administrators:

- Avoid the use of coercive power: coercion alienates.
- Use organizational power to develop personal power.
- Use personal power to motivate and create commitment.

Power need not be thought of as a constraining force on subordinates. **Empowerment** is the process by which administrators share power and help others use it in constructive ways to make decisions affecting themselves and their work (Schermerhorn, Hunt, and Osborn, 1994). More than ever before, administrators and reformers are trying to empower teachers (Conley and Bacharach, 1990; Midgley and Wood, 1993; Rice and Schneider, 1994; Marks and Louis, 1997; Rinehart, Short, and Johnson, 1997; Rinehart, Short, Short, and Eckley, 1998). Empowerment gets translated into shared decision making, delegation of authority, teamwork, and site-based management (see

Chapter 9). Rather than viewing power as the domain of administrators, it is increasingly seen as something to be shared by everyone in more collegial organizations (Lugg and Boyd, 1993). When teachers are empowered, principals are less likely to boss and push them around (use coercive power) and more likely to serve as facilitators who guide teams of teachers using their knowledge and expertise (expert power). Principals will increasingly be less able to rely on their position (legitimate power) to direct subordinates; in fact, as teachers are empowered, expertise will become the most significant element in power relationships between teachers and principals. Finally, evidence is beginning to emerge that shows empowering teachers in curricular matters is related to improving student performance (Sweetland and Hoy, 2000a).

Mintzberg's Perspective on Power

Henry Mintzberg (1983a) proposes another way to analyze power in and around organizations. In his view, power in organizations stems from control over a *resource,* a *technical skill,* or a *body of knowledge.* In all cases, however, to serve as a basis for power the resource, skill, or knowledge has to be important to the functioning of the organization; it must be in short supply; and it must not be readily replaceable. In other words, the organization must need something that only a few people can supply. For example, the principal who has primary responsibility for determining tenure for teachers has resource power. The assistant principal who has the interpersonal skills to deal effectively with irate parents, students, and teachers has power, as does the teacher who alone in the school understands the elements of a new curriculum thrust.

A fourth general basis of power derives from *legal prerogatives,* which gives some individuals the exclusive right to impose choices. School boards have the legal right to hire and fire administrators and teachers; they are vested with such power through state statute. School administrators in turn are often required by state law to evaluate the competence of nontenured teachers. Moreover, they are delegated the right to issue orders to employees, which are tempered by other legal prerogatives that grant power to teachers and their associations.

Finally, power often comes to those who have *access* to power holders. Many principals' secretaries have power because of their access to and influence with those who wield power. Similarly, friends of the board president or superintendent or principal often change the course of organizational decision making.

Mintzberg also proposes a set of four internal power systems that are the basic sources for controlling organizational life: the system of authority, the system of ideology, the system of expertise, and the system of politics. The system of authority contributes to attainment of the formal goals as defined by the organization; the system of ideology contributes to the achievement of informal objectives that emerge as the organization develops its culture; and the system of expertise controls the behavior of professionals as they subject themselves to the standards of their professional training. These three systems of control typically contribute to the needs of the organization; that is, they are legitimate. But those with power also have personal needs. In the process of striving to accomplish the broader organizational needs, individuals find they have discretion, and discretion opens the way to political power. Thus a system of political power emerges that is not sanctioned by the formal authority, ideology, or certified expertise; in fact, it is typically divisive, parochial, and illegitimate.

The **system of authority** is the formal flow of power through legitimate channels. There are two subsystems of control here, personal and bureaucratic. *Personal control* is wielded by giving orders, setting decision premises, reviewing decisions, and allocating resources. Together these four personal means of controlling give administrators considerable power to orient the decisions and actions of their faculties. *Bureaucratic control,* on the other hand, rests with the imposition of impersonal standards that are established to guide the general behavior of teachers across a whole range of areas—for example, the time they are expected to be at school each day, cafeteria duty, and grading and homework requirements.

The **system of ideology** is the informal agreements among teachers about the school and its relationships to other groups. The character of the work group in terms of climate and culture are the terms we use in this text (see Chapter 5) to capture the essence of the system of ideology. The openness of the climate and the basic values of the school culture provide powerful sources of power and control.

The **system of expertise** is the interplay among experts or professionals to solve critical contingencies that the organization confronts. Faced with the complex tasks of teaching and learning, schools hire specialists (e.g., teachers, counselors, psychologists, and administrators) to achieve their basic goals. The need for autonomy to make professional decisions often conflicts with the system of formal authority, perhaps an inevitable consequence of professionals working in bureaucratic structures (see Chapter 3). As teachers continue to become increasingly professional, the demand for greater autonomy and power seems likely, and the granting of such power will likely be at the expense of the formal authority system.

The **system of politics** is the network of organizational politics, which lacks the legitimacy of the other three systems of power. It is a system that also lacks the consensus and order found in the other systems. There is no sense of unity or pulling together for a common good. This system can be described as a set of political games that power holders play. The games can coexist with the legitimate systems, be antagonistic to the systems, or substitute for the legitimate systems of control.

School administrators must recognize these systems of influence and must know how to tap into and use them. Clearly the system of authority is the beginning point for school administrators. Their positions are vested with power, but the personal and bureaucratic control of the position is not usually sufficient to motivate teachers to expend extra effort or to be creative in their service to the school and students. The danger to the school administrator is exclusive reliance on the system of authority. To do so is to limit commitment to the school and to risk producing resistance and alienation among teachers.

What Mintzberg calls the system of ideology is akin to what others refer to as the culture or climate of the school (see Chapter 5). Organizational ideology can produce a sense of mission among members. First-level administrators, such as principals, are key actors in the development of ideology. The goal is to create a belief among teachers and students that there is something special about their school, that it has a distinctive identity or unique culture. We have already discussed some of the ways that principals can tap into the informal organization, develop loyalty and trust, and enlarge the scope of their authority. Informal authority, however, is another beginning, not an end. Ultimately, the principal must go beyond commanding personal loyalty and generate an organizational commitment in which teachers give loyalty to the school and take pride and identity from it. Of course, the consequence of a strong ideology is to redistribute power; that is, power becomes more evenly distributed among educators.

Although the systems of authority and ideology promote coordination and compliance, they are rarely sufficient. When work is complex, experts or professionals are required, and with them come demands for autonomy to make decisions on the basis of professional considerations, not on the basis of authority or ideology. The power of the administrators needs to be shared with professionals. As teaching becomes more fully professionalized as an occupation, teacher empowerment will likely become a reality rather than merely a slogan, and many more schools will move toward organizational structures that are professional bureaucracies (see Chapter 3).

Our discussion of Mintzberg's systems of power makes one thing clear for school administrators: they must be ready to share power. Those who hoard power are likely to become victims of teacher and student dissatisfaction, alienation, and hostility. Moreover, the inadequacy of their systems of control is likely to open the way in schools for the play of informal power of a more clandestine nature—that is, political power, a topic to which we will return later in this chapter. We summarize this section with four imperatives for effective administrators:

- Extend your system of authority; formal authority is not sufficient for leadership.
- Tap into the system of ideology; the organization culture is another source of authority.
- Tap into the system of expertise; share power with your teachers.
- Know and understand the system of politics and limit it.

A Comparison and Synthesis of Power Perspectives

Our analysis of authority and power has covered a number of conceptual views (see Table 6.2). The perspectives can be compared in terms of the extent

TABLE 6.2

Comparison of Sources of Power and Authority

	Peabody (1962)	**Blau and Scott (1962)**	**Weber (1947)**	**French and Raven (1968)**	**Mintzberg (1983a)**
Legitimate Formal Power	Formal authority	Formal authority	Bureaucratic authority	Reward power and legitimate power	System of authority
Legitimate Informal Power	Functional authority	Informal authority	Charismatic authority and traditional authority	Referent power and expert power	System of ideology and system of expertise
Illegitimate Formal Power				Coercive power*	
Illegitimate Informal Power					System of politics*

*The power can be legitimate, but it is typically not.

to which the power is legitimate or illegitimate and formal or informal. By definition, the three formulations of authority consider only legitimate power. In contrast, the perspectives on power deal with both legitimate and illegitimate control as well as formal and informal power, but none of the frameworks is so comprehensive as to consider all four combinations of power; hence, we propose a synthesis. The French and Raven (1968) typology provides a classic analysis of interpersonal power, whereas Mintzberg (1983a) focuses his analysis on organizational power, and he develops four systems of influence to explore the power configurations in and around organizations. Only Mintzberg's formulation, however, considers power that is both illegitimate and informal—the system of internal politics. We propose a synthesis of power relations to include formal and informal authority (legitimate power), and coercive and political power (illegitimate). See Figure 6.2.

In analyzing power, a structural perspective calls attention to authority—the legitimate, formal power of the office or position (see Chapter 3). A cultural perspective underscores the legitimate, informal power of the organizational culture (see Chapter 5). An individual perspective emphasizes the legitimate, informal role of expertise and knowledge in generating power (see Chapter 4). But it is the political perspective that calls attention to the illegitimate, informal power that is inherent in organizations.

		Source of Power	
		Formal	Informal
Legitimacy of Power	Legitimate	Formal Authority	Informal Authority
	Illegitimate	Coercive Power*	Political Power*

*The power can be legitimate, but is typically not.

FIGURE 6.2 *Synthesis of Power Relations*

Power and Rationality: A Critical View

Power often blurs the difference between rationality and rationalization. Rationality is the application of reason to make decisions and solve problems whereas rationalization is an attempt to make a decision seem rational after it has been made. Rationalization masquerading as rationality can be a principal strategy in the exercise of power. Kant (1794) was one of the first to argue that the possession of power spoils the free use of reason, a proposition that has been demonstrated many times in a variety of contexts. Many of us have experienced how the view from the top (superintendent, dean, or principal) gets interpreted, sometimes reinterpreted, as the "truth." Power has a way of defining reality; indeed, people in power frequently varnish and spin the truth to suit their own purposes (Sweetland and Hoy, 2000b).

On the basis of an in-depth case study of politics, administration, and planning in the Danish town of Aalborg, Bent Flyvbjerg (1998) advances a theory of power and rationality that is both intriguing and instructive. The essence of his theory can be summarized in 10 propositions and is built on the practical politics of Machiavelli (1984), the philosophy of Nietzsche (1968), and the antienlightenment and post-modern thought of Foucault (1984). Although the propositions derive from a case study and are in need of further testing and refinement, they do provide a set of guidelines and challenging issues that both administrators and organizational participants should face. Let's take a brief look.

Proposition 1: *Power delimits reality.* Power concerns itself with defining rather than discovering reality. Power defines what counts as rationality and knowledge and hence reality itself. Evidence is always interpreted and sometimes reinterpreted by those in power. Nietzsche

(1968) said it well, "interpretation is itself a means of becoming master of something and subduing and becoming masters involves a fresh interpretation "(p. 342). When the chief interprets, the tribe listens.

Proposition 2: *Rationality is context-dependent, and the context of rationality is power, which blurs the distinction between rationality and rationalization.* Because rationality is penetrated by power, it is meaningless or misleading for administrators to act as if power were not part of rationality. What the superintendent or principal believes is an important part of school decision making. Hidden control, rationalization, and using power are typically more forceful tactics than rational argument. Indeed, when powerful participants need rationalization, it is rationalization and not rationality that prevails.

Proposition 3: *Rationalization presented as rationality is a basic strategy in the exercise of power.* In the world of practice, it is difficult to distinguish between rationality and rationalization. For public purposes, rationality dominates but frequently only as a front. Rationality is more legitimate and acceptable. But this "front behavior" is not the whole story and usually not the most important. Backstage, hidden from public scrutiny, power and rationalization dominate. A rationalized front is not necessarily dishonest because many individuals and organizations believe their own rationalizations. In fact, this self-delusion may be part of the will to power (Nietzsche, 1968). Not surprisingly, many administrators are true believers of their own rationalizations; they convince themselves of both the merit and the rationality of their rationalizations.

Proposition 4: *The greater the power, the less the rationality of actions.* Machiavelli asserts that, "We must distinguish between . . . those who to achieve their purpose can force the issue and those who must use persuasion. In the second case, they always come to grief." (1984: 51–52). These are strong words, but power does enable the leader to define and construct reality; hence, the greater the power, the less the need to discover reality because the leader can construct it. Moreover, the greater the power, the greater the temptation to construct both rationality and reality and the more likely it will be accepted. A leader's unwillingness to present rational argument or documentation may simply be an indicator of his or her power to act and to create reality. Power often finds ignorance, deception, rationalization, and lies more useful than the truth or rationality. Sometimes the creation of reality based on deception and lies creates grief but not always. That is, some leaders use politics successfully to create the reality they prefer. The distinction between what "should be" and "what is" is a fact of political life.

Proposition 5: *Stable power relations are more common in politics and administration than antagonistic confrontations.* Although Foucault characterizes power relations as dynamic and reciprocal, stable power relations in organizations are more common than antagonistic ones in part because of the pain and extra effort demanded of antagonism. In fact, antagonistic confrontations are actively avoided most of the time, and when they do occur, they are quickly transformed into stable power relations (Flyvbjerg, 1998). Conflict and antagonism get attention because they are not common and they cause organizational excitement, which is fodder for rumor and innuendo. Most administrators prefer harmony and stability to antagonism and instability, and they work to avoid conflict and gain a steady equilibrium of relative harmony.

Proposition 6: *Power relations are constantly being developed and redeveloped.* Even the most stable power relations are not immutable; they change. Power demands maintenance, cultivation, and reproduction. New leaders emerge, new coalitions develop, and new compromises occur. New arrangements and different power figures will likely soon surprise the administrator who is not attentive to power relations in the organization. Power is dynamic.

Proposition 7: *The rationality of power has a much longer history than the power of rationality.* From a historical perspective, the notions of rationality and democracy are young and fragile compared to the tradition of class and privilege. Policy and administration in most organizations are marked as much by the traditions of class and privilege as they are by rationality and democracy. The former are so firmly entrenched in the daily practices of our social institutions that attempts to eliminate or attenuate them are largely unsuccessful. The power of rationality and democracy are in large part ideals that are never implemented once and for all. The rationality of power, however, is strong and active in all contemporary organizations. Power and politics are inevitable aspects of organizational lives.

Proposition 8: *In open confrontation, power inevitably triumphs over rationality.* In open, antagonistic confrontation, there is no contest. Power is the victor. Knowledge and rationality carry little weight in these kinds of confrontations; indeed, the proverb that "Truth is the first casualty of war" is confirmed. Flyvbjerg captures the essence of the proposition when he explains that in such confrontations, "use of naked power tends to be more effective than any appeal to objectivity, facts, knowledge, or rationality, even though feigned versions of the latter, that is, rationalization, may be used to legitimate naked power (p. 232)." Naked power can be exercised freely and efficiently.

Proposition 9: *Rationality-power relations are more typical of stable power relations than of antagonistic confrontations.* The interaction of rationality and power tend to stabilize power relations because rationality produces legitimacy and a higher degree of consensus than the naked exercise of power. Stable power relations, however, are not typically equal or balanced power relations, that is, situations where individuals act as equal parties. Stability implies neither justice nor noncoerciveness; in fact, stability may be no more than a working consensus with unequal relations of dominance. But where rational considerations do play a role, they do so in the context of stable power relations. Thus, stability in power relations does not guarantee rationality, but rationality is more common in stable power relations. In stable situations, administrators are likely to be more open to rational argument than they are in antagonistic or confrontational ones.

Proposition 10: *The power of rationality (force of reason) is embedded in stable power relations rather than in confrontational situations.* This proposition may be seen as a corollary to the previous one. Confrontations are a natural part of the rationality of power, but not of the power of rationality. The power of rationality, that is, the force of reason, is most effective in stable power relations that demand negotiation and consensus. In fact, reason can be maintained only as long as power relations are stable and not antagonistic. Administrators are more likely to listen to reason when relationships with others (e.g., teachers or the union) are not hostile. The power of rationality is most effective and emerges most frequently in the absence of confrontation; naked power makes such rationality appear fragile—the power of rationality is weak in antagonistic situations.

In brief, this perspective reveals power as both rational and irrational. We cannot escape the fact that much organizational behavior is irrational and that in fact power and politics often undermine rationality. Although Bacon's (1597) famous dictum that "knowledge is power" is true, it is also the case that "power is knowledge." Power procures the knowledge that supports its purposes and ignores or suppresses that which does not. It is argued that the power-is-knowledge view is more important in determining behavior in organizations than the knowledge-is-power view. Flyvbjerg's perspective on power and rationality raises a host of intriguing questions, for example:

- Is rationality such a weak form of power that organizations built on rationality will fail?
- Under what conditions can democracy and rationality succeed in organizations?
- Does an emphasis on rationality leave us ignorant about how politics and power work in schools?
- Does a democratic emphasis make school participants more vulnerable to manipulation by those in power?
- Are democracy and rationality insufficient ways to solve problems in schools?

Let us return to Machiavelli's (1984: 91) warning concerning the dangers and reality of power: "A man who neglects what is actually done for what should be done learns the way to self-destruction." We need to see and understand organizational life as it is so that we have some chance to move it toward what we believe it should be. Power and politics are critical elements in such an undertaking.

Organizational Power and Politics[1]

Politics is "individual or group behavior that is informal, ostensibly parochial, typically divisive, and above all, in the technical sense, illegitimate—sanctioned neither by formal authority, accepted ideology, nor certified expertise" (Mintzberg, 1983a: 172). Although there are powerful individuals, the political arenas of organizations are composed of **coalitions** of individuals—groups who bargain among themselves to determine the distribution of power (Cyert and March, 1963). Despite all attempts to integrate individual needs in the service of the organization's goals, individuals have their own needs to fulfill. Inevitably, they get caught up in attempts to satisfy their more parochial needs and, in the process, they form coalitions with others who have similar aspirations. These major interest groups are varied and diverse; for example, they represent departmental, professional, gender, and ethnic groups as well as internal and external interests. Moreover, there are enduring differences in values, beliefs, knowledge, and perceptions among the coalitions. These differences are stable, change slowly, and are sources of much tension and conflict. Many of the most important organizational decisions concern allocating scarce resources. Thus a critical question becomes: How does each coalition articulate its preferences and mobilize its power to obtain resources (Bolman and Deal, 1997)?

External Coalitions

Significant outside influencers of schools include a myriad of groups such as teacher associations, unions, parent-teacher associations, taxpayer groups, state departments of education, consortia of colleges and universities, professional organizations, the media, and other organized special interest groups (see Chapter 7). Most of these outside-influence groups are trying to bring their own interests and external power to bear on the activities of the school. Their problem, of course, is figuring out how to achieve the outcomes they desire when they are functioning outside the official decision-making structure of the school. Mintzberg (1983a) notes that the impact of the external coalition on the organization varies dramatically, and he proposes a continuum of three external coalitions—dominated, divided, and passive.

A **dominated external coalition** is composed of one sole, powerful influencer or a set of external influencers acting in concert. In such cases the external coalition is so powerful that it dominates not only the internal coalition but also the board of education and the superintendent. Indeed, the board and superintendent are simply tools for the external coalition. For example, on occasion, a community issue such as "back to basics" can become so popular that a concerted effort by an organized group of external influencers can come to dominate not only curriculum change but, if left unchallenged, the basic policy and activities of the school.

Dominant coalitions do not remain unchallenged; in fact, it seems only a matter of time until other groups and individuals will coalesce and act. Without a dominant external power coalition, the power system of an organization changes in fundamental ways. When the external coalition is divided among independent and competing external individuals and groups of influencers, the organization is pushed in different directions as it attempts to respond to conflicting pressures.

A **divided external coalition** exists when a few, usually two or three, different sets of influencers emerge such that there is a rough balance of influence among the conflicting groups. For example, in school communities the balance can be between two external coalitions, one conservative and the other progressive. The curriculum and instructional programs often are battlegrounds for control as the coalitions compete. Their power struggles are reflected on the board of education and inevitably spill over into the internal coalitions within the school. In fact, Mintzberg (1983a) claims a divided external coalition often has the effect of politicizing the board as well as the internal coalition.

A **passive external coalition** is reached when the number of outside groups of external influencers continues to increase to the point where the power of each is diffuse and limited. The external coalition becomes passive and power is concentrated within the organization. Apathy becomes the natural strategy for the large, dispersed group (Olsen, 1965, 1968). The external environment is relatively stable and calm as influencers remain dispersed and passive; such an environment is welcomed by many administrators.

Internal Coalitions

Just as the organization can be influenced by external coalitions, it is also affected by internal groups of influencers that band together in common cause—internal coalitions. The external coalition shapes the kind of internal coalitions that emerge. A dominated external coalition tends to weaken internal coalitions; a divided external coalition tends to politicize them; and a passive external coalition gives internal coalitions a chance to flourish. But regardless of the kind of external coalition, it is through the efforts of the internal coalitions that the organization functions. Five dominant types of internal coalitions can develop—personalized, bureaucratic, ideologic, professional, and politicized (Mintzberg, 1983a).

The **personalized internal coalition** is one in which power is concentrated in the hierarchy of authority in the person of the chief executive officer, who rules the internal coalition. The superintendent, for example, controls the critical decisions and functions of the school in such a situation. There is little political game playing by insiders here.

In a **bureaucratic internal coalition,** power is also concentrated in the formal system of authority, but here its focus is on bureaucratic controls—rules, regulations, and procedures. Although bureaucratic controls tend to limit politics, political games arise—for example, between line and staff or among principals as they try to build empires and enlarge their own school budgets, usually at the expense of other schools in the district.

An **ideologic internal coalition** sometimes controls the organization; the system of ideology is so pervasive it dominates. For example, if the culture of a school is sufficiently strong and unified, teaches do not simply accept the goals and objectives, they share them as their very own. The administrator may seem to have great power because he or she embodies the culture, but the fact is that in sharing beliefs everyone shares power. Collegiality and egalitarianism prevail (Sergiovanni, 1992), and internal politics is very limited because of the strong sharing of beliefs.

In a **professional internal coalition,** the system of expertise dominates the organization. Highly trained experts—professionals—surrender a great deal of power to their organizations and the institutions that train them (Mintzberg, 1983a). Here politics is usually substantial because of the conflict between the systems of authority and expertise—what we have discussed as professional-bureaucratic conflict in Chapter 3. The professional internal coalition then is a playing field for a wide assortment of political games, yet politics is held in check by expertise.

In a **politicized internal coalition** power rests on politics. Here antagonistic, political games dominate the organization and either substitute for or drive out legitimate power. Whether the organization, however, is politicized or not, the game of politics is played in all organizations, and schools are not an exception.

THE POWER GAME

Power matters; it is an important aspect of what an organization does and it affects what its members do. Hirschman (1970), in his classic book, *Exit, Voice, and Loyalty,* observes that participants in any system have three basic options:

- Leave; find another place—exit.
- Stay and play; try to change the system—voice.
- Stay and contribute as expected; be a loyal member—loyalty.

Those members who leave the organization cease to be influencers; those who are loyal choose not to participate as active influencers; but those who choose to stay and speak out become players in the power game. Access to power itself, however, is not sufficient. Power players must also have the *will* to play, which means they must be willing to expend the energy to be successful, as well as the *skill* to act strategically and tactically when necessary. Power is an elusive blend of negotiating advantages and then willingly and skillfully exploiting those bargaining advantages (Allison, 1971).

Politics is a fact of organization life. Mintzberg (1983 a,b) argues that internal politics is typically clandestine and illegitimate because it is designed to benefit the individual or group, usually at the expense of the organization; therefore, the most common consequences of politics are divisiveness and conflict. Conflict is not necessarily bad; in fact, it sometimes calls attention to problems in the legitimate systems of control. Remember, however, that politics is not typically sanctioned by formal authority, ideology, or certified expertise; in fact, it arises because of default, weakness in the other systems of influence, or by design to resist or exploit others in control. Notwithstanding its lack of legitimacy, politics, like all forms of power, can solve important organizational problems (Mintzberg, 1983a):

- Politics ensures that the strongest members of the organization are brought into positions of leadership.
- Politics ensures that all sides of an issue are debated; the systems of authority, ideology, and sometimes even expertise tend to promote only one side.
- Politics are often needed to promote change blocked by the formal organization.
- Politics can ease the execution of decisions; administrators play political games to get their decisions implemented.

There is no guarantee that those who gain power will use it rationally or justly, but power and politics are not always demeaning and destructive. Politics can be a vehicle for achieving noble purposes (Bolman and Deal, 1997).

Where the formal system is usually a highly organized structure, George Strauss (1964) observes that the political system is a mass of competing power groups, each seeking to influence organizational policy for its own interests, or at least, in terms of its own distorted image of the organization's interest. Successful politics requires organizational members to bargain, negotiate, jockey for position, and engage in a myriad of political games, strategies, and tactics to influence the goals and decisions of their organization. As we have already noted, these politics can coexist with other more legitimate forms of power, array themselves in opposition to the legitimate power, or become substitutes for weak legitimate systems of control. With this view in mind, we turn to three important topics—political tactics, political games, and conflict management.

Political Tactics

All members of an organization can engage in organizational politics. In fact, it seems likely that, regardless of level or position, everyone is a player in the game of politics. Thus, we turn to a set of political tactics that are commonly used by employees at all levels (Vecchio, 1988).

Ingratiating is a tactic used to gain the goodwill of another through doing favors, being attentive, and giving favors. It is based on what sociologists call the "norm of reciprocity," a pervasive norm in American society. Help a colleague or superior and the person feels obliged to return the favor or repay the positive action. Teachers often attempt to gain the goodwill and obligation of their colleagues and principals by going beyond their duty in helping others. Daniel Griffiths and his colleagues (1965), in a study of teacher mobility in New York City, described how this tactic was used by teachers to become administrators. A sizable number of teachers volunteered for jobs that were perceived to be irritants by most teachers: teacher in charge of the lunchroom, administrator of the annual field day, school coordinator for student teachers, or trainer of the school track team. None of these jobs was paid, but they earned the teachers the goodwill and attention of superiors and frequently gained them more important positions such as assistant principal or acting chair.

Networking is the process of forming relationships with influential people. Such people may or may not be in important positions, but they often have access to useful information. Teachers who have close, friendly relations with the teachers' union representative or principal usually have access to important information. Likewise, teachers who have contacts with the spouse of the board president or who have an indirect link to the superintendent or who know the union head are also likely to gain valuable inside information.

Information management is a tactic used by individuals who want to control others or build their own status. Although having critical information is useful in itself, the techniques used to spread the information can enhance one's position in both the formal and informal organizations. Releasing information when it has full impact can promote self-interest and defeat the ambitions of others. The key to information management is first to get crucial information (networking) and then to use it skillfully, making things known to others in ways that increase their dependence and build your reputation as one who "really knows" what is happening. Teachers who have networks that garner them important information are typically major actors in the political life of the school, and their careful nurturing and managing of that knowledge usually enhances their roles as important players in the political games of the school.

Impression management is a simple tactic that most everyone uses from time to time to create a favorable image. The tactic includes dressing and behaving appropriately, underscoring one's accomplishments, claiming credit whenever possible, and creating the impression of being important, if not indispensable. The key is to build an image such that others see you as knowledgeable, articulate, sensible, sensitive, and socially adept.

Coalition building is the process of individuals banding together to achieve common goals. Teachers often join forces to oppose a proposed policy, to resist a proposed change, or to initiate change. A change in the curriculum is often successful depending on which teacher coalitions support or oppose it. Individuals alone are much less effective at influencing than groups; and relatively powerless groups become stronger if they can act together in coalition. Those teachers who are effective at organizing internal coalitions are often the political power players in a school.

Scapegoating is blaming and attacking others when things go wrong or badly. Principals often try to blame teachers when their statewide proficiency test scores are not high, and teachers seek to find someone to blame too, the administration, the school board, the parents, or another teacher. Blaming others for shortcomings is common in all organizations and schools are no exception. Finding a scapegoat can allow politically astute individuals an opportunity to shift attention and "get off the hook" by finding someone else to take the fall.

Some tactics are natural and legitimate; others are devious and illegitimate. When the tactics are based on dishonesty, deceit, and misinformation, they are hard to justify on moral grounds. Robert Vecchio (1988) argues that on the grounds of self-defense, one should be familiar with such devious political tactics as scapegoating, nurturing conflict by spreading false rumors, excluding rivals from important meetings, and making false promises. Although political tactics are a fact of organizational life, not all are viewed as legitimate (Cox, 1982). Moreover, there are a number of common blunders that are costly political mistakes: violating the chain of command, losing your temper in public, saying no too often to superiors, and challenging cherished beliefs (Vecchio, 1988). Such tactics, as we have discussed, are the bases of organizational politics.

Political Games

One way to describe more fully organizational politics is to conceive of it as a set of political games that are played by organizational participants. The games are complex, with intricate and subtle tactics played according to the rules. Some rules are explicit, others implicit. Some rules are quite clear, others fuzzy. Some are very stable; others are ever-changing. But the collection of rules, in effect, defines the game. First, rules establish position, the paths by which people gain access to positions, the power of each position, and the action channels. Second, rules constrict the range of decisions and actions that are acceptable. Third, rules can sanction such moves as bargaining, coalitions, persuasion, deceit, bluff, and threat while making other moves illegal, immoral, or inappropriate (Allison, 1971).

Mintzberg (1983a) identifies five general kinds of games that organizational members play: games to resist authority, games to counter that resistance, games to build power bases, games to defeat opponents, and games to change the organization. Relying heavily on Mintzberg's work, each will be discussed.

Insurgency games usually are played to resist formal authority. They range from resistance to sabotage to mutiny. When an order is issued, there is typically some discretion in executing the order. Because there is no guarantee that the order will be carried out to the letter, the individual served the order can manipulate the action to serve his or her ends. For decisions supported, one can go beyond the spirit, if not the letter. For those not supported, Graham Allison (1971: 173) notes that one can "maneuver, to delay implementation, to limit implementation to the letter but not the spirit, and even to have the decision disobeyed."

Participants at the bottom of the structure have little power over the organization; hence, they sometimes attempt control by circumventing, sabotaging, and manipulating the formal structure (Mechanic, 1962). Teacher professionals can and do resist formal actions of the administration. A rule requiring teachers to stay 15 minutes after school each day to help students with their work can easily be undermined by all teachers staying exactly 15 minutes—that is, by meeting the letter but not the spirit of the rule. If the climate of the school (see Chapter 5) is not healthy, then most likely the insurgency is symptomatic of more endemic problems rather than the particular issue itself. Administrators, however, often use more authority to fight resistance to authority. For example, when rules are ignored or undermined, a typical administrative response is to develop further rules and buttress their enforcement with close supervision and punishment for those who do not comply. The attempted solution usually fails because it does not deal with the cause of the problem, only the symptom. Thus, if administrators are to successfully counter insurgency, they must expend a great deal of their own political skill together with the power and authority of their position "to persuade, cajole, and bargain with operators to get what they want" (Mintzberg 1983a: 193). They end up bargaining and making informal deals with key actors in the system.

Power-building games are used by participants to build a power base. Superiors, peers, or subordinates can be used in the process. The *sponsorship game* is a simple one in which a subordinate attaches himself or herself to a superior and then professes absolute loyalty in return for a piece of the action. For example, the young teacher who would be principal sometimes tries to enlist the sponsorship of an influential vice principal or principal. Rosabeth M. Kanter (1977) notes that such sponsors provide three important services for their protégés. They fight for them and stand up for them in meetings; they enable them to get information and bypass formal channels; and they provide a signal to others, a kind of reflective power. Of course, there are costs in the sponsorship game. When the sponsor falls, the protégé is also in danger, and there is great danger if the young teacher goes against the sponsor or does not show proper deference. Sponsorship is a vulnerable means of power, yet it is a frequent power game played by many at virtually all levels in the organization. Principals, assistant principals, teachers, and secretaries all can play if they can find a sponsor and are willing to provide a service in return for a share of the power.

The power-base game is also played among colleagues; here it becomes an *alliance-building game.* Mintzberg (1983a) describes the process in the following way: Either an individual develops a concern and seeks supporters, or a group of individuals concerned about an issue seek out an informal leader who can effectively represent their position and around whom they can coalesce. Thus the nucleus of an interest group is formed. Some interest groups disappear as the issue is resolved, but others persist because the players have a number of common issues; they become factions. Interest groups and factions often lack the power to win an issue on their own. Consequently, they enlist the aid of other interest groups or factions to enlarge their power base. Thus alliances are formed. Groups are enticed, threatened, and cajoled to join the alliance. Kanter (1977: 185) notes, "Peer alliances often worked through direct exchange of favors. On lower levels information was traded; on higher levels bargaining and trade often took place around good performers and job openings." The alliance continues to grow until no more players are willing to join, or until it dominates or runs into a rival alliance. Over time, issues are won and lost and there is a gradual shifting of membership, but there is a basic stability in the membership of an alliance.

The *empire-building game* is the attempt of an individual, usually in middle management, to enhance his or her power base by collecting subordinates and groups. Empire building is fought over territory. In most school systems, empire building takes place as a budgeting game. Principals want a disproportionate share of the total budget. There is rivalry and feuding among principals as they compete for scarce resources; they want more teachers, more support staff, more computers, more space, more of everything than their competitors have. The goal of the game is simple: Get the largest possible allocation for your school. The strategies are fairly clear: always request more than you need because the request will be cut; highlight all rational arguments that support a large budget and suppress those that do not; and always spend the entire budget for the year, even if some is wasted. In fact, some administrators like to go a "little in the red" to demonstrate that their allocations were inadequate, a risky strategy that may cause scrutiny of expenditures.

Expertise is another base upon which to build power. The *expertise game* is usually played by professionals who really have developed skills and expertise needed by the organization. They play the power game aggressively by exploiting their knowledge to the limit. They emphasize the uniqueness and importance of their talents as well as the inability of the organization to replace them. At the same time, they strive to keep their skills and talents unique by discouraging any attempts to rationalize them. Occasionally a master teacher will develop a reputation in a district as a truly outstanding teacher. Such a teacher has an edge in developing a power base not only on the basis of expertise, but also in terms of playing the alliance and sponsorship games. Moreover, principals who demonstrate rare administrative and leadership skills can use that power as a base to engage in alliance and empire building as well as in sponsorship. Indeed, principals who are successful in building a strong power base become formidable candidates for the superintendency.

The last of the power-building games is *lording,* in which those who have legitimate power "lord it over" those who are their subordinates, thus exploiting them in illegitimate ways. Individuals with limited power are tempted to play the lording game. Kanter (1977: 189) asserts, "When a person's exercise of power is thwarted or blocked, when people are rendered powerless in the larger arena, they tend to concentrate their power needs on those over whom they have even a modicum of authority." Teachers who are frustrated by the full weight of strong bureaucratic control and an authoritarian principal may displace control downward to students, demonstrating that they too can flex their power as they boss their students around. In like fashion, the principal who is ruled with an iron fist by the superintendent may be tempted to lord it over the teachers. Although such behavior may give the players a sense of power over someone, it is no way to build a substantial power base.

Rival games are those to defeat competitors. The *line and staff game* is a classic confrontation between middle-line managers with formal authority and staff advisors with specialized expertise. In schools it often is a conflict between the principal of a school and a districtwide curriculum coordinator. The curriculum coordinator reports directly to the superintendent and so does the principal. In a sense the players are peers. The object of the game is to control behavior in the school. The curriculum coordinator is the expert, but the principal is the formal authority. The game becomes one of the formal authority of the line against the informal authority of expertise. The battles arise over issues of change. Staff is concerned with change and improvement. The curriculum coordinator wants changes in the curriculum. But change often produces conflict and turmoil. Principals as line administrators are responsible for smoothly running organizations; principals have a vested interest in relative stability. The battle lines are drawn. The superintendent will likely get involved, but there is usually no simple solution as each party in the game develops its respective case and mobilizes political allies.

The *rival-camps game* occurs when there are two and only two major alliances facing each other. These are generally vicious games in which all the stops are pulled, and in which there are winners and losers. The game can be between two personalities, between two units, or between forces for stability and change. Proposed changes, for example, can split the organization into two factions—the Old Guard and the New Guard. Normally, the battle is resolved with one group winning and the organization moving ahead with its work. But occasionally no group can win decisively. Schools often have to balance the traditional goals of teaching basic skills with the progressive goals of social and emotional development. So while the balance sometimes shifts one way or the other, the battles continue.

Change games are designed to alter the organization or its practices. The *strategic-candidates game* can be played by anyone in the organization. All it takes is an individual or group to seek a strategic change by using the legitimate system of authority to promote a proposal or project—its "strategic candidate." Those who are successful in initiating an important change gain a large amount of power in the organization. Because many strategic decisions get made in ways that are fundamentally unstructured, they invite political gamesmanship as different alliances and factions champion their cause—that is, their candidates for change (Mintzberg, Raisinghani, and Theoret, 1976). The strategic-candidates game combines the elements of most of the other games. Mintzberg (1983a) describes the process as follows:

> Strategic candidates are often promoted in order to build empires, and they often require alliances; rivalries frequently erupt between line and staff or between rival camps during the game; expertise is exploited in this game and authority is lorded over those without it; insurgencies sometimes occur as byproducts [sic] and are countered; capital budgets often become the vehicles by which strategic candidates are promoted; and sponsorship is often a key to success in this game. (p. 206)

The *whistle-blowing game* has become increasingly more common in all organizations. It is designed to use inside information on particular behavior that an individual believes violates an important norm or perhaps the law. The player blows the whistle by informing an external authority of the foul play. Because the informer is circumventing the legitimate channels of control and is subject to reprisal, the player typically attempts to keep the contact a secret. For example, the story may be published in the newspaper and attributed to an unidentified source. Whistle-blowing is often a dramatic affair that does cause change in the organization, but it is a high-risk game. Whistle-blowers are typically not admired.

Perhaps the most intense of all the games is the *Young Turks game.* The stakes are high; the goal is not simple change or change to counter authority, but rather "to effect a change so fundamental that it throws the legitimate power into question" (Mintzberg, 1983a: 210). The Young Turks challenge the basic thrust of the organization by seeking to overturn its mission, displace a major segment of its expertise, replace its basic ideology, or overthrow its leadership. This is major rebellion and the consequences are severe. Curriculum reform is one area in schools where the Young Turks game is played. Alliances develop and the showdown comes in an intense struggle in which teachers, staff, and administrators find themselves in one of two rival camps, either "for" or "against" the change. If the existing legitimate power yields to the Young Turks, the Old Guard will never have the same authority; indeed, the organization will never be the same because it is quite likely that the Young Turks will take over leadership. If the Young Turks lose, on the other hand, they are permanently weakened. They frequently leave the organization, and sometimes a schism is created within the organization. This is often an all-or-nothing game—win it all or lose it all.

Mintzberg's system of political games is summarized in Table 6.3. There is virtually no research literature that examines the relationships among political games, but there are a number of studies of noneducational organiza-

TABLE 6.3

Summary of Political Games

Game	Purpose	Primary Players
Insurency	Resist authority	Administrators/teachers/staff
Counterinsurgency	Counter resistance to authority	Administrators
Sponsorship	Build power base	Upwardly mobile administrators/teachers
Alliance Building	Build power base	Administrators/teachers
Empire Building	Build power base	Administrators
Budgeting	Build power base	Administrators
Expertise	Build power base	Administrators/teachers
Lording	Build power base	Administrators/teachers
Line versus Staff	Defeat rivals	Administrators/staff
Rival Camps	Defeat rivals	Administrators/teachers
Strategic Candidates	Produce change	Administrators/teachers
Whistle-blowing	Produce change	Administrators/teachers/staff
Young Turks	Produce change	Administrators/teachers

tions that probe into specific political games commonly played (Kanter, 1977; Zald and Berger, 1978). There is little doubt that much game playing occurs in school organizations; however, usually the system of politics coexists with the legitimate means of authority without dominating it. In Mintzberg's (1983a: 217) words, "Here the System of Politics seems to consist of a number of mild political games, some of which exploit the more legitimate systems of influence, and in the process actually strengthen them, others which weaken them, but only to a point, so that politics remains a secondary force."

Conflict Management

Because power and organizational politics inevitably produce conflict, we conclude our analysis of power with a brief discussion of conflict management. Administrators are faced with the classic confrontation between individual needs and organizational expectations; consequently, they spend a substantial amount of time attempting to mediate conflict. Kenneth Thomas (1976) provides a useful typology for examining five **conflict-management styles.** He identifies two basic dimensions of behavior that can produce conflict: attempting to satisfy one's concerns (organizational demands in the case of administrators), and attempting to satisfy others' concerns (individual needs of the members). Attempting to satisfy organizational demands can be viewed along an assertive-unassertive continuum; attempting to satisfy individual needs can be conceptualized from uncooperative to cooperative. Figure 6.3 shows the five conflict-management styles that are generated.

An *avoiding style* is both unassertive and uncooperative. Here the administrator ignores conflicts hoping that they will remedy themselves. Problems are simply put on hold. When they are considered, drawn-out procedures are used to stifle the conflict and secrecy is used as a tool to avoid

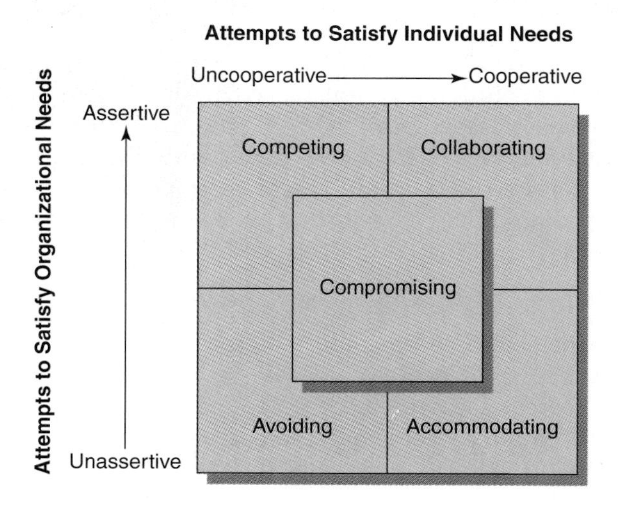

FIGURE 6.3 *Conflict-Management Styles*

confrontation. Often the administrator will turn to bureaucratic rules to resolve the conflict.

A *compromising style* is a balance between the needs of the organization and those of the individual. The focus of this style is on negotiating, looking for the middle ground, trade-offs, and searching for solutions that are satisfactory or acceptable to both parties.

The use of a *competitive style* creates win–lose situations. The administrator is assertive and uncooperative in attempts to resolve conflict. Invariably, competition produces rivalry, with the objective being to achieve the goals at the expense of others. Power is used to achieve submission—to win.

The *accommodating style* is unassertive and cooperative. The administrator gives in to the demands of the subordinates; it is a submissive and compliant approach.

The *collaborating style* is assertive and cooperative. This is a problem-solving approach. Problems and conflicts are seen as challenges. Differences are confronted and ideas and information are shared. There is a concerted effort to find integrative solutions, those in which everyone wins.

Thomas (1977) proposes that each of the five styles may be effective depending on the situation; in fact, using data collected from a set of chief executives, he matches the five conflict-management styles with the appropriate situations:

Competing

- When quick, decisive action is essential—e.g., emergencies.
- When critical issues require unpopular action—e.g., cost cutting.
- When issues are vital to the welfare of the organization.
- Against individuals who take unfair advantage of others.

Collaborating

- When both sets of concerns are so important that only an integrative solution is acceptable; compromise is unsatisfactory.
- When the goal is to learn.
- To integrate insights from individuals with different perspectives.
- When consensus and commitment are important.
- To break through ill feelings that have hindered relationships.

Compromising

- When the objectives are important, but not worth the potential disruption.
- When there is a "standoff."
- To gain temporary settlements to complex problems.
- To expedite action when time is important.
- When collaboration or competition fails.

Avoiding

- When the issue is trivial.
- When the costs outweigh the benefits of resolution.
- To let the situation "cool down."
- When getting more information is imperative.
- When others can solve the problem more effectively.
- When the problem is a symptom rather than a cause.

Accommodating

- When you find you have made a mistake.
- When the issues are more important to others.
- To build goodwill for more important matters.
- To minimize losses when defeat is inevitable.
- When harmony and stability are particularly important.
- To allow subordinates a chance to learn from their mistakes.

As with so many things, there is no one best way to manage conflict. Rather, successful conflict management is likely by carefully matching the style with the situation, a topic to which we will return in our discussion of leadership (see Chapter 11).

THEORY INTO PRACTICE

Litigation, Religion, and Politics[2]

The Washington School District is a K–12 system with 4,500 students, which was formed as a result of a lengthy desegregation law case. The commissioner of education ordered the forced merger of the wealthy and white Washington Township school system with the heavily minority Washington City schools. The case was triggered by the K–8 Washington Township attempt to withdraw its high school–age population from Washington High School and build its own high school. The consequence would have been an increase in Washington High School's minority population from 20 to 70 percent. The commissioner of education not only denied Washington Township's withdrawal request but also determined that the best interests of the children would be served by merging both school systems into one desegregated K–12 school system, a decision upheld by the state supreme court.

The first reactions from many of the parents and from the board of education of Washington Township were anger and threats to boycott the new school system. In fact over 20 percent of the parents did withdraw their children and enrolled them in private or parochial schools. Because the students in the Washington Township schools were almost all white, a state desegregation plan was implemented that created four elementary school zones, each with four public and four Catholic elementary schools.

New Superintendent

Dr. Lawrence Epstein had just been appointed the superintendent of the merged district following the retirement of the former superintendent, who had been instrumental in the creation of the new district. Although this is Dr. Epstein's first superintendency, he came to Washington with a strong background, having served as a teacher, guidance director, principal, and assistant superintendent;

THEORY INTO PRACTICE (Continued)

in fact, he has both urban and suburban school experience during his 21 years as a public school teacher and administrator.

The Board of Education

Because this is a merged school district, the composition of the board is determined by the percentage of students who attend the district from either Washington Township or Washington City. Superintendent Epstein inherited a board with five members from Washington Township and the other four from the city. The merger is now 10 years old and many of the fears that caused parents to pull their children from the then new school district never materialized, and the reputation of the school district has improved significantly. Washington High School is considered one of the best in the state and is proud of its ethnic and racial diversity. The board members are also proud of their schools and pleased with their selection of the new superintendent. Board members no longer vote to represent where they live, but they see their responsibility to the entire district. Although they are a diverse group, they are all college educated, successful in their careers, and have or have had children in the merged school district. They function well together and present a united front to the public and staff.

The Problem

Three months after Dr. Epstein took over the reins as superintendent, he received a telephone call from an irate parochial school parent protesting a notice from the district's transportation coordinator that his children would no longer be entitled to receive "courtesy busing." The state's requirement for busing students is primarily based on a minimum distance of two miles from a student's home to the assigned elementary school. Many of the students attending the elementary schools live less than two miles from their schools, but they are transported under the board of education policy called "courtesy busing." When a board of education decides to provide transportation for students who live less than two miles from their schools, the district does not receive any financial reimbursement from the state for these students. "Courtesy busing" is further complicated by a series of decisions by commissioners of education in this state that ordered public boards of education to provide transportation to private and parochial students on the same basis as their public school students.

The superintendent listened patiently to the parent's complaint and promised that he would investigate the case and get back to him. Superintendent Epstein called Marilyn Ricco, his transportation coordinator, to his office to provide him with the rationale or policy that supported the decision to remove this parent's children from the eligible list of students provided transportation. Marilyn Ricco explained that Jim Ryan, the parent who was protesting the decision, was no longer eligible for courtesy busing. Mr. Ryan had removed his children from one parochial school and enrolled them in another one because of a dispute with the parochial school principal. The decision by the parent to remove his children from the parochial school in one of the elementary school districts created by the desegregation plan and enroll them in another parochial school resulted in forfeiting his right to "courtesy busing." The explanation seemed reasonable to the superintendent, particularly when Ricco indicated that all similar cases were handled the same way, and this was strong past practice in the district.

Armed with this information, Superintendent Epstein called Jim Ryan back to tell him why he was supporting the decision by his transportation coordinator. Ryan exploded and angrily threatened a lawsuit because he claimed that he had evidence that there were a number of parochial school students being transported under similar circumstances. Dr. Epstein tried to calm the situation by suggesting that if names and addresses of these other students were produced, then he would consider reversing his decision. The parent, however, refused to inform on his friends. "Just take my word," he said. The conversation ended congenially with both agreeing to keep an open mind.

THEORY INTO PRACTICE (Continued)

Dr. Epstein immediately and discretely launched an investigation into the facts, and what he found, he didn't like. First, it was true that there were many such cases; the parent was correct. Second, the parent was influential in the community and was mobilizing a parental action group. Third, Marilyn Ricco, his transportation coordinator, had not been fair in her administration of the busing policy. When confronted with more than a dozen cases of parochial school students who had been receiving transportation in violation of board policy, she admitted the variance but tried to justify her decision. Finally, this case proved to be only the tip of the iceberg. More than 130 students were subsequently identified who were not eligible for transportation; yet they had been receiving it at a substantial cost to the district.

Faced with this information, the superintendent asked the board president to call a special closed session of the board. The session was closed because of the potential of litigation. The board members expressed their dismay about a practice that has been going on for many years and unanimously agreed that the 100+ parochial students who were not eligible for transportation should be removed from the buses. The board directed the superintendent to do two things: take disciplinary action with Marilyn Ricco and inform the parents of these parochial students that "courtesy busing" for their children would stop.

The superintendent sensed a major challenge that, if not handled effectively, would undermine his leadership. He called a meeting of all the parochial school principals to give them advance notice of the board's intentions and listened carefully to their reactions and suggestions. Although the meeting was cordial, he understood that litigation was inevitable. He alerted both the board attorney and members about the outcome of the meeting. The attorney advised the board that the history of these cases suggested that the board's position might not be upheld; however, he promised to review the state supreme court's prior decisions in similar cases and report at the next board meeting. Meanwhile the superintendent was directed to notify the parents by letter that in the following school year busing would not be provided.

It took only a week after the letters were sent for the board of education to receive notice that the parents of the affected students had retained an attorney and litigation to reverse the board's decision was being filed. The reaction came as no surprise, but the report of the board's attorney was intriguing. He advised the board that his research had convinced him that not only would the board prevail in the impending litigation, but that "courtesy busing" for any private or parochial student was not a requirement. He indicated that all the transportation being provided for all private and parochial students was not required except for those who attend schools more than two miles from their homes.

His findings were a surprise because the board thought that the issue had been settled in the state by a number of decisions from the commissioner of education and state board of education. The attorney informed the board that the issue of "courtesy busing" for private and parochial students had never been appealed to the state's supreme court, and he was convinced that the board would be successful if they determined to proceed with the case. Board members were elated because a saving of over $600,000 a year was a possibility if the attorney was correct in his assessment. Some of the board members were enthusiastic for other reasons beyond the financial reward. They believed that the board would gain widespread support from other boards who would now have the opportunity to save significant money without negatively affecting their programs. The Washington District and its board of education would again gain statewide attention as it did when the district was the first and only to be formed to resolve the desegregation dilemma.

Superintendent Epstein pondered the prospect of spending the next year or two preparing for litigation as well as dealing with the daily impact of the negative reactions that were sure to come from the parochial schools and churches as well as parents and teachers in the district. He knew that both he and the board members would

THEORY INTO PRACTICE (Continued)

be the targets of ugly rhetoric and vicious attacks. The board turned to him for his recommendations as they sought the safety of a superintendent's advice. Because he and four board members were not Catholic, they would be special targets during the next few months. He also was concerned that the board members who were Catholic would be pressured in church and by many of their friends. Would they buckle under the impending assault? He knew that he and the board had to make a momentous decision and soon. Oh yes, and then there was his transportation coordinator, Marilyn Ricco; he was under pressure to fire her. He needed a plan and a timetable to act. Assume you are the superintendent.

- Is there a way to prevent this issue from polarizing the community?
- Is litigation inevitable? If not, how can it be avoided?
- What kind of external coalition is likely? What are the consequences?
- Is this issue likely to spill into the school and affect students and teachers? How?
- What kind of political games and tactics are likely to get played out?
- What kind of conflict-management styles are needed? Why?
- How should you deal with Marilyn Ricco?
- Formulate a thoughtful plan of action. What are your short-term goals? Long-term goals?

Summary and Suggested Readings

Power is a basic element of organizational life. It can be legitimate and willingly accepted by subordinates or it can be coercive, illegitimate, and resisted. Our analysis begins by examining legitimate power—authority. Weber identifies three types of authority based on the source of legitimacy: charisma, tradition, or the law. Peabody extends the notion by distinguishing the bases of formal authority—legitimacy and position—from the bases of functional authority—competence and personal or human relations skills. Finally, Blau and Scott simplify the foundations of legitimate power in organizations by classifying authority as formal or informal.

Next, a general analysis of power is undertaken using French and Raven's bases of interpersonal power—reward, coercion, legitimacy, reference, and expertise—and extending their framework to the organizational level. In another formulation of power, Mintzberg provides another perspective on power and describes four systems of power: authority, ideology, expertise, and politics. His framework makes explicit the importance of organizational politics. In brief, four basic kinds of organizational power exist: two forms of legitimate power—formal and informal authority—and two kinds of illegitimate power—coercive and political.

A critical perspective on power suggests that power defines reality by stating what counts as rationality and knowledge. Evidence is reinterpreted by those in power in ways that are to their advantage. We cannot escape the fact that power is both rational and irrational and that power and politics undermine rationality.

Politics is a fact of organizational life. Although there are powerful individuals, the political arenas of organizations are composed of coalitions of individuals and groups, which bargain among themselves to determine the distribution of resources. External as well as internal coalitions influence organizational politics. Political tactics are the bases of a system of political games played to resist authority, to counter resistance, to build power bases, to defeat opponents, and to change the organization. The system of politics typically coexists with the more legitimate systems of influence without dominating. Because power and politics often generate conflict, our analysis concludes with a model of conflict management.

All students of administration should read Niccolo Machiavelli's classic, *The Prince.* Lee Bolman and Terry Deal (1997) present a nice overview of the political frame of organizations in their book, *Reframing Organizations.* Two comprehensive analyses of power in organizations are Amitai Etzioni's (1975) *A Comparative Analysis of Complex Organizations* and Henry Mintzberg's (1983a) *Power In and Around Organizations.* Etzioni uses the concept of power to create a comprehensive theory of organizations. Mintzberg develops a theory of power and politics in organizations. In our view, Mintzberg's treatment of power and politics is the most comprehensive of its kind. No one interested in organizations should miss it. Finally, Rosabeth Moss Kanter (1977) examines organizational politics in her insightful analysis of *Men and Women of the Corporation,* and Bent Flyvbjerg (1998) presents a critical and post-modern approach to power in *Rationality and Power: Democracy in Practice.*

Notes

1. This section draws heavily on the power analysis of Mintzberg (1983a).
2. This case was written for this book by Dr. Harry Galinsky, Paramus, NJ.

Key Concepts and Ideas

Authority
Bureaucratic internal coalition
Change games
Charismatic authority
Coalition building
Coalitions
Coercive power
Conflict-management styles
Divided external coalition
Dominated external coalition
Empowerment
Expert power
Formal authority
Functional authority
Ideologic internal coalition
Impression management
Informal authority
Information management
Ingratiating
Insurgency games
Legal authority
Legitimate power
Networking
Passive external coalition
Personalized internal coalition
Politicized internal coalition
Politics
Power
Power-building games
Professional internal coalition
Referent power
Reward power
Rival games
Scapegoating
System of authority
System of expertis
System of ideology
System of politics
Traditional authority

CHAPTER 7

EXTERNAL ENVIRONMENTS OF SCHOOLS

It becomes evident that the choices of expanding organizations about what units to add are not random but are, rather, partially determined by conditions in the institutional environment.

Brian Rowan
"Organizational Structure and the Institutional Environment: The Case of Public Schools"

PREVIEW

1. Schools are open systems and depend on exchanges with environmental elements to survive.
2. Multiple environmental influences come from different levels of society and affect what happens in schools.
3. Two general perspectives of environment are analyzed—task and institutional.
4. The task perspective includes both the information and the resource-dependency theories, which define task environment, as the aspects of the external setting that are potentially relevant for goal setting, goal achievement, effectiveness, and survival.
5. The information perspective treats the external environment as a source of information for decision makers. Complexity, stability, and uncertainty are the major concepts of the model.
6. The resource-dependence perspective views the environment as a place to gain scarce resources (e.g., fiscal, personnel, information and knowledge, and products and services) for support of the technical processes of schools.
7. In contrast to the task perspectives, institutional theory assumes that the environment encourages schools to conform to powerful sets of rules and requirements that are imposed by the legal, social, professional, and political contexts of organizations.
8. Institutional theory asserts that school structures and processes mirror the norms, values, and ideologies institutionalized in society. The essence of the theory is that institutional environments of schools press more for form than for substance.
9. School organizations do not have to be passive instruments of the

external environment; both internal and external coping strategies can be used to manage the environment.

10. Environments for schools may be shifting their emphasis from primarily institutional to more task concerns. If a shift is occurring, it represents fundamental change in the environments of schools that will have profound effects.

The open-systems concept (see Chapter 1) highlights the vulnerability and interdependence of organizations and their environments. External environments are important because they affect the inputs, internal structures and processes, and outputs of organizations; hence, one is forced to look both inside and outside the organization to explain behavior within school organizations. Indeed, the larger social, cultural, economic, demographic, political, and technological trends all influence the internal operations of schools and districts. Because school organizations are conceptualized as part of a larger universe or environment, an argument can be made that anything that happens in the larger environment may affect the school and vice versa. For example, one needs only to observe the race by school districts to purchase personal computers and other information technologies to see the effects that recent technology has had on the internal processes of schools. Similarly, the incidents of violence that have occurred in a number of schools, but especially in Littleton, Colorado, have fixated the national media and national and state political leaders. As a result schools far away from the violent episodes are preparing various contingency plans, hiring security officers, and installing weapon detectors.

As shown in Figure 7.1, multiple environmental influences come from different levels of society and affect what happens in schools. Technological and informational developments, political structures and patterns of legal norms, social conditions and cultural values, economic and market factors, and population and demographic characteristics influence school structures and processes. Within a specific locality, myriad stakeholder groups play key roles in affecting educational practices—for example, individual parents, taxpayer associations, business groups, legislatures, and accrediting agencies influence school policy.

Administrators tend to focus monitoring and planning processes on local environmental elements and often fail to recognize that environmental factors in the larger society also have the potential to influence not only their schools but local environments as well. Changing demographics—for example, age, sex, race, and ethnicity distributions in the population—will likely bring tremendous pressures for change in virtually all American schools. For example, the increasing percentage of educationally disadvantaged children entering and remaining in the schools has significant implications for educational attainment (Pallas, Natriello, and McDill, 1989). These are the students whose schools have traditionally been unable to serve in highly effective ways. That is, low achievement levels and high absenteeism and dropout rates have

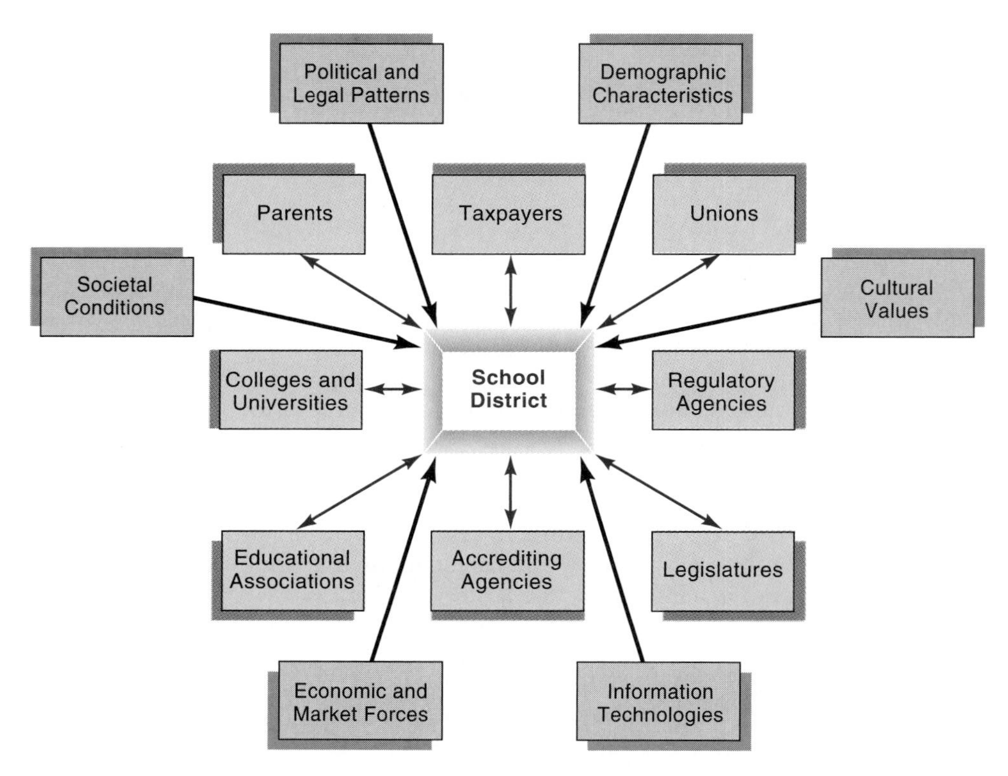

FIGURE 7.1 *Selected External Influences and Constituencies for School Districts*

characterized the academic careers of the educationally disadvantaged. Without fundamental changes in the ways schools and other organizations educate children, the problems of school effectiveness and the pressures on schools will increase. Thus, demographic trends suggest that external environments of schools are characterized by growing uncertainty and importance.

The emphasis on the external environments of school organizations is not new. However, the extent to which organizations are connected to and affected by the larger environment has been underestimated (Scott and Meyer, 1991). In fact, W. Richard Scott (1998) stresses that a central understanding emerging from open-systems theory is that all organizations are incomplete and depend on exchanges with other organizations in the environment as a condition of their survival. William R. Dill (1958) proposed task environment as a useful concept in understanding external influences on organizations. **Task environments** include all aspects of the external environment that are potentially relevant to goal setting, goal achievement, effectiveness, and survival. This conception emphasizes that most organizations are created to perform some type of work and to achieve goals. As Scott (1998) indicates, features in task environments emphasize that organizations such as schools are productive systems—they convert inputs into outputs—and in doing so require material and energy inputs and markets or buyers that will provide resources in exchange for what is produced. Therefore, organizations are not self-sufficient and must enter into exchanges with the external environment to gain the needed information and resources for survival. Information and resource-dependency perspectives are the best-known examples of task-environment theories. In these models, environments are seen as sources of information and stocks of information, respectively. They also emphasize ways that organizations succeed by developing effective structures to coordinate and control work processes and to regulate environmental demands (Scott, 1992; Meyer, Scott, and Deal, 1992). A second approach to understanding external environments is the institutional perspective. In this formulation, little emphasis is placed on task goals, effectiveness, and efficiency. Instead, the basic premise is that the chances of organizational survival are highest when school structures and processes mirror the norms, values, and ideologies institutionalized in society (Rowan, 1993). The information, resource-dependence, and institutional perspectives will be reviewed, evaluated, and applied to school settings.

Information Perspective

In the **information perspective,** the external environment is a source of information that decision makers use in maintaining or changing the internal structures and processes of their organizations. In this framework, the **external environment** is defined as information about external factors as perceived by organizational participants. Perceptions of information by decision makers link the external environment to actions taken by participants in the organization (Aldrich and Mindlin, 1978). Stated as a hypothesis, organizational changes are explained by variations in perceived information of decision makers about the external environment (Koberg and Ungson, 1987). For instance, how important a superintendent perceives the information from officials in state departments of education to be concerning the need to implement new state curriculum frameworks will partially determine how much effort the district will expend to change their instructional programs.

Although it is true that actions are based on administrator and teacher perceptions of the environment, such perceptions are not likely to be completely idiosyncratic to a particular person or school setting (Aldrich and Pfeffer, 1976). A variety of social processes combine to create similar perceptions. For instance, hiring educators with similar backgrounds, imitating programs from other schools, and following professional norms and governmental regulations promote the development of a common frame of reference for perceiving environmental information.

A Typology of Information Environments

Specific formulations of the information perspective have typically been based on typologies using a variety of seemingly similar dimensions, concepts, or continuums of complexity, stability, and uncertainty. Examples include typologies constructed by Fred E. Emery and Eric L. Trist (1965),

James D. Thompson (1967), Paul R. Lawrence and Jay W. Lorsch (1967), Robert B. Duncan (1972), and Ray Jurkovich (1974). To increase the clarity and ease in dealing with their ideas, we have grouped the concepts under two continuums: environmental complexity (simple to complex) and environmental stability (stable to unstable).

Environmental complexity, ranging from simple to complex, is the number, similarity, and linkage among the elements to which organizations must relate. Simple environments have relatively small numbers of homogeneous, unlinked elements that exercise comparatively little influence on organizations; complex environments have large numbers of diverse, linked entities that exert significant influence on organizations. As the complexity of the environment increases, so does the number of positions and units within organizations, which increases their internal complexity (Daft, 1989). In schools, for example, the number and types of at-risk children are indicators of environmental complexity. As schools have adapted to educate an increasingly diverse array of children, several categories of special teachers, speech therapists, school psychologists and counselors, and social workers have evolved.

Environmental stability, ranging from stable to unstable, is the extent to which elements in the environment are shifting or dynamic. Stable environments experience little and slow change; unstable environments experience abrupt and rapid change. Stability occurs in situations where the set of relationships among elements remain constant and in situations that are either unchanging or changing slowly. Instability arises in situations that are loose and erratic. In unstable conditions, both the value and kinds of environmental elements are changing unpredictably (Jurkovich, 1974). For administrators in schools, creating a sense of stability is critical in order to maintain an image of effective leadership and is an ongoing social pressure (McCabe and Dutton, 1993).

Different theorists have used slightly different terms to designate each dimension. Examples include:

- *Simple to complex axis:* Homogeneous to diverse, unlinked to linked, random to clustered, and few to many elements.
- *Stable to unstable axis:* Static to shifting, placid to unstable, not dynamic to dynamic, calm to turbulent, predictable to unpredictable, and unchanging/changing.

Combining the two dimensions—complexity and stability—produces the four-category typology shown in Figure 7.2. Each category also depicts the degree of uncertainty expected in the environment.

Environmental Uncertainty

A primary concern of the information perspective is uncertainty. **Environmental uncertainty** is the inability of decision makers in an organization to make accurate predictions because existing conditions in the external environment prevent them from having adequate information (Milliken, 1987; McCabe and Dutton, 1993). Uncertainty is a fundamental problem for organ-

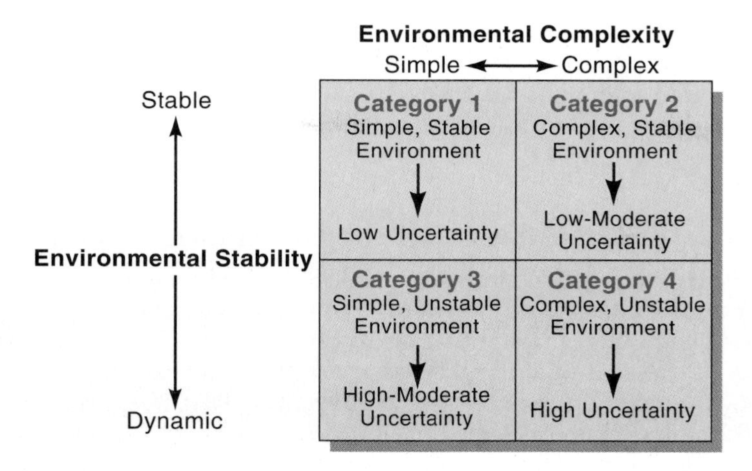

FIGURE 7.2 *Integrated Typology of Organizational Environments and Uncertainty*

izations, and dealing with it is the essence of the administrative process (Thompson, 1967). As shown in Figure 7.2, Duncan (1972) hypothesized that as environments are classified from category 1 (simple, stable) to category 4 (complex, unstable), the degree of uncertainty increases. Information generated by unstable and complex environments, for example, is likely to be in the form of questionable, suspicious, and ambiguous communications. Hence, as the environment becomes more complex and unstable, uncertainty for the organization increases.

The level of uncertainty is determined by the kind, clarity, and amount of information that organizational decision makers have about trends and changes in environmental conditions. Thus, when uncertainty is high, at least five problematic situations might arise for administrators.

- Additional or new information categories are needed to make sense of the information from the environment.
- Preferences regarding possible outcomes become less clear.
- Alternative courses of action and their outcomes become increasingly unpredictable and risky.
- Strategies and tactics become relatively difficult to communicate and implement.
- Potential outcomes from a decision are not known.

When confronted with environmental uncertainty, educators and schools often attempt to cope by creating special units or programs specifically to deal with the problem (Thompson, 1967). The idea is that schools adapt to produce environmental fit—that is, school organizations match their structures and processes to their perceived external environments (Miller, 1992; Pennings, 1992). As more and diverse groups become interested in education, for example, special units, such as offices of public information, government relations, community involvement, special education, information technology, and business partnerships are created to monitor their activities, report perceived information about their goals and behaviors to key administrators, and engage the groups in information exchanges in an effort to gain their support.

Research and Evaluation of the Information Perspective

Jane H. Karper and William Lowe Boyd (1988) studied state educational policy making during a period of increasing environmental instability. Specifically, they examined policy making that resulted from the statewide movement to increase educational quality that was sparked by the *Nation at Risk* report (National Commission on Excellence in Education, 1983). Karper and Boyd observe that many governors seized the initiative on educational reform. Hence, environmental uncertainty for schools and educational agencies increased dramatically. The researchers found that, by the mid-1980s, an extraordinary shift had taken place in the relationships among the key educational special-interest groups. These groups had moved from conflict and competition to collaboration and cooperation, forming a broad new coalition to advance and protect funding levels. As the environment became turbulent (category 4), the organizations adjusted to the new conditions by making the transition from competitive operations to multilateral agreements.

To study different conditions of environmental stability, Lawrence and Lorsch (1967) investigated the perceptions of organizational decision makers about the environment in three different industries. The researchers were interested in perceived environmental complexity and effectiveness. Their findings and conclusions supported the earlier findings of Dill (1958). When organizations are confronted with complex and dynamic environments, they are able to maintain or increase their effectiveness through additional flexibility in their structural configurations. Similarly, decentralization is an appropriate response to increased uncertainty because, as the environment becomes more uncertain, more information is needed (Govindarajan, 1988). An effective way to deal with the situation is to move the level of decision making to where the information exists rather than upward in the hierarchy.

Robert B. Duncan (1972) elaborated and empirically tested the typologies of Thompson and Lawrence and Lorsch. He found support for the general hypothesis that the levels of uncertainty for organizations increase significantly across each category from 1 to 2 to 3 to 4 (see Figure 7.2). The simple, stable environment creates the most certainty for organizations, and the complex, unstable, the most uncertainty. Moreover, low stability in the environment was a more important contributor to uncertainty than was high complexity. Both dimensions, however, interact to produce enhanced environmental uncertainty. Similarly, a consistent finding is that organizational innovation is positively related to environmental uncertainty. Explanations for this finding are that higher levels of uncertainty generate more innovation through opportunity seeking and adaptation to change, and increased levels of innovation create the perception of uncertainty among administrators (Russell and Russell, 1992). Moreover, perceptions of uncertainty or certainty have less impact on entrepreneurial than on conservative administrators (Dickson and Weaver, 1997).

In sum, the central characteristics of the information perspective are threefold:

- The focus is on the decision makers' perceptions of their environments rather than on the actual characteristics. Consequently, internal structures and processes will be influenced but not totally determined by the external environment.
- Perceived environmental uncertainty affects the degree of flexibility and bureaucratic nature of organizations. As the environment becomes more uncertain, organizations become more flexible and organic—that is, less formalized and less centralized.
- Empirical studies based on the information perspective typically measure environmental factors using subjective perceptions of organizational members. The research findings have been generally supportive of the information perspective.

Resource-Dependence Perspective

In contrast to the information perspective, the **resource-dependence perspective** views the environment as a place to gain scarce resources for the task and technical processes of the organization. Four general types of environmental resources are typically identified—fiscal, personnel (e.g., students, teachers, administrators, school volunteers, and board members), information and knowledge (e.g., outcomes from research, development, and evaluation projects), and products and services (e.g., instructional materials and test scoring services) (Aldrich, 1972; Benson, 1975). Organizations both compete for and share the environmental resources.

Environmental resources are commonly conceptualized on a continuum of **scarcity** to **munificence**—that is, the extent or capacity of the environment to provide resources that support the stability and sustained growth of the organization. The relative abundance of resources in the environment is the ultimate determinant of sufficient input for any organization. When resources are munificent, survival is relatively easy and the pursuit of wide-ranging task goals becomes possible (Castrogiovanni, 1991). For example, school districts in wealthy environments might have high property evaluations that produce relatively large tax revenues with small tax levies. In environments with abundant capacity, school districts would likely offer wide-ranging curricular and extracurricular programs. Under conditions of limited capacity or scarcity, competition for resources among subgroups can take the form of a zero-sum game with each subgroup caring more about its share of finite resources than for the overall welfare of the organization. For example, school districts in impoverished environments would be limited to a basic academic curriculum with extracurricular programs competing for what might be left over.

Dependence is defined both by the extent of need for a resource and its availability (i.e., scarcity/munificence) in the environment. For educational settings, dependence is directly related to the school organizations' need for resources controlled by other organizations, and inversely related to the resource availability from other organizations. That is, if school organizations cannot accomplish their goals without the resources controlled by other organizations and are unable to secure them elsewhere, they become dependent on the other organizations. Conversely, as resources are provided, the suppliers gain power over the schools. With this power, supplying organizations have two general means of control—deciding whether the schools get the resources they need and determining whether the schools can use the resources the way they want (Froosman, 1999). A major consequence of competition for resources is the development of dependencies among organizations in the environment. Notice that dependence is an attribute of the relationship between the organizations and not an attribute of individual organizations in isolation (Aldrich and Mindlin, 1978; Sutcliffe, 1994). It follows that the greater the resource dependence, the more the organizations communicate with each other (Van de Ven and Ferry, 1980).

Events in school finance illustrate the dependence concept. As fiscal resources from local property taxes and federal grants decline, school districts have an increased need to secure additional appropriations from state legislatures. Because greater percentages of their budgets are supplied by the state, the dependence of school districts on state governments grow dramatically. In a parallel fashion, the power of the state over local school districts expands and state legislatures and offices of education are able to dictate educational reforms to school districts—for example, curriculum standards and testing programs.

The fundamental proposition of resource-dependence theory is that if organizations are unable internally to generate the resources to maintain themselves, they must enter into exchanges with environmental elements to acquire the needed resources.[1] In exchange for resources, the external organizations may not only consume the organization's outputs but demand certain actions or changes from the organization. In other words, organizations lose some autonomy and become constrained by a network of interdependencies with other organizations. For example, individuals who have been educated and trained in the schools contribute their efforts to society, and society demands that schools offer particular types of educational programming. Hence, a basic hypothesis is that organizational changes are explained by the abilities of competing organizations to acquire and control critical resources (Koberg and Ungson, 1987).

Because all organizations are dependent on their environments, external control of organizational behavior is possible and constraint inevitable. If they are not responsive to the demands of their environments, organizations cannot thrive and may not survive. Hence, the resource-dependence model emphasizes that organizations adapt to their environments and that they can act to improve their chances of survival (Scott, 1998). But demands often conflict; thus, organizations cannot thrive or even survive by simply responding to every environmental demand. The challenge for school decision makers is to determine the extent to which their schools can and must adapt to various environmental demands and the implications of those responses for their organizations.

Whereas organizations must depend on their environments, they strive to gain control over resources in order to avoid becoming dependent on others and to make others dependent on them. Therefore, the resource-dependence model also portrays organizations as active and capable of changing as well as responding to their environments. Administrators manage their environments as well as their organizations; in fact, Pfeffer (1976) maintains that managing the environment may be more important than managing the organization. Members of the organization make active, planned, and conscious responses to environmental contingencies. Organizations attempt to absorb uncertainty and interdependence either completely, as through merger or consolidation, or partially, as through cooptation or the movement of personnel among organizations. Attempts are made to stabilize relations with other organizations, using tactics ranging from tacit collusion to legal contracts. Educational organizations, for example, establish external advisory groups composed of leading individuals from related organizations or publics to stabilize their relationships with other important parties.

Research and Evaluation of the Resource-Dependency Perspective

In a study based on resource-dependency theory, Michael Aiken and Jerald Hage (1968) hypothesized that, as interdependence is established between organizations, problems of internal coordination and control increase. Their findings indicate that organizations with more joint programs, and thus a higher degree of dependence on the environment, are more complex themselves, have somewhat less centralized decision-making processes, are more innovative, have greater frequency of internal communication, and tend to be less formalized than organizations with fewer joint programs. Support for the work of Aiken and Hage is provided by the findings of Mindlin and Aldrich (1975) that the higher the dependence on other organizations, the lower the formalization and standardization of organizational structure.

A study by John H. Freeman (1979) demonstrates the impact of resource changes on decision making. When enrollments or budgets plunge, rational decisions should be made about the programs and personnel that are to be trimmed or eliminated. Freeman found, however, that rationality was not the prime decision-making criterion. Categorical programs from the federal government and programs of importance to special interest groups, even those with limited demand, could not be cut. The decisions in the local school districts reflected external pressures, rather than the rational decisions that school officials might have made themselves.

In sum, three generalizations capture the essence of resource-dependency theory (Aldrich and Mindlin, 1978):

- As organizations become increasingly dependent on their environments for securing resources, they require and tend to exhibit more flexible and adaptive structures that are more informal, less standardized, and decentralized.
- Dependence on external elements for resources often leads to interorganizational relationships such as joint programs and cooptation.
- Research based on this perspective uses archival, observational, and other "objective" methods to gather data.

Combining these statements from resource dependence with the ideas from the information perspective, the essential question for administrators is: "How can environmental uncertainty be reduced without increasing dependence?" (Wood and Gray, 1991:141).

Administering Information and Resource Environments

Because environmental factors can threaten or constrain school autonomy and effectiveness, administrators often try to minimize external effects on internal school operations. Such attempts raise questions about the extent to which school organizations control, or even create, their own environments (Bowditch and Buono, 1985). Do organizations react to their environments, coping as best they can? Alternatively, do they control their environments, imposing structure on disorder, achieving dominance and predictability? The answers to these questions are not simple. Although it is tempting to say yes to both, situations are so dynamic that even when control is achieved, it is easily lost (Gross and Etzioni, 1985). Attempts to reduce environmental influence from these task perspectives can be grouped as internal or interorganizational coping strategies. Both sets of strategies are designed to protect key processes from environmental influences by increasing certainty and gaining additional resources.

Internal Coping Strategies

Environments seek to impose task or technical constraints on organizations such as schools. By adapting to task-environmental pressures, organizations reap rewards for effective control and coordination of work processes (Fennell and Alexander, 1987). In addition, organizations try to isolate their technical cores—for example, teaching and learning activities in schools—from external influences. Buffering, planning and forecasting, spanning organizational boundaries, and adjusting internal operations are coping strategies widely applicable to school organizations.

Buffering This strategy of isolation is based on the assumption that efficiency can be maximized only when the technical core, for example, teaching in schools, is not disturbed by external uncertainties. **Buffering** uses structures and processes to insulate or surround internal activities and absorb environmental disturbances. Buffering creates a protective layer between the organization and its environment (Miner, Amburgey, and Stearns, 1990; Pennings, 1992). Therefore, specific departments, roles, and processes are created in schools to deal with uncertainty and dependence from a variety of environmental elements. Purchasing, planning, human resource, curriculum, and facilities departments are created to buffer teachers from factors in the school's environment. These departments transfer materials, services, information, money, and other resources between the environment and school. In addition, a primary role of principals is dealing with parental complaints about teachers. The goal of buffering is to make the technical core as near to a closed system as possible and, thereby, enhance efficiency (Daft, 1989).

Planning and Forecasting In unstable environments and at high levels of dependence, buffering strategies probably cannot provide adequate protection for the instructional program. Under the conditions of high uncertainty and dependence, school organizations can attempt to control environmental fluctuations by **planning and forecasting strategies.** These strategies anticipate environmental changes and take actions to soften their adverse effects. Under these circumstances, a separate planning department is frequently established. In uncertain and dependent situations, planners must identify the important environmental elements, and analyze potential actions and counteractions by other organizations. Planning must be extensive and forecast a variety of scenarios. As conditions continue to change, the plans must be updated. To the extent that educators can accurately forecast environmental fluctuations, they have an opportunity to reduce uncertainty (Robbins, 1983).

Spanning Organizational Boundaries **Boundary spanning** creates internal roles for cross-organizational boundaries and links schools with elements in the external environment. This is also an important strategy for coping with environmental uncertainty and dependence. Two classes of functions are typically performed by boundary-spanning roles: detecting information about changes in the external environment and representing the organization to the environment (Aldrich and Herker, 1977).

For the detection function, boundary roles concentrate on the transfer of information between the environment and schools. Boundary personnel scan and monitor events in the environment that can create abrupt changes and long-term trends, and communicate the information to decision makers (Daft, 1989). By identifying new technological developments, curricular innovations, regulations, and funding patterns, boundary personnel provide data that enable schools to make plans and adjust programs. In contrast to buffering personnel, boundary spanners act to keep school organizations open systems in harmony with their environments. A number of individuals in schools—for example, superintendents and principals—play both buffering and boundary-spanning roles. Other school boundary-spanning roles include administrators in public information, government relations and research, evaluation, and development departments.

For the representation function, boundary-spanning personnel send information into the environment from the organization. The idea is to influence other people's perceptions of the organization. Schools often have offices of public information whose express purpose is to communicate information to significant stakeholders. Other district offices also can serve this function. For example, community and adult education programs, which primarily attract taxpaying patrons, can exemplify the quality of instruction that is available to students. Business and legal departments can inform legislators about the school needs or views on political matters. Similarly, the boards of education and school advisory committees link their schools to important constituencies in the environment in highly visible ways to create the impression, if not always the opportunity, for interests to be expressed. Thus, women, minority group members, and students are appointed in increasing numbers to a variety of advisory committees (Aldrich and Herker, 1977). Promoting a positive image of the school can reduce uncertainty and dependence on the various elements in the environment. Hence, boundary spanners play key roles in interorganizational relations (Friedman and Podolny, 1992) and can be highly influential with key decision makers in the organization (At-Twaijri and Montanari, 1987).

Adjusting Internal Operations The information and resource-dependence perspectives suggest a structural contingency approach to organizational design (Aldrich and Mindlin, 1978; Pennings, 1992). The way an organization should be designed depends in part on its environment. In other words, no one best way exists to organize schools. Rather, the most effective school structure is one that adjusts to its important environmental elements.

The first researchers to indicate that different types of organizational structure might be effective in different environments were Tom Burns and G. M. Stalker (1961). They found that the types of structure that existed in dynamic environments were different from the types that existed in stable environments. When the external environment was stable, the internal organization was "mechanistic" or highly bureaucratic—that is, characterized by formal rules and regulations, standard operating procedures, and centralized decision making; interpersonal relationships were formal, impersonal, rigid, and clear-cut. Relying heavily on programmed behaviors, mechanistic organizations performed routine tasks effectively and efficiently, but responded relatively slowly to unfamiliar events.

In highly unstable environments, the internal organization was "organic" or informal—that is, it exhibited few rules, informal agreements about operating procedures, and decentralized decision making; interpersonal relations were informal, personal, flexible, and somewhat ambiguous. Burns and Stalker did not conclude that the mechanistic model was inferior to the organic model, but rather, that the most effective structure is one that adjusts to the requirements of the environment—a mechanistic design in a stable environment and an organic form in an unstable environment. Danny Miller (1992) found considerable support for the contingency or environmental fit model. Organizations that achieve the best fit with external uncertainty exhibit the least number of interdependencies among internal structures and processes. In contrast, organizations showing the poorest fit with uncertainty have the strongest associations among structures and processes.

Organizational arrangements to fit each environmental condition of the typology on the basis of uncertainty have also been proposed. A synthesis of the proposed configurations is summarized in Figure 7.3. Duncan (1979) and Mintzberg (1979), have made similar recommendations.

Taken separately, the two dimensions suggest different organizational configurations. When the environment is simple, internal structures and processes are also simple. As complexity increases, however, organizations need more departments to analyze and relate to the increased elements and information in their environments. When environments are stable, internal arrangements tend to be routine, formal, and centralized—that is, more mechanistic. As instability increases, the structures and processes tend to become less formal and more decentralized—that is, more organic. Moreover, planning assumes added importance because the organization reduces uncertainty by anticipating future changes.

Simple, stable environments yield centralized bureaucratic structures that rely on standardized work processes. In simple, stable environments, for example, school districts would have extensive curricular frameworks and all teachers would be expected to follow the guides using similar teaching behaviors. By contrast, complex, stable environments lead to somewhat decentralized structures. School districts in complex, stable environments try to coordinate the instructional program through standard skills of teachers. These

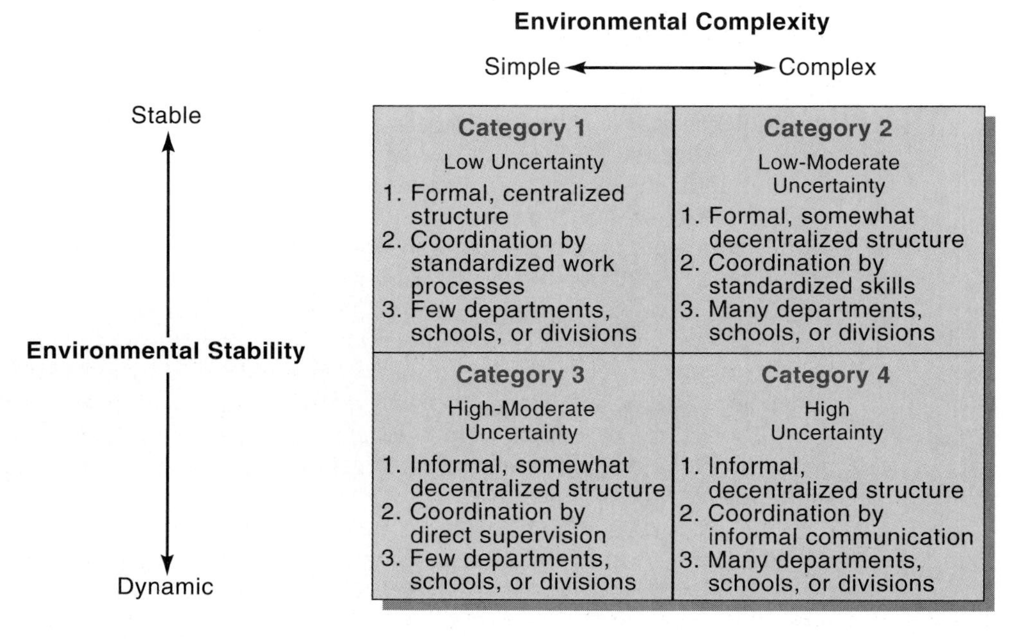

FIGURE 7.3 *Contingency Model for Environmental Uncertainty and School Structure*

schools become bureaucratic because of the standard knowledge and procedures learned in formal training programs and imposed on the organization by certification and accrediting agencies (Mintzberg, 1979).

Simple, unstable environments also produce some flexibility in the bureaucratic structure, but decisions tend to remain centralized. Schools in this type of environment use direct supervision to coordinate the instructional program—that is, administrators emphasize classroom observation and evaluation procedures. Complex, unstable environments lead to flexible, informal, and decentralized structures. In complex, unstable environments, school organizations must decentralize decisions to administrators, specialists, and teachers who can comprehend the issues. The school must be responsive to unpredictable changes. Informal communication becomes the prime coordinating mechanism as individuals and groups cope with the uncertain environment. Therefore, the basic postulate is that as complexity and instability increase, so do the number of positions and departments within the school organization. As suggested by open-systems theory, each major element in the environment requires an employee or department to deal with it (Daft, 1989). For example, personnel departments hire people who want to work in the district; government-relations employees negotiate with state legislators and education officials; and finance people deal with bankers.

Just as the information perspective suggests a structural contingency approach, so does the resource-dependence model. According to resource-dependence theory, the environment does not impose strict requirements for survival. Therefore, a wide range of possible actions and organizational structures are possible; hence, criteria guiding decisions and determining structures become both important and problematic. Internal power differences are important because no single optimal structure or set of actions aligns the organization with its environment. Instead, a range of choices or strategies of alignment are available. The influence of a variety of internal stakeholders may determine, in interaction with the demands of external constituencies, the response of the organization. Resource-dependence theory highlights the importance of environmental factors in promoting and restraining organizational decisions and actions, yet at the same time leaves room for the operation of strategic choice on the part of organizational members as they maneuver through known and unknown contexts. In other words, the resource-dependence model posits that although environmental influences are important, environmental constraints do not reduce the feasible set of structures to only one form. Rather, a variety of internal structures and actions are consistent with the survival of the organization, which means that although the organization may have the goal of survival, survival does not imply only a single or very limited set of structural forms (Aldrich and Pfeffer, 1976).

As a note of caution in applying the findings from contingency research, structural and process variations occur across schools as a result of active alternative generation and search procedures to adapt and change the environment. In fact, Boyd (1976) argues that schools are neither "mirror images" of the communities they serve nor completely insulated bastions dominated by unresponsive and self-serving professional educators. To a considerable extent, school organizations can shape their environments to fit their capabilities.

Interorganizational Coping Strategies

Thus far we have described ways in which school organizations can adapt internally to the external environment. Schools also reach out and change their environments. James G. March (1981) even asserts that, in part, organizations create their environments. Two types of strategies are used to manage the external environment—establishing favorable linkages and shaping environmental elements. A point to be remembered about attempts to control the environment is that it, too, has some organized character and the ability to fight back (Katz and Kahn, 1978).

Establishing Favorable Linkages A way organizations seek to control their environments is by establishing linkages with other organizations (Gross and Etzioni, 1985). Interorganizational linkages are important because they increase organizational power, reduce uncertainty, increase performance by ensuring a stable flow of critical resources, and protect the organizations from adverse effects of environmental uncertainty and scarcity (Stearns, Hoffman, and Heide, 1987). Moreover, strong ties with other organizations promote adaptation and innovation by increasing communication, sharing information, and learning flexibility strategies (Goes and Park, 1997; Kraatz, 1998). The connections are often in complex networks that try to regularize the flow of information and reduce uncertainty. The primary social process is believed to be some form of social exchange. Organizations create links by exchanging information, personnel, funds, equipment, and other needed items. In short, resources are exchanged in an effort to control the environment.

In business organizations a favorite mechanism to reduce competition and dependence is the merger. If a source of raw material is uncertain, buying the supplier removes the dependence on the external element. Although educational organizations cannot rely on mergers, they do enter into joint ventures with other organizations. School districts form *partnerships* with private foundations, universities, and federal and state governments to share the risks and costs associated with large-scale innovations and research projects. Current examples of joint ventures include Headstart, Follow Through, Individually Guided Education, special education programs, and vocational education. The number of joint ventures may be the best predictor of organizational influence on the environment (Boje and Whetten, 1981). Given the recent emphasis on market models of change such as charter schools, public school districts may link with parent groups to create their own charter schools as a way to reduce the number established by non–school district groups.

Cooptation represents another strategy of developing favorable linkages. Cooptation means bringing leaders from important elements in the environment into the policy and decision structures of the school organization. Cooptation occurs when influential citizens are appointed to boards of education or to advisory committees. When cooptation cannot be established directly, Pfeffer (1997) indicates that building favorable linkages with others who in turn can affect influence is sometimes an effective strategy. The evidence is mixed, however, for increasing the influence of organizations through advisory councils. Some research is supportive (Pfeffer, 1972); others are not (Boje and Whetten, 1981).

Another typical example of cooptation is the hiring of militant teachers or other activists to administrative positions. In these roles the coopted individuals have an interest in the school and are introduced to the needs of the district. As a result they are more likely to include the district's interests in their decision making and less likely to be critical of the decision in which they participated.

Shaping Environmental Elements Politicking is a primary method of shaping environmental elements for school districts and other interest groups. Using a relatively large but common set of tools or tactics to promote their interests, school officials and paid lobbyists express their views to local, state, and federal policy makers (Kollman, 1998). As shown in Table 7.1, Baumgartner and Leech (1998) describe 12 types of **influence tactics.** Modern information technologies such as e-mail, Internet search engines and websites, and computerized fax machines enhance both the urgency and pervasiveness of these influence efforts. Using these tactics with the intent of influencing public policy is lobbying.

Rather than trying to control the outcomes of educational policy, educators and other interest groups frequently attempt to influence its formulation using both positive and negative methods (Heinz, Laumann, Nelson, and Salisbury, 1993). **Interest groups** not only promote and advocate new issues or agenda items related to their interests, they also work to block unfavorable alternatives. For example, public schools have engaged in extensive efforts to block state and federal support to private schools. Intense lobbying campaigns have been leveled against proposals concerning such initiatives as tuition tax credits, schools of choice, and educational vouchers.

TABLE 7.1

Influence Tactics of Interest Groups

- Testifying at legislative or agency hearings
- Contacting legislators and other officials directly
- Making informal contacts with legislators and government officials
- Generating constituent influence
- Litigating
- Protesting and demonstrating
- Presenting research results
- Monitoring, influencing appointments, and doing favors for officials
- Drafting legislation and regulations and serving on commissions
- Engaging the mass media
- Electing and endorsing policy allies
- Forming coalitions

Pooling resources is a related strategy to shape the external environment. Educational associations usually have both professional and political missions. Examples include the Parent-Teacher Association, National Education Association, American Federation of Teachers, American Association of School Administrators, Council for American Private Education, Council of Exceptional Children, and Council of Chief State School Officers. A complete list is very long. Moreover, the individual groups do not remain isolated in the policy environment. They actively seek allies for support and leverage of their ideas. Government personnel dealing with education policy and education interest groups seek each other out for consultation and advice (Baumgartner and Walker, 1989). However, Hugh Heclo (1978) asserts that small circles of participants no longer control policy making. With the growth in both the government bureaucracy and the interest group system, policy making now takes place within relatively open issue or policy networks. These networks—as communication webs of people knowledgeable about some policy area—frequently include government officials, legislators, businesspeople, lobbyists, academics, and journalists (McFarland, 1992). By pooling resources, individual educators or educational organizations can afford to pay people to carry out activities such as lobbying legislators, influencing new regulations, promoting educational programs, and presenting public relations campaigns.

Karper and Boyd (1988) describe how the formation of coalitions and lobbying activities increases during periods of increasing uncertainty. Education interest groups in Pennsylvania responded to challenging circumstances during the mid-1980s by increasing the number, specialization, and sophistication of their lobbyists, and by forming a grand coalition to maximize their strength. As would be suggested by the information perspective, the findings indicate that the groups believed they had to increase the amount of information they had and could share. In turn, the need for information fostered increasing specialization and sophistication within the lobbying groups. The groups increased their research capacity, engaged in policy analysis, and employed higher levels of technology.

Tim L. Mazzoni and Betty Malen (1985) detail a successful attempt to shape educational policy. They analyzed a series of case studies dealing with constituency mobilization to impact state educational policy. In essence, an alliance consisting of the Minnesota Catholic Conference and the Citizens for Educational Freedom wanted the legislature to provide tax concessions for private school parents. Using both electoral and lobbying tactics, the alliance was able to persuade the legislature to endorse a tax concession package. The alliance kept the issue continuously on the legislative agenda, energized sympathetic lawmakers to carry its bills, and, most important, mobilized grassroots constituency pressure to sway votes among legislators. Mazzoni and Malen concluded that the political strategy of constituency mobilization had a significant impact on this policy issue.

The overall implication for practice is that school organizations do not have to be simple, passive instruments of the external environment. Both internal and external coping strategies can be used to buffer environmental influences and actually to change the demands. Structures, programs, and processes can be developed by educational administrators to manage the environments of their school organizations.

Institutional Perspective

Although the important elements of task environments for organizations are material and resource based, the primary factors in institutional environments are symbolic and cultural in nature (Scott, 1998). Moreover, the **institutional perspective** has become a leading approach to understanding organizations and their environments (Mizruchi and Fein, 1999). Brian Rowan (1993) characterizes it as one of the most vital formulations in organizational theory today. The roots of institutional theory are found in the works of Philip Selznick (1949, 1957). His ideas were revitalized and elaborated by Meyer and Rowan (1977) to create a "new" institutional theory. Since the late 1970s institutional theory has generated widespread interest among scholars and provides valuable conceptual and practical insights about schools.

According to Rowan and Miskel (1999), the goal of institutional theory is to explain how socially organized environments arise and how they influence social action. In essence, social actors of all kinds—individuals, administrators, teachers, interest groups, and schools—are seen as embedded in socially organized environments that generate rules, regulations, norms, and definitions of the situation that constrains and shapes behavior and other actions. Institutional arrangements are found at virtually all levels of social systems (e.g., societal, individual organizations, and small groups); have regulative, normative, cognitive roots (Scott, 1995); and have activities and functions that occur in a stable and recurring fashion.

Institutions can be formal organizations, but they do not have to be. Some institutions are based on formal, written codes of conduct—that is, laws, constitutions, standard operating procedures, and so forth—that are enforced by the coercive power of social agencies. Other institutions endure less formally as norms and values—that is, as strongly felt obligations that have been internalized through socialization. Still others persist as cognitive schema—that is, as relatively tacit, taken for granted, rulelike understandings of a situation. Objects that are commonly thought of as institutions, for example, include marriage, family, voting, the handshake, formal organizations, schools, attending school, teaching, teaching profession, academic tenure, the school principal, labor unions, and schooling (Rowan and Miskel, 1999). To capture this diversity of institutional structures, Peter Abell (1995) defines the **institution** as a more or less agreed-upon set of rules that carry meaning for and determine the actions of some population of actors.

Jepperson (1991) further observes that all institutions simultaneously empower and control; they are vehicles for activity within constraints. All institutions are frameworks of programs and rules establishing identities and activity schemes for such identities. For instance, a school considered as an institution is a packaged social technology, with accompanying rules and instructions for its incorporation and employment in a social setting. Institutions, then, embody common actions or standardized activities in situations that become taken for granted. Schools as institutions are taken for granted in the sense that they are treated as fixtures in a social environment and are explained as performing a function in that environment.

The **institutional environment,** therefore, is characterized by the elaboration of rules and requirements to which individual organizations must conform if they are to receive support and legitimacy. In modern societies, the environmental requirements (e.g., rules, norms, values, and ideologies) are rational in form, with the chief sources of rationalization being governments and professions. State or federal education agencies like to create bureaucratic arrangements that centralize discretion and allow limited autonomy to local practitioners. Professionals and their associations prefer weaker and more decentralized structures that locate maximum discretion in the hands of local educators. Whatever the source, however, organizations are rewarded for conforming to these institutional rules, beliefs, and ideologies (Meyer and Rowan, 1977; DiMaggio and Powell, 1991; Scott, 1995; Scott and Meyer, 1991).

In fact, rationalized myth is commonly used in discussions of institutions and their environments. Myths are widely held beliefs that cannot be or typically are not objectively tested. They are true because they are believed. Myths become rationalized when they take the form of bureaucratic or professional rules specifying procedures necessary to accomplish a given end (Scott, 1992). **Rationalized myths,** then, are rules specifying procedures to accomplish an outcome on the basis of beliefs that are assumed to be true or are taken for granted. For example, a rationalized myth is the use of psychological tests and classification systems to place students in special education classes. These diagnostic approaches are rational because they provide procedures for assessing intellectual and emotional processes. They are myths because their use depends heavily on endorsements by professional associations, accrediting bodies, and funding agencies (D'Aunno, Sutton, and Price, 1991).

Conceptual Foundations

Institutional theory is similar to the task-environmental theories, information, and resource dependence. Both institutional and task-environment theories focus on organization-environment relations rather than on internal influences. The task-environment theories, however, concentrate on task or technical environments to gain information and resources from the external environment. In contrast, institutional environments encourage conformity to powerful sets of rules and requirements that are imposed by the legal, social, professional, and political contexts of organizations (Fennell and Alexander, 1987). Both task-environmental and institutional theories promote "rational" organizational forms.

Technical environments emphasize a rationality that incorporates a set of prescriptions for matching means and ends in ways that produce desirable and predictable outcomes. Meyer, Scott, and Deal (1992) conclude that from the technical perspective, schools are peculiarly ineffective organizations.

Schools do not have clear, efficacious technologies and do not control their work processes adequately, particularly those involved in teaching and learning. By comparison, institutional environments press "rationales" as rationality. That is, institutional rationality provides an explanation that makes past actions understandable, acceptable, and seemingly accountable.

Recent versions of institutional theory have moved well beyond the simplistic assertion that institutional rules always conflict with organizational efficiency (Rowan and Miskel, 1999). Hence, task and institutional environments should not be viewed as mutually exclusive factors because they can and do coexist. In other words, technical and institutional factors are not dichotomous, but instead are separate dimensions along which environments can vary. Schools operate in relatively strong institutional but weak technical environments (Powell, 1991; Scott, 1998; Scott and Meyer, 1991). As a consequence, schools tend to be rewarded primarily for their conformity to professional standards and legal requirements rather than for the quality of their outputs. With the current emphasis on linking curriculum frameworks and testing programs, the relative strength of the task environment may be increasing and placing added pressure on schools to meet minimal output criteria (Scott, 1998). Important ideas in institutional theory include conformity, diversity, and stability.

Conformity and Institutional Environments

Institutional theory emphasizes that organizations are open systems, which are strongly influenced by their environments. Moreover, many of the most decisive forces are not rational pressures for more effective performance but social pressures to conform to conventional beliefs (Scott, 1992). Hence, a basic premise of institutional theory is that organizational structures and processes mirror the norms, values, and ideologies institutionalized in society. Accordingly, organizations conform to institutionalized rules and procedures to gain legitimacy—that is, cultural support for the organization. In other words, institutional conformity promotes the apparent success and long-term survival of the organization, independent of any effects that conformity might have on technical productivity. By designing a formal structure that conforms to the prescriptions of the institutional environment, an organization demonstrates that it is acting on collectively valued purposes in a proper and adequate fashion (Meyer and Rowan, 1977; Rowan, 1993). This thesis is particularly salient to educators because organizations lacking clear technologies and not operating in competitive markets—that is, public school systems—are especially likely to adopt institutionalized elements and conform to the institutional environment (DiMaggio, 1988).

Similarly, Paul J. DiMaggio and Walter W. Powell (1983, 1991) contend that organizational change in institutional environments makes organizations more alike without making them more efficient. Organizations within the same institutional environments tend to become homogenized. Public schools within a given country, for example, resemble each other. Their buildings and pedagogies are similar, with classrooms designed for a teacher, a set of students, and similar ways of engaging in teaching and learning processes. DiMaggio and Powell identify three mechanisms that promote institutional conformity.

Coercive conformity stems from political influence and problems of legitimacy. Coercive conformity results when organizations follow the rules and regulations promulgated by government agencies and thereby produce similar structures or processes (Rowan and Miskel, 1999). Common and visible coercive pressures or policy instruments for school change include government mandates and inducements. On the basis of both federal and state regulations, for example, schools now hire special education teachers to serve special-needs children, develop curriculum materials to meet standards or frameworks, and give students achievement tests that conform to government standards. A major problem with coercive policy instruments is that they often increase enforcement costs without producing the predicted gains in efficiency and effectiveness.

Imitative conformity results from adopting standard responses from other sources to reduce uncertainty. This process is similar to Meyer and Rowan's (1977) concept of rationalized myths, where organizations mimic successful or prestigious organizations. In other words, when organizations such as schools have weak technologies and ambiguous goals, they may model themselves on other organizations that they perceive to be more legitimate and successful. Rodney T. Ogawa (1992) offers the following example of an imitative process: A school adopts a new structure to enhance efficiency. If the new structure is perceived to improve performance, others may copy it. Over time, schools may adopt the new structure, not for the technical purpose of improving efficiency but for the institutional purpose of gaining legitimacy with constituents by mimicking a successful organization. A specific instance is the adoption of school-based management by a few urban school districts, an idea designed to deal with a multitude of problems, such as low academic achievement and tight budgets. As word spread of the successes enjoyed by these "innovative" districts, other districts uncritically implemented the innovation, even though they did not share the problems encountered by the original adopters. Betty Malen (1993) similarly concludes that school-based management is tied to a belief that attaches virtue to innovation and helps school districts retain their reputations as progressive systems.

Normative conformity arises when personnel who have been socialized and educated to follow professional standards spread professional codes across organizations (Rowan and Miskel, 1999). Two aspects of professionalism are particularly important in producing conformity in school organizations. The first rests on formal education and cognitive knowledge. Professionals learn standard methods of practice and normative rules about appropriate behavior. The second comes from the growth and elaboration of professional networks and associations that span organizations and allow new models to diffuse rapidly. Associations or labor unions of teachers and administrators, for example, facilitate the exchange of information among professionals and provide policies and practices that can be copied throughout education.

Through these conformity forces, schools produce similar structures and services and begin to resemble each other. Schools tend to look very much alike (Ogawa, 1992). In fact, pressures for conformity probably produce a surprising level of homogeneity within the American public school system. Meyer, Scott, and Deal (1992) found that schools go to great lengths to maintain their legitimate status as schools. They seek accreditation by conforming to a set of rules that are professionally specified or legally mandated. They hire licensed teachers who are assigned carefully defined students. Students are classified in grades that are given standardized meanings throughout the country. Finally, the teachers and students engage a curriculum that in turn is organized in fairly standardized categories of science, English, and mathematics. In other words, individual schools conform to and are constrained by institutional rules of what society defines a school to be; schools are expected to reflect the goals, values, and culture of broader society (Bacharach and Mundell, 1993).

Educational Diversity and Multiple Institutional Environments

While there are strong environmental pressures for conformity, considerable diversity is also evident within the larger K–12 educational sector. In contrast to highly centralized national systems in many countries, the institutional environments of American schools are complex and have many layers. American schools operate amid pressures from parents, community groups, and local governments, many agencies of the federal and state governments, and a wide array of professional and special-interest groups at all levels of society (Meyer, Scott, and Strang, 1987).

Many policy makers, citizens, parents, scholars, and educators probably have not recognized and taken seriously the diversity of the K–12 educational sector. When considering K–12 education in the United States, they see primarily the pervasive public school system. Yet well-developed subsectors of private, vocational, day-care, and alternative approaches also coexist with or within the public subsector of K–12 education. In fact, the persistence and increasing frequency of calls for market approaches to education (e.g., public and private choice, alternative schools, and voucher plans) may signal an increasing interest in private and alternative forms of education. An important point of speculation about this diversity and moves to strengthen the various subsectors is that different institutional environments may not only exist for each subsector of the K–12 system but also produce different educational structures and processes.

Rowan (1993) asserts that a strong case can be made that each subsector has a relatively unique institutional environment. He also proposes that by virtue of their institutional location, public schools have had to define a broad mission and are heavily penetrated by rationalizing forces. Conversely, private schools have been able to define narrow missions and are not subject to the kinds of pressures faced by the public schools. Therefore, a reasonable hypothesis is that in comparison to public schools, private schools have different institutional environments and reflect different structures andprocesses—

for example, smaller size, less bureaucratization, little or no vocational education, fewer curriculum offerings, a communal learning and support environment, and different governance arrangements. Empirical support for this hypothesis is provided by the work of Anthony S. Bryk, Valerie E. Lee and Peter B. Holland (1993).

Stability and Institutional Environments

In contrast to the common belief that uncertainty is increasing, Meyer and Rowan (1977) theorize that institutional environments tend to stabilize both internal and external relationships. They reason that centralized governments, professional associations, and coalitions among organizations provide for standardized operating procedures and stability. Environmental demands, characteristics of inputs and outputs of schools, and technical processes are brought under the jurisdiction of institutional meanings and control. Support is guaranteed by agreements instead of depending on performance. Regardless of whether schools educate students, for instance, people remain committed to schools and continued funding almost becomes automatic. Moreover, Meyer and Rowan argue that institutional environments buffer organizations from turbulence and allow conformance relationships to remain stable. Changes occur more slowly as the number of agreements increases. In fact, pervasive collective agreements among organizations grant near monopolies and ensure clienteles for organizations such as schools and professional associations. Thus, American school districts are near monopolies and have experienced high stability. The price for this legitimacy has been to conform to ever-widening rules about classifications and credentials of students and teachers, and the official content of the curriculum. In return, school districts are protected by rules that make education, as defined by the institutional classifications, compulsory. As a point of speculation, the institutional environment may be changing. The increased calls by citizens, policy makers, and business representatives for alternative schools and heightened technical performance suggest that previous institutional agreements are being questioned. We will return to this possibility later in this chapter.

In sum, institutional theory offers a substantially different perspective on the school organization-environment relationships rather than information and resource-dependence theories. Schools maintain conformity with institutionalized rules and ideologies and expend little effort in controlling and coordinating instructional processes and outcomes. The image conveyed is form over substance (Ingersoll, 1993). Since the reemergence of institutional theory in the mid-1970s, a substantial body of research in educational settings has developed.

Research and Evaluation of Institutional Perspective

Samual Bacharach and Brian Mundell (1993) believe that the research literature on the politics of educational policy can be reinterpreted using institutional theory. Many of the studies dealing with local, state, and federal interest groups can be explained by their desire to impose a particular set of rules and ideologies on schools, and in turn how the schools adopted or buffered themselves from the rationalized myths. In addition to research on political processes, a number of studies that explicitly use institutional theory have been conducted in educational settings.

Meyer (1992) observes that American education is distinctive in the decentralization of its funding and control to state and local levels. The federal government has little constitutional authority to regulate education and attempts to build such authority have largely been unsuccessful. Although the federal role has expanded, the role is largely restricted to funding and authority in various special educational programs spread across multiple federal agencies. Consequently, the institutional environment of public education at the federal level involves the centralization of funding without substantive authority; and the linkages at local, state, and national levels tend to be loose, circuitous, and indirect. Meyer calls this pattern *fragmented centralization.* Extending this reasoning, Meyer, Scott and Strang (1987) assert that school districts have an obvious interest in gaining funds by meeting the federal legal requirements for participation. One response is to develop an administrative system with the competence to search out funding prospects, learn how to conform to program and reporting requirements, and smooth the whole process. Support was found for the hypothesis that increments in federal funding produced larger additions to the administrative staffs of school districts than did increments in state or local revenues, a finding consistent with underlying institutional theory.

Institutional theory also offers an explanation of school district consolidation (i.e., merging of two or more districts into one). David Strang (1987) studied school district consolidation from 1938 through 1980. During this period over 100,000 school districts failed to survive. To a substantial extent, these deaths were affected by changes in the institutional environment—that is, the ideology about the appropriate size and structure of schools changed. Consolidation does preserve local control, albeit in larger, more bureaucratic districts. At the same time, however, local school administrators in consolidated districts now must attend to state and national policies to a greater extent than before they were merged. Strang found, for instance, that the more centralized the state's control was over education, the more extensive the consolidation. The new consolidated districts were larger and more complex organizations that were more susceptible to central initiatives across a range of state and national policy issues.

On the basis of the assumption that structural elements are first legitimated in the environment and then adopted by local organizations, Rowan (1982) traced the incorporation of three occupations into California school district structures. He charted how health, psychological, and curriculum services and occupations were created and institutionalized by the rules and ideologies of state agencies, legislatures, and professional groups, and were then incorporated into the structure of local school districts. As early as 1909, the legislature passed legislation permitting school personnel to make medical inspections of children. The original purpose of the inspections was to combat the spread of infectious diseases. After the legislation passed, crusaders engaged in institution building. The result was that by 1935, yearly medical inspections were mandated by the *School Code.* Moreover, larger school districts were always more likely than small districts to incorporate occupations, but that independent of size, districts added and subtracted occupations as support for an occupation ebbed and flowed in the institutional environment. In addition, the most successful adoption was health services and the least successful was curriculum services. This is interesting because health services are the most removed from the technical core of instruction and curriculum is the closest.

Ogawa (1994) believes that the aim of the current wave of reform in the United States is not to renew and enhance existing structures, but to make fundamental changes in them. Using institutional theory, he studied a widely popular reform called school-based management. The basic idea in this reform is to delegate important decisions from the district to the school level. His findings suggest that the movement to school-based management was institutionalized. The primary proponents—National Governors' Association, Carnegie Forum on Education and the Economy, American Federation of Teachers, and various academics—basically represented the interests of the education profession. The groups articulated two overarching goals: first, to improve the effectiveness of public schools; and second, to enhance the professional status of teachers. Ogawa observes that the goals seek to shift greater control to teachers and emphasize the importance of public education, which has been compared unfavorably with private education by proponents of school choice. At face value, these goals could be taken as a move to promote a task or technical effectiveness. However, when asked to explain their advocacy for school-based management, the groups invoked broad societal interests and ignored more parochial or personal goals. Hence, Ogawa concludes that the findings are consistent with institutional theory. The proponents justified their preferred structural elements by linking them to widely shared cultural beliefs or institutions.

Using David Cohen and James Spillane's (1992) analysis of the influence of institutionalized rules on teachers' work, Spillane and Nancy Jennings (1997) investigated curricular reforms in a school district that had carefully aligned its instructional policies to support an ambitious, new model of literacy instruction. They found that when the policies were unambiguous and clear, implementation was reliable with limited variation in teachers' practices. When the policies about practice were ambiguous, however, implementation was not consistent because teachers' practices were influenced more by their prior experience and individual interpretations of the policies. This study suggests that clarity and consistency in institutional rule making can produce genuine effects on the technical core of schools.

A criticism of institutional theory is that its broad emphasis on processes of conformity has led to downplaying the role of active agency and resistance in organization-environment relations (Goodstein, 1994). A narrow focus on conformity processes deflects theoretical interest away from explaining the circumstances in which institutionalization is contested or incomplete. Organizations such as schools can exercise some choice in responding to institutional pressures. For example, school districts vary widely in their responses to state policy initiatives (Firestone, Rosenblum, Bader and Massell, 1991). Nonetheless, the criticism of institutional theory, that it portrays organizations as relatively passive actors that simply conform to their environments, does suggest an important area needing additional conceptual development and empirical testing.

Nonetheless, a substantial body of research confirms the central insight of institutional theory. Over time, an institutional sector in America and around the world has developed to define and standardize educational organizations (Rowan and Miskel, 1999). In other words, research supports the basic premise of institutional theory that organizational structures respond to trends in the institutional environment. Perhaps the most important contribution of institutional theory, however, has been providing an alternative conceptualization of organizational environments. Meyer and Rowan's (1977) article called attention to a neglected facet of environments: institutionalized or symbolic elements such as beliefs, rules, and roles are capable of affecting organizational forms independent of resource flows and technical requirements.

Administering Institutional Environments

Scott (1992) indicates that there are clear differences in the way organizations respond to technical (i.e., information and resource) and institutional aspects of the environment. Most links with technical environments involve exchanges of information and resources. Although some ties to institutional environments involve exchanges, especially information, the institutional perspective postulates that organizations are constituted by elements drawn from their environments. Because institutional environments are different from technical and resource-dependent environments, and because of the recent development of institutional theory, less is known about how organizations relate to their institutional environments (Scott, 1992). The basic and ubiquitous notion in administering institutional environments is that school organizations will be rewarded for having a legitimate reputation (Elsbach and Sutton, 1992). As with information and resource-dependence models, variations of buffering and boundary-spanning strategies also appear useful in managing institutional environments.

Buffering Strategies

Recall from our earlier discussion that buffers are structures and processes that insulate or surround internal activities and absorb environmental disturbances. Buffering essentially creates a protective layer between the organization and its environment. A major problem to resolve by buffering mechanisms is conflicts between pressures for technical efficiency and institutional rules. From an institutional perspective, decoupling and managing the image are two ways to buffer school organizations from their environments.

Decoupling Meyer and Rowan (1977) say that organizations designed for efficiency ideally attempt to maintain a close alignment between their structures and their technical activities. Close alignment in institutionalized organizations makes public a record of inefficiency and inconsistency. As a consequence, organizations functioning in institutionalized environments attempt to decouple their institutional structures from their technical structures and activities. **Decoupling** is intentionally neglecting to provide adequate control of work processes (Ingersoll, 1993). Decoupling divides organizations into two parts: one primarily links to the institutional environment and one produces the technical activities. Thus, the technical portion faces inward to its technical core and turns its back on the environment, whereas the institutional part turns its back on the technical core in order to focus on conforming to its institutional environment (Meyer, Scott, and Deal, 1992).

Decoupled school organizations exhibit a number of characteristics. For example, activities are performed beyond the purview of administrators and professionalism is actively encouraged. Goals are made ambiguous and categorical ends are substituted for technical ends—that is, schools produce students, not academic learning (Meyer and Rowan, 1977). Organizations decouple for several reasons. Decoupling masks or buffers inconsistencies, irrationalities, and poor task performance that might undermine public faith in the organization. Moreover, decoupled organizations can incorporate and display structural elements that conform to institutionalized conventions and yet preserve some autonomy of action. In inconsistent or conflicting environments, decoupling represents a particularly useful strategy (Scott, 1992).

Managing the Image This strategy involves impression management to portray structures and actions in ways that garner endorsement (Elsbach and Sutton, 1992). Impression management makes extensive use of symbolic categories and coding rules. Similar to cognitive schema (see Chapter 4), symbolic categories are created to select, identify, classify, and label the things or people being processed by the organization. Coding rules are the essence of institutional frameworks; they provide the distinctions among things and people that allow standard operating or taken-for-granted procedures to be employed (Scott, 1992). Meyer and Rowan (1977), for instance, state that using cost analysis to justify school projects in an institutional norm can provide a rationale if a project fails. Administrators whose plans have failed can demonstrate to other administrators, teachers, the board of education, and the public that the procedures were prudent and that their decisions were made rationally. Hence, institutionalized practices and impression management help justify their actions and portray a positive image to constituents. Such symbolic activities can produce shared meanings and value that in turn result in commitments, support, and legitimacy of the school organization (Ogawa, 1992).

Boundary-Spanning Strategies

Earlier in this chapter, boundary spanning, or bridging, was defined as activities that create internal roles to cross-organizational boundaries and link the school organization with elements in the external environment. Meyer and Rowan (1977), DiMaggio and Powell (1991), and Scott (1992) propose conformity as the central boundary-spanning strategy in institutional environments. By incorporating institutional rules, beliefs, and ideologies into their own structures, organizations become more homogeneous and gain legitimacy. Scott proposes three types of bridging strategies that can be used to manage institutional environments.

Categorical Conformity According to Scott (1992), this is a broad and general strategy. It basically is a process whereby institutional rules become taken-for-granted distinctions and provide organizations with a basis to pattern their structures. These distinctions are examples of widely shared cognitive schema. The cognitive structures become built into our language and become widely believed. Meyer and Rowan (1978) refer to this as a system of ritual categories. There are elaborate rules for classifying teachers—for example, elementary or secondary—and each category has its own specifications and credentials. Students, similarly, are categorized by grade level, ability level, and courses completed. Standard categories and ritual classification procedures involve not only educators and students, but also curriculum topics and schools (e.g., alternative and traditional). Schools that incorporate these shared cognitive belief systems—that is, exhibit categorical conformity—enhance their legitimacy and increase their resource capacities.

Structural Conformity Sometimes institutional environments impose very specific structural requirements on schools as a condition of acceptance and support (Scott, 1992). External mandates cause schools to implement new programs. In the past three decades, many special-education programs—for example, programs for those who are mildly learning disabled to severely and profoundly retarded, and for those who have hearing, visual, and other impairments—have been incorporated into educational organizations to meet various legislative laws, administrative rules, and parental beliefs. Using various arrangements, schools have developed structures to conform to the special-need categories designated in the institutional environments. Administrators know the score—success comes with meeting the demands for institutional conformity rather than with instructional efficiency (Rowan, 1981). As mentioned earlier, schools often borrow or imitate successful structural forms when they confront uncertainty. Thus, by choice and coercion, schools frequently use structural conformity as a mechanism for adapting to the environment (Scott, 1992).

Procedural Conformity Meyer and Rowan (1977) observe that despite the lack of coordination and control of the technical activities, schools are not anarchies. Day-to-day activities occur in an orderly fashion. In fact, institutional environments pressure schools to carry out activities in specified ways. School organizations can respond with rational myths that detail the steps to be followed in carrying out certain types of procedures. For example, schools tightly control such processes as hiring teachers with proper credentials, assigning students to classes, and scheduling events (Meyer and Rowan, 1978). Adherence to procedural specifications is a method by which stable school forms can be created and legitimated to work in institutional environments. By using socially acceptable procedures to execute controversial activities, schools can maintain the impression that they are rational and legitimate (Scott, 1992).

In sum, practical methods for administering the institutional environments of schools remain somewhat undeveloped. The foregoing sets of buffering and bridging strategies appear to offer substantial insights for developing specific tactics to manage the institutional environments of schools.

Policy Making and the Changing Environments for Education

The web of multiple levels of government rules, norms of professional associations, and ideological consensus of the public about what schools look like and do has produced a relatively stable institutional environment for public K–12 education. Current activities may indicate that the institutional environment for education is changing in the United States. That is, existing institutional explanations are being questioned. Worried about economic competitiveness in world markets, American businesspeople and policy makers are challenging the decoupling and rationalized myths about teaching and instruction. The longevity, intensity, and diversity of calls for educational reform may indicate that the public consensus is declining and destablizating the institutional environment. For example, Susan H. Fuhrman, Richard F. Elmore, and Diane Massell (1993) assert that pressure for increased and more consistent results from schools will continue to mount. In particular, the calls for systemic reform and competitive markets in K–12 education may reflect a shift in school environments from primarily institutional to task or technical.

Since the early 1980s, the reform movement in the United States has been characterized by a wave metaphor—first, second, and third waves. As conceptualized by Marshall Smith and Jennifer O'Day (1990), the current wave, called systemic reform, is a strong force for educational change. **Systemic reform** is a comprehensive change program designed to modify schools in an integrated, coordinated, and coherent fashion to achieve clearly stated educational outcomes (Fuhrman, Elmore, and Massell, 1993). The enactment of the Goals 2000 program by the federal government gave powerful impetus to a systemic reform movement in the United States. Powerful coalitions of business, policy, and governmental groups continue to support systemic reform programs. The basic priority of systemic reform is to define ambitious curriculum content and achievement standards in core academic subjects and to tightly couple the goals with an assessment program. The alignment of curriculum content and achievement standards with assessment procedures creates an accountability system for monitoring the efficiency and effectiveness of K–12 schools. Systemic reform proponents plan to augment the accountability system with changes in educator preparation and practices, instructional materials, governance, and finance. From the perspective of environmental theory, we hypothesize that a goal of systemic reform of K–12 education is to increase the influence of technical and decrease the influence of institutional environments.

As Ogawa's (1994) work indicates, a crucial point in systemic reform is whether the current initiatives promote technical efficiency and effectiveness or societal arguments, further governmental standardization, and professional control. If the goals of systemic reformers are to be achieved, technical environments must become the dominant form for schools and tight linkages must develop for accountability, efficiency, and effectiveness. If the switch to technical environments does not occur, the systemic reform efforts may produce a new, thicker web of rationalized myths and further institutionalize the environments of public K–12 education. Alternatively, further reliance on rationalized myths in the face of intense public calls for reform might force a break in the near monopoly of public education and produce a competitive market for K–12 education.

Paul E. Peterson (1989) maintains that the quasi monopoly of K–12 public education is so pervasive a fact in the United States that its existence is pretty much taken for granted. During the last century public education has captured a powerful set of legitimating symbols—social democracy, equal opportunity, and a common homogenizing experience in a pluralistic society. In other words, the schools have been institutionalized and have assumed a near-monopoly position.

Intense criticism of the academic performance of American public schools and popular presentations of the positive achievements of private and foreign schools (Stevenson and Stigler, 1992; Bryk, Lee, and Holland, 1993) have led many to question the monopolistic position of public K–12 schools. John E. Chubb and Terry M. Moe (1990) have been particularly articulate in arguing that the best way to improve American schools is to set them free in a competitive marketplace. **Competitive market** means that people choose the school and type of education that they think best meet their educational needs. Free-market proponents believe that competitive forces produce better educational services than do monopolized responses and unleash strong incentives for school reform. In a competitive market, it is reasoned that parents and students will opt for the public or private schools they think are most efficient and effective. If consumers are not satisfied with the outcomes, they can just walk away and thereby send clear signals to educators about the level of school performance. Without such feedback, stimuli for improvement remain weak and monopolistic indifference reigns (Boyd and Walberg, 1990). Methods commonly proposed to produce a competitive educational market include establishing parental choice and alternative schools in both public and private settings, creating charter schools, and offering government-issued tuition vouchers or scholarships that can be used to pay for the students' cost of schooling.

As is the case with systemic reform, the rationale for competitive-market strategies is to place technical environments ahead of institutional environments. Competitive-market supporters are hypothesizing that parents and students will choose schools with ambitious academic goals, excellent teachers and administrators, motivating instructional materials, high efficiency and effectiveness, and strong accountability systems. Even if market-driven schools are established on a relatively widespread basis, forces in the institutional environment, however, will likely counter the drive to enhance their technical environments. For example, market-driven schools will likely develop their own rationalized myths, will operate in environments institutionalized by government agencies and professional associations, and will be strongly resisted by the current holders of the K–12 education monopoly.

In sum, we agree with Rowan and Miskel's (1999) conclusion. Concerted institution building over the past three decades by professional associations, government agencies, and private sector organizations is increasing the intensity of technical environments for schooling. This enhanced technical environment includes a model of educational productivity and the technical capacity to inspect educational outcomes of schools. Consequently, schools are facing stronger demands for technical performance than they have in the past, but without also encountering a decline in demands for institutional conformity. Hence, shifting the environment from primarily institutional to both institutional and technical represents fundamental change and will likely have profound effects on how schools operate.

THEORY INTO PRACTICE

A Reading War

You have been principal at Goodlion Elementary for nearly seven years. The school has 720 students in grades K–5. Your staff includes 32 teachers, 6 teacher aides, an assistant principal, and 2 secretaries. With expenditures at the 75 percentile on a statewide per pupil basis, Goodlion is one of six elementary schools in a middle-class suburban school system in the Southwest. The parents tend to be upwardly mobile and place a high priority on their children's achievement. You had been a fifth grade teacher for 10 years and an assistant principal in the district for one year prior to taking the job at Goodlion. During your service as a teacher and assistant principal, you completed a master's degree and other advanced graduate study in educational administration, curriculum, and philosophy. You especially liked the ideas of John Dewey. As a teacher and graduate student, you prided yourself on being a successful and progressive educator. You employed project-based methods and other constructivist approaches in your teaching and classroom. Your principal, fellow teachers, district administrators, and parents recognized you as an exemplary teacher. When the opportunity presented itself, you applied, and were hired as principal of Goodlion Elementary. You were eager to work with the teachers to establish a school where the best constructivist practices of teaching and learning were used.

After four years, Goodlion's early reading program had all of the best features of whole language approaches. You are particularly proud that your school has a literacy rich environment that is characterized by bountiful amounts of reading aloud to children, oral discussions about authentic topics, immersion in individual reading and writing projects, invented spelling, and reading selected books. In this environment, children can learn to read naturally. The program places minimal reliance on basal readers and achievements tests. Phonics instruction is implicit and embedded in the authentic rich literature. From your observations and reports from the teachers, the children are highly motivated to read, although some students seem to be having

THEORY INTO PRACTICE, (Continued)

some difficulty learning to read. From your perspective, you have successfully realigned the relations between the students, teachers, and yourself. The children have been empowered to direct their own learning; the teachers have been empowered to direct teaching without interference from you or basal readers. From your perspective and that of the teachers, the new approach to reading is working and its continuation and refinement could more or less be taken for granted.

As this new reading program was being developed, ominous clouds were boiling up in the state political environment, however. A moderately conservative governor had been elected. A central campaign plank had been a return to basic education through a model of systemic reform. The primary components of the governor's program are high standards and high-stake tests. In the fall of your seventh year as principal and three years after the reading program was fully implemented, the new state test was given in all the public schools of the state. The test result for Goodlion Elementary placed it at the 50 percentile.

Given your view that standardized tests are not valid indicators of student learning and school performance, you were not particularly concerned about the results. You assured yourself that your qualitative assessments had found that the students were motivated to read, enjoyed their reading in school, and had attained levels of comprehension not measured by the quantitative test. Your positive conclusions were reinforced by teacher expressions of satisfaction and support for the whole language program.

You are somewhat taken aback when you see a front-page story in the metropolitan newspaper about the test results and find that the test scores for all the schools in the area are listed and ranked within districts. Moreover, the governor's website contains a complete statewide listing of the scores in a report card format. Goodlion ranked fifth of the six elementary schools in the district and is given a C grade by the governor. You brace yourself for calls from parents demanding an explanation for the low scores. You are surprised when you are accused by some of the parents of harming the children through the whole-language program. Abetted by the local chamber of commerce and the realtors' association, the parents quickly organize and petition the superintendent and board of education to change Goodlion's reading program to emphasize the following principles: teach phonemic awareness directly in kindergarten; teach each sound-spelling relationship systematically; show children exactly how to sound out words; balance but do not mix comprehension and decoding instruction. If you agree to these principles, your progressive program in reading will be destroyed.

- How did this problem arise without your being aware of the potential problem?
- Who are the constituents or stakeholders of Goodlion Elementary?
- In what respects has the environmental uncertainty for Goodlion Elementary increased? Or has it?
- Can the information perspective be used to understand how this set of events arose?
- What resources might you gain/lose by meeting/ignoring the demands of the parents?
- What tactics might be used to limit the influence of the parents?
- What tactics might be used to minimize the effects on the teachers?
- Is it time to re-evaluate your reading program?
- Is it time to deinstitutionalize the reading program? Was it ever institutionalized?

Summary and Suggested Readings

Open-systems theory highlights the vulnerability and interdependence of school organizations and their environments. External environment is important because it affects the internal structures and processes of organizations. In this chapter, three perspectives of the environment have been presented. The first two—information and resource-dependence theory—are primarily concerned with the task or technical elements of the external environment that are potentially relevant to goal setting, goal achievement, effectiveness, and survival. These models emphasize that schools are created to perform some type of work and to achieve goals. The information perspective assumes that the environment is a source of information to be used by organizational decision makers. The resource-dependence approach assumes that organizations cannot generate internally the needed resources and that resources must come from the environment. In contrast, the third perspective—institutional theory—assumes that environments encourage schools to conform to powerful sets of rules and requirements that are imposed by the legal, social, professional, and political contexts of organizations. The essence of institutional theory is that the environment of schools presses more for form than substance. Nevertheless, technical and institutional environments do coexist; schools now function in relatively strong institutional but weak technical environments. Current drives for systemic reform and competitive markets suggest that worried businesspeople and policy makers may be seeking to place a heightened emphasis on task environments. A shift from primarily institutional to technical environments would shatter the rationalized myths and lead to fundamental changes in schools, a shift that will be bitterly fought by current institutional forces.

Because external environments can threaten organizational autonomy and effectiveness, administrators often try to minimize external effects on internal school operations. Their responses can be classified as either internal or interorganizational coping strategies. Internal coping strategies include buffering the technical core, planning and forecasting, adjusting internal processes, conforming to environmental expectations, and spanning organizational boundaries. Interorganization coping strategies include establishing favorable linkages with important external constituencies and shaping environmental elements through political action. By using the coping strategies, administrators can, to some degree, manage the environments of their schools.

To explore the information perspective in greater depth, a number of classic sources should be consulted—for example, Emery and Trist (1965), Thompson (1967), Lawrence and Lorsch (1967), and Terreberry (1968). To understand resource-dependence theory, one must read the work of Pfeffer (1972, 1981, 1982). Probably the most widely cited source for this perspective is by Pfeffer and Salancik (1978). To enter the literature on interest groups and influence processes, we recommend Baumgartner and Leech (1998) and Kollman (1998). Excellent sources for institutional theory are anthologies by Meyer and Scott (1983) and Powell and DiMaggio (1991). The latter collection includes the classic article by Meyer and Rowan (1977) and an updated version of a classic by DiMaggio and Powell (1983). In education, works by Rowan (1981, 1982, 1993), Rowan and Miskel (1999), Ogawa (1994), and Malen (1993) are particularly useful. Although scholarly work is evident for all three models, theoretical development and research seem most active for institutional theory.

Note

1. The primary proponent of resource-dependence theory has been Jeffrey Pfeffer. References to his work include the following: Pfeffer (1972, 1981, 1982, 1997); Pfeffer and Salancik (1978); Pfeffer and Leblebici (1973); and Aldrich and Pfeffer (1976). The present discussion of resource-dependence theory draws heavily from these sources.

Key Concepts and Ideas

Boundary spanning
Buffering
Coercive conformity
Competitive market
Decoupling
Dependence
Environmental complexity
Environmental stability
Environmental uncertainty
External environment
Imitative conformity
Influence tactics
Information perspective
Institution
Institutional environment
Institutional perspective
Interest groups
Munificence
Normative conformity
Planning and forecasting strategies
Rationalized myths
Resource-dependence perspective
Scarcity
Systemic reform
Task environment

CHAPTER 8

EFFECTIVENESS AND QUALITY OF SCHOOLS

From the position 30 years ago that "schools make no difference". . . there is now a widespread assumption internationally that schools affect children's development, that there are observable regularities in the schools that "add value" and the task of educational policies is to improve schools. . . .

David Reynolds and Charles Teddlie
The International Handbook of School Effectiveness

PREVIEW

1. Organizational effectiveness and quality are key concepts in open-systems theory.
2. The goal model and the system-resource model are two theoretical bases for making judgments and for taking actions necessary to work toward school effectiveness.
3. Within a goal model, schools are effective if the outcomes of their activities meet or exceed their organizational goals.
4. Within a system-resource model, schools are effective when they secure an advantageous bargaining position and acquire a disproportionate share of scarce and valued resources.
5. An integrated goal and system-resource model of organizational effectiveness emphasizes both the effectiveness and the quality of all aspects of the system. Time and multiple constituencies are also important dimensions of the model.
6. Three important performance outcome indicators of schools are academic achievement, job satisfaction, and perceived organizational effectiveness.
7. Pragmatic discussions of quality have begun to replace theoretical analyses of organizational effectiveness, but the constructs are complementary, not opposites.
8. The most popular approach to quality is total quality management or TQM.
9. Quality schools have as their purpose the continual improvement of learning and teaching.
10. Quality school administrators lead their schools by transforming their culture into one that emphasizes cooperation, trust, openness, and continuous improvement.

Issues of organizational effectiveness and quality represent fundamental challenges to practice in school administration. When educators, school patrons, or policy makers gather, school quality and effectiveness frequently drive the conversation. Terms such as "accountability," "academic achievement," "performance standards," "test scores," "teaching performance," "student dropout rates," "job satisfaction," and "productive learning culture" infuse these conversations. Education is certainly not devoid of effectiveness and quality indicators. Educators and the public acknowledge that different schools achieve different levels of success, even with similar student populations. On the basis of real or imagined information, parents decide, for example, to locate in a given area because they know that William Bennett Elementary emphasizes basic skills, and high academic expectations and standards, whereas John Dewey Elementary uses high-quality motivational and hands-on teaching methods. Moreover, schools report results to the public that educators believe represent their accomplishments and innovative practices. Patrons are invited to art shows, music performances, science fairs, and athletic events because these activities illustrate school quality and productivity. At the level of practice, effectiveness and quality indicators are known and used.

The practical interest in school effectiveness and quality issues intensified significantly during the 1980s. The *Nation at Risk* report in 1983 crystallized the performance problems of schools in the minds of Americans, especially business officials and policy makers. The public came to the clear recognition that the world economy had become intensely competitive, interdependent, and knowledge driven, that academic achievement levels in America's schools were not competitive internationally, and that societal demographics for the United States were changing in fundamental ways—for example, an aging population and an emerging multicultural citizenry. As a consequence the focus on school performance intensified and the concern continues today.

Issues of organizational effectiveness and quality also constitute key concepts in open-systems theory. In Chapter 1 (see Figures 1.2 and 1.5), we proposed an open social-systems framework of school organization using input, process, and output components. In Chapters 2 through 7, we made detailed analyses of five internal process elements—learning and teaching, structural, individual, cultural, and political—and the external environment of schools. As an overall generalization of open-systems theory, we stated that outputs of schools are a function of the interaction of structure, individual, culture, and politics as shaped and constrained by environmental forces. Moreover, school outputs constitute the performance outcomes of students, teachers, and administrators that can be used as indicators of organizational effectiveness and can be assessed for their quality.

During the last two decades of the twentieth century, organizational effectiveness became a premier concept in organizational theory. Kim S. Cameron and David A. Whetten (1996) observed, however, that the dominance of effectiveness in organizational sciences is being challenged by the construct of quality. As a fashionable, perhaps faddish, organizational performance concept, Cameron and Whetten document a fundamental shift away from effectiveness to quality. This shift can be seen in such popular books as *Theory Z* (Ouchi, 1981); *Out of Crisis* (Deming, 1986); and *In Search of Excellence* (Peters and Waterman, 1982). These books emphasize words such as "quality," "excellence," "continuous improvement," and "transformation" rather than organizational effectiveness. According to Cameron and Whetten, this shift in emphasis can be partly explained by a basic change of focus from abstract theoretical formulations of effectiveness to practical applications of quality in organizational studies. For example, concerns about a loss of economic competitiveness and unsatisfactory academic achievement in schools fueled the drive to find the best practices and ways to improve the quality of schools.

However, it is only the phrase "organizational effectiveness" that is getting less attention in contemporary scholarship and administrative practice and not the need to assess outcomes and to make appraisals about admirable practices. Indeed, the recent emphasis on standards and assessments as part of systemically reforming schools suggests that the drive for effectiveness has in fact intensified for educational organizations. Although "effectiveness" and "quality" are not synonyms, both are ways to describe and explain organizational performance. Therefore, we believe the concepts are complementary perspectives on school performance. Hence, we will use an open social-systems framework to present the major theoretical formulations and associated research for the concepts of both organizational effectiveness and quality.

Organizational Effectiveness of Schools

The concept of effectiveness is both the apex and the abyss in organizational analysis. It is the apex because all theories of organizational and administrative practices are ultimately aimed at identifying and producing effective performance. It is an abyss because the theories of organizational effectiveness and lists of criteria are neither necessary nor sufficient to evaluate the concept (Cameron, 1984). Both the importance and the confusion surrounding organizational effectiveness are apparent for schools. For example, when specific questions about effectiveness are raised, the controversy intensifies: What criteria? How are the criteria to be defined? Who determines the criteria? How are the indicators to be measured? Is effectiveness a short-term or a long-term phenomenon? How do you create effective schools?

To ask global questions about whether a school is effective or ineffective, however, is of limited value. Effectiveness is not one thing; hence, a one-dimensional definition is not adequate. Rather, a school or any other organization can be effective and ineffective. Without a theoretical guide, it is meaningless to claim that one school is more effective than another, to say that a given indicator is a measure of effectiveness, or to design ways to enhance school effectiveness. The goal model and the system-resource model are two theoretical guides for making these judgments and for taking the action necessary to work toward school effectiveness.[1]

Goal Model of Organizational Effectiveness

Traditionally organizational effectiveness has been defined in terms of the degree of goal attainment. Similar to the definition of individual goals in Chapter 4, organizational goals are simply the desired states that the organization is trying to attain. Within this model, goals and their relative accomplishment are essential in defining organizational effectiveness. Goals provide direction and reduce uncertainty for participants and represent standards for assessment of the organization. In a **goal model,** a school is effective if the outcomes of its activities meet or exceed its goals.

Types of Goals

In a goal model of organizational effectiveness, a distinction must be made between official and operative goals (Steers, 1977). **Official goals** are formal declarations of purpose by the board of education concerning the nature of the school's mission. These statements usually appear in board of education publications and faculty and staff handbooks. Official goals typically are abstract and ambitious (e.g., all students will achieve their full potential). They are usually timeless, and serve the purpose of securing support and legitimacy from the public for schools rather than for guiding the behavior of professional educators.

In contrast, **operative goals** reflect the true intentions of a school organization. That is, operative goals mirror the actual tasks and activities performed in the school irrespective of its claims. Hence, official goals in schools may be operative or inoperative depending on the extent to which they accurately represent actual educational practices. Some operative goals are widely published (e.g., efforts to place students with handicaps in regular classrooms), whereas others are not (e.g., efforts to provide custodial care of students for six to eight hours per day). In fact, attractive official goals in some districts act as expedient covers to less attractive operative goals such as racism and sexism.

Assumptions and Generalizations

Assumptions of the goal model of organizational effectiveness include the following.

- A rational group of decision makers sets the goals.
- The number of goals are few enough to be administered.
- The goals are clearly defined and understood by participants.
- The goals supply the criteria for evaluating effectiveness (Campbell, 1977; Scott, 1992).

Although decision makers obviously are not completely rational, these assumptions and the generalizations that flow from them should not be rejected without careful consideration. In fact, administrative practices have been developed to enhance goal specification and goal achievement. For example, setting individual goals (see Chapter 4) and instructional objectives for courses are used to specify the goals and criteria to judge their achievement. Similarly, state and local boards of education and administrators attempt to enhance goal attainment by centralizing and formalizing school organizations, by mandating curriculum standards, and by using assessment criteria and criterion-referenced tests. However, shortcomings of the goal concept and the goal model should be noted.

Criticisms of the Goal Approach

Cameron (1978) details the following criticisms of using goals to assess organization effectiveness:

- Too often the focus is on the administrators' goals rather than those set by teachers, students, parents, and other constituencies.
- The contradictory nature of multiple goals is frequently overlooked. For instance, educators are expected to maintain secure and orderly environments in schools, and at the same time, to develop the values of trust, group loyalty, and caring among students.
- Organizational goals are retrospective. They merely serve to justify school and educator action, not to direct it.
- Organizational goals are dynamic, whereas the goal model is static. Goals change as the situation and behavior vary, but the model remains the same.
- Official goals of the organization may not be its operative goals.

Given such strong criticisms, a persuasive argument can be formulated that a goal model of organizational effectiveness is inadequate. Indeed, a system-resource model has been proposed as an alternative approach to organizational effectiveness.

System-Resource Model of Organizational Effectiveness

Similar to the resource-dependence view of external environments (see Chapter 7), the **system-resource model** defines effectiveness as the organization's ability to secure an advantageous bargaining position in its environment and to capitalize on that position to acquire scarce and valued resources (Yuchtman and Seashore, 1967). The concept of bargaining position implies the exclusion of specific goals as ultimate effectiveness criteria. Rather, the system-resource model directs attention toward the more general capacity of the organization to procure assets. Consequently, this definition of effectiveness emphasizes the continuous, never-ending processes of exchange and competition for scarce and valued resources. This process is visible each time a state legislature meets to appropriate tax monies for schools. Educational organizations compete in an environment of state politics with transportation, social welfare, correctional, and other agencies and organizations to acquire the valued commodity of state aid. With the proposals for vouchers, charter schools, and alternative and choice schools, competition between public and private schools is likely to increase. When public school enrollments decline and the employment prospects weaken for educators, competition for students intensifies. According to the system-resource model, the most effective schools sustain growth or minimize decline by advantageous bargaining with parents, students, and legislators. Hence, the criterion for effectiveness becomes the organization's ability to acquire resources.

Assumptions and Generalizations

The system-resource model contains several implicit assumptions (Yuchtman and Seashore, 1967; Campbell, 1977; Goodman and Pennings, 1977):

- The organization is an open system that exploits its external environment.
- Harmony within the system improves performance.
- Organizations compete for scarce resources.
- An organization of any size faces such complex demands that defining a small number of meaningful goals may be impossible.

It follows that for the organization to increase its effectiveness, the internal elements of bureaucratic expectations, group culture, political expectations, and individual need to work more harmoniously to exploit the environment. Educational administrators, for instance, place great importance on maintaining harmony because conflict impedes the system's ability to garner resources. In schools, as in all organizations, the quality levels of internal processes and performance outputs are clearly connected (Cameron and Whetten, 1996).

Because of their dependence on environmental forces, organizations must concentrate on adaptive functions to compete successfully for resources. From the system-resource perspective, effective organizations are those with sensitive monitoring mechanisms that provide information about new behavior that can lead to the acquisition of more assets. Hence, the primary criteria for assessing organizational effectiveness from a system-resource perspective are the consistency of the internal processes and structures and the ability to monitor and adapt to environmental constraints.

Criticisms of the System-Resource Approach

The system-resource model of organizational effectiveness also has alleged defects, especially when applied to educational organizations (Cameron, 1978; Scott, 1977; Steers, 1977; Kirchhoff, 1977):

- Too much emphasis on acquiring resources may have damaging effects on outcomes. For example, in order to stem declining enrollments, public and private schools might engage in intense and expensive competition for students that compromises program rigor and quality.
- Too much stress on inputs masks the importance of outcomes.

- The system-resource model is actually a goal model in which the operative goal is acquiring resources. Thus, the differences between the goal and the system-resource approaches may represent an argument over goals and semantics.

In other words, the system-resource model actually verifies the operative goal concept and the two approaches are complementary (Steers, 1977). Indeed, a possible, even highly desirable approach is to combine the two perspectives.

An Integrated Goal and System-Resource Model of Effectiveness

Both the goal and system-resource models share the crucial assumption that it is possible and desirable to develop a single set of evaluative criteria, and therefore, a single statement of organizational effectiveness (Connolly, Conlon, and Deutsch, 1980). In the goal model, effectiveness is defined in terms of the relative attainment of feasible objectives that can be exchanged for other resources. The resource model, based on the open-systems perspective, places great value on the harmonious operations of the organization's internal components; the ability to monitor and adapt to the environment; and the optimization of such administrative processes as deciding, communicating, motivating and leading people.

Several theorists (Goodman and Pennings, 1977; Steers, 1977; Campbell, 1977) have attempted to integrate the two approaches, and although their ideas differ slightly, they agree that the use of goals cannot be avoided. Behavior is explicitly or implicitly goal directed, and organizational functioning is no exception. However, from a system-resource framework, goals become more diverse and dynamic; they are not static, ultimate states, but are subject to change over relatively short periods of time. Moreover, the attainment of some short-term goals can represent new resources to achieve subsequent goals. Thus, when a systems framework is used, a cyclic nature characterizes goals.

In order to convey an understanding of the subtle nuances of organizational effectiveness, an integrated model must address three important characteristics—time, multiple constituencies, and multiple criteria.

Time

A neglected factor in the study of organizations and the assessment of their effectiveness is time. Yet issues of time are absolutely of central importance (Bluedorn and Denhardt, 1988). Martin Burlingame (1979) speaks of the rhythm of seasons; that is, clear cycles characterize the school calendar—the year begins in the fall, breaks for a holiday in the winter, and ends in the late spring. Educators know that certain times of the school year hold greater potential for crises, disruption of the system, and reduced goal attainment. The last few days of the school year, for example, provide conditions for chaos. Knowing this, educators develop coping mechanisms to handle these short-term performance problems, such as strict interpretation of discipline rules, field trips, and other special activities.

The time dimension in a model of organizational effectiveness can be conceptualized with a continuum of success ranging from the short to the long term. For schools, representative indicators of short-term effectiveness include student scores on achievement tests, faculty morale, and job satisfaction. Criteria for intermediate success encompass adaptability of the school organization and instructional programs, career advancement of educators, and success of the former students. From the system-resource framework, the ultimate long-term criterion is survival of the organization. Declining enrollments, school closings, and consolidation of small school districts represent long-term problems of survival. To illustrate this point, Emil J. Haller and David H. Monk (1988) found that between 1930 and 1988 the number of school districts in the United States declined from 128,000 to 14,000. Just during the 1960s, the number of school districts was halved.

Another influence of time is that the criteria for organizational effectiveness do not remain constant. As constituencies change their preferences, new constraints and expectations evolve to define school effectiveness. During the 1970s, for example, schools emphasized socioemotional growth of students and equity, but with the reform reports of the early 1980s, the public started to demand that efficiency, academic achievement, and employment skills be emphasized (Bacharach, 1988; Wimpelberg, Teddlie, and Stringfield, 1989). Based on state-mandated curriculum standards and tests, many schools currently emphasize basic skills, thinking, and problem-solving abilities so that their graduates can advance the nation's pragmatic economic goals well into the twenty-first century.

In sum, performance that is effective today is likely to be ineffective tomorrow as preferences and constraints change (Cameron, 1984). Therefore, the goal of the effective school is, continually, to *become* effective rather than *be* effective (Zammuto, 1982). Hence, when discussing school effectiveness, the dimension of time is an essential component.

Multiple Constituencies

A **constituency** is a group of individuals within or outside who hold similar preferences or interests about the activities and outcomes of an organization (Cameron, 1978; Tsui, 1990). Effectiveness criteria always reflect the values and biases of multiple constituencies or stakeholders. For organizations like schools, with multiple constituencies, effectiveness criteria typically are drawn from many interest groups. That is, multiple stakeholders play critical roles in defining and assessing the goals (Connolly, Conlon, and Deutsch, 1980). The debate to define school effectiveness has been joined by parents, administrators, students, teachers, school board members, businesspeople, politicians, governmental officials, news media, and taxpayers. To say the least, this list depicts a diverse set of interest groups. In terms of a political model of organizations (Kanter and Brinkerhoff, 1981), schools can be viewed as battlegrounds where stakeholders compete to influence the criteria for effectiveness in ways that will advance their own interests. Consequently, effectiveness becomes less a scientific and more a political concept.

As a further complicating factor, constituent groups actively prefer different criteria (Hall, 1980; Kanter and Brinkerhoff, 1981; Scott, 1992). For example, administrators and board of education members emphasize input resources and structural indicators of effectiveness such as available facilities and their use, amount of financial resources, and personnel practices. These are important in part because they are factors under administrative control. In contrast, teachers emphasize the processes of educational effectiveness. They argue that effectiveness must be conceived in terms of the quality and appropriateness of their instructional methods. Students, taxpayers, and politicians, however, focus primarily on outcomes and efficiency measures. They evaluate schools in terms of academic achievement, the values of graduates, and cost per student.

Therefore, a combination of the goal and system-resource models requires the inclusion of multiple constituencies who define and evaluate school effectiveness using a variety of criteria. The relativistic approach (Keeley, 1984) assumes that multiple statements about organizational effectiveness are not only possible but also necessary because stakeholders in and around schools require different kinds of effectiveness measures. No single effectiveness indicator, or a simple, general list, will suffice (Kanter and Brinkerhoff, 1981), and power and politics affect both the definition and the measurement of effectiveness.

Multiple Criteria

A basic assumption throughout this discussion has been that organizational effectiveness is a many-faceted concept—that is, models must include multiple criteria. No single ultimate criterion such as student achievement or overall performance can capture the complex nature of school effectiveness. Choosing the most appropriate and representative effectiveness variables can be an overwhelming task. For instance, John P. Campbell (1977) used 30 categories for a comprehensive list of organizational effectiveness indicators. Similarly, Steers (1975) found 15 different criteria in a sample of only 17 studies of effectiveness.

The development of a multidimensional index or composite measure of organizational effectiveness requires the selection of key concepts. The open-systems perspective developed in Chapter 1 can be employed to guide the choice of effectiveness criteria or goals in the combined goal and system-resource approach. Effectiveness indicators can be derived for each phase of the open-systems cycle—inputs (human and financial resources), transformations (internal processes and structures), and outputs (performance outcomes).[2] This point is illustrated by considering each phase of the open-systems cycle as a category of effectiveness indicators.

Performance outcomes constitute the quantity of the school's services and products for students, educators, and other constituents and the quality of each output. These are the effects of the organization. Examples of outcome indicators are academic achievement, job satisfaction, teacher and student attitudes, student dropout rates, teacher absenteeism levels, employee commitment to the organization, and society's perceptions of school effectiveness. Scott (1992) observes that outcomes are frequently considered the quintessential criteria of effectiveness.

Structure and process criteria are the quantity, quality, and harmony of the internal processes and structures that transform the inputs to outcomes. System harmony among the internal elements is a key in acquiring external resources and transforming the resources to performance outcomes. Performance outcomes reflect effects; transformation resonates effort (Scott, 1992; Cameron and Whetten, 1996). Examples of structural criteria include congruence among the organizational, individual, cultural, and political systems. Process criteria include the health of the interpersonal climate, motivation levels of students and teachers, teacher and administrator leadership, and quality-control procedures such as the number of tests given, quality of teaching, use of instructional technology, and personnel evaluations. These throughput criteria are directly related to performance outcomes. Thus, schools characterized by positive internal criteria should produce high-performance outcomes (Ostroff and Schmitt, 1993).

Input criteria (see Figure 1.5) are the school's beginning capacity and potential for effective performance. These include all environmental constraints such as state and local educational policies and standards, organizational features, or participant characteristics understood to influence organizational effectiveness (Scott, 1992). Examples of input criteria are wealth of the school district, abilities of students, capabilities of the faculty and administration, parental support, number of volumes in the library, quality and quantity of instructional technology, and condition of the physical facilities. Input criteria do not indicate either the amount or quality of the work performed, but rather they set the limits for the transformation and outcomes of the system.

Virtually every input, transformation, or outcome variable can be and has been used as an indicator of goal or resource effectiveness. The next step is to combine the time, constituency, and effectiveness criteria into a coherent formulation.

Integrating Time, Multiple Constituencies, and Multiple Criteria: A Goal and System-Resource Model

The results of merging the general dimensions, specific criteria or indicators, and other perspectives of effectiveness are summarized in Figure 8.1. Consequently, an integrated **goal and system-resource model** uses specific indicators of the input, throughput, or outcome concepts as operative goals and combines them with the time frame and constituencies applicable to each indicator.

As illustrated in Figure 8.1, the result is a more comprehensive theoretical formulation for defining the quality and effectiveness of schools. To apply this model of organizational effectiveness to schools, a series of steps must be taken.

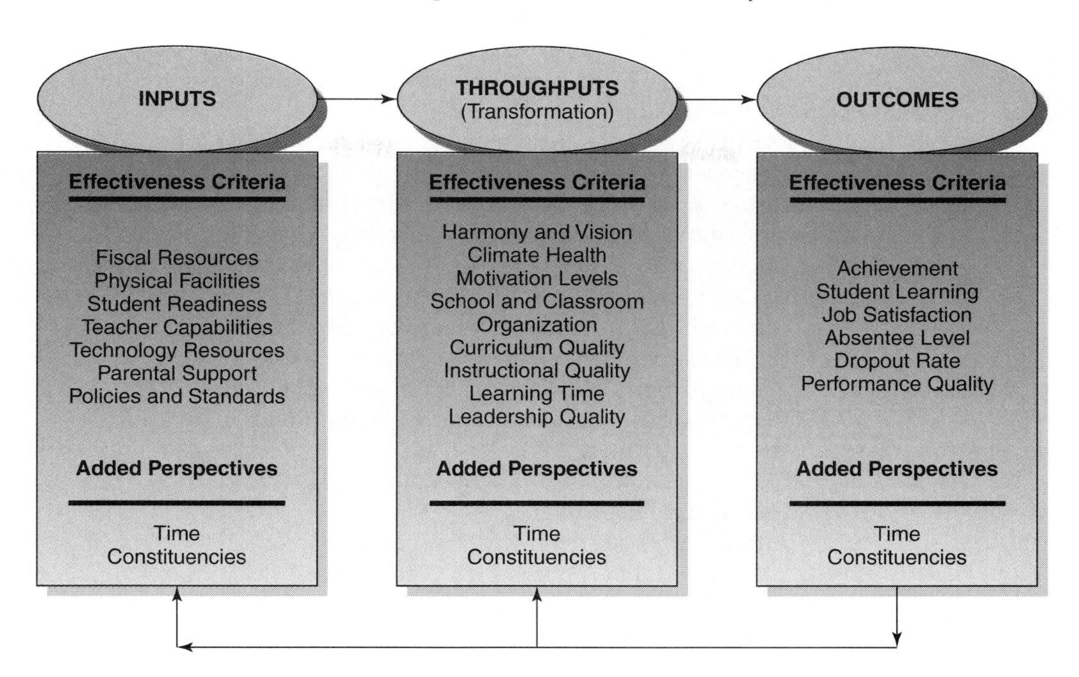

FIGURE 8.1 *Integrated Model of Organizational Effectiveness*

- Constituencies who would define the important operative goals must be identified.
- Time dimensions (e.g., short term, medium term, long term) must be specified.
- Criterion indicators for each of the three systems' phases must be selected.

For example, an assessment of short-term and intermediate-term school effectiveness from the perspective of students might be teacher quality, strength of culture, academic achievement, and student satisfaction with instruction.

THREE OUTCOME CRITERIA

Several of the concepts that have been suggested as indicators of organizational effectiveness have been given detailed attention in earlier chapters. Three important performance outcome indicators of schools have not yet been discussed—academic achievement, job satisfaction, and overall perceptions of school effectiveness. These concepts will now be considered systematically.

Academic Achievement

Many parents and other citizens, government policy makers, and scholars define organizational effectiveness narrowly; they equate school effectiveness with academic achievement. Although most acknowledge other criteria, they typically ignore the school's role in developing creativity, self-confidence, aspirations, and expectation—all of which are needed for future success in school and adult life.

Two apparent reasons help explain the overreliance on standardized test scores as measures of achievement. The first is political and the second practical. On the political side, a number of important educational constituencies—students, parents, and business leaders—see test scores as having intrinsic value. On the practical side, with the emphasis by policy makers on curriculum standards and assessments, student achievement data are readily available and widely and publicly measured. Even though expediency, rather than theory, has too often guided research on school effectiveness, student achievement remains one of the important performance indicators and should not be neglected. Two research approaches dominate the study of cognitive achievement.

Input-Output Research

Input-output, or production-function, research became popular in the mid-1960s. Developed by economists to predict the output of a system using sets of input variables, the underlying model is forthright (Hanushek, 1989). The **production-function model** assumes that performance output of the educational process is related directly to a series of inputs. For schools, the input groups usually are classified as family resources, school resources, community characteristics, student resources, and peer group characteristics, whereas the outputs are scores on achievement tests (Lau, 1978). The purpose of production-function research is to predict an outcome rather than to explain how the result was produced. In terms of the open-systems model, production-function research ignores the system's internal transformational process and uses only inputs to predict outputs.

James S. Coleman and his associates (1966) conducted the most influential educational study reflecting this approach, *Equality of Educational Opportunity.* Popularly known as the Coleman Report, it remains the largest survey of American public education ever undertaken. Nationally, 645,000 students completed standardized ability and achievement tests as well as forms to describe their family backgrounds. Approximately 60,000 teachers responded to questionnaires about their educational experiences, teaching tenure, attitudes, and verbal ability. Finally, data on a variety of organizational input or capacity variables, including class size, school organization, libraries, and laboratory facilities, were collected from over 4,000 schools. The most surprising finding was the role the school-capacity variables had in predicting pupil achievement. When home background variables were controlled, school factors showed limited relationships to test scores. What mattered most were not the characteristics of the school but the students' home backgrounds before entering the school and their peers in school.

Since the Coleman Report, a large number of additional production-function studies have been conducted and several excellent reviews of this literature are available.[3] Eric A. Hanushek (1989) concludes that two decades of production-function research in education has produced startlingly consistent results—variations in school expenditures are not systematically related to variations in student performance. The factors that he examined were: teacher/pupil ratio, teacher education, experience, salary, expenditures per pupil, administrative inputs, and facilities. After updating his earlier findings, Hanushek (1997) came to the same conclusion—schools are inefficient organizations because there is no strong or consistent relationship between variations in school resources and student performance. Stated simply, production-function research finds little evidence to support the idea that spending additional money on current schools will improve student learning.

In an effort to clarify or counter Hanushek's conclusions, Albert Shanker (1989) maintains that the "facts" in this type of research do not necessarily speak for themselves. In response to the finding that pupil/teacher ratio does not make a difference, Shanker explains that this ratio is not the same thing as class size. Large numbers of teachers do not regularly work with children because they are assigned to duties that make little difference to student achievement. Indeed, J. D. Finn and Charles M. Achilles (1999) report that powerful findings from Tennessee's Project STAR clearly show that small classes in kindergarten through the third grade are academically beneficial, especially to minority and inner-city children. In regard to production-function studies, Shanker makes two conclusions: they do not make the case that money and other resources do not matter in education; and they should not be dismissed. Rather, he believes that the research should give pause to those who insist that more money for doing the same things the same way will improve student achievement. Instead, Shanker and Hanushek contend that to improve organizational effectiveness significantly, fundamental changes must occur in the way schools are organized and operated.

Although production-function research has been plagued by inconsistent and insignificant results (Monk, 1992), the studies still leave little doubt that learning in the home is extremely important. No matter how they are measured, differences in socioeconomic background of the family lead to significant differences in student achievement. A reasonable interpretation is that measures of socioeconomic status are proxies for the quality of the learning environment in the home—nutrition, physical surroundings, parental attitudes, education, and so forth. Even so, little room for doubt exists that differences among schools and teachers also produce important changes in academic achievement. Schools are not homogeneous in their effects on students; schools differ in the effectiveness of their efforts to influence achievement test scores. As Steven T. Bossert (1988) maintains, input-output studies typically do not consider how students actually use resources that are available in the school. On the basis of reasoning similar to Shanker's and Bossert's, a new line of inquiry emerged that was designed to explain how home, school, and internal-system factors influence academic achievement.

Input-Throughput-Output Research

If the findings are accepted from production-function research that home factors explain as well as predict student achievement, building a case for additional resources from the external environment to provide more teachers, better facilities, new curricula, and staff development becomes exceedingly difficult. Reacting to this realization and wanting to improve academic achievement in low-income, largely minority schools, educational researchers developed a new line of inquiry during the mid-1970s (Cuban, 1984; Reynolds and Teddlie, 2000). Using a system's perspective, input-throughput-output research not only considers inputs but relates such throughputs as classroom practices (instructional methods, classroom organization, opportunities to learn, time to learn), school climate or culture, organizational operations, and political relationships to a variety of outputs, including student achievement on standardized tests. This general approach has been called various names, including process-product research, systems research, and organizational research, but the most commonly used designation is **effective-schools research.** A number of excellent descriptions, analyses, and reviews of this literature have been published.[4]

Scholars have deduced what they believe are the few critical school factors for enhancing scores on standardized tests. As popularized by Ronald Edmonds (1979), most educators became familiar with his five-factor effective-schools formula:

- Strong leadership by the principal, especially in instructional matters.
- High expectations by teachers for student achievement.
- An emphasis on basic skills.
- An orderly environment.
- Frequent, systematic evaluations of students.

Bossert (1988); Terry A. Astuto and David L. Clark (1985b); and Wimpelberg, Teddlie, Stringfield (1989); and Jaap Scheerens and Roel Bosker (1997) derive similar lists from the research. S. C. Purkey and Marshall S. Smith (1983) suggest a larger number of school factors. The factors from the reviews by Edmonds, Purkey and Smith, and Scheerens and Bosker are summarized in Table 8.1.

Stated simply, effective-schools research had a tremendous impact on school practice during the 1980s and its influence continues to be strongly felt. Good and Brophy (1986) and Stedman (1987) provide summaries of a number of the school improvement programs—for example, Project RISE in Milwaukee and School Improvement Project in New York City—that are based on this body of research. Other programs were initiated in Atlanta, Chicago, Minneapolis, Pittsburgh, San Diego, St. Louis, Washington, D.C., and many, many other smaller school districts (Cuban, 1984). Nevertheless, the results of these efforts to apply a formula for changing a limited number of school factors to improve academic performance has produced mixed results. According to Brophy and Good, Project RISE appears to have achieved some success. The scores on the achievement tests did improve to an extent, especially in some schools and in the area of mathematics. Stedman takes a more critical stance on Project RISE. Although some schools did improve their math scores, most RISE schools continued to do poorly in reading.

TABLE 8.1

Three Sets of Factors in the Effective-Schools Formula

Edmonds	Smith and Purkey	Scheerens and Bosker
• Principal leadership	• Instructional leadership	• Achievement orientation
• Emphasis on basic skills	• Planned and purposeful curriculum	• Educational leadership
• High expectations for student achievement	• Clear goals and high expectations	• Consensus and cohesion
• Frequent and systematic evaluation of students	• Time on task	• Curriculum quality/opportunity to learn
• Orderly environment	• Recognition of academic success	• School climate
	• Orderly climate	• Classroom climate
	• Sense of community	• Parental involvement
	• Staff development	• Evaluative potential
	• Staff stability	• Effective learning time
	• Collegial and collaborative planning	• Structured instruction
	• School site management	• Independent learning
	• Parental support and involvement	• Adaptive instruction
	• Direct support	• Feedback and reinforcement

Moreover, those schools that achieved success often did so by teaching to the test. In a similar vein, Cuban (1983, 1984) cautioned that rushing to implement the changes called for by the effective-schools advocates would produce significant problems and unanticipated consequences.

During the last decade, Charles Teddlie and David Reynolds (2000) report that substantial conceptual and empirical progress has been made in understanding and explaining effective schools. The emergent theoretical models add specificity about inputs and transformational processes, how they interact in schools, and how their relationships with outcomes vary across different settings or contexts. In particular, the concept of context has been broadened. Instead of considering only urban inner-city school settings, the contexts of effective-schools research now include public and private elementary, middle, and secondary schools from communities with all social classes in rural, urban, and suburban settings, and levels of support. The current effective-school models and research not only focus on schools serving all types of students in all types of contexts, but also emphasize school improvement across all contexts. Moreover, with the improved research methods, the findings clearly show that schools can make a difference.

Indeed, school effectiveness is starting to be conceptualized as sets of interacting variables such as those shown in our integrated model of organizational effectiveness (see Figure 8.1) and a number of similar models reviewed by Scheerens and Bosker (1997). For example, we all know that schools serve students who differ enormously on factors such as initial educational attainments, family structure, and social and economic status. Peter Mortimore (1998) contends that effectiveness models and research must account fully for these initial differences when comparing the effects of individual schools on the progress and development of their students. Because recent research developments can now account for initial student differences, he asserts that effective schools are those that succeed with their students whatever their initial characteristics. That is, Mortimore (1993) defines effective schools as ones in which students progress further than might be expected from their characteristics at entry. Similarly, transformational processes have been elaborated to explain how they can promote learning. For example, instructional or teaching quality of schools depends on factors such as teacher expectations for achievement and how well knowledge (e.g., subject matter, curriculum, pedagogical) and skills (e.g., presentational, classroom management, assessment) are used in the classrooms. Likewise, strong, positive leadership is important. However, the effects of leaders such as principals on school effectiveness are not as direct as early writers such as Edmonds have portrayed them.

Principal Effects

Bossert (1988) identified four characteristics that are typically associated with principals who administer effective schools. These factors are goals and production emphasis, power and strong decision making, effective management, and strong human relations skills. The results are not as clear as some proponents of the effective-schools programs claim. For instance, Good and Brophy (1986) assert that nearly all studies of effective schools support the importance of principal leadership, but limited accord exists on the behaviors and practices that characterize leadership for enhanced academic achievement. In an even stronger assessment, Bossert (1988) maintains that effective-schools studies have tried to resurrect the bureaucratic ideal by stating that strong principal leadership is needed in order to structure schools for effectiveness. However, the research is silent on which processes must be structured and which structures need to be created to produce success. Similarly, Philip Hallinger and Ronald H. Heck (1996, 1998) conclude that principal leadership has measurable influence on student achievement. The effects, however, are indirect and occur when principals manipulate internal school structures, processes and visions that are directly connected to student learning. They further assert that just because the effects of principals are mediated by other school factors does not diminish the importance of principal contributions to school effectiveness.

From the effective-schools research, two generalizations regarding principals are supported—administrative behaviors are important to school effectiveness, and no single style of leadership appears appropriate for all schools (Bossert, Dwyer, Rowan, and Lee, 1982). Effectiveness depends on the appropriate matching of such situational variables as the shape of the administrative hierarchy and organization of the curricular program with the leadership style of the principal. More specifically, Valerie E. Lee, Anthony S. Bryk, and Julia B. Smith (1993) propose three functional roles principals play in effective secondary schools:

- *Administration:* Allocating resources, developing and enforcing policies and procedures, and supervising professional development.
- *Mediation:* Helping communication to internal and external constituencies and buffering the teachers from environmental disturbances.
- *Leadership:* Shaping school goals and guiding instructional processes.

Although standardized achievement tests contain conceptual, empirical, and political traps for educators, they constitute essential ingredients of school effectiveness. Moreover, the interrelationships among school inputs, transformation, and such outcomes as academic achievement are highly complex. Another performance outcome, job satisfaction, is less controversial than student achievement, although it too is little understood.

Job Satisfaction

The formal study of job satisfaction did not start until the Hawthorne studies in the early 1930s (see Chapter 1). However, even prior to those studies, scientific managers had implicitly recognized the concept in conjunction with worker fatigue. Since the 1930s, job satisfaction probably has been the most extensively and enthusiastically studied concept in organizational science. C. J. Cranny, Patricia Cain Smith, and Eugene F. Stone (1992) estimate that over 5,000 articles, books, and dissertations have been published on the subject. From 1984 to 1996, more than 300 works per year were published (Spector, 1997).

Why does job satisfaction continue to attract so much interest? Paul E. Spector (1997) gives three reasons—utilitarian, humanitarian, and organizational effectiveness. Early human relations proponents held that happy workers behave positively and are productive. During the 1960s and 1970s, a general concern for the quality of working life emerged with the proposition that people deserve to be treated fairly and with respect (U.S. Department of Health, Education and Welfare, 1973). To some extent, job satisfaction is an indicator of good treatment. Finally, job satisfaction can reflect how well the school organization is functioning. Differences among schools in job satisfaction levels of teachers can be diagnostic of potential trouble spots.

Definition

The classic attempt to define job satisfaction was made in 1935 by Robert Hoppock. He cautioned about the difficulty of formulating an adequate definition because of the limited amount of knowledge then available on the subject. Nevertheless, he defined job satisfaction as any combination of psychological, physiological, and environmental circumstances that cause a person to say, "I am satisfied with my job." That is, job satisfaction is the extent to which people like their jobs (Spector, 1997). Among scholars, general agreement seems to have emerged that **job satisfaction** is an affective or emotional reaction to a job that results from the employee's comparing actual outcomes to desired, expected, or deserved outcomes (Cranny, Smith, and Stone, 1992).

Situational Model of Job Satisfaction

The **situational model of job satisfaction** relates combinations of task, organizational, and personal variables to indicators of job satisfaction (Glisson and Durick, 1988; Quarstein, McAfee, and Glassman, 1992; Agho, Mueller, and Price, 1993). As shown in Figure 8.2, this contingency perspective generally divides the variables into three groups: (1) characteristics of the work organization (e.g., centralization, professionalism, leadership, feedback, culture, communication); (2) characteristics of the job tasks (e.g., autonomy, pay and other benefits, significance, challenge, variety); and (3) characteristics of the employees (e.g., age, gender, education, motivation, ability, predisposition to be happy). The general hypothesis explains job satisfaction by combining the critical variables suggested in the social-systems model (see Chapter 1). Several excellent reviews of the research testing the general situational model are available (e.g., Locke 1976; Holdaway 1978a, 1978b; Rice 1978). David P. Thompson, James F. McNamara, and John Hoyle (1997) found support for the situational model of job satisfaction. A brief review of selected findings follows.

After reviewing the literature, Ratsoy (1973) concluded that teacher job satisfaction, in general, is lower in schools where the teachers perceive a high degree of bureaucracy. Other evidence, however, suggests that this statement is too general. When specific bureaucratic dimensions of schools are related to job satisfaction, a complex picture emerges. Bureaucratic factors that enhance status differences among the professionals, such as the hierarchy of authority and centralization, produce low satisfaction levels. But factors that clarify the job and yield equal applications of school policy promote high levels of satisfaction (Carpenter, 1971; Gerhardt, 1971; Grassie and Carss, 1973;

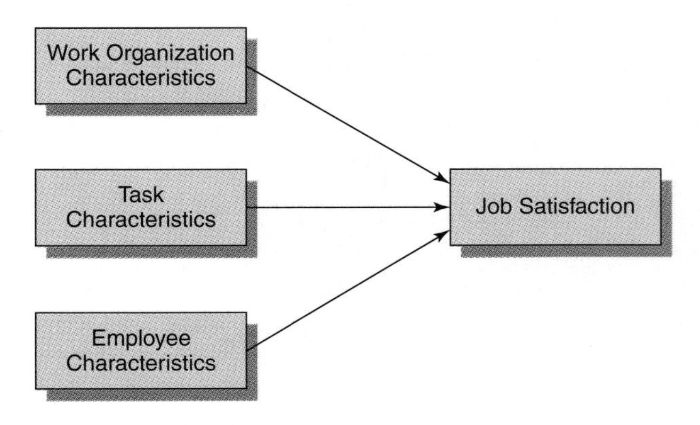

FIGURE 8.2 ***Situational Model of Job Satisfaction***

Miskel, Fevurly, and Stewart, 1979). Findings from a recent review indicate that role conflict and role ambiguity are the strongest and negative predictors of educator job satisfaction (Thompson, McNamara, and Hoyle, 1997). Indeed, Richard R. Verdugo and his colleagues (1997) found that as teachers' perceptions of legitimacy of their schools' governance structure increases, their job satisfaction increases.

Leadership, decision making, and communication processes also influence job satisfaction. The nature of the relationships between teachers and administrators and the quality of leadership correlate highly with teacher satisfaction. Greater participation in decision making, especially concerning instructional methods, yields enhanced teacher job satisfaction (Belasco and Allutto, 1972; Mohrman, Cooke, and Mohrman, 1978). Moreover, the lack of opportunities to participate in decision making is the greatest source of teacher dissatisfaction (Holdaway, 1978b). Finally, the quality of the communication processes also relates to overall teacher job satisfaction (Nicholson, 1980). Communicating clearly to employees the scope of the job, how their contributions are related to the school's goals, and how they are being judged, for instance, are positively correlated with job satisfaction.

The jobs and tasks of both teachers and administrators have long been characterized as offering variety, complexity and the potential to be interesting and satisfying. In educational settings, studies of specific job characteristics and job satisfaction are rare. Spector (1997) notes, however, Hackman and Oldham's (1976, 1980) theory (see Chapter 4) offers a good way to link job characteristics and satisfaction. Relatively strong support has been found for the hypothesis that the five job characteristics listed by Hackman and Oldham—autonomy, feedback, skill variety, task identity, and task significance—are positively related to job satisfaction.

Work motivation is also consistently correlated with job satisfaction. Expectancy motivation is related to teacher job satisfaction; teachers who believe that they have the capabilities to do the job and envision positive consequences for their efforts will generally have high levels of satisfaction (Miskel, DeFrain, and Wilcox, 1980; Miskel, McDonald, and Bloom, 1983). Similarly, as the organizational climates of schools become more open or participative (see Chapter 5), the level of teacher satisfaction increases (Grassie and Carss, 1973; Miskel, Fevurly, and Stewart, 1979). Similar to the conclusions of Spector (1997), Thompson, McNamara, and Hoyle (1997) found only limited relationships between demographic variables (e.g., age, gender) and job satisfaction.

We conclude from this brief overview that interest in job satisfaction has been high among scholars in educational administration. Moreover, useful models and widely applicable findings for job satisfaction are available to guide research and to inform administrative practice.

Perceived Organizational Effectiveness

To formulate a model of **perceived organizational effectiveness,** Paul E. Mott (1972) combined several important performance outcomes—quantity of the product, quality of the product, efficiency, adaptability, and flexibility.

Mott reasoned that these five criteria define the ability of an organization to mobilize its centers of power for action to achieve goals and to adapt. Effective schools produce higher student achievement, generate more positive student attitudes, adapt better to environmental constraints, and deal more potently with internal problems. Clearly, Mott's perspective is consistent with the integrated goal and system-resource model of organizational effectiveness developed in this chapter.

Although we have cautioned against single indicators, a short global measure based strongly in a theoretical model and used with other instruments can begin to improve our understanding of organizational effectiveness. Mott developed an eight-item measure for use in a variety of organizational settings, which has been modified for studies in schools (Miskel, Fevurly, and Stewart 1979; Miskel, Bloom, and McDonald, 1983). The resultant *index of perceived organizational effectiveness* (IPOE) is shown in Table 8.2. Its careful adaptation to school situations makes it a strong candidate for use as an overall measure in future studies; in fact, Mott concludes that the subjective evaluations of employees provide a fairly valid measure of organizational effectiveness. Supporting this conclusion, Wayne K. Hoy and Judith Ferguson (1985) found that perceived overall effectiveness of secondary schools was significantly related to four sets of school output variables.

Mott (1972) has made extensive use of the index of perceived organizational effectiveness. In highly centralized organizations, effectiveness tended to be lower. Moreover, effectiveness was greater when the leaders provided more structure for the tasks to be done and when the climate was open. Findings in the school setting by Miskel, Fevurly, and Stewart (1979) support Mott's conclusions. Formalization and complexity of the school structure and participative climates are conducive to organizational effectiveness. Similarly, Miskel, McDonald, and Bloom (1983) found that high organizational effectiveness as perceived by teachers is associated with strong linkages to the principal in the area of student discipline, support from special-education experts, time for classroom activities, and high-expectancy motivation. Supportive of the foregoing results, Connie S. Logan, Chad D. Ellett, and Joseph Licata (1993) found that structural coupling, robustness, academic achievement, and student attendance were related to perceived organizational effectiveness as measured by the IPOE. Finally, Cynthia L. Uline, Daniel M. Miller, and Megan Tschannen-Moran (1998) found that expressive activities (i.e., teacher trust in colleagues and principals and healthy school climate) and instrumental activities (i.e., achievement in reading, math, and writing) are related to perceived organizational effectiveness of schools.

It is clear from what has been said thus far that many variables are needed to assess adequately the complex effects of organizational and administrative processes on school effectiveness. Although the knowledge of organizational effectiveness remains somewhat limited, it is being indirectly expanded by the tremendous attention on organizational quality.

TABLE 8.2

The Index of Perceived Organizational Effectiveness

Every educator produces something during work. It may be a "product" or a "service." The following list of products and services are just a few of the things that result from efforts in schools:

Lesson plans	Student learning	Athletic achievements
Community projects	Instruction	Art and music programs
New curricula	Teacher-parent meetings	Classroom activities

Please indicate your responses by checking the appropriate line for each item.

1. Of the various things produced by the people you know *in your school,* how *much* are they producing?
   _____ Low production _____ Moderate
   _____ High _____ Fairly low
   _____ Very high production
2. How good is the *quality* of the products or services produced by the people you know in your school?
   _____ Poor quality _____ Fair quality
   _____ Good quality _____ Low quality
   _____ Excellent quality
3. Do the people in your school get maximum output from the available resources (money, people, equipment, etc.)? That is, how *efficiently* do they do their work?
   _____ Not efficiently
   _____ Fairly efficiently
   _____ Not too efficiently
   _____ Very efficiently
   _____ Extremely efficiently
4. How good a job is done by the people in your school in *anticipating* problems and preventing them from occurring or minimizing their effect?
   _____ A poor job _____ A fair job
   _____ A very good job _____ An adequate job
   _____ An excellent job
5. How *informed* are the people in your school about innovations that could affect the way they do their work?
   _____ Uninformed _____ Very informed
   _____ Informed _____ Somewhat informed
   _____ Moderately informed
6. When changes are made in the methods, routines, or equipment, how *quickly* do the people in your school accept and adjust to the changes?
   _____ Very slowly _____ Fairly rapidly
   _____ Rapidly _____ Rather slowly
   _____ Immediately
7. How *many* of the people in your school readily accept and adjust to the changes?
   _____ Many less than half
   _____ Nearly everyone
   _____ The majority
   _____ Less than half
   _____ Many more than half
8. How good a job do the people in your school do in *coping* with emergencies and disruptions?
   _____ A poor job _____ A fair job
   _____ A good job _____ An adequate job
   _____ An excellent job

Quality of Schools

Depending on your perspective, models of quality either have begun to replace or add to theories of organizational effectiveness. The most widely used definition of **quality** is the extent to which a product or service meets or exceeds customer or client expectations (Reeves and Bednar, 1994). From a policy maker's point of view, an example for educational settings would be the degree to which schools are meeting or exceeding state standards for academic achievement. Similar to the integrated model of effectiveness (see Figure 8.1), the notion of quality is more than just outcomes or products. Rather, it deals with the quality of the system and all its components; hence, researchers and practitioners are interested in the quality of inputs and processes as well as the quality of outputs. **Total quality management (TQM)** is the most popular example of the quality movement.

Total Quality Management

Barbara A. Spencer (1994) characterizes TQM as a comprehensive set of management ideas, which emphasize or promote quality in organizations. Its goal is to make quality enhancement the governing priority of the organizations and one that is vital for their long-term survival and effectiveness, a position compatible with the system-resource model of organizational effectiveness. TQM also blurs the boundaries between organizations and their environments and assumes that constituents who were previously considered outsiders (e.g., parents, policy makers) are included in organizational processes.

Prominent leaders of the TQM movement include W. Edwards Deming (1986), Joseph M. Juran (1989), and Kaoru Ishikawa (1985). J. Richard Hackman and Ruth Wageman (1995) believe that these proponents agree that the primary goal of organizations is survival. By surviving, organizations can advance stability in community, generate useful products and services for clients and customers, and provide satisfaction and growth of employees. The TQM strategy for attaining these normative results relies on four highly related assumptions. These assumptions, as derived by Hackman and Wageman, follow:

- Quality is less costly to the organization than poor workmanship.
- If employees are provided with appropriate training and technology, they naturally care about the quality of work and will take initiatives to improve it.
- As systems with highly interdependent parts, the central problems of organizations involve crossing traditional functional lines. To ensure high-quality instructional materials, for example, curriculum specialists must work closely and collaboratively with teachers.
- Quality is ultimately and inescapably the responsibility of top management. Hence, TQM is a top-down approach to administering schools.

James W. Dean and David E. Bowen (1994) further organize the separate and sometimes divergent ideas of TQM in a helpful manner. They view the approach as a philosophy involving three principles of change—customer or client focus (most important), continuous improvement, and teamwork. Each principle is implemented through related sets of practices and techniques. Applying Dean and Bowen's ideas to education yields the following examples of principles, practices, and techniques:

- *Client focus* in schools is satisfying the academic and emotional needs of the students. Using *techniques* such as surveys and focus groups, *practices* of school administrators and teachers would include gathering information about student needs and using the information to modify existing or designing new instructional and extracurricular programs.
- *Continuous improvement* means enhancing instructional and administrative processes through regular or constant examinations. Employing *techniques* such as statistical analyses and flowcharts, *practices* of school administrators and teachers would include analyzing and reengineering their instructional and management processes and programs, and solving problems.
- *Teamwork* is collaboration among school administrators and teachers, between school units such as grade levels and departments, and between students and school employees. Using *techniques* such as organizational development methods (e.g., group processing) and team-building exercises (e.g., role clarification and group feedback), *practices* of school administrators and teachers would include searching for arrangements that would benefit all units and forming teams or task forces. These principles and practices are closely related and mutually reinforcing.

Some TQM techniques have evolved as favorites among practitioners. Hackman and Wageman (1995) found that when administrators implement TQM, they use five techniques most frequently—short-term problem-solving teams, training, top-down implementation, collaboration with suppliers, and obtaining data about clients. Competitive benchmarking and employee involvement are also prominent features of TQM programs in the United States. Some findings are at odds with the TQM philosophy. Administrators place great emphasis on group process techniques and interpersonal skills and only limited reliance on the scientific methods of TQM. In addition, they link the organization's performance evaluation and reward systems to the achievement of specific quality goals, a practice Deming condemns.

Deming's (1983, 1986, 1993) work has been exceptionally important. After World War II, Deming and his philosophy of management are credited with turning around Japanese industry and helping make Japan a dominant business force in the postwar world. Japan set a new standard for industry and business success, and by the 1980s, more and more American business, governmental, and service organizations were turning to Deming's teachings, philosophy, and principles of total quality management. By the 1990s, total quality management had become an important focus in the management of both business (Scherkenbach, 1991, 1992) and educational organizations (AASA, 1991) in the United States. His approach (1986) is summarized by his 14 principles for transforming and improving organizations and their administration. These principles of transformation represent a complex, prescriptive set of interrelated rules stated in terms of a series of commands. The 14 principles are shown in Table 8.3.

Five propositions summarize some of the critical ideas of Deming's approach. These propositions can be used to develop a tentative theoretical scheme to explain the success of total quality management (Anderson, Rungtusanatham, and Schroeder, 1994), as follows:

Proposition 1: Transformational leadership enables the simultaneous creation of a cooperative and a learning organization.

Proposition 2: An organization that simultaneously facilitates cooperation and learning enhances opportunities for process-management practices and limits management by results.

Proposition 3: Process-management practices simultaneously produce a press toward continuous improvement and employee fulfillment.

Proposition 4: An organization's simultaneous efforts at continuous improvement and employee fulfillment lead to higher client gratification.

Proposition 5: An organization's simultaneous efforts at continuous improvement and employee fulfillment lead to quality in processes, services, and products.

Do the Deming principles apply to schools? Many educational administrators and commentators believe so (Glaub, 1990; Rhodes, 1990; AASA,

TABLE 8.3

Deming's 14 Principles of TQM

- Create a constancy of purpose for improvement
- Adopt a new philosophy
- Cease dependence on inspection and ratings to achieve quality
- Stop awarding business on the basis of price tag alone
- Constantly improve every system in the organization to enhance the quality of products and services
- Institute training on the job
- Institute leadership
- Remove barriers that rob people of pride of workmanship
- Break down barriers between departments
- Eliminate slogans, exhortations, and targets for the workforce
- Eliminate work standards and management by numbers
- Remove barriers that rob people of pride of workmanship
- Institute a program of education and self-improvement
- Put everyone to work transforming the organization

1991; Leonard, 1991; Meany, 1991; Bonstingl, 1992), but some remain skeptical (Capper and Jamison, 1993; Pallas and Neumann, 1993). Deming's principles of management seem applicable to schools. The principles are consistent with the systems approach taken in this text; in fact, they reinforce many of the concepts we have developed—for example, the importance of systems thinking, involvement, motivation, rational decision making, culture, and transformational leadership. The close link between total quality management (TQM) and systems theory has been noted (Spencer, 1994). TQM does not abandon a rational systems approach in favor of a natural one, but rather, blends both in an open-systems perspective. For example, the Deming perspective describes organizations as systems embedded in a broader environment, which at the same time are concerned about making rational decisions as well as establishing a culture of participation and trust among employees.

Theory, Research, and Practice: Some Observations

Since the introduction of the core ideas in the mid-1980s, TQM has become something of a social movement. It has spread across nearly all sectors of the economy, including education; has become prominent in the popular press; and has amassed a horde of trainers, consultants and organizations promoting TQM. At the same time, TQM has also become controversial with many skeptics, especially scholars, questioning its effects and asking if TQM is not another fad like t-groups, quality circles, MBO, and job enrichment (Hackman and Wageman, 1995).

Although some scholars (Gartner and Naughton, 1988) describe Deming's approach to management as his "theory of management," most agree that Deming's 14 points are more aptly termed a "management philosophy" (Lawler, 1994; Dean and Bowen, 1994) or a "management method" for improving administrative practice (Anderson, Rungtusanatham, and Schroeder, 1994). Nevertheless, the TQM and quality formulations by Deming, Juran, and Ishikawa and others suggest concepts and processes that might be developed into a theory of management. The challenge is to engage in empirical research to discover, or perhaps to invent, the underlying theory of quality management; such a theory will describe, explain, and predict the effects of adopting quality management methods (Anderson, Rungtusanatham, and Schroeder, 1994).

Systematic research on the quality management approach has been neither as abundant nor as uncritical as its widespread acceptance might suggest (Lawler, 1994). Hackman and Wageman (1995) conclude that research on the effects of TQM has focused mostly on global outcomes, shown highly positive results, and been based primarily on case studies. They contend that the findings are of limited value because nearly all the studies are fundamentally flawed. For Hackman and Wageman, an adequate assessment of TQM must respond to three questions. How much of the full TQM package has actually been implemented? Have the work process criteria of effectiveness (e.g., effort, knowledge and skill, and performance strategy) been improved? Have the outcome criteria of effectiveness (e.g., academic achievement and dropout rates) been enhanced? In one of the few large-sample studies,

Thomas C. Powell (1995) found that the organizational characteristics commonly associated with TQM programs do not produce significant increases in effectiveness.

Support for total quality management comes primarily from practicing administrators. For instance, managers of business corporations tell amazing success stories about the effects of TQM. There is little doubt that such Japanese corporations as Honda, Toyota, and Sony were highly successful in producing quality products in the 1980s. More recently, TQM has become a popular management approach in many of the Fortune 500 companies in America, including winners of the prestigious Malcolm Baldrige National Quality Award (Blackburn and Rosen, 1993; Lawler, 1992, 1994). Nonetheless, research scholars are skeptical and believe that rhetoric about TQM is defeating substance. In too many settings, pale imitations of Deming, Juran, and Ishikawa's powerful ideas about improving quality are being implemented (Hackman and Wageman, 1995). Similarly, others (e.g., Westphal, Gulati, and Shortell, 1997; Zbaracki, 1998) note technical and rhetorical versions of TQM in their studies. They generally conclude that institutional theory best explains their findings about the implementation of TQM programs. Early adopters, seeking to improve the effectiveness of their organizations, tend to be faithful to ideas of TQM. In contrast, late adopters (being less concerned about effectiveness) focus on gaining legitimacy by imitating accepted and desirable management practices.

In brief, total quality management provides a renewed emphasis on a systems approach to organizations. The perspective shifts attention away from the effectiveness of results to the quality of all aspects of the system. Although systematic research on the formulation is sparse, it remains a popular formulation, especially among practitioners. Finally, the concepts that underlie TQM provide researchers and theorists with conceptual capital to formulate a theory of management.

THEORY INTO PRACTICE

A Mandate for Higher Test Scores

You have recently been appointed as the principal of New Central High School (NCHS), which is to open next fall. This new school is located in the inner corridor of a large urban city in Northeast. The new building was awarded a prize for its architectural design and is equipped with the latest instructional and security technology. The school is projected to have 2,500 students who have been attending two nearby schools—East and West High Schools—that are being closed at the end of the academic year. The students come primarily from low-income, minority families. Both schools have been experiencing declining enrollments, high dropout rates, and low scores on state-mandated tests. To further complicate the situation, East and West High Schools are in many ways quite different. East uses mixed-ability grouping of students and the principal runs the school with an inclusive style. West tracks its students into classes on the basis of ability and the principal manages with an authoritarian approach. Because a federal court has mandated that the state provide special compensatory programs

THEORY INTO PRACTICE, (Continued)

with small class sizes, NCHS will open with a professional staff of 150. You have been able to select your administrative staff and to influence the selection of the teachers. However, the contract with the teachers' union specified that many of the teachers would be assigned to NCHS on the basis of seniority. Even with the history of substantial performance problems in the existing high schools, the large investment in the new facility with its state of the art equipment, the court mandates for quality educational programs, and the vision of a new start by the students and parents have significantly raised the expectations for NCHS. Obviously, the pressure is on you to produce a highly effective school.

- Which outcomes would be the most important in the short term? Medium term? Long term?
- Who should be involved in establishing the importance of the effectiveness outcomes?
- Which context factors would likely have the most effects on the outcome criteria? Which ones can you influence?
- Given your analysis of the outcome and context factors, which throughput or transformational characteristics should be given highest priority? What actions on your part might promote the effectiveness of these processes?
- What are the pros and cons of implementing a total quality management program in the New Central High School?

SUMMARY AND SUGGESTED READINGS

Organizational effectiveness and quality now play such central roles in the theory and practice of education that thorough understandings of the concepts are essential. Two general approaches, a goal perspective and a system-resource model, dominate the study of organizational effectiveness. Quality, like effectiveness, is a multidimensional construct that refers to continuous improvement in all phases of a system. Discussions on quality have begun to replace those on organizational effectiveness. This new emphasis in the organizational literature can be traced to the work of W. Edwards Deming and the success of Japanese industry during the 1980s. Effectiveness is a more abstract and theoretical concept, whereas quality seems to be a more pragmatic approach to the success of organizations; effectiveness and quality are two sides of the same coin.

Our review of the theory and research on quality and effectiveness leads us to conclude that simple measures of organizational outcomes are insufficient indicators of either effectiveness or quality. This should come as no surprise to those who use a systems approach to understand organizational behavior. Outcomes are only one part of the system and perhaps not the most important element. The inputs as well as the transformational process of the system are equal partners in determining both quality and effectiveness of schools.

We have proposed an integrated goal and system-resource model of school performance. The perspective addresses the importance of all aspects of a social system, including the effectiveness and quality of inputs, transformation processes, and outcomes. This system sequence and the elements of environment, structure, individual, culture, and politics were first presented in Chapter 1. In Chapters 2 to 7, these system elements were elaborated. The concepts of effectiveness and quality in this chapter complete the sequence and provide the ends for which the elements of the system are the means.

School administrators can improve the quality and effectiveness of schools by using a number of other critical processes—decision making, communication, and leadership. These are administrative processes that educators must employ effectively if they are to help develop quality schools. Thus, Chapters 9 to 11 provide in-depth examinations of the theory, research, and practice of these areas.

Several sources are recommended to further your exploration of organizational effectiveness. Two classic treatments are Goodman and Penning's (1977) *New Perspectives on Organizational Effectiveness* and Cameron and Whetten's (1983) *Organizational Effectiveness.* They provide excellent sets of readings on the theoretical underpinning of the construct. For contemporary reviews of job satisfaction, works by Cranny, Smith, and Stone (1992) and Paul E. Spector (1997) are valuable resources. The roots of quality as a substitute for effectiveness can be traced to the work of W. Edwards Deming (1986). His *Out of Crisis* has become the bible for advocates of total quality management. The *Academy of Management Review,* 19(3), 1994, devoted an entire issue to total quality. S. C. Purkey and Marshall Smith's (1983) review of the literature remains a must reading for students interested in school effectiveness. Recent reports by Scheerens and Bosker (1997) and Mortimore (1998) are excellent sources. We especially recommend the recent book by Teddlie and Reynolds (2000). It provides a comprehensive, in-depth, and comparative review of the school effectiveness literature. Finally, Kim Cameron and David Whetten (1996) provide a recent comprehensive preview of the next generation of effectiveness and quality studies.

Notes

1. Cameron and Whetten (1996) list seven common models of organization effectiveness. Our integrated model of organizational effectiveness uses four of the seven—goal, system resource, internal processes, and strategic constituencies.
2. The employment of input, transformation, and output phases of open-systems theory to identify effectiveness indicators seems to parallel Scott's (1992) use of structural capabilities, processes, and outcomes for the same purpose.
3. The following reviews of the production-function literature are recommended: Averich et al. (1972); Jamison, Suppes, and Wells (1974); Hanushek (1989, 1997); Murnane (1981); MacKensie (1983); Rowen, Bossert, and Dwyer (1983); Monk (1992); Teddlie and Reynolds (2000).
4. See, for example, the following sources: Brookover et al. (1978); Edmonds (1979); Madaus, Airasian, and Kellaghan (1980); Purkey and Smith (1983); Clark, Lotto, and Astuto (1984); Brophy and Good (1986); Good and Brophy (1986); Bossert (1988); Bryk (1993); Lee, Bryk, and Smith (1993); Mortimore (1998); and Scheerens and Bosker (1997).

Key Concepts and Ideas

- Constituency
- Effective-schools research
- Goal and system-resource model
- Goal model
- Input criteria
- Job satisfaction
- Official goals
- Operative goals
- Perceived organizational effectiveness
- Performance outcomes
- Production-function model
- Quality
- Situational model of job satisfaction
- Structure and process criteria
- System-resource model
- Total quality management (TQM)

CHAPTER 9

DECISION MAKING IN SCHOOLS

The task of "deciding" pervades the entire administrative organization. . . . A general theory of administration must include principles of organization that will insure correct decision making, just as it must include principles that will insure effective action.

Herbert A. Simon
Administrative Behavior

PREVIEW

1. Administrative decision making is a dynamic process that solves some organizational problems and, in the process, often creates others.
2. Decision making is a general pattern of action found in the rational administration of all functional and task areas in organizations.
3. Values are an integral part of decision making.
4. The classical decision-making model uses a strategy of optimizing to maximize the achievement of goals, but the model is an ideal rather than an actual description of practice.
5. Satisficing is a pragmatic decision-making strategy that some administrators use to solve the problems of practice.
6. Most administrators probably use an incremental model of deciding; they muddle through.
7. An adaptive strategy of deciding unites the rationalism and comprehensiveness of satisficing with the flexibility and utility of the incremental model.
8. Like most complex processes, however, there is no single best way to decide; the best approach is the one that best fits the circumstances: a contingency approach is proposed.
9. Not all organizational decisions are rational; the garbage can model helps explain nonrational decision making.
10. Irrationality in decision making is often produced by stress; the Janis-Mann conflict model describes the pitfalls of defective decision making.
11. Sometimes participation improves the quality of decisions; sometimes it does not. The Hoy-Tarter model suggests when and how to involve subordinates in decision making.

12. One of the dangers of group decision making is groupthink, shared illusions about the correctness and invulnerability of the group.
13. Groupthink can be avoided by understanding its causes and by appropriately structuring group decision making.

Decision making is a major responsibility of all administrators, but until decisions are converted into action they are only good intentions. Deciding is a sine qua non of educational administration because the school, like all formal organizations, is basically a decision-making structure. Our analysis begins with an examination of classical decision making.

The Classical Model: An Optimizing Strategy

Classical decision theory assumes that decisions should be completely rational; it employs an **optimizing** strategy by seeking the best possible alternative to maximize the achievement of goals and objectives. According to the classical model, the decision-making process is a series of sequential steps:

1. A problem is identified.
2. Goals and objectives are established.
3. *All* the possible alternatives are generated.
4. The consequences of each alternative are considered.
5. All the alternatives are evaluated in terms of the goals and objectives.
6. The *best* alternative is selected—that is, the one that maximizes the goals and objectives.
7. Finally, the decision is implemented and evaluated.

The **classical model** is an ideal (a normative model), rather than a description of how most decision makers function (a descriptive model). Most scholars, in fact, consider the classical model an unrealistic ideal, if not naive. Decision makers virtually never have access to all the relevant information. Moreover, generating all the possible alternatives and their consequences is impossible. Unfortunately, the model assumes information-processing capacities, rationality, and knowledge that decision makers simply do not possess; consequently, it is not very useful to practicing administrators.

The Administrative Model: A Satisficing Strategy

Given the severe limitations of the classical model, it should not be surprising that more realistic conceptual approaches to decision making in organizations have evolved. The complexity of most organizational problems and the limited capacity of the human mind make it virtually impossible to use an optimizing strategy on all but the simplest problems. Herbert Simon (1947) was the first to introduce the **administrative model** of decision making to provide a more accurate description of the way administrators both do and should make organizational decisions.[1] The basic approach is **satisficing**—that is, finding a satisfactory solution rather than the best one. Before analyzing the satisficing strategy in detail, we examine the basic assumptions upon which the model rests.

Some Basic Assumptions

Assumption 1. *Administrative decision making is a dynamic process that solves some organizational problems and creates others.*

Specific decisions that foster the achievement of the organization's purposes frequently interfere with other conditions that are also important. Peter M. Blau and W. Richard Scott (1962: 250–51) explain that the process of decision making is dialectical: "problems appear, and while the process of solving them tends to give rise to new problems, learning has occurred which influences how the new challenges are met." Thus at best, decision making by thoughtful and skillful executives and their staffs should lead to more rational decisions, but it typically will not result in final decisions. The complex nature of organizations usually precludes that possibility.

Assumption 2. *Complete rationality in decision making is impossible; therefore, administrators seek to satisfice because they have neither the ability nor the cognitive capacity to maximize the decision-making process.*

Effective administration requires rational decision making. Decisions are rational when they are appropriate for accomplishing specific goals, and people typically try to make rational decisions (Tversky, 1969; Payne, Bettman, and Johnson, 1988). Administrative decisions, however, are often extremely complex, and rationality is limited for a number of reasons:

- All the alternatives cannot be considered because there are too many options that do not come to mind.
- All the probable consequences for each alternative cannot be anticipated because future events are exceedingly difficult to predict and evaluate.
- Finally, rationality is limited not only by the administrators' information-processing capacities, but also by their unconscious skills, habits, and reflexes as well as their values and conceptions of purpose that may deviate from the organization's goals (Simon, 1947, 1991).

Because individuals are not capable of making completely rational decisions on complex matters, they are concerned with the selection and implementation of satisfactory alternatives rather than optimal ones. To use Simon's words, administrators "satisfice" rather than "optimize." Nonetheless, administrators continue to talk about finding the best solutions to problems. What is meant, of course, is the best of the satisfactory alternatives.

Administrators look for solutions that are "good enough." They recognize that their perception of the world is a drastically simplified model of the complex interacting forces that constitute the real world. They are content with this oversimplification because they believe that most real-world facts are not important to the particular problem(s) they face and that most significant chains of cause and effect are short and simple. Consequently, they ignore many aspects of reality and make choices using a simplified picture of reality that accounts for only a few of the factors that they consider most relevant and important (Simon, 1947). That is, they limit the scope of the decisions so that rationality can be approached.

Organizations provide members with an environment of goals, objectives, and purposes. This environment narrows and defines the roles, thereby limiting the number of alternatives. According to Simon (1947), rational behavior consists of a means-ends chain. Given certain ends, appropriate means are selected, but once those ends are achieved, they in turn become means for further ends, and so on. After organizational objectives are agreed on, the administrative structure serves as a basis for the means-ends chains. To illustrate, once the ends for organizational members are defined by the directives from a superior, the subordinate's responsibility is primarily to determine the "best" means for attaining those ends. That pattern, along with procedural regulations, narrows the alternatives and establishes **bounded rationality.**

An individual's decision is rational if it is consistent with the values, alternatives, and information that were analyzed in reaching it. An organization's decision is rational if it is consistent with its goals, objectives, and information. Therefore, the organization must be constructed so that a decision that is rational for the individual remains rational for the organization when reassessed from the organizational perspective (Simon, 1957b).

Assumption 3. *Decision making is a general pattern of action found in the rational administration of all major tasks and functional areas in organizations.*

In deciding, those with the responsibility generally go through a general pattern of action that includes the following:

- Recognize and define the problem or issue.
- Analyze the difficulties in the situation.
- Establish criteria for a satisfactory solution.
- Develop a strategy for action.
- Initiate a plan of action.
- Evaluate the outcomes.

Although the process is conceptualized as a sequential pattern because each step serves as a logical basis for the next, the process is also cyclical. Thus, decision making may be entered into at any stage. Moreover, the steps are taken again and again in the process of administering organizations. The cyclical evolution of rational, deliberate, purposeful action—beginning with the development of a decision strategy and moving through implementation and appraisal of results—occurs in all types of organizations (Litchfield, 1956).

The structure of the process is the same, for example, in military, industrial, educational, or health services organizations. The universality of rational decision making calls attention to the fact that essentially it is the same regardless of specific context. Educational organizations are different from industrial organizations in a great many important ways. For example, the technologies and the products are quite different, but the decision-making process is not.

The specific tasks of school administration can be described in a number of ways. School administrators are responsible for curriculum and instruction, negotiations, physical facilities, finance and business, pupil personnel, evaluation and supervision, recruitment and selection of employees, and public relations. Regardless of the task, decision making is essential not only in each of these task areas but also in the broader functional areas of administration—policy, resources, and execution (Litchfield, 1956).

A **policy** is a general statement of objectives that guides organizational actions. The policy function is often termed "policy making" or "policy formulation," but it is substantially more.[2] Policies are not only formulated but also programmed, communicated, monitored, and evaluated. Policy making is a special instance of decision making in which issues revolve around policy matters.

The key resources of administration are people, money, authority, and materials. The rational process of deciding also is the vehicle for resource allocation. In determining the need for personnel, supplies, physical facilities, and monies, the administrator is confronted with difficulties and problems that require both deliberate and reflective choice and implementation—the use of the action cycle of the decision-making process.

Finally, the cycle is used in the execution of administration. In order to allocate and integrate the resources consistent with policy mandates and to accommodate conflicting values and tendencies, the executive attempts to administer the system through a continuous series of the cyclical actions that constitute the decision-making process (Litchfield, 1956).

Assumption 4. *Values are an integral part of decision making.*

Decisions are not value free. Values and moral choice are critical in systematic and deliberate decision making. When administrators pursue actions that they believe will attain a valued outcome, they are making judgments of value between competing goods or the lesser of evils.[3] But action requires more than good intention. For example, educational administrators often must weigh compassion for students against the judgments of teachers. Teachers may be threatened by students and react strongly to reestablish their authority. In the process, students may be punished for infractions that challenge the teacher's position. Most administrators value the welfare of both teachers and students, and yet administrators often must make decisions that favor one over the other. Judgments of value are inextricably tied to judgments of fact. The same kind of scanning and assessing used by decision makers to consider their options can abet moral choices (Willower, 1991;Willower and Licata, 1997).

Science and rationality, and ethics and practice should not be sharply separated (Dewey, 1938; Evers and Lakomski, 1991; Willower, 1993). One goes through the same process to make an ethical judgment or a rational decision. Whether making ethical judgments or rational decisions, the reflective examination of alternative courses of action and their consequences is necessary. Hence, both moral choice and rational decisions require the formulation of hypotheses concerning probable consequences and outcomes. The practice of administrative decision making is a continuing exercise in both rationality and valuation; it is both a rational and ethical activity. To separate the activities is foolhardy and impossible. Values and rationality are symbiotic not antithetical. The separation of ethics and the reflective methods of science promote ritualism and mechanistic administration. Decision making is about moral choice, and thoughtful moral choice depends on informed explanation and inference (Hoy and Tarter, 1995).

Decision-Making Process: An Action Cycle

The specific sequence of steps in the decision-making process has already been outlined. The action cycle of that process is illustrated in Figure 9.1. Many decision-making action cycles may be occurring simultaneously. One elaborate cycle, regarding fundamental goals and objectives (strategic planning), may be proceeding at the level of the board of education, whereas smaller and related sequential cycles, regarding curriculum and instruction, pupil personnel services, finance and business management, and facilities planning, may be progressing at the district level.

Let us turn to a more detailed analysis of each step in the action cycle.[4]

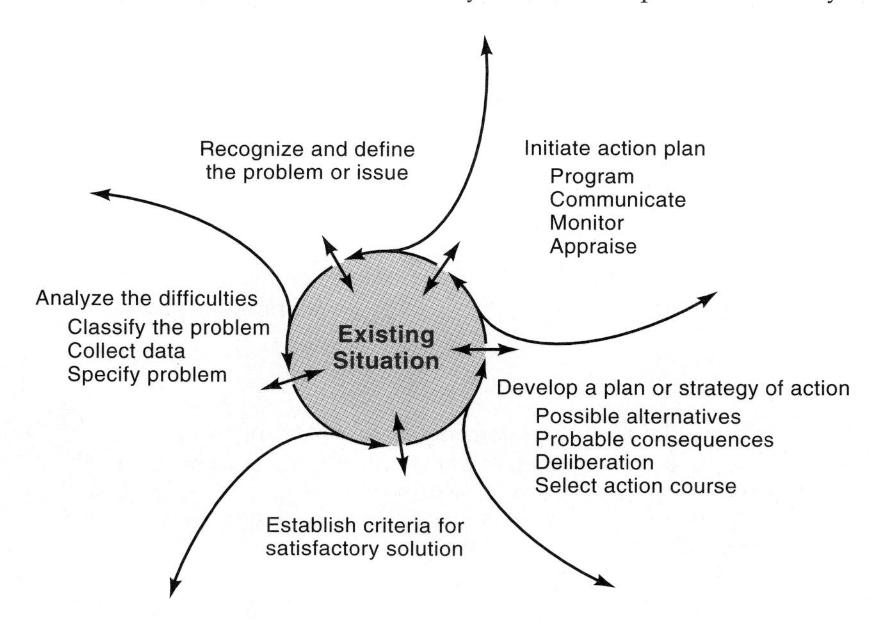

FIGURE 9.1 ***Decision-Making Action Cycle***

Step 1. Recognize and Define the Problem or Issue

The recognition of a difficulty or disharmony in the system is the first step in the decision-making process. Effective administrators are sensitive to organizational actions and attitudes that do not measure up to the prescribed standards. The common retort, "We don't have problems; we have answers," is symptomatic of insensitive administrators who are headed for trouble. Although it may be possible for them to maintain equilibrium in the organization over the short run, the likelihood of organizational chaos over the long run seems great.

The recognition and definition of a problem are crucial to deciding and often do not receive adequate attention. The way a problem is conceptualized is important to subsequent analysis and solution. Not only are sensitivity and perceptual acuteness in the administrator necessary, but a rich conceptual background and a thorough understanding of formal and informal organizations are desirable in framing the problem. Too often administrators define problems quickly and narrowly and, in so doing, restrict their options. They treat only the symptoms of the problems, not the problem itself. For example, the response to a request from a teacher group for more autonomy in selecting curricular materials can be seen by a principal as an attempt to undermine administrative authority. The problem so conceived yields a set of alternatives that likely will be unduly narrow and restrictive. Such a teacher request, however, can open up a host of positive, creative possibilities for long-range curriculum development. This example, coincidentally, underscores the importance of security and confidence; the secure and confident administrator is unlikely to view such a teacher request as a threat to his or her authority.

During this first stage in the process, it is important to place the problem in perspective. If the problem is complex, its definition likewise will be complicated, perhaps multidimensional. The problem may need to be broken down into subproblems, with each subproblem cycled through the decision-making process. Furthermore, the problem may require several solutions. For instance, the problem of districting in a school system, where large numbers of parents want their children in school X rather than Y, may be settled in the short run by a policy statement indicating that a child will be assigned to a school solely on the basis of geographic location. The long-run solution, however, might well involve equalizing educational opportunities and improving the program of instruction in one or more schools.[5] Two guides for defining the problem:

- First, define the immediate problem.
- Then, define the long-term problem.

In deciding, the executive does not necessarily merely react to existing problems. Effective administrators are constantly alert to issues that might become problems. In that way they can adopt a course of action that will prevent problems as well as promote organizational health and growth.

Step 2. Analyze the Difficulties in the Existing Situation

This stage of the decision-making process is directly related to the first stage; in fact, some writers prefer to combine definition and analysis. However, analysis calls for the classification of the problem. Is the problem unique? Or is it a new manifestation of a typical difficulty for which a pattern of action has already been developed?

Chester I. Barnard (1938) distinguished three kinds of decisions based on where the need for them originates:

- Intermediary decision arise from authoritative communications from superiors that relate to the interpretation, application, or distribution of instruction.
- Appellate decisions grow out of cases referred by subordinates.
- Creative decisions originate in the initiative of the executive concerned.

In contrast, Peter F. Drucker (1966) proposed two basic kinds of decisions—generic or unique. **Generic decisions** arise from established principles, policies, or rules. Indeed, recurring problems are routinely solved by formulaic rules and regulations. A great many of the intermediary or appellate decisions that confront school principals (indeed, all middle-level administrators) are generic. That is, the organization has established mechanisms and procedures for dealing with problems. This does not mean, however, that they are unimportant; it simply means that they belong to a general group of organizational problems that frequently occur and that the organization wants to be prepared to deal with. Such decisions are needed when a principal implements policy mandated by the board, monitors absenteeism among teachers, mediates student-teacher conflicts, and interprets disciplinary procedures. All these generic decisions can be intermediary or appellate decisions (originating from above or below the principal in the hierarchy). In all cases the principal should be able to handle the situation by applying the appropriate rule, principle, or policy to the concrete circumstances of the case.

Unique decisions, however, are probably creative decisions that require going beyond established procedures for a solution; in fact, they may require a modification of the organizational structure. Here the decision maker deals with an exceptional problem that is not adequately answered by a general principle or rule. Creative decisions quite often change the basic thrust or direction of an organization. In order to seek a creative solution, decision makers explore all ideas that are relevant to the problem.

A unique decision might arise when principal and staff work to resolve a curricular issue where there are no established guidelines. The superintendent may specifically request an innovative solution. Completely unique events are rare; nevertheless, the distinction between problems that are routine and those that are unique is an important one in terms of deciding. Two common mistakes administrators need to guard against are:

- Treating a routine situation as if it were a series of unique events.
- Treating a new event as if it were just another old problem to which old procedures should be applied.

Once the problem has been classified as generic or unique, the administrator is in a position to address a number of other questions. How important is the problem? Can the problem be more fully specified? What information is needed to specify the problem? The original definition of a problem is usually global and general. After classifying and determining the importance of the problem, the decision maker begins to define more precisely the problem and issues involved. This entails the need for information. The amount of information that should be collected depends on a number of factors, including the importance of the problem, time constraints, and existing procedures and structure for data collection. The more important the problem, the more information the decision maker gathers. Time, of course, is almost always a constraint. Finally, the existing procedures for data collection may facilitate or prohibit the search for relevant information.

In brief, decision makers need relevant facts. What is involved? Why is it involved? Where is it involved? When? To what extent? Answers to these questions provide information to map the parameters of the problem. Such information can be collected in formal, sophisticated ways, making use of operations research and computer facilities, as well as in informal ways, through personal contacts, by telephone, or in conversations.

Step 3. Establish Criteria for a Satisfactory Solution

After the problem has been analyzed and specified, the decision maker must decide what constitutes an acceptable solution. What are the minimum objectives that are to be achieved? What are the musts compared to the wants? It is not unusual for the perfect solution in terms of outcomes to be unfeasible. What is good enough? Answers to such questions help the decision maker establish his or her aspiration level. That is, what are the criteria for a satisfactory decision? At this point, sometimes the decision maker will rank possible outcomes along a continuum from minimally satisfying to maximally satisfying; a completely satisfactory outcome usually does not remain after compromise, adaptation, and concession. It is also useful to consider what is satisfactory in both the short and long term.

Criteria of adequacy need to be specified early so that the decision maker knows that a "right" decision is being made and not just one that will be accepted. In general, the criteria used to judge the decision should be consistent with the organization's mission. What we have referred to as criteria of adequacy, scientists often refer to as **boundary conditions**—the limits that the decision maker must meet if the decision is to be judged satisfactory.

Step 4. Develop a Plan or Strategy of Action

This is the central step in the process. After recognizing the problem, collecting data, and specifying the problem and its boundary conditions, decision makers develop a systematic and reflective plan of action. The process involves at least the following steps:

- Specify alternatives.
- Predict the consequences of each alternative.
- Deliberate.
- Select a plan of action.

Before we proceed to analyze each of these steps, several limitations need to be reiterated. Administrators base their plans of action on simplified pictures of reality; they choose the factors that they regard as most relevant and crucial; and thus they are able to come to some general conclusions and take actions without becoming paralyzed by the facts that "could be" indirectly related to the immediate problems. In describing the art of administrative decision making, Barnard (1938) warns:

- Do not decide questions that are not pertinent.
- Do not decide prematurely.
- Do not make decisions that cannot be effective.
- Do not make decisions that others should make.

The search for alternatives to solve a particular organizational problem is called **problemistic search.** It is distinguished from random curiosity and from the search for understanding per se (Cyert and March, 1963; Bass, 1985b). Problemistic search is straightforward, usually reflecting simplified notions of causality, and based on two simple rules:

- Search in the area of the problem symptom(s).
- Search in the area of the current alternative(s).

When these two rules do not produce enough reasonable alternatives, expand the search. Problemistic search probably is the dominant style of administrators; hence, most decision making is reactive.

But deciding need not be reactive. James D. Thompson (1967) has suggested that it is possible to develop behavior-monitoring procedures to search the environment for opportunities that are not activated by a problem. He calls this process **opportunistic surveillance;** it is the organizational counterpart of curiosity in the individual. Obviously, a decision-making structure that encourages opportunistic surveillance is more desirable than one that allows for only problemistic search.

Specifying Alternatives A preliminary step in formulating an intention to act is to list all possible alternatives. In actuality, only some of the options are specified because, as we have noted earlier, people do not have the information-processing capacity to think of all alternatives. Nonetheless, advancing a greater number of choices increases the likelihood of finding satisfactory alternatives that meet the already-specified conditions.

Creative decision makers are able to develop unique, viable alternatives, an often time-consuming task. Unfortunately, too many administrators do not take the time to develop a comprehensive set of possible options; they see the solution as a simple dichotomy—it is either this or that. Don't be overly impressed with speed in deciding; it is often a symptom of sloppy thinking. The impact of a solution is much more important than the technique. Educational organizations need sound decisions, not clever techniques.

Time is necessary to develop a comprehensive set of alternatives, yet time is limited. Consider as your first alternative doing nothing. Once in a great while, such an alternative turns out to solve the problem; things work themselves out. Unfortunately, most problems do not just work themselves out, but the decision not to decide should always be reflectively considered. Even if "doing nothing" does not solve the problem, sometimes it buys time for further thinking and information gathering, that is, it becomes a short-term strategy. In fact, it is useful to consider other temporary alternatives that do not really solve the problem but that provide more time for deliberation. Temporary alternatives, once refined and more completely thought through, are often the basis for more elaborate proposals. The key in developing preliminary and temporary alternatives is that, if successful, they buy time without creating hostility. There is always the danger that options that buy time will be seen as stalling; hence, buying time should be used sparingly and adroitly.

Routine decisions often can be handled quickly and effectively. Unique decisions demand more thoughtful and creative decision making. Creative thinking is of particular value in generating options. To think creatively, individuals must be able to reduce external inhibitions on the thinking process, to make relativistic and nondogmatic distinctions, to be willing not only to consider but also to express irrational impulses, and to be secure and amenable to brainstorming. Of course, the climate and culture (see Chapter 5) of the organization can either inhibit or facilitate creative thinking.

In brief, the development of effective solutions typically requires:

- A willingness to make fewer black-and-white distinctions.
- The use of divergent and creative thinking patterns.
- Time to develop as many reasonable alternatives as possible.

Predicting Consequences For each alternative that is developed, probable consequences should be proposed. Although for analytic purposes we have treated specifying alternatives and predicting consequences as separate operations, they usually occur simultaneously. The formulation of alternatives and probable consequences is a good place to use groups—pooling brainpower and experience to make predictions as accurately as possible. By and large, predicting consequences to proposed alternatives is hazardous. On some issues—for example, those involving financial costs—accurate predictions of consequences can be made; however, when trying to anticipate the reactions of individuals or groups, the results typically are much more problematic.

Predicting consequences underscores the need for a good management-information system, and those school structures that have built-in capacities to collect, codify, store, and retrieve information have a distinct advantage in the decision-making process. In addition, consulting with a number of individuals who are in a position to know improves one's predictive power. For each decision alternative, the consequences can be predicted only in terms of probable rather than certain outcomes.

Deliberating on And Selecting the Course of Action The final phase of developing a strategy for action involves a reflective analysis of the alternatives and consequences. Sometimes it is helpful to list all the alternatives with their accompanying probable consequences in a probability-event

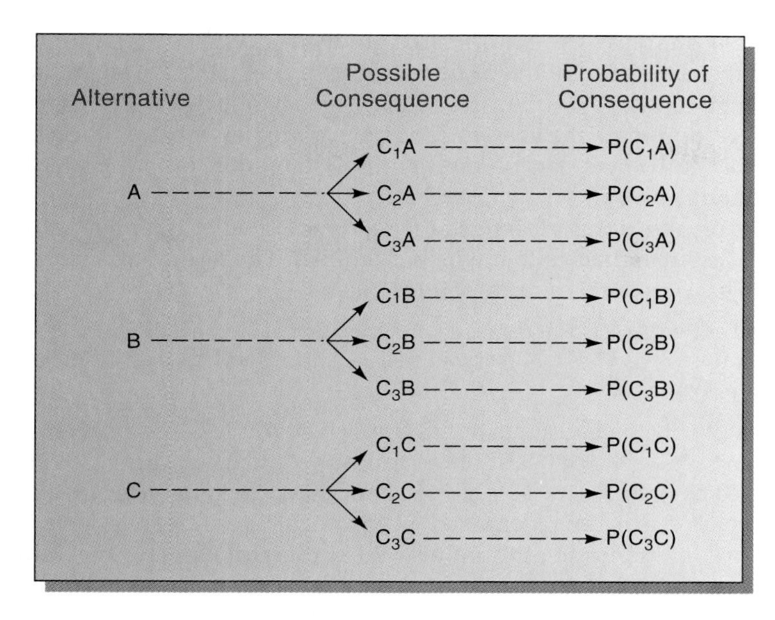

FIGURE 9.2 ***Example of Probability Event Chain***

chain (see Figure 9.2). The figure is read as follows: Alternative A has three possible consequences (C_1A, C_2A, C_3A), and the probability of each of these consequences occurring is designated $P(C_1A)$, $P(C_2A)$, $P(C_3A)$. Although this procedure may not be completed for each problem-solving issue, every option typically has a number of consequences, each with a certain probability that should be considered.

In the deliberation, prior to selecting the appropriate alternatives, decision makers carefully weigh the probable consequences of each alternative in light of the criteria for a satisfactory solution. After such reflection, they choose the "best" alternative or select a series of alternatives that are linked in some sequential order, which provides a strategy and plan of action; the more problematic the issue, the more likely a complex course of action.

To illustrate the planning of strategy, let us simplify the procedure. It may be possible to set up a strategy several moves in advance, just as a good chess player does. Alternative A may result in a positive and acceptable solution; however, if it does not, the decision maker goes to alternative B and, if need be, to alternative C, and so on, provided the probable consequences are still satisfactory. Of course, unanticipated consequences may require a rethinking of viable alternatives. Occasionally decision makers cannot find an acceptable alternative. A reduction in the aspiration level may be necessary; that is, the criteria for a satisfactory solution are reconsidered (return to step 3). A new set of objectives, new alternatives, new data, and a new and more feasible strategy may have to be formulated.

In the process of searching for satisfactory alternatives, decision makers seek to keep the activity manageable by using simplified decision rules called

heuristics—simple rules of thumb that guide the decision making and enable us to make decisions in a rapid and efficient manner.[6] For example, rules about when to take a "hit" in blackjack ("hit on 16, stick on 17") or how to play chess (dominate the center of the board) are heuristics. Some heuristics are useful, but others can be misleading (Gigerenzer, Todd, and ABC Research Group, 1999).

The **recognition heuristic** is the tendency to infer a higher value (e.g., stronger, faster, higher) to that which is familiar. The recognition heuristic for a two-object problem is simply stated:

> If one of two objects is recognized and the other is not, then infer that the recognized object has a higher value (Gigerenzer, Todd, and ABC Research Group, 1999).

For example, "Which city has a larger population: Munich or Dortmund?" The person who has not heard of Dortmund would infer Munich to be larger and would be correct. The recognition heuristic should only be applied when one of the objects is not recognized, but in such cases research demonstrates that the recognition rule of thumb is quite powerful (Gigerenzer, Todd, and ABC Research Group, 1999).

The **availability heuristic** is the tendency for decision makers to base their judgments on information already available to them (Abelson and Levi, 1985). Although such a strategy is quick and efficient, it is limited by what is known and what first comes to mind. Moreover, this heuristic can cause people to make errors (Tversky and Kahneman, 1974) and to overestimate the frequencies of events. In short, what is available in the decision maker's memory is often inadequate and sometimes misleading.

The **representative heuristic** is the tendency to view others as the typical stereotype that they represent; for example, an accountant is seen as bright, mild-mannered, and precise (Tversky and Kahneman, 1974: Greenberg and Baron, 1997). The representative heuristic applies to events and objects as well as people—the more closely an item represents the most typical occurrence, the more likely it will be judged to be that prototype. Even though such quick judgments are incomplete and prone to error, they are quite common in decision making (Tversky and Kahneman, 1974, 1981).

The **anchoring-and-adjustment heuristic** is a mental rule of thumb in which existing information is accepted as a reference point for decision making but is adjusted as new information becomes available (Baron, 1998). For example, a principal may evaluate teacher performance during an observation as satisfactory, but when confronted with new information from the teacher may make an adjustment on the rating. Such a process is more likely if the principal does not have a good basis for judging the quality.

The influence of heuristics on decision making is strong and often occurs unconsciously; in fact, recent evidence suggests that arbitrary numbers can anchor people's judgments even when the numbers are irrelevant to the decision (Wilson, Houston, Etling, and Brekke, 1996). The bad news is that the potential sources of errors of some heuristics are strong; but the good news is that such errors can be reduced by experience and expertise (Frederick and Libby, 1986; Northcraft and Neale, 1987; Smith and Kida, 1991).

Obviously, a large number of factors mediate the choice of a preferred alternative or alternatives. The values of the administrator, the cultural context in which the decision is made and implemented, the perceptions of those involved, the importance of the situation, the pressure on the decision maker, heuristics, and the importance of the goal—all of these and other factors intervene in the selection of a final course of action. Nonetheless, deliberate, rational, and reflective decisions generally result from following a systematic sequence of steps.

Step 5. Initiate the Plan of Action

Once the decision has been made and a plan of action formulated, the decision needs to be implemented—the final element in the decision-making cycle. The initiation of the plan of action requires at least four steps: programming, communicating, monitoring, and appraising.

Programming Decisions must be translated and interpreted into specific programs—that is, the mechanics and specific details for implementing the plan must be specified. For example, the plan to change the system of grading elementary school students contains a specific and detailed set of operations that require answers to a number of questions. Who has to have information about the plan? What actions need to be taken and by whom? What preparation is needed so that those who have to take action can do so? The action that is to be programmed must be appropriate to the abilities of the people involved. In brief, the program must be realistic and capable of implementation.

What we call "programming" others have called "program planning"—the activity designed to implement decisions. Program planning can be accomplished through a wide range of specific methods and techniques. Which ones are used depends on the sophistication and capabilities of the school organization. Programming may include budgeting, setting behavioral objectives, using network-based management techniques, and specifying other ways of translating a decision into specific programs for allocating authority and human resources.

Communicating Once the plan has been programmed, it is necessary that each involved individual become aware of his or her responsibilities. Channels of communication among the individuals as well as opportunities for communicating both horizontally and vertically must be given careful attention. For a program to be successful, individuals need to know clearly not only what their own roles are, but also the roles of others as they relate to the total plan. Otherwise, efforts may be duplicated, counterproductive, or ineffective. The communication system developed to implement the plan in large part can and should be a crucial mechanism to initiate action and to enhance coordination of the program. Communicating is discussed in detail in Chapter 10.

Monitoring The process of overseeing the implementation of the plan of action is monitoring. Evaluation and reporting must be built into the action cycle to provide continuous assessment of actual outcomes as compared to expected ones. Monitoring is a control process using systematic feedback. Standards of performance, once they are set, need to be enforced. Enforcement does not necessarily mean coercive control. There are many techniques of control such as rewards and incentives, persuasion, and identification with organizational goals. Different modes of control and enforcement are more or less effective depending on the situation and the individuals involved. Continuous feedback is necessary to evaluate the progress of implementing the plan of action.

Appraising Once the decision has been programmed, communicated, and monitored, the outcomes still need to be appraised to determine how successful the decision has been. Has the decision been a satisfactory one? What new issues or problems have arisen? Decisions commonly are made in situations where probabilities, not certainties, are weighed. Even the most carefully conceived and executed decisions can fail or become obsolete. Organizational decisions are made in a context of change—facts, values, and circumstances change. Therefore, a fully articulated decision—one that has been reflectively made, programmed, communicated, and monitored—in itself brings about sufficient change to necessitate its own further reevaluation and appraisal (Litchfield, 1956). Hence, the appraisal stage is both an end and a new beginning in the action cycle of decision making. Clearly, there are no ultimate solutions—only satisfactory decisions and solutions for the moment.

The Incremental Model: A Strategy of Successive Limited Comparisons

Although the satisficing strategy that we have just described in detail is well suited to dealing with many problems in educational administration, occasionally some situations require an incremental strategy. When relevant alternatives are difficult to discern or the consequences of each alternative are so complicated as to elude prediction, even satisficing does not work well (Grandori, 1984). For example, to what new activities should a school administrator allocate more resources? The answer to this question is probably more adequately addressed by considering only alternatives that differ marginally from existing conditions. The underlying assumption of the strategy is that small incremental changes will not produce major unanticipated negative consequences for the organization.

Charles Lindblom (1959, 1965, 1968, 1980; Braybrook and Lindblom 1963; Lindblom and Cohen, 1979) first introduced and formalized the incremental strategy. He characterizes this method of deciding as the science of **muddling through** and argues that it may be the only feasible approach to systematic decision making when the issues are complex, uncertain, and riddled with conflict. The process is best described as a method of successive limited comparisons. Deciding does not require objectives, exhaustive analysis of alternatives and consequences, or a priori determination of either optimum or satisfactory outcomes. Instead only a small and limited set of alternatives, similar to the existing situation, is considered by successively comparing their consequences until decision makers come to some agreement on a course of action.

This incremental approach has a number of important features. First, the setting of objectives and the generation of alternatives are not separate activities. Goals and objectives are not established prior to decision analysis. Rather, a feasible course of action emerges as alternatives and consequences of action are explored. The more complex the problems, the more likely objectives will change as the decision evolves. Thus, the marginal differences in value among alternative courses of action rather than any prior objectives serve as the basis for deciding.

The **incremental model** also greatly reduces the number of alternatives. The strategy considers only alternatives that are very similar to the existing situation, analyzes only differences between the current state and proposed outcomes, and ignores all outcomes that are outside the decision maker's narrow range of interest. With this approach, the complexity of the decision making is dramatically reduced and made manageable. Lindblom (1959) argues that this simplification of analysis, achieved by concentrating on alternatives that differ only slightly, is not capricious; simplifying by limiting the focus to small variations from existing situations merely makes the most of available knowledge. Administrators who limit themselves to a reasonable set of alternatives on the basis of their experiences can make predictions of consequences with accuracy and confidence. Moreover, by emphasizing only differences among alternatives, time and energy are conserved. The narrow focus on outcomes avoids possible paralysis caused by attempts to predict and analyze all possible outcomes of a specific course of action.

Finally, successive comparison is often an alternative to theory. In both the classical and the administrative models, theory is viewed as a useful way to bring relevant knowledge to bear on specific problems. As problems become increasingly complex, however, the inadequacies of our theories to guide decisions become more prevalent. The strategy of successive limited comparisons suggests that, in such complex situations, decision makers make more progress if they successively compare concrete practical alternatives rather than emphasize more abstract, theoretical analyses.

In brief, the incremental approach has the following distinctive features:

- Means-end analysis is inappropriate because setting objectives and generating alternatives occur simultaneously.
- Good solutions are those upon which decision makers agree regardless of objectives.
- Alternatives and outcomes are drastically reduced by considering only options similar to the current state of affairs.
- Analysis is restricted to differences between the existing situation and proposed alternatives.
- The incremental method eschews theory in favor of successive comparisons of concrete, practical alternatives.

The Mixed-Scanning Model: An Adaptive Strategy

Although widely used, muddling through has its limitations: it is conservative and aimless (Hoy and Tarter, 1995). Yet most administrators make decisions with only partial information and under the press of time. Amitai Etzioni (1967, 1986, 1989) offers a model of decision making that is a pragmatic approach to complexity and uncertainty. His adaptive model, or **mixed-scanning model,** is a synthesis of the administrative and incremental models that we have just described (Thomas, 1984; Wiseman, 1979a, 1979b).

Mixed scanning involves two questions:

- What is the organization's mission and policy?
- What decisions will move the organization toward its mission and policy?

Mixed scanning seeks to use partial information to make satisfactory decisions without either getting bogged down examining all the information or proceeding blindly with little or no information.[7] This **adaptive strategy** is "a mixture of shallow and deep examination of data—generalized consideration of a broad range of facts and choices followed by detailed examination of a focused subset of facts and choices" (Etzioni, 1989: 124). Higher-order, fundamental decision making (mission or policy decisions) is combined with lower-order, incremental decisions that work out the higher-order ones (Etzioni, 1986; Goldberg, 1975; Haynes, 1974). Mixed scanning unites the rationalism and comprehensiveness of the administrative model with the flexibility and utility of the incremental model.

As we have suggested, there are times when alternatives are difficult to discern and when consequences are hard to predict. In these situations, administrators often muddle through. Their incremental decisions are tentative or remedial—small steps taken in directions not far afield from the existing state. Such decision making has its downside, however; it is patently conservative and often without direction. That is, unless decision makers evaluate these incremental decisions in terms of some broad, fundamental policy, drift is likely. Broad guidelines, however, are not incrementally formulated; in fact, they have all the trappings of grand, a priori, decisions, which incrementalism seeks to avoid (Etzioni, 1989).

The mixed-scanning model has its roots in medicine. It is the way effective physicians make decisions. Unlike incrementalists, doctors know what they are trying to achieve and on which parts of the organism to focus attention. Moreover, unlike decision makers who seek to optimize, they do not engage all their resources on the basis of an initial diagnosis, or wait for every conceivable bit of personal history and scientific data before beginning treatment. Doctors survey the symptoms of a patient, analyze the difficulty, initiate a tentative treatment, and, if it fails, they try something else (Etzioni, 1989).

The principles for mixed scanning are straightforward; in fact, Etzioni (1989) advances seven basic rules for a mixed-scanning strategy, which Wayne Hoy and John Tarter (1995) have summarized as follows:

1. *Use focused trial and error.* First, search for reasonable alternatives; then select, implement, and test them; and finally, adjust and modify as the outcomes become clear. Focused trial and error assumes that, despite the fact that important information is missing, the administrator must act. Thus decisions are made with partial information and then carefully monitored and modified in light of new data.
2. *Be tentative; proceed with caution.* Be ready to modify a course of action as necessary. It is important that administrators view each decision as experimental, expecting to revise it.
3. *If uncertain, procrastinate.* Waiting is not always bad. When the situation is ambiguous, delay as long as possible so that more information can be collected and analyzed before taking action. Complexity and uncertainty frequently justify delay.
4. *Stagger your decisions.* Commit to a decision in stages, evaluating the outcomes of each phase before proceeding to the next phase.
5. *If uncertain, fractionalize decisions.* Staggered decisions can be tested in parts. Do not invest all your resources to implement a decision, but instead use partial resources until the consequences are satisfactory.
6. *Hedge your bets.* Implement several competing alternatives, provided that each has satisfactory outcomes. Then make adjustments on the basis of the results.
7. *Be prepared to reverse your decision.* Try to keep decisions tentative and experimental. Reversible decisions avoid overcommitment to a course of action when only partial information is available.

Educational administrators can skillfully employ all of these adaptive techniques; all illustrate flexibility, caution, and a capacity to proceed with partial knowledge.

In sum, the mixed-scanning model has the following distinctive features:

- Broad, organizational policy gives direction to tentative incremental decisions.
- Good decisions have satisfactory outcomes that are consistent with organizational policy and mission.
- The search for alternatives is limited to those close to the problem.
- Analysis is based on the assumption that important information is missing but action is imperative.
- Theory, experience, and successive comparisons are used together.

The major differences in the four models of decision making—classical, administrative, incremental, and mixed scanning—are compared in Table 9.1.

The Right Strategy for the Situation

We have proposed four decision-making models thus far. Which is the best way to decide? There is no best way to decide just as there is no best way to organize, to teach, to do research, or to do myriad other tasks. As in most complex tasks, the best approach is the one that best matches the circumstances—a contingency approach.

TABLE 9.1

Comparison of the Classical, Administrative, Incremental, and Mixed-Scanning Models of Decision Making

Classical	Administrative	Incremental	Mixed Scanning
Objectives are set prior to generating alternatives	Objectives are usually set prior to generating alternatives.	Setting objectives and generating alternatives are intertwined.	Broad policy guidelines are set prior to generating alternatives.
Decision making is a means-ends analysis: first, ends are determined, and then the means to obtain them are sought.	Decision making is typically means-ends analysis; however, occasionally ends change as a result of analysis.	Because means and ends are not separable, means-ends analysis is inappropriate.	Decision making is focused on broad ends and tentative means.
The test of a good decision is that it is shown to be the best means to achieve the end.	The test of a good decision is that it can be shown to result in a satisfactory means to achieve the end; it falls within the established boundary conditions.	The test of a good decision is that decision makers can agree an alternative is in the "right" direction when the existing course proves to be wrong.	The test of a good decision is that it can be shown to result in a satisfactory decision that is consistent with the organization's policy.
(Optimizing)	(Satisficing)	(Successive comparing)	(Adaptive satisficing)
Engage in comprehensive analysis; all alternatives and all consequences are considered.	Engage in "problemistic search" until a set of reasonable alternatives is identified.	Drastically limit the search and analysis: focus on alternatives similar to the existing state. Many alternatives and important outcomes are ignored.	Limit the search and analysis to alternatives close to the problem, but evaluate tentative alternatives in terms of broad policy. More comprehensive than incrementalism.
Heavy reliance on theory.	Reliance on both theory and experience.	Successive comparisons reduce or eliminate the need for theory.	Theory, experience, and successive comparisons used together.

The decision strategies can be ordered according to their capacity to deal with complexity and conditions of increasing uncertainty and conflict (Grandori, 1984). When decisions are simple, information complete and certain, and a collective preference (no conflict) exists, then an optimizing strategy is most appropriate. As we have already noted, however, organizational problems are almost never simple, certain, and without conflict in preferences. Even in the case of the traditional application of the classical model—the economic theory of competitive decision—questions abound concerning its suitability.

When uncertainty and conflict prevail, as is typically the case in administrative decision making, a satisficing strategy becomes appropriate. The administrative model is flexible and heuristic. Decisions are based on comparisons among consequences of alternatives and the decision maker's aspiration level. Only a partial exploration of the alternatives is performed until a satisfactory course of action is discovered. If satisfactory solutions are not found, then the aspiration level is lowered.

When alternatives are difficult if not impossible to discern or consequences are so complicated as to elude prediction, even a satisficing strategy has its limits. In such situations an incremental strategy may be appropriate because it deals with both uncertainty and conflict of interest by assuming that small changes will not produce large negative consequences for the organization (Grandori, 1984). Thus, when the organization is in turmoil and without direction, the incremental approach may be the appropriate short-run strategy.

Some students of organization (Starkie, 1984; Etzioni, 1989), however, argue that even when the decisions are complex and outcomes are difficult to predict, incrementalism is too conservative and self-defeating. Small, incremental decisions made without guidelines lead to drift—to action without direction. Instead, mixed scanning or adaptive decision making is recommended to deal with exceedingly complex decisions. Mixed scanning combines the best of both the satisficing and the incremental models; a strategy of satisficing is combined with incremental decisions guided by broad policy. Full scanning is replaced by partial scanning of a set of satisfactory options, and tentative and reversible decisions are emphasized in an incremental process that calls for caution as well as a clear sense of destination.

We have suggested that the appropriate decision model depends on the amount of information and the complexity of the situation. A summary guide for matching the appropriate decision models with situations is found in Table 9.2.

The Garbage Can Model: Nonrational Decision Making

Individuals and institutions sometimes need ways of doing things for which there are no good reasons. Not always, not even usually, but occasionally people need to act before they think (March, 1982, 1994). The so-called **garbage can model** describes this tendency, which is most likely to occur in organizations that experience extremely high uncertainty. Michael Cohen,

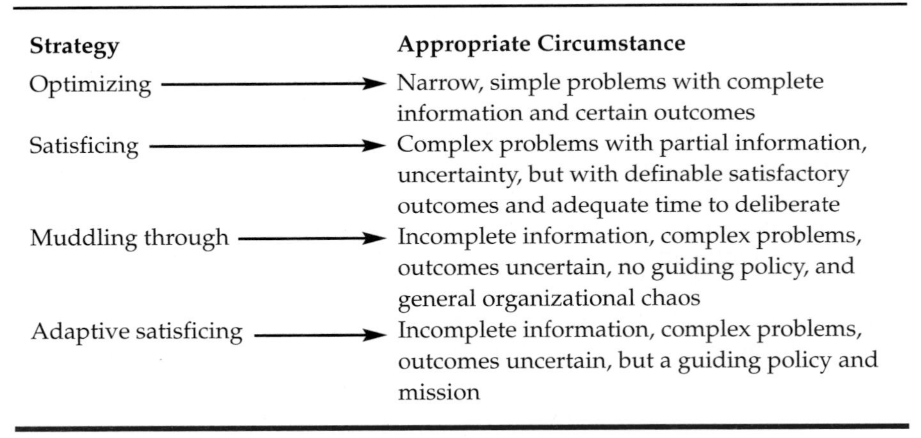

TABLE 9.2

Matching the Right Decision Strategy with the Appropriate Circumstance

Strategy		Appropriate Circumstance
Optimizing	→	Narrow, simple problems with complete information and certain outcomes
Satisficing	→	Complex problems with partial information, uncertainty, but with definable satisfactory outcomes and adequate time to deliberate
Muddling through	→	Incomplete information, complex problems, outcomes uncertain, no guiding policy, and general organizational chaos
Adaptive satisficing	→	Incomplete information, complex problems, outcomes uncertain, but a guiding policy and mission

James March, and Johan Olsen (1972), the originators of the model, call such organizations organized anarchies. These organizations are characterized by *problematic preferences, unclear technology, and fluid participation.* That is, ambiguity accompanies each step of the decision process; cause-and-effect relationships within the organization are virtually impossible to determine; and there is a rapid turnover in participants and time is limited for any one problem or decision. Although no organization fits this extremely organic and loosely coupled system all the time, the model is often useful for *understanding* the pattern of decisions for situations of organized anarchy.

The basic feature of the garbage can model is that the decision process does not begin with a problem and end with a solution; rather, decisions are a product of independent streams of events in the organization (Cohen, March, and Olsen, 1972; Cohen and March, 1974; March, 1982; Estler, 1988; Daft, 1989; Tarter and Hoy, 1998; Slater and Boyd, 1999). The following four streams are particularly relevant for organizational decision making in organized anarchies:

- *Problems* are points of dissatisfaction that need attention; however, problems are distinct from solutions and choices. A problem may or may not lead to a solution and problems may or may not be solved when a solution is adopted.
- *Solutions* are ideas proposed for adoption, but they can exist independently of problems. In fact, the attractiveness of an idea can produce a search for a problem to justify the idea. Cohen and colleagues (1972: 3) argue, "Despite the dictum that you cannot find the answer until you have formulated the question well, you often do not know what the question is in organizational problem solving until you know the answer."

- *Participants* are organizational members who come and go. Because personnel are fluid, problems and solutions can change quickly.
- *Choice opportunities* are occasions when organizations are expected to make decisions—for example, contracts must be signed, people hired and fired, money spent, and resources allocated.

Within these four streams of events, the overall pattern of organizational decision making takes on a quality of randomness. Organizational decision makers do not perceive that something is occurring about which a decision is necessary until the problem matches one with which they already have had some experience (Hall, 1987). When problems and solutions happen to match, a decision may occur. An administrator who has a good idea may suddenly find a problem to solve. When a problem, solution, and participant just happen to connect at one point, a decision may be made and the problem may be solved, but it will not be solved if the solution does not fit the problem. In the garbage can model, organizations are viewed as a set of choices looking for problems, issues and feelings looking for decision arenas in which they might be aired, solutions looking for questions to which they might be answers, and decision makers looking for work (Cohen, March, and Olsen, 1972).

The garbage can model helps explain why solutions may be proposed to problems that don't exist; why choices are made without solving problems; why problems persist without being solved; and why few problems are solved. Events may be so poorly defined and complex that problems, solutions, participants, and choice opportunities act as independent events. When they mesh, some problems are solved, but in this chaotic decision process many problems are not solved—they simply persist (Daft, 1989). Undoubtedly the garbage can metaphor contains elements of truth, and it appears to be an apt description of the way decisions are reached in some situations but not in others. The model has received support in a number of studies of different kinds of organizations (Sproull, Weiner, and Wolf, 1978; Bromily, 1985; Levitt and Nass, 1989), but other recent research has questioned its utility as a *general* model of decision making, even in organizations of complexity, uncertainty, discontinuity, and power politics (Janis and Mann, 1977; Padgett, 1980; Hickson et al., 1986; Pinfield, 1986; Heller, Drenth, Koopman, and Rus, 1988).

In brief, the garbage can model has the following distinctive features:

- Organizational objectives emerge spontaneously; they are not set beforehand.
- Means and ends exist independently; chance or happenstance connects them.
- A good decision occurs when a problem matches a solution.
- The decision relies more on chance than rationality.
- Administrators scan existing solutions, problems, participants, and opportunities looking for matches.

The garbage can metaphor is a description of how decisions sometimes occur; it is not a suggestion for action.

Janis-Mann Conflict Theory: Stress and Irrationality in Decision Making

Regardless of which decision-making strategy is employed, the pressures of the situation and the decision-making process itself often produce stress. Irving Janis and Leon Mann (1977) have developed an insightful model of conflict that answers the following two questions: Under what conditions does stress have unfavorable effects on the quality of decision making? Under what conditions will individuals use sound decision-making procedures to avoid choices that they would quickly regret?[8]

People handle psychological stress in different ways as they make vital decisions. The main sources of such stress are the fear of suffering from the known losses that will occur once an alternative is selected, worry about unknown consequences when a critical decision is at stake, concern about making a public fool of oneself, and losing self-esteem if the decision is disastrous (Janis, 1985). Critical decisions usually involve conflicting values; therefore, decision makers face the unsettling dilemma that any choice they make will require sacrificing ideals or other valued objectives. Thus, the decision makers' anxiety, shame, and guilt rise, which increases the level of stress (Janis, 1985).

There is no question that errors in decision making are a result of many causes, including poor analysis, ignorance, bias, impulsiveness, time constraints, and organizational policies. But another major reason for many poorly conceived and implemented decisions is related to the motivational consequences of conflict—in particular, attempts to overcome stress produced by extremely difficult choices of vital decisions. As a result, people employ a variety of defensive mechanisms as they try to cope with the stress of the decision-making situation, most of which impede the efficiency of the process.

Janis (1985) identified five basic patterns of coping with psychological stress:

- **Unconflicted adherence:** The decision maker ignores information about risks and continues what has begun.
- **Unconflicted change:** The decision maker uncritically accepts whatever course of action is most salient or popular, without concern for costs or risks.
- **Defensive avoidance:** The decision maker evades the conflict by procrastinating, shifting the responsibility elsewhere, constructing wishful rationalizations, minimizing expected unfavorable consequences, and remaining selectively inattentive to corrective feedback.
- **Hypervigilance:** The decision maker panics and searches frantically for a solution, rapidly vacillating back and forth between alternatives, and then impulsively seizes upon a hastily contrived solution that promises immediate relief. The full range of alternatives and consequences is neglected because of emotional excitement, repetitive thinking, and cognitive schema that produce simplistic ideas and a reduction in immediate memory span.

- **Vigilance:** The decision maker searches carefully for relevant information, assimilates the information in an unbiased manner, and then evaluates the alternatives reflectively before making a choice.

The first four patterns are typically dysfunctional and lead to defective decisions. Although vigilance is no panacea, it is most likely to lead to effective decisions.

Even when decision makers are vigilant, however, they sometimes make mistakes by taking cognitive shortcuts to deal with the multiplicity of judgments that are essential. All kinds of people, including scientists and statisticians, make cognitive errors such as overestimating the likelihood that events can be easily imagined, giving too much weight to information about representativeness, relying too much on small samples, and failing to discount biased information (Tversky and Kahneman, 1973; Nisbet and Ross, 1980; Janis, 1985). Moreover, these kinds of errors probably increase when decision makers are under psychological stress.

The coping strategies of unconflicted adherence or unconflicted change promote sloppy and uncritical thinking because of a lack of motivation to engage in careful decision analysis. Defensive avoidance is used to elude the work required for vigilant decision making. If the decision maker cannot pass the buck or postpone the decision, the defensively avoidant person usually makes a quick choice to "get it over with" and then engages in wishful thinking and rationalization—playing up the positive reasons and playing down the negative ones. Hypervigilance produces a paniclike state in which the decision maker temporarily is overwhelmed by information as a result of being overly attentive to both relevant and trivial data. The informational overload and sense of imminent catastrophe contribute to the hypervigilant decision maker's tendency to use such simple-minded decision rules as "do whatever the first expert advises" (Janis, 1985).

The vigilant decision maker is most effective because he or she avoids many of the traps of the other four patterns and also because vigilance requires (Janis and Mann, 1977):

- A careful survey of a wide range of alternatives.
- An analysis of the full range of objectives to be fulfilled and the values implicated by the choice.
- An analysis of the risks and drawbacks of the choice.
- Intensive search for new information relevant to further evaluation of alternatives.
- Conscientious evaluation of new information or expert judgment, even when such information does not support the initial preferred course of action.
- Reexamination of both positive and negative consequences of alternatives, including those originally regarded as unacceptable.
- Detailed plans for implementing the selected course of action with special attention to contingency plans that might be required if various anticipated risks were to develop.

Notice the similarity of these seven criteria for vigilant information processing and the satisficing strategy that we have already discussed.

What are the conditions that make for vigilance? When confronted with a decision, reflective decision makers either consciously or unconsciously consider four issues (Janis and Mann, 1977).

Issue 1: Once the process begins, the decision maker's first question to himself or herself is: Are the risks serious if I don't change? If it is determined that the risks of not changing anything are not serious, then the result is a state of unconflicted adherence. The decision maker simply adheres to the current situation and avoids stress and conflict.

Issue 2: If the answer to the first question is affirmative, however, then the level of stress increases slightly, and the decision maker is likely to ask a second question: Are the risks serious if I do change? Here the emphasis is on losses associated with changing. If the anticipated losses of changing are minimal, then the risks are not serious and the decision maker is predicted to accept uncritically the first reasonable alternative—that is, to opt for a state of unconflicted change. Again stress is limited.

Issue 3: If the answer to the second question is yes, then stress builds because there are serious risks in both changing and not changing. The anxiety typically produces the next question: Is it realistic to hope to find a better solution? If the decision maker believes there is no realistic hope of finding a better solution, then the result is a state of defensive avoidance. In order to escape from the conflict and reduce the stress, the individual avoids making the decision by either passing the buck or rationalizing the current situation.

Issue 4: If, however, there is some perceived hope for a better solution, then the decision maker inquires: Is there sufficient time to search and deliberate? If the decision maker perceives insufficient time, then a state of hypervigilance may occur. Panic sets in and the individual seizes upon a hastily contrived solution that promises immediate relief. If time is ample, then the decision maker is much more likely to engage in vigilant information processing, a process that enhances the effectiveness of the decision making through careful search, appraisal, and contingency planning.

Clearly, administrators should avoid unconflicted adherence, unconflicted change, defensive avoidance, and hypervigilance; however, the forces of labor, time, and stress are operating against vigilance. Nevertheless, knowing the dangers of defective decision making and when they are most likely to occur should help avoid them.

Participation in Decision Making

In 1948 Lester Coch and John R. P. French conducted a classic study on the effects of participation in decision making, using a series of field experiments at the Harwood Manufacturing Corporation. The results were clear and conclusive: employee participation in decision making improved productivity. Other studies also have supported the desirability and influence of participation in decision making, both in business and in educational organizations.[9] The following generalizations summarize much of the research and theoretical literature on teacher participation in decision making.

- The opportunity to share in formulating policies is an important factor in the morale of teachers and in their enthusiasm for the school.
- Participation in decision making is positively related to the individual teacher's satisfaction with the profession of teaching.
- Teachers prefer principals who involve them in decision making.
- Decisions fail because of poor quality or because they are not accepted by subordinates.
- Teachers neither expect nor want to be involved in every decision; in fact, too much involvement can be as detrimental as too little.
- The roles and functions of both teachers and administrators in decision making need to be varied according to the nature of the problem.

Should teachers be involved in decision making and policy formulation? Wrong question! Sometimes they should. Other times they should not. Involvement can produce either positive or negative consequences. The appropriate questions are: Under what conditions should subordinates be involved in decision making? To what extent? How?

There are a number of models of shared decision making that are useful in answering these questions. The most well-known model is one originally developed by Victor Vroom and Phillip Yetton (1973) and refined by Vroom and Jago (1988). The Vroom-Jago model matches participation in decision making with the nature of the problem and situation. From the extant research, a set of eight rules is developed to improve the quality and acceptance of a decision. In addition, the constraints of time and development are formulated as two additional rules. In brief, these 10 rules provide a complicated model of participation that requires the use of a complex set of decision trees or a computer (Vroom and Jago, 1988). The model has its limitations for practice, in that it is initially difficult to learn and then challenging to apply; nonetheless, students of administration would be well advised to examine the formulation in some depth (Vroom and Jago, 1988; Hoy and Tarter, 1995). We focus our attention on a simplified model of shared decision making developed by Hoy and Tarter (1992, 1993a, 1993b, 1995).

Hoy-Tarter Model of Shared Decision Making

Subordinates accept some decisions without question because they are indifferent to them. As Barnard (1938: 167) explains, there is a **zone of indifference** "in each individual within which orders are accepted without conscious questioning of their authority." Simon prefers the more positive term of **zone of acceptance,** but the terms are used interchangeably in the literature. The subordinates' zone of acceptance is critical in deciding under what conditions to involve or not involve subordinates in the decision making.

Zone of Acceptance: Its Significance and Determination

Drawing on the work of Barnard (1938), Simon (1947), and Chase (1951), Edwin M. Bridges (1967) advances two propositions about shared decision making:

1. As subordinates are involved in making decisions located within their zone of acceptance, participation will be less effective.
2. As subordinates are involved in making decisions located outside their zone of acceptance, participation will be more effective.

The problem for the administrator is to determine which decisions fall inside and which outside the zone. Bridges suggests two tests to answer this question:

- *The test of relevance:* Do the subordinates have a personal stake in the decision outcomes?
- *The test of expertise:* Do subordinates have the expertise to make a useful contribution to the decision?

The answers to these two questions define the four situations pictured in Figure 9.3. When subordinates have both expertise and a personal stake in the outcomes, then the decision is clearly outside their zone of acceptance. But if subordinates have neither expertise nor a personal stake, then the decision is inside the zone. There are, however, two marginal conditions, each with different decisional constraints. When subordinates have expertise but no personal stake, or have a personal stake but no particular expertise, the conditions are more problematic. Hoy and Tarter (1995) propose two additional theoretical propositions for guidance:

3. As subordinates are involved in making decisions for which they have marginal expertise, their participation will be marginally effective.
4. As subordinates are involved in making decisions for which they have marginal interest, their participation will be marginally effective.

		Do Subordinates Have a Personal Stake?	
		Yes	No
Do Subordinates Have Expertise?	Yes	Outside Zone of Acceptance (Probably Include)	Marginal with Expertise (Occasionally Include)
	No	Marginal with Relevance (Occasionally Include)	Inside Zone of Acceptance (Definitely Exclude)

FIGURE 9.3 *The Zone of Acceptance and Involvement*

Trust and Situations

One more consideration is useful if we are to be successful in applying the model to actual problems. Trust of subordinates should sometimes moderate their degree of involvement.[10] When subordinates' personal goals conflict with organizational ones, it is ill-advised to delegate decisions to them because of the high risk that decisions will be made on personal bases at the expense of the overall welfare of the school.[11] Thus subordinate trust is important, and to gauge trust, we propose a final test.

- *The test of trust:* Are subordinates committed to the mission of the organization? And can they be trusted to make decisions in the best interests of the organization?

If the decision is outside the zone of acceptance and if subordinates can be trusted to make decisions in the best interest of the organization, then participation should be extensive. We call this a *democratic situation* because the only issue is whether the decision should be made by consensus or majority rule. But if the decision is outside the zone and there is little trust in the subordinate, then we have a *conflictual situation* and participation should be restricted. To do otherwise invites moving in directions inconsistent with the overall welfare of the organization.

If the decision issue is not relevant to subordinates and they have no expertise, however, then the decision clearly falls within their zone of acceptance and involvement should be avoided; this is a *noncollaborative situation.* Indeed, participation in such cases will likely produce resentment because subordinates typically are not interested.

When subordinates have a personal stake in the issue but little expertise, we have a *stakeholder situation* and subordinate participation should be limited and only occasional. To do otherwise courts trouble. If subordinates have nothing substantive to contribute, the decision ultimately will be made by those with the expertise (not subordinates), and a sense of frustration and hostility may be generated. Subordinates, in fact, may perceive the experience as an empty exercise in which the decisions have "already been made." Daniel L. Duke, Beverly K. Showers, and Michael Imber (1980) conclude from their research that shared decision making is often viewed by teachers as a formality or attempt to create the illusion of teacher influence. On the other hand, occasionally it may be useful to involve teachers in a limited way. When involvement is sought under these circumstances, it must be done skillfully. Its major objectives should be to open communication with subordinates, to educate them, and to gain support for the decision.

Finally, when there is an *expert situation*—when subordinates have no personal stake in the outcomes but do have the knowledge to make a useful contribution. Should subordinates be involved? Only occasionally! To involve them indiscriminately in decisions of this type is to increase the likelihood of alienation. Although involvement under these circumstances increases the administrator's chances of reaching a higher-quality decision, subordinates too often are likely to wonder aloud "what the administrator gets paid for." These decision situations and appropriate responses are summarized in Figure 9.4.

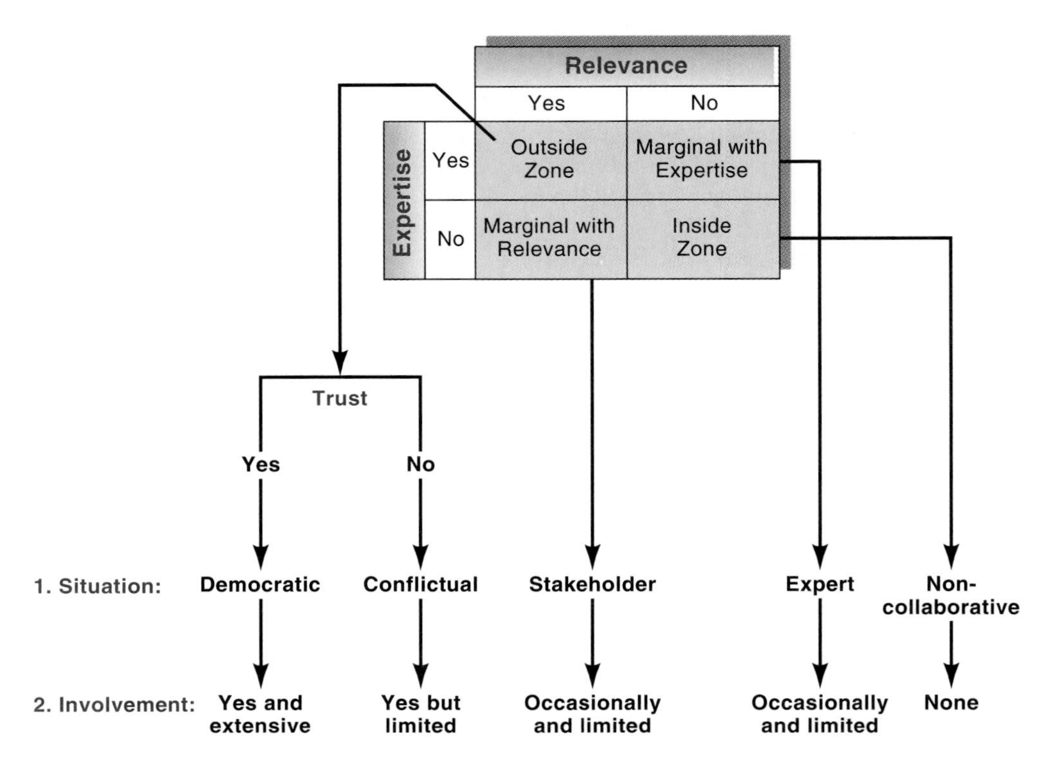

FIGURE 9.4 *Decision Situation and Subordinate Involvement*

Decision-Making Structures

Once the administrator has determined that subordinates should be involved in deciding, the next question becomes how the process should proceed. Hoy and Tarter (1995) suggest five decision-making structures:

1. *Group consensus:* The administrator involves participants in the decision making, then the group decides. All group members share equally as they generate and evaluate a decision, but total consensus is required before a decision can be made.
2. *Group majority:* The administrator involves participants in the decision making, then the group decides by majority rule.
3. *Group advisory:* The administrator solicits the opinions of the entire group, discusses the implications of group suggestions, then makes a decision that may or may not reflect subordinates' desires.
4. *Individual advisory:* The administrator consults with subordinates individually who have expertise to inform the decision, then makes a decision that may or may not reflect their opinions.
5. *Unilateral decision:* The administrator makes the decision without consulting or involving subordinates in the decision.

TABLE 9.3

Administrative Roles for Shared Decision Making

Role	Function	Aim
Integrator	Integrates divergent positions	To gain consensus
Parliamentarian	Promotes open discussion	To support reflective group deliberation
Educator	Explains and discusses issues	To seek acceptance of decisions
Solicitor	Solicits advice	To improve quality of decisions
Director	Makes unilateral decisions	To achieve efficiency

Leader Roles

Thus far we have focused on subordinates in shared decision making. Now we turn to the administrator and define five leadership roles: integrator, parliamentarian, educator, solicitor, and director. The *integrator* brings subordinates together for consensus decision making. Here the task is to reconcile divergent opinions and positions. The *parliamentarian* facilitates open communication by protecting the opinions of the minority and leads participants through a democratic process to a group decision. The *educator* reduces resistance to change by explaining and discussing with group members the opportunities and constraints of the decisional issues. The *solicitor* seeks advice from subordinate-experts. The quality of decisions is improved as the administrator guides the generation of relevant information. The *director* makes unilateral decisions in those instances where the subordinates have no expertise or personal stake. Here the goal is efficiency. The function and aim of each role is summarized in Table 9.3.

Putting It Together: A Model for Shared Decision Making

Administrators are too often exhorted to involve teachers in all decisions. The more appropriate stance is to reflect upon the question: When should others be involved in decision making and how? We have proposed a model that answers this question.

The key concept in the model, drawn from Barnard (1938) and Simon (1947), is the zone of acceptance. There are some decisions that subordinates simply accept and, therefore, in which they need not be involved. The administrator identifies those situations by asking two questions:

1. *Relevance question:* Do the subordinates have a personal stake in the outcome?

2. *Expertise question:* Can subordinates contribute expertise to the solution?

If the answer to both these questions is yes, the subordinates have both a personal stake in the outcome and the expertise to contribute, then the situation is outside the zone of acceptance. Subordinates will want to be involved, and their involvement should improve the decision. However, one must next evaluate their commitment to the organization by asking the following question:

3. *Trust question:* Can subordinates be trusted to make a decision in the best interests of the organization?

If they are committed, their involvement should be extensive as the group tries to develop the "best" decision. In the process, the role of the administrator is to act either as an integrator (if consensus is essential) or as a parliamentarian (if a group majority is sufficient). If subordinates are not committed (conflictual situation), their involvement should be limited. In this situation the administrator acts as an educator, and the group serves to advise and identify pockets of resistance.

If, however, subordinates have only a personal stake in the decision but no expertise (stakeholder situation), their involvement should be occasional and limited. Subordinates are interested in the outcome, but they have little knowledge to bring to bear on the decision. The reason for occasional involvement in this situation is to lower resistance and educate participants. If the involvement is more than occasional, the danger is alienation as teachers feel manipulated because their wishes are not met. At the outset, all parties should know that the group is clearly advisory to the leader. The administrator's role is to decide and educate.

If subordinates have expertise but no personal stake (expert situation), their involvement should also be occasional and limited as the administrator attempts to improve the decision by tapping the expertise of significant individuals who are not normally involved in this kind of action. At first blush, one might think that expertise should always be consulted in a decision, but if workers have no personal stake in the outcomes, their enthusiasm will quickly wane. They may well grumble, "This isn't my job."

In noncollaborative situations the teachers have neither the interest nor the expertise to contribute to the decision. Yet there is such a strong norm about involving teachers in all sorts of decisions that school administrators often feel constrained to involve teachers regardless of their knowledge or interest. Such ritual is dysfunctional and illogical. Why would you involve someone in a decision when that person doesn't care and can't help? The model suggests that administrators make direct unilateral decisions when the issue is within the zone of acceptance of subordinates. The entire model is summarized in Figure 9.5.

This model for shared decision making is not a panacea. It is not a substitute for sensitive and reflective administrative thought and action; it simply provides some guidelines for determining when and how teachers and

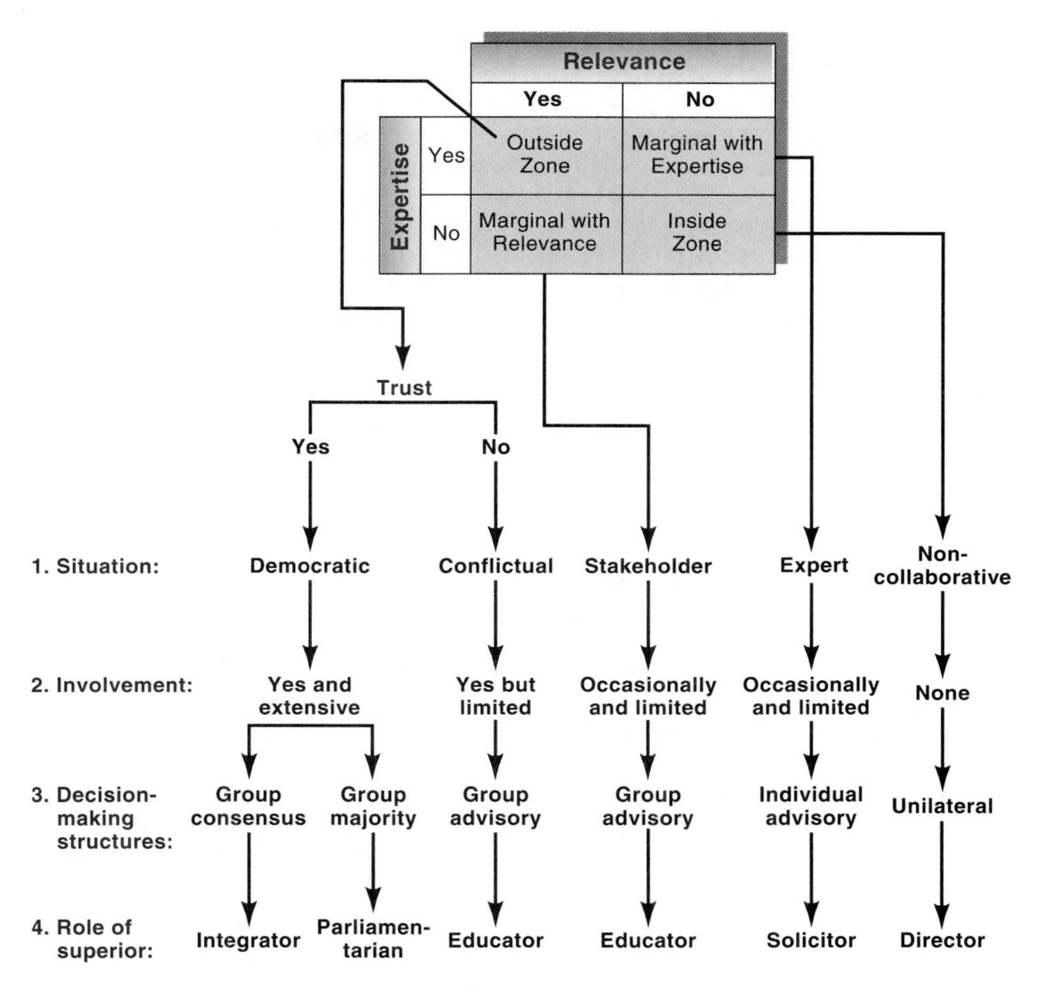

FIGURE 9.5 *A Normative Model for Participative Decision Making*

principals should be involved in joint decision making. The effectiveness of decisions is determined by both the quality of the decision and the acceptance and commitment of subordinates to implement the decision.

A Caution on Group Decision Making: Groupthink

There is little question that group decision making can be an effective process, but there are some dangers even when the conditions call for a group decision. Time is always a potential constraint on participation in decision making, and group decisions typically require more time than individual decisions. Participation involves discussion, debate, and often conflict; in fact, as the number of actors increases in the process, coordination becomes more important and difficult. Speed and efficiency are not basic advantages of group decision making.

Although participation in decision making can produce rampant conflict in the group, success in group problem solving often produces a strong cohesiveness, especially among members of smaller "in" groups. Too much cohesiveness can be as dangerous as conflict. Conflict prevents action; strong cohesiveness promotes uniformity within the group. The problem with uniformity is that it can produce a like-mindedness that is uncritical. Janis (1985) highlights this concurrence-seeking tendency among moderately or highly cohesive groups. When the tendency is dominant, the members use their collective cognitive resources to develop rationalizations consistent with the shared illusion about the invulnerability of their organization; that is, they display the **groupthink syndrome.**

The following eight main symptoms of groupthink characterize historic decision-making fiascoes (Janis and Mann, 1977; Janis, 1982):

- *Illusion of invulnerability:* Members ignore obvious danger, take extreme risks, and are overly optimistic.
- *Collective rationalization:* Members discredit and explain away warning contrary to group thinking.
- *Illusion of morality:* Members believe their decisions are morally correct, ignoring the ethical consequences of their decisions.
- *Excessive stereotyping:* The group constructs negative stereotypes of rivals outside the group.
- *Pressure for conformity:* Members pressure any in the group who express arguments against the group's stereotypes, illusions, or commitments, viewing such opposition as disloyalty.
- *Self-censorship:* Members withhold their dissenting views and counterarguments.
- *Illusion of unanimity:* Members perceive falsely that everyone agrees with the group's decision; silence is seen as consent.
- *Mindguards:* Some members appoint themselves to the role of protecting the group from adverse information that might threaten group complacency.

Conditions That Foster Groupthink

Janis (1985) provides a comprehensive analysis of the conditions that encourage groupthink. The likelihood that groupthink will occur in cohesive groups depends on a number of conditions. One of the most potent conditions is insulation from direct contact with others in the same organization who are not members of the "in" group of policy makers. As Janis (1985) explains:

> For example, an insulated group of executives is likely to receive only brief and unimpressive summaries of warning about the insurmountable difficulties of implementing a strategic reorganization or a new method of production that is under consideration. The top commanders of the organization may end up concurring on a course of action that many

> middle-level and lower-level personnel on the firing line could have informed them in advance would not be feasible. (p. 174)

Lack of impartial leadership also will encourage concurrence seeking, especially when the leader is strong and charismatic. Followers seek to please such leaders, and knowing a leader's initial preferences channels their thinking. Moreover, lack of norms requiring systematic analysis as well as homogeneity of members' social background and ideology contribute to like-mindedness.

Similarly, the situational context may nurture groupthink. We have already discussed the negative consequences produced by stress. High stress from external threats combined with little hope that the leader will advance a better solution pushes the group toward uncritical consensus. Furthermore, low self-esteem of the group, temporarily induced by recent failures, excessive difficulties, and moral dilemmas, fosters groupthink. All these antecedent conditions promote a tendency toward concurrence seeking, which in turn produces the consequences of groupthink—overestimation of the group, closed mindedness, and pressure of unanimity. Such behavior makes for low vigilance in decision making, which ultimately results in defective decision making with a low probability of a successful outcome.

Avoiding Groupthink

There are a number of ways to prevent groupthink. The following 10 recommendations are a tentative set of prescriptions for counteracting the conditions that foster groupthink (Janis, 1985).

1. The group should be made aware of the causes and consequences of groupthink.
2. The leader should be neutral when assigning a decision-making task to a group, initially withholding all preferences and expectations. This practice will be especially effective if the leader consistently encourages an atmosphere of open inquiry.
3. The leader should give high priority to airing objections and doubts, and be accepting of criticism.
4. Groups should always consider unpopular alternatives, assigning the role of devil's advocate to several strong members of the group.
5. Sometimes it is useful to divide the group into two separate deliberative bodies as feasibilities are evaluated.
6. The group should spend a sizable amount of time surveying all warning signals from rival groups and organizations.
7. After reaching a preliminary consensus on a decision, all residual doubts should be expressed and the matter reconsidered.
8. Outside experts should be included in vital decision making.
9. Tentative decisions should be discussed with trusted colleagues, not in the decision-making group.
10. The organization should routinely follow the administrative practice of establishing several independent decision-making groups to work on the same critical issue or policy.

THEORY INTO PRACTICE

Anonymous Letter[12]

Jack Garner is the principal of Dewey Elementary School. Dewey is one of five elementary schools in Pleasantville, a community of 30,000 in a middle Atlantic state.

Pleasantville is an interesting cross section of America. It is a working-class community in transition to a different kind of workforce. The old work of farms, mills, and mines has given way to newer occupations in a small aircraft plant and in the emergence of the state college (recently renamed the State University at Pleasantville). The paper mill, a carpet factory, a chemical plant, a small steel mill, and a coal mine were formerly the major employers of the townspeople. But recently, much to the dismay of the working people in Pleasantville, most of the factories and mills are in decline. Unemployment is up to 13 percent and not getting better. The people blame the government. In the old days, there had been no EPA and no environmentalists and no interference from the state and federal bureaucrats. In those days, people worked hard and made a decent living.

With the advent of environmental protection regulations and changes in the marketplace, the steel mill employs only half the people it employed 15 years ago. So too with the paper mill and the coal mine. The chemical plant is on the verge of bankruptcy because newer dyes are imported from abroad and expensive chemical cleanup projects have plagued the plant for the past three years. In fact, there seems to be only one major industry that is thriving in Pleasantville—the state university. It is growing, from an enrollment of 2,000 10 years ago to nearly 10,000 students today. Although construction of the expanding campus produced many jobs during the past five years, it did not offset the decline of the old industries. Moreover, many of the jobs that were produced by the state university were professional positions that required employment of outsiders rather than townspeople.

Some people resent the intrusion from the outside and harken back to the halcyon days of the past. Others in the community, especially businesspeople, welcome the expansion of the school and are proud of the fact that Pleasantville has become sophisticated.

Jack Garner is no stranger to Pleasantville. At 35, his entire life has been spent in and around Pleasantville. He went to elementary school, junior high, and high school in town. Upon graduation, he went to the local state college and majored in education. His first job was as a science teacher at Pleasantville High. During his first year of teaching, Jack Garner decided that he wanted an expanded role in education down the road. He began taking curriculum classes in the summers at the main campus of the state university, 65 miles from Pleasantville.

Taking courses at the main campus was Garner's first real exposure to life outside Pleasantville. A chronic bad knee had kept him out of the service, and perhaps just as well. Thinking back, Garner judged the experience at the main campus to be an eye-opener for a country boy, as he sometimes refers to himself. Ten years later, he had completed his doctorate in educational curriculum, served as districtwide elementary science curriculum coordinator, and as a result of his success in working with people and his genuine good sense, he was promoted to principal of the new Dewey Elementary School. Some might think that Dewey is a progressive school, but the Dewey this elementary school was named after was Thomas, the former governor of New York, not the educator. Therein lay a substantial difference. Dewey Elementary School is not a place hospitable to change. Former students who grew up in the system send their children to Dewey. They want the same good education they had received—no frills, no life adjustment, no multiculturalism, no debates on right to life or the nature of families, just basic learning in reading, math, science, writing, and history.

There is no question that the surrounding neighborhood of Dewey is conservative, but it is slowly changing as more and more college professors buy houses in Dewey Heights. In fact, the Dewey neighborhood is becoming a choice residential area for young professionals in the community.

THEORY INTO PRACTICE, (Continued)

As a curriculum person and skillful administrator, Garner has been able to initiate a strong elementary school curriculum. He has combined many of the elements of cooperative learning and mastery education in order to engage students individually and collectively in the pursuit of math, science, and reading. His whole-language approach to the teaching of English and composition is a model that is frequently observed by students from the local college. (Garner has a hard time thinking of his undergraduate school as a state university; he still thinks of it as his college.) Five years as curriculum coordinator and five years as principal have produced a school of which he is proud. The elementary school students continue to do well and parents are generally supportive of his initiatives, even though some complain that he is getting away from the basics.

It is Monday morning. As Jack reviews his mail, he is shocked by the third letter he opens and reads.

May 11

Dear Dr. Garner:

You should know that your science curriculum supervisor is a homo. He lives with another man and I have seen them fondling each other in the tavern in Greenville. I don't care what people do in their private lives, but teachers are different. I don't want my son endangered by this guy. Of course, there is always the question of AIDS, and I don't want him abusing my child. There is a rumor that Jenkins has not been well. Frankly, we're worried for the safety of our children.

We know that you are with us on this issue. After all, you are one of us. Why don't you do something about this? Everyone is talking about it. And if you don't do something, I can't be responsible for what some hotheads might do. Jenkins is in some danger.

I am not going to sign this letter because I don't want to be involved in this, but I think you ought to know about the situation. Someone is going to get hurt. Do something before it becomes a police matter.

Sincerely,

A Concerned Parent

Matt Jenkins had been Garner's new elementary science supervisor for the past three years. Although Garner had not hired Jenkins directly, the former superintendent, who had thought highly of Jenkins, consulted him. Garner had called one of his former professors in curriculum at the state university and the professor had said, "He is a little peculiar but without question he is one of the brightest and most creative students I have known. He will be an asset to your program." Without much further ado, Jenkins was hired, even though he was an outsider and a segment of the community was opposed to hiring from the outside.

There is no question in Garner's mind that Jenkins had shown strong leadership in improving the science curriculum at Dewey. Other teachers like him because he is low-key, supportive, sensitive, and nurturing. He has a few odd mannerisms, but they don't seem to bother anyone. He stays to himself and lives 10 miles outside the city, in a small suburb of Pleasantville called Greenville. No one seems to know much about Jenkins or his personal life. Rumor has it that Jenkins spends a lot of his time at University Station, the main campus of the state university. Many of the townspeople take a dim view of the liberal goings-on in University Station, but it is a world away. Only one time could Garner remember any negative comments about Jenkins. One of the parents had complained that he was always touching her son. Garner had discreetly looked into this matter and found nothing substantial. Rather, he found that Jenkins had grabbed the student in question a number of times to correct his aggressive behavior with the other children. The student in question was a little on the wild side.

Garner was a bit surprised to discover that Jenkins lives with a new high school English teacher, Brad Korbus. Garner had been instrumental in the recruitment and selection of Korbus, and now the two teachers were roommates in Greenville. Garner is inclined to believe that whatever people do privately is their own business. His policy for dealing with anonymous letters is to file them in the circular file. Yet the implied threat of this letter troubles him.

He felt constrained to do something, but what? He thought about turning the matter over to the

THEORY INTO PRACTICE, (Continued)

local police. Should he talk to his superintendent? Is this a crank letter from an isolated individual? Does he have a right to make inquiries—even if done discreetly? Should he talk to Jenkins? What would he say, if he did? Suppose Jenkins is gay and living with another man, would it matter? Is there a problem? A potential problem? Is this a time for preventive action? Or will any action simply exacerbate the situation? Is it time for the district to develop a policy on private behavior or alternative lifestyles?

Assume the role of principal.

- What are the short-term and long-term problems in this case?
- Is this a case for satisficing, muddling through, or adaptive scanning?
- What are your immediate and long-term plans?
- Who should be involved in this decision and how?
- No matter what your eventual strategy, make sure it includes a plan to address the dysfunctional consequences of your actions.

Summary and Suggested Readings

An understanding of the decision-making process is vital to successful administration. Four basic strategies of managerial decision making are identified and described. The optimizing strategy of the classical model is found not to be useful to administrators because it assumes perfect information, rationality, and human capacity not found in the actual world of administration.

Although completely rational decision making is impossible, administrators need a systematic process to enhance the selection of satisfactory solutions. Thus, a strategy of satisficing is central to decision making in the administrative model. Here decision making is a cycle of activity that includes recognition and definition of the problem, analysis of difficulties, establishment of criteria for a satisfactory resolution, development of a plan of action, and initiation of the plan. Because of its cyclical nature, the decision-making action cycle may be entered at different stages and the stages are gone through again and again in the process of administration.

The satisficing strategy is well suited for dealing with many problems in educational administration; however, when the set of alternatives is indefinable or the consequences of each alternative are unpredictable, then an incremental strategy may seem more appropriate. This process is a method of successive limited comparisons; only a limited set of alternatives, similar to the existing situation, is considered by successively comparing their consequences until agreement is reached on a course of action. It is assumed that small changes are not likely to produce large negative consequences for the organization.

Incrementalism, however, can be too conservative and self-defeating. Incremental decisions made without fundamental guidelines can lead to action without direction. Thus, the mixed-scanning model of decision making is proposed for complex decisions. Mixed scanning unites the best of both the administrative and the incremental models. A strategy of satisficing is used in combination with incremental decision making guided by broad policy.

Full scanning is replaced by partial scanning and tentative decisions are made incrementally in a process that is guided by a clear sense of destination.

As in most complex tasks, however, there is no single best approach to deciding; the best strategy is the one that best matches the circumstances. We have proposed a set of guidelines that matches the right strategy with the situation.

The garbage can model of organizational decision making is useful for understanding nonrational decisions. In this model, the decision does not begin with a problem and end with a solution; rather, organizations are viewed as sets of choices looking for problems, issues and feelings seeking opportunities, solutions searching for problems, and administrators looking for work. Problems, solutions, participants, and choice opportunities act as independent events. When they mesh, some problems are solved, but in this chaotic decision process many problems are not solved—they simply persist. The model explains why solutions may be proposed to problems that do not exist and why irrelevant choices are made.

Regardless of the strategy, decision making often causes stress, which produces irrationality. The conditions under which stress has unfavorable effects on the quality of decision making are discussed, and five coping mechanisms that decision makers are most likely to use in stressful situations are analyzed.

It is not always beneficial for administrators to involve subordinates in decision making. A simplified model of shared decision making is proposed to help administrators determine under what conditions subordinates should and should not participate in the decision-making process. The framework uses the tests of relevance, expertise, and commitment as guides for participation. Administrators, depending on the circumstances, use the roles of integrator, parliamentarian, educator, solicitor, and director. Finally, the conditions that foster groupthink are analyzed, and suggestions are proposed for avoiding them.

Decision making is a complex process. Ideas and theories are drawn from such diverse disciplines as cognitive science, economics, political science, psychology, and sociology. Several supplementary books are useful to beginning students. James G. March (1994) provides a primer on decision making; his book is concerned with how decisions actually happen rather they how they should; his ideas are simple and straightforward. Amitai Etzioni (1988) reminds us of the moral dimension of decision making and the centrality of moral issues in economic thought. Two edited selections are worth perusing: Mary Zey's (1992) collection pursues alternatives to the rational-choice models, and the March (1988) selections examine decision making under ambiguity. For those students who want a sophisticated treatment of participation in decision making, Victor Vroom and Arthur Jago (1988) provide an excellent and comprehensive model. Hoy and Tarter (1995) use case studies to link decision theory to problems of practice; they demonstrate the utility of good theory in solving actual administrative problems in schools. Finally, Willower and Licata (1997) discuss values and valuation in educational decision making and demonstrate the use of "consequence analysis" to solve the problems of practice.

NOTES

1. Research suggests that many administrators ignore normative methods prescribed by scholars for effective decision making and persist in questionable decision tactics. See Nutt (1984).
2. What has been termed policy making in the public sector is often discussed as strategic formulation in the private sector; for example, see Henry Mintzberg (1978) and Johannes Pennings (1985).
3. For an excellent discussion and application of values and valuation in the practice of educational administration, see Willower and Licata (1997).
4. Iterations of this cycle occur frequently in the organizational literature. For example, see Griffiths (1959) and Daft (1989).
5. The problem is much more complex, however, if it also involves the integration of minority students into segregated schools.
6. A critical and interesting analysis of heuristics is made by a group of cognitive psychologists called the *prospect school.* Their main thesis is that individuals cope with their limited cognitive abilities by using heuristic devices to solve complex problems. Although the heuristics help, they themselves sometimes introduce systematic biases that may subvert decision making. For example, see Nisbett and Ross (1980) and Kahneman, Solvic, and Tversky (1982).
7. Etzioni (1967) reports that 50 articles and Ph.D. dissertations have been written on mixed scanning since his original article. For his synthesis, see Etzioni (1986).
8. This section draws heavily on the work of Janis (1985) and Janis and Mann (1977).
9. For studies that support the desirability of participation in decision making, see Sharma, 1955; Guest, 1960; Vroom, 1960, 1976; Belasco and Allutto, 1972; Allutto and Belasco, 1973; Conway, 1976; Hoy, Newland, and Blazovsky, 1977; Driscoll, 1978; Mohrman, Cooke, and Mohrman, 1978; Moon, 1983. For a comprehensive and somewhat critical review of participation in decision making, see Locke and Schweiger (1979). Likewise, for a review of participative decision making in education, see Conway (1984). The effects of subordinate participation in decision making, however, are neither simple nor unambiguous; for example see Imber, 1983; Conway, 1984; Imber and Duke, 1984; Vroom and Jago, 1988; Conley, Bower, and Bacharach, 1989; Bacharach, Bamberger, Conley, and Bauer, 1990; Conley, 1990.
10. In earlier versions of this model, this third test was called commitment; we believe trust is a better word to capture the meaning of the test.
11. For a useful distinction between shared decision making and delegation of decision making, see Hoy and Sousa (1984), and for a critical analysis on participation in schools, see Keith (1996).
12. Hoy and Tarter (1995) illustrate the application of decision theory to practice with actual contemporary cases and then provide 30 new cases

from educational settings for consideration. The anonymous letter was written by Hoy and Tarter for this chapter. From Hoy and Tarter Administrators Solving the Problems of Practice. Copyright © 1995 by Allyn & Bacon. Adapted by permission.

Key Concepts and Ideas

Adaptive strategy
Administrative model
Anchoring-and-adjustment heuristic
Availability heuristic
Boundary conditions
Bounded rationality
Classical model
Defensive avoidance
Garbage can model
Generic decisions
Groupthink syndrome
Heuristics
Hypervigilance
Incremental model
Mixed-scanning model
Muddling through
Opportunistic surveillance
Optimizing
Policy
Problemistic search
Recognition Heuristic
Representative heuristic
Satisficing
Unconflicted adherence
Unconflicted change
Unique decisions
Vigilance
Zone of acceptance
Zone of indifference

CHAPTER 10

Communication in Schools

Humans live by communication, and many of the practices that we think define us as human are a direct outgrowth of the ways in which we communicate: our language, our reasoning, our morality, and our social organization.

Nicholas C. Burbules
Dialogue in Teaching

Preview

1. Communication pervades virtually all aspects of school life. It does not, however, provide all the answers to the problems confronting educational administrators.
2. Current conceptions of communication rely on notions that communication involves meaningful exchanges of symbols between at least two people.
3. One-way communication is unilateral, initiated by a speaker, and terminated at a listener.
4. Two-way communication is a reciprocal, interactive process with all participants in the process initiating and receiving messages. Interactive communication is transactional; it has no necessary beginning or ending.
5. Conversation, inquiry, debate, and instruction are four types of two-way communication.
6. Humans use two major symbol systems in their efforts to communicate—verbal and nonverbal.
7. As the content of communication becomes more ambiguous, richer media can improve communication performance.
8. Each new communication technology imposes its own special requirements on how messages are composed. Technology also governs the speed and convenience of sending messages and influences the ways receivers reconstruct meaning.
9. Formal channels are communication networks sanctioned by the organization and directed toward organizational goals.
10. Individuals bypass formal channels of communication by using informal networks or "grapevines."
11. The degree of centralization, shape of the hierarchy, and level of information technology influence how the formal communication system operates in schools.
12. Although the formal network is usually larger and better developed than the informal, they are closely related, can be complementary, and are critical to the organization.

Even though educators and students are barraged with hundreds of messages and pieces of information every day that seem to demand attention (Sanchez, 1999), communication is complex, subtle, and ubiquitous; it permeates every aspect of school life. Teachers instruct, using oral, written, and other media such as videotapes, computers, and art forms. Students demonstrate their learning through similar media. And superintendents and principals spend the majority of their time communicating. Given this importance, educational administrators simply must understand communication because it underlies or infuses the interpersonal, organizational, and administrative processes and structures of schools. Communication skills, therefore, are essential tools for an effective administrator. However, before concluding that communication provides all the answers to the problems confronting educational administrators, four caveats must be observed.

- Communication is difficult to isolate from such other administrative processes as deciding, motivating, and leading.
- Not all school problems involve unsuccessful communication. Problems commonly attributed to poor interactions may reflect breakdowns in other fundamental components of school life.
- Communication reveals and hides as well as eliminates problems (Katz and Kahn, 1978). It can surface conflicts in values among teachers, students, and administrators that may otherwise go unnoticed, and it also may obscure existing problems by glossing over issues with empty rhetoric.
- Communication is a process that evokes action, but it is far from being the substance of good administration. It is no substitute for faulty ideas and misguided educational programs.

Even though these cautions are limitations, communication does serve several pervasive and integrative functions in schools. To claim that communication is either the universal problem or problem solver oversimplifies and limits both the analysis and the solution of educational problems. In this chapter, we will discuss a variety of conceptual approaches while attempting to keep both the important functions and the cautionary guides in proper perspective.

Theoretical Approaches to Communication

In everyday usage, communication is the process that people use to exchange significant messages and share meaning about their ideas and feelings with one another (Porter and Roberts, 1976; Manning, 1992). **Communication,** in other words, is sharing messages, ideas, or attitudes in ways that produce a degree of understanding between two or more people (Lewis, 1975). Using face-to-face or technological media, individuals interact and influence each other through communication (Craig, 1999). Practically all conceptions of communication contain explicit or implicit notions that involve meaningful interactions between at least two people. For example, educators do not communicate in a vacuum but with other educators, citizens, and students; and successful exchange does not occur unless both parties develop shared interpretations of the information.

Kathleen J. Krone, Fredric M. Jablin, and Linda L. Putnam (1987) observe that virtually all perspectives dealing with communication processes recognize and use the same concepts. Although each term varies somewhat across different theoretical perspectives, we agree with the definitions summarized by Krone and her colleagues.

- **Message** is typically the verbal or nonverbal cues or symbols that each communicator conveys. It is the idea that an individual hopes to communicate.
- **Channel** is the vehicle, medium, or form in which a message travels. Form can range from light waves of nonverbal cues to sound waves of talking face-to-face, to electronic signals in telephones and e-mail.
- **Sender** is the person or a generalized source (e.g., office of the superintendent) sending a message; **receiver** marks the destination of the message or the individual who deciphers it.
- **Transmission** is the actual sending and receiving of messages through designated channels or media.
- **Encoding** and **decoding** involve cognitive structures and processes to create, transform, and decipher messages. Encoding is converting the intended message to symbolic form by the sender. Decoding is retranslating the message by the receiver. Through encoding and decoding processes, individuals compose **meanings** by interpreting or making sense of the message.
- **Feedback** is the message sent in response to the initial message or, as defined in Chapter 1, it is information that enables corrections to be made. Using feedback facilitates interpretation of a message.
- **Communication effects** are the outcomes or general results of the message exchange process—for example, new knowledge, different attitudes, culture, and satisfaction.

Hence, a more elaborate definition is that human communication is a process during which source individuals initiate messages using symbols, signs, and contextual cues to express meaning by transmitting information in ways so that similar understandings are constructed by the receiving individual(s) (DeFleur, Kearney, and Plax, 1993). This definition incorporates the concepts defined above and produces the general model shown in Figure 10.1.

A sender encodes a message with certain intentions and transmits it by some channel to a receiver who then decodes the message and provides feedback to the original sender (see Figure 10.1). Both the source and the receivers are communicators in this process. Note the process is interactive and transactional (Adler and Rodman, 1991); it flows back and forth, often going both ways simultaneously as both talk or as one talks and the other listens and gives feedback through nonverbal cues. Hence Thomas E. Harris (1993) con-

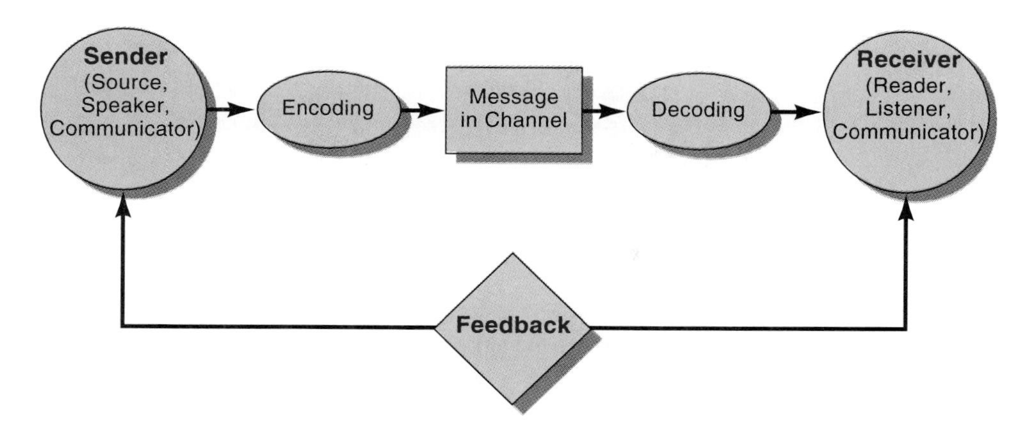

FIGURE 10.1 *A General Model of the Communication Process*

cludes that the process is complex, dynamic, and with no necessary beginning or end. In fact, designating participants as senders and receivers is a subjective but sometimes useful decision.

As important as communication is to the effective operation of schools and other institutions, few comprehensive theories of interpersonal or organizational communication have been developed (Jablin, Putnam, Roberts, and Porter, 1987). For present purposes, we will first describe important components of a general process model (see Figure 10.1) and then use a network framework to analyze organizational communication in schools. These two approaches are amalgams of several models and perspectives.

Components of a General Model of the Communication Process

Michele Tolela Myers and Gail E. Myers (1982) posit that communication can be viewed as a transactional process where people construct meaning and develop expectations about what is happening around them through the exchange of symbols. In constructing meanings, people use **symbols** (i.e., objects or words that stand for ideas, feelings, intentions, and other objects) to describe their experiences and develop a common symbol system or language for sharing their experiences with others. Learning symbols or a language and associating learning symbols with experiences come about by interacting with people and observing what they do when they use symbols. As a result of these interactions and observations, individuals not only learn to construct meanings that are reasonably similar to those of people around them, but also develop expectations or make predictions about what people will do and think. Every day individuals in schools exchange symbols using several different verbal and nonverbal forms (e.g., lecturing, exhorting, explaining, visiting, arguing, negotiating, discussing, dressing, making visual displays). These transactions to gain shared meanings can be conceptualized as a continuum from one-way to two-way communication.

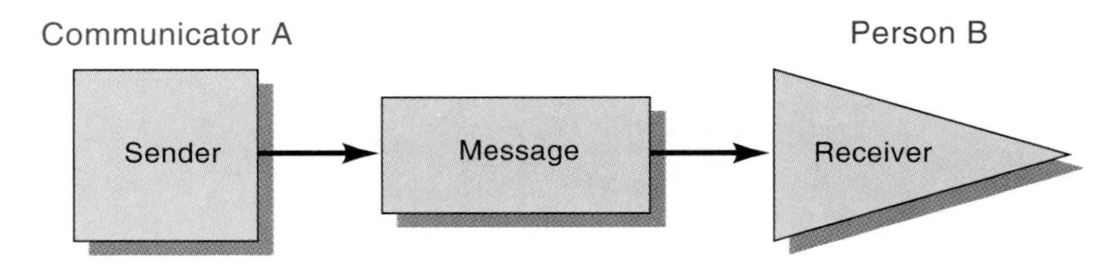

FIGURE 10.2 *Model of One-Way Communication*

One-Way Communication

As shown in Figure 10.2, **one-way communication** occurs when one person tells another person something. This type of communication is unilateral; it is initiated by a speaker and terminated at a listener (Schmuck and Runkel, 1985). Lectures in classrooms about subject matter or exhortations in the principal's office about appropriate demeanor represent widespread applications of one-way communication in schools. Other examples include announcements over the public address system in a school or during meetings. A metaphor for one-way communication as shown in Figure 10.2 is the hypodermic needle approach of injecting information into another person (Broms and Gahmberg, 1983).

The advantages of one-way communication are twofold (Clampitt, 1991). First, it emphasizes the skills of the message sender and encourages administrators and teachers to think through their ideas, accurately articulate them, and provide specificity in their instructions, explanations, and descriptions. Second, one-way strategies typically imply strong linkages between communication behavior and action. Teachers and administrators who use one-way communication discourage idle chatter, discussions of personal problems, and unnecessary information sharing. In other words, it conveys a strong emphasis on efficiency and goal achievement.

Given the need for shared understandings in schools, one-way communication many times is inadequate. For instance, Philip G. Clampitt (1991) asserts that the basic flaw in one-way communication lies in the belief that effective expression equals effective communication. Even if the message sender effectively articulates an idea, it does not necessarily guarantee that it will be understood as intended. Clampitt believes that two faulty assumptions explain the continued reliance on one-way communication. First, receivers are seen as passive information processors. Instead of being passive processing machines, however, people actively reconstruct messages and create their own meanings. Second, words are seen as containers of meaning. Language works against this assumption. For example, meaning depends on how the words are used, the context in which the statement is made, and the people involved. Words do not serve so much as containers of meaning as stimulators of meaning. Therefore, the need for understanding in schools suggests that additional or other forms of communication are required for goal achievement, change, and social purposes.

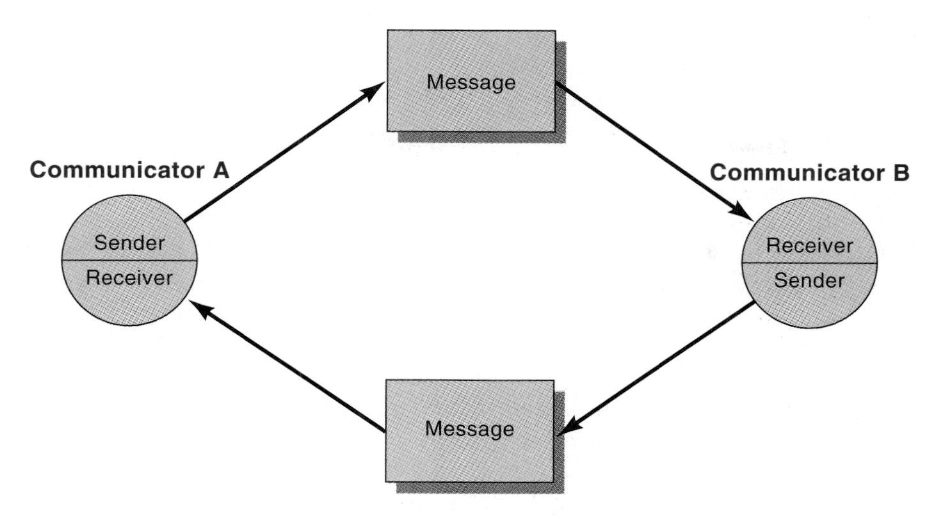

FIGURE 10.3 *Model of Two-Way Communication*

Two-Way Communication

By **two-way communication** we mean a reciprocal, interactive process; all participants in the process initiate and receive messages. In contrast to the one-way approach, two-way communication requires continuous exchanges and transactions. As shown in Figure 10.3, this means that each participant initiates messages and that each message affects the next one. Such interactive exchanges can improve the communication process by reducing the chance of major disparities between the information or idea received and the one intended.

A special case is **autocommunication,** or communicating with oneself. A number of instances of sharing symbols and images with oneself are evident. Examples include keeping a diary, writing an autobiography, engaging in a monologue, reflecting, and meditating. These are instances of a person turning inward to pacify and clarify the mind. Similarly, when writing a memorandum, the individual is *both* informing the other person and building communication schema within his or her cognitive structure (Broms and Gahmberg, 1983).

We conceive of two-way communication as being very similar to the concept of dialogue as defined and discussed by Burbules and Bruce (1993, 2000).[1] From a perspective of dialogue, two-way communication also is an activity directed toward discovery and new understandings; it advances knowledge, insights, and sensitivity. In other words, two-way interactions help the participants learn and change. According to Burbules, the process is a continuous and developmental interchange through which the participants gain a fuller awareness of education, themselves, and each other.

An information-processing perspective provides an explanation of communication, learning, and understanding. Schemas represent organized knowledge about given concepts or types of experience in an individual's memory. They are internal models of the outside world and arise from a variety of sources, including interpersonal communication. Hence, understanding or encoding/decoding involves creating new schemas and incorporating new information into existing schema. Moreover, schemas serve as criteria against which newly encountered messages are judged. As such, schemas are extremely powerful screens; they often cause people to misperceive messages or to misremember them. Whereas existing schemas can be called upon to interpret or decode messages that may be unfamiliar to less experienced people, entrenched schemas may prevent people from making fresh and uncontaminated interpretations about messages they may encounter. For example, educators holding stereotypes (one type of cognitive schema) of certain ethnic, gender, or ability groups will screen new information against their current criteria and probably distort the intent of the message.

Two-way communication is a reciprocal, interactive process directed toward discovery and new understandings through speaking and listening. It offers promise for creating similar schemas (mutual understanding, shared meanings) and for modifying stereotypical schemas. An important corollary of the information-processing model of learning is that merely presenting new information without adequate attention to current schemas virtually guarantees that the new material will be forgotten or misunderstood. Burbules (1993) also gives the cognitive explanation an explicit political interpretation. He explains that in communication encounters, we do not change people; they change themselves. In other words, people construct their own understandings, change their own minds, decide on alternative courses of action, and define their own goals.

Principles of Two-Way Communication Burbules (1993) elaborates his ideas for dialogue by positing three principles or normative standards.

- *The principle of participation* maintains that engagement in a dialogue relationship must be voluntary and open to active involvement by all of its participants in such activities as questioning, trying out new ideas, and hearing diverse points of view.
- *The principle of commitment* holds that engagement must allow the flow of conversation to be persistent and extensive across a range of shared concerns, even when they are difficult and divisive.
- *The principle of reciprocity* proposes that engagement in two-way exchanges must be undertaken in a spirit of mutual respect and concern, and must not take for granted the role of privilege or expertise.

These three principles, then, provide guidelines developing and using two-way communication strategies and communication with creativity, spontaneity, and understanding.

Types of Two-Way Communication Burbules (1993, 2000) also describes four types or patterns of two-way interaction—conversation, inquiry, debate, and instruction.

Conversation is distinguished by two traits—a generally cooperative, tolerant spirit and a direction toward mutual understanding. This form is used when individuals are interested in understanding each other's perspectives and experiences. An example would be two students talking about how they spent their summer vacations and what they learned as a result.

Inquiry involves a coinvestigation to answer a question, resolve a disagreement, or formulate a compromise that is agreeable to all. Dialogue of this nature typically investigates alternatives and examines possible answers within a structure that encourages a range of perspectives and approaches to the problem. An example would be a group of science teachers exploring why some students are thriving in classes using a new project-based curriculum, whereas others are failing.

Debate exhibits sharp questioning, a skeptical spirit, and no necessary need for agreement among the participants. The potential benefit of debate is that the participants see their alternative ideas and positions receive the most intense challenge possible. The aim is that alternative positions can be clarified and strengthened through such an exchange. An example would be seeing policy makers discuss the relative merits of providing public tax support to private schools.

Instruction, as dialogue, involves an intentional process in which a teacher leads students to certain answers or understandings. It generally uses critical questions and other statements to move a discussion to a definite conclusion. The exemplar of this type of two-way communication is the *Socratic method.* A good example of instruction as dialogue is reciprocal teaching. In reciprocal teaching, teachers and students engage in a highly interactive process in which participants take turns assuming the role of teacher (Palincsar, 1986).

In sum, the many types of one-way and two-way communication clearly show that none of the models shown in Figures 10.1, 10.2, and 10.3 is a single technique. An administrator who is a skillful communicator will have a repertoire of communication strategies from which to draw and will be creative and flexible in moving from one approach to another as people, situations, and content change (Burbules and Bruce, 2000).

Channels of Communication: Methods of Exchanging Symbols

In their efforts to communicate, humans use two major symbol systems—verbal and nonverbal (Dahnke and Clatterbuck, 1990). Verbal symbols include:

- Human speech—direct, face-to-face conversation or electronic exchanges via telephone, radio, or television.
- Written media—memos, letters, electronic mail, and newspapers.

Nonverbal symbols include:

- Body language or gestures—facial expressions, posture, and arm movements.
- Physical items or artifacts with symbolic value—office furnishings, clothing, and jewelry.
- Space—territoriality and personal space.

- Touch—hugging.
- Time.
- Other nonverbal symbols—intonation, accents, pitch, intensity of the voice, and rate of speech.

Hence, messages can be communicated in a variety of channels, ways, forms, or media.

Verbal Channels Richard L. Daft and Robert H. Lengel (1984, 1986) hypothesize that media determine the richness of communication, where **richness** is the medium's potential to carry information and resolve ambiguity. Four criteria define media richness: speed of feedback, variety of communication channels, personalness of source, and richness of language. Rich media combine multiple cues, rapid or timely feedback, tailoring the messages to personal circumstances, and a variety of language (Huber and Daft, 1987). Rich media are characterized by high touch and qualitative data; they are best for lessening ambiguity. Lean media are suitable for technology-based, high-volume data exchanges and are best for conveying quantitative data with precision and accuracy to large audiences (Daft, Bettenhausen, and Tyler, 1993). Using these four criteria, Daft and his colleagues place communication media and richness on the parallel continua as shown in Figure 10.4.

The face-to-face medium is the richest form because it provides immediate feedback through verbal and visual cues. Although verbal feedback is rapid, the telephone medium is less rich than face-to-face because the visual cues are absent. Written communication is described as being moderate or low in richness because feedback is slow and only written information is

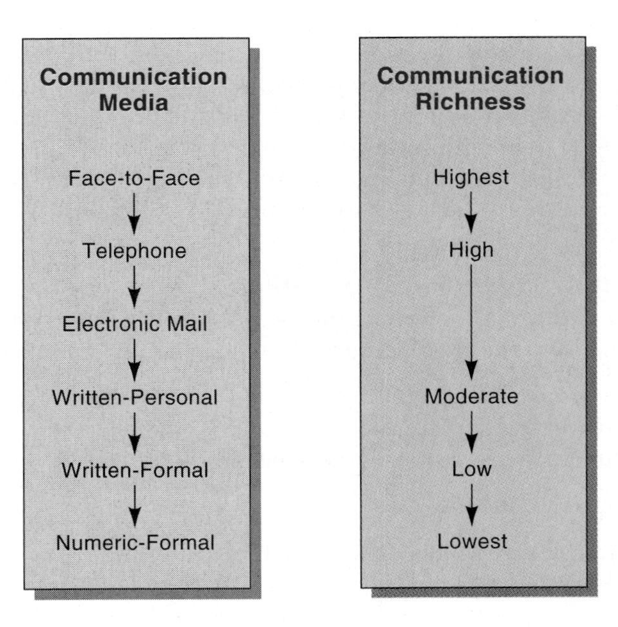

FIGURE 10.4 *Continua for Communication Media and Richness*

conveyed. Addressed correspondence is personal in character and somewhat richer than general memos and bulletins, which are anonymous and impersonal. Formal numeric documents—for example, computer printouts containing quantitative data such as achievement test scores—convey the least-rich information because numbers do not have the information-carrying capacity of natural language. Electronic messaging can be placed between telephone and written personal media on the richness continuum (Steinfield and Fulk, 1986).

The basic hypothesis is that as the content of communication becomes more ambiguous or uncertain, richer media will be selected to improve communication performance. A number of studies have tested the hypothesis with the number supporting and not supporting being about equal (Schmitz and Fulk, 1991). Studies by Daft and his colleagues (Trevino, Lengel, and Daft, 1987; Russ, Daft, and Lengel, 1990) are generally supportive of the basic richness hypothesis. Other studies (Steinfield and Fulk, 1986; Rice, 1992) have found weak or mixed support. Overall, the results are more supportive of the media richness hypothesis when applied to traditional (e.g., face-to-face) rather than newer media (e.g., computers and other electronic devices) (Fulk and Boyd, 1991).

As might be expected from the discussion of richness, when the effects of written and oral media are compared, a problem faces the communicator (Porter and Roberts, 1976). Comprehension is higher when information is presented in written form. However, opinion change or persuasiveness is greater in face-to-face interactions. The appropriate medium thus depends on the purpose—that is, understanding or persuading.

Redundancy in media increases both the richness of the information and the accuracy of message transmission (Redding, 1972). Generally, the most effective and accurate communication efforts use a combination of written and oral media; the next most effective is oral alone; and written is least powerful (Level, 1972). The combination of written and oral media is seldom inappropriate. Written communication alone can be effective in two situations—where information requires future action or where it is general. The oral medium by itself also can be effective in two situations demanding immediate feedback—for administering reprimands and settling disputes.

Nonverbal Channels of Communication Although redundancy in media usually leads to better understanding, vocal and written media carry only a portion of the information that administrators convey when they interact with others. At least as important as verbal signals are the less fully understood nonverbal symbols. **Nonverbal communication** is all behavior of communicative value done in the presence of another that does not use words. The raised eyebrow, the firm handshake, and the impatient tapping of the fingers are well-known actions of nonverbal media that convey meaning. Even silence and rigid inactivity may signal anger, annoyance, depression, or fear. Although this definition of nonverbal communication suggests a rather all-inclusive domain, a gray area still exists between verbal and nonverbal forms. Paralanguage is vocal but not strictly oral. It includes stress, inflection, and speed of speech, as well as nonword vocalizations such as grunts, laughter, sighs, and coughs (Knapp, 1972; Wietz, 1974).

Research on nonverbal communication often explores the meanings of paralanguage, body motion, and spatial cues. For example, a combination of five types of nonverbal behaviors consistently exert the strongest positive influence on one individual's attempts to build rapport with another person: smiling, touching, affirmative head nods, immediacy behavior (e.g., leaning forward), and eye behavior. These behaviors are essential in communicating a sense of warmth, enthusiasm, and interest (Heintzman, Leathers, Parrot, and Adrian Bennett Cairus, 1993).

The face is the most obvious nonverbal conveyor of feelings (McCaskey, 1979). Most feeling is communicated through facial expression. Without formal training, observers of facial expression can distinguish a variety of human emotions such as excitement, humiliation, and fear (Harris, 1993). Eye-to-eye contact is one of the most direct and powerful ways people communicate nonverbally. In mainstream American culture, the social rules indicate that in most situations eye contact for a short period is appropriate. Direct eye contact is also seen as an indication of honesty and credibility. Prolonged eye contact is usually taken to be either threatening or, in another context, a sign of romantic interest. Speakers know that a way to enhance the impact of their presentations is to look directly at individual members of the audience and establish eye contact.

In regard to workspace, Michael B. McCaskey (1979) notes that an office represents personal territory, which separates what belongs to one person from what belongs to others. Where a meeting is held may intimate the purpose of the meeting. To conduct an adversarial discussion, to emphasize hierarchy and authority, or to give directions, McCaskey advises the supervisor to hold the meeting in his or her own office. The office arrangement itself might communicate the intended nature of the interactions. For example, many administrators arrange their offices with two different areas. In one, the administrator talks across the desk to a person seated at the other side. This layout emphasizes the administrator's authority and position. In the second area, chairs are in a circle at a round table. Because the arrangement signals a willingness to downplay hierarchical differences, freer exchanges are encouraged. Hence, an office arrangement with a center for informal conversations, a display of personal memorabilia and decorations, and a relatively close distance between the chairs and desk, represents nonverbal symbols that transmit powerful messages of welcome to visitors. In one of the few studies of nonverbal meaning in educational administration, James M. Lipham and Donald C. Francke (1966) confirmed these propositions in schools.

Congruence of Verbal and Nonverbal Messages Verbal and nonverbal messages must be consistent for effective understanding. An illustration of this generalization usually occurs when a new administrator meets with the staff. A typical verbal statement is, "If you have any questions or problems, please come by my office, and we'll discuss the situation. My door is always open." When a staff member interprets the words literally and does visit the principal, the nonverbal messages probably will determine the meaning of the verbal message. If the person is met at the door, ushered to a chair, and a productive conference results, the verbal message is reinforced and the meaning is understood. If, however, the administrator remains in the chair behind the desk, leaves the staff member standing or seats him or her across the room, and continues to write, the verbal message is contradicted. When verbal and nonverbal message conflict, a problem of meaning results.

New and Emerging Technologies A plethora of rapidly developing information technologies are coming to society and education. Information technologies include all types of computing and communications hardware and software (Harris, 1993). For example, high-speed personal computers, computer networks, e-mail, fax machines, voice mail, CD-ROMs, digitized audio and video information storage and retrieval devices, and their use in combination as multimedia interactive units are already having significant impacts on communication forms in schools. The current revolution is more than just replacing traditional paper-based media with computer screens and other technological marvels. The change to new communication technologies promises to have personal, social, and pedagogical consequences. The widespread adoption of new technologies has altered the communication process itself. Each new medium imposes its own special requirements on how messages are composed, governs the speed and convenience of message transmission, and influences the ways receivers reconstruct meaning (DeFleur, Kearney, and Plax, 1993). In terms of pedagogy, the potential seems almost unlimited. Teachers and students can access vast stores of information almost instantly, interact with colleagues around the world with computer or videoconferences, and create new knowledge in many different media forms. The new technologies can change the emphasis from passive to active learning and they may even replace the physical school with distance learning and virtual schools.

Sources in the Communication Process: Senders and Receivers

The source of a message does not have to be a person. It can be organizations, supervisors, co-workers, or the task itself (Northcraft and Earley, 1989; Bantz, 1993). In considering the source, credibility and cognitive capacities are important factors.

Credibility The credibility or believability (Adler and Rodman, 1991) of the sender influences the effectiveness of a message. Two characteristics that influence credibility are expertness and trustworthiness (Shelby, 1986; Becker and Klimoski, 1989). Credibility consists of the trust and confidence that the receiver has in the words and actions of the sender. The level of credibility, in turn, influences the reactions of the receiver to the words and actions of the communicator (Gibson, Ivancevich, and Donnelly, 1976). In some cases the identity and reputation of the sender, far from authenticating the message, lead instead to the receiver distorting the information or ignoring the message completely (Bowers, 1976). For example, faculty members who view the principal as less than competent, dishonest, or both probably will distort all communications from him or her.

Being prepared to speak can show expertise. It starts by organizing the idea into a series of symbols such as words or pictures that will communicate the intended meaning. These symbols are arranged for rationality, coherence, and compatibility with the methods of delivery, or media. An e-mail message, for instance, usually is worded differently from a formal letter of reprimand, and both are different from face-to-face conversation. In other words, a message that is well researched, organized, written, or presented will greatly increase the receiver's assessment of the sender's competence and hence credibility.

Cognitive Capacities Psychological characteristics limit an individual's ability to communicate. Information-processing capacity (e.g., schemas for communication skills and knowledge of the subject) and personality and motivation factors (e.g., attitudes, values, interests, and expectations) combine to limit and filter the content and the quality of the message (Berlo, 1970). Cognitive schemas significantly influence not only what information is attended to, conveyed, and interpreted but also how the information is processed (Krone, Jablin, and Putnam, 1987). For example, the assistant superintendent for instruction when communicating with principals screens out information that he or she thinks is not pertinent to building administrators; principals filter information to the assistant superintendent that might reflect negatively on their performance.

Cognitive structures and processes also influence the recipient's ability to understand or decode the message. If the listener is effective, cooperative, and knowledgeable, he or she attempts to interpret the message as intended by the sender. However, as is the case with the sender, the receiver has communication capacities, knowledge of the subject, interests, values, and motivational characteristics that combine to limit qualitatively what is decoded. Consequently, the meaning the receiver applies is not exactly what the sender intended. Meanings may, of course, be relatively comparable, but they are never identical. The receiver's cognitive schemas and processes limit the range of response alternatives. Based on experience as represented by cognitive structures and processes, the receiver selects how to act or respond to the message. The actions serve as feedback to the sender.

Feedback

In all types of communication environments, there is a significant probability that what we say will be ambiguous and misinterpreted. For example, "I'll be there in a minute" and "Call me later and we'll talk about it" make vague references to time. How long a "minute" or "later" is varies greatly across individuals and cultures. Through the use of feedback, however, even unclear statements can become part of specific effective communications (Alessandra and Hunsaker, 1993).

Feedback is a response from a person who has received a message. It provides knowledge about the meaning and impact of the message for the receiver and an opportunity for the sender to correct any problems. Hence, if a dialogue is to continue for any length of time and still have meaning, feedback is important. This process provides at least two benefits. First, it supplies clues about the success of the communication and improves the accuracy and clarity of a message. Asking questions and paraphrasing what the speaker has said are forms of verbal feedback (Adler and Rodman, 1991). Statements such as "What do you mean by . . .?" or "Let me review what you have said. . . ." check for mutual understanding (Alessandra and Hunsaker, 1993). Second, the knowledge of results forms a basis for correcting or modifying future communications (Ashford, 1986). The point is—feedback increases the accuracy and clarity of communication.

Communicating in Context

Communication among people also depends on a combination of contextual, cultural, or environmental factors. The process is clouded by contextual factors that are typically called *noise* or *barriers.* **Noise** is any distraction that interferes with the communication process. Noise can be so intense that it becomes more important than the content of the message itself (Reilly and DiAngelo, 1990).

In schools, noise resulting from social and personal factors can produce more troublesome problems than physical interference. For example, closed organizational climates, punishment-centered bureaucratic structures, cultural and gender differences, and authoritarian leaders create distortions in the communication processes. In such cases, group membership becomes important. Militant teachers cannot hear arbitrary administrators and vice versa; bureaucratic educators do not pay attention to demanding parents.

Prejudices toward age, gender, race, social class, and ethnic group differences constitute barriers in the communication process that distort messages. In a multicultural society, demographic attributes such as race, occupation, and gender provide surrogate indicators for the common experiences and background attributes that shape language development and communication abilities (Zenger and Lawrence, 1989). For example, a man who believes that his particular work can be done effectively only by a man is predisposed to deny facts, information, and messages that suggest that a woman can do the work equally well or better. Every message is filtered through barriers, predispositions, or cognitive schemas (Reilly and DiAngelo, 1990).

Similarly, both the written and spoken language used by American women and men has traditionally been somewhat different (Tannen, 1990; Gray, 1992). Women tend to adopt upper-class speech patterns, certain words (e.g., "darling" as an adjective) and expressive language (e.g., "adorable," "lovely"). Men tend to be more comfortable with slang expressions. In comparison to men, women tend to hedge or use qualified constructions (e.g., "perhaps," "seem," "could"), shy away from universal pronouncements, and employ language that encourages community building, politeness, cheerfulness, and concern

(Shakeshaft, 1986). In taking turns in speaking, women in social settings and professional meetings talk less, are interrupted more, and are challenged more than are men. However, gender differences in taking turns appear to be related more to women's concern for permitting others to speak than in expressing their own opinions. Thus, language characteristics such as expressiveness, hedging, and taking turns make women appear more collegial or interpersonally oriented than men (Baker, 1991).

Brenda M. Wilkins and Peter A. Andersen (1991) note that research seeking to identify gender differences in communication styles of managers has become very popular. They found women and men managers do differ in their communication behaviors, but that the amount of variance was so small that the statistical differences appear to have little social value. In her review, Charol Shakeshaft (1986) concludes that the traditional and stereotypical styles of women are more like those of good administrators than are the styles of traditional and stereotypical men. She observes that the communication styles of women respond to needs for less autocratic downward communication, noncoercive motivational and persuasive skills, humanized feedback, and threat-reducing strategies. To become effective school administrators, she believes, men would be well advised to watch how women speak and listen and try to make those styles their own rather than pushing women to modify their language to mimic men.

Within education, male and female educators and students frequently have very different socioeconomic, ethnic, educational, and work backgrounds. These differences can be expected to produce contextual noise as women and men administrators, teachers, and students communicate in schools. However, where females achieve a more equal status with males, the differences in language usage may diminish. Young men and women today are much more likely to have similar vocabularies and speech patterns than was the case 50 years ago (McNall and McNall, 1992).

Hence, context noise of all types—for example, physical, social, and personal—may produce language disparities that constrain communication within schools even further. Given the growing diversity and other changes of school contexts (e.g., in economic wealth, ethnicity, gender in administrative positions, and with at-risk children), the challenge of communicating accurately and clearly will surely increase. As shown in Figure 10.1, creating shared meaning through the communication process depends on the individuals involved, content of the message, methods used, and context. Succinctly stated, the relationship is shown with the following formula:

Meaning = Information + Communicators + Media + Context

The essence of the formula and approach can be understood by considering the following questions:

- Who is speaking to whom and what roles do they occupy? Administrators? Administrator and teacher? Teachers? Men and women? Teacher and student? Administrator and parent?
- Is the language or set of symbols able to convey the information and be understood by both the sender and receiver?

- What is the content and effect of the communication? Positive or negative? Relevant or irrelevant?
- What methods or media are being used?
- What is the context in which the communication is taking place? What factors are creating noise that might block or distort the message?

As a general conclusion, the lack of two-way communication, the use of conflicting media and messages, and the existence of situational noise constitute the most serious problems for understanding in educational organizations.

ORGANIZATIONAL PERSPECTIVES OF COMMUNICATION

Organizations are information-processing systems. Information flows through organizations and influences virtually all structures and processes. Moreover, organizations are processing an increasing volume of data and the preferred media are becoming face-to-face discussion and group participation (Daft, Bettenhausen, and Tyler, 1993). Consequently, the escalating volume and change to richer media make understanding organizational communication in schools even more important than previously thought.

Organizational Communication and Networks

The earlier general definition can be adapted to define **organizational communication** as the sending of messages through both formal and informal networks that results in the construction of meaning and influences both individuals and groups (DeFleur, Kearney, and Plax, 1993). In other words, organizational communication is a collective and interactive process that creates and interprets messages. Coordinated activities and relationships among participants within and outside the organization produce networks of understanding (Stohl, 1995). For example, staff development activities are held for teachers and administrators across a school district to communicate information about new curriculum standards. As a result of these coordinated activities, networks within and between schools develop among the educators and shared understandings about the standards are created.

Networks are formal or informal patterns or channels of communication that have become regularized. **Formal channels** are methods sanctioned by the organization and are related to such organizational goals as regulation and innovation. When individuals communicate through **informal channels** and networks, they are using **grapevines** (Harris, 1993). These forms of communication are part of the organizational structure of schools, even though they are not shown on the hierarchical chart (Lewis, 1975). The direction of formal and informal channels can be vertical (up and down) and horizontal as well as one- or two-way. Hence, networks and channels are simply methods, vehicles, or forms a message travels in organizations such as schools; they are lines of communication.

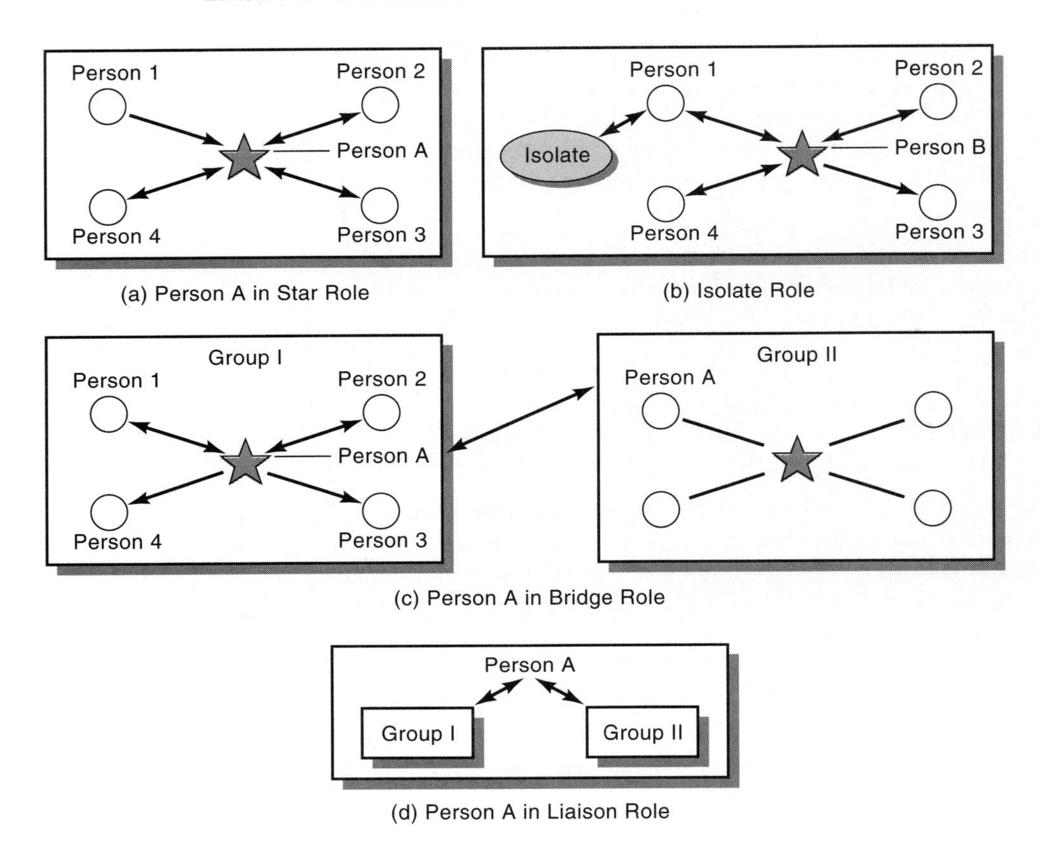

FIGURE 10.5 *Examples of Star, Isolate, Bridge, and Liaison Roles in Communication Networks*

The general notions of a network and channels are familiar because we all have had extensive experience with physical networks and channels, such as rivers, streets and highways, telephone lines, and sewer pipes (Monge, 1987). In contrast, communication networks in organizations are more difficult to identify because they comprise abstract human behaviors over time rather than physical materials such as pavement, streams, and pipes. Nevertheless, communication networks are regular patterns of person-to-person contacts that can be identified as people exchange information in schools. By observing the communication behavior over time, inferences can be made about which individuals are connected to other individuals through the exchange of information.

As shown in Figure 10.5, the members within communication networks assume a variety of roles. The communication role that a person serves within a communication network is important because it can influence the person's attitudes and behaviors. A **star role** is where a large number of people communicate with an individual. The star is a nexus within the network. Having a central role, the star is potentially powerful because he or she has greater access to and possible control over group resources (McElroy and Shrader, 1986; Yamagishi, Gillmore, and Cook, 1988). Hence, a star can be thought of as a leader in the network.

In contrast, an **isolate role** is one where individuals are involved in communication with others only infrequently (see Figure 10.5). Isolates are loosely coupled or even decoupled from the network—that is, removed from the regular flow of communication and out of touch with the rest of the network. Isolates are a concern because their lack of communication activity is often accompanied by feelings of alienation, low job satisfaction, little commitment to the work organization, and low performance. Active participation in communication networks seems to produce positive outcomes, whereas isolation is associated with disaffection (Harris, 1993). However, programs designed to lessen educator isolation in schools may produce a situation in which the individuals who should benefit the most will resist and benefit little (Bakkenes, de Brabander, and Imants, 1999).

Patrick Forsyth and Wayne Hoy (1978) found that, without exception, being isolated in one instance carries over to other instances. The results of a subsequent study were similar, except that isolation from friends was not related to isolation from formal authority (Zielinski and Hoy, 1983). In other words, communication isolates in schools tend to be separated from perceived control, respected co-workers, the school's control structure, and sometimes friends. The potentially destructive aspect of this isolation is alienation. To counteract this negative effect, administrators must devise alternative communication processes because the isolates are not reachable by existing channels.

Exchanges occur across networks through individuals who fill special roles as bridges and liaisons. For example, people who belong to more than one group are called **bridges.** By belonging to a district curriculum committee and the department within a school, an English teacher serves in a bridging role for the two groups and will likely pass information between them (see Figure 10.5). **Liaisons** are individuals who link groups to which they do not belong. Liaisons serve as intermediaries among various groups within schools. In other words, they perform the vital function of keeping groups informed about each other's activities. Interactions among liaisons and group members do not occur with great frequency or formality, but when communication occurs regularly, the members usually know what the others are doing. As described in Chapter 3, these important linkages are weak ties or loose couplings. Liaisons many times are formally assigned by the organization to link different departments or committees and ensure accurate communication among them. By supervising the English curriculum committees in two schools, for example, the assistant superintendent for curriculum and instruction is a liaison for the two groups. There are formal as well as informal liaisons. Cynthia Stohl (1995) concludes that highly effective groups have more links with other groups in the organization or the external environment than less effective groups. However, the most cohesive and highly satisfied groups interact infrequently with outside constituents.

Purposes of Communication in School Organizations

Communication in organizations such as schools serves a number of key purposes—for example, production and regulation, innovation, and individual socialization and maintenance (Myers and Myers, 1982). Production and regulation purposes include activities aimed at doing the primary work of the organization, such as teaching and learning in schools. They include setting goals and standards, transmitting facts and information, making decisions, leading and influencing others, and assessing outcomes. Innovation purposes include messages about generating new ideas and changing programs, structures, and procedures in the school. Finally, socialization and maintenance purposes of communication affect the participants' self-esteem, interpersonal relationships, and motivation to integrate their individual goals with the school's objectives. The capacity of a school to maintain such complex, highly interdependent patterns of activity is limited by its ability to handle communication for these purposes.

To serve the multiple purposes of production, regulation, innovation, socialization, and maintenance in schools, communication must promote high levels of shared understandings. Human action is needed to accomplish goals in schools. Goal-directed behavior is elicited through communication; hence, the greater the clarity and understanding of the message, the more likely the administrator, teacher, and student actions will proceed in fruitful, goal-oriented directions. Within an effectively operating school, for example, administrators, teachers, and students want to understand and accept each other's ideas and to act on them. School goals and guidelines for their accomplishment are developed through extensive dialogue. One innovative goal might be to implement a project-based approach of instruction. The accompanying guidelines to accomplish the goal would include the development of new curricula, new interactive instructional strategies, socializing and training teachers, portfolio-assessment procedures, and plans for maintaining the programs. As group leaders, the principal, teachers, parents, and students emphasize the validity of the goal, stress the usefulness of the new procedures, promote shared understandings, encourage collective actions to implement the program, and assist in implementation and continuation. The extent and success of the actions depend in large measure on how effectively communication about the goal and accompanying procedures are initiated and maintained by the school organization.

Formal Communication Networks in Schools

According to Scott (1998) one explanation of why organizations develop is their superior capacity to manage flows of information. The hierarchal structure of schools (see Chapter 3) incorporates several features, e.g., status and power differences among positions, but among the most important is a centralized communication system. Communication is embedded in all school structures. Formal communication channels, or networks, traverse the organization through the hierarchy of authority. Barnard (1938) calls these formal networks "the communication system." According to Barnard, several factors must be considered when developing and using the formal communication system:

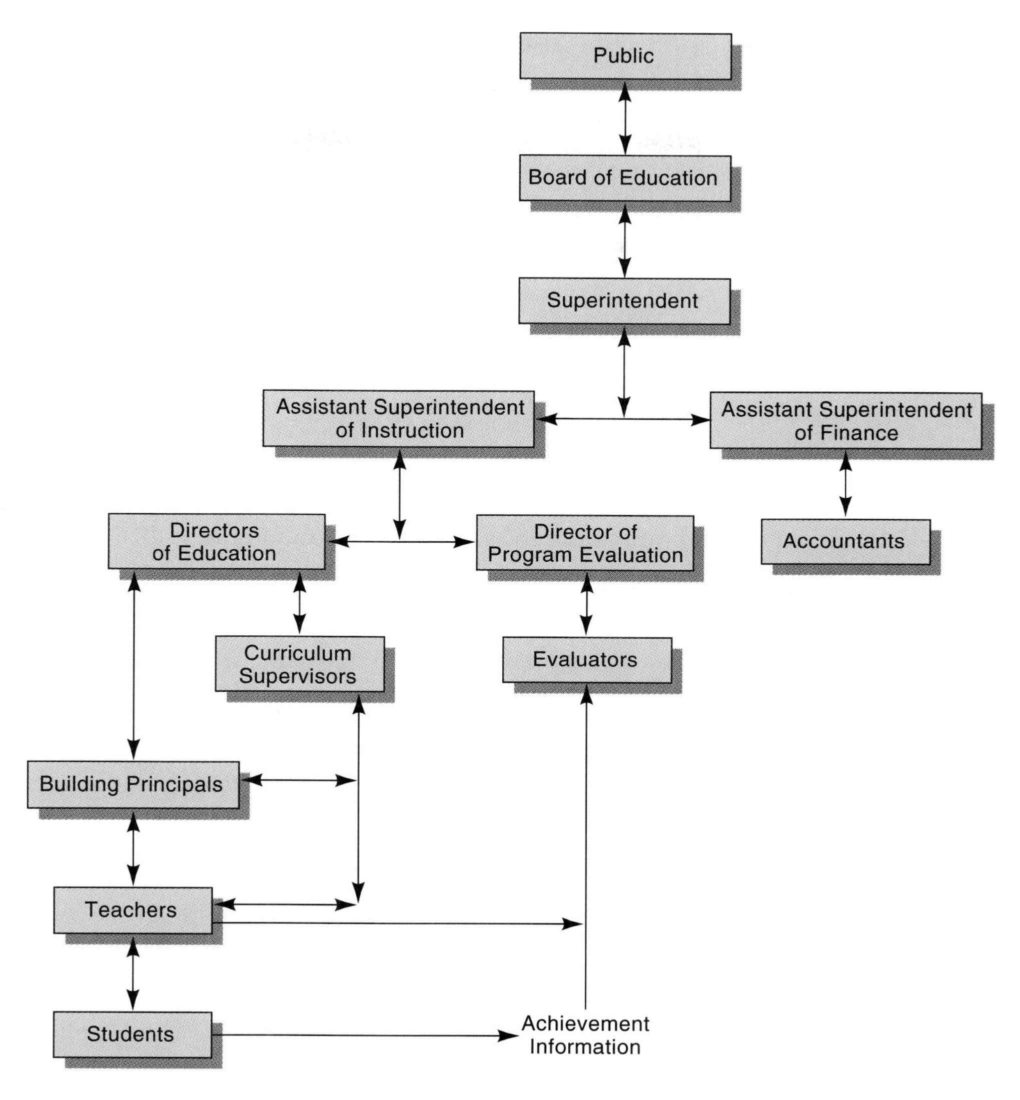

FIGURE 10.6 ***Formal Communication Channels for Program Implementation in a School District***

- The channels of communication must be known.
- The channels must link every member of the organization.
- Lines of communication must be as direct and as short as possible.
- The complete network of communication typically is used.
- Every communication is authenticated as being from the correct person occupying the position and within his or her authority to issue the message.

Figure 10.6 illustrates a school district's formal communication network using Barnard's descriptive statements. Note that the chart delineates the formal communication channels and that every member reports to someone. The directors report to the assistant superintendent for instruction, who, with the assistant superintendent for finance, report to the superintendent. The line of communication from the superintendent to the teachers goes through five hierarchical levels. This is reasonably short and direct for a large school district. Adding specific names and the bureaucratic rules and regulations that define the jobs places this system in compliance with Barnard's suggestions.

Within all organizations, formal restrictions on the communication process are apparent. "Making certain to go through proper channels" and "following the chain of command" are two common expressions that reflect a demand for control and structure of communication in organizations (Harris, 1993). Three characteristics of school bureaucracies seem particularly critical to the formal system of communication. They are centralization in the hierarchy, the organization's shape or configuration, and the level of information technology.

Centralization—the degree to which authority is not delegated but concentrated in a single source in the organization—is important to the effectiveness of communication systems (Porter and Roberts, 1976). In centralized schools, a few positions in the structure have most of the information-obtaining ability. For example, the superintendent and two assistant superintendents pictured in Figure 10.6 would gather most of the information for the formal system of communication. If the district is decentralized or loosely coupled (see Chapter 3), however, the information-obtaining potential is more or less spread across all of the positions. Research examining the different information-obtaining abilities supports the finding that centralized structures are more efficient communicators when the problems and tasks are relatively simple and straightforward. When the problems and tasks become more complex, however, decentralized hierarchies appear to be more efficient (Argote, Turner, and Fichman, 1989).

Shape—the number of hierarchical levels or tallness versus flatness of the school organization—also affects the communication processes. Hierarchical levels and size are structural characteristics that are commonly associated with shape. A school district with five levels, such as the one depicted in Figure 10.6, differs from systems with more or fewer levels in its ability to communicate across levels and from top to bottom. The number of levels can be seen as the distance a message must travel. As the distance increases, the chance for message distortion increases and the satisfaction with the quality and quantity of communication decreases (Clampitt, 1991; Zahn, 1991). Teachers will generally express less satisfaction with messages from superintendents than from principals. In addition, organizational size is negatively related to communication quality; as the district becomes larger, communication becomes more impersonal or formal and quality declines (Jablin, 1987).

Technology also appears to have a significant effect on organizational communication, though that effect remains somewhat speculative. As we noted in Chapter 3, writers subscribing to the position that schools are loosely coupled systems argue that educational organizations have a relatively low level of technology. However, as communication technology becomes more sophisticated in schools, its use will dramatically alter the communication that takes place in both the formal and informal networks (Huseman and Miles, 1988).

We are living in a creative and dynamic era that is producing fundamental changes, as is apparent in such advances as computer networks, the World Wide Web, electronic mail, computer conferences, communication satellites, and data-handling devices. Until recently, electronic information exchange has largely been adapted to convey voice, vision, text, and graphics as distinct and separate types of communication. Now, simultaneous and instantaneous transmission of voice, vision, text, and graphics to many locations are becoming common. Even while imagining the tremendous changes yet to come, the usual descriptions of the forthcoming power of electronic technologies together with the geographic distribution of participants do not adequately capture the differences between these and traditional media. Consequently, the potential influence of such technologies on all aspects of communication in schools—administrative, instructional, and social—is probably underestimated.

Informal Communication Networks in Schools

Informal networks or grapevines exist in all organizations regardless of how elaborate the formal communication system happens to be. One generalization that has been observed repeatedly by researchers and by participants in organizations is that people who are in groups, cliques, or gangs tend to reach an understanding on things or issues very quickly. They communicate easily and well among themselves. Facts, opinions, attitudes, suspicions, gossip, rumors, and even directives flow freely and rapidly through the grapevine. Built around social relationships among the school members, informal channels develop for such simple reasons as common office areas, similar duties, shared coffee breaks, carpools, and friendships. Social relationships and communication channels arise at all organizational levels of the school. Returning to Figure 10.6, informal communication patterns exist at the central office. One central office group might include some of the directors, an assistant superintendent, some supervisors, an evaluator, and an accountant. Certainly, informal communication channels thrive among school principals and within teacher groups and the student body.

The communication patterns among principals in elementary and secondary schools are quite different (Licata and Hack, 1980). Secondary school principals form informal groups that are guildlike. That is, the communication patterns are based on common professional interests and the need for mutual aid and protection. In contrast, elementary principals cluster into clanlike groups in which their communications revolve around social ties with mentors, friends, neighbors, and relatives. In brief, secondary principals structure the grapevine around professional survival and development, whereas elementary principals communicate informally about social matters.

Although a major disadvantage of grapevines is the spread of rumors, informal networks serve a number of purposes in formal school organization. First, they reflect the quality of activities in a school. Communication through informal sources provides vital feedback to administrators and other school leaders. Moreover, active informal networks are indicative of a school's culture and leaders can learn a great deal by listening to them. Second, informal channels may satisfy social or affiliation needs not met by formal channels. Third, grapevines fill an information void by carrying a great deal of information. No matter how elaborate, formal communication networks simply cannot carry all of the information required in contemporary schools. Informal networks provide outlets when formal channels are clogged. Informal channels are particularly helpful during periods of change, when the information is new, and when face-to-face or electronic communication is relatively easy. Fourth, informal networks provide meaning for activities within the school. As messages travel through informal networks, the messages are translated with surprising accuracy into terms that make sense to the participants. The accuracy is 75 to 90 percent for noncontroversial information. When distortions occur, they generally reflect an incorrect emphasis that is based on incomplete information. A problem is that even a small distortion or error can have dramatic consequences (Clampitt, 1991; Harris, 1993).

Complementary Networks: Formal and Informal Communication

As we have noted, formal and informal communication networks exist in all educational organizations. The results from research studying networks across a variety of settings indicate that communication patterns in organizations are extraordinarily complex. Within schools, there is not a single unitary network, but rather a series of overlapping and interrelated networks (Jablin, 1980). A large majority of all participants interact consistently with many other individuals and in far greater numbers than is suggested by formal organizational charts. Although the task network is larger and better developed than the social network, both are closely related to each other and critical to the organization (O'Reilly and Pondy, 1979). Generally, communication groups form along task-focused lines. Task structures of work groups act to improve or detract from the accuracy and openness of the transmitted message. Groups with specialized skills and high status are more open in information exchanges than other groups (O'Reilly and Roberts, 1977). Further, accuracy and openness have a positive impact on performance, but the frequency of communication among educators is not high (Miskel, McDonald, and Bloom, 1983). In sum, both the substance and the direction of communication can make the two systems complementary.

Substance

In terms of content, communication can be thought of as instrumental or expressive (Etzioni, 1960). Instrumental communication distributes information and knowledge that affect cognitive structures and processes. Administrative directives, policies, curricular objectives and materials, and attendance data are typical examples. The purpose of instrumental communication is to develop consensus about methods and procedures. Expressive communication, on the other hand, attempts to change or reinforce attitudes, norms, and values. Appropriate affective orientations toward students, militancy, discipline, and organizational rewards are typical examples of the substance of expressive communication.

Formal communication channels carry both instrumental and expressive content. The informal network can enhance both. For example, the grapevine serves as a barometer of opinion and sentiment. School administrators can often tap the informal flow for information about the morale of students, teachers, and other administrators. They also can float trial balloons to test the receptivity of a new procedure or program. For instance, an administrator may want to introduce a new in-service program for teacher preparation. Before making a final decision, the hypothetical possibilities are discussed informally with some staff members. As the information flows through the grapevine, the sentiment can be monitored. Depending on the reaction, the administrator uses the formal communication system to announce plans for the new program, allows the program to remain hypothetical, or formally quashes the rumor. Barnard (1938) suggests that this type of communication flows without interruption in the informal networks, but would be either inconvenient or raise issues calling for premature decisions in the formal channels. Hence, informal can complement formal instrumental communication by serving as a testing ground for possible courses of action. In terms of expressive communication, the informal network can be a positive vehicle for personal expression by allowing participants to communicate and interact socially. Informal networks then provide gratification of the social needs of many school members at little financial cost to the district.

Direction

Messages do not sit around waiting to be discovered, nor do they float around randomly to be picked up by some lucky accident (Myers and Myers, 1982). Communication in organizations flows directionally through the formal and informal networks. The direction of information flow also demonstrates the possible complementary nature of formal and informal communication networks. Information flows vertically and horizontally in both networks.

Vertical flow refers to the upward and downward direction of communication through the different levels of the school's hierarchy. Information is passed down or up the line of authority through memos, directions, policies, and programs of action. An important point about the vertical flow of organizational communication is that messages moving in the formal network are extremely important to the people who send them and those who receive them. The jobs of individuals can depend on the messages they receive about such matters as directives, assessments, requests, and instructions (DeFleur, Kearney, and Plax, 1993).

In formal downward communication, information passes through the chain of command—that is, through the hierarchical status structure. These messages typically reaffirm the chain of command and reinforce control (Harris, 1993). Five types of communications from superior to subordinate include (Katz and Kahn, 1978):

- Instructions about specific tasks.
- Rationale about why the task needs to be done and how it relates to other tasks.
- Information about organizational procedures and practices.
- Feedback about the performance levels of individuals.
- Information regarding the organization's goals.

Downward communication is relatively easy to send, but subordinates often may misunderstand the message. To ensure that the intended meanings are understood, administrators must develop two-way communication channels and use extensive feedback processes up and down the hierarchy.

Communication from the lower levels of the hierarchy to the upper levels is upward communication. Upward communication provides four types of messages (Katz and Kahn, 1978; DeFleur, Kearney, and Plax, 1993):

- Routine operational messages.
- Reports on problems.
- Suggestions for improvement.
- Information on how subordinates feel about each other and the job.

Upward communication is one means by which subordinates are made accountable to superiors. Such communication is often viewed as an instrument of administrative control. Consequently, subordinates have a tendency to emphasize positive information, withhold negative data, and communicate what they think the "boss wants to hear." Because many decisions are made at the top of the hierarchy, the quality of the decisions will depend on the accuracy and timeliness of the communication that moves through the formal system. In general, the more tangible and the more objective the information, the more likely that subordinates will communicate accurately with their superiors. Frequent two-way exchanges also improve accuracy (Porter and Roberts, 1976).

A well-developed informal network can help administrators gain timely information and assess the accuracy of formal upward communication. In exchange for the information, however, teachers influence administrator behavior. Some teachers gain influence and power because they have information about how to get things accomplished or who can resolve specific problems. Similarly, department chairs, committee members, and teachers with specialized skills possess valued information. As a result of their knowledge and positions in the communication network, they can exert considerable influence on administrator decisions (Barnett, 1984).

Horizontal flow indicates that communication moves across organizational members at the same hierarchical level. A principal, for instance, may provide information to another principal, who in turn, passes it to still other principals. Such communication is the strongest and most easily understood (Lewis, 1975). Horizontal communication can be either formal or informal. In Figure 10.6, the lateral communication link between the two assistant superintendents would be formal when they are working on ways to finance the introduction of a new curriculum. Another common example is teachers talking with each other in a lounge or planning room during class periods when they are not teaching. The major purposes of horizontal communication are coordinating tasks, problem solving, sharing information with colleagues, resolving conflicts, and building rapport (Harris, 1993). For example, principals communicate so that their activities or curriculum emphases will be similar in different schools, and to share information about content, avoid potential conflicts, and build friendly relationships with peers. The direction affects the ease, content, and accuracy of organizational communication.

In studying horizontal communication, W. W. Charters, Jr. (1967), found substantial differences between elementary and high schools. Elementary schools exhibited a much larger volume, with most teachers in direct contact with one another. In contrast, only 15 percent of the high school staff interacted regularly. This difference in communication volume is partially explained by staff size. The average number of contacts per staff member declined with increasing faculty size. Larger facilities and physical dispersion along with specialized personnel (guidance counselors or special teachers) who are not in the main flow of classroom instruction help explain the impact of size on communication volume. Charters did note, however, that size alone does not account for the entire difference. Elementary school staffs communicate more than high school staffs. Finally, Charters found that stability in the communication patterns is related to the division of labor and physical proximity. Teachers in the same subject specialty and, to a lesser extent, those in closer physical proximity form enduring communication networks. Thus, three factors—level and size of school, specialization, and proximity—affect the horizontal communication patterns in schools.

External Environment and Organizational Communication

Schools can continually collect, interpret, create, and use information from the external environment to become knowing organizations. Chun Wei Choo (1998) asserts that knowing organizations are effective because they continually evolve with their changing environments, renew their knowledge resources, and practice vigilant information processing in making decisions. Developing the capacity to be a knowing organization is exceedingly important because, as we discussed in Chapter 7, schools with greater environmental turbulence and complexity face two problems with respect to internal information processing: a larger volume and greater ambiguity (i.e., multiple meanings) of information. Schools must deal with this heightened volume and ambiguity through their internal communication networks and media (Daft, Bettenhausen, and Tyler, 1993).

As ambiguity and volume increase, two factors emerge that require heightened information processing. First, in situations of high ambiguity, strategies must be developed to obtain some degree of clarity of meaning. When information from the environment is muddled, people in the organization can reach very different, but defensible conclusions, even when observing the same objective information. Probably the most powerful way to resolve ambiguity is through debate, clarification, and discussion. In this way, educators can construct meanings on which they can agree. Hence, in ambiguous situations, the appropriate response is characterized by low technology and high touch. People need to use rich media—that is, face-to-face interactions—to build shared understandings based on previously shared assumptions and experiences.

Second, in conditions of high volume, the communication capacity must be enhanced to meet increasing demands. Fast-changing and complex environments can generate huge amounts of information for organizations. To stay informed, school organizations develop specialized monitoring and boundary-spanning units, special teams to integrate the incoming information, and computer technologies to store and retrieve information quickly (Daft, Bettenhausen, and Tyler, 1993).

Improving Communication Processes

Communication does not have an opposite. There is no way for people not to behave and all behaviors have communication value (Myers and Myers, 1982). Similarly, totally planned and accurate communication is impossible. Accuracy in sending messages, however, is significantly associated with leader and organization performance (Penley, Alexander, Jernigan, and Heuwood, 1991). Using knowledge from communication theory can improve the efficiency and effectiveness of individual and organizational communication. For example, improvement guidelines can be drawn from the steps of the general process described in Figure 10.1. General guides suggested by Sayles and Strauss (1966) are still applicable:

- Determine the objective of the planned communication.
- Identify the intended receivers and characteristics that might facilitate or complicate constructing a shared understanding.
- Encode the message to fit the relationship between the sender and receiver.
- Determine ways to establish a mutual interest with the receiver and design the media for sending the message.
- Assess the results with feedback.

Improving school communication requires a planned program of organizational development. Suggestions for this approach to improving school communication include the following:

- Assess the organizational design of the communication system against criteria suggested earlier in this chapter by Barnard.
- Develop mechanisms to facilitate the process—for example, close proximity of personnel, convenient sites for formal and informal interaction, mechanical links such as telephones and computers, and a committee system to accomplish tasks and make decisions.
- Establish information storage and retrieval systems.
- Select personnel with good communication skills.
- Develop a training program to improve communication skills.

Despite the many barriers to effective communication, these general guidelines can be incorporated with a number of techniques to minimize inaccuracies, add clarity, and enhance richness in the process. Three sets of skills stand out: sending, listening, and feedback.

Sending skills are the abilities to make oneself understood. As a key to effective communication, sending skills of educators can be enhanced through the following five methods. First, appropriate and direct language should be used. Educational jargon and complex concepts should be avoided when simpler words will do. However, to establish credibility, the language must demonstrate that the sender is knowledgeable about educational issues. Second, clear and complete information should be provided to the listener. Information is needed to build or reorganize the listener's cognitive schemas. Third, noise from the physical and psychological environments should be minimized. During parent conferences, for example, steps need to be taken to eliminate telephone interruptions and to reduce stereotypes held by either the professional educator or parent. Fourth, multiple and appropriate channels of media should be employed. Being skillful in matching richness of media to situational and communication needs may be a key factor in administrator performance (Alexander, Penley, and Jernigan, 1991). Fifth, face-to-face communication and redundancy should be used when communicating complex or equivocal messages. Richness, repetition, and feedback enhance the likelihood that the intended effect of gaining a shared meaning for the message will occur.

Listening skills are the abilities of individuals to understand others. Listening is a form of behavior in which individuals attempt to comprehend what is being communicated to them through the use of words, actions, and things by others (DeFleur, Kearney, and Plax, 1993). In active listening, a listener reflects back to the speaker what he or she has heard—content, feeling, and meaning—from the speaker's perspective (Elmes and Costello, 1992). Listening skills are required for relatively accurate, two-way exchanges. Listening to a person shows respect, interest, and concern for one's fellow communicator. When it is an active effort, listening can encourage others to develop and express their own points of view (Burbules, 1993).

Developing important listening skills, however, is frequently neglected. How many times have you been asked a question by someone only to get disturbing nonverbal cues that the questioner is not really interested or, worse, not listening to your response? How often are your responses not truly heard or misinterpreted? Allen Ivey and Mary Ivey (1999) suggest a number of critical elements in effective listening skills—attending, questioning, encouraging, paraphrasing, reflecting feeling, and summarizing.

Attending is the process of being attentive to the conversation. It involves appropriate eye contact, receptive body language, and staying focused and on task. Making eye contact and looking at the person doing the talking communicates interest and attentiveness just as looking away communicates disinterest. Leaning forward, maintaining an open posture, smiling, and looking pleasant are the kinds of nonverbal cues that communicate interest. Finally the effective listener stays with the other person, that is, pays attention and does not zone out. Effective listening demands attention.

Questioning is often essential to understanding the message. The message may not be as clear as the communicator thinks; some messages are vague. They require questions for clarification. Some factual questions are direct, clear, and simple and are answered by a yes or no. Other questions are more open and call for speculation and development, for example, "Why do you think the conflict occurred?" Skillful questions clarify and elaborate and are a natural part of careful listening.

Encouraging is also part of skillful listening. There are a few minimal "encouragers" that can facilitate communication (Morse and Ivey, 1996). Silence is a powerful, nonverbal message. Saying nothing but remaining interested suggests to the communicator that you want to hear more. Empathic acknowledgement also adds communication. Verbal cues like "yes," "um-hum," and "I see" encourage especially when they are linked to such nonverbal cues of nodding and smiling. There are also a number of encouragers that are short sentences that stimulate communication, such as, "Tell me more," "Give me an example," and "Say a little more about that."

Paraphrasing is another way to show that you are paying attention and understanding what is being said. It helps the listener respond effectively to people, and it provides feedback to the speaker that you understand the essence of the message. Paraphrasing also serves as a correction mechanism. Skillful listeners paraphrase, provide feedback, and make sure they have the correct message.

Reflecting feeling is a positive way to embrace the speaker. The listener should be attentive to the feelings and emotions of the communicator. Acknowledging feelings is a good place to begin the reflecting process because it paces the other individual's emotional state but does not get the listener overly involved (Morse and Ivey, 1996). Acknowledging feelings focuses on labeling the feeling and communicating it back to the speaker, and often tempers the emotion and puts it under control. Statements like "You feel that way because . . ." and "I sense you are disappointed," reflect emotion and create empathy. Also using the person's name from time to time is helpful. Skillful listeners sort out facts from emotions and acknowledge and reflect feelings.

Summarizing is quite similar to paraphrasing except that the summary covers a longer period of time and it typically comes near the end of the conversation. The goal of summary is to organize the facts and feelings into a coherent, accurate, and brief synopsis.

We should not be surprised that effective communication involves listening as well as speaking. Communication, after all, is an interactive process. Blocking out external distractions, attending to verbal and nonverbal cues, probing and encouraging, differentiating between the intellectually and emotional content of a message, and summarizing and making inferences about the speaker's meaning and feelings are critical to effective communication (Woolfolk, 2000).

Giving and seeking feedback is a special case of two-way communication. In work settings, we usually think of feedback as involving information about task performance or how others perceive and evaluate an individual's behavior (Ashford, 1986; Cusella, 1987). Two types of feedback are possible. When feedback reinforces, accentuates, or adds to the direction being taken by the person or school, it is positive. Feedback is negative when it corrects a deviation (Harris, 1993). It can be communicated either verbally or nonverbally, consciously or unconsciously. For example, a student who falls asleep during a class lecture may provide as much feedback to the teacher as the student who responds to examination questions.

Susan J. Ashford (1986) defines the concept of feedback-seeking behavior as the conscious devotion of effort to determining the correctness and adequacy of behaviors for attaining goals. Individuals should develop feedback-seeking behaviors because such actions will help them adapt and be successful employees. Two strategies for seeking feedback are suggested. The first is monitoring the environment by observing naturally occurring informational cues, other individuals, and how others respond. In other words, monitoring involves receiving feedback vicariously through watching how others are responded to and reinforced. The second strategy is to inquire directly about how others perceive and evaluate your behavior. As a caution, feedback-seeking actions can be hard on an individual's self-esteem because it potentially increases the chances of hearing information that one would rather not know or confront. In fact, individuals who suspect that they are performing poorly tend to use feedback-seeking strategies to minimize the amount of negative information they receive (Larson, 1989).

A number of criteria or guidelines have been proposed for developing **feedback skills** (Anderson, 1976; Harris, 1993).

- Feedback should be intended to be helpful to the recipient.
- Feedback should be specific rather than general and recent rather than old.
- Feedback should be directed toward behavior that the person could change.
- Feedback should be timely—the more immediate, the better.

Although circumstances always exist that make the acceptance of negative feedback difficult, Anderson (1976) argues that acceptance is dependent on trust within the group, expression of wanting to help, use of descriptive rather than evaluative information, and appropriate timing of the meeting. When these criteria for giving and receiving feedback are met, the likelihood of successful communication increases substantially.

Unfortunately, feedback is not always useful. Three points are important in this regard. First, feedback must be pursued vigorously because people do not always give it voluntarily. In many situations, administrators, teachers, or students would rather risk doing the task incorrectly than ask for clarification. Second, feedback consists of nonverbal as well as verbal messages; people sometimes speak loudest with their feet (i.e., they walk away to avoid contact). Third, bogus feedback is common (Downs, 1977). People are reluctant to give negative feedback (Becker and Klimoski, 1989; Larson, 1989). Neutral or positive feedback is easier to give than negative assessments, even when holding negative reactions. Most of us are fairly adept at sending back messages that do not really represent our true reactions. Some people rationalize such behavior as tact, human relations, or survival. Consequently, both personal skill and preparation are critical to give and receive helpful feedback (Anderson, 1976; Rockey, 1984).

Because communication plays such a central role in schools, the key issue is not whether administrators, teachers, and students engage in communication but whether they communicate effectively. People must exchange information in schools, but to develop shared meanings requires the effective use of sending, listening, and feedback skills in a situation with minimal noise or barriers.

THEORY INTO PRACTICE

Scandal at Placido High: Coincidence or Conspiracy?[2]

Placido is a small, bedroom community with a population of nearly 12,000. Its public schools enjoy a fine reputation. Parents are interested and involved in the education of their children. Last week, during the high school graduation ceremonies, the president of the board of education spoke proudly of the recognition the district has received for high student scores at all grade levels on statewide tests.

The superintendent of schools, Debra Bass, has just completed her third year in Placido. The members of the community have been very pleased with her performance and members of the board of education recently renewed her contract. Dr. Bass is a student-centered educator who has attempted to heighten the sensitivity of the professional staff to the needs of all students. She had just concluded a regular Monday meeting with her administrative team when she received a phone call from a representative of the National Testing Corporation (NTC).

Robert Bender, the NTC representative, informed Superintendent Bass that he had received a letter from three recent graduates of Placido High School. In their letter, the students claimed to have had an unfair advantage over the thousands of students in other high schools all over the country who were administered a University Placement Exam on May 13. They noted that they had received prior knowledge of four of the five reading passages on the interpretative section of the exam and two of the three passages on the translation section several days prior to the exam from their teacher, Mr. Will Johnson. The students enclosed photocopies of the passages in question with their letter. They explained that they waited until after graduation to reveal the impropriety for fear of jeopardizing final course grades and their graduation, even though they did nothing wrong or dishonest.

Dr. Bass requested a meeting with Mr. Bender to discuss the situation and to determine jointly how the investigation of the allegations would proceed. Mr. Bender politely informed Dr. Bass that NTC had an established procedure to investigate these situations, but he would be pleased to meet with her to discuss how NTC planned to proceed. He made it clear to the superintendent that NTC would safeguard the identity of the graduates who sent the letter and assured her that no other contacts would be made until after their meeting, scheduled for the next morning.

The superintendent immediately called Hal Curry, the high school principal. Principal Curry was appointed principal January 1, upon the retirement of his predecessor. He served as assistant principal for 12 years prior to the appointment and he knew the faculty, students, and community well. The superintendent arranged to meet Principal Curry in 30 minutes to brief him and to plan a course of action.

Dr. Bass knew that the director of student services, Lorna Leonard, was responsible for both test security and test administration. NTE is an independent organization that contracts with school districts to have their exams administered during normal school hours by school employees. Exam packets are delivered to each site by courier to the designated test coordinator, who has the responsi-

THEORY INTO PRACTICE, (Continued)

bility to keep them secure until their administration on a specified day and time.

Lorna, the designated coordinator for Placido, has been in the district for 28 years and was currently on vacation and not due to return for 10 days. Will Johnson, the teacher of that particular university placement course, already had departed for summer break with the rest of the nonadministrative professional staff. Superintendent Bass placed a phone call to the president of the board to inform him of the situation and promised to report back after she had met the NTC representative the next day.

Principal Curry was visibly shaken as the superintendent conveyed the allegations. He felt responsible for the actions of his staff and often reminded staff members that, "the buck stopped at his desk." The possibility that innocent students would suffer negative consequences as a result of inappropriate behavior by one of their teachers really upset both the principal and superintendent.

A search of the records revealed that 15 students, 9 seniors and 6 juniors, were administered the exam at the high school in May. Superintendent Bass reminded the principal that it was important to conduct a thorough investigation while safeguarding the privacy and rights of all parties. They agreed that Principal Curry would call the 15 students who took the exam to request a private meeting with each student and his/her parents. He also would attempt to contact Will Johnson, the teacher, and Lorna Leonard, director of student services, immediately.

By late afternoon, the principal had made contact with six of the students. He provided his home phone number and requested that each have a parent call him later that evening. He left a message for Lorna Leonard at her vacation home. There was no response to the call to Will Johnson's home. A check of the teacher's contact card revealed a summer address in a resort community several hours away by auto, but no other phone number. The principal planned to make calls from his home that night with hopes of contacting Will Johnson and all involved students.

During their meeting the following morning, Robert Bender gave the superintendent a copy of the letter with names removed, and copies of the passages that he received. Although the students never saw a copy of the exam prior to its administration, they claimed that during the review process, Mr. Johnson specifically reviewed and focused on four reading passages and two translation passages, which comprised the vast majority of the exam. Mr. Bender described the procedures that the NTC would follow in the investigation. He explained that all the individual tests of the students from Placido had been analyzed and that none of their scores would be reported. Students would be given an opportunity to retake another form of the exam at no cost, as soon as a mutually convenient time could be arranged. Superintendent Bass was surprised by the hasty decision, but offered complete cooperation and expressed the desire of the district to get to the truth.

She suggested that NTC use offices in the school to meet with students and any staff members they wished to interview. Mr. Bender thanked the superintendent and informed her that his staff would begin contacting the students immediately. He asked the superintendent to arrange interviews with the high school principal, guidance counselors, Lorna Leonard, and Will Johnson. Dr. Bass explained that some of the individuals were on vacation, but she would attempt to contact them and make arrangements for the interviews as soon as possible.

The superintendent was upset. She knew that it was just a matter of time before the local newspaper got wind of the "scandal." Parents of innocent students would be outraged that their children were being required to retake the exam. To make matters worse, the high school principal was not able to make contact with the teacher. Lorna Leonard had returned the principal's call last evening and promised to return to Placido by the beginning of next week. Principal Curry had made appointments to meet with 11 of the students beginning that evening, determined that two were on vacation for the week, and left a message for the other two students.

A call to the board president only generated questions. Were the testing materials secured?

THEORY INTO PRACTICE, (Continued)

Who had access to the keys to the storage area? Was it possible that the allegations were untrue? What should be done about the public relations nightmare that was emerging? All these questions had run through the superintendent's mind, along with dozens of others. The president of the board agreed to brief all other board members and instructed the superintendent to have a special board meeting advertised for next Monday evening.

Superintendent Bass prepared a press release and called the editor of the local paper and arranged to meet. She drafted a letter to Will Johnson and sent a copy to his home and vacation addresses via Express Mail. The teacher has been the instructor of the university placement course every year since its inception at Placido High. He attended annual summer training sessions and boasted that his students always performed well. However, Will Johnson's performance in his other classes was not stellar. The superintendent really needed to speak with him.

During the meetings that followed, the principal assured each of the students and their parents that he expected them to tell the truth. No matter what they revealed to him or during interviews with NTC, there would be no reprisals. The principal assured them that everyone wanted to know what happened and that he would deal with anyone, student or faculty member, who had done anything dishonest or inappropriate.

Wednesday morning brought the anticipated headline "Honest Students Report Unfair Advantage" as well as dozens of calls from concerned parents and community members. It also brought some very disturbing information conveyed to the principal during meetings with two of the students.

One of the students, a junior, claimed to have received an exam packet that was torn open. At that time, he verbally expressed that fact loud enough for others in the room to hear. The student noted that Ms. Leonard did not respond to his statement, continued to give test instructions, and reminded the students that they were on a tight schedule. The other student reported that within a day of the exam, she and at least five other students had gone to a teacher "they trusted," Mrs. Anne Bishop, to express their concern that they "knew more than they should" when they took the exam.

The phone rang. The president of the board of education asked for a report on findings. He also expressed the collective opinion of several board members, including his own, that the teacher should be dismissed. The scandal was the talk of the community. Honest students were being punished by having to take another exam because of Johnson's actions. Will Johnson had gone too far and perhaps he had not acted alone. The superintendent's requests to "not to jump to conclusions" had fallen on deaf ears. She urged the board president to be patient and give her the opportunity to get to the facts of the incident.

As Dr. Bass hung up, her secretary gave her a message from the local newspaper editor requesting a return call as soon as possible. She placed the call and much to her chagrin was asked to verify the charge that, during the test administration, one of the students had been given an examination packet that had previously been opened.

Things were really spinning out of control. Priorities must be established and decisions must be made! Assume that you are the superintendent:

- Do circumstances suggest a conspiracy? How can the principal and superintendent find out? What are key communication channels?
- What happens to communication within the organization during the summer when schools are closed for vacation? How can some of the impediments to effective communication be overcome?
- What should the superintendent communicate to the board? How? When?
- Discuss the superintendent's public relations strategy. Is public relations the same as communication?
- What other groups should be involved in the communication process? When? How?
- What are the political ramifications of the incident? How can the negative

THEORY INTO PRACTICE, (Continued)

consequences be anticipated and controlled?

- Develop two scenarios, one in which the teacher is innocent of the charges and one in which he is not. If true, are the charges grounds for dismissal of a tenured teacher?
- What should the superintendent do if she finds that all the evidence is circumstantial and the teacher and director deny any wrongdoing?
- What is the appropriate stance with the media?
- How can such a situation be avoided in the future? Are new district policies and procedures about testing required?

SUMMARY AND SUGGESTED READINGS

Communication is so pervasive in schools that it is a fundamental and integrative process in educational administration. Communication means sharing messages, ideas, or attitudes to produce understanding or shared meanings among people. Four conclusions seem clear. First, to be a good communicator is to know the various types of communication, their particular characteristics, how to choose among them, and how to apply them skillfully. Second, individuals exchange symbols with other persons when interacting in social situations; the people who interpret them in a given situation construct the meanings of those symbols. This means that direct transmission of an intended meaning is not always straightforward. Third, messages traverse formal and informal channels, using a variety of verbal and nonverbal media. Although the formal network is usually larger and better developed than the informal, they are closely related, can be complementary, and are critical to the organization. Fourth, to ensure a high level of shared understanding, feedback is essential. Although perfection is impossible, several techniques are available to measure and improve the communication process at both the individual and organizational levels.

Chester Barnard (1938) proposed an early and still important set of ideas about individual and organizational communication. This is an excellent source to consult on communication and other concepts. Two excellent general sources dealing with the communication literature are the textbooks by DeFleur, Kearney, and Plax (1993) and Harris (1993). They provide relatively comprehensive and in-depth coverage of the various theories and applications in the communication field. Clampitt's (1991) book is useful because he presents the models of communication in a context of administrative applications, myths, and tactics. For an excellent review of the literature and suggestions for further research on gender and communication, we suggest the article by Baker (1991).

Notes

1. Probably the most intense form of two-way communication is what Nicholas C. Burbules (1993) designates as dialogue. Burbules develops an extensive and excellent scholarly treatise on the concept of dialogue in schools, particularly as it relates to teaching. Although the narrative dealing with two-way and interpersonal communication in this section relies heavily on the ideas advanced by Burbules regarding dialogue, we primarily employ the term "two-way communication." Although "two-way communication" and "dialogue" are not exactly the same, we think that the two terms share enough common characteristics for the theoretical foundations of dialogue (as advanced by Burbules) to be applied to our usage of two-way communication. Moreover, "two-way communication" is a more commonly used term in organization analysis than dialogue.
2. The author of this case, Michael F. DiPaola, Ed.D., is a former high school principal and district superintendent. He is currently an associate professor in the Educational Policy, Planning and Leadership Program of the School of Education at the College of William and Mary in Virginia. This case is from DiPaola (1999). "Scandal at Placido High: Coincidence or Conspiracy?" *Journal of Cases in Educational Leadership* [on-line].2(3).

Key Concepts and Ideas

Autocommunication
Bridges
Channel
Communication
Communication effects
Conversation
Debate
Decoding
Encoding
Feedback
Feedback skills
Formal channels
Grapevines
Informal channels
Inquiry
Instruction
Isolate role
Liaisons
Listening skills
Meanings
Message
Networks
Noise
Nonverbal communication
One-way communication
Organizational communication
Receiver
Richness
Sender
Sending skills
Star role
Symbols
Transmission
Two-way communication

CHAPTER 11

LEADERSHIP IN SCHOOLS

Who can say that government is not about charismatic leadership after watching Ronald Reagan. It is important to build consensus but leadership must first be bold and have a direction.

Jesse Jackson, 1990

The effective functioning of social systems from the local PTA to the United States of America is assumed to be dependent on the quality of their leadership.

Victor H. Vroom,
"Leadership"

PREVIEW

1. Leaders are important because they serve as anchors, provide guidance in times of change, and are responsible for the effectiveness of organizations.
2. Leadership is a social influence process that is comprised of both rational and emotional elements.
3. Leader and administrator refer to individuals who occupy positions in which they are expected to exert leadership.
4. The work of leaders exhibits similar patterns across different countries and organizational settings.
5. Personality, motivation, and skill traits appear to be systematically related to leadership in schools.
6. Critical situational factors in educational leadership are environment, leader roles, nature of subordinates, and characteristics of the organization.
7. Task-oriented, relations-oriented, and change-oriented behaviors are fundamental classes of leader behavior.
8. Leader effectiveness can be conceptualized as having three dimensions—personal, organizational, and individual.
9. Contingency models attempt to explain the relationships among traits, situations, behaviors, and effectiveness. Two well-known contingency theories are the least preferred co-worker and leadership substitutes.
10. Interest in the traditional contingency models waned in the 1970s. Visionary and change-oriented ideas emerged to drive the "new leadership" theories and gave a new impetus to the field during the 1980s and 1990s.

11. Both the leader and the followers are key actors in constructing a charismatic relationship.
12. Transformational leaders use idealized influence, inspirational motivation, intellectual stimulation, and individualized consideration to change their schools.
13. Educating potential leaders, selecting new administrators, changing administrators (succession), engineering the situation, and transforming organizational culture are ways to improve schools.

Leadership evokes highly romanticized, emotional, and courageous images for many of us. When we think of specific leaders, names such as Gandhi, Churchill, Kennedy, King, Mandela, Mao Zedong, Meir, Napoleon, Reagan, Roosevelt, and Thatcher come to mind. According to Gary Yukl (1998), the term itself projects images of powerful, dynamic individuals who command victorious armies, build wealthy and influential empires, or alter the course of nations. Stated succinctly, people commonly believe that leaders make a difference and want to understand why. Indeed, leadership is often regarded as the single most important factor in the success or failure of institutions such as schools (Bass, 1990). With a primary focus on administrative leadership in schools, we will build on the premise that leaders are important to educational organizations, and we will select and develop useful theoretical perspectives.

Defining Leadership

As a word from our everyday language, **leadership** has been incorporated into the technical vocabulary of organizational studies without being precisely redefined (Yukl, 1998). Therefore, it is not surprising that definitions of the concept are almost as numerous as the scholars engaged in its study. Bennis (1989), for example, opined that leadership is like beauty—it is hard to define, but you know it when you see it. Martin M. Chemers (1997:1) offers the following typical definition: "leadership is a process of social influence in which one person is able to enlist the aid and support of others in the accomplishment of a common task." The only assumption shared by this and most definitions is that leadership involves a social influence process in which one individual exerts intentional influence over others to structure activities and relationships in a group or organization. Disputes about definitions remain, however, over whether leadership is a specialized role or social influence process; over the kind, basis, and purpose of influence attempts; and over leadership versus management (Yukl, 1998).

One view is that all groups have a specialized leadership role that includes some responsibilities and functions that cannot be shared without jeopardizing the effectiveness of the group (Yukl, 1998). The individual who has the most influence and who is expected to carry out the leadership role is the leader; other members are followers. An alternative concept is that leadership is a social process that occurs naturally within a social system and is shared among its members. Leadership, then, is a process or property of the organization rather than of the individual. Rodney T. Ogawa and Steven T. Bossert (1995) contend that leadership is a quality of school organizations, which flows broadly through social networks and roles. Similarly, Mark A. Smylie and Ann W. Hart (1999) note recent empirical support for leadership as an organizational property of schools. Katz and Kahn (1978) identify three major components of leadership that clarify the controversy: (1) an attribute of an office or position, (2) a characteristic of a person, and (3) a category of actual behavior. Hence, both views can be useful—leadership can profitably be examined as a property of individuals or as roles and processes of the social system.

A second set of controversies involves how much to circumscribe the kind, basis, and purpose of influence attempts. Yukl (1998) delineates dichotomous perspectives on these issues. In regard to the type and outcome of influence processes used by leaders, some theorists include only strategies that produce willing commitment by followers and exclude those that result in neutral or reluctant conformity. Other scholars contend that this is too restrictive because the same kind of influence attempts can produce different results across different situations. Similarly, some theorists restrict influence processes of leaders to those related to task goals and group maintenance, that is, to what is ethical and favorable to the organization and its people. Others place no restrictions on the definition and include all attempts to influence followers, regardless of the intended purpose or actual beneficiary, because acts of leadership frequently have multiple motives. Finally, traditional definitions of leadership tend to emphasize rational processes in which leaders influence followers to believe that it is in their best interest to cooperate and achieve shared task goals. Recent formulations of charismatic and transformational leadership use definitions that recognize the importance of emotions as a basis of influence. In other words, leaders inspire their followers to sacrifice their selfish interests for a larger cause.

Another debate involves distinctions between leaders and administrators and what and how they try to influence (Yukl, 1994). Obviously, individuals can be leaders without being administrators (e.g., an informal leader); conversely, individuals can be administrators without being leaders. Some argue that leadership and administration are fundamentally different concepts. The basis of the dispute appears to be that **administrators** emphasize stability and efficiency, whereas **leaders** stress adaptive change and getting people to agree about what needs to be accomplished. For example, administrators plan and budget, organize and staff, and control and solve problems; leaders establish direction, align people, and motivate and inspire (Kotter, 1990). In school settings, Kenneth Leithwood and Daniel Duke (1999) conclude that justifying a conceptual distinction between leadership and management is difficult. Although no one suggests that administering or managing and leading schools are equivalent, the degree of overlap is disputed.[1] Rather than argue about the specific amount of overlap, we will use both terms to refer to individuals (e.g., administrators, teachers, school board members, students) who occupy positions in which they are expected to exert leadership for subordinates or followers, but without the assumption that they actually do so.

Thus, we agree with Yukl (1998). Leadership should be defined broadly as a social process in which a member of a group or organization influences the interpretation of internal and external events, the choice of goals or desired outcomes, organization of work activities, individual motivation and abilities, power relations, and shared orientations. Moreover, as a specialized role and social influence process, leadership is comprised of both rational and emotional elements with no assumptions about the purpose or outcome of the influence efforts. Employing such a broad definition opens an abundance of useful conceptual and empirical capital for both practitioners and scholars of school administration and leadership.

The Nature of Administrative Work

Given the intense and long-standing interest in leaders and leadership, what is it that leaders do that is so intriguing? Can describing the nature of leaders' work advance our understanding of leadership? Certainly, partial responses to these questions can be gained by observing leaders as they administer and lead their organizations. A number of studies have used a structured observation approach to describe what managers, administrators, and leaders do in their everyday jobs.[2] These studies provide detailed and vivid pictures of what business managers and school administrators do in their jobs, and with whom and where they spend their time. Given the regularities in the research, Kyung Ae Chung and Cecil Miskel (1989) summarize the major findings.

- Managerial work is feverish and consuming in both business and educational organizations; school administrators work long hours at an unrelenting, physically exhausting pace.
- School leaders rely on verbal media; they spend a great deal of time walking around the building and talking to individuals and groups.
- Administrator activities vary widely; hence, administrators constantly change gears and tasks.
- Managerial work is fragmented; for school administrators, the pace is rapid and frenzied, discontinuity prevalent, and the span of concentration short.

Overall, the descriptions of administrative work are similar across different countries and organizational settings. Administrators work primarily in their offices or school buildings. Their jobs are characterized by long hours and brief verbal encounters across a wide range of issues with diverse individuals and groups. Structured observation studies are useful because they respond descriptively and clearly to the question: What do school administrators and leaders do in their jobs? Nevertheless, it is not clear how individuals engaged in work characterized as consuming, reactive, and fragmented can actually provide leadership to their organizations. Moreover, technological advances, demands for reform and accountability, and environmental competition from new forms of schools are changing the nature of work for school administrators. Although the results from these studies are important and interesting, they largely fail to answer the key question, How do we understand the nature of this work in terms of leading schools? To respond to this question, we will summarize the dominant theoretical approaches to understanding leadership.

Traits and Leadership

Many individuals still believe, as Aristotle did centuries ago, that from the hour of birth, some are marked for subjection, others for rule. Aristotle thought that individuals are born with characteristics that would make them leaders. The conception that the key factors in determining leadership are inherited produced the so-called **trait approach of leadership.** Bass (1990) observes that early in this century, leaders were generally regarded as superior individuals who, because of fortunate inheritance or social circumstance, possessed qualities and abilities that differentiated them from people in general. Until the 1950s investigations to find the traits that determine who will be leaders dominated the study of leadership. Researchers attempted to isolate unique traits or characteristics of leaders that differentiated them from their followers. Frequently studied traits included physical characteristics (height, weight), a host of personality factors, needs, values, energy and activity levels, task and interpersonal competence, intelligence, and charisma. Over time, recognition grew that traits can generally be affected by inheritance, learning, and environmental factors.

Early Trait Research

Pure trait approaches—that is, the view that only traits determine leadership capacity—were all but put to rest with the publication of literature reviews during the 1940s and 1950s. In particular, Ralph M. Stogdill (1948) reviewed 124 trait studies of leadership that were completed between 1904 and 1947. He classified the personal factors associated with leadership into the following five general categories:

- Capacity—intelligence, alertness, verbal facility, originality, judgment.
- Achievement—scholarship, knowledge, athletic accomplishments.
- Responsibility—dependability, initiative, persistence, aggressiveness, self-confidence, desire to excel.
- Participation—activity, sociability, cooperation, adaptability, humor.
- Status—socioeconomic position, popularity.

Although Stogdill found a number of traits (e.g., above-average intelligence, dependability, participation, and status) that consistently differentiated leaders from nonleaders, he concluded that the trait approach *by itself* had yielded negligible and confusing results. He asserted that a person does not become a leader by virtue of the possession of some combination of traits because the impact of traits varies widely from situation to situation. As a consequence,

Stogdill added a sixth factor associated with leadership—situational components (e.g., characteristics of followers and goals to be achieved). R. D. Mann's (1959) later review produced similar conclusions.

Recent Perspectives on Leadership Traits

Notwithstanding the lack of success in identifying general leadership traits, research persisted. More recent trait studies, however, use improved and a wider variety of measurement procedures, including projective tests and assessment centers; and they focus on managers and administrators rather than other kinds of leaders. Yukl (1981, 1998) explains that although Stogdill's 1948 literature review greatly discouraged many researchers from studying leader traits, industrial psychologists interested in improving managerial selection continued to conduct trait research. Their emphasis on selection focused trait research on the relationship between leader traits and leader effectiveness, rather than on the comparison of leaders and nonleaders. This distinction is a significant one. Predicting who will become leaders and predicting who will be more effective are quite different tasks. Hence, the so-called trait studies continue, but they now tend to explore the relationship between traits and leadership effectiveness of administrators in particular types of organizations and settings.

This second generation of studies has produced a more consistent set of findings; in fact, in 1970, after reviewing another 163 new trait studies, Stogdill (1981) concluded that a leader is characterized by the following traits: a strong drive for responsibility and task completion, vigor and persistence in pursuit of goals, venturousness and originality in problem solving, drive to exercise initiative in social situations, self-confidence and sense of personal identity, willingness to accept consequences of decision and action, readiness to absorb interpersonal stress, willingness to tolerate frustration and delay, ability to influence other persons' behavior, and capacity to structure interaction systems to the purpose at hand. Similarly, Glenn L. Immegart (1988) concluded that the traits of intelligence, dominance, self-confidence, and high energy or activity level are commonly associated with leaders. Nevertheless, the evidence does support the conclusion that the possession of certain traits increases the likelihood that a leader will be effective (Yukl, 1998), but it does not represent a return to the original trait assumption that "leaders are born, not made." Rather, it is a more sensible and balanced view, one that acknowledges the influence of both traits and situations.

Given the plethora of concepts and for ease of discussion, we will classify the trait variables that currently are associated with effective leadership into one of three groups. The categories are: personality, motivation, and skills (see Table 11.1). We will discuss selected traits within each group.[3]

Personality Traits According to Yukl (1998), **personality traits** are relatively stable dispositions to behave in a particular way. The list of personality factors associated with effective leadership is quite long. Four seem particularly important.

TABLE 11.1

Traits Associated with Effective Leadership

Personality	Motivation	Skills
Self-confidence	Task and interpersonal needs	Technical
Stress tolerance	Achievement orientation	Interpersonal
Emotional maturity	Power needs	Conceptual
Integrity	Expectations	Administrative

- Self-confident leaders are more likely to set high goals for themselves and their followers, to attempt difficult tasks, and to persist in the face of problems and defeats.
- Stress-tolerant leaders are likely to make good decisions, to stay calm, and to provide decisive direction to subordinates in difficult situations. As shown by the structured observation studies, the pace, long hours, fragmentation, and demands for decisions place leaders under intense pressure that can best be addressed by stress-tolerant individuals.
- Emotionally mature leaders tend to have an accurate awareness of their strengths and weaknesses, to be oriented toward self-improvement; they do not deny their shortcomings or fantasize about success. Consequently, emotionally mature administrators can maintain cooperative relationships with subordinates, peers, and supervisors.
- Integrity means that the behaviors of leaders are consistent with their stated values and that they are honest, ethical, responsible, and trustworthy. Yukl believes that integrity is an essential element in building and retaining loyalty and obtaining cooperation and support of others.

Hence, self-confidence, stress tolerance, emotional maturity, and integrity are personality traits associated with leader effectiveness.

Motivational Traits Motivation is a set of energetic forces that originate both within as well as beyond an individual to initiate work-related behavior and to determine its form, direction, intensity, and duration. A basic postulate is that motivation factors play key roles in explaining both the choice of action and its degree of success. Generally, highly motivated leaders are likely to be more effective than individuals with low expectations, modest goals and limited self-efficacy. Drawing from the works of several scholars (e.g., Fiedler, 1967; McClelland, 1985; Yukl, 1998), four **motivational traits** are especially critical for leaders.

- Task and interpersonal needs are two underlying dispositions that motivate effective leaders. Effective leaders are characterized by their drive for the task and their concern for people.
- Power needs refer to motives of individuals to seek positions of authority and to exercise influence over others.
- Achievement orientation includes a need to achieve, desire to excel, drive to succeed, willingness to assume responsibility, and a concern for task objectives.
- High expectations for success of school administrators refers to their belief that they can do the job and will receive valued outcomes for their efforts.

In addition to these motivation traits, the physical traits of energy and activity levels allow individuals to exhibit competence through active engagement with others.

Skills Other important components, which are often neglected in the leadership literature, are skills and experience. Competence, or having a mastery of task-relevant knowledge and skills to accomplish a goal in an effective fashion, is mandatory for a leader. Yukl (1998) discusses four types of **skills** associated with leader effectiveness.

- Technical skills deal with specialized knowledge, procedures, and techniques to accomplish the task. High levels of technical skill are especially important for administrators at the lower levels of the organization such as principals and others who supervise followers with high skill levels such as teachers.
- Interpersonal skills focus on the ability to understand feelings and attitudes of others and to establish cooperative work relationships. To be effective this skill must occur naturally, unconsciously, and consistently in a leader's behavior.
- Conceptual skills involve developing and using ideas and concepts to plan, to organize, and to solve complex problems. Given the greater scope of activities and complexity of relationships of jobs higher in the hierarchy, conceptual skills are particularly important in contributing to the effectiveness of administrators who are at the upper levels of the organization.
- Administrative skills include knowledge about specific kinds of such managerial activities as planning, mentoring, delegating, supervising, and handling meetings. Administrative skills usually combine technical, interpersonal, and conceptual skills to assist in the performance of managerial functions.

These four skills must be developed in the context of practice. Experience represents an opportunity to learn the job and apply the skills; experience has been found to be central in determining job performance of professional and managerial employees (Schmidt and Hunter, 1992).

We have identified three sets of traits—personality, motivational, and skills—that are related to leadership effectiveness. Hence, it is fundamentally

TABLE 11.2

Situational Factors of Educational Leadership

Subordinate	Organizational	Internal Environment	External Environment
Personality	Size	Climate	Social
Motivation	Hierarchy	Culture	Economic
Abilities	Formalization		
	Leader role		

important for educational administrators to determine their strengths and weaknesses, to enhance the skills that are deficient, and to compensate for weaknesses (Yukl, 1998). Our summary of the most important of these traits is shown in Table 11.1.

Situations and Leadership

Reaction, or perhaps more appropriately overreaction, to the trait approach was so intense during the late 1940s and 1950s that for a time it seemed that scholars had substituted a strictly situational analysis for the then-questionable trait approach. The view that leaders are born was rejected (Bass, 1990). Researchers sought to identify distinctive characteristics of the setting to which the leader's success could be attributed; they attempted to isolate specific properties of the **leadership situation** that had relevance for leader behavior and performance (Campbell, Dunnette, Lawler, and Weick, 1970; Lawler, 1985; Vecchio, 1993). As shown throughout this book and summarized in Table 11.2, a number of variables have been postulated to influence behavior in schools and, hence, can be viewed as situational determinants of leadership. A few general examples follow:

- Structural properties of the organization—size, hierarchical structure, formalization, technology.
- Role characteristics—type and difficulty of task, procedural rules, content and performance expectations, power.
- Subordinate characteristics—education, age, knowledge and experience, tolerance for ambiguity, responsibility, power.
- Internal environment—climate, culture, openness, participation levels, group atmosphere, values, and norms.
- External environment—complexity, stability, uncertainty, resource dependency, institutionalization.

John P. Campbell and his colleagues (1970) came to an interesting conclusion about the situational phase of leadership study. Everyone believed that the need for research was great, but actual empirical activity was scarce. Consequently, the jump from "leaders are born, not made" to "leaders are made by the situation, not born," was short-lived. Bass (1990) maintains that the situational view overemphasized the situational and underemphasized the personal nature of leadership. To restrict the study of leadership to either traits or situations is unduly narrow and counterproductive.

Behaviors and Leadership

Early conceptualizations of leadership typically relied on two distinct categories of **leader behavior**—one concerned with people, interpersonal relations, and group maintenance, and the other with production, task completion, and goal achievement (Cartwright and Zander, 1953). Similar findings were reflected in other early studies of leadership. We now turn to a description of an early program of research and a more recent perspective on leader behavior.

The Ohio State and Related Leadership Studies

To students of educational administration, probably the most well-known leader research inquiries are the leader behavior description questionnaire (LBDQ) studies started at Ohio State University in the 1940s. Originally developed there by John K. Hemphill and Alvin Coons (1950), the LBDQ was later refined by Andrew Halpin and B. J. Winer (1952). It measures two basic dimensions of leader behavior—initiating structure and consideration.

Initiating structure includes any leader behavior that delineates the relationship between the leader and subordinates and, at the same time, establishes defined patterns of organization, channels of communication, and methods of procedure. **Consideration** includes leader behavior that indicates friendship, trust, warmth, interest, and respect in the relationship between the leader and members of the work group (Halpin, 1966). Using the LBDQ, subordinates, superiors, or the individuals themselves can describe the leader behavior of themselves and each other.

Four major findings emerged from the Ohio State University LBDQ studies (Halpin, 1966).

- Initiating structure and consideration are fundamental dimensions of leader behavior.
- Effective leader behavior tends most often to be associated with frequent behaviors on both dimensions.
- Superiors and subordinates tend to evaluate the contributions of the leader behavior dimensions oppositely in assessing effectiveness. Superiors tend to emphasize initiating structure; subordinates are more concerned with consideration.
- Only a slight relationship exists between how leaders say they should behave and how subordinates describe that they do behave.

Hoy and his colleagues (Kunz and Hoy, 1976; Leverette, 1984; Hoy and Brown, 1988) investigated the relationship between the leadership styles of principals and the "zone of indifference or acceptance" (Barnard, 1938; Simon, 1957a) of teachers—that is, the range of behavior within which subordinates are ready to accept the decisions made by their leaders. The LBDQ findings suggest that principals who exhibit frequent behaviors on both initiating structure and consideration produce situations that are conducive to relatively broad zones of acceptance by teachers. The results indicate that the relationships between the leadership behaviors of elementary and secondary principals and the zone of acceptance of teachers differ slightly. Similar to the secondary schools, both initiating structure and consideration were positively related to the zone of acceptance. But *both* dimensions had significant independent effects on the professional zone of acceptance of teachers. Unlike the secondary schools, the consideration of the elementary principals had a significant independent relationship with the zone of acceptance of teachers.

The findings of Kunz, Hoy, and Leverette support the conclusions made by other scholars (Vroom, 1976; House and Baetz, 1979; Mitchell, 1979). Consideration is typically related to subordinate satisfaction with work and with the leader. While the evidence is somewhat mixed, initiating structure has been identified as a source of subordinate performance. However, situational variables apparently affect the relationship between consideration and initiating structure and affect the criteria of organizational effectiveness as well. Consideration has its most positive effect on the satisfaction of subordinates who work in structured situations or who work on stressful, frustrating, or dissatisfying tasks. In contrast, initiating structure has the greatest impact on group performance when subordinates' tasks are ill defined.

The implications of these findings are fairly clear to us. To neglect initiation of structure limits the leader's impact on the school; to ignore consideration reduces the satisfaction of the subordinates. Certainly, leader behavior that integrates strength on both initiating structure and consideration into a consistent pattern is desirable. Nevertheless, the converse also seems likely; there are situations especially favorable to considerate leadership style that are characterized by strong consideration and limited initiating structure. The matching of leadership style with the appropriate situation in order to maximize effectiveness is a knotty problem to which we will return throughout this chapter.

A Recent Perspective on Leader Behavior

Yukl (1994) also cautions not to interpret the results of the early studies as universal theories of effective leader behavior. In other words, concluding that the same style of leader behavior is optimal across all situations is not warranted. Blake and Mouton's (1985) managerial grid is a well-known universal theory. Its basic hypothesis is that the most effective leaders are high on both production and people concerns. Production and people concerns are similar to the earlier models using terms such as "task" or "initiating structure" and "relationship" or "consideration." Yukl notes that Blake and Mouton suggest a situational aspect with the idea that the behaviors must be relevant to the situation to be effective. However, they never actually state specific generalizations linking appropriate behaviors to different situations. As we have shown in our discussion of the earlier studies, situational factors do affect the effectiveness of leader behavior, even when an individual is high on both people and task dimensions.

Although we have limited our discussion to structured observations and the Ohio State studies, many listings of leader behavior are found in the literature. To integrate the many typologies and taxonomies, Yukl (1998) developed a three-category framework of leader behavior. His categories and brief descriptions follow.

- Task-oriented behaviors encompass clarifying roles, planning and organizing operations, and monitoring organizational functions. These actions emphasize accomplishing tasks, using personnel and resources efficiently, maintaining stable and reliable processes, and making incremental improvements.
- Relations-oriented behaviors include supporting, developing, recognizing, consulting, and managing conflict. These activities focus on improving relationships and helping people, increasing cooperation and teamwork, and building commitment to the organization.
- Change-oriented behaviors consist of scanning and interpreting external events, articulating an attractive vision, proposing innovative programs, appealing for change, creating a coalition to support and implement changes. These acts concentrate on adapting to change in the environment, making major changes in goals, policies, procedures and programs, and gaining commitment to the changes.

Task-oriented and relations-oriented behaviors are similar to initiating structure and consideration, respectively, but are defined more broadly.

Leaders will typically engage in all three types of behaviors. Yukl (1998) believes, however, that the external environment plays a particularly important role in determining the appropriate mix for leader effectiveness. In stable environments, task-oriented behavior should be used more frequently than change-oriented behavior. For example, when the programs of a school are appropriate to its stable community, the emphasis needs to be such task-oriented behaviors as increasing efficiency and maintaining stable operations. Some change-oriented behaviors are needed in monitoring the environment and diffusing new knowledge. Similarly, relations-oriented behaviors are more feasible in simple stable environments than in complex unstable environments. In complex unstable environments, change-oriented behavior is likely to be the most effective. In sum, appropriately applying or balancing different types of behaviors for varying situations is fundamental to enhancing leader performance.

Leadership Effectiveness

The final set of concepts in a contingency model is the criteria used to judge leadership effectiveness. To both practicing administrators and scholars, effectiveness is a complicated, multifaceted, and subtle topic. Three types of effectiveness outcomes are suggested in Table 11.3.

- Personal—other perceptions of reputation and self-assessments.
- Individual member satisfaction.
- Organizational goal attainment.

TABLE 11.3

Effectiveness Indicators for Educational Leaders

Personal	**Organizational**	**Individual**
Perceived reputation	Goal attainment	Satisfaction
Self-assessment		Performance

Perceived evaluations of performance are important: subjective judgments of the leader by himself or herself, subordinates, peers, and superiors within the school and by members of the public outside the school yield measures of effectiveness. In schools, the opinions, for example, respect, admiration, commitment, held by students, teachers, administrators, and patrons are highly significant. However, these groups may view the performance levels quite differently. A second indicator of leadership effectiveness is the satisfaction of organizational participants. Finally, the relative levels of school goal achievement also define the effectiveness of educational leaders (see Chapter 8). **Leadership effectiveness,** then, can be defined as having a more objective dimension—accomplishment of organizational goals—and two subjective dimensions—perceptual evaluations of significant reference groups and overall job satisfaction of subordinates.

Contingency Models of Leadership

Hitting their zenith in the 1970s, contingency approaches such as the general model shown in Figure 11.1 were the most influential models of leadership into the 1980s. At their best, **contingency approaches** include the four sets of concepts that we have just considered—traits of leaders, characteristics of the situation, behaviors of the leader, and effectiveness of the leader. Two basic hypotheses are shown in Figure 11.1. First, traits of the leaders and characteristics of the situation combine to produce leader behavior and effectiveness. Second, situational factors have direct impacts on effectiveness. For example, the motivation and ability levels of teachers and students are related to the goal attainment of schools. Moreover, the socioeconomic status of individuals attending a school is strongly related to student achievement on standardized tests. From a short-range perspective, at least, the situational characteristics of the school may have a greater influence on leader effectiveness than a leader's own behavior. Contingency approaches also seek to specify the conditions or situational variables that moderate the relationship among leader traits, behaviors, and performance criteria (Bryman, 1996). The evidence indicates that in one set of circumstances, one type of leader is effective; under another set of circumstances, a different type of leader is effective. Although at least six contingency models appear in the literature (Yukl, 1998), we will briefly review three—least preferred co-worker, substitutes for leadership, and path-goal theories.[4]

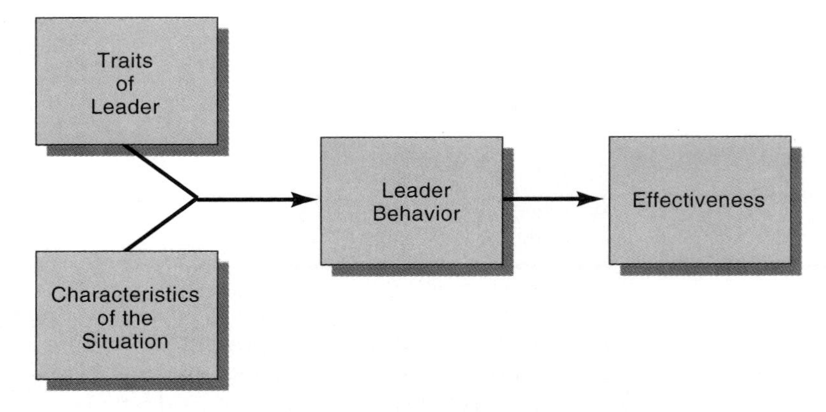

FIGURE 11.1 *A Contingency Schema for Understanding Leadership.*

Least Preferred Co-worker Theory

Fiedler (1967) constructed the first major theory to propose specific contingency relationships in the study of leadership. Lacking a behavior component, the least preferred co-worker model uses leader style as a trait, three indicators of the situational control, and effectiveness.[5]

Leadership style is determined by the motivational system of the leader, that is, the underlying needs structure that motivates behavior in various interpersonal situations. The least preferred co-worker (LPC) scale is used to measure this trait. Using the LPC, a respondent selects the person with whom he or she works least well (least preferred co-worker) and then describes that individual on the scale. A person scoring high on the LPC describes the least preferred co-worker positively, as being pleasant, loyal, warm, kind, efficient, and so forth. In contrast, the individual scoring low on the LPC describes the least preferred co-worker negatively, as being unpleasant, backbiting, cold, unkind, inefficient, and so forth. The LPC score indicates the extent to which the individual sets a higher priority or value on task accomplishment (task-motivated) or on maintaining good interpersonal relations (relationship-motivated) (Fiedler and Garcia, 1987).

Situational control is the degree of power and influence that leaders have to implement plans, decisions, and action strategies (Fiedler and Garcia, 1987). Situational control is determined by three factors. First, *position power* is the power that the organization confers on the leader for the purpose of getting the job done. Examples include the extent to which a leader can reward and punish members and whether the group can depose the leader. Second, *task structure* is the extent to which the task has clearly specified goals, methods, and standards of performance. The more structured the task, the more control the leader has in directing the group. Third, *leader-member relations* is the extent to which the leader is accepted and respected by group members. Two factors are important with respect to leader-member relations: the quality of interpersonal relations between the leader and subordinates, and the level of informal authority granted to the leader. The quality of leader-member relations is the most important factor in determining the leader's influence over group members, followed by task structure and position power. Fiedler formed eight situations by dichotomizing the three factors—that is, good or bad leader-member relations, structured or unstructured tasks, and high or low position power. The eight combinations or octants map the range of situations from high control to low control. The basic contention is that the leader has more control and influence when the group is supportive, the leader knows exactly what to do and how to do it, and the organization gives the leader means to reward and punish the group members.

Effectiveness in this theory is straightforward—namely, the extent to which the group accomplishes its primary task. In many of Fiedler's studies, objective measures of group effectiveness are used—net profit, cost per unit, percentage of wins, number of problems solved. If a reliable objective measure of group performance is not available, then performance ratings by the supervisor of the leader or group are used. But in all cases, leader effectiveness is determined by the degree to which the task is judged to be achieved.

From data collected before 1962, Fiedler developed three propositions for his contingency theory.

- In high-control situations, task-oriented leaders are more effective than relationship-oriented leaders.
- In moderate-control situations, relationship-oriented leaders are more effective than task-oriented leaders.
- In low-control situations, task-oriented leaders are more effective than relationship-oriented leaders.

Since then, the model has been used to predict group performance in a large variety of social settings (Fiedler, 1967, 1973; Fiedler and Garcia, 1987). Two studies provide rigorous and complete tests of the model—that is, investigations that meet the criteria set by Fiedler and include leaders from all eight situations. One study was supportive (Chemers and Skrzypek, 1972); one was not (Vecchio, 1977). Moreover, three meta-analyses (Strube and Garcia, 1981; Peters, Hartke, and Pohlman, 1985; Crehan, 1985) of research testing the contingency model provide some support, but not for all octants and not as strongly for field studies as for laboratory studies. In school settings, findings from a number of studies also support Fiedler's theory (McNamara and Enns, 1966; Williams and Hoy, 1973; Martin, Isherwood, and Lavery, 1976).

The LPC theory has been subjected to several criticisms. Probably the most persistent objection is that the definition has changed over the years concerning what the LPC measures. At first, it was seen simply as a measure of an emotional reaction to individuals with whom the leader found it difficult to work; then it was thought to differentiate between individuals who had a task orientation as opposed to an interpersonal one; later the LPC score was interpreted as an indicator of a leader's motivational hierarchy. Overall, Fiedler's theory represents an ambitious and laudable effort to build a powerful contingency theory of leadership. Although interest has waned, the model demonstrates that a combination of situational and individual characteristics partly explains the leadership phenomenon. Like most pioneering efforts, it undoubtedly is incorrect in detail if not in substance. Yet Fiedler's contingency model was the first and, to date, the longest-lasting attempt to answer the question: What particular style in what special situation?

Substitutes for Leadership Model

An assumption of contingency models other than this one is that some kind of formal leadership is needed and important in organizations such as schools (Howell, 1997). Steven Kerr and John M. Jermier (1978) questioned this assumption and created the **substitutes for leadership model.** The primary concepts of this contingency model are supportive and instrumental leader behaviors, situational variables that act as substitutes and neutralizers for leadership, and outcome variables. *Substitutes* are persons or things that make person-oriented or task-oriented behavior unnecessary and redundant. In other words, substitutes are situational aspects that replace or reduce a leader's ability to influence the attitudes, perceptions, or behaviors of followers. In contrast, *neutralizers* do not replace leader behaviors but are situational factors that prevent a leader from acting in a particular way or that nullify the effects of the leader's actions. For example, a principal's lack of authority to reward effective performance of a teacher is situational constraint on the leader behavior, whereas the teacher's lack of interest in an incentive offered by the principal is a condition that makes the behavior pointless (Yukl, 1998).

Kerr and Jermier (1978) identify three categories of situational variables that have the potential to act as leader substitutes. First, characteristics of subordinates include their abilities, training, experience and knowledge, professional orientation, and indifference toward rewards. Second, task characteristics comprise structured routine tasks, intrinsically satisfying tasks, and feedback provided by the task. Third, organizational characteristics consist of such things as formalization of roles and procedures, flexibility of rules and policies, work group cohesiveness, and spatial distance between the administrator and followers. The substitutes for leaders model sees performance as dependent on subordinate, task, and organizational characteristics rather than on those of the leader. For example, when the subordinates have high ability, are experienced and knowledgeable, or the task is unambiguous and routine, task-oriented leadership is not needed. Similarly, when the task is intrinsically satisfying or the work group is closely knit and cohesive, relationship or supportive leadership is of limited usefulness. Taken to its logical conclusion, knowledge of these substitutes would enable the design of a situation that permits free information flow, effective decision making, and exercise of authority without a designated leader (Fiedler and Garcia, 1987). However, Kerr and Jermier do not take their theory to this extreme and note that substitutes exist for some leader activities but not for others. Jon P. Howell (1997) elaborates this point when he asserts that substitutes for leadership will not make all leadership insignificant because some substitute variables may neutralize or replace one leader behavior and enhance one or more other behaviors.

Philip M. Podsakoff and his colleagues (1993) conclude that the theory has generated substantial interest because it helps explain why leader behaviors have significant effects in some situations and may have no effects in others. Although results from recent attempts to test the model have not been particularly supportive, Podsakoff and his colleagues conclude that it is necessary to consider both leader behaviors and substitutes to understand how employee attitudes, behaviors, and role perceptions are determined. In sum, they believe that the leadership substitutes model should receive additional attention.

Reformulated Path-Goal Theory

House (1971, 1973) initially developed the path-goal theory of leadership and House and Mitchell (1974) refined it. With 40–50 studies lending mixed support for the model, House (1996) recently made a major overhaul of the theory. He expanded the leader behaviors from 4 to 10 classes, modernized the conceptions of subordinate motivation and abilities and task characteristics as situational variables, and expanded the outcomes to include subordinate satisfaction and individual and work unit effectiveness. The major concepts—leader behavior, situational factors, and effectiveness, but not leader traits—comprising the reformulated path-goal theory are shown in Table 11.4. House believes that the new version specifies leader behaviors that promote positive outcomes. The general or meta proposition is that to be effective, leaders engage in behaviors that complement the subordinate's environments and abilities in ways that compensate for deficiencies and enhance subordinate satisfaction and individual and work unit effectiveness. Moreover, 26 specific propositions link the concepts together. To illustrate the specific propositions of this complex theory, five leader behaviors will be defined and then related to the situational and outcome variables through five specific propositions.

First, under certain conditions, **path-goal clarifying behaviors** of a leader are capable of making subordinates' needs and preferences contingent on effective performance. These include clarifying the following: performance goals, means to carry out the tasks, standards of performance, expectations of others, rewards and punishments for subordinates. This leads to the

TABLE 11.4

Concepts in the Reformulated Path-Goal Theory of Leadership

Leader Behaviors		Situation	Outcomes
Path-goal clarifying	Group decision process	Subordinate motivation	Subordinate satisfaction
Achievement oriented	Representation		Subordinate empowerment
Work facilitation	Networking	Subordinate abilities	Subordinate effectiveness
Supportive	Value based		
Interaction facilitation	Shared	Task demands	Work unit effectiveness

proposition that when task demands of subordinates are satisfying but ambiguous, path-goal clarifying behaviors by superiors will be a source of clarification and subordinate satisfaction will be motivational.

Second, **achievement-oriented leader behavior** is behavior that encourages excellent performance, sets challenging goals, seeks improvement, and shows confidence that subordinates will attain high performance standards. More than merely emphasizing performance or goals, it depends on the motivational orientations of the subordinates. Hence, House (1996) proposes that achievement-oriented leader behavior will be effective when performed by superiors who administer subordinates who have individual responsibility and control over their work.

Third, **supportive leader behavior** displays a concern for subordinates' welfare, creates a friendly and psychologically supportive work environment, and takes into account subordinates' needs and preferences. Such behavior is particularly needed when the situation is dangerous, monotonous, stressful, or frustrating. Conversely, House (1996) proposes that when tasks are intrinsically satisfying or the situation is not stressful, supportive leader behavior will have limited effect on follower satisfaction, motivation, or performance.

Fourth, **value-based leader behavior** appeals to followers' treasured values, enhances their self-efficacy and sense of consistency, and makes their self-worth contingent on contributing to the leaders' mission. Behaviors include articulating a vision or ideological goal for a better future for the followers, displaying passion for the vision, and using symbolic behaviors to emphasize the values contained in collective vision. Because ideological visions often challenge the status quo, their expression is often suppressed. Hence, the proposition is when the values inherent in the vision of a value-based leader are in conflict with the dominant coalition or prevailing culture of the organization, value-based leadership will induce substantial intergroup conflict.

Finally, **shared leadership** occurs when the formally appointed leader shares the leader behaviors with members of the work group. Based on research finding that peer leadership is often more strongly related to effectiveness than leadership exercised by formal administrators, the following proposition is offered by House (1996): When the work is interdependent within the work unit, encouragement by the leader of collaborative shared responsibility for performing leader behaviors will enhance work unit cohesiveness and performance.

Any given leader is unlikely to have the ability to engage in all or even most of the 10 sets of behavior. On the basis of their personalities and inventories of abilities, House (1996) contends that effective leaders will select the behaviors with which they are most comfortable. In addition, some of the behaviors are probably substitutable for each other. For example, articulating a vision coupled with modeling appropriate behaviors may be substitutable path-goal clarifying behaviors. Some of the moderating variables may substitute for each other. Task-relevant knowledge may substitute for task structure.

Although the reformulated path-goal theory of leadership has not yet been tested empirically, House (1996) maintains that it is consistent with and integrates the predictions from other current leadership theories and empirical generalizations. It is limited, however, in not dealing with emergent informal leadership, political behavior of leaders, leadership as it affects several levels of administrators or subordinates in organizations, or leadership for change.

Changing Leadership Perspectives

In presenting the trait, behavior, situational, and contingency approaches, we have tended to follow a historical sequence of knowledge development for leadership. Most of the theory development and research on these traditional models occurred before 1980. The accumulated knowledge from these approaches is substantial and provides significant insights about leadership. Nevertheless, James G. Hunt (1999) describes the development of a sense of "doom and gloom" about the study of leadership during the 1970s. A number of scholars questioned the usefulness of the leadership concept (e.g., Lieberson and O'Connor, 1972; Salancik and Pfeffer, 1977; McCall and Lombardo, 1978; Kerr and Jermier (1978). Scholars saw little new conceptual capital being created and thought the massive number of leadership studies had produced a field that was rigorous, boring, and static. Most important, the research examined more and more the inconsequential questions and provided little new knowledge. Amid these cries of catastrophe, two bright spots appeared to save the day—charismatic and transformational leadership (Hunt, 1999). With new ideas of visionary and change-oriented leadership, the doom and gloom atmosphere was transformed during the 1980s to a burst of enthusiasm for the "new leadership."

The New Leadership

By the early 1990s, charismatic and transformational leadership theories were evoking high levels of interest among scholars and practitioners (Carey, 1992; House and Howell, 1992; Howell and Avolio, 1993). The interest only seems to increase and by the end of the decade, dozens of diverse research studies had been completed (Conger, 1999). As new approaches, this genre of theory differs from traditional approaches in at least three ways.

- Leaders are managers of meaning who exhibit inspirational, visionary, and symbolic or less rationalistic aspects of behavior (House, Spangler, and Woycke, 1991; Bryman, 1996).
- Leaders emphasize the importance of the followers' emotional responses to their leader's inspiring vision.
- Charismatic and transformational theories tend to focus on leaders at the upper levels of the organization rather than on the earlier emphasis on leaders at lower levels who have face-to-face relationships with followers (Hunt, 1999).

Jay A. Conger (1999) observes that even though House first articulated the basic formulation of charismatic theory in 1977, transformational leadership theory as proposed by Bass (1985a) quickly became the darling of the field and overshadowed the charismatic paradigm. By the early 1990s, however, House and other leadership scholars such as Conger began to build more comprehensive models and to test them empirically. As a result variations on both approaches became highly popular during the 1990s. The basic concepts of the models are leader traits, leader behaviors, facilitating conditions, and effects, characteristics that to some degree parallel the traits, situation, behavior, and performance ideas of contingency models.

Charismatic Leadership

In the study of leadership, the origins of charisma are usually attributed to Max Weber (1947). Weber saw charisma as a mode of influence based on followers' perceptions that the leader displayed exceptional characteristics. He believed that during a time of crisis, charisma emerges as a leader with an extraordinary spirit who comes forth with a radical vision. Seeing a potential solution, a striking vision, and a leader with overwhelming personal appeal, followers are attracted to the leader. Typically, a common value orientation develops within the group to produce an intense normative commitment to and identification with the leader. Although advocates see charisma as a remarkable form of leadership, such intense loyalty by subordinates and some characteristics of these leaders have combined throughout history to reveal a frightening dark side (Conger, 1999). The negative consequences of Stalin and Hitler show the depths of the possible darkness. Plainly, charisma is a term that does not distinguish between good and evil or moral and immoral leadership (House and Howell, 1992). Although several theories of charismatic leadership have been developed (Yukl, 1998), we will consider the initial model and its refinements as developed by House and his colleagues.

House's Charismatic Leadership

Adapting Weber's ideas to the organizational settings, House's (1977) theory of **charismatic leadership** differentiates the personality and behavioral characteristics of charismatic and noncharismatic leaders. Charismatic leaders are distinguished by dominance, self-confidence, need to influence, and strong convictions in the moral correctness of their beliefs. House and Howell (1992) expanded and refined the inventory of personality traits of charismatic leaders to include the following.

- Achievement orientation.
- Strong tendencies to be creative, innovative, and inspirational.
- High levels of energy and involvement.
- Self-confidence.
- High need for social influence coupled with a strong concern for the moral and nonexploitive use of power.

- High levels of work involvement and risk propensity.
- Tendencies to be nurturing, socially sensitive, and considerate of followers.

House, Spangler, and Woycke (1991) argue that charisma is not a personality trait of specific leaders, but that personality characteristics such as these contribute to the formation of charismatic relationships.

Charisma refers to the ability of a leader to exercise both intense and diffuse influence over the beliefs, values, behaviors, and performance of others. It arises through actual behavior and personal example of the leader or the attributions made to the leader by followers; that is, a leader is not charismatic unless described by subordinates as being charismatic (House, Spangler, and Woycke, 1991). This perspective views both the leader and the followers as key actors in constructing a charismatic relationship. Hence, House and his colleagues see charisma as residing in the relationship between a leader who has charismatic traits and followers who are open to charisma. This suggests that within a charismatic relationship, followers attribute certain qualities or traits to the leader who is then esteemed and given their loyalty and admiration (Gardner and Avolio, 1998).

The attributions of charisma form as followers observe a leader's behavior (Conger and Kanungo, 1988). In addition to communicating appealing ideological goals and high performance expectations, charismatic leaders also engage in behaviors that create a sense of leader success and competence among followers. Behaviors include the following.

- Visioning the future.
- Managing impressions.
- Making self-sacrifices.
- Taking personal risks.
- Modeling behavior for followers to imitate.
- Engaging in unconventional behavior.
- Sharing power.

These behaviors arouse motives related to the group's task mission. For example, appealing visions of the future give the work added meaning and inspire enthusiasm and excitement among followers. Impression management increases trust in the leader's decisions and increases willing compliance by followers (Yukl, 1998).

In comparison to traditional leadership approaches that depend on rational and instrumental aspects such as expectancies and cognitions, House (1977) hypothesizes that the impacts of charismatic leaders are greatest on follower emotions. Such leaders transform the needs, values, preferences, and aspirations of followers from self-interests to collective interests. In other words, a charismatic leader causes followers to become highly committed to the leader's vision and to perform far above the usual expectations. As a result, charismatic leaders have profound and unusual effects on their followers. In attempting to explain the profound motivational effects, Boas Shamir, R. J. House and Michael B. Arthur (1993) contend that people behave in ways to establish and affirm their sense of identity or self-concept. Charismatic leaders wield influence by behaving in ways that bind the self-concepts of the followers to the leader and the leader's goals. At least five sets of behaviors are hypothesized to activate leader influence—offering an appealing future vision, intensifying personal identification of followers with the leader, developing a deep social or collective identity among followers, changing follower perceptions of work so that values are linked to task objectives, and heightening the self-efficacy of individuals and the collective (Yukl, 1998; Conger, 1999). In a recent study, the findings provide only partial support for the theory and suggest a need for greater sensitivity to situational features (Shamir, Zakay, Breinin, and Popper, 1998).

Situational Factors in Charismatic Leadership

Boas Shamir and Jane M. Howell (1999) declare that most writings about charismatic and transformation leadership create the impression that they apply across all organizational settings. If this were the case, the new leadership paradigm would simply represent a return to the "one best way" or "leaders are born" attitudes of the trait and behavioral approaches. Even when references are made to the situation, the ideas are not well developed. Similar to earlier contingency theories, Shamir and Howell contend that the emergence and effectiveness of charismatic leadership are facilitated by some contexts and inhibited by others. They believe that incorporating the concept of situational strength would substantially increase the efficacy of charismatic leadership theory.

Strong situations are structured and clear. A setting with structure and clarity directs the participants to interpret the context the same way, promotes uniform expectations about the appropriate responses, provides clear incentives for performing certain behaviors, and requires skills that everyone has. In contrast, weak situations are less structured and more ambiguous. A weak context exerts few pressures for conformity and provides few social and organizational cues about what constitutes appropriate and potentially effective behavior. Consequently, the behavior of people may be guided primarily by their self-concepts. Weak situations with their ambiguity and lack of clarity and the tendency of individuals to seek external cues to guide their behavior create opportunities for the emergence and influence of charismatic leaders.

A basic proposition of Shamir and Howell (1999) is that charismatic leadership is more likely to emerge and be effective in weak situations than in strong situations. Circumstances that promote weak situations in school organizations may include the following:

- The external environment is characterized by crisis and upheaval, uncertainty (dynamic and complex), or high demands and opportunities for change.
- The goals, tasks, and technology are ambiguous, complex, and challenging.
- The structure is organic rather than mechanistic.
- The culture emphasizes adaptability.

How different situations can affect the emergence of charismatic leaders is shown by the research of N. C. Roberts and R. T. Bradley (1988). They observed the same leader as a superintendent of a public school district and later as a state commissioner of education. As a superintendent, she was perceived as a highly charismatic and effective leader. She successfully implemented a large, mandated budget cut and started a number of innovative educational programs. As superintendent, she was not initially seen as a charismatic leader, but her reputation as a charismatic leader developed over a two-year period and only after her success in promoting educational change. The perception of charisma did not transfer to or develop in the commissioner's position, however. Although she was evaluated as an effective administrator, little evidence was found that she was either perceived as being a charismatic commissioner or generated widespread support for substantial changes in the state system. Roberts and Bradley attributed the different perceptions of charisma to a variety of situational factors. First, in contrast to state agency, the school district faced a financial crisis that called for creative solutions. Second, as district superintendent, she had much more autonomy and authority than as commissioner. Third, strong political opposition and a culture of bureaucratic resistance thwarted her efforts to restructure the department of education and to build her own administrative team. In sum, the relatively week situation in the district helped her inspire strong trust and affection with constituents as superintendent and the relatively strong situation in the department restricted such relationships and thus, the emergence of charismatic leadership.

Research and Evaluation

Yukl (1998) observes that charismatic leadership theories are quite new and are supported by a limited amount of research. Nonetheless, they provide a better explanation for the exceptional influence some leaders have on followers than earlier trait and behavior models. Theories based on charisma also recognize the importance of emotional reactions of subordinates to leaders and of symbolic behavior in making events meaningful to followers. Finally, Yukl concludes that charisma is not necessary to achieve major changes in organizations and their performance. Rather, successful change is usually a product of transformational leadership by administrators not perceived as being overly charismatic.

Transformational Leadership

On the basis of James MacGregor Burns's (1978) ideas of transactional and transformational political leaders, Bernard M. Bass (1985a) explicitly developed a transformational leadership theory. For Burns, transactional political leaders motivate followers by exchanging rewards for services rendered—for example, jobs for votes and influence for campaign contributions. When subordinates are doing their work in organizations such as schools, transactional leaders recognize what followers want from work and try to provide them with what they want, exchange rewards and promises of reward for effort, and respond to employees' immediate self-interests. Transactional leaders pursue a cost-benefit, economic exchange to meet followers' current material and psychological needs in return for contracted services rendered by the subordinate (Bass, 1985a). Stated differently, transactional leadership is a form of contingent reinforcement (Bass, 1998). Reinforcement takes the form of a leader's promise and rewards or threats and disciplinary actions; reinforcing behavior is contingent on the follower's performance. In other works, transactional leaders give followers things they want in exchange for things leaders want (Kuhnert and Lewis, 1987).

In sharp contrast, **transformational leadership** goes well beyond exchanging inducements for desired performance (Bennis and Nanus, 1985; Tichy and Devanna, 1986; Howell and Frost, 1989; Howell and Avolio, 1993). Transformational leaders build commitment to the organization's objectives and empower followers to achieve these objectives (Yukl, 1998). For example, they are expected to:

- Define the need for change.
- Create new visions and muster commitment to the visions.
- Concentrate on long-term goals.
- Inspire followers to transcend their own interests to pursue higher-order goals.
- Change the organization to accommodate their vision rather than work within the existing one.
- Mentor followers to take greater responsibility for their own development and that of others. Followers become leaders and leaders become change agents, and ultimately transform the organization.

Nonetheless, Bass (1998) and Avolio (1999) contend that transactional leadership forms the basis of a sustainable leadership system. For instance, if leaders stand by their many transactions with followers, over time the people come to trust their leaders. It is this higher level of trust and identification that transformational leaders use as a foundation for achieving exemplary performance. Transformational leadership does not replace transactional leadership but does augment or expand its effects on follower motivation, satisfaction, and performance. Hence, they can be represented as points on the same leadership continuum.

The source of transformational leadership is in the personal values and beliefs of leaders. By expressing their personal standards, transformational leaders are able to both unite followers and change their goals and beliefs in ways that produce higher levels of performance than previously thought possible (Kuhnert and Lewis, 1987). Indeed, Thomas J. Sergiovanni (1994) argues that the heart of leadership talk is conceptions, values, and ideas. House (1988) further maintains that transformational leadership depends on leaders effectively expressing their need for power by using metaphors and other imagery to represent socially desirable examples of change and outcomes.

Similarly, Bass (1985a, 1998) observes that transformational leadership is seen when leaders stimulate others to view their work from new perspectives, generate an awareness of the mission or vision of the organization, develop colleagues and followers to higher levels of ability and potential, and motivate them to look beyond their own interests toward those that will benefit the group. Transformational leaders set more challenging goals and typically achieve higher performances than transactional leaders. Bass views transformational leadership as an expansion of transactional leadership that goes beyond simple exchanges and agreements by employing one or more of the four I's—*i*dealized influence, *i*nspirational motivation, *i*ntellectual stimulation, and *i*ndividualized consideration.

Idealized influence represents the building of trust and respect in followers and provides the basis for accepting radical and fundamental changes in the ways individuals and organizations do their work. The leaders are admired, respected, and trusted. Followers identify with their leaders and want to emulate them. Without such trust and commitment to the leaders, attempts to change and redirect the organization's mission are likely to be met with extreme resistance (Avolio, 1994). Idealized influence results from transformational leaders behaving as role models for their followers. Among the behaviors that transformational leaders exhibit in exerting idealized influence are (Bass and Avolio, 1994):

- Demonstrating high standards of ethical and moral conduct.
- Sharing risks with followers in setting and attaining goals.
- Considering the needs of others over their own.
- Using power to move individuals or groups toward accomplishing their mission, vision and cause, but never for personal gain.

In the earlier formulations and measures, idealized influence was referred to as charismatic leadership (see Bass, 1990).

Inspirational motivation changes the expectations of group members to believe that the organization's problems can be solved (Atwater and Bass, 1994). It also plays a central role in developing the vision to guide the organization goals and how it will operate (Avolio, 1994). Inspirational motivation comes primarily from leader behaviors that provide meaning and challenge for followers. Transformational leaders get people involved in creating visions and attractive futures for the organization and clearly communicate expectations that followers want to meet. Hence, team spirit, enthusiasm, optimism, goal commitment, and a shared vision arise and coalesce within the work group or organization (Bass and Avolio, 1994).

Intellectual stimulation addresses the problem of creativity (Atwater and Bass, 1994). Transformational leaders stimulate followers to be innovative and creative by questioning assumptions, reframing problems, and approaching old situations in new ways. Transformational leaders encourage creativity in new procedures, programs, and problem solving; foster unlearning and eliminate the fixation on old ways of doing things; and do not publicly criticize individual members for mistakes (Bass and Avolio, 1994).

Leaders insist on constant open examination of everything and total receptivity to change (Avolio, 1994). In turn, followers stimulate their leaders to reconsider their own perspectives and assumptions. Nothing is too good, too fixed, too political, or too bureaucratic that it cannot be contested, changed, or cleared out (Avolio, 1999).

Individualized consideration means that transformational leaders pay particular attention to each individual's needs for achievement and growth. The purpose of individualized consideration is to determine the needs and strengths of others (Atwater and Bass, 1994). Using this knowledge and acting as mentors, transformational leaders help followers and colleagues develop to successively higher levels of potential and to take responsibility for their own development (Avolio, 1994). Creating new learning opportunities in a supportive climate, recognizing and accepting individual differences in needs and values, using two-way communication, and interacting with others in a personalized fashion are necessary behaviors to accomplish individualized consideration. The individually considerate leader listens actively and effectively.

Avolio (1999) concludes that idealized influence and inspirational leadership are the most effective and satisfying; intellectual stimulation and individualized consideration have somewhat less effect. All four I's are more effective than transactional leadership. Overall, then, transformational leadership is close to what people have in mind when they describe their ideal leader. Practically, it means that leaders develop in their followers an expectation of high performance rather than merely spending time in transactional activities. In other words, the leader must be a developer of people and a builder of teams (Bass, 1990).

Situational Factors in Transformational Leadership

Similar to the charismatic approaches, proponents of transformational leadership models tend to deemphasize the importance of the setting. Bass (1997), for example, argues that the transformational leadership model is valid across situations and cultures. Bass (1998) does recognize crisis situations as being highly important. He asserts that for leaders to be effective in crisis conditions, they must be transformational and rise above what their followers see as their immediate needs and appropriate responses. Only transformational leaders can arouse their followers to see the threats and their lack of preparedness and provide goals to transcend self-interests and to provide confident direction. Bass (1998) further acknowledges that a number of situational conditions (e.g., environment, organization, task and goals, and distribution of power between the leaders and followers) will likely influence the emergence and success of both transactional and transformational leadership. B. S. Pawar and Kenneth K. Eastman (1997) propose four situational factors that influence the receptivity to organizational change and transformational leadership. These include adaptive or efficiency orientation, dominance of technical core or boundary-spanning units, type of organizational structure (e.g., simple structure or professional bureaucracy), and clan or bureaucratic modes of governance.

Research and Evaluation

Empirical research to date has predominantly dealt with models of transactional leadership, but the body of research dealing with transformational leadership is expanding rapidly (Bass, 1998). Most research studies testing transformational leadership theory have used the multifactor leadership questionnaire (MLQ) to measure various aspects of transformational and transactional leadership. Early versions of MLQ received severe criticism (Sashkin and Burke, 1990). Since its introduction, the content of the MLQ has changed and been refined to increase the items describing observable leader behaviors, but it still lacks some important transformational behaviors (Yukl, 1999). In addition, some instability in the number of factors has been evident and other psychometric issues remain to be resolved (Bass, 1998). Even so, findings from studies using the MLQ indicate that transformational leaders receive higher ratings, are perceived as leading more effective organizations, and have subordinates who exert greater effort than transactional leaders (Yukl, 1999). Likewise, Bass (1998) concludes that research evidence clearly demonstrates that transformational leadership can move followers to exceed expected performance. In comparison to transactional leadership, he believes that transformational leadership generates greater subordinate effort, commitment, and satisfaction. Other scholars tend to be positive about the model as well.

In a four-year study of schools making a variety of structural changes, Keith Leithwood (1994) assessed the effects of transformational leadership. His conceptual framework is based on two assertions. First, transformational leadership in schools directly affects such school outcomes as teacher perceptions of student goal achievement and student grades. Second, transformational leadership indirectly affects these outcomes by influencing three critical psychological characteristics of staff—perceptions of school characteristics, teacher commitment to change, and organizational learning—which in turn affect the outcomes. From his research, Leithwood draws the following generalizations:

- Transformational leadership depends on attending to all aspects of leadership—for example, in the terms of Bass, idealized influence, inspirational motivation, intellectual stimulation, and individualized consideration.
- School organizations may require unique formulations of transformational leadership with its base being individualized consideration.
- Except for expert thinking, transformational leadership represents a contingency approach.
- Distinctions between management and leadership cannot be made in terms of observed behavior.

Hence, Leithwood concludes that reasonably robust support exists for the claim that transformational forms of leadership are of significant value in restructuring schools. Similarly, H. C. Silins (1992) found that transformational leaders have greater positive effects on schools than transactional leaders.

James G. Hunt (1991) criticizes Bass's approach to theory development and testing on three bases. First, he believes that questionnaires were used before sufficient knowledge of transformational leadership was available. Early reliance on descriptive interviews and observational methods would have advanced the theory's development more powerfully than immediate use of questionnaires such as the MLQ. Second, leadership outcomes were confused with leader behavior. For example, inspirational behavior on the part of the leader might be used as a criterion variable instead of followers' emotional attachment to the leader. And third, insufficient attention is given to the two-way aspects of leader-follower interactions that were very important to Burns's original approach.

Yukl (1999) asserts that transformational and charismatic models share at least three conceptual weaknesses. First, the focus on leader-individual follower relationships is too narrow and needs to be broadened to include influence processes at the group and organizational levels. Second, although the models have wide applicability, they need to enhance the emphasis on situational variables that both limit and facilitate transformational and charismatic leadership. Third, the approaches have reasonable differences that should be recognized. As an overall assessment, however, Yukl concludes that transformational and charismatic leadership models seem to be making important contributions to the explanation of leadership processes and outcomes. In particular, they rely on important symbolic aspects and are more than just the technical and interpersonal aspects of efficient management. It rests upon meanings as well as actions and leaders make meanings.

In sum, leadership in schools is a complex process, which includes balancing technical and symbolic demands (Deal and Peterson, 1994). It involves more than mastering a set of skills, finding the right situation, exhibiting a certain style of behavior, combining these factors in a contingency approach, or even deciding to become a transformational leader. Matching the appropriate leader traits and behaviors with a specific situation is important, but so too is the symbolic and cultural side of leadership. The issue is not one of choosing between leadership as an instrumental and behavioral activity and leadership as a symbolic and cultural one; it is clearly both. Hence, many models of leadership call for diverse sets of applications for enhancing the leadership capacity in schools.

Improving Leadership in Schools

Theory and research suggest several ways to advance leadership in schools. Steps can be taken to enhance the trait and situational factors related to effectiveness. Examples include selecting individuals with the desired personality, motivational, and skill traits and placing them in situations that will benefit from their talents. Education and experience can improve the skill levels of potential and practicing administrators. Although the application possibilities are numerous, we will discuss five general applications—education, selection, succession, situational engineering, and transformations.

Educating Future Leaders

As elaborated throughout this chapter, school administrators must deal with a wide array of problems, situations, and people. To lead effectively, they must have a range of abilities and skills. To enhance their abilities and learn the needed skills, prospective leaders typically complete administrator preparation or training programs. Griffiths, Stout, and Forsyth (1988) believe that such preparation programs should emphasize theoretical and clinical knowledge, applied research, and supervised practice. To include these ideas, they propose that administrator education programs should include the following five strands for **educating leaders.**

Strand 1: Study theoretical models. Administration and leadership actions have an intellectual and value basis found in administrative theory, the behavioral sciences, philosophy, and experience.

Strand 2: Learn the technical core of school administration. Every profession, including school leadership, has a core of technical knowledge that practitioners must possess or at least be familiar with. Typical core areas include finance, law, personnel, information systems, curriculum theory and design, and teaching pedagogy.

Strand 3: Develop problem-solving skills through the use of applied and active methods. This strand can best be taught through the collaboration of universities and schools. By working on authentic problems in schools (e.g., low student achievement, organizational change), essential problem-solving skills can be developed (e.g., creating visions, effective speaking, conducting meetings, research design, negotiating).

Strand 4: Practice leadership under supervised conditions. Prospective leaders need clinical experiences that begin early in their preparation and gradually increase in responsibility throughout the training.

Strand 5: Demonstrate competence. This could take such forms as creating computer simulations, building portfolios, conducting a field test of a new program, or handling a difficult case study.

Exactly how these strands are blended together will vary from program to program because the goals of each strand can be achieved in a variety of ways. Combining these five strands to produce a comprehensive program of preparation can help develop school administrators as effective leaders.

Selecting New Administrators Through Assessment Centers

Our knowledge about leader traits and skills holds high potential for use in **selecting leaders** (Yukl, 1994). However, impressionistic measurements such as simple interviews and application forms lack the power and accuracy to assess the desired characteristics of prospective leaders. Rather intensive, systematic measurement procedures such as those used in assessment centers provide relatively accurate information about motivation, communication skills, cognitive skills, and personality factors.

An **assessment center** is a standardized set of procedures and activities that are designed to evaluate individuals for selection, placement, development, or promotion, usually in administrative positions. A fundamental task in constructing an assessment center is to identify trait and skill dimensions that are related to the job (Wendel, Kelley, Kluender, and Palmere, 1983). On the basis of trait and situational theories of leadership, the key is to choose personal factors that are job related—that is, defined by the situation. To evaluate the traits and skills, a variety of activities can be included in assessment centers that evoke samples of behavior. Examples include such assessment center activities as in-baskets, leaderless group discussions, case studies, negotiations, and management games. Although not all types of activities are employed in a given assessment center, multiple exercises are used.

In the United States, the National Association of Secondary School Principals (NASSP) has made an extensive effort to develop a reliable and valid assessment center program. According to Hersey (1982), the NASSP Assessment Center process requires participants who are candidates for administrative selection, promotion, or development to complete simulated activities commonly expected of principals. The simulations include leaderless group activities, fact-finding and stress exercises, and in-basket tasks dealing with typical school problems. While completing the assessment exercises, each participant is observed by trained assessors who record behavior relating to 12 dimensions. Example categories are problem analysis, judgment, leadership, stress tolerance, and oral communication. The team of assessors discusses each participant's observed behavior and skills and a comprehensive assessment report is prepared describing strengths, improvement needs, and development suggestions for each candidate.

Overall ratings made in the assessment centers were reliable, relevant to the principal's job, and related to subsequent measures of performance and school climate (Hersey, 1982). Hence, assessment centers offer some promise in identifying and selecting potential school administrators who have and display the desired personality, motivation, and ability traits associated with future leadership effectiveness.

Assuming a New Position: Succession

Leader succession is the process of replacing key officials in organizations (Grusky, 1961). This generic phenomenon of changing leaders produces naturally occurring instabilities in the organization and offers challenging opportunities for individuals. The replacement of principals or superintendents is disruptive because it changes the lines of communication, realigns relationships of power, affects decision making, and generally disturbs the equilibrium of normal activities. Administrative succession substantially raises the level of consciousness among organizational participants about the importance of school leaders (Hart, 1993). Those who appoint new leaders, individuals who work with them, and those who may be affected by their actions watch for signs that change will occur. In other words, new leaders face high performance expectations to maintain or improve existing levels of organizational effectiveness (Miskel and Cosgrove, 1985). A number of factors in the succession process are important in affecting the probability of being hired and one's success after being appointed as an administrator. Three situational factors seem particularly important in school settings—selection process, reason for the succession, and source of the new leader.

Selection Process

Understanding who participates and the methods of recruitment used in the selection process is important for aspiring administrators. In school districts, participants in the selection process for principals typically include the superintendent, senior administrators, personnel directors, long-term principals, and school board members. Superintendents play a primary role in choosing future principals because the management of their school systems depends on principals' carrying out their districts' decisions and plans. Teacher candidates for principalships usually come to the attention of their superintendents through the support of their principals. As teachers volunteer for committees, handle discipline problems, and spend extra time in schools, the principal becomes a mentor, encouraging the teacher to pursue administrative certification and providing opportunities to become visible at the district level (Griffiths, Goldman, and McFarland, 1965). Having obtained a broad reputation, the career path to a principalship is often through being a vice principal or curriculum coordinator. Then as vacancies occur for school principals, the candidate can apply and, if patient enough, will eventually obtain an appointment. Assessment centers or outside agencies may be used in the recruitment of potential candidates. Their purpose is to provide rigor, structure, and standardization to the evaluation of the candidate's potential as an administrator (Baltzell and Dentler, 1983).

Reason for the Succession

A number of reasons account for changing administrators. Succession can be environmentally controlled, as in death, illness, or movement to a better position; or succession can be directly controlled by the organization, as in promotion, demotion, or dismissal (Grusky, 1960). The successor confronts a different set of circumstances depending on the reason for the vacancy. For instance, death prevents the transfer of accumulated knowledge of the predecessor to the new leader, and consequently, discontinuity may result, accompanied by rapid policy changes. In contrast, if the predecessor remains in the organization, his or her presence acts as a stabilizing influence. In the case of the predecessor's advancing to a superior position, the outside recognition of administrator performance is an indicator of successful policies. The successor may feel a reluctance to initiate immediate changes, and because of the apparent inheritance of a well-managed school, may not receive due credit for improvements that are made.

Source of the New Leader

The source of leaders can be divided into two categories—insiders and outsiders. Depending on situational factors, either an insider or an outsider can be the best choice for an administrative position. When conflict within the organization is high, a candidate from within may better understand and be able to cope than an outsider. An outsider joining a school at a difficult time may unintentionally "step on toes" or be unable to discern the source of problems because he or she lacks the appropriate historical perspective. Inside succession can lead to problems as well. When an educational organization trains several people to fill future vacancies, a surplus often results. The qualified but unchosen individuals often either leave the organization or remain as frustrated and unsupportive employees. To reduce this type of conflict, the selection process might avoid vertical promotions from within the organization in an attempt to prevent unproductive competition among prospective candidates and their supporters. Instead, candidates can be selected from similar institutions whose characteristics would result in comparable socializing experiences for potential leaders and thus facilitate the smooth assimilation of the new leader in the organization (Birnbaum, 1971).

Mandate for Action

During the selection process, new administrators often are given, or perceive that they are given, a mandate either to maintain the existing stability or to initiate change and innovation (Grusky, 1960; Gordon and Rosen, 1981). They may be told to get rid of "dead wood,""clean house," reorganize the administrative staff, or essentially maintain the status quo. The type of mandate may depend on whether the successor is an insider or an outsider. Superintendents, and to a lesser degree principals, recruited from the outside often receive a mandate to break established patterns and make structural or personnel changes. For insiders the mandate typically is to continue present operations with only minor changes. In a study of principal succession by Dorothy Cosgrove (1985), little evidence was found that the principals in her study received a mandate from the superintendent or other district officials. However, Rodney T. Ogawa (1991) also found a general expectation among teachers that the succession would bring changes to the school. A potentially important extension of the work by Cosgrove and Ogawa would be to examine the mandates given to transformational leaders. To date succession issues for transformational leaders have received very limited attention (Conger, 1999).

In sum, truly critical phenomena occur for prospective leaders before they arrive on the scene and shortly after arrival. Knowing the workings of the selection process and being aware that instability arises during the succession period makes the new leader particularly visible and can be used to enhance the success in getting and keeping an administrative position.

Engineering the Situation

Another approach for applying knowledge to improve leadership in schools is **situational engineering.** Instead of trying to select or train leaders to fit an existing condition, the situation is changed to be more congruent with the traits of the leader. For example, the upper-level administrators of a school district could modify the conditions within the school building by changing the responsibilities and scope of authority of the principal, by transferring certain personnel, or by creating an in-service training program to improve the interpersonal climate among the professional staff members. Taking this idea further, Fiedler, Chemers, and Mahar (1976) proposed that administrators such as principals could be trained to modify certain aspects of their situation. They have developed a programmed textbook to teach leaders how to analyze their situation in terms of leader-member relations, task structure, and position power of the leader, and based on the analysis, to change the conditions that will improve group performance. A major limitation of the studies supporting situational engineering is their failure to determine how much change actually occurred during the experiments (Yukl, 1994). Nevertheless, the approach can be of some value in designing situations to enhance the level of leadership in schools.

Transforming Schools and Strengthening Their Cultures

Yukl (1998) concludes that the knowledge base is good enough to suggest a number of guidelines for leaders who seek to transform their organizations and the cultures within them. An essential first step in **transforming schools** is to create a clear and appealing vision of what the school can achieve or become. Before educators and the public will make a commitment to fundamental change, they need an image of a better future that is attractive enough to justify changing their routine ways of doing tasks. The vision should be simple and idealistic. For instance, the vision might call for becoming the best school in the district. A next step is to develop a strategy for accomplishing the vision. Clear links must be made between the vision and the strategies to attain the vision. Yukl (1994) believes that these links are easier to establish if the strategy uses three or four lucid themes that epitomize the shared values of the participants. For example, a theme might be to "improve the academic achievement of all the school's students." Then the vision must be communicated to others with explanations of how the vision can be attained. In addition, leaders must act confident and optimistic, express confidence in followers, ensure opportunities for early successes, celebrate successes, employ exciting symbolic actions to stress central values, lead by example, and empower people to accomplish the vision (Yukl, 1998).

Similarly, Jay A. Conger (1991) proposes that two distinct skills are required to effectively communicate strategic visions for organizations. The first is a "framing skill," or simply stating the vision clearly and logically. The second is "rhetorical crafting," or the leader's ability to use symbolic language to give emotional power to the vision. In other words, rhetorical crafting of the vision laces the message with metaphors, stories, symbols, and other forms of colorful and emotional language. The leader must act confidently, lead by example, and express confidence in the followers as they work together to implement the strategy and attain the vision of transforming the organization. Early successes should be used to build confidence and the successes should be celebrated in ways that emphasize key values of the school.

On the basis of the work of Trice and Beyer (1993), Yukl (1994) also developed several guidelines for strengthening the existing culture of schools. The key first step is to identify aspects of the culture that are essential and worthy of preservation—that is, the ideologies that inspire commitment and persist as conditions change. Another way to strengthen school culture is to eliminate components of the culture that are inconsistent with the core values of the ideology. For instance, most schools have old rules and policies that are no longer useful and are inconsistent with core values. These can be identified and eliminated. Leaders can then articulate the ideology lucidly and persistently through a variety of media. In other words, school culture can be strengthened by repeatedly publicizing the core ideology in speeches at meetings and ceremonies, statements in newsletters, and distribution or display of physical symbols. Leaders must then keep decisions and actions consistent with the ideology and emphasize the ideology through rituals, ceremonies, and rites of passage.

THEORY INTO PRACTICE

District Leadership and Systemic Reform

For the past five years, you have been the superintendent of Camargo Unified School District. Located in the Southwest, the school district enrolls about 5,000 students. As a consolidated district, the students come from the surrounding rural areas and from city neighborhoods. The average expenditure per student is about $6,000 per year. Other than the typical variations in family income and rural-city attendance area, the district is rather homogeneous. About 5 percent of the students are Hispanic and about 2 percent are Native American. During your tenure, you have worked energetically to establish trust with many constituencies, including the board of education, other administrators, teachers, business leaders, and parents from the rural and city areas. In a real sense, you have become a respected member of the community. As superintendent, you have set high expectations for school improvement and performance. The other educators and students have responded positively and Camargo School District now is seen as high achieving and well managed. In a front-page story, the local newspaper recently asserted that the district had been transformed under your leadership.

During the fall of your fifth year at Camargo, the president of a national search firm approached you about applying for the position of superintendent of the Willow Tree School District. This relatively affluent district of about 15,000 students is located in a large metropolitan area in the upper Midwest. Being ambitious and wanting to try new challenges, you investigate the district by visiting Willow Tree School District's website and other websites for area businesses, governments, and media outlets. You find that the district has 20 elementary, 6 middle, 3 comprehensive high schools and 3 other special and alternative schools. The teaching staff is highly qualified with about 75 percent of them holding master's degrees and above. In addition, the average expenditure is about $8,400 per student. Although the district appears rather homogeneous and wealthy, you note that minority students, mostly African American and Hispanic, comprise about 15 percent of the enrollment. By consulting the school report card at Governor's website, you find the district's scores on the state achievement test to be relatively high at about the 65 percentile and stable over the past five years.

THEORY INTO PRACTICE, (Continued)

With encouragement from the search firm and the tremendous professional opportunity for you, you apply for the position in Willow Tree and are invited for an interview, along with four other candidates. The interview process is a whirlwind. During the formal interview sessions and in follow-up meetings and discussions, you meet individually and collectively with the seven school board members, several members of the administration, teachers and their union representatives, parents and members of the public. It seems that the overriding concern is student achievement. First, parents in this relatively affluent school district hold high ambitions for their children and business leaders see high test scores as essential for the area's continued economic development. The school board clearly wants rapid improvements on the state test scores. Moreover, they seem committed to a systemic reform approach that is based on aligning the district's curriculum with the state standards and testing program. Second, there is an achievement gap between minority and majority students. In a variety of interview settings, parents of minority children and five school board members, two of whom are African American and one of whom is Hispanic, asked repeated questions about what actions you would propose to close the achievement gap.

After returning to Camargo and reflecting on the prospects, you start asking yourself questions about whether the Willow Tree job is for you.

- What are my strengths and weaknesses as a leader? Self-confidence? Preferred behaviors? Communication abilities? Values and beliefs?
- What are the situational constraints and facilitators in Willow Tree? How strong and clear is the situation for a new superintendent?
- How do my strengths and weaknesses match the situation? Are there substitutes to help with my weaknesses?
- Can the situation be changed or engineered to fit my strengths?
- How will the board's likely mandates for implementing systemic reform and closing the achievement gap affect my ability to transform the district?
- Can I be successful in Willow Tree?

SUMMARY AND SUGGESTED READINGS

Leadership remains an important topic for students of educational administration. Given the fact that leadership is an extremely complex and elusive concept, some conceptual confusion and empirical shortcomings are to be expected. Nevertheless, substantial progress has been made in building a solid body of knowledge about leadership. General agreement exists that leadership involves a social influence process in which an individual exerts intentional influence over others to structure activities and relationships in a group or organization. To explain the influence process, a number of leadership models have been proposed and tested. Contingency theories reached their peak popularity in the 1970s. The approach has been illustrated by Fiedler's postulate that leadership effectiveness is contingent upon matching leadership style with the appropriate situation. As interest in contingency theory waned, exciting new models became dominant during the 1980s. Charismatic and transformational leadership approaches have been receiving extensive attention from scholars and practitioners. These new leadership theories incorporated emotional responses of followers and visionary, change-oriented behaviors. Transformational leadership, for example, has four critical elements—idealized influence, inspirational motivation, intellectual stimulation, and individualized consideration. From these conceptual frameworks, useful practical applications for selecting and educating leaders, assuming new leadership positions, and transforming schools have been created. It is our conclusion that all of these developments attest to an enhanced understanding of the leadership phenomenon.

The leadership literature is huge with over 5,000 published studies and the number continues to increase by the hundreds each year (Yukl, 1994). Within this expansive body of knowledge, rich sources of theories, empirical studies, and practical applications of leadership can be found in the four editions of Yukl's (1981, 1989, 1994, 1998) book, *Leadership in Organizations*. The editions take moderately different approaches to the leadership concept and each contains some unique insights not found in the other editions or in other works. Probably the most complete review of the leadership literature is found in *Bass and Stogdill's Handbook of Leadership* (Bass, 1990). For an extensive and interesting discussion of specific measures of leadership, the book by Clark and Clark (1990) should be consulted. If you want to explore leadership preparation, the work by Griffiths, Stout, and Forsyth (1988) contains some very good chapters. The journal *Leadership Quarterly* publishes only papers focusing on leadership. For those interested in transformational leadership, the following sources are recommended—Bass and Avolio (1994), Leithwood (1994), Avolio (1999), and Bass (1998). Many other worthy publications could have been given as examples, but our recommendation to individuals interested in exploring leadership in detail is to review this chapter, consult the references we cite, and then plunge yourself into a very deep pool of literature.

Notes

1. John P. Kotter (1990) provides a detailed analysis of the distinction between management and leadership. We consider the term "administration" as commonly used in educational settings to be essentially synonymous with "management."
2. Structured observation techniques typically observe and question leaders intensively as they perform their work. Mintzberg (1973) and Kotter (1982) conducted two of the best-known investigations in business organizations. A number of investigations using structured observation procedures also have been conducted in school settings across a number of countries on superintendents (O'Dempsey, 1976; Friesen and Duignan, 1980; Duignan, 1980; Pitner and Ogawa, 1981); on principals (Peterson, 1977–78; Willis, 1980; Martin and Willower, 1981; Morris and his associates, 1981; Kmetz and Willower, 1982; Phillips and Thomas, 1982; Chung, 1987; Chung and Miskel, 1989); and on educational innovators (Sproull, 1981). In addition to providing a

fascinating glimpse of their work, the findings are important because the behaviors of school administrators have been described systematically and found to be consistent across organizational types—businesses and schools—across organizational roles—superintendents, supervisors, and principals—and across countries—Australia, Canada, and the United States.

3. For readers interested in a detailed consideration of the traits associated with effective leadership, a comprehensive treatment can be found in Bass (1990). Although less extensive, Yukl (1998) provides an insightful discussion of traits and leader effectiveness.
4. The other three contingency models that Yukl (1998) describes are the cognitive-resource theory (Fiedler, 1984; Fiedler and Garcia, 1987), situational leadership theory (Hershey and Blanchard, 1977), and the multiple-linkage model (Yukl, 1971).
5. Fiedler and a number of colleagues (e.g., Fiedler, 1967, 1971; Fiedler and Chemers, 1974; Fiedler, Chemers, and Mahar, 1976; Fiedler and Garcia, 1987) describe the least preferred co-worker model and review the related research.

Key Concepts and Ideas

Achievement-oriented leader behavior
Administrators
Assessment center
Charismatic leadership
Consideration
Contingency approach
Educating leaders
Effectiveness
Idealized influence
Individualized consideration
Initiating structure
Inspirational motivation
Intellectual stimulation
Leader behavior
Leaders
Leadership
Leadership effectiveness
Leadership situation
Leader succession
Leadership style
Motivational traits
Path-goal clarifying behaviors
Personality traits
Selecting leaders
Shared leadership
Situational control
Situational engineering
Skills
Substitutes for leadership model
Supportive leader behavior
Trait approach of leadership
Transformational leadership
Transforming schools
Value-based leader behavior

CHAPTER 12

One Last Time: A Review of the School as a Social System

Systems thinking is the fifth discipline. It is the discipline that integrates the disciplines, fusing them into a coherent body of theory and practice. . . . It continually reminds us that the whole can exceed the sum of its parts.

Peter M. Senge

The Fifth Discipline

The preceding chapters present a substantial body of knowledge that constitutes a strong argument for the value of an open social-systems approach to educational administration. In this chapter, we review the social-systems model that serves as a theoretical guide to the ideas developed in our work. Intrinsic dilemmas of the model will then be considered.

A Model of Synthesis

Open-systems theory is organic rather than mechanical. As a conceptual language, it is useful in describing the recurring structures and dynamic processes in educational organizations to make their full patterns clearer and to help us change successfully. According to the social-systems model for schools, organizational performance is determined by at least four sets of key elements—structure, the individual, culture and climate, and power and politics—as they interact with the teaching-learning process. These elements take inputs from the environment and transform them. The elements and their interactions form the transformation system, which is constrained by the opportunities and demands from the environment. In addition, internal and external feedback mechanisms enable the system to evaluate the quality of all its systems and inputs. As discrepancies between actual and expected performance are detected, feedback enables the system to adjust.

In brief, the model in Figure 12.1 (first developed in Chapter 1) summarizes the major external and internal features of organizations conceived as open social systems. Of course, the figure cannot capture the dynamic movement of a system as it responds to its environment through internal

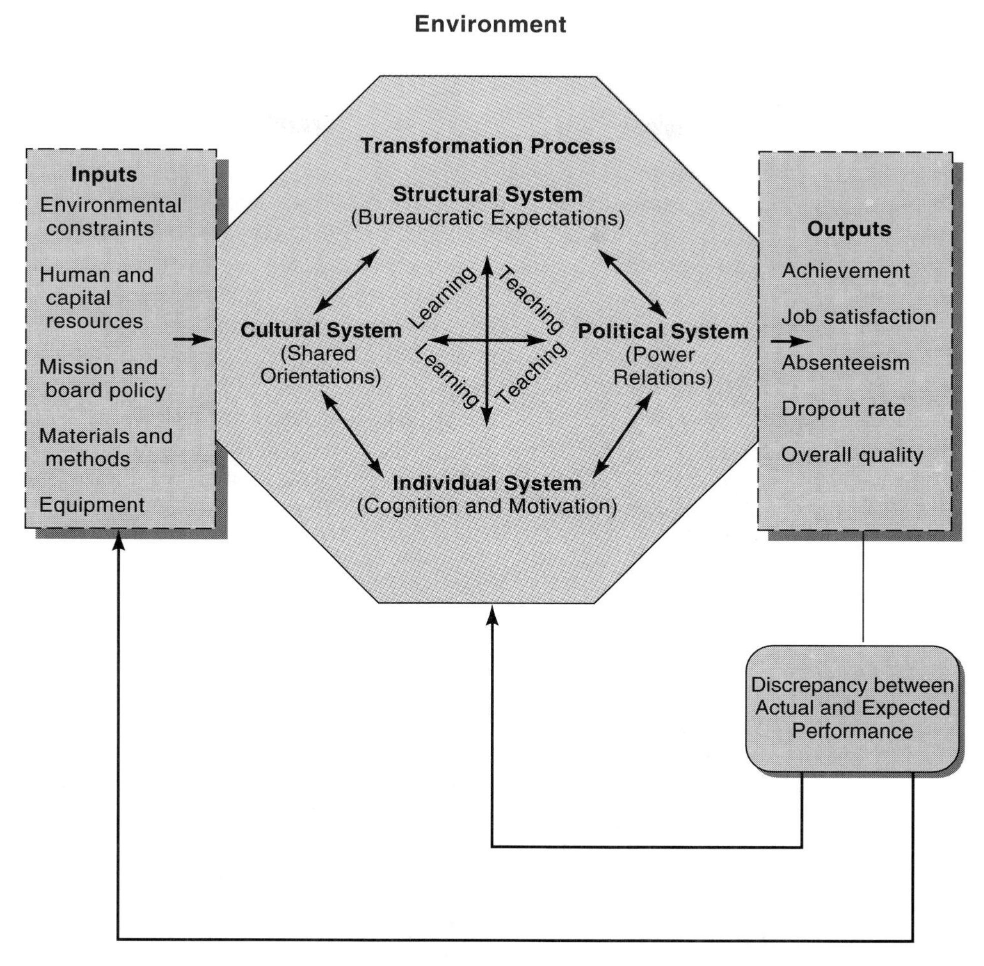

FIGURE 12.1 *Social System Model for Schools.*

processes and as it produces such products as student learning or employee satisfaction. Although we examine the parts of the system, do not lose sight of the fact that the system is a working whole.

Structure in Schools

Bureaucratic structure (see Chapter 3) is the formal organization specifically established to achieve explicit goals and carry out administrative tasks. Whatever the organizational goals, such structural properties as rules, regulations, hierarchy, and division of labor are consciously designed to attain those goals. In Weber's analysis of ideal types, bureaucracy employs authority through these means to achieve rational decision making and maximize efficiency. Division of labor and specialization produce impersonal experts who make technically correct, rational decisions based on fact. Once these decisions have been made, the hierarchy of authority implements a disciplined, coordinated compliance to directives through rules and regulations. Career-oriented employees have an incentive to be loyal and productive.

Although probably the best known, Weber's is not the only theory of organizational structure. Henry Mintzberg provides still another framework for examining bureaucratic structure. He describes structure simply as the ways in which an organization divides its labor into tasks and then achieves coordination among them. Mutual adjustment, direct supervision, and standardization are basic coordinating mechanisms—the glue that holds the organization together. His analysis yields five ideal types. Mintzberg describes organizations as structures that are influenced by their environments—that is, open systems.

The concept of loose coupling in schools calls attention to ambiguity in goals, unclear educational technologies, fluid participation, coordination problems, and a structure often disconnected from educational outcomes. The distinctive combination of bureaucracy and structural looseness has important consequences for organizational performance and quality in schools (see Chapter 3).

Individuals in Schools

The fact that an organization has been formally established does not mean that all its activities and interactions conform to structural requirements. The individual is also a key element of all social systems. Students, teachers, and administrators bring with them individual (Chapter 4) needs, goals, and beliefs and develop their own personal orientations and intellectual understanding of their roles. Just as structure helps shape behavior in schools so too do the needs, goals, and beliefs of individuals.

Maslow describes a hierarchy of basic needs that motivate behavior ranging from biological to self-actualization needs, and Herzberg distinguishes between needs that produce worker satisfaction and those that cause dissatisfaction. The need for achievement and the need for autonomy are two other powerful motivating forces within individuals, which moderate teacher and administrator behavior in schools.

Work motivation is a set of energetic forces that originate both within as well as beyond an individual's being. Individual goals and goal setting are key ingredients of personal motivation, especially when the goals are embraced by the individual and are specific, challenging, and attainable. These forces initiate work-related behavior and determine the form, direction, intensity, and duration of motivation. Similarly, beliefs are important motivational forces. Administrators, teachers, and students are likely to work hard if they believe that success is primarily due to their ability and effort, that causes of outcomes are under their control, that extra effort will improve performance, that good performance will be noticed and rewarded, that the rewards are valued, and that they have been treated fairly and with respect by their superiors. Moreover, effective performance is closely related to self-efficacy, the belief that one has the capability to organize and execute a course of action that is required to attain the desired level of performance.

Motivation that comes from the interest and challenge of the activity itself is intrinsic, whereas extrinsic motivation is based on rewards and punishment. Although both can motivate, intrinsic motivation is typically more effective. Merit pay and management by objectives are two attempts to build motivational systems on the basis of extrinsic rewards. The job-characteristics model is a good example of job design based on the application of intrinsic motivation. Finally, a career-ladder program for teachers is an attempt to wed intrinsic and extrinsic strategies of motivation into a plan to redesign and reform the school workplace.

Culture and Climate in Schools

Our analysis of the internal atmosphere of schools focused on two related concepts—culture and climate (see Chapter 5). Each of these notions goes beyond the formal and individual aspects of organizational life. Each suggests a natural, spontaneous, and human side to organization; each suggests that the whole is greater than the sum of its parts; and each deals with shared meanings and unwritten rules that guide organizational behavior.

Organizational culture is the set of shared orientations that holds a unit together and gives it a distinctive identity. Although climate tends to focus on shared perceptions, culture is defined in terms of shared assumptions, values, and norms. These three levels of culture—assumptions, values, and norms—are explored as alternative ways of describing and analyzing schools. Research on business organizations suggests that effective systems have strong corporate cultures: cultures characterized by intimacy, trust, cooperation, egalitarianism, a bias for action, and orientations that stress quality, innovation, and people. Yet, in many respects, culture is like structure; both can improve or impede the effective functioning of the school depending on the mission and environmental conditions.

Organizational climate is a relatively enduring quality of the school environment that is experienced by teachers, affects their behavior, and is based on their collective perceptions of behavior in schools. A climate emerges through the interaction of members and exchange of sentiments among them. The climate of a school is its "personality." Three different conceptualizations of climate were described and analyzed.

When schools have an open climate, we find that principals and faculty are acting authentically, but when the climate is closed, everyone simply goes through the motions of education without dedication and commitment. As might be expected, research has shown that such affective characteristics as positive student and faculty attitudes are related to openness of climate.

The climate of schools can also be examined in terms of organizational health. A healthy school is one that is meeting both its instrumental and its expressive needs, while successfully coping with disruptive outside forces as it directs its energies toward its mission. The healthier the organizational dynamics of a school, the greater are the trust and openness in member relations and the greater the student achievement.

Finally, social climate of schools was conceived along a continuum of pupil-control orientation ranging from custodial to humanistic. This formulation is based on the dominant expectations teachers and principals have of how their methods will control student behavior. Schools with custodial expectations are rigidly controlled settings in which the primary concern is order. In contrast, humanistic schools are characterized by an emphasis on student self-discipline and cooperative student-teacher actions and experiences. A humanistic climate is associated with less student alienation and goal displacement than a custodial climate. Changing the culture and climate of schools is a long-term objective: there are no simple, quick fixes.

Power and Politics in Schools

Even before joining an organization, individuals grant the use of formal authority to the system when they voluntarily agree to comply with legitimate commands. Once in the organization, however, power relations expand; in fact, power becomes a central aspect of relations within the system.

Power is a broad construct that includes both legitimate and illegitimate and formal and informal methods of ensuring compliance (see Chapter 6). Hence, four basic kinds of organizational power exist: two forms are legitimate—formal and informal authority—and two kinds are illegitimate—coercive and political power.

The legitimate system of authority promotes coordination and compliance, and contributes to attainment of the formal goals. Legitimate power comes from the formal organization by virtue of position, from informal norms and values of the culture, and from the expertise of individuals in the system. These three systems of control typically contribute to the needs of the organization; that is, they are legitimate. But those with power also have personal needs. In the process of striving to accomplish the broader organizational needs, individuals find they have discretion, and discretion opens the way to political power. Thus a system of political power emerges that is not sanctioned by the formal authority, culture, or certified expertise; in fact, it is typically divisive, parochial, and illegitimate. Politics is illegitimate because it is a means to serve personal ends at the expense of the overall organization. That does not mean that politics never produces positive results. To the contrary, politics can promote change blocked by the formal organization, can ensure that strong members acquire leadership roles, can encourage debate among diverse positions, and can help in the execution of decisions.

Politics is a fact of organizational life. Although there are powerful individuals, the political arenas of organizations are composed of coalitions of individuals and groups, which bargain among themselves to determine the distribution of resources. External as well as internal coalitions influence organizational politics. Political tactics are the bases of a system of political games played to resist authority, to counter resistance, to build power bases, to defeat opponents, and to change the organization. The system of politics typically coexists with the more legitimate systems of influence without dominating them, but power and politics generate conflict. Thus, conflict management is a useful administrative tool.

Teaching and Learning in Schools

The teaching-learning process is the technical core of the school (Chapter 2). Other activities are secondary to the basic mission of teaching and learning; in fact, the process shapes many of the administrative decisions that must be made in schools. Indeed, teaching and learning provide a crucial set of internal opportunities and constraints.

Both teaching and learning are elaborate processes that need careful attention. Learning occurs when there is a stable change in an individual's knowledge or behavior. Although most experts on learning would agree with this general definition of learning, some would emphasize behavior and others, knowledge. Learning is a complex cognitive process and there is no one best explanation of learning. Different theories of learning offer more or less useful explanations depending on what is to be explained. We examined three general theories of learning—behavioral, cognitive, and constructivist—each with a different focus.

Behavioral theories of learning stress observable changes in behaviors, skills, and habits. The focus of this perspective is clearly on behavior. Learning is defined as a change in behavior brought about by experience with virtually no concern for the mental or internal processes of thinking. Behavior is simply what a person does in a given situation. The intellectual underpinnings of this perspective rest with Skinner's (1950) operant conditioning. Learning objectives, mastery learning, direct instruction, and basic skills are teaching strategies that evolve from this perspective. When specific skills and behaviors need to be learned, teaching approaches consistent with behavioral learning theory are quite effective.

Cognitive theories of learning focus on thinking, remembering, creating, and problem solving. How information is remembered and processed as well as how individuals use their own knowledge to monitor and regulate their cognitive processes are critical in this perspective. Some of the most important teaching applications of cognitive theories are teaching students how to learn and remember by using learning tactics such as note taking, mnemonics, and use of visuals. Teaching strategies based on cognitive views of learning, particularly information processing, highlight the importance of attention, organization, practice, and elaboration in learning and provide ways to give students more control over their own learning by developing and improving their own self-regulated learning strategies. The emphasis of the cognitive approach is on what is happening "inside the head" of the learner.

Constructivist theories of learning are concerned with how individuals make meaning of events and activities; hence, learning is seen as the construction of knowledge. In general, constructivism assumes that people create and construct knowledge rather than internalize it from the external environment, but there are a variety of different approaches to constructivism. Some constructivist views emphasize the shared and social construction of knowledge, whereas others see social forces as less important. Constructivist perspectives on learning and teaching, which are increasingly influential today, are grounded in the research of Piaget, Brunner, Dewey, and Vygotsky. Inquiry and problem-based learning, cooperative learning, and cognitive apprenticeships are typical teaching strategies that are grounded in the constructivist approach. The essence of the constructivist approach is that it places the students' own efforts at the center of the educational process.

External Environments of Schools

Schools are open systems, which must adapt to changing environmental conditions to be effective and, in the long term, to survive. The environments of schools (see Chapter 7) affect their internal structures and processes. Social, economic, political, and technological trends influence the internal operations of schools, as do more specific aspects such as unions, taxpayer associations, and state legislatures.

Environments are complex and difficult to analyze, but two general perspectives are useful—task and institutional. The task perspective includes both information and resource-dependency theories, which define the task environment as all aspects of the external setting that are potentially relevant for goal setting, goal achievement, effectiveness, and survival.

The information model treats the external environment as a source of information for decision makers. Three general dimensions of this framework are complexity, stability, and uncertainty. The more complex and unstable the environment, the greater the uncertainty for the organization. Perceived organizational uncertainty in turn affects the flexibility and bureaucratic configuration of organizations. Like all organizations, schools strive for certainty because they are under pressure to demonstrate rationality.

The resource-dependency approach assumes that organizations cannot generate internally the needed resources; resources must come from the environment. Thus, schools must enter into exchanges and competition with environmental units to obtain the requisite products and services. Scarcity produces competition with other organizations for resources.

Because environmental uncertainty and scarcity of resources threaten organizational autonomy and effectiveness, administrators often attempt to develop strategies to gain more control over the environment. Internal coping strategies include buffering the technical core, planning or forecasting, adjusting internal operations on the basis of contingency theory, and spanning organizational boundaries. Interorganizational coping strategies include establishing favorable linkages with important external constituencies and shaping environmental elements through political actions.

In contrast to the task perspectives, institutional theory assumes that the environment encourages schools to conform to powerful sets of rules and requirements that are imposed by the legal, social, professional, and political institutions. The theory asserts that school structures and processes mirror the norms, values, and ideologies institutionalized in society. The essence of the theory is that the environment of schools presses more for form than for substance.

Nevertheless, technical and institutional environments do coexist; schools function in relatively strong institutional but weak technical environments. Current drives for systemic reform and competitive markets suggest that worried businesspeople and policy makers may be seeking to place heightened emphasis on task environments. A shift from primarily institutional to technical environments would shatter the rationalized myths and lead to fundamental changes in schools, a shift that will be bitterly fought by current institutional forces.

Effectiveness and Quality of Schools

Outputs of schools are a function of the interaction of structure, individuals, culture, and politics as constrained by environmental forces. Issues of organizational effectiveness and quality represent fundamental challenges to school administration (Chapter 8). In our open-systems model, school outputs are the performances of students, teachers, and administrators. All can be used as indicators of organizational effectiveness and can be assessed for their quality. Although effectiveness and quality are not synonyms, they both are terms used to assess all aspects of the system.

Simple measures of organizational outcomes are insufficient indicators of either effectiveness or quality. This should come as no surprise to those who use a systems approach to understand organizational behavior. Outcomes are only one part of the system and perhaps not the most important element. The inputs as well as the transformational process of the system are equal partners in determining both the quality and effectiveness of schools.

We have proposed an integrated goal and system-resource model of school performance. The perspective underscores the importance of all the aspects of a social system, especially the quality of inputs, transformation processes, and outcomes. Each of these system phases needs to be assessed over the short term as well as the long term, using a variety of such constituencies as students, teachers, and administrators. Teacher quality, internal harmony, effort, student achievement, job satisfaction, and overall performance quality are examples of indicators of organizational effectiveness and quality.

Feedback Loops

The knowledge of the outcomes enters two different types of feedback loops. Internally, the relative level of goal achievement serves as an indicator of the need to adjust one or more of the elements of the transformation process. Externally, different constituencies in the community evaluate the school's products. This assessment provides information that also influences the structural, cultural, individual, and political subsystems.

Put bluntly, administrators are responsible for school effectiveness and quality of student learning and teaching. On the one hand, they must respond to the expectations and information carried in the feedback loops; on the other hand, they must maintain or increase goal-directed behavior of teachers, students, and other employees. One of the major administrative problems—control of performance—requires not only the allocation of resources, but also the integration of the basic organizational dimensions (structure, culture, individuals, and politics). Fulfillment of administrative functions requires deciding, motivating, communicating, and leading.

Decision Making in Schools

Deciding means selecting and implementing a course of action from among alternatives (see Chapter 9). This behavior affects the total organization, including the system phases of inputs, throughputs, and outputs.

Although completely rational decision making is impossible, administrators need systematic ways to enhance the selection of satisfactory solutions; hence, a strategy of satisficing is central to administrative decision making. The process is conceptualized as being cyclical with distinct phases: recognition and definition of a problem, analysis of difficulties, establishment of criteria of success, development of an action plan, and initiation and appraisal of the plan. Owing to its cyclical nature, administrators go through the stages repeatedly.

This administrative strategy is well suited to dealing with most problems. Occasionally, however, the set of alternatives is undefinable or the consequences of each alternative are unpredictable with respect to a given aspiration level; here an incremental strategy is more appropriate. This process is a method of successive limited comparisons; only a limited set of alternatives, similar to the existing situation, is considered by successively comparing their consequences until agreement is reached on a course of action. Incrementalism, however, can be too conservative and self-defeating. Incremental decisions made without fundamental guidelines can lead to action without direction. Thus, the mixed-scanning model of decision making is proposed for complex decisions. Mixed scanning unites the best of both the administrative and the incremental models. A strategy of satisficing is used in combination with incremental decision making guided by broad policy.

Research suggests that the quality of administrative action can be judged by the amount of preparation for implementing a course of action and by the amount of work done in making the decision. Effective decision makers engage in substantial preliminary work; they seek more information, differentiate between fact and opinion, and frequently encourage subordinate participation in the process. Sometimes participation improves the quality of decisions; sometimes it does not. We have proposed a model that suggests when and how to involve subordinates in decision making. In complex organizations, motivation, communication, and leadership are necessary to translate the decisions into concrete action.

Communication in Schools

Verbal and nonverbal interactions pervade virtually all aspects of school life. Good communication does not, however, provide all the answers to the problems confronting educational administrators. Nearly all current conceptions of information exchange rely on the notion that communication involves meaningful exchanges of symbols between at least two people (see Chapter 10). The process is dynamic because it continually influences the transformation and environmental elements of the social system.

One-way communication is unilateral, initiated by a speaker and terminated at a listener. In contrast, two-way communication is reciprocal and interactive with all participants initiating and receiving messages. It has no necessary beginning or ending. Messages flow through formal and informal channels of the school. Although the formal network is usually larger and better developed than the informal, they are closely related, can be complementary, and are critical to the organization.

Leadership in Schools

Leaders are important because they serve as anchors, provide guidance in times of change, and are responsible for the effectiveness of organizations (see Chapter 11). General agreement exists that leadership involves a social influence process. The leader exerts intentional influence over others to structure activities and relationships in a group or organization. The most influential theories of leadership are contingency models, which explain the interrelationships among traits, situations, behaviors, and effectiveness. We developed a schema to categorize and link together these four sets of concepts. Contingency theory was further illustrated by expanding Fiedler's postulate that leadership effectiveness is contingent upon matching leadership styles with the appropriate situation.

Transformational leadership is an approach that currently is receiving extensive attention from scholars and practitioners. It has four critical elements—idealized influence, inspirational motivation, intellectual stimulation, and individualized consideration.

Leadership in schools is a complex process. It involves more than the mastering of a set of leadership skills or the matching of the appropriate leader behavior with a specific situation. Useful methods to improve school leadership are selecting and educating leaders, assuming new leadership positions, engineering the situation, and transforming schools. Leadership is not only an instrumental and behavioral activity, but also a symbolic and cultural one.

Administrative Behavior

We have been arguing that administrative behavior in the context of teaching and learning should be analyzed in relation to the primary elements of the school social system. Structure, individuals, culture, and politics represent "leverage points" that can be used to influence the performance of organizational members. A number of observations are important and bear repeating. First, deciding, communicating, and leading are key processes that modify school performance. If a leader consciously manipulates one dimension of the system, a "ripple effect" is created; the other dimensions are affected, and a new combination of expectations and behaviors results. Second, a variety of means are available to reach desired goals: there is no one best way to organize, lead, decide, motivate, or teach. Rather, the means to achieve goals depend on many factors including the community, complexity, and culture as well as opportunities and constraints in the situation. Administration is a complex process that requires careful reflection and continuous vigilance to changing conditions. Finally, complexity and connectedness in schools require "systems thinking"—recognition of the importance of the whole rather than a focus on parts; the school is a social system in which the whole is always greater than the sum of its parts. We conclude our examination of schools as social systems by looking at some of the continuing dilemmas that teachers and administrators must face.

Organizational Dilemmas

Both change and dilemmas will always be with us, but dilemmas, unlike change, need not accelerate. Peter M. Blau and W. Richard Scott (1962) maintain that the concept of dilemma contributes to our understanding of internal pressures for change. A dilemma arises when one is confronted by decision alternatives in which any choice sacrifices some valued objectives in the interest of other objectives. Daniel Katz and Robert L. Kahn (1978) have elaborated on this definition by distinguishing between problems and dilemmas. Problems are difficulties that can be solved by past precedents or by the application of existing theory or policy. Dilemmas are unsolvable within the existing framework. Solutions and perfect adjustments are impossible. Because dilemmas are endemic to organizations, they serve as perpetual sources of change.

The fundamental dilemma facing formal organizations is order versus freedom. Both order and freedom are desirable and necessary conditions for high levels of effectiveness and quality, but increasing one decreases the other. The tension between order and freedom is manifested in at least four operational dilemmas in schools: coordination and communication, bureaucratic discipline and professional expertise, administrative planning and individual initiative, and learning as behavior and cognition.

Coordination and Communication

Based on the work of Blau and Scott (1962), two-way communication with unrestricted exchange of ideas, criticism, and advice contributes to effective problem solving in at least three ways: it furnishes social support to individual participants; it provides an error-correcting mechanism; and it fosters a healthy competition for respect.

Problem-solving situations often produce stress and anxiety for individual participants and lead to mental blocks that interfere with effective development of their thinking. However, when individuals communicate openly, good ideas are likely to receive the approval of others (thus reducing anxiety) and to promote further participation, development, and refinement of ideas; hence, the social support derived from an unrestricted exchange of ideas aids in problem solving.

It is not easy for a person to detect mistakes in his or her own thinking. An individual takes a set framework to the problem-solving situation that makes it difficult to see the problem from a different perspective. Open and free-flowing communication brings a variety of perspectives, experiences, and information to bear on the common task; hence, the chances of identifying an error in thinking are increased. Other members of the group are more prone to spot inconsistencies and blind spots than the individual; therefore, two-way communication facilitates error correction. Finally, open, two-way communication motivates members of a group to make expert suggestions in order to win the respect and esteem of fellow participants.

Whereas the free flow of information improves problem solving, it also impedes coordination. Unrestricted communication may drown effective action in a sea of conflicting ideas. True, information helps in the selection of good ideas, but too many ideas hinder agreement, and coordination requires agreement on a single master plan.

Coordination in organizations is accomplished primarily through hierarchical differentiation, but such structure impedes decision making because it interferes with the free flow of information (see Chapter 3). In fact, differentiation, centralized direction, and restricted communication appear essential for effective coordination. In brief, those very things that enhance the coordination process also hinder the free flow of communication. Organizations require both effective coordination and effective problem solving. But the hierarchical structure in organizations that facilitates efficient coordination also impedes communication and problem solving. The dilemma seems inherent in the conflicting requirements of coordination and problem solving because there is the simultaneous need for restricted and unrestricted communication. The conflict, which causes adaptation and change, cannot be readily resolved and needs continuing attention.

Bureaucratic Discipline and Professional Expertise

The similarities and differences in the characteristics of professional and bureaucratic orientations (see Chapter 3) lead to a second dilemma. Although both orientations stress technical competence, objectivity, impersonality, and service, the unique structure of the professions is a basic source of conflict. Professionals attempt to control themselves through self-imposed standards and group surveillance. In contrast, bureaucratic employees are expected to adhere to rules and regulations and to subordinate themselves to the hierarchy. The ultimate basis for a professional act is the professional's knowledge; the ultimate justification of a bureaucratic act is its consistency with organizational rules and regulations and approval by a superior. The conflict is between professional expertise and autonomy, and bureaucratic discipline and control. The significance of the discord is brought into sharp focus when we examine employees who are subject to both forms of social control: professionals working in bureaucracies.

There are different ways to resolve the strain created by the merger of these two institutional means of control. In some organizations, major structural changes have been instituted through the development of two separate authority lines—one professional and one administrative. Nonetheless, when professional considerations conflict with bureaucratic ones, dividing authority seems to be a partial solution at best. Without organizational change some individuals attempt to accommodate themselves to the conflict by developing role orientations that are compatible with the bureaucracy or the profession, and some adopt orientations that are compatible with both. Although accommodation is made, the conflict remains a continuing dilemma and thus a fundamental issue.

Professional expertise and bureaucratic discipline are alternative modes of coping with uncertainty. Discipline restricts its scope, whereas expertise provides knowledge and social support to cope with uncertainty. Blau and Scott held that the struggle will remain as long as professionals are employed in bureaucratic organizations. It seems likely that the professional-bureaucratic dilemma will become an even more significant internal one in schools as teachers and administrators become more professionalized and continue to function in school organizations that are essentially bureaucratic in nature.

Administrative Planning and Individual Initiative

A third manifestation of the tension between order and freedom is the need for both administrative planning and individual initiative. The disharmony between them poses a major difficulty in the administrative process, which includes not only the development of plans to solve problems but their subsequent implementation and appraisal. The setting of organizational decision making is the organization as a collectivity. The exercise of any independent judgment must be compatible with the thrust of the formal organization. There is continuous pressure from the formal organization through its elaborate bureaucratic machinery to subordinate individual initiative to organizational directives. The organization is, of course, interested in creative, individual efforts, but only when they do not conflict with formal plans.

How can the organization encourage individual initiative without confounding administrative planning? We have suggested a number of organizational responses. A model for shared decision making has been introduced that delineates under what conditions the individual should be involved in the decision-making process (see Chapter 9). The arrangement calls for harnessing the creative initiative of individuals in a constructive way that is beneficial to both the organization and the person. We have sketched the characteristics of a professional organizational structure in which emphasis is placed on shared decision making rather than on autocratic bureaucracy (see Chapter 3). Further, we described a number of organizational climates—open, healthy, and humanistic—that would tend to lessen the conflict between compliance and initiative (see Chapter 5).

In brief, organizations can be structured and organizational climates and cultures can be developed to minimize the conflict between administrative planning and individual initiative. This is not to suggest that the dilemma can be resolved. The best that we can probably hope for is a healthy balance between compliance and initiative, a balance continually disrupted by the conflicting needs for order and freedom.

Learning as Behavior and Cognition

Finally, the tension between behaviorism and cognitive approaches to teaching and learning ripple through virtually all administrative decisions in schools. On the one hand, there is strong research to support the use of principle of reinforcement in teaching and classroom management. Learning objectives, mastery learning, and direct instruction are examples of teaching applications that are effective in certain situations. On the other hand, cognitive theories, especially constructivism, put the student at the center of the teaching-learning and the teacher in the indirect role of assistant and coach. Inquiry and problem-based learning are critical aspects of teaching in this approach. Constructivists and most cognitive approaches eschew the research and practice of the behaviorists. Indeed, many of the contemporary conflicts about teaching are manifestations of the behavior-cognitive dilemma, for example, "phonics" versus "whole reading," "basic skills" versus "critical thinking," "direct instruction" versus "discovery," and "core knowledge" versus "authentic knowledge."

How can school administrators encourage the use of cognitive and constructivist approaches without denigrating or eliminating behaviorist approaches. We argue that first, administrators and teachers must understand the basic theory and research that undergird each approach (see Chapter 2). Understanding is essential if we are to avoid the negative consequences of choosing sides in the most current educational controversy. For example, when the goal is to learn new behaviors or explicit information or when learning is sequential or factual, a behavioral approach to teaching and learning is usually quite effective. If, however, the goal is problem solving or critical thinking, then a cognitive approach is a more effective teaching-learning strategy, one, for example, which uses scaffolding, coaching, and stresses meaning rather than memory. The point is that the kind of outcome is related to the kind of teaching that is most effective. There is no one best way to teach because teaching and learning depend on the goal of instruction. Effective teachers and administrators need to incorporate sound behavioral as well as cognitive principles in their practice.

Balance and knowledge are the keys to coping successfully with this dilemma. We do not suggest that the behavioral and cognitive learning dilemma can ever be finally resolved, but rather the answer to success rests with knowing when and how to use each approach. An "either-or" approach to teaching and learning is bound to be counterproductive. A learning environment that encourages freedom while tempering it with order is likely to be most successful in schools. The balance between freedom and order, however, is dynamic. Continuous assessment and change are necessary.

THEORY INTO PRACTICE

Controversial Speaker

"I can't stand those guys."

Juan Rodriquez looked up from a note just handed to him by a student messenger. "What guys?" he asked.

"Queers, Mr. Rodriquez. If one ever came up to me, I'd punch him out."

Before Rodriquez could respond, the bell rang and the students quickly left the classroom to go to lunch.

"It was right at the end of class this morning," said Rodriquez speaking to Lisa Pagan, another teacher in the social studies department. "One of the runners came by from the office to drop off an announcement. After he left, one of the kids told me he couldn't stand him because he was queer."

"What did you do?" asked Pagan.

"Nothing, I was saved by the bell."

"Do you deal with the topic of homosexual behavior in your Minority Studies class?" asked Pagan.

"No," replied Rodriquez. "I deal mostly with racial minorities, you know, African Americans, Chicanos, and Indians. I have enough trouble getting students to deal rationally with race without getting into the problems of gays and lesbians."

Rodriquez and Pagan continued their discussion over lunch. Pagan explained that she was dealing with a section on civil rights in her Problems of Democracy course and had touched on the problem of sexual discrimination toward women, but she admitted that she had only briefly considered homosexual discrimination, and she, too, had noticed the evident hostility toward homosexuals. She chalked it up to the normal fears of suburban adolescents.

Over the course of that week, the two teachers talked about the problem again and decided to use homosexual discrimination as a topic in their respective classes, although only as a small two- or three-day unit. Early in the next week, Pagan told Rodriquez that she had contacted the public information office of the Society of Individual Rights (SIR), a national homosexual organization, and that SIR furnished speakers and would send, if requested, a speaker to the school.

"I don't know about the speaker," Rodriquez ventured cautiously, "I certainly don't want some raving drag queen in here. Really what I would like is someone to talk about the problems of discrimination in a legal sense; I absolutely don't want anyone giving 15 minutes on the joys of being gay."

"Don't worry," said Pagan. "I met the speaker that would be sent here. I had some reservations of my own about his being an ex-marine who was in Viet Nam, but he said he would only speak on the legal problems faced by homosexuals. He seemed all right to me."

"Well, OK," said Rodriquez. "Let's ask him to speak to both classes."

Rodriquez and Pagan then talked with Tom Norcera, the department chairman. Satisfied that the speaker would aid in the class objectives and was thus justified, Norcera told the teachers to clear the speaker with the principal, Richard Rego.

Rego was proud of his high school. It was the smaller of the two high schools in Silicon Heights but, he believed, the better. Richard was hired as principal before the school was built and, consequently, had been in the enviable position of staffing the school as he chose and, with his staff, participating in the design of the buildings. Although the local townspeople were interested primarily in the athletic activities, the school district was the most pervasive institution in the town of 34,000. Most of the parents had attended the local school district. Rego heard the teachers out and agreed with them that the speaker would fit the nature of their classes. He gave permission for the speaker with two provisions: student attendance would be voluntary, and no one would be penalized for nonattendance of class the day of the SIR speaker. Second, Rego wanted teachers to apprise the parents about the class and receive parental permission slips from each youngster in the class. A student without a slip would not be allowed in class that day. It was true that parents had already given permission to their children to be in these

THEORY INTO PRACTICE, (Continued)

two senior elective classes, but Rego thought that the alteration in the class justified a reaffirmation of parental consent.

Although Rego was no stranger to controversy, he did not openly court it. He had in the past defended a teacher accused of teaching Marxism in his history class. Rego was quick to defend the teacher, although the fact that the class was one in Russian history made the defense easy. In general, the community was favorably disposed toward Rego and Silicon Heights High. The school district had a good reputation; nearly 80 percent of the graduates went on to college, with a surprisingly high number being accepted at schools of national reputation. Richard Rego saw no major problem in having a homosexual speaker in this setting.

"What are you trying to do, Richard? Do you want the parents to rise as one and descend on us with tar and feathers?" It was superintendent Jeff Cruz on the phone to Rego.

"What's the problem?" asked Rego.

"One of the school board members, John Sloan, told me that you were turning the school over to some gay activist group for the day."

"Well, I know what he is talking about. But that's not quite right. We have a couple of senior classes—Minority Studies and Problems of Democracy—and the teachers of these two classes are going to have a homosexual speaker talk to both classes about civil rights, legal problems, and that sort of thing. Both of the classes are senior electives, and parental permission slips in both cover us. According to Rodriquez, one of the teachers, the guy seems pretty normal and we should be OK."

"Well, look Richard, I'll get back to Sloan, and then I'll get back to you. Actually, I wish you would have bounced the idea off of me before going ahead with the speaker."

"Normally, I don't check with you about curriculum issues," rejoined Rego. "But, you know," he continued, "we probably should have some kind of policy for controversial speakers. In fact, that might be something for the next roundtable."

"It probably would be a good idea," Superintendent Cruz responded, but you know, I try to keep a low profile on rules and regulations. I'm buried in paper as it is. Look, I'll get back to you, but in the meantime, don't get us in over our heads."

"No problem."

Superintendent Cruz had hoped the issue was restricted to a couple of crank calls. But his hope was not fulfilled. In the next two days he had a dozen or so people call to complain about the proposed speaker, although none of the callers was a parent with a student in the affected classes. Later in the week, after two other members of the board called to protest a homosexual speaker at Silicon Heights High, Cruz decided to call his principal.

"Richard, the natives are restless. I have three board members who are edgy. They keep asking what is happening with the homosexual speaker. The whole thing may be getting out of hand. Do you think this talk is really worth the trouble?"

After a slight pause, the principal responded, "I did tell my teachers they could have the speaker, and I don't like to renege. These are dedicated teachers whom I respect. Of course, I've had some calls, too. I just don't know if it is going to be a big issue or not."

"You know my policy, Richard. I don't interfere with my principals. And, God knows, you are doing a great job there. But I see a potential catastrophe. We are still going to be in business after the speaker has come and gone. And if I can't bargain with the community here and there, I really can't do my job the way it should be done. Remember, it's you and I who have to live with these people, not the two teachers. I trust your judgment to do the right thing. Keep me posted."

"There really ought to be a policy about this," Rego thought to himself as he hung up the phone. "The speaker is coming tomorrow, and I may end up looking like George Wallace at the schoolhouse door. George Wallace! God, I'm getting old." With that thought he left for the day.

As was his habit, Principal Rego got to school early the next day. He put a note in John Rodriquez's box telling him to stop by in the morning during his break. When Rodriquez came by, Rego told him only that there was a little trouble about the speaker and that he wanted the speaker to report to the principal's office before he went to

THEORY INTO PRACTICE, (Continued)

the classes. Rodriquez said he would get in touch with the speaker.

About a half an hour before he was scheduled to speak, a well-dressed young man in a pinstriped gray suit walked into the administration building and asked the principal's secretary where he could find Mr. Rego. "My name is Samuel Sheldon, and I am going to give a talk for Mr. Rodriquez and Mrs. Pagan today. John Rodriquez asked me to stop in and see the principal for a minute before I went over to the social studies office."

"Have a seat, Mr. Sheldon. Mr. Rego will be with you in a minute."

- Assume the role of the principal in this case.
- What kind of decision-making model is most appropriate? Satisficing? Muddling? Mixed scanning? Other?
- Define the short-term and long-term problems.
- Develop a strategy of action. Be sure to consider the structural, political, individual, and cultural elements.
- What are the environmental constraints? How will your actions affect teaching and learning?
- Is it too late to renege?
- What is the line between professional responsibility and community accountability?
- No matter what your eventual strategy, make sure that it includes a plan to address the dysfunctional consequences of your actions.

From Hoy, Wayne K. and Tarter, C. John. *Administrators Solving the Problems of Practice* (c) 1995 by Allyn and Bacon. Reprinted and adapted by permission.

CONCLUSION

The position that we have held throughout this book embodies two related perspectives: what Peter F. Drucker (1968) calls reality and what Peter M. Senge (1990) calls "systems thinking." Knowledge has become a central resource. The systematic acquisition of knowledge—that is, organized formal education—must supplement experience as the foundation for increasing productive capacity and improving performance. But knowledge and experience themselves are not enough. Events must be seen as a whole pattern of change, not isolated snapshots. Increasingly, successful performance will depend on the ability to use concepts and theories as well as skills acquired through experience to make the full patterns clearer and help us to cope with them.

The dilemmas we have explored demand basic changes in administrators. They require new training, knowledge, policies, and a readiness to shed deeply entrenched practices. The practice of administration can become one of deepened dilemmas or of heightened achievements. We hold that a path to the latter is through reflective leadership anchored in sound theory and research in educational organizations.

Bibliography

AASA. (1991). *An Introduction to Total Quality Management: A Collection of Articles on the Concepts of Total Quality Management and W. Edwards Deming*. Arlington, VA: American Association of School Administrators.

Abbott, M. (1965a). Hierarchical Impediments to Innovation in Educational Organizations. In M.Abbott and J. Lovell (Eds.), *Change Perspectives in Educational Administration* (pp. 40–53). Auburn, AL: Auburn University.

Abbott, M. (1965b). Intervening Variables in Organizational Behavior. *Educational Administration Quarterly, 1,* 1–14.

Abbott, M., and Caracheo, F. (1988). Power, Authority, and Bureaucracy. In N. J. Boyan (Ed.), *Handbook of Research on Educational Administration* (pp. 239–57). New York: Longman.

Abelson, R. P., and Levi, A. (1985). Decision-Making and Decision Theory. In G. Lindzey and E. Aronson (Eds.), *Handbook of Social Psychology* (3rd ed., Vol. 1, pp. 231–309). Reading, MA: Addison-Wesley.

Abell, P. (1995). The New Institutionalism and Rational Choice Theory. In W. R. Scott and T. Christiansen (Eds.), *The Institutional Construction of Organizations: International and Longitudinal Studies* (pp. 3–14). Thousand Oaks, CA: Sage.

Abramowitz, S., and Tenenbaum, E. (1978). *High School '77*. Washington, DC: National Institute for Education.

Adler, P. S., and Borys, B. (1996). Two Types of Bureaucracy: Enabling and Coercive. *Administrative Science Quarterly, 41,* 61–89.

Adler, R. B., and Rodman, G. (1991). *Understanding Human Communication.* Fort Worth, TX: Holt, Rinehart and Winston.

Adler, S., Skov, R. B., and Salvemini, N. J. (1985). Job Characteristics and Job Satisfaction: When Cause Becomes Consequence. *Organizational Behavior and Human Decision Processes, 35,* 266–78.

Agho, A. O., Mueller, C. W., and Price, J. L. (1993). Determinants of Employee Job Satisfaction: An Empirical Test of a Causal Model. *Human Relations, 46*(8), 1007–27.

Aiken, M., and Hage, J. (1968). Organizational Interdependence and Intra-Organizational Structure. *American Sociological Review, 33,* 912–30.

Aldrich, H. E. (1972). An Organization-Environment Perspective on Cooperation and Conflict between Organizations in the Manpower Training System. In A. R. Negandi (Ed.), *Conflict and Power in Complex Organizations* (pp. 11–37). Kent, OH: Center for Business and Economic Research, Kent State University.

Aldrich, H. E. (1979). *Organizations and Environment.* Englewood Cliffs, NJ: Prentice Hall.

Aldrich, H. E., and Herker, D. (1977). Boundary-Spanning Roles and Organization Structure. *Academy of Management Review, 2,* 217–30.

Aldrich, H. E., and Mindlin, S. (1978). Uncertainty and Dependence:Two Perspectives on Environment. In L. Karpik (Ed.), *Organization and Environment: Theory, Issues and Reality* (pp. 149–70). Beverly Hills, CA: Sage.

Aldrich, H. E., and Pfeffer, J. (1976). Environments of Organizations. *Annual Review of Sociology, 2,* 79–105.

Alessandra, T., and Hunsaker, P. (1993). *Communicating at Work.* New York: Simon & Schuster.

Alexander, E. R., Penley, L. E., and Jernigan, I. E. (1991).The Effect of Individual Differences on Managerial Media Choice. *Management Communication Quarterly, 5*(2), 155–73.

Alexander, P. A. (1996). The Past, Present, and Future of Knowledge Research: A Reexamination of the Role of Knowledge in Learning and Instruction. *Educational Psychologist, 31,* 89–92.

Alinsky, S. (1971). *Rules for Radicals.* New York: Random House.

Allen, R. F., and Kraft, C. (1982). *The Organizational Unconscious: How to Create the Corporate Culture You Want and Need.* Englewood Cliffs, NJ: Prentice Hall.

Allinder, R. M. (1994). The Relationship between Efficacy and the Instructional Practices of Special Education Teachers and Consultants. *Teacher Education and Special Education, 17,* 86–95.

Allison, G. T. (1971). *Essence of Decision: Explaining the Cuban Missile Crisis.* Boston: Little, Brown.

Allutto, J. A., and Belasco, J. A. (1973). Patterns of Teacher Participation in School System Decision Making. *Educational Administration Quarterly, 9,* 27–41.

Anderman, E. M., and Maehr, M. L. (1994). Motivation and Schooling in the Middle Grades. *Review of Educational Research, 64,* 287–310.

Anderson, B. (1971). Socioeconomic Status of Students and Schools Bureaucratization. *Educational Administration Quarterly, 7,* 12–24.

Anderson, C. S. (1982). The Search for School Climate: A Review of the Research. *Review of Educational Research, 52,* 368–420.

Anderson, D. P. (1964). *Organizational Climate of Elementary Schools.* Minneapolis: Educational Research and Development Council.

Anderson, J. (1976). Giving and Receiving Feedback. In P. R. Lawrence, L. B. Barnes, and J. W. Lorsch (Eds.), *Organizational Behavior and Administration* (pp. 103–11). Homewood, IL: Irwin.

Anderson, J. C., Rungtusanatham, M., and Schroeder, R. G. (1994). A Theory of Quality Management Underlying the Deming Management. *Academy of Management Review, 19* (3), 472–509.

Anderson, J. R. (1990). *Cognitive Psychology and Its Implications* (3rd ed.). New York: Freeman.

Anderson, J. R. (1993). Problem Solving and Learning. *American Psychologist, 48,* 35–44.

Anderson, J. R. (1995). *Cognitive Psychology and Its Implications* (4th ed.). New York: Freeman.

Anderson, J. R., Reder, L. M., and Simon, H. A. (1995). Applications and misapplication of cognitive psychology to mathematics education. Unpublished manuscript (accessible at *http://www.psy. cmu.edu/~mm4b/misapplied.html*).

Anderson, L. M. (1989a). Learners and Learning. In M. Reynolds (Ed.), *Knowledge Base for Beginning Teachers* (pp. 85–100). New York: Pergamon.

Anderson, M. B. G., and Iwanicki, E. F. (1984). Teacher Motivation and Its Relationship to Burnout. *Educational Administration Quarterly, 20,* 109–32.

Andrews, J. H. M. (1965). School Organizational Climate: Some Validity Studies. *Canadian Education and Research Digest, 5,* 317–34.

Appleberry, J. B., and Hoy, W. K. (1969). The Pupil Control Ideology of Professional Personnel in "Open" and "Closed" Elementary Schools. *Educational Administration Quarterly, 5,* 74–85.

Arches, J. (1991). Social Structure, Burnout, and Job Satisfaction. *Social Work, 36*(3), 202–6.

Argote, L., Turner, M. E., and Fichman, M. (1989). To Centralize or Not to Centralize: The Effects of Uncertainty and Threat on Group Structure and Performance. *Organizational Behavior and Human Performance, 43,* 58–74.

Aristotle (1883). *Politics.* Book I, Chapter 5. London: Macmillan.

Armbruster, B. B., and Anderson, T. H. (1981). Research Synthesis on Study Skills. *Educational Leadership, 39,* 154–56.

Armor, D., Conry-Oseguera, P., Cox, M., King, N., McDonnell, L., Pascal, A., Pauly, E., and Zellman, G. (1976). *Analysis of the School Preferred Reading Program in Selected Los Angeles Minority Schools* (No. R-2007-LAUSD). Santa Monica, CA: Rand.

Arnold, H. J., and House, R. J. (1980). Methodological and Substantive Extensions to the Job Characteristics Model of Motivation. *Organizational Behavior and Human Performances, 25,* 161–83.

Ashford, S. J. (1986). Feedback-Seeking in Individual Adaptation: A Resource Perspective. *Academy of Management Journal, 29,* 465–87.

Ashforth, B. E. (1985). Climate Formations: Issues and Extensions. *Academy of Management Review, 10,* 837–47.

Ashton, P. T., Olejnik, S., Crocker, L., and McAuliffe, M. (1982, April). *Measurement Problems in the Study of Teachers' Sense of Efficacy.* Paper presented at the annual meeting of the American Educational Research Association, New York.

Ashton, P. T., and Webb, R. B. (1986). *Making a Difference: Teachers' Sense of Efficacy.* New York: Longman.

Astuto, T. A., and Clark, D. L. (1985a). *Merit Pay for Teachers.* Bloomington: School of Education, University of Indiana.

Astuto, T. A., and Clark, D. L. (1985b). Strength of Organizational Coupling in the Instructionally Effective School. *Urban Education, 19,* 331–56.

At-Twaijri, M. I. A., and Montanari, J. R. (1987). The Impact of Context and Choice on the Boundary-Spanning Process: An Empirical Study. *Human Relations, 40,* 783–98.

Atwater, D. C., and Bass, B. M. (1994). Transformational Leadership in Teams. In B. M. Bass and B. J. Avolio (Eds.), *Improving Organizational Effectiveness Through Transformational Leadership* (pp. 48–83). Thousand Oaks, CA: Sage.

Audia, G., Kristof-Brown, A., Brown, K. C., and Locke, E. A. (1996). Relationship of Goals and Microlevel Work Processes to Performance on a Multipath Task. *Journal of Applied Psychology,* 81, 483–97.

Aupperle, K. E., Acar, W., and Booth, D. E. (1986). An Empirical Critique of *In Search of Excellence:* How Excellent Are the Excellent Companies? *Journal of Management, 12,* 499–512.

Ausubel, D. P. (1963). *The Psychology of Meaningful Verbal Learning.* New York: Grune and Stratton.

Averich, H. A., Carroll, S. J., Donaldson, T. S., Kiesling, H. J., and Pincus, J. (1972), *How Effective Is Schooling: A Critical Review and Synthesis of Research Findings.* Santa Monica, CA: Rand.

Avolio, B. J. (1994). The Alliance of Total Quality and the Full Range of Leadership. In B. M. Bass and B. J. Avolio (Eds.), *Improving Organizational Effectiveness Through Transformational Leadership* (pp. 121–45). Thousand Oaks, CA: Sage.

Avolio, B. J. (1999). *Full Leadership Development.* Thousand Oaks, CA: Sage.

Babbie, E. R. (1990). *Survey Research Methods* (2nd ed.). Belmont, CA:Wadsworth Publishing.

Bacharach, S. B. (1988). Four Themes of Reform: An Editorial Essay. *Educational Administration Quarterly, 24,* 484–96.

Bacharach, S. B. (1989). Organizational Theories: Some Criteria for Evaluation. *Academy of Management Review, 14,* 496–515.

Bacharach, S. B., Bamberger, P., Conley, S. C., and Bauer, S. (1990). The Dimensionality of Decision Participation in Educational Organizations: The Value of Multi-Domain Educative Approach. *Educational Administration Quarterly, 26,* 126–67.

Bacharach, S. B., Conley, S., and Shedd, J. (1986). Beyond Career Ladders: Structuring Teacher Career Development Systems. *Teachers College Record, 87,* 565–74.

Bacharach, S. B., and Mundell, B. L. (1993). Organizational Politics in Schools: Micro, Macro, and Logics of Action. *Educational Administration Quarterly, 29*(4), 423–52.

Bacon, F. (1597). *Meditationes Sacrae.*

Baddeley, A. D. (1986). *Working Memory.* Oxford, UK: Claredon Books.

Baker, M. A. (1991). Gender and Verbal Communication in Professional Settings: A Review of Research. *Management Communication Quarterly, 5*(1), 36–63.

Bailyn, L. (1985). Autonomy in the R & D Lab. *Human Resource Management,* 24 (2), 129–46.

Bakkenes, I., de Brabander, C., and Imants, J. (1999). Teacher Isolation and Communication Network Analysis. *Educational Administration Quarterly, 35*(2), 166–202.

Baltzell, D. C., and Dentler, R. A. (1983). *Selecting American School Principals: A Sourcebook for Educators.* Cambridge, MA: Abt Associates.

Bandura, A. (1977). Self-Efficacy: Toward a Unifying Theory of Behavioral Change. *Psychological Review, 84,* 191–215.

Bandura, A. (1986). *Social Foundations of Thought and Action.* Englewood Cliffs, NJ: Prentice Hall.

Bandura, A. (1991). Social Cognitive Theory of Self-Regulation. *Organizational Behavior and Human Decision Processes, 50,* 248–87.

Bandura, A. (1993). Perceived Self-Efficacy in Cognitive Development and Functioning. *Educational Psychologist, 28,* 117–48.

Bandura, A. (1997). *Self-Efficacy: The Exercise of Control.* New York: Freeman.

Bantz, C. R. (1993). *Understanding Organizations: Interpreting Organizational Communication Cultures.* Columbia: University of South Carolina Press.

Barnabe, C., and Burns, M. L. (1994). Teachers' Job Characteristics and Motivation. *Educational Research, 36*(2), 171–85.

Barnard, C. I. (1938). *Functions of an Executive.* Cambridge, MA: Harvard University Press.

Barnard, C. I. (1940). Comments on the Job of the Executive. *Harvard Business Review, 18,* 295–308.

Barnes, R. M. (1949). *Motion and Time Study.* New York: Wiley.

Barnes, K. M. (1994). The organizational health of middle schools, trust and decision participation.

Doctoral diss., Rutgers University, New Brunswick.

Barnett, B. G. (1984). Subordinate Teacher Power in School Organizations. *Sociology of Education, 57,* 43–55.

Baron, R. A. (1998). *Psychology* (4th ed.). Boston: Allyn and Bacon.

Bass, B. M. (1985a). *Leadership and Performance Beyond Expectation.* New York: Free Press.

Bass, B. M. (1985b). *Organizational Decision Making.* Homewood, IL: Irwin.

Bass, B. M. (1990). *Bass and Stogdill's Handbook of Leadership* (3rd ed.). New York: Free Press.

Bass, B. M. (1997). Does the Transactional-Transformational Paradigm Transcend Organizational and National Boundaries? *American Psychologist, 52,* 130–39.

Bass, B. M. (1998). *Transformational Leadership: Industrial, Military, and Educational Impact.* Mahwah, NJ: Erlbaum.

Bass, B. M., and Avolio, B. J. (1994). Introduction. In B. M. Bass and B. J. Avolio (Eds.), *Improving Organizational Effectiveness Through Transformational Leadership* (pp. 1–10). Thousand Oaks, CA: Sage.

Bates, R. (1987). Conceptions of School Culture: An Overview. *Educational Administration Quarterly, 23,* 79–116.

Baumgartner, F. R., and Leech, B. L. (1998). *Basic Interests: The Importance of Groups in Politics and in Political Science.* Princeton, NJ: Princeton University Press.

Baumgartner, F. R., and Walker, J. L. (1989). Educational Policymaking and the Interest Group Structure in France and the United States. *Comparative Politics, 21,* 273–88.

Becker, T. E., and Klimoski, R. J. (1989). A Field Study of the Relationship Between the Organizational Feedback Environment and Performance. *Personnel Psychology, 42,* 343–58.

Becker, W. C., Engelmann, S., and Thomas, D. R. (1975). *Teaching 1: Classroom Management.* Chicago: Science Research Associates.

Belasco, J. A., and Allutto, J. A. (1972). Decisional Participation and Teacher Satisfaction. *Educational Administration Quarterly, 8,* 44–58.

Ben-Peretz, M., and Schonmann, S. (1998). Informal Learning Communities and Their Effects. In K. Leithwood and K. S. Louis (Eds.), *Organizational Learning in Schools* (pp. 47–66). Lisse: Swets and Zeitlinger.

Bennis, W. G. (1959). Leadership Theory and Administrative Behavior. *Administrative Science Quarterly, 4,* 259–301.

Bennis, W. G. (1966). *Changing Organizations.* New York: McGraw-Hill.

Bennis, W. G. (1989). *On Becoming a Leader.* Reading, MA: Addison-Wesley.

Bennis, W., and Nanus, B. (1985). *Leaders: The Strategies for Taking Charge.* New York: Harper & Row.

Benson, J. K. (1975). The Interorganizational Network as a Political Economy. *Administration Science Quarterly, 20,* 229–49.

Berg, C. A., and Clough, M. (1991). Hunter Lesson Design: The Wrong One for Science Teaching. *Educational Leadership, 48*(4), 73–78.

Berlo, D. K. (1970). *The Process of Communication.* New York: Holt, Rinehart & Winston.

Berman, P., McLaughlin, M., Bass, G., Pauly, E., and Zellerman, G. (1977). *Federal Programs Supporting Educational Change: Factors Affecting Implementation and Continuation* (Vol. 7, No. R-1589/7-HEW). Santa Monica, CA: Rand.

Betz, E. L. (1984). Two Tests of Maslow's Theory of Need Fulfillment. *Journal of Vocational Behavior, 24,* 204–20.

Beyer, J. M., and Trice, H. M. (1987). How an Organization's Rites Reveal Its Culture. *Organizational Dynamics, 15,* 4–24.

Bhagat, R. S., and Chassie, M. B. (1980). Effects of Changes in Job Characteristics on Some Theory-Specific Attitudinal Outcomes: Results from a Naturally Occurring Quasi-Experiment. *Human Relations, 33,* 297–313.

Bidwell, C. E. (1965). The School as a Formal Organization. In J. G. March (Ed.), *Handbook of Organization* (pp. 972–1022). Chicago: Rand McNally.

Bimber, B. (1993). *School Decentralization: Lessons from the Study of Bureaucracy.* Santa Monica, CA: Rand.

Birnbaum, R. (1971). Presidential Succession: An Interinstitutional Analysis. *Educational Record, 52,* 133–45.

Blackburn, R., and Rosen, B. (1993). Total Quality and Human Resources Management: Lessons Learned from Baldrige Award-Winning Companies. *Academy of Management Executive, 2* (3), 49–66.

Blake, R. R., and Mouton, J. S. (1985). *The Managerial Grid III.* Houston, TX: Gulf.

Blau, P. M. (1955). *The Dynamics of Bureaucracy.* Chicago: University of Chicago Press.

Blau, P. M. (1956). *Bureaucracy in Modern Society.* New York: Random House.

Blau, P. M., and Scott, W. R. (1962). *Formal Organizations: A Comparative Approach.* San Francisco: Chandler.

Bloom, B. S. (1968). Learning for Mastery. *Evaluation Comment,* 1(2). Los Angeles: University of California, Center for the Study of Evaluation of Instructional Programs.

Bluedorn, A. C., and Denhardt, R. B. (1988). Time and Organizations. *Journal of Management, 4,* 299–320.

Blumberg,A. (1984). The Craft of School Administration and Some Other Rambling Thoughts. *Educational Administration Quarterly, 20,* 24–40.

Blumberg,A. (1989). *School Administration as a Craft: Foundations of Practice.* Needham Heights, MA: Allyn and Bacon.

Bobbit, F. (1913). Some General Principles of Management Applied to the Problems of City School Systems. *The Supervision of City Schools, Twelfth Yearbook of the National Society for the Study of Education, Part I* (pp. 137–96). Chicago: University of Chicago Press.

Boje, D. M., and Whetten, D. A. (1981). Effects of Organizational Strategies and Contextual Constraints on Centrality and Attributions of Influence in Interorganizational Networks. *Administrative Science Quarterly, 26,* 378–95.

Bok, D. (1993). *The Cost of Talent.* New York: Free Press.

Bolman, L. G., and Deal, T. E. (1991). *Reframing Organizations: Artistry, Choice, and Leadership.* San Francisco: Jossey-Bass.

Bolman, L. G., and Deal, T. E. (1997). *Reframing Organizations: Artistry, Choice, and Leadership* (2nd ed.). San Francisco, CA: Jossey-Bass.

Bonstingl, J. J. (1992). The Quality Revolution in Education. *Educational Leadership, 50,* 4–9.

Bose, C., Feldberg, R., and Sokoloff, N. (1987). *Hidden Aspects of Women's Work.* New York: Praeger.

Bossert, S. T. (1988). School Effects. In N. J. Boyan (Ed.), *Handbook of Research on Educational Administration* (pp. 341–52). New York: Longman.

Bossert, S. T., Dwyer, D. C., Rowan, B., and Lee, G. V. (1982). The Instructional Management Role of the Principal. *Educational Administration Quarterly, 18,* 34–64.

Bowditch, J. L., and Buono, A. F. (1985). *A Primer on Organizational Behavior.* New York. Wiley.

Bowers, D. G. (1976). *Systems of Organizations: Management of the Human Resource.* Ann Arbor: University of Michigan Press.

Boyan, N. J. (1951). A study of the formal and informal organization of a school faculty: the identification of the systems of interactions and relationships among the staff members of a school and an analysis of the interplay between these systems. Doctoral diss. Harvard University, Cambridge.

Boyd, W. L. (1976). The Public, the Professional, and Educational Policy Making: Who Governs? *Teachers College Record, 77,* 539–77.

Boyd, W. L., and Walberg, H. J. (1990). Introduction and Overview. In W. L. Boyd and H. J. Walberg (Eds.), *Choice in Education: Potential and Problems* (pp. ix–xiii). Berkeley, CA: McCutchan.

Brady, L. (1985). The "Australian" OCDQ: A Decade Later. *Journal of Educational Administration, 23,* 53–58.

Braybrook, D., and Lindblom, C. E. (1963). *The Strategy of Decision.* New York: Free Press.

Bridges, E. M. (1967). A Model for Shared Decision Making in the School Principalship. *Educational Administration Quarterly, 3,* 49–61.

Bromily, P. (1985). Planning Systems in Large Organizations: Garbage Can Approach with Applications to Defense PPBS. In J. G. March and R. Weissinger-Baylon (Eds.), *Ambiguity and Command: Organization Perspectives on Military Decision Making* (pp. 120–39). Marshfield, MA: Pitman.

Broms, H., and Gahmberg, H. (1983). Communication to Self in Organizational Cultures. *Administrative Science Quarterly, 28*(3), 482–95.

Brookover, W. B., Schweitzer, J. H., Schneider, J. M., Beady, C. H., Flood, P. K., and Wisenbaker, J. M. (1978). Elementary School Social Climate and School Achievement. *American Educational Research Journal, 15,* 301–18.

Brooks, J. G., and Brooks, M. G. (1993). Becoming a Constructivist Teacher. *In Search of Understanding: The Case for Constructivist Classrooms.* Alexandria, VA: The Association for Supervision and Curriculum Development.

Brophy, J. E., and Good, T. L. (1986). Teacher Behavior and Student Achievement. In M. C. Wittrock (Ed.), *Handbook of Research on Teaching* (3rd ed., pp. 328–75). New York: Macmillan.

Brown, A. (1987). Metacognition, Executive Control, Self-Regulation, and Other More Mysterious Mechanisms. In F. Weinert and R. Kluwe (Eds.), *Metacognition, Motivation, and Understanding* (pp. 65–116). Hillside, NJ: Erlbaum.

Brown, A. F. (1965). Two Strategies for Changing Climate. *CAS Bulletin, 4,* 64–80.

Brown, A. L., Bransford, J., Ferrara, R., and Campione, J. (1983). Learning, Remembering, and Understanding. In P. Mussen (Ed.), Handbook of Child Psychology (Vol. 3). New York: Wiley.

Brown, D. (1990). *Decentralization and School-Based Management.* New York: Falmer Press.

Brown, J. S. (1990). Toward a New Epistemology for Learning. In C. Frasson and G. Gauthier (Eds.) *Intelligent Tutoring Systems: At the Crossroads of Artificial Intelligence and Education* (pp. 266–82). Norwood, NJ: Ablex.

Bruner, J. S. (1966). *Toward a Theory of Instruction.* New York: Norton.

Bruner, J. S., Goodnow, J. J., and Austin, G. A. (1956). *A Study of Thinking.* New York: Wiley.

Bruning, R. H., Schraw, G. J., and Ronning, R. R. (1995). *Cognitive Psychology and Instruction* (2nd ed.). Englewood Cliffs, NJ: Merrill/Prentice Hall.

Bryk, A. S. (1993). Educational Indicator Systems: Observations on Their Structure Interpretation, and Use. *Review of Research in Education, 19,* 451–84.

Bryk, A. S., Lee, V. E., and Holland, P. (1993). *Catholic Schools and the Common Good.* Cambridge, MA: Harvard University Press.

Bryman, A. (1996). Leadership in Organizations. In S. R. Clegg, C. Hardy, and W. R. Nord (Eds.), *Handbook of Organizational Studies.* Thousand Oaks, CA: Sage.

Burbules, N. C. (1993). *Dialogue in Teaching: Theory and Practice.* New York: Teachers College Press.

Burbules, N. C., and Bruce, B. C. (2000). Theory and Research on Teaching as Dialogue. In V. Richardson (Ed.), *Handbook of Research on Teaching* (4th ed.). Washington, DC: American Educational Research Association.

Burlingame, M. (1979). Some Neglected Dimensions in the Study of Educational Administration. *Educational Administration Quarterly, 15,* 1–18.

Burns, J. M. (1978). *Leadership.* New York: Harper & Row.

Burns, T., and Stalker, G. M. (1961). *The Management of Innovation.* London: Travistock.

Burrell, G., and Morgan, G. (1980). *Sociological Paradigms and Organizational Analysis.* London: Heinemann.

Calas, M. B., and Smircich, L. (1997). *Postmodern Management Theory.* Brookfield, VE: Ashgate Publishing.

Callahan, R. E. (1962). *Education and the Cult of Efficiency.* Chicago: University of Chicago Press.

Cameron, K. S. (1978). Measuring Organizational Effectiveness in Institutions of Higher Education. *Administrative Science Quarterly, 23,* 604–32.

Cameron, K. S. (1984). The Effectiveness of Ineffectiveness. *Research in Organizational Behavior, 6,* 235–85.

Cameron, K. S., and Quinn, R. E. (1999). *Diagnosing and Changing Organizational Climate.* New York: Addison-Wesley.

Cameron, K. S., and Whetten, D. A. (1983). *Organizational Effectiveness: A Comparison of Multiple Models.* New York: Academic.

Cameron, K. S., and Whetten, D. A. (1996). Organizational Effectiveness and Quality: The Second Generation. *Higher Education Handbook of Theory and Research, 11,* 265–306.

Campbell, J. P. (1977). On the Nature of Organizational Effectiveness. In P. S. Goodman and J. M. Pennings (Eds.), *New Perspectives on Organizational Effectiveness* (pp. 13–55). San Francisco: Jossey-Bass.

Campbell, J. P., Dunnette, M. D., Lawler, E. E. III, and Karl E. Weick, J. (1970). *Managerial Behavior, Performance, and Effectiveness.* New York: McGraw-Hill.

Campbell, J. P., and Pritchard, R. D. (1976). Motivation Theory in Industrial and Organizational Psychology. In M. D. Dunnette (Ed.), *Handbook of Industrial and Organizational Psychology* (pp. 63–130). Chicago: Rand McNally.

Campbell, R. (1971). *NCPEA—Then and Now.* National Conference of Professors of Educational Administration Meeting, University of Utah, Salt Lake City.

Campbell, R., Fleming, T., Newell, L. J., and Bennion, J. W. (1987). *A History of Thought and Practice in Educational Administration.* New York: Teachers College Press.

Capper, C. A., and Jamison, M. T. (1993). Let the Buyer Beware: Total Quality Management and Educational Research and Practice. *Educational Researcher, 22*(8), 25–30.

Carey, M. R. (1992). Transformational Leadership and the Fundamental Option for Self-Transcendence. *Leadership Quarterly, 3* (3), 217–36.

Carlson, R. O. (1962). *Executive Succession and Organizational Change.* Chicago: University of Chicago, Midwest Administration Center.

Carlson, R. O. (1964). Environmental Constraints and Organizational Consequences: The Public School and Its Clients. In D. E. Griffiths (Ed.), *Behavioral Science and Educational Administration* (pp. 262–76). Chicago: University of Chicago Press.

Carnegie Task Force on Teaching as a Profession (1986). *A Nation Prepared: Teachers for the 21st Century.* New York: Carnegie Corporation, Carnegie Forum on Education and the Economy.

Carpenter, H. H. (1971). Formal Organizational Structural Factors and Perceived Job Satisfaction of Classroom Teachers. *Administrative Science Quarterly, 16,* 460–65.

Carroll, S. J. (1986). Management by Objectives: Three Decades of Research and Experience. In S. L. Rynes and G. T. Milkovich (Eds.), *Current Issues in Human Resource Management.* Plano, TX: Business Publications.

Cartwright, D., and Zander, A. (1953). *Group Dynamics: Research and Theory.* Evanston, IL: Row, Peterson.

Casner-Lotto, J. (1988). Expanding the Teacher's Role: Hammond's School Improvement Process. *Phi Delta Kappan, 69,* 349–53.

Castrogiovanni, G. J. (1991). Environmental Munificence: A Theoretical Assessment. *Academy of Management Review, 16*(3), 542–65.

Chandler M. (1997). Stumping for Progress in a Post-modern World. In E. Amsel and K. A. Renninger (Eds.). *Change and Development: Issues of Theory, Method, and Application* (pp. 1–26). Mahwah, NJ: Erlbaum.

Chapman, D. W., and Hutcheson, S. M. (1982). Attrition from Teaching Careers: A Discriminant Analysis. *American Educational Research Journal, 19,* 93–105.

Charters, W. W., Jr. (1967). Stability and Change in the Communication Structure of School Faculties. *Educational Administration Quarterly, 3,* 15–38.

Chase, F. S. (1951). Factors for Satisfaction in Teaching. *Phi Delta Kappan, 33,* 127–32.

Chatman, J. A., and Jehn, K. A. (1994). Assessing the Relationship Between Industry Characteristics and Organizational Culture: How Different Can You Be? *Academy of Management Journal, 37* (3), 522–53.

Chemers, M. M. (1997). *An Integrative Theory of Leadership.* Mahwah, NJ: Erlbaum.

Chemers, M. M., and Skrzypek, G. J. (1972). Experimental Test of Contingency Model of Leadership Effectiveness. *Journal of Personality and Social Psychology, 24,* 172–77.

Cherrington, D. J. (1991). Need Theories of Motivation. In R. M. Steers and L. W. Porter (Eds.), *Motivation and Work Behavior* (pp. 31–44). New York: McGraw-Hill.

Chisolm, G. B., Washington, R., and Thibodeaux, M. (1980). Job Motivation and the Need Fulfillment Deficiencies of Educators. Annual Meeting of the American Educational Research Association, Boston.

Choo, C. W. (1998). *The Knowing Organization.* New York: Oxford.

Chubb, J. E., and Moe, T. M. (1990). *Politics, Markets, and America's Schools.* Washington, DC: Brookings Institution.

Chung, K. A. (1987). A comparative study of principals' work behavior. Doctoral diss., University of Utah, Salt Lake City.

Chung, K. A., and Miskel, C. (1989). A Comparative Study of Principals' Administrative Behavior. *Journal of Educational Administration, 27,* 45–57.

Clampitt, P. G. (1991). *Communicating for Managerial Effectiveness.* Newbury Park, CA: Sage.

Clark, D. L., Astuto, T. A., Foster, W. P., Gaynor, A. K., and Hart, A. W. (1994). Organizational Studies: Taxonomy and Overview. In W. K. Hoy, T.A.Astuto, and P. B. Forsyth (Eds.), *Educational Administration: The UCEA Document Base.* New York: McGraw-Hill Primus.

Clark, D. L., Lotto, L. S., and Astuto, T. A. (1984). Effective Schools and School Improvement: A Comparative Analysis of Two Lines of Inquiry. *Educational Administration Quarterly, 20,* 41–68.

Clark, K. E., and Clark, M. B. (Eds.). (1990). *Measures of Leadership.* West Orange, NJ: Leadership Library of America.

Clune, W. H., and White, J. F. (Eds.). (1990). *Choice and Control in American Education. Volume 2: The Practice of Choice, Decentralization and School Restructuring.* New York: Falmer Press.

Coch, L., and French, J. R. P., Jr. (1948). Overcoming Resistance to Change. *Human Relations, 1,* 512–32.

Cognition and Technology Group at Vanderbilt. (1990). Some Thoughts about Constructivism and Instructional Design. *Educational Technology, 31*(5), 16–18.

Cognition and Technology Group at Vanderbilt. (1993). Anchored Instruction and Situated Learning Revisited. *Educational Technology, 33*(3), 52–70.

Cohen, D. K. (1987). Schooling More and Liking It Less: Puzzles of Educational Improvement. *Harvard Educational Review, 57,* 174–77.

Cohen, D. K., and Spillane, J. P. (1992). Policy and Practice: The Relations Between Governance and Instruction. *Review of Research in Education,* 18, 3–49.

Cohen, M. D., and March, J. G. (1974). *Leadership and Ambiguity.* New York: McGraw-Hill.

Cohen, M. D., March, J. G., and Olsen, J. P. (1972). A Garbage Can Model of Organizational Choice. *Administrative Science Quarterly, 17,* 1–25.

Cohen, M. D., and Sproull, L. S. (Eds.). (1996). *Organizational Learning.* Thousand Oaks, CA: Sage.

Coleman, J. S. (1990). *Foundations of Social Theory.* Cambridge, MA: Belknap.

Coleman, J. S. (1961). *The Adolescent Society.* New York: Free Press.

Coleman, J. S. (1974). *Power and Structure of Society.* New York: Norton.

Coleman, J. S., Campbell, E. Q., Hobson, C. J., McPartland, J., Mood, A. M., Weinfeld, F. D., and York, R. L. (1966). *Equality of Educational Opportunity.* Washington, DC: U.S. Government Printing Office.

Collins, A., Brown, J. S., and Holum, A. (1991). Cognitive Apprenticeship: Making Thinking Visible. *American Educator, 15*(3), 38–39.

Collins, A., Brown, J. S., and Newman, S. E. (1989). *Cognitive Apprenticeship: Teaching the Crafts of Reading, Writing, and Mathematics.* In L. B. Resnick (Ed.), Knowing, Learning, and Instruction: Essays in Honor of Robert Galser. Hillsdale, NJ: Erlbaum.

Commons, J. R. (1924). *Legal Foundations of Capitalism.* New York: Macmillan.

Conant, J. B. (1951). *Science and Common Sense.* New Haven: Yale University Press.

Conger, J. A. (1991). Inspiring Others: The Language of Leadership. *Academy of Management Executive, 5*(1), 31–45.

Conger, J. A. (1999). Charismatic and Transformational Leadership in Organizations: An Insider's Perspective on These Developing Streams of Research. *Leadership Quarterly, 10*(2), 145–79.

Conger, J. A., and Kanungo, R. N. (1988). The Empowerment Process: Integrating Theory and Practice. *Academy of Management Journal, 13,* 471–82.

Conley, S. C. (1990). A Metaphor for Teaching: Beyond the Bureaucratic-Professional Dichotomy. In S. B. Bacharach (Ed.), *Educational Reform: Making Sense of It All* (pp. 313–24). Boston: Allyn and Bacon.

Conley, S. C., and Bacharach, S. B. (1990). From School Site-Management to Participatory Site-Management. *Phi Delta Kappan, 72,* 539–44.

Conley, S. C., Bower, S., and Bacharach, S. B. (1989). The School Work Environment and Teacher Career Satisfaction. *Educational Administration Quarterly, 25,* 58–81.

Conley, S., and Levinson, R. (1993). Teacher Work Redesign and Job Satisfaction. *Educational Administration Quarterly, 29*(4), 453–78.

Connolly, T., Conlon, E. J., and Deutsch, S. J. (1980). Organizational Effectiveness: A Multiple-Constituency Approach. *Academy of Management Review, 5,* 211–17.

Constas, H. (1958). Max Weber's Two Conceptions of Bureaucracy. *American Journal of Sociology, 63,* 400–9.

Conway, J. A. (1976). Test of Linearity Between Teachers' Participation in Decision Making and Their Perceptions of Schools as Organizations. *Administrative Science Quarterly, 21,* 130–39.

Conway, J. A. (1984). The Myth, Mystery, and Mastery of Participative Decision Making in Education. *Educational Administration Quarterly, 3,* 11–40.

Cook, S. D., and Yanon, D. (1996). Culture and Organizational Learning. In M. D. Cohen and L. S. Sproull (Eds.). *Organizational Learning* (pp. 430–59). Thousand Oaks, CA: Sage.

Cordery, J. L., and Sevastos, P. P. (1993). Responses to the Original and Revised Job Diagnostic Survey: Is Education a Factor in Responses to Negatively Worded Items? *Journal of Applied Psychology, 78* (1), 141–43.

Corwin, R. G. (1965). Professional Persons in Public Organizations. *Educational Administration Quarterly, 1,* 1–22.

Corwin, R. G., and Borman, K. M. (1988). School as Workplace: Structural Constraints on

Administration. In N. J. Boyan (Ed.), *Handbook of Research on Educational Administration* (pp. 209–37). New York: Longman.

Corwin, R. G., and Herriott, R. E. (1988). Occupational Disputes in Mechanical and Organic Social Systems: An Empirical Study of Elementary and Secondary Schools. *American Sociological Review, 53,* 528–43.

Cosgrove, D. (1985). The effects of principal succession on elementary schools. Doctoral diss., University of Utah, Salt Lake City.

Cox, A. (1982). *The Cox Report on the American Corporation.* New York: Delacorte.

Craig, R. T. (1999). Communication Theory as a Field. *Communication Theory, 9*(2), 119–61.

Craig, T. (1995). Achieving Innovation Through Bureaucracy. *California Management Review, 38*(10), 8–36.

Craik, F. I. M., and Lockhart, R. S. (1972). Levels of Processing: A Framework for Memory Research. *Journal of Verbal Learning and Verbal Behavior, 11,* 671–84.

Cranny, C. J., Smith, P. C., and Stone, E. F. (1992). *Job Satisfaction.* New York: Lexington.

Crehan, E. P. (1985). A meta-analysis of Fiedler's contingency model of leadership effectiveness. Doctoral diss., University of British Columbia, Vancouver.

CTGV (*see* Cognition and Technology Group at Vanderbilt)

Cuban, L. (1983). Effective Schools: A Friendly but Cautionary Note. *Phi Delta Kappan, 64,* 695–96.

Cuban, L. (1984). Transforming the Frog into a Prince: Effective Schools Research, Policy, and Practice at the District Level. *Harvard Educational Review, 54,* 129–51.

Cunningham, W. G., and Gresso, D. W. (1993). *Cultural Leadership.* Boston: Allyn and Bacon.

Cusella, L. P. (1987). Feedback, Motivation, and Performance. In F. M. Jablin, L. L. Putnam, K. Roberts, and L. W. Porter (Eds.), *Handbook of Organizational Communication: An Interdisciplinary Perspective* (pp. 624–78). Newbury Park, CA: Sage.

Cusick, P. A. (1981). A Study of Networks among Professional Staffs in Secondary Schools. *Educational Administration Quarterly, 17,* 114–38.

Cusick, P. A. (1987). Organizational Culture and Schools. *Educational Administration Quarterly, 23,* 3–117.

Cyert, R. M., and March, J. G. (1963). *A Behavioral Theory of the Firm.* Englewood Cliffs, NJ: Prentice Hall.

D'Aunno, T., Sutton, R. L., and Price, R. H. (1991). Isomorphism and External Support in Conflicting Institutional Environments: A Study of Drug Abuse Treatment Units. *Academy of Management Journal, 34*(3), 636–61.

Daft, R. L. (1989). *Organization Theory and Design* (3rd ed.). St. Paul, MN: West.

Daft, R. L. (1994). *Organizational Theory and Design.* St. Paul, MN: West.

Daft, R. L., Bettenhausen, K. R., and Tyler, B. B. (1993). Implications of Top Managers' Communication Choices for Strategic Decisions. In G. P. Huber and W. H. Glick (Eds.), *Organizational Change and Redesign.* New York: Oxford University Press.

Daft, R. L., and Lengel, R. H. (1984). Information Richness: A New Approach to Managerial Behavior and Organizational Design. *Research in Organizational Behavior, 6,* 191–233.

Daft, R. L., and Lengel, R. H. (1986). Organizational Information Requirements, Media Richness, and Structural Design. *Management Science, 32,* 554–71.

Dahnke, G. L., and Clatterbuck, G. W. (Eds.). (1990). *Human Communication: Theory and Research.* Belmont, CA: Wadsworth.

Dalton, M. (1959). *Men Who Manage.* New York: Wiley.

Damanpour, F. (1991). Organizational Innovation. *Academy of Management Journal, 34,* 555–91.

Dansereau, D. F. (1985). Learning Strategy Research. In J. Segal, S. Chipman, and R. Glaser (Eds.), *Thinking and Learning Skills. Volume I: Relating Instruction to Research.* Hillsdale, NJ: Erlbaum.

Darling-Hammond, L. (1984). *Beyond the Commission Reports: The Coming Crisis in Teaching.* Santa Monica, CA: Rand.

Darling-Hammond, L. (1985). Valuing Teachers: The Making of a Profession. *Teachers College Record, 87,* 205–18.

Darling-Hammond, L., and Wise, A. (1985). Beyond Standardization: State Standards and School Improvement. *Elementary School Journal, 85,* 315–36.

David, J. L., Purkey, S., and White, P. (1989). *Restructuring in Progress: Lessons from Pioneering Districts.* Washington, DC: Center for Policy Research, National Governor's Association.

Deal, T. E. (1985). The Symbolism of Effective Schools. *Elementary School Journal, 85,* 601–20.
Deal, T. E., and Celotti, L. D. (1980). How Much Influence Do (and Can) Educational Administrators Have on Classrooms? *Phi Delta Kappan, 61,* 471–73.
Deal, T. E., and Kennedy, A. A. (1982). *Corporate Cultures: The Rites and Rituals of Corporate Life.* Reading, MA: Addison-Wesley.
Deal, T. E., and Peterson, K. D. (1990). *The Principal's Role in Shaping School Culture.* Washington DC: U.S. Government Printing Office.
Deal, T. E., and Peterson, K. D. (1994). *The Leadership Paradox.* San Francisco, CA: Jossey-Bass.
Deal, T., and Wise, M. (1983). Planning, Plotting, and Playing in Education's Era of Decline. In V. Baldridge and T. Deal (Eds.), *The Dynamics of Educational Change.* San Francisco: McCutchan.
Dean, J. W., and Bowen, D. E. (1994). Management Theory and Total Quality. *Academy of Management Review, 19* (3), 392–418.
deCharms, R. (1976). *Enhancing Motivation.* New York: Irvington.
deCharms, R. (1983). Intrinsic Motivation, Peer Tutoring, and Cooperative Learning: Practical Maxims. In J. Levine and M. Wang (Eds.), *Teacher and Student Perceptions: Implications for Learning* (pp. 391–98). Hillsdale, NJ: Erlbaum.
Deci, E. and Ryan, R. M. (1985). *Intrinsic Motivation and Self-Determination in Human Behavior.* New York: Plenum.
Deci, E., Vallerand, R. J., Pelletier, L. G., and Ryan, R. M. (1991). Motivation and Education: The Self-Determination Perspective. *Educational Psychologist, 26,* 325–46.
DeFleur, M. L., Kearney, P., and Plax, T. G. (1993). *Mastering Communication in Contemporary America.* Mountain View, CA: Mayfield.
Deming, W. E. (1983). *Quality, Productivity, and Competitive Advantage.* Cambridge: Massachusetts Institute of Technology, Center for Advanced Engineering.
Deming, W. E. (1986). *Out of Crisis.* Cambridge: Massachusetts Institute of Technology, Center for Advanced Engineering.
Deming, W. E. (1993). *The New Economics for Economics, Government, Education.* Cambridge: Massachusetts Institute of Technology, Center for Advanced Engineering.
Denhardt, R. B., and Perkins, J. (1976). The Coming Death of Administrative Man. *Women in Public Administration, 36,* 379–84.
Denison, D. R. (1990). *Corporate Culture and Organizational Effectiveness.* New York: Wiley.
Denison, D. R. (1996). What Is the Difference Between Organizational Culture and Organizational Climate? A Native's Point of View on a Decade of Paradigm Wars. *The Academy of Management Review,* 3, 619–54.
Derry, S. J. (1989). Putting Learning Strategies to Work. *Educational Leadership, 47*(5) 4–10.
Derry, S. J. (1992). Beyond Symbolic Processing: Expanding Horizons for Educational Psychology. *Journal of Educational Psychology, 84,* 413–19.
Dewey, J. (1933). *How We Think.* Boston: Heath.
Dewey, J. (1938). *Experience and Education.* New York: Collier Books.
Dickson, P. H., and Weaver, K. M. (1997). Environmental Determinants and Individual-Level Moderators of Alliance Use. *Academy of Management Journal, 40*(2), 404–25.
Diebert, J. P., and Hoy, W. K. (1977). Custodial High Schools and Self-Actualization of Students. *Educational Research Quarterly, 2,* 24–31.
Dill, R. W. (1958). Environment as an Influence on Managerial Autonomy. *Administrative Science Quarterly, 2,* 409–43.
DiMaggio, P. J. (1988). Interest and Agency in Institutional Theory. In L. G. Zucker (Ed.), *Institutional Patterns in Organizations: Culture and Environments* (pp. 3–21). Cambridge, MA: Ballinger.
DiMaggio, P. J. (1995). Comments on "What Theory is Not." *Administrative Science Quarterly, 40,* 391–97.
DiMaggio, P. J., and Powell, W. W. (1983). The Iron Cage Revisited: Institutional Isomorphism and Collective Rationality in Organizational Fields. *American Sociological Review, 48,* 147–60.
DiMaggio, P. J., and Powell, W. W. (1991). The Iron Cage Revisited: Institutional Isomorphism and Collective Rationality. In W. W. Powell and P. J. DiMaggio (Eds.), *The New Institutionalism in Organizational Analysis* (pp. 41–62). Chicago: University of Chicago Press.
DiPaola, M. F. (1999). Scandal at Placido High: Coincidence or Conspiracy? *Journal of Cases in Educational Leadership* [www.ucea.org]. 2 (3).

DiPaola, M. F., and Hoy, W. K. (1994). Teacher Militancy: A Professional Check on Bureaucracy. *The Journal of Research and Development in Education, 27,* 78–82.

Donmoyer, R. B. (1999). The Continuing Quest for a Knowledge Base: 1976–1998. In J. Murphy and K. S. Louis (Eds.), *Handbook of Research on Educational Administration* (2nd ed., pp. 25–44). San Francisco: Jossey-Bass.

Donmoyer, R. B., Schurich, J., and Imber, M. L. (Eds.). (1994). *The Knowledge Base in Educational Administration: Multiple Perspectives.* Albany: SUNY Press.

Downs, C. W. (1977). *Organizational Communicator.* New York: Harper & Row.

Driscoll, J. W. (1978). Trust and Participation in Decision Making as Predictors of Satisfaction. *Academy of Management Journal, 1,* 44–56.

Driscoll, M. P. (1999). *Psychology of Learning for Instruction.* Boston: Allyn and Bacon.

Drucker, P. F. (1954). *The Practice of Management.* New York: Harper & Row.

Drucker, P. F. (1966). *The Effective Executive.* New York: Harper & Row.

Drucker, P. F. (1968). *The Age of Discontinuity.* New York: Harper & Row.

Dubin, R. (1969). *Theory Building.* New York: Free Press.

Duchastel, P. (1979). Learning Objectives and the Organization of Prose. *Journal of Educational Psychology, 71,* 100–6.

Duignan, P. (1980). Administrative Behavior of School Superintendents: A Descriptive Study. *Journal of Educational Administration, 18,* 5–26.

Duke, D. L., Showers, B. K., and Imber, M. (1980). Teachers and Shared Decision Making: The Costs and Benefits of Involvement. *Educational Administration Quarterly, 16,* 93–106.

Duncan, R. B. (1972). Characteristics of Organizational Environments and Perceived Environmental Uncertainty. *Administrative Science Quarterly, 17,* 313–27.

Duncan, R. B. (1979). What Is the Right Organizational Structure? Decision Free Analysis Provides the Answer. *Organizational Dynamics, 7,* 59–80.

Dweck, C. S., and Bempechat, J. (1983). Children's Theories on Intelligence: Consequences for Learning. In S. Paris, G. Olson, and W. Stevenson (Eds.), *Learning and Motivation in the Classroom* (pp. 239–56). Hillsdale, NJ: Erlbaum.

Dyer, W. G. (1985). The Cycle of Cultural Evolution in Organization. R. H. Kilmann, M. J. Saxton, and R. Serpa (Eds.) *Gaining Control of the Corporate Culture.* (pp. 200–30). San Francisco: Jossey-Bass.

Ebmeier, H., and Hart, A. W. (1992). The Effects of a Career-Ladder Program on School Organizational Process. *Educational Evaluation and Policy Analysis, 14*(3), 261–81.

Edmonds, R. (1979). Some Schools Work and More Can. *Social Policy, 9,* 28–32.

Einstein, A., and Infeld, L. (1938). *The Evolution of Physics.* New York: Simon & Schuster.

Elmes, M. B., and Costello, M. (1992). Mystification and Social Drama: The Hidden Side of Communication Skills Training. *Human Relations, 45*(5), 427–45.

Elmore, R. F. (1988). *Early Experiences in Restructuring Schools: Voices from the Field.* Washington, DC: Center for Policy Research, National Governor's Association.

Elsbach, K. D., and Sutton, R. I. (1992). Acquiring Organizational LegitimacyThrough Illegitimate Actions: A Marriage of Institutional and Impression Management Theories. *Academy of Management Journal, 35*(4), 699–738.

Emery, F. E., and Trist, E. L. (1965). The Causal Texture of Organization Environments. *Human Relations, 18,* 21–32.

English, F. W. (1994). *Theory in Educational Administration.* New York: HarperCollins.

English, F. W. (1998). The Cupboard Is Bare: The Postmodern Critique of Educational Administration. *Journal of School Leadership, 7,* 4–26.

Enoch, Y. (1989). Change of Values During Socialization for a Profession: An Application of the Marginal Man Theory. *Human Relations, 42,* 219–39.

Erez, M., and Zidon, I. (1984). Effects of Goal Acceptance on the Relationship of Goal Difficulty to Performance. *Journal of Applied Psychology, 69,* 69–78.

Estler, S. E. (1988). Decision Making. In N. J. Boyan (Ed.), *Handbook of Research on Educational Administration* (pp. 304–20). New York: Longman.

Etzioni, A. (1960). Two Approaches to Organizational Analysis: A Critique and Suggestion. *Administrative Science Quarterly, 5,* 257–78.

Etzioni, A. (1964). *Modern Organizations.* Englewood Cliffs, NJ: Prentice Hall.

Etzioni, A. (1967). Mixed Scanning: A Third Approach to Decision Making. *Public Administration Review, 27,* 385–92.

Etzioni, A. (1975). *A Comparative Analysis of Complex Organizations.* New York: Free Press.

Etzioni, A. (1986). Mixed Scanning Revisited. *Public Administration Review, 46,* 8–14.

Etzioni, A. (1988). *The Moral Dimension: Toward a New Economics.* New York: Free Press.

Etzioni, A. (1989). Humble Decision Making. *Harvard Business Review, 67,* 122–26.

Evans, M. G., Kiggundu, M. N., and House, R. J. (1979). A Partial Test and Extension of the Job Characteristics Model of Motivation. *Organizational Behavior and Human Performance, 24,* 354–81.

Evers, C. W., and Lakomski, G. (1991). *Knowing Educational Administration.* Oxford, England: Pergamon Press.

Farnaham-Diggory, S. (1994). Paradigms of Knowledge and Instruction. *Review of Educational Research, 64,* 463–77.

Fennell, M. L., and Alexander, J. A. (1987). Organizational Boundary Spanning in Institutionalized Environments. *Academy of Management Journal, 30*(3), 456–76.

Ferguson, K. E. (1984). *The Feminist Case Against Bureaucracy.* Philadelphia: Temple University Press.

Feynman, R. P. (1985). *Surely You're Joking Mr. Feynman.* New York: Norton.

Fiedler, F. E. (1967). *A Theory of Leadership Effectiveness.* New York: McGraw-Hill.

Fiedler, F. E. (1971). Validation and Extension of the Contingency Model of Leadership Effectiveness: A Review of Empirical Findings. *Psychological Bulletin, 76,* 128–48.

Fiedler, F. E. (1973). The Contingency Model and the Dynamics of the Leadership Process. *Advances in Experimental Social Psychology, 11,* 60–112.

Fiedler, F. E. (1984). *The Contribution of Cognitive Resources and Leader Behavior to Organizational Performance.* Organization Research Technical Report No. 84-4. Seattle: University of Washington.

Fiedler, F. E., and Chemers, M. M. (1974). *Leadership and Effective Management.* Glenview, IL: Scott, Foresman.

Fiedler, F. E., Chemers, M. M., and Mahar, L. (1976). *Improving Leadership Effectiveness: The Leader Match Concept.* New York: Wiley.

Fiedler, F. E., and Garcia, J. E. (1987). *New Approaches to Effective Leadership: Cognitive Resources and Organizational Performance.* New York: Wiley.

Finkelstein, R. (1998). The effects of organizational health and pupil control ideology on the achievement and alienation of high school students. Doctoral diss., St. John's University.

Finn, J. D., and Achilles, C. M. (1999). Tennessee's Class Size Study: Findings, Implications, and Misconceptions. *Educational Evaluation and Policy Analysis, 21*(2), 97–109.

Firestone, W. A. (1991). Merit Pay and Job Enlargement as Reforms: Incentives, Implementation, and Teacher Response. *Educational Evaluation and Policy Analysis, 13*(3), 269–88.

Firestone, W. A., and Bader, B. D. (1992). *Redesigning Teaching: Professionalism or Bureaucracy.* Albany, NY: State University of New York Press.

Firestone, W. A., and Herriott, R. E. (1981). Images of Organization and the Promotion of Change. *Research in the Sociology of Education and Socialization, 2,* 221–60.

Firestone, W. A., and Herriott, R. E. (1982). Two Images of Schools as Organizations: An Explication and Illustrative Empirical Test. *Educational Administration Quarterly, 18,* 39–60.

Firestone, W. A., and Louis, K. L. (1999). Schools as Cultures. In Murphy, J. and Louis, K. S. (Eds.), *Handbook on Research of Educational Administration* (pp. 297–322). San Francisco: Jossey-Bass.

Firestone, W. A., and Pennell, J. (1993). Teacher Commitment, Working Conditions, and Differential Incentives. *Review of Educational Research, 63*(4), 489–526.

Firestone, W. A., Rosenblum, S., Bader, B. D., and Massell, D. (1991). *Education Reform from 1983–1990: State Action and District Response.* New Brunswick, NJ: Consortium for Policy Research in Education.

Firestone, W. A., and Wilson, B. L. (1985). Using Bureaucratic and Cultural Linkages to Improve Instruction: The Principal's Contribution. *Educational Administration Quarterly, 21,* 7–31.

Flavell, J. H. (1985). *Cognitive Development* (2nd ed.). Englewood Cliffs, NJ: Prentice Hall.

Flavell, J. H., Friedrichs, A. G., and Hoyt, J. D. (1970). Developmental Changes in Memorization Processes. *Cognitive Psychology,* 1,324–40.

Flavell, J. H., Green, F. L., and Flavell, E. R. (1995). *Young Children's Knowledge about Thinking.* Monographs of the Society for Research in Child Development, 60(1) (Serial No. 243).

Flyvbjerg, B. (1998). *Personality and Power: Democracy in Practice.* Chicago: University of Chicago Press.

Follett, M. P. (1924). *Creative Experience.* London: Longman and Green.

Ford, M. E. (1992). *Motivating Humans: Goals, Emotions, and Social Agency Beliefs.* Newbury Park, CA: Sage.

Forsyth, P. B., and Hoy, W. K. (1978). Isolation and Alienation in Educational Organizations. *Educational Administration Quarterly, 14,* 80–96.

Foster, W. (1986). *Paradigms and Promises.* Buffalo, NY: Prometheus.

Foucault, M. (1984). Nietzsche, Genealogy, History. In P. Rabinow (Ed.), *The Foucault Reader.* New York: Pantheon.

Fox, S., and Feldman, G. (1988). Attention State and Critical Psychological States as Mediators Between Job Dimensions and Job Outcomes. *Human Relations, 41,* 229–45.

Frase, L. E., and Heck, G. (1992). Restructuring in the Fort McMurray Catholic Schools: A Research-Based Approach. *The Canadian School Executive, 11*(8), 3–9.

Frase, L. E., and Matheson, R. R. (1992). Restructuring: Fine-Tuning the System in Fort McMurray Catholic Schools. *Challenge, 29* (1), 16–22.

Frase, L. E., and Sorenson, L. (1992). Teacher Motivation and Satisfaction: Impact on Participatory Management. *NASSP Bulletin, 76,* 37–43.

Frederick, D., and Libby, R. (1986). Expertise and Auditors' Judgment of Conjunctive Events. *Journal of Accounting Research, 24,* 270–90.

Freeman, J. H. (1979). Going to the Well: School District Administrative Intensity and Environmental Constraint. *Administrative Science Quarterly, 24,* 119–133.

French, J. R. P., and Raven, B. H. (1968). Bases of Social Power. In D. Cartwright and A. Zander (Eds.), *Group Dynamics: Research and Theory* (pp. 259–70). New York: Harper & Row.

Friedman, R. A., and Podolny, J. (1992). Differentiation of Boundary-Spanning Roles: Labor Negotiations and Implications for Role Conflict. *Administrative Science Quarterly, 37,* 28–47.

Friesen, D., and Duignan, P. (1980). How Superintendents Spend Their Working Time. *Canadian Administrator, 19,* 1–5.

Fromm, E. (1948). *Man for Himself.* New York: Farrar & Rinehart.

Froosman, J. (1999). Stakeholder Influence Strategies. *Academy of Management Review, 24*(2), 191–205.

Frost, P. J., Moore, L. F., Louis, M. R., Lundberg, C. C., and Martin, J. (Eds.). (1991). *Reframing Organizational Culture.* Newbury Park, CA: Sage.

Fuhrman, S. H., Elmore, R. F., and Massell, D. (1993). School Reform in the United States: Putting It into Context. In S. L. Jacobson and R. Berne (Eds.), *Reforming Education: The Emerging Systemic Approach* (pp. 3–27). Thousand Oaks, CA: Corwin.

Fulk, J., and Boyd, B. (1991). Emerging Theories of Communication in Organizations. *Journal of Management, 17*(2), 407–46.

Gagné, E. D., Yekovich, C. W., and Yekovich, F. R. (1993). *The Cognitive Psychology of School Learning* (2nd ed.). New York: HarperCollins.

Gagné, R. M. (1985). The Conditions of Learning and Theory of Instruction (4th ed.). New York: Holt, Rinehart & Winston.

Galbraith, J., and Cummings, L. L. (1967). An Empirical Investigation of the Motivational Determinants of Task Performance: Interactive Effects Between Instrumentality-Valence and Motivation-Ability. *Organization Behavior and Human Performance, 2,* 237–57.

Ganz, H. J., and Hoy, W. K. (1977). Patterns of Succession of Elementary Principals and Organizational Change. *Planning and Changing, 8,* 185–96.

Gardner, D. G., and Cummings, L. L. (1988). Activation Theory and Job Design: Review and Reconceptualization. *Research in Organizational Behavior, 10,* 81–122.

Gardner, W. L., and Avolio, B. J. (1998). The Charismatic Relationship: A Dramaturgical Perspective. *Academy of Management Review, 23*(1), 32–58.

Garner, R. (1990). When Children and Adults Do Not Use Learning Strategies: Toward a Theory

of Settings. *Review of Educational Psychology, 60,* 517–30.
Garrison, J. (1995). Deweyan Pragmatism and the Epistemology of Contemporary Social Constructivism. *American Educational Research Journal, 32,* 716–41.
Gartner, W. B., and Naughton, M. J. (1988). The Deming Theory of Management. *Academy of Management Review, 17,* 138–42.
Geertz, C. (1973). *The Interpretation of Cultures.* New York: Basic.
Gerhardt, E. (1971). Staff conflict, organizational bureaucracy, and individual satisfaction in selected Kansas school districts. Doctoral diss., University of Kansas, Lawrence.
Gerth, H. H., and Mills, C. W. (Eds.). (1946). *From Max Weber: Essays in Sociology.* New York: Oxford University Press.
Getzels, J. W., and Guba, E. G. (1957). Social Behavior and the Administrative Process. *School Review, 65,* 423–41.
Getzels, J. W., Lipham, J. M., and Campbell, R. F. (1968). *Educational Administration as a Social Process: Theory, Research, and Practice.* New York: Harper & Row.
Gibson, J. L., Ivancevich, J. M., and Donnelly, J. H. (1976). *Organizations: Behavior, Structure, and Processes* (Rev. ed.). Dallas, TX: Business Publications.
Gibson, S., and Dembo, M. (1984). Teacher Efficacy: A Construct Validation. *Journal of Educational Psychology, 76* (4), 569–582.
Gigerenzer, G., Todd, P. M., and ABC Research Group. (1999). *Simple Heuristics that Make Us Smart.* New York: Oxford University Press.
Gilligan, C. (1982). *In a Different Voice: Psychological Theory and Women's Development.* Cambridge, MA: Harvard University Press.
Gilmer, B. H. (1966). *Industrial Psychology* (2nd ed.). New York: McGraw-Hill.
Gilovich, T. (1991). *How We Know What Isn't So: The Fallibility of Human Reason in Everyday Life.* New York: Free Press.
Gist, M. E. (1987). Self-Efficacy: Implications for Organizational Behavior and Human Resource Management. *Academy of Management Review, 12* (3), 472–85.
Gist, M. E., and Mitchell, T. R. (1992). Self-Efficacy: A Theoretical Analysis of Its Determinants and Malleability. *Academy of Management Review, 17* (2), 183–211.
Glaub, J. (1990). Made in Japan. *Illinois School Board Journal, 58,* 5–7.
Glisson, C., and Durick, M. (1988). Predictors of Job Satisfaction and Organizational Commitment in Human Service Organizations. *Administrative Science Quarterly, 33,* 61–81.
Goddard, R. D., Hoy, W. K., and Woolfolk Hoy, A. (in press). Collective Teacher Efficacy: Its Meaning, Measure, and Impact on Student Achievement. *American Educational Research Journal.*
Goddard, R. D., Sweetland, S. R., and Hoy, W. K. (2000). Academic Emphasis and Student Achievement in Urban Elementary Schools. Annual Meeting of the American Educational Association, New Orleans.
Goes, J. B., and Park, S. O. (1997). Interorganizational Links and Innovation: The Case of Hospital Services. *Academy of Management Journal, 40*(3), 673–96.
Goffman, E. (1957). The Characteristics of Total Institutions. *Symposium on Prevention and Social Psychiatry* (pp. 43–84). Washington, DC: Walter Reed Army Institute of Research.
Goldberg, M. A. (1975). On the Efficiency of Being Efficient. *Environment and Planning, 7,* 921–39.
Goldring, E. B., and Chen, M. (1992). Preparing Empowered Teachers for Leadership. *Planning and Changing, 23,* 3–15.
Good, T. L. (1996). Teaching Effects and Teacher Evaluation. In J. Sikula (Ed.), *Handbook of Research on Teacher Education* (pp. 617–65). New York: Macmillan.
Good, T. L. (1983). Classroom Research: A Decade of Progress. *Educational Psychologist, 18,* 127–44.
Good, T. L., and Brophy, J. E. (1986). School Effects. In M. C. Wittrock (Ed.), *Handbook of Research on Teaching* (pp. 570–602). New York: Macmillan.
Good, T. L., Grouws, D., and Ebmeier, H. (1983). *Active Mathematics Teaching.* New York: Longman.
Goodman, P. S., and Pennings, J. M. (1977). Toward a Workable Framework. In P. S. Goodman and J. M. Pennings (Eds.), *New Perspectives on Organizational Effectiveness* (pp. 147–84). San Francisco: Jossey-Bass.
Goodstein, J. D. (1994). Institutional Pressures and Strategic Responsiveness: Employer Involvement in Work-Family Issues. *Academy of Management Journal, 37*(2), 350–82.
Gordon, C. W. (1957). *The Social System of the High School.* New York: Free Press.

Gordon, G. E., and Rosen, N. (1981). Critical Factors in Leadership Succession. *Organizational Behavior and Human Performance, 27,* 227–54.

Gorsuch, R. A. (1977). An Investigation of the Relationships Between Core Job Dimensions, Psychological States, and Personal Work Outcomes among Public School Teachers (Doctoral diss., University of Maryland, 1976). *Dissertation Abstracts International, 38,* 1779A.

Gouldner, A. (1950). *Studies in Leadership.* New York: Harper.

Gouldner, A. (1954). *Patterns of Industrial Bureaucracy.* New York: Free Press.

Gouldner, A. (1958). Cosmopolitans and Locals: Toward an Analysis of Latent Social Roles—II. *Administrative Science Quarterly, 3,* 444–79.

Gouldner, A. (1959). Organizational Analysis. In R. K. Merton, L. Broom, J. Leonard, and S. Cottrell (Eds.), *Sociology Today* (pp. 400–28). New York: Basic Books.

Govindarajan, V. (1988). A Contingency Approach to Strategy Implementation at the Business-Unit Level: Integrating Administrative Mechanisms with Strategy. *Academy of Management Journal, 31,* 828–53.

Grabe, M., and Latta, R. M. (1981). Cumulative Achievement in a Mastery Instructional System: The Impact of Differences in Resultant Achievement Motivation and Persistence. *American Educational Research Journal, 18,* 7–14.

Graen, G. (1963). Instrumentality Theory of Work Motivation: Some Experimental Results and Suggested Modifications. *Journal of Applied Psychology Monograph, 53,* 1–25.

Graham, L. L. (1980). Expectancy theory as a predictor of college student grade point average, satisfaction, and participation. Doctoral diss., University of Kansas, Lawrence.

Graham, S. (1991). A Review of Attribution Theory in Achievement Contexts. *Educational Psychology Review, 3*(1), 5–39.

Graham, S., and Weiner, B. (1996). Theories and Principles of Motivation. In D. Berliner and R. Calfee (Eds.), *Handbook of Educational Psychology* (pp. 63–84). New York: Macmillan.

Grandori, A. (1984). A Prescriptive Contingency View of Organizational Decision Making. *Administrative Science Quarterly, 29,* 192–208.

Grassie, M. C., and Carss, B. W. (1973). School Structure, Leadership Quality, Teacher Satisfaction. *Educational Administration Quarterly, 9,* 15–26.

Gray, J. (1992). *Men Are from Mars, Women Are from Venus.* New York: HarperCollins.

Greenberg, J. (1993a). The Social Side of Fairness: Interpersonal and Informational Classes of Organizational Justice. In R. Cropanzano (Ed.), *Justice in the Workplace* (pp. 79–103). Hillsdale, NJ: Erlbaum.

Greenberg, J. (1993b). Stealing in the Name of Justice: Informational and Interpersonal Moderators of Theft Reactions to Underpayment Inequity. *Organizational Behavior and Human Decision Processes, 54,* 81–103.

Greenberg, J., and Baron, R. A. (1997). *Behavior in Organizations* (6th ed.). Englewood Cliffs, NJ: Prentice Hall.

Greenberg, J., and Scott, K. S. (1995). Why Do Workers Bite the Hands That Feed Them? Employee Theft as a Social Exchange Process. In B. M. Staw and L. L. Cummings (Eds.), *Research in Organizational Behavior* (Vol. 18). Greenwich, CT: JAI Press.

Greene, C. N., and Podsakoff, P. M. (1981). Effects of Withdrawal of a Performance Contingent Reward of Supervisory Influence and Power. *Academy of Management Journal, 24,* 527–42.

Greenfield, T. B., and Ribbins, P. (Eds.). (1993). *Greenfield on Educational Administration: Towards a Human Science.* London: Routledge.

Greeno, J. G., Collins, A. M., and Resnick, L. B. (1996). Cognition and Learning. In D. Berliner and R. Calfee (Eds.), *Handbook of Educational Psychology* (pp. 15–46). New York: Macmillan.

Griffeth, R. W. (1985). Moderation of the Effects of Job Enrichment by Participation: A Longitudinal Field Experiment. *Organizational Behavior and Human Decision Processes, 35,* 73–93.

Griffin, R. W. (1987). Toward an Integrated Theory of Task Design. *Research in Organizational Behavior, 9,* 79–120.

Griffin, R. W. (1991). Effects of Work Redesign on Employee Perceptions, Attitudes, and Behaviors: A Long-Term Investigation. *Academy of Management Journal, 34*(2), 425–35.

Griffiths, D. E. (1959). *Administrative Theory.* New York: Appleton-Century-Crofts.

Griffiths, D. E. (1988). Administrative Theory. In N. Boyan (Ed.), *Handbook of Research on Educational Administration* (pp. 27–51). New York: Longman.

Griffiths, D. E., Goldman, S., and McFarland, W. J. (1965). Teacher Mobility in New York City. *Educational Administration Quarterly, 1,* 15–31.
Griffiths, D. E., Stout, R. T., and Forsyth, P. B. (1988). The Preparation of Educational Administrators. In D. E. Griffiths, R. T. Stout, and P. B. Forsyth (Eds.), *Leaders for America's Schools* (pp. 284–304). Berkeley, CA: McCutchan.
Gross, E., and Etzioni, A. (1985). *Organizations in Society.* Englewood Cliffs, NJ: Prentice Hall.
Grusky, O. (1960). Administrative Succession in Formal Organizations. *Social Forces, 39,* 105–15.
Grusky, O. (1961). Corporate Size, Bureaucratization, and Managerial Succession. *American Journal of Sociology, 67,* 261–69.
Guest, R. H. (1960). *Organizational Change: The Effect of Successful Leadership.* Homewood, IL: Dorsey.
Guidette, M. R. M. (1982). The relationship between bureaucracy and staff sense of powerlessness in secondary schools. Doctoral diss., Rutgers University, New Brunswick.
Gulick, L. (1937). Notes on the Theory of Organization. In L. Gulick and L. F. Urwick (Eds.), *Papers on the Science of Administration* (pp. 3–45). New York: Institute of Public Administration, Columbia University.
Guskey, T. R. (1987). Context Variables That Affect Measures of Teacher Efficacy. *Journal of Educational Research, 81*(1), 41–47.
Guskey, T. R., and Gates, S. L. (1986). Synthesis of Research on Mastery Learning. *Education Leadership, 43,* 73–81.
Guskey, T. R., and Passaro, P. (1994). Teacher Efficacy: A Study of Construct Dimensions. *American Educational Research Journal, 31,* 627–43.
Hackman, J. R., and Oldham, G. R. (1975). Development of the Job Diagnostic Survey. *Journal of Applied Psychology, 60,* 159–70.
Hackman, J. R., and Oldham, G. R. (1976). Motivation Through the Design of Work: A Test of a Theory. *Organizational Behavior and Human Performance, 16,* 250–79.
Hackman, J. R., and Oldham, G. R. (1980). *Work Redesign.* Reading, MA: Addison-Wesley.
Hackman, J. R., and Suttle, J. L. (1977). *Improving Life at Work.* Santa Monica, CA: Goodyear.
Hackman, J. R., and Wageman, R. (1995). Total Quality Management: Empirical, Conceptual, and Practical Issues. *Administrative Science Quarterly, 40*(2), 309–42.
Hage, J. (1980). *Theories of Organizations.* New York: Wiley.
Hajnal, V. J., and Dibski, D. J. (1993). Compensation Management: Coherence Between Organization Directions and Teacher Needs. *Journal of Educational Administration, 31*(1), 53–69.
Hall, R. H. (1962). The Concept of Bureaucracy: An Empirical Assessment. *American Sociological Review, 27,* 295–308.
Hall, R. H. (1980). Effectiveness Theory and Organizational Effectiveness. *Journal of Applied Behavioral Science, 16,* 536–45.
Hall, R. H. (1987). *Organizations: Structures, Processes, and Outcomes* (4th ed.). Englewood Cliffs, NJ: Prentice Hall.
Hall, R. H. (1991). *Organizations: Structures, Processes, and Outcomes* (5th ed.). Englewood Cliffs, NJ: Prentice Hall.
Hallahan, D. P., and Kauffman, J. M. (1997). *Exceptional Learners: Introduction to Special Education* (7th ed.). Boston: Allyn and Bacon.
Haller, E. J., and Monk, D. H. (1988). New Reforms, Old Reforms, and the Consolidation of Small Rural Schools. *Educational Administration Quarterly, 24,* 470–83.
Hallinger, P., and Heck, R. H. (1996). Reassessing the Principal's Role in Effectiveness: A Review of Empirical Research, 1980–1995. *Educational Administration Quarterly, 32*(1), 5–44.
Hallinger, P., and Heck, R. H. (1998). Exploring the Principal's Contribution to School Effectiveness, 1980–1995. *School Effectiveness and School Improvement, 9*(2), 157–91.
Halpin, A. W. (1966). *Theory and Research in Administration.* New York: Macmillan.
Halpin, A. W., and Croft, D. B. (1962). *The Organization Climate of Schools.* Contract #SAE 543-8639. U.S. Office of Education, Research Project.
Halpin, A. W., and Croft, D. B. (1963). *The Organization Climate of Schools.* Chicago: Midwest Administration Center of the University of Chicago.
Halpin, A. W., and Winer, B. J. (1952). *The Leadership Behavior of the Airplane Commander.* Washington, DC: Human Resources Research Laboratories, Department of the Air Force.
Hamilton, R. J. (1985). A Framework for the Evaluation of the Effectiveness of Adjunct Questions and Objectives. *Review of Educational Research, 55,* 47–86.
Hannum, J. (1994). The organizational climate of middle schools, teacher efficacy, and student achievement. Doctoral diss., Rutgers University, New Brunswick.

Hanson, E. M. (1991). *Educational Administration and Organizational Behavior.* Boston: Allyn and Bacon.

Hanushek, E. A. (1989). The Impact of Differential Expenditures on School Performance. *Educational Researcher, 18,* 45–51, 62.

Hanushek, E. A. (1997). Assessing the Effects of School Resources on Student Performance: An Update. *Educational Evaluation and Policy Analysis, 19*(2), 141–64.

Harder, J. W. (1992). Play for Pay: Effects of Inequity in Pay-for-Performance Contest. *Administrative Science Quarterly, 37,* 321–35.

Harris, T. E. (1993). *Applied Organizational Communication.* Hillsdale, NJ: Erlbaum.

Hart, A. W. (1987). A Career Ladder's Effect on Teacher Career and Work Attitudes. *American Educational Research Journal, 24*(4), 479–503.

Hart, A. W. (1990a). Impacts of the School Social Unit on Teacher Authority During Work Redesign. *American Education Research Journal, 27*(3), 503–32.

Hart, A. W. (1990b). Work Redesign: A Review of Literature for Education Reform. *Advances in Research and Theories of School Management, 1,* 31–69.

Hart, A. W. (1993). *Principal Succession: Establishing Leadership in Schools.* Albany, NY: State University of New York Press.

Hart, A. W. (1995). Reconceiving School Leadership: Emergent Views. *The Elementary School Journal, 96,* 9–28.

Hart, A. W., and Murphy, M. J. (1990). New Teachers React to Redesigned Teacher Work. *American Journal of Education, 93*(3), 224–50.

Hart, D. K., and Scott, W. G. (1975). The Organizational Imperative. *Administration and Society, 7,* 259–85.

Hartley, M., and Hoy, W. K. (1972). Openness of School Climate and Alienation of High School Students. *California Journal of Educational Research, 23,* 17–24.

Hatry, H. P., and Greiner, J. M. (1985). *Issues and Case Studies in Teacher Incentive Plans.* Washington, DC: Urban Institute Press.

Hayes, A. E. (1973). A Reappraisal of the Halpin-Croft Model of the Organizational Climate of Schools. Annual Meeting of the American Educational Research Association, New Orleans.

Haymond, J. E. (1982). Bureaucracy, climate, and loyalty: an Aston study in education. Doctoral diss., Rutgers University, New Brunswick.

Haynes, P. A. (1974). Towards a Concept of Monitoring. *Town Planning Review, 45,* 6–29.

Heclo, H. (1978). Issue Networks and the Executive Establishment. In A. King (Ed.), *The New American Political System* (pp. 87–124). Washington, D.C.: AEI Press.

Heinz, J. P., Laumann, E. O., Nelson, R. L., and Salisbury, R. H. (1993). *The Hollow Core: Private Interests in National Policymaking.* Cambridge, MA: Harvard University Press.

Heintzman, M., Leathers, D. G., Parrot, R. L., and Adrian Bennett Cairns, I. (1993). Nonverbal Rapport-Building Behaviors' Effects on Perceptions of a Supervisor. *Management Communication Quarterly, 7*(2), 181–208.

Heller, F., Drenth, P., Koopman, P., and Rus, V. (1988). *Decisions in Organizations.* Beverly Hills, CA: Sage.

Hellriegel, D., Slocum, J. W., and Woodman, R. W. (1992). *Organizational Behavior* (6th ed.). St. Paul, MN: West.

Hemphill, J. K., and Coons, A. E. (1950). *Leader Behavior Description Questionnaire.* Columbus: Personnel Research Board, Ohio State University.

Henderson, J. E., and Hoy, W. K. (1983). Leader Authenticity: The Development and Test of an Operational Measure. *Educational and Psychological Research, 2,* 123–30.

Heneman, H. G. I., and Schwab, D. P. (1972). An Evaluation of Research on Expectancy Theory Predictions of Employee Performance. *Psychological Bulletin, 78,* 1–9.

Hernshaw, L. S. (1987). *The Shaping of Modern Psychology: A Historical Introduction from Dawn to Present Day.* London: Routledge and Kegan Paul.

Herrick, H. S. (1973). *The Relationship of Organizational Structure to Teacher Motivation in Multiunit and Non-multiunit Elementary Schools No. 322.* Madison: Wisconsin Research and Development Center for Cognitive Learning, University of Wisconsin.

Herriott, R. F., and Firestone, W. A. (1984). Two Images of Schools as Organizations: A Refinement and Elaboration. *Educational Administration Quarterly, 20,* 41–58.

Hersey, P. W. (1982). *The NASSP Assessment Center: Validation and New Development.* Reston, VA: National Association of Secondary School Principals.

Hershey, P., and Blanchard, K. H. (1977). The Management of Organizational Behavior (3rd ed.). Englewood Cliffs, NJ: Prentice Hall.

Herzberg, F. (1982). *The Managerial Choice: To Be Efficient and to Be Human* (Rev. ed.). Salt Lake City, UT: Olympus.

Herzberg, F., Mausner, B., and Snyderman, B. (1959). *The Motivation to Work.* New York: Wiley.

Hickson, D., Butler, R., Gray, D., Mallory, G., and Wilson, D. (1986). *Top Decisions: Strategic Decision Making in Organizations.* Oxford: Basil Blackwell.

Hill, P. T., and Bonan, J. (1991). *Decentralization and Accountability in Public Education.* Santa Monica, CA: Rand.

Hirschhorn, L. (1997). *Reworking Authority: Leading and Following in a Post-Modern Organization.* Cambridge, MA: MIT Press.

Hirschman, A. O. (1970). *Exit, Voice, and Loyalty: Responses to the Decline in Firms, Organizations, and States.* Cambridge, MA: Harvard University Press.

Hitt, M. A., and Ireland, R. D. (1987). Peters and Waterman Revisited: The Unended Quest for Excellence. *Academy of Management Executive, 1,* 91–98.

Hodgkinson, C. (1991). *Educational Leadership: The Moral Art.* Albany, NY: State University of New York Press.

Hoffman, A. J. (1999). Institutional Evolution and Change: Environmentalism and the U.S. Chemical Industry. *Academy of Management Journal, 42*(4), 351–71.

Hoffman, J. D. (1993).The organizational climate of middle schools and dimensions of authenticity and trust. Doctoral diss., Rutgers University, New Brunswick.

Hoffman, J. D., Sabo, D., Bliss, J., and Hoy, W. K. (1994). Building a Culture of Trust. *Journal of School Leadership, 3,* x.

Holdaway, E. A. (1978a). Facet and Overall Satisfaction of Teachers. *Educational Administration Quarterly, 14,* 30–47.

Holdaway, E. A. (1978b). *Job Satisfaction: An Alberta Report.* Edmonton: University of Alberta.

Holdaway, E. A., Newberry, J. F., Hickson, D. J., and Heron, R. P. (1975). Dimensions of Organizations in Complex Societies: The Educational Sector. *Administrative Science Quarterly, 20,* 37–58.

Holmes Group. (1986). *Tomorrow's Teachers.* East Lansing, MI: Holmes Group.

Homans, G. C. (1950). *The Human Group.* New York: Harcourt, Brace and World.

Hoppock, R. (1935). *Job Satisfaction.* New York: Harper.

House, R. J. (1971). A Path-Goal Theory of Leadership Effectiveness. *Administrative Science Quarterly, 16,* 321–38.

House, R. J. (1973). A Path-Goal Theory of Leader Effectiveness. In E.A. Fleishman and J. G. Hunt (Eds.), *Current Developments in the Study of Leadership* (pp. 141–77). Carbondale, IL: Southern Illinois University Press.

House, R. J. (1977). A 1976 Theory of Charismatic Leadership. In J. G. Hunt and L. L. Larson (Eds.), *Leadership: The Cutting Edge* (pp. 189–207). Carbondale, IL: Southern Illinois University Press.

House, R. J. (1988). Leadership Research: Some Forgotten, Ignored, or Overlooked Findings. In J. G. Hunt, B. R. Baliga, H. P. Dachler, and C.A. Schriesheim (Eds.), *Emerging Leadership Vistas* (pp. 245–60). Lexington, MA: Lexington.

House, R. J. (1996). Path-Goal Theory of Leadership: Lessons, Legacy, and a Reformulated Theory. *Leadership Quarterly, 3*(2), 323–52.

House, R. J., and Baetz, M. L. (1979). Leadership: Some Empirical Generalizations and New Research Directions. *Research in Organizational Behavior, 1,* 341–423.

House, R. J., and Howell, J. M. (1992). Personality and Charismatic Leadership. *Leadership Quarterly, 3*(2), 81–108.

House, R. J., and Mitchell, T. R. (1974). Path-Goal Theory and Leadership. *Journal of Contemporary Business, 3,* 81–97.

House, R. J., Spangler, W. D., and Woycke, J. (1991). Personality and Charisma in the U.S. Presidency: A Psychological Theory of Leader Effectiveness. *Administrative Science Quarterly, 36,* 364–96.

Howell, J. M., and Avolio, B. J. (1993). Transformational Leadership, Transactional Leadership, Locus of Control, and Support of Innovation: Key Predictors of Consolidated Business-Unit Performance. *Journal of Applied Psychology, 78*(6), 891–902.

Howell, J. M., and Frost, P. J. (1989). A Laboratory Study of Charismatic Leadership. *Organizational Behavior and Human Decision Processes, 43,* 243–69.

Howell, J. P. (1997). Substitutes for Leadership: Their Meaning and Measurement—An Historical Assessment. *Leadership Quarterly, 8*(2), 113–16.

Hoy, W. K. (1967). Organizational Socialization: The Student Teacher and Pupil Control Ideology. *Journal of Educational Research, 61,* 153–55.

Hoy, W. K. (1968). Pupil Control and Organizational Socialization: The Influence of Experience on the Beginning Teacher. *School Review, 76,* 312–23.

Hoy, W. K. (1969). Pupil Control Ideology and Organizational Socialization: A Further Examination of the Influence of Experience on the Beginning Teacher. *School Review, 77,* 257–65.

Hoy, W. K. (1972). Dimensions of Student Alienation and Characteristics of Public High Schools. *Interchange, 3,* 38–51.

Hoy, W. K. (1978). Scientific Research in Educational Administration. *Educational Administration Quarterly, 14,* 1–12.

Hoy, W. K. (1990). Organizational Climate and Culture: A Conceptual Analysis of the School Workplace. *Journal of Educational and Psychological Consultation, 1,* 149–68.

Hoy, W. K (1996). Science and Theory in the Practice of Educational Administration: A Pragmatic Perspective. *Educational Administration Quarterly, 32,* 366–78.

Hoy, W. K. (1997). A Few Quibbles with Denison, *The Academy of Management Review, 22*(1), 13–14.

Hoy, W. K., and Aho, F. (1973). Patterns of Succession of High School Principals and Organizational Change. *Planning and Changing, 2,* 82–88.

Hoy, W. K., and Appleberry, J. B. (1970). Teacher Principal Relationships in "Humanistic" and "Custodial" Elementary Schools. *Journal of Experimental Education, 39,* 27–31.

Hoy, W. K., Astuto, T. A., and Forsyth, P. B. (Eds.). (1994). *Educational Administration: The UCEA Document Base.* New York: McGraw-Hill Primus.

Hoy, W. K., Blazovsky, R., and Newland, W. (1980). Organizational Structure and Alienation from Work. Annual Meeting of the American Educational Research Association, Boston.

Hoy, W. K., Blazovsky, R., and Newland, W. (1983). Bureaucracy and Alienation: A Comparative Analysis. *The Journal of Educational Administration, 21,* 109–21.

Hoy, W. K., and Brown, B. L. (1988). Leadership Behavior of Principals and the Zone of Acceptance of Elementary Teachers. *Journal of Educational Administration, 26,* 23–39.

Hoy, W. K., and Clover, S. I. R. (1986). Elementary School Climate: A Revision of the OCDQ. *Educational Administration Quarterly, 22,* 93–110.

Hoy, W. K., and Feldman, J. (1987). Organizational Health. The Concept and Its Measure. *Journal of Research and Development in Education, 20,* 30–38.

Hoy, W. K., and Feldman, J. (1999). Organizational Health Profiles for High Schools. In J. Freiberg (Ed.)., *School Climate: Measuring, Sustaining, and Improving.* Philadelphia: Falmer Press.

Hoy, W. K., and Ferguson, J. (1985). A Theoretical Framework and Exploration of Organizational Effectiveness in Schools. *Educational Administration Quarterly, 21,* 117–34.

Hoy, W. K., and Forsyth, P. B. (1986). *Effective Supervision: Theory into Practice.* New York: Random House.

Hoy, W. K., and Forsyth, P. B. (1987). Beyond Clinical Supervision: A Classroom Performance Model. *Planning and Changing, 18,* 210–23.

Hoy, W. K., and Hannum, J. (1997). Middle School Climate: An Empirical Assessment of Organizational Health and Student Achievement. *Educational Administration Quarterly, 33,* 290–311.

Hoy, W. K., Hannum, J., and Tschannen-Moran, M. (1998). Organizational Climate and Student Achievement: A Parsimonious and Longitudinal View. *Journal of School Leadership, 8,* 1–22.

Hoy, W. K., and Henderson, J. E. (1983). Principal Authenticity, School Climate, and Pupil-Control Orientation. *Alberta Journal of Educational Research, 2,* 123–30.

Hoy, W. K., Hoffman, J., Sabo, D., and Bliss, J. (1994). *The Organizational Climate of Middle Schools: The Development and Test of the OCDQ-RM.* Journal of Educational Administration, 34, 41–59.

Hoy, W. K., and Miskel, C. G. (1991). *Educational Administration: Theory, Research, and Practice* (4th ed.). New York: McGraw-Hill.

Hoy, W. K., Newland, W., and Blazovsky, R. (1977). Subordinate Loyalty to Superior, Esprit, and Aspects of Bureaucratic Structure. *Educational Administration Quarterly, 13,* 71–85.

Hoy, W. K., and Rees, R. (1974). Subordinate Loyalty to Immediate Superior: A Neglected Concept in the Study of Educational Administration. *Sociology of Education, 47,* 268–86.

Hoy, W. K., and Rees, R. (1977). The Bureaucratic Socialization of Student Teachers. *Journal of Teacher Education, 28,* 23–26.

Hoy, W. K., and Sabo, D. (1998). *Quality Middle Schools: Open and Healthy.* Thousand Oaks, CA: Corwin Press.

Hoy, W. K., and Sousa, D. (1984). Delegation: The Neglected Aspect of Participation in Decision

Making. *Alberta Journal of Educational Research, 30,* 320–31.
Hoy, W. K., and Sweetland, S. R. (2000). Bureaucracies that work: Enabling, not coercive. Unpublished research paper, The Ohio State University.
Hoy, W. K., and Tarter, C. J. (1990). Organizational climate school health and student achievement: a comparative analysis. Unpublished paper.
Hoy, W. K., and Tarter, C. J. (1992). Collaborative Decision Making: Empowering Teachers. *Canadian Administration, 32,* 1–9.
Hoy, W. K., and Tarter, C. J. (1993a). A Normative Model of Shared Decision Making. *Journal of Educational Administration, 31,* 4–19.
Hoy, W. K., and Tarter, C. J. (1993b). Crafting Strategies, Not Contriving Solutions: A Response to Downey and Knight's Observations on Shared Decision Making. *Canadian Administration, 32,* 1–6.
Hoy, W. K., and Tarter, C. J. (1995). *Administrators Solving the Problems of Practice: Decision-Making Concepts, Cases, and Consequences.* Boston: Allyn and Bacon.
Hoy, W. K., and Tarter, C. J. (1997a). *The Road to Open and Healthy Schools: A Handbook for Change, Secondary Edition.* Thousand Oaks, CA: Corwin Press.
Hoy, W. K., and Tarter, C. J. (1997b). *The Road to Open and Healthy Schools: A Handbook for Change, Elementary Edition.* Thousand Oaks, CA: Corwin Press.
Hoy, W. K., Tarter, C. J., and Kottkamp, R. (1991). *Open Schools/Healthy Schools: Measuring Organizational Climate.* Beverly Hills, CA: Sage.
Hoy, W. K., Tarter, C. J., and Wiskowskie, L. (1992). Faculty Trust in Colleagues: Linking the Principal with School Effectiveness. *Journal of Research and Development in Education, 26*(1), 38–58.
Hoy, W. K., and Williams, L. B. (1971). Loyalty to Immediate Superior at Alternate Levels in Public Schools. *Educational Administration Quarterly, 7,* 1–11.
Hoy, W. K., and Woolfolk, A. E. (1989). Socialization of Student Teachers. Annual Meeting of the American Educational Research Association, San Francisco.
Hoy, W. K., and Woolfolk, A. E. (1990). Socialization of Student Teachers. *American Educational Research Journal, 27*(2), 279–300.
Hoy, W. K., and Woolfolk, A. E. (1993). Teachers' Sense of Efficacy and the Organizational Health of Schools. *Elementary School Journal, 93*(4), 355–72.
Huber, G. P. (1996). Organizational Learning: The Contributing Processes and Literatures. In Cohen, M. D., and Sproull, L. S. (Eds.). *Organizational Learning* (pp. 124–62). Thousand Oaks, CA: Sage.
Huber, G. P., and Daft, R. L. (1987). The Information Environments of Organizations. In F. M. Jablin, L. L. Putnam, K. Roberts, and L. W. Porter (Eds.), *Handbook of Organizational Communication: An Interdisciplinary Perspective* (pp. 130–64). Newbury Park, CA: Sage.
Huber, V. L. (1981). The Sources, Uses, and Conservation of Managerial Power. *Personnel, 51,* 66–67.
Hunt, J. G. (1991). *Leadership: A New Synthesis.* Newbury Park, CA: Sage.
Hunt, J. G. (1999). Transformational/Charismatic Leadership's Transformation of the Field: An Historical Essay. *Leadership Quarterly, 10*(2), 129–44.
Hunter, M. (1982). *Mastery Teaching.* El Segundo, CA: TIP Publications.
Huseman, R. C., and Miles, E. W. (1988). Organizational Communication in the Information Age: Implications of Computer-Based Systems. *Journal of Management, 14,* 181–204.
Iannaccone, L. (1962). Informal Organization of School Systems. In D. Griffiths, D. L. Clark, R. Wynn, and L. Iannaccone (Eds.), *Organizing Schools for Effective Education* (pp. 227–93). Danville, IL: Interstate.
Imber, M. (1983). Increased Decision Making Involvement for Teachers: Ethical and Practical Considerations. *Journal of Educational Thought, 17,* 36–42.
Imber, M., and Duke, D. L. (1984). Teacher Participation in School Decision Making: A Framework for Research. *Journal of Educational Administration, 22,* 24–34.
Immegart, G. L. (1988). Leadership and Leader Behavior. In N. J. Boyan (Ed.), *Handbook of Research on Educational Administration* (pp. 259–77). New York: Longman.
Ingersoll, R. M. (1993). Loosely Coupled Organizations Revisited. *Research in the Sociology of Organizations, 11,* 81–112.

Irwin, J. W. (1991). *Teaching Reading Comprehension* (2nd ed.). Boston: Allyn and Bacon.

Isaacson, G. (1983). Leadership behavior and loyalty. Doctoral diss., Rutgers University, New Brunswick.

Isherwood, G., and Hoy, W. K. (1973). Bureaucracy, Powerlessness, and Teacher Work Values. *Journal of Educational Administration, 9,* 124–38.

Ishikawa, K. (1985). *What Is Total Quality Control? The Japanese Way.* Englewood Cliffs, NJ: Prentice Hall.

Ivey, A. E., and Ivey, M. B. (1999). *Intentional Interviewing and Counseling: Facilitating Client Development in a Multicultural Society.* Pacific Grove, CA: Brooks/Cole Publishing.

Jablin, F. M. (1980). Organizational Communication Theory and Research: An Overview of Communication Climate and Network Research. *Communication Yearbook, 4,* 327–47.

Jablin, F. M. (1987). Formal Organization Structure. In F. M. Jablin, L. L. Putman, K. Roberts, and L. W. Porter (Eds.), *Handbook of Organizational Communication: An Interdisciplinary Perspective* (pp. 389–419). Newbury Park, CA: Sage.

Jablin, F. M., Putnam, L. L., Roberts, K., and Porter, L. W. (Eds.). (1987). *Handbook of Organizational Communication: An Interdisciplinary Perspective.* Newbury Park, CA: Sage.

Jackson, J. (1990, January 28). Interview with Jesse Jackson. *Parade,* 5.

Jackson, S., and Schuler, R. S. (1985). A Meta-Analysis and Conceptual Critique of Research on Role Ambiguity and Role Conflict in Work Settings. *Organizational Behavior and Human Decision Processes, 36,* 17–78.

James, W. (1983). *Talks to Teachers on Psychology and to Students on Some of Life's Ideals.* Cambridge, MA: Harvard University Press.

Jamison, D., Suppes, P., and Wells, S. (1974). The Effectiveness of Alternative Instructional Media: A Survey. *Review of Educational Research, 44,* 1–67.

Janis, I. L. (1982). *Groupthink: Psychological Studies of Policy Decisions and Fiascoes.* Boston: Houghton Mifflin.

Janis, I. L. (1985). Sources of Error in Strategic Decision Making. In J. M. Pennings (Ed.), *Organizational Strategy and Change* (pp. 157–97). San Francisco: Jossey-Bass.

Janis, I. L., and Mann, L. (1977). *Decision Making: A Psychological Analysis of Conflict, Choice, and Commitment.* New York: Free Press.

Jepperson, R. L. (1991). Institutions, Institutional Effects, and Institutionalism. In W. W. Powell and P. J. DiMaggio (Eds.), *The New Institutionalism in Organizational Analysis* (pp. 164–82). Chicago: University of Chicago Press.

Johns, G., Xie, J. L., and Fang, Y. (1992). Mediating and Moderating Effects in Job Design. *Journal of Management, 18*(4), 657–76.

Johnson, S. M. (1986). Incentives for Teachers: What Motivates, What Matters. *Educational Administration Quarterly, 22,* 54–79.

Juran, J. A. M. (1989). *Juran on Leadership and Quality.* New York: Free Press.

Jurden, F. H. (1995). Individual Differences in Working Memory and Complex Cognition. *Journal of Educational Psychology, 87,* 93–102.

Jurkovich, R. (1974). A Core Typology of Organizational Environments. *Administrative Science Quarterly, 19,* 380–94.

Kagan, S. (1994). *Cooperative Learning.* San Juan Capistrano, CA: Kagan Cooperative Learning.

Kahneman, D., Solvic, P., and Tversky, A. (1982). *Judgment under Uncertainty: Heuristics and Biases.* Cambridge, England: Cambridge University Press.

Kahneman, D., and Tversky, A. (1973). On the Psychology of Prediction. *Psychological Review,* 80, 251–73.

Kakabadse, A. (1986). Organizational Alienation and Job Climate. *Small Group Behavior, 17,* 458–71.

Kanfer, R. (1990). Motivation Theory and Industrial Organizational Psychology. In M. D. Dunnette and L. M. Hough (Eds.), *Handbook of Industrial and Organizational Psychology* (pp. 75–170). Palo Alto, CA: Consulting Psychologists Press.

Kanigel, R. (1997). *The One Best Way.* New York: Viking.

Kanner, L. (1974). Machiavellianism and the secondary schools: teacher-principal relations. Doctoral diss., Rutgers University, New Brunswick.

Kant, I. (1794). *Kritik der Reinen Vernunft* [Critique of Pure Reason] (4th ed.). Riga, Latvia: J. R. Hartknoch.

Kanter, R. (1977). *Men and Women of the Corporation.* New York: Basic Books.

Kanter, R., and Brinkerhoff, D. (1981). Organizational Performance: Recent Developments in Measurement. *Annual Review of Sociology, 7,* 321–49.

Karper, J. H., and Boyd, W. L. (1988). Interest Groups and the Changing Environment of State Educational Policymaking: Developments in Pennsylvania. *Educational Administration Quarterly, 24,* 21–54.

Katz, D., and Kahn, R. L. (1966). *The Social Psychology of Organizations.* New York: Wiley.

Katz, D., and Kahn, R. L. (1978). *The Social Psychology of Organizations* (2nd ed.). New York: Wiley.

Katzell, R. A., and Thompson, D. E. (1990). Work Motivation: Theory and Practice. *American Psychologist, 45*(2), 144–53.

Keeley, M. (1984). Impartiality and Participant-Interest Theories of Organizational Effectiveness. *Administrative Science Quarterly, 29,* 1–25.

Keith, N. V. (1996). A Critical Perspective on Teacher Participation in Urban Schools. *Educational Administration Quarterly, 32,* 45–79.

Kelly, J. (1992). Does Job Re-Design Theory Explain Job Re-Design Outcomes? *Human Relations, 45* (8), 753–74.

Kelsey, J. G. T. (1973). Conceptualization and instrumentation for the comparative study of secondary school structure and operation. Doctoral. diss., University of Alberta, Edmonton.

Kerlinger, F. N. (1986). *Foundations of Behavioral Research* (3rd ed.). New York: Holt, Rinehart & Winston.

Kerr, S., and Jermier, J. M. (1978). Substitutes for Leadership: Their Meaning and Measurement. *Organizational Behavior and Human Performance, 22,* 375–403.

Kets de Vries, M. F. R., and Miller, D. (1986). Personality, Culture, and Organization. *Academy Management Review, 11,* 266–79.

Kiewra, K. A. (1985). Investigating Notetaking and Review: A Depth of Processing Alternatives. *Educational Psychologist, 20,* 23–32.

Kiewra, K. A. (1988). Cognitive Aspects of Autonomous Note Taking: Control Processes, Learning Strategies, and Prior Knowledge. *Educational Psychologist, 23,* 39–56.

Kiewra, K. A. (1989). A Review of Note-taking: The Encoding Storage Paradigm and Beyond. *Educational Psychology Review, 1,* 147–72.

Kiggundu, M. N. (1980). An Empirical Test of the Theory of Job Design Using Multiple Job Ratings. *Human Relations, 33,* 339–51.

Kilmann, R. H. (1984). *Beyond the Quick Fix.* San Francisco: Jossey-Bass.

Kilmann, R. H., and Saxton, M. J. (1983). *The Kilmann-Saxton Culture Gap Survey.* Pittsburgh, PA: Organizational Design Consultant.

Kilmann, R. H., Saxton, M. J., and Serpa, R. (1985). *Gaining Control of the Corporate Culture.* San Francisco: Jossey-Bass.

Kirchhoff, B. A. (1977). Organization Effectiveness Measurement and Policy Research. *Academy of Management Review, 2,* 347–55.

Kmetz, J. T., and Willower, D. J. (1982). Elementary School Principals' Work Behavior. *Educational Administration Quarterly, 18,* 62–78.

Knapp, M. L. (1972). *Nonverbal Communication in Human Interaction.* New York: Holt, Rinehart, & Winston.

Koberg, C. S., and Ungson, G. R. (1987). The Effects of Environmental Uncertainty and Dependence on Organizational Structure and Performance: A Comparative Study. *Journal of Management, 13,* 725–37.

Kofman, F., and Senge, P. M. (1993). Communities of Commitment: The Heart of Learning Organizations. *Organizational Dynamics, 22,* 5–23.

Kolesar, H. (1967). An empirical study of client alienation in the bureaucratic organization. Doctoral diss., University of Alberta, Edmonton.

Kollman, K. (1998). *Outside Lobbying: Public Opinion and Interest Group Strategies.* Princeton, NJ: Princeton University Press.

Kondrasuk, J. N. (1981). Studies in MBO Effectiveness. *Academy of Management Review, 6,* 419–30.

Kotter, J. P. (1978). Power, Success, and Organizational Effectiveness. *Organizational Dynamics, 6,* 27–40.

Kotter, J. P. (1982). *The General Managers.* New York: Free Press.

Kotter, J. P. (1985). *Power and Influences: Beyond Formal Authority.* New York: Free Press.

Kotter, J. P. (1990). *A Force for Change: How Leadership Differs from Management.* New York: Free Press.

Kottkamp, R. B., and Mulhern, J. A. (1987). Teacher Expectance Motivation, Open to Closed Climate and Pupil Control Ideology in High Schools. *Journal of Research and Development in Education, 20,* 9–18.

Kottkamp, R. B., Mulhern, J., and Hoy, W. K. (1987). Secondary School Climate: A Revision of the OCDQ. *Educational Administration Quarterly, 23,* 31–48.

Kraatz, M. S. (1998). Learning by Association? Interorganizational Networks and Adaptation to Environmental Change. *Academy of Management Journal, 41*(6), 621–43.

Krone, K. J., Jablin, F. M., and Putnam, L. L. (1987). Communication Theory and Organizational Communication: Multiple Perspectives. In F. M. Jablin, L. L. Putnam, K. Roberts, and L. W. Porter (Eds.), *Handbook of Organizational Communication: An Interdisciplinary Perspective* (pp. 18–40). Newbury Park, CA: Sage.

Kuhlman, E., and Hoy, W. K. (1974). The Socialization of Professionals into Bureaucracies: The Beginning Teacher in the School. *Journal of Educational Administration, 8,* 18–27.

Kuhnert, K. W., and Lewis, P. (1987). Transactional and Transformational Leadership: A Constructive/Developmental Analysis. *Academy of Management Review, 12*(4), 648–57.

Kulik, C. T., and Ambrose, M. L. (1992). Personal and Situational Determinants of Referent Choice. *Academy Management Review, 17,* 212–37.

Kulik, C. L., Kulik, J. A., and Bangert-Drowns, R. L.(1990). Effectiveness of Mastery Learning Programs: A Meta-analysis. *Review of Educational Research, 60,* 265–99.

Kunz, D., and Hoy, W. K. (1976). Leader Behavior of Principals and the Professional Zone of Acceptance of Teachers. *Educational Administration Quarterly, 12,* 49–64.

Landy, F. J., and Becker, W. S. (1987). Motivation Theory Reconsidered. *Research in Organizational Behavior, 9,* 1–38.

Larson, J. R. J. (1989). The Dynamic Interplay Between Employee's Feedback-Seeking Strategies and Supervisors' Delivery of Performance Feedback. *Academy of Management Review, 14,* 408–22.

Latham, G., and Baldes, J. (1975). The Practical Significance of Locke's Theory of Goal Setting. *Journal of Applied Psychology, 60,* 122–24.

Latham, G. P., and Locke, E. A. (1991). Self-Regulation Through Goal Setting. *Organizational Behavior and Human Decision Processes, 50,* 212–47.

Latham, G. P., and Yukl, G. A. (1975). A Review of Research on the Application of Goal Setting in Organizations. *Academy of Management Journal, 18,* 824–45.

Lau, L. J. (1978). Education Production Functions. Conference on School Organization and Effects, National Institute of Education, Washington, DC.

Lave, J. (1988). *Cognition in Practice: Mind, Mathematics, and Culture in Everyday Life.* New York: Cambridge University Press.

Lave, J., and Wenger, E. (1991). *Situated Learning: Legitimate Peripheral Participation.* Cambridge, MA: Cambridge University Press.

Lawler, E. E., III. (1973). *Motivation in Work Organizations.* Monterey, CA: Brooks/Cole.

Lawler, E. E., III. (1985). Education, Management Style, and Organizational Effectiveness. *Personnel Psychology, 38,* 1–26.

Lawler, E. E., III. (1992). *The Ultimate Advantage.* San Francisco, CA: Jossey-Bass.

Lawler, E. E., III. (1994). Total Quality Management and Employee Involvement: Are They Compatible? *Academy of Management Executive, 8*(1), 68–76.

Lawrence, P. R., and Lorsch, J. W. (1967). *Organization and Environment: Managing Differentiation and Integration.* Boston: Graduate School of Business Administration, Harvard University.

Leavitt, H. J., Dill, W. R., and Eyring, H. B. (1973). *The Organizational World.* New York: Harcourt Brace Jovanovich.

Lee, V. E., Bryk, A. S., and Smith, J. B. (1993). The Organization of Effective Secondary Schools. *Review of Research in Education, 19,* 171–267.

Lefkowitz, J., Somers, M. J., and Weinberg, K. (1984). The Role of Need Level and/or Need Salience as Moderators of the Relationship between Need Satisfaction and Work Alienation-Involvement. *Journal of Vocational Behavior, 24,* 142–58.

Leithwood, K. (1994). Leadership for School Restructuring. *Educational Administration Quarterly, 30*(4), 498–518.

Leithwood, K., and Duke, D. L. (1999). A Century's Quest to Understand School Leadership. In J. Murphy and K. S. Louis (Eds.), *Handbook of Research on Educational Administration* (pp. 45–72). San Francisco, CA: Jossey-Bass.

Leithwood, K., Jantzi, D., and Steinbach, R. (1998). Leadership and Other Conditions Which Foster Organizational Learning in Schools. In K. Leithwood and K. S. Louis (Eds.), *Organizational Learning in Schools* (pp. 67–90). Lisse: Swets and Zeitlinger.

Leithwood, K., and Louis, K. S. (1998). *Organizational Learning in Schools.* Lisse: Swets and Zeitlinger.

Leonard, J. F. (1991). Applying Deming's Principles to Our Schools. *South Carolina Business, 11,* 82–87.

Lepper, M. R., and Greene, D. (1978). *The Hidden Costs of Rewards: New Perspectives on the Psychology of Human Motivation.* Hillsdale, NJ: Erlbaum.

Level, D. A., Jr. (1972). Communication Effectiveness: Method and Situation. *Journal of Business Communication, 9,* 19–25.

Leverette, B. B. (1984). Professional zone of acceptance: Its relation to the leader behavior of principals and socio-psychological characteristics of teaching. Doctoral diss., Rutgers University, New Brunswick.

Levin, J. R. (1985). Educational Applications of Mnemonic Pictures: Possibilities Beyond Your Wildest Imagination. In A. A. Sheikh (Ed.), *Imagery in the Educational Process.* Farmingdale, NY: Baywood.

Levitt, B. L., and March, J. G. (1996). In Cohen, M. D., and Sproull, L. S. (Eds.), *Organizational Learning* (pp. 516–40). Thousand Oaks, CA: Sage.

Levitt, B. L., and Nass, C. (1989). The Lid on the Garbage Can: Institutional Constraints on Decision Making in The Technical Core of College-Text Publishers. *Administrative Science Quarterly, 34,* 190–207.

Lewis, P. V. (1975). *Organizational Communications: The Essence of Effective Management.* Columbus, OH: Grid.

Liao, Y. M. (1994). School climate and effectiveness in Taiwan's secondary schools. Doctoral diss., St. John's University, Queens.

Licata, J. W., and Hack, W. G. (1980). School Administrator Grapevine Structure. *Educational Administration Quarterly, 16,* 82–99.

Lieberson, S., and O'Connor, J. F. (1972). Leadership and Organizational Performance: A Study of Large Corporations. *American Sociological Review, 37,* 117–30.

Lindblom, C. E. (1959). The Science of Muddling Through. *Public Administrative Review, 19,* 79–99.

Lindblom, C. E. (1965). *The Intelligence of Democracy: Decision Making Through Mutual Adjustment.* New York: Free Press.

Lindblom, C. E. (1968). *The Policy-Making Process.* Englewood Cliffs, NJ: Prentice Hall.

Lindblom, C. E. (1980). *The Policy-Making Process* (2nd ed.). Englewood Cliffs: Prentice Hall.

Lindblom, C. E., and Cohen, D. K. (1979). *Usable Knowledge: Social Science and Social Problem Solving.* New Haven, CT: Yale University Press.

Lipham, J. A. (1988). Getzel's Model in Educational Administration. In N. J. Boyan (Ed.), *Handbook of Research on Educational Administration* (pp. 171–84). New York: Longman.

Lipham, J. A., and Francke, D. C. (1966). Nonverbal Behavior of Administrators. *Educational Administration Quarterly, 2,* 101–9.

Litchfield, E. H. (1956). Notes on a General Theory of Administration. *Administrative Science Quarterly, 1,* 3–29.

Litwin, G. H., and Stringer, R. A., Jr. (1968). *Motivation and Organizational Climate.* Boston: Harvard University Press.

Locke, E. A. (1968). Toward a Theory of Task Motivation and Incentives. *Organizational Behavior and Human Performance, 3,* 157–89.

Locke, E. A. (1976).The Nature and Causes of Job Satisfaction. In M. D. Dunnette (Ed.), *Handbook of Industrial and Organizational Psychology* (pp. 1297–349). Chicago: Rand McNally.

Locke, E. A. (1991). The Motivation Sequence, the Motivation Hub, and the Motivation Core. *Organizational Behavior and Human Decision Processes, 50,* 288–99.

Locke, E. A., and Latham, G. P. (1984). *Goal Setting: A Motivational Technique That Works.* Englewood Cliffs, NJ: Prentice Hall.

Locke, E. A., and Latham, G. P. (1990). *A Theory of Goal Setting and Task Performance.* Englewood Cliffs, NJ: Prentice Hall.

Locke, E. A., Latham, G. P., and Erez, M. (1988). The Determinants of Goal Commitment. *Academy of Management Review, 13,* 23–39.

Locke, E. A., and Schweiger, D. M. (1979). Participation in Decision Making: One More Look. *Research in Organizational Behavior, 1,* 265–339.

Logan, C. S., Ellet, C. D., and Licata, J. W. (1993). Structural Coupling, Robustness, and Effectiveness of Schools. *Journal of Educational Administration, 31*(1), 19–32.

Lorsch, J. W. (1985). Strategic Myopia: Culture as an Invisible Barrier to Change. In R. H. Kilmann, M. J. Saxton, and R. Serpa (Eds.), *Gaining Control of the Corporate Culture* (pp. 84–102). San Francisco: Jossey-Bass.

Lortie, D. C. (1969). The Balance of Control and Autonomy in Elementary School Teaching. In A. Etzioni (Ed.), *The Semiprofessions and Their Organization* (pp. 1–53). New York: Free Press.

Lortie, D. C. (1975). *Schoolteacher: A Sociological Study.* Chicago: University of Chicago Press.

Louis, K. S., and Kruse, S. D. (1998). Creating Community in Reform: Images of Organizational Learning in Inner-city Schools. In K. Leithwood and K. S. Louis (Eds.), *Organizational Learning in Schools* (pp. 17–45). Lisse: Swets and Zeitlinger.

Lugg, C. A., and Boyd, W. L. (1993). Leadership for Collaboration: Reducing Risk and Fostering Resilience. *Phi Delta Kappan, 75,* 252–58.

Lunenburg, F. C. (1983). Pupil Control Ideology and Self-Concept as a Learner. *Educational Research Quarterly, 8,* 33–39.

Lunenburg, F. C., and Schmidt, L. J. (1989). Pupil Control Ideology, Pupil Control Behavior, and Quality of School Life. *Journal of Research and Development in Education, 22,* 35–44.

Machiavelli, N. (1984). *The Prince.* Harmondsworth: Penguin.

MacKay, D. (1964). An empirical study of bureaucratic dimensions and their relations to other characteristics of school organization. Doctoral diss., University of Alberta, Edmonton.

MacKensie, D. E. (1983). Research for School Improvement: An Appraisal and Some Recent Trends. *Educational Research, 12,* 5–17.

MacKinnon, J. D., and Brown, M. E. (1994). Inclusion in Secondary Schools: An Analysis of School Structure Based on Teachers' Images of Change. *Educational Administration Quarterly, 30,* 126–52.

Madaus, G. F., Airasian, P. W., and Kellaghan, T. (1980). *School Effectiveness: A Reassessment of the Evidence.* New York: McGraw-Hill.

Maeroff, G. I. (1988). *The Empowerment of Teachers: Overcoming the Crisis of Confidence.* New York: Teachers College Press.

Mager, R. (1975). *Preparing Instructional Objectives* (2nd ed.). Palo Alto, CA: Fearon.

Malen, B. (1993). Enacting site based management: a political utilities analysis. Unpublished paper, College of Education, University of Washington.

Malen, B., Murphy, M. J., and Hart, A. W. (1988). Restructuring Teacher Compensation Systems: An Analysis of Three Incentive Strategies. In K. Alexander and D. H. Monk (Eds.), *Eighth Annual Yearbook of the American Educational Finance Association* (pp. 91–142). Cambridge, MA: Ballinger.

Malen, B., and Ogawa, R. T. (1992). Site-Based Management: Disconcerting Policy Issues, Critical Policy, and Choices. In J. J. Lane and E. G. Epps (Eds.), *Restructuring the Schools: Problems and Prospects* (pp. 185–206). Berkeley, CA: McCutchan.

Malen, B., Ogawa, R. T., and Kranz, J. (1990). What Do We Know About School-Based Management? A Case Study of the Literature—A Call for Research. In W. H. Clune and J. F. White (Eds.), *Choice and Control in American Education. Volume 2: The Practice of Choice, Decentralization and School Restructuring* (pp. 289–342). New York: Falmer Press.

Mann, R. D. (1959). A Review of the Relationships Between Personality and Performance. *Psychological Bulletin, 56,* 241–70.

Manning, P. K. (1992). *Organizational Communication.* New York: Aldine De Gruyer.

March, J. G. (1981). Footnotes to Organizational Change. *Administrative Science Quarterly, 26,* 563–77.

March, J. G. (1982). Emerging Developments in the Study of Higher Education. *Review of Higher Education, 6,* 1–18.

March, J. G. (1988). *Decisions and Organizations.* Oxford: Blackwell.

March, J. G. (1994). *A Primer of Decision Making.* New York: Free Press.

March, J. G., and Olsen, J. P. (1976). *Ambiguity and Choice in Organization.* Bergen, Norway: Universitetsforlaget.

March, J. G., and Simon, H. (1958). *Organizations.* New York: Wiley.

March, J. G., and Simon, H. (1993). *Organizations* (2nd ed.). Cambridge, MA: Blackwell.

Marjoribanks, K. (1977). Bureaucratic Orientation, Autonomy and Professional Attitudes of Teachers. *Journal of Educational Administration, 15,* 104–13.

Mark, J. H., and Anderson, B. D. (1985). Teacher Survival Rates in St. Louis, 1969–1982. *American Educational Research Journal, 22,* 413–21.

Marks, H. M., and Louis, K. S. (1997). Does Teacher Empowerment Affect the Classroom? The Implications of Teacher Empowerment for Instructional Practice and Student Academic Performance. *Educational Evaluation and Policy Analysis, 19,* 245–75.

Markman, E. M. (1977). Realizing That You Don't Understand: A Preliminary Investigation. *Child Development,* 48, 986–92.

Markman, E. M. (1979). Realizing That You Don't Understand: Elementary School Children's Awareness of Inconsistencies. *Child Development, 50,* 643–55.

Martin, J. (1985). Can Organizational Culture Be Managed? In P. J. Frost, L. F. Moore, M. R. Lousi, C. C. Lundberg, and J. Martin (Eds.), *Organizational Culture* (pp. 95–98). Beverly Hills, CA: Sage.

Martin, J. (1990a). Deconstructing Organizational Taboos: Suppression of Gender Conflict in Organizations. *Organizational Science, 1,* 339–59.

Martin, J. (1990b). Rereading Weber: Searching for Feminist Alternatives to Bureaucracy. Annual Meeting of the Academy of Management, San Francisco.

Martin, J. (1992). *Cultures in Organizations.* New York: Oxford University Press.

Martin, J., and Knopoff, K. (1999). The Gendered Implications of Apparently Gender-Neutral Theory: Rereading Weber, in *Ruffin Lectures Series.* Volume 3: *Business Ethics and Women's Studies*, Eds. E. Freeman and A. Larson. Oxford: Oxford University Press.

Martin, W. J., and Willower, D. J. (1981). The Managerial Behavior of High School Principals. *Educational Administration Quarterly, 17,* 69–90.

Martin, Y. M., Isherwood, G. B., and Lavery, R. G. (1976). Leadership Effectiveness in Teacher Probation Committees. *Educational Administration Quarterly, 12,* 87–99.

Marx, K. (1963). *Karl Marx: Early Writings.* T. Bottomore (Trans. and Ed.). London: Watts.

Maslow, A. H. (1965). *Eupsychian Management.* Homewood, IL: Irwin.

Maslow, A. H. (1970). *Motivation and Personality* (2nd ed.). New York: Harper & Row.

Maxey, S. J. (1995). *Democracy, Chaos, and New School Order.* Thousand Oaks, CA: Corwin Press.

Mayo, E. (1945). *The Social Problems of an Industrial Civilization.* Boston: Graduate School of Business Administration, Harvard University.

Mazzoni, T. L., and Malen, B. (1985). Mobilizing Constituency Pressure to Influence State Education Policy Making. *Educational Administration Quarterly, 21,* 91–116.

McCabe, D. L., and Dutton, J. E. (1993). Making Sense of the Environment: The Role of Perceived Effectiveness. *Human Relations, 46*(5), 623–43.

McCall, M. W., Jr., and Lombardo, M. M. (Eds.). (1978). *Leadership: Where Else Can We Go?* Durham, NC: Duke University Press.

McCaskey, M. B. (1979). The Hidden Messages Managers Send. *Harvard Business Review, 57,* 135–48.

McClelland, D. C. (1961). *The Achieving Society.* Princeton, NJ: Van Nostrand.

McClelland, D. C. (1965). Toward a Theory of Motive Acquisition. *American Psychologist, 20* (5), 321–33.

McClelland, D. C. (1985). *Human Motivation.* Glenview, IL: Scott, Foresman.

McConkie, M. L. (1979). A Clarification of the Goal Setting and Appraisal Process in MBO. *Academy of Management Review, 4,* 29–40.

McCormick, C. B., and Levin, J. R. (1987). Mnemonic Prose-Learning Strategies. In M. Pressley and M. McDaniel (Eds.), *Imaginary and Related Mnemonic Processes.* New York: Springer-Verlag.

McElroy, J. C., and Schrader, C. B. (1986). Attribution Theories of Leadership and Network Analysis. *Journal of Management, 12,* 351–62.

McFarland, A. S. (1992). Interest Groups and the Policymaking Process: Sources of Countervailing Power in America. In M. P. Petracca (Ed.), *The Politics of Interests* (pp. 58–79). Boulder, CO: Westview.

McNall, S. G., and McNall, S. A. (1992). *Sociology.* Englewood Cliffs, NJ: Prentice Hall.

McNamara, V., and Enns, F. (1966). Directive Leadership and Staff Acceptance of the Principal. *Canadian Administrator, 6,* 5–8.

McNeil, L. M. (1986). *Contradictions of Control: School Structure and School Knowledge.* New York: Routledge & Kegan Paul.

McNeil, L. M. (1988a). Contradictions of Control, Part 1: Administrators and Teachers. *Phi Delta Kappan, 69,* 333–39.

McNeil, L. M. (1988b). Contradictions of Control, Part 2: Administrators and Teachers. *Phi Delta Kappan, 69,* 432–38.

Meany, D. P. (1991). Quest for Quality. *California Technology Project Quarterly, 2,* 8–15.

Mechanic, D. (1962). Sources of Power of Lower Participants in Complex Organizations. *Administrative Science Quarterly, 6,* 349–64.

Meichenbaum, D., Burland, S., Gruson, L., and Cameron, R. (1985). Metacognitive Assessment. In S. Yussen (Ed.), *The Growth of Reflection in Children.* Orlando, FL: Academic Press.

Mendell, P. R. (1971). Retrieval and Representation in Long-Term Memory. *Psychonomic Science, 23,* 295–96.

Mennuti, N., and Kottkamp, R. B. (1986). Motivation Through the Design of Work: A

Synthesis of the Job Characteristics Model and Expectancy Motivation Tested in Middle and Junior High Schools. Annual Meeting of the American Educational Research Association, San Francisco.

Mento, A. J., Locke, E. A., and Klein, H. J. (1992). Relationship of Goal Level to Valence and Instrumentality. *Journal of Applied Psychology, 77,* 395–405.

Merton, R. (1957). *Social Theory and Social Structure.* New York: Free Press.

Metz, M. H. (1986). *Different by Design: The Context and Character of Three Magnet Schools.* New York: Routledge and Kegan Paul.

Meyer, J. W. (1992). Centralization of Funding and Control in Educational Governance. In J. W. Meyer and W. R. Scott (Eds.), *Organization Environments: Ritual and Rationality* (pp. 179–97). Newbury Park, CA: Sage.

Meyer, J. W., and Rowan, B. (1977). Institutionalized Organizations: Formal Structure as Myth and Ceremony. *American Journal of Sociology, 83,* 440–63.

Meyer, J. W., and Rowan, B. (1978). The Structure of Educational Organizations. In M. W. Meyer (Ed.), *Environments and Organizations* (pp. 78–109). San Francisco: Jossey-Bass.

Meyer, J. W., and Scott, W. R. (1983). *Organizational Environments: Ritual and Rationality.* Beverly Hills, CA: Sage.

Meyer, J. W., Scott, W. R., and Deal, T. E. (1992). Institutional and Technical Sources of Organizational Structure: Explaining the Structure of Educational Organizations. In J. W. Meyer and W. R. Scott (Eds.), *Organization Environments: Ritual and Rationality* (pp. 45–67). Newbury Park, CA: Sage.

Meyer, J. W., Scott, W. R., and Strang, D. (1987). Centralization, Fragmentation, and School District Complexity. *Administrative Science Quarterly, 32,* 186–201.

Meyer, M. W. (1978). Introduction: Recent Developments in Organizational Research and Theory. In M. W. Meyer (Ed.), *Environments and Organizations* (pp. 1–19). San Francisco: Jossey-Bass.

Michaels, R. E., Cron, W. L., Dubinsky, A. J., and Joachimsthaler, E. A. (1988). Influence of Formalization on the Organizational Commitment and Work Alienation of Salespeople and Industrial Buyers. *Journal of Marketing Research, 25,* 376–83.

Michels, R. (1949). *Political Parties.* E. and C. Paul (Trans.). Glencoe, IL: Free Press (first published in 1915).

Midgley, C., Feldlaufer, H., and Eccles, J. S. (1989). Change in Teacher Efficacy and Student Self- and Task-Related Beliefs in Mathematics During the Transition to Junior High School. *Journal of Educational Psychology, 81*(2), 247–58.

Midgley, C., and Wood, S. (1993). Beyond Site-Based Management: Empowering Teachers to Reform Schools. *Phi Delta Kappan, 75,* 245–52.

Miles, M. B. (1965). Education and Innovation: The Organization in Context. In M. Abbott and J. Lovell (Eds.), *Changing Perspectives in Educational Administration* (pp. 54–72). Auburn, AL: Auburn University Press.

Miles, M. B. (1969). Planned Change and Organizational Health: Figure and Ground. In F. D. Carver and T. J. Sergiovanni (Eds.), *Organizations and Human Behavior* (pp. 375–91). New York: McGraw-Hill.

Milgram, S. (1963). Behavioral Study of Obedience. *Journal of Abnormal and Social Psychology, 17,* 371–78.

Milgram, S. (1973). The Perils of Obedience. *Harper's* (December), 62–66, 75–77.

Milgram, S. (1974). *Obedience to Authority.* New York: Harper & Row.

Miller, D. (1992). Environmental Fit versus Internal Fit. *Organization Science, 3*(2), 159–78.

Miller, G. A. (1956). The Magical Number Seven, Plus or Minus Two: Some Limits on Our Capacity for Processing Information. *Psychological Review, 63,* 81–97.

Miller, G. A., Galanter, E., and Pribram, K. H. (1960). *Plans and the Structure of Behavior.* New York: Holt, Rinehart & Winston.

Miller, L. E., and Grush, J. E. (1988). Improving Predictions in Expectancy Theory Research: Effects of Personality, Expectancies, and Norms. *Academy of Management Journal, 31,* 107–22.

Miller, P. (1993). *Theories of Developmental Psychology.* New York: Freeman.

Milliken, F. J. (1987). Three Types of Perceived Uncertainty about the Environment: State, Effect, and Response Uncertainty. *Academy of Management Review, 12,* 133–43.

Mindlin, S. E., and Aldrich, H. (1975). Interorganizational Dependence: A Review of the Concept and a Reexamination of the Findings of the Aston Group. *Administrative Science Quarterly, 20,* 382–92.

Miner, J. B. (1980). *Theories of Organizational Behavior.* Hinsdale, IL: Dryden.
Miner, J. B. (1988). *Organizational Behavior.* New York: Random House.
Miner, A. S., Amburgey, T. L., and Stearns, T. M. (1990). Interorganizational Linkages and Population Dynamics: Buffering and Transformational Shields. *Administrative Science Quarterly, 35,* 689–713.
Mintzberg, H. (1973). *The Nature of Managerial Work.* New York: Harper & Row.
Mintzberg, H. (1978). Patterns in Strategy Formulation. *Management Science, 24,* 934–48.
Mintzberg, H. (1979). *The Structuring of Organizations.* Englewood Cliffs, NJ: Prentice Hall.
Mintzberg, H. (1980). Organizational Structure and Alienation from Work. Annual Meeting of the American Educational Research Association, Boston.
Mintzberg, H. (1981). The Manager's Job: Folklore and Fact. *Harvard Business Review, 53*(4), 49–61.
Mintzberg, H. (1983a). *Power In and Around Organizations.* Englewood Cliffs, NJ: Prentice Hall.
Mintzberg, H. (1983b). *Structure in Fives.* Englewood Cliffs, NJ: Prentice Hall.
Mintzberg, H. (1989). *Mintzberg on Management.* New York: Free Press.
Mintzberg, H., Raisinghani, D., and Theoret, A. (1976). The Structure of "Unstructured" Decision Processes. *Administrative Science Quarterly, 23,* 246–75.
Miskel, C., and Cosgrove, D. (1985). Leader Succession in School Settings. *Review of Educational Research, 55,* 87–105.
Miskel, C., DeFrain, J., and Wilcox, K. (1980). A Test of Expectancy Work Motivation Theory in Educational Organizations. *Educational Administration Quarterly, 16,* 70–92.
Miskel, C., Fevurly, R., and Stewart, J. (1979). Organizational Structures and Processes, Perceived School Effectiveness, Loyalty, and Job Satisfaction. *Educational Administration Quarterly, 15,* 97–118.
Miskel, C., McDonald, D., and Bloom, S. (1983). Structural and Expectancy Linkages Within Schools and Organizational Effectiveness. *Educational Administration Quarterly, 19,* 49–82.
Miskel, C., and Ogawa, R. (1988). Work Motivation, Job Satisfaction, and Climate. In N. J. Boyan (Ed.), *Handbook of Research on Educational Administration* (pp. 279–304). New York: Longman.
Mitchell, T. R. (1974). Expectancy Models of Job Satisfaction, Occupational Preference, and Effort: A Theoretical, Methodological and Empirical Appraisal. *Psychological Bulletin, 81,* 1053–77.
Mitchell, T. R. (1979). Organization Behavior. *Annual Review of Psychology, 30,* 243–81.
Mitroff, I. I., and Kilmann, R. H. (1978). *Methodological Approaches to Social Science: Integrating Divergent Concepts and Theories.* San Francisco: Jossey-Bass.
Mizruchi, M. S., and Fein, L. C. (1999). The Social Construction of Organizational Knowledge: A Study of the Uses of Coercive, Mimetic, and Normative Isomorphism. *Administrative Science Quarterly, 44*(4), 653–83.
Moeller, G. H., and Charters, W. W., Jr. (1966). Relation of Bureaucratization to Sense of Power among Teachers. *Administrative Science Quarterly, 10,* 444–65.
Mohan, M. L. (1993). *Organizational Communication and Cultural Vision.* Albany, NY: State University of New York Press.
Mohrman, A. M., Jr., Cooke, R. A., and Mohrman, S. A. (1978). Participation in Decision Making: A Multidimensional Perspective. *Educational Administration Quarterly, 14,* 13–29.
Monge, P. R. (1987). The Network Level of Analysis. In C. R. Berger and S. H. Chaffee (Eds.), *Handbook of Communication Science* (pp. 239–70). Newbury Park, CA: Sage.
Monk, D. H. (1992). Education Productivity Research: An Update and Assessment of Its Role in Education Finance Reform. *Educational Evaluation and Policy Analysis, 14*(4), 307–32.
Moon, N. J. (1983). The construction of a conceptual framework for teacher participation in school decision making. Doctoral diss., University of Kentucky, Lexington.
Moran, E. T., and Volkwein, J. F. (1992). The Cultural Approach to the Formation of Organizational Climate. *Human Relations, 45*(1), 19–47.
Morgan, G. (1986). *Images of Organizations.* Beverly Hills, CA: Sage.
Morgan, G. (1997). *Images of Organizations* (New Ed.). Thousand Oaks, CA: Sage.
Morris, P. F. (1990). Metacognition. In M. W. Eysenck, (Ed.), *The Blackwell Dictionary of Cognitive Psychology* (pp. 225–29). Oxford, UK: Basil Blackwell.
Morris, V. C., Crowson, R. L., Hurwitz, E. Jr., and Porter-Gehrie, C. (1981). *The Urban Principal.*

Chicago: College of Education, University of Illinois at Chicago.

Morse, P. S., and Ivey, A. E. (1996). *Face to Face: Communication and Conflict Resolution in Schools.* Thousand Oaks, CA: Sage.

Mortimore, P. (1993). School Effectiveness and the Management of Effective Learning and Teaching. *School Effectiveness and School Improvement, 4*(4), 290–310.

Mortimore, P. (1998). *The Road to Improvement: Reflections on School Effectiveness.* Lisse: Swets and Zeitlinger.

Moshman, D. (1982). Exogenous, Endogenous, and Dialectical Constructivism. *Developmental Review, 2,* 371–84.

Moshman, D. (1997). Pluralist Rational Constructivism. *Issues in Education* (3), 235–44.

Mott, P. E. (1972). *The Characteristics of Effective Organizations.* New York: Harper & Row.

Mowday, R. T. (1978). The Exercise of Upward Influence in Organizations. *Administrative Science Quarterly, 23,* 137–56.

Mowday, R. T., Porter, L. W., and Steers, R. M. (1982). *Employee-Organizational Linkages: The Psychology of Commitment, Absenteeism, and Turnover.* New York: Academic Press.

Mullins, T. (1983). Relationships among teachers' perception of the principal's style, teachers' loyalty to the principal, and teachers' zone of acceptance. Doctoral diss., Rutgers University, New Brunswick.

Murnane, R. J. (1981). Interpreting the Evidence on School Effectiveness. *Teachers College Record, 83,* 19–35.

Murnane, R. J. (1987). Understanding Teacher Attrition. *Harvard Educational Review, 57,* 177–82.

Murphy, M. J. (1985). Testimony before the California Commission on the Teaching Profession. Sacramento.

Myers, I. B., and Briggs, K. C. (1962). *The Myers-Briggs Type Indicator.* Princeton: NJ: Educational Testing Service.

Myers, M. T., and Myers, G. E. (1982). *Managing by Communication: An Organizational Approach.* New York: McGraw-Hill.

Nadler, D. A., and Lawler, E. E., III. (1977). Motivation: A Diagnostic Approach. In J. R. Hackman, E. E. Lawler III, and L. W. Porter (Eds.), *Perspectives on Behavior in Organizations* (pp. 26–38). New York: McGraw-Hill.

Nadler, D. A., and Tushman, M. L. (1983). A General Diagnostic Model for Organizational Behavior Applying a Congruence Perspective. In J. R. Hackman, E. E. Lawler III, and L. W. Porter (Eds.), *Perspectives on Behavior in Organizations* (pp. 112–24). New York: McGraw-Hill.

Nadler, D. A., and Tushman, M. L. (1989). Organizational Frame Bending: Principles for Managing Reorientation. *Academy of Management Executive, 3,* 194–203.

National Commission on Excellence in Education. (1983). *A Nation at Risk.* Washington, DC: U.S. Government Printing Office.

National Commission on Excellence in Educational Administration. (1987). *Leaders for America's Schools.* Tempe, AZ: University Council for Educational Administration.

National Council of Teachers of Mathematics (NCTM). (1989). *Curriculum and Evaluation Standards for School Mathematics.* Reston, VA: Author.

Needles, M., and Knapp, M. (1994). Teaching Writing to Children Who Are Undeserved. *Journal of Educational Psychology, 86,* 339–49.

Nelson, T. O. (1996). Consciousness and Metacognition. *American Psychologist, 51,* 102–16.

Nespor, J. (1987). The Role of Beliefs in the Practice of Teaching. *Journal of Curriculum Studies, 19,* 317–28.

Newberry, J. F. (1971). A comparative analysis of the organizational structures of selected post-secondary educational institutions. Doctoral diss., University of Alberta, Edmonton.

Nicholls, J. G., and Miller, A. (1984). Conceptions of Ability and Achievement Motivation. In R. Ames & C. Ames (Eds.), *Research on Motivation in Education. Volume 1: Student Motivation* (pp. 39–73). New York: Academic Press.

Nicholson, J. H. (1980). Analysis of communication satisfaction in an urban school system. Doctoral diss., George Peabody College for Teachers of Vanderbilt University, Nashville, TN.

Nietzsche, F. (1968). *The Will to Power.* New York: Vintage Books.

Nietzsche, F. (1968). *Twilight of the Idols.* Harmondsworth: Penguin.

Nietzsche, F. (1969). *Ecce Homo.* New York: Vintage Books.

Nisbett, R. E., and Ross, L. (1980). *Human Interferences: Strategies and Shortcomings in Social Judgments.* Englewood Cliffs, NJ: Prentice Hall.

Northcraft, G. B., and Earley, P. C. (1989). Technology, Credibility, and Feedback Use. *Organizational Behavior and Human Performance, 44,* 83–96.

Northcraft, G. B., and Neale, M. A. (1987). Experts, Amateurs, and Real Estate: An Anchoring-and –Adjustment Perspective on Property Pricing in Decision. *Organizational Behavior and Human Decision Processes, 39,* 84–97.

Nutt, P. C. (1984). Types of Organizational Decision Processes. *Administrative Science Quarterly, 29,* 414–50.

O'Dempsey, K. (1976). Time Analysis of Activities, Work Patterns and Roles of High School Principals. *Administrator's Bulletin, 7,* 1–4.

Odiorne, G. S. (1979). *MBO II: A System of Managerial Leadership for the 80s.* Belmont, CA: Pitman.

O'Donnell, A. M., and O'Kelly, J. (1994). Learning from Peers: Beyond the Rhetoric of Positive Results. *Educational Psychology Review, 6,* 321–50.

Ogawa, R. T. (1991). Enchantment, Disenchantment, and Accommodation: How a Faculty Made Sense of the Succession of a Principal. *Educational Administration Quarterly, 27*(1), 30–60.

Ogawa, R. T. (1992). Institutional Theory and Examining Leadership in School. *International Journal of Educational Management, 6* (3), 14–21.

Ogawa, R. T. (1994). The Institutional Sources of Educational Reform: The Case of School-Based Management. *American Educational Research Journal, 31*(3), 519–48.

Ogawa, R. T., and Bossert, S. T. (1995). Leadership as an Organizational Property. *Educational Administration Quarterly, 31,* 224–43.

Okeafor, K. R., and Teddlie, C. (1989). Organizational Factors Related to Administrator's Confidence in Teachers. *Journal of Research and Development in Education, 22,* 28–36.

Oldham, G. R., and Kulik, C. T. (1984). Motivation Enhancement Through Work Redesign. In J. L. Bess (Ed.), *College and University Organization* (pp. 85–104). New York: New York University Press.

Oldham, G. R., and Miller, H. E. (1979). The Effect of Significant Other's Job Complexity and Employee Reactions to Work. *Human Relations, 32,* 247–60.

Olsen, M. E. (1965). *The Logic of Collective Action: Public Goods and the Theory of Groups.* Cambridge, MA: Harvard University Press.

Olsen, M. E. (1968). A Theory of Groups and Organizations. In B. M. Russett (Ed.), *Economic Theory of International Politics.* Chicago: Markham.

O'Reilly, C. A. I., Chatman, J. A., and Caldwell, D. (1991). People and Organizational Culture: A Q-sort Approach to Assessing Person-Organization Fit. *Academy of Management Journal, 34*(3), 487–516.

O'Reilly, C. A. I., and Pondy, L. R. (1979). Organizational Communication. In S. Kerr (Ed.), *Organizational Behavior* (pp. 119–50). Columbus, OH: Grid.

O'Reilly, C. A. I., and Roberts, K. H. (1977). Task Group Structure, Communication, and Effectiveness in Three Organizations. *Journal of Applied Psychology, 62,* 674–81.

Orpen, C. (1979). The Effects of Job Enrichment on Employee Satisfaction, Motivation, Involvement, and Performance: A Field Experiment. *Human Relations, 32,* 189–217.

Ostroff, C., and Schmitt, N. (1993). Configurations of Organizational Effectiveness and Efficiency. *Academy of Management Journal, 36*(6), 1345–61.

Ouchi, W. (1981). *Theory Z.* Reading, MA: Addison-Wesley.

Ouchi, W., and Wilkins, A. L. (1985). Organizational Culture. *Annual Review of Sociology, 11,* 457–83.

Pace, C. R., and Stern, G. C. (1958). An Approach to the Measure of Psychological Characteristics of College Environments. *Journal of Educational Psychology, 49,* 269–77.

Packard, J. S. (1988). The Pupil Control Studies. In N. J. Boyan (Ed.), *Handbook of Research on Educational Administration* (pp. 185–207). New York: Longman.

Packard, J. S., and Willower, D. J. (1972). Pluralistic Ignorance and Pupil Control Ideology. *Journal of Educational Administration, 10,* 78–87.

Padgett, J. F. (1980). Managing Garbage Can Hierarchies. *Administrative Science Quarterly, 25,* 583–604.

Page, C. H. (1946). Bureaucracy's Other Face. *Social Forces, 25,* 88–94.

Pajares, F. (1996). Current Directions in Self Research: Self-Efficacy. Paper presented at the annual meeting of the American Educational Research Association, New York.

Pajares, F. (1997). Current Directions in Self-Efficacy Research. In M. L. Maehr and P. R. Pintrich

(Eds.), *Advances in Motivation and Achievement* (pp. 1–49). Greenwich, CT: JAI Press.

Palincsar, A. S. (1986). The Role of Dialogue in Providing Scaffolding Instruction. *Educational Psychologist, 21,* 73–98.

Palinscar, A. M. (1998). Social Constructivist Perspectives on Teaching and Learning. In. J. T. Spence, J. M. Darley, D. J. Foss (Eds.), *Annual Review of Psychology* (pp. 345–76). Palo Alto, CA: Annual Reviews.

Pallas, A. M., Natriello, G., and McDill, E. L. (1989). The Changing Nature of the Disadvantaged Population: Current Dimension and Future Trends. *Educational Researcher, 18,* 16–22.

Pallas, A. M., and Neumann, A. (1993). Blinded by the Light: The Applicability of Total Management to Educational Organizations. Annual Meeting of the American Educational Research Association, Atlanta, GA.

Paris, S. G., and Cunningham, A. E. (1996). Children Becoming Students. In D. Berliner and R. Calfee, (Eds.), *Handbook of Educational Psychology* (pp. 117–46). New York: Macmillan.

Paris, S. G., Lipson, M. Y., and Wixson, K. K. (1983). Becoming a Strategic Reader. *Contemporary Educational Psychology, 8,* 293–316.

Parsons, T. (1947). Introduction. In Max Weber, *The Theory of Social and Economic Organization* (pp. 3–86). A. M. Henderson and T. Parsons (Trans.). New York: Free Press.

Parsons, T. (1960). *Structure and Process in Modern Societies.* Glencoe, IL: Free Press.

Parsons, T. (1967). *Sociological Theory and Modern Society.* New York: Free Press.

Parsons, T., Bales, R. F., and Shils, E. A. (1953). *Working Papers in the Theory of Action.* New York: Free Press.

Parsons, T., and Shils, E. A. (Eds.). (1951). *Toward a General Theory of Action.* Cambridge, MA: Harvard University Press.

Pasch, M., Sparks-Langer, G., Gardner, T. G., Starko, A. J., and Moody, C. D. (1991). *Teaching as Decision Making: Instructional Practices for the Successful Teacher.* New York: Longman.

Pastor, M. C., and Erlandson, D. A. (1982). A Study of Higher Order Need Strength and Job Satisfaction in Secondary Public School Teachers. *Journal of Educational Administration, 20,* 172–83.

Pawar, B. S., and Eastman, K. K. (1997). The Nature and Implications of Contextual Influences on Transformational Leadership: A Conceptual Examination. *Academy of Management Review, 22*(1), 80–109.

Payne, J. W., Bettman, J. R., and Johnson, E. J. (1988). Adaptive Strategy Selection in Decision Making. *Journal of Experimental Psychology: Learning, Memory, and Cognition, 14,* 534–52.

Peabody, R. L. (1962). Perceptions of Organizational Authority: A Comparative Analysis. *Administrative Science Quarterly, 6,* 463–82.

Penley, L. E., Alexander, E. R., Jernigan, I. E., and Henwood, C. I. (1991). Communication Abilities of Managers: The Relationship to Performance. *Journal of Management, 17*(1), 57–76.

Pennings, J. M. (1985). *Organizational Strategy and Change.* San Francisco: Jossey-Bass.

Pennings, J. M. (1992). Structural Contingency Theory: A Reappraisal. *Research in Organizational Behavior, 14,* 267–309.

Perkins, D. N. (1991, May). Technology Meets Constructivism: Do They Make a Marriage? *Educational Technology, 31,* 18–23.

Perrow, C. (1978). Demystifying Organization. In R. Saari and Y. Hasenfeld (Eds.), *The Management of Human Services* (pp. 105–20). New York: Columbia University Press.

Perrow, C. (1986). *Complex Organizations: A Critical Essay* (3rd ed.). Glencoe, IL: Scott, Foresman.

Peters, L. H., Hartke, D. D., and Pohlmann, J. T. (1985). Fiedler's Contingency Theory of Effectiveness: An Application of the Meta-Analysis Procedures of Schmidt and Hunter. *Psychological Bulletin, 97,* 274–85.

Peters, T. J., and Waterman, R. H., Jr. (1982). *In Search of Excellence.* New York: Harper & Row.

Peterson, K. D. (1977–78). The Principal's Tasks. *Administrator's Notebook, 26,* 1–4.

Peterson, P. E. (1989). The Public Schools: Monopoly or Choice? Conference on Choice and Control in American Education. Robert M. LaFollette Institute of Public Affairs, University of Wisconsin, Madison.

Pfeffer, J. (1972). Size and Composition of Corporate Boards of Directors: The Organization and Its Environment. *Administrative Science Quarterly, 17,* 218–28.

Pfeffer, J. (1976). Beyond Management and the Worker: The Institutional Function of Management. *Academy of Management Review, 1,* 36–46.

Pfeffer, J. (1981). *Power in Organizations.* Boston: Pitman.

Pfeffer, J. (1982). *Organizations and Organization Theory.* Boston: Pitman.
Pfeffer, J. (1997). *New Directions for Organization Theory.* New York: Oxford University Press.
Pfeffer, J., and Leblebici, H. (1973). The Effect of Competition on Some Dimensions of Organizational Structure. *Social Forces, 52,* 268–79.
Pfeffer, J., and Salancik, G. (1978). *The External Control of Organizations: A Resource Dependence Perspective.* New York: Harper & Row.
Phillips, D. C., and Thomas, A. R. (1982). Principals' Decision Making: Some Observations. In W. S. Simpkins, A. R. Thomas, and E. B. Thomas (Eds.), *Principal and Task: An Australian Perspective* (pp. 74–83). Armidale, NSW, Australia: University of New England.
Phillips, D. C. (1997). How, Why, What, When, and Where: Perspectives on Constructivism in Psychology and Education. *Issues in Education, 3,* 151–94.
Pinder, C. C. (1984). *Work Motivation: Theory, Issues, and Applications.* Dallas: Scott, Foresman.
Pinfield, L. T. (1986). A Field Evaluation of Perspectives on Organizational Decision Making. *Administrative Science Quarterly, 31,* 365–88.
Pintrich, P. R. (1988). A Process-Oriented View of Student Motivation and Cognition. In J. S. Stark and L. A. Mets (Eds.), *Improving Teaching and Learning Through Research* (pp. 65–79). San Francisco: Jossey-Bass.
Pintrich, P. R., and Garcia, T. (1991). Student Goal Orientation and Self-Regulation in the College Classroom. In M. Maehr and P. R. Pintrich (Eds.), *Advances in Motivation and Achievement* (pp. 371–402). Greenwich, CT: JAI.
Pintrich, P. R., Marx, R. W., and Boyle, R. A. (1993). Beyond Cold Conceptual Change: The Role of Motivational Beliefs and Classroom Contextual Factors in the Process of Conceptual Change. *Review of Educational Research, 63*(2), 167–99.
Pitner, N., and Ogawa, R. T. (1981). Organizational Leadership: The Case of the Superintendent. *Educational Administration Quarterly, 17,* 45–65.
Podgurski, T. P. (1990). School effectiveness as it relates to group consensus and organizational health of middle schools. Doctoral diss., Rutgers University, New Brunswick.
Podsakoff, P. M., Niehoff, B. P., MacKenzie, S. B., and Williams, M. L. (1993). Do Substitutes for Leadership Really Substitute for Leadership? An Empirical Examination of Kerr and Jermier's Situational Leadership Model. *Organizational Behavior and Human Decision Processes, 54,* 1–44.
Poole, M. S. (1985). Communication and Organizational Climates: Review, Critique, and a New Perspective. In R. D. McPhee and P. K. Tompkins (Eds.), *Organizational Communications: Traditional Themes and New Directions* (pp. 79–108). Beverly Hills, CA: Sage.
Porter, L. W. (1961). A Study of Perceived Need Satisfactions in Bottom and Middle Management Jobs. *Journal of Applied Psychology, 45,* 1–10.
Porter, L. W., and Lawler, E. E., III. (1968). *Managerial Attitudes and Performance.* Homewood, IL: Dorsey.
Porter, L. W., and Roberts, K. H. (1976). Communication in Organizations. In M. D. Dunnette (Ed.), *Handbook of Industrial and Organizational Psychology* (pp. 1533–89). Chicago: Rand McNally.
Powell, T. C. (1995). Total Quality Management as Competitive Advantage: A Review and Empirical Study. *Strategic Management Journal, 16,* 15–37.
Powell, W. W. (1991). Expanding the Scope of Institutional Analysis. In W. W. Powell and P. J. DiMaggio (Eds.), *The New Institutionalism in Organizational Analysis* (pp. 183–203). Chicago: University of Chicago Press.
Powell, W. W., and DiMaggio, P. J. (1991). Introduction. In W. W. Powell and P. J. DiMaggio (Eds.), *The New Institutionalism in Organizational Analysis* (pp. 1–38). Chicago: University of Chicago Press.
Prawat, R. S. (1992). Teachers Beliefs about Teaching and Learning: A Constructivist Perspective. *American Journal of Education, 100,* 354–95.
Pressley, M., Levin, J., and Delaney, H. D. (1982). The Mnemonic Keyword Method. *Review of Research in Education, 52,* 61–91.
Prestine, N. A. (1991). Shared Decision Making in Restructuring Essential Schools: The Role of the Principal. *Planning and Changing, 22,* 160–78.
Pugh, D. S., and Hickson, D. J. (1976). *Organizational Structure in Its Context.* Westmead, Farnborough, Hants., England: Saxon House, D. C. Heath.
Pugh, D. S., Hickson, D. J., and Hinings, C. R. (1968). Dimensions of Organizational Structure. *Administrative Science Quarterly, 13,* 56–105.

Pugh, D. S., Hickson, D. J., Hinings, C. R., and Turner, C. (1969). The Context of Organizational Structure. *Administration Science Quarterly, 14,* 91–114.

Purkey, S. C., and Smith, M. S. (1983). Effective Schools: A Review. *Elementary School Journal, 83,* 427–52.

Quarstein, V. A., McAfee, R. B., and Glassman, M. (1992). The Situational Occurrences Theory of Job Satisfaction. *Human Relations, 45*(8), 859–72.

Rachlin, H. (1991). *Introduction to Modern Behaviorism* (3rd ed.). New York: Freeman.

Raffini, J. P. (1996). *150 Ways to Increase Intrinsic Motivation in the Classroom.* Boston: Allyn and Bacon.

Ratsoy, E. W. (1973). Participative and Hierarchical Management of Schools: Some Emerging Generalizations. *Journal of Educational Administration, 11,* 161–70.

Raudenbush, S., Rowen, B., and Cheong, Y. (1992). Contextual Effects on the Self-Perceived Efficacy of High School Teachers. *Sociology of Education, 65,* 150–67.

Rauschenberger, J., Schmitt, N., and Hunter, J. E. (1980). A Test of the Need Hierarchy Concept by a Markov Model of Change in Need Strength. *Administrative Science Quarterly, 25,* 654–70.

Recht, D. R., and Leslie, L. (1988). Effect of Prior Knowledge on Good and Poor Readers' Memory of Text. *Journal of Educational Psychology, 80,* 16–20.

Redding, W. C. (1972). *Communication Within the Organization.* West Lafayette, IN: Purdue Research Council.

Reder, L. M., and Anderson, J. R. (1980). A Comparison of Texts and Their Summaries: Memorial Consequences. *Journal of Verbal Learning and Verbal Behavior, 19*(2), 121–34.

Reeve, J. (1996). *Motivating Others: Nurturing Inner Motivational Resources.* Boston: Allyn and Bacon.

Reeves, C. A., and Bednar, D. A. (1994). Defining Quality: Alternatives and Implications. *Academy of Management Review, 19*(3), 419–45.

Reilly, B. J., and DiAngelo, J. A. (1990). Communication: A Cultural System of Meaning and Value. *Human Relations, 43*(2), 129–40.

Reiss, F. (1994). Faculty loyalty in and around the urban elementary school. Doctoral diss., Rutgers University, New Brunswick.

Reiss, F., and Hoy, W. K. (1998). Faculty Loyalty: An Important but Neglected Concept in the Study of Schools. *Journal of School Leadership, 8,* 4–21.

Resnick, L. B. (1981). Instructional Psychology. *Annual Review of Psychology, 32,* 659–704.

Reynolds, D., and Teddlie, C. (with Creemers, B., Scheerens, J., and Townsend, T.). (2000). An Introduction to School Effectiveness Research. In C. Teddlie, and D. Reynolds, (Eds.), *The International Handbook on School Effectiveness Research* (pp. 3–25). New York: Falmer.

Reynolds, P. D. (1971). *A Primer in Theory Construction.* Indianapolis, IN: Bobbs-Merrill.

Rhodes, L. A. (1990). Why Quality Is Within Our Grasp . . . If We Reach. *The School Administrator, 47*(10), 31–34.

Rice, A. W. (1978). Individual and work variables associated with principal job satisfaction. Doctoral diss., University of Alberta, Edmonton.

Rice, R. E. (1992). Task Analyzability, Use of New Media, and Effectiveness: A Multi-Site Exploration of Media Richness. *Organization Science, 3*(4), 475–500.

Rice, M. E., and Schneidner, G. T. (1994). A Decade of Teacher Empowerment: An Empirical Analysis of Teacher Involvement in Decision Making, 1980–1991. *Journal of Educational Administration, 32,* 43–58.

Rinehart, J. S., Short, P. M, and Johnson, P. E. (1997). Empowerment and Conflict at School-Based and Non-School-Based Sites in the United States. *Journal of International Studies in Educational Administration, 25,* 77–87.

Rinehart, J. S., Short, P. M., Short, R. J., and Eckley, M. (1998). Teacher Empowerment and Principal Leadership: Understanding the Influence Process. *Educational Administration Quarterly, 24,* 608–30.

Robbins, S. P. (1983). *The Structure and Design of Organizations.* Englewood Cliffs, NJ: Prentice Hall.

Robbins, S. P. (1991). *Organizational Behavior: Concepts, Controversies, and Applications* (5th ed.). Englewood Cliffs, NJ: Prentice Hall.

Robbins, S. P. (1998). *Organizational Behavior: Concepts, Controversies, Applications.* Upper Saddle, NJ: Allyn and Bacon.

Roberts, K. H., Hulin, C. L., and Rousseau, D. M. (1978). *Developing an Interdisciplinary Science of Organizations.* San Francisco: Jossey-Bass.

Roberts, N. C., and Bradley, R. T. (1988). Limits of Charisma. In J. A. Conger and R. N. Kanungo (Eds.), *Charismatic Leadership: The Elusive Factor in Organizational Effectiveness* (pp. 253–75). San Francisco, CA: Jossey-Bass.

Robinson, D. H., and Kiewra, K. A. (1995). Visual Argument: Graphic Outlines Are Superior to Outlines in Improving Learning from Text. *Journal of Educational Psychology, 87,* 455–67.

Rockey, E. H. (1984). *Communication in Organizations.* Lanham, MD: University Press of America.

Roethlisberger, F. J., and Dickson, W. J. (1939). *Management and the Worker.* Cambridge: Harvard University Press.

Rogers, R. C., and Hunter, J. E. (1989). The impact of management by objectives on organizational productivity. Unpublished paper, School of Public Administration, University of Kentucky, Lexington.

Rosenau, P. M. (1992). *Post-Modernism and the Social Sciences: Insights, Inroads, and Intrusions.* Princeton, NJ: Princeton University Press.

Rosenshine, B. (1979). Content, Time, and Direct Instruction. In P. Peterson and H. Walberg (Eds.), *Research on Teaching: Concepts, Findings, and Implications* (pp. 28–56). Berkeley, CA: McCutchan.

Rosenshine, B. (1988). Explicit Teaching. In D. Berliner and B. Rosenshine (Eds.), *Talks to Teachers* (pp. 75–92). New York: Random House.

Rosenshine, B., and Stevens, R. (1986).). Teaching functions. In M. Wittrock (Ed.) *Teaching Research on Teaching* (3rd ed., pp. 376–91). New York: Macmillan.

Ross, J. A., Cousins, J. B., and Gadalla, T. (1996). Within-Teacher Predictors of Teacher Efficacy. *Teaching and Teacher Education, 12,* 385–400.

Rossman, G. B., Corbett, H. D., and Firestone, W. A. (1988). *Change and Effectiveness in Schools: A Cultural Perspective.* Albany, NY: State University of New York Press.

Rotter, J. B. (1954). *Social Learning and Clinical Psychology.* Englewood Cliffs, NJ: Prentice Hall.

Rotter, J. B. (1966). Generalized Expectancies for Internal versus External Control of Reinforcement. *Psychological Monographs, 80* (1, Whole No. 609).

Rousseau, D. M. (1978). Characteristics of Departments, Positions, and Individuals: Contexts for Attitudes and Behavior. *Administrative Science Quarterly, 23,* 521–40.

Rowan, B. (1981). The Effects of Institutionalized Rules on Administrators. In S. B. Bacharach (Ed.), *Organizational Behavior in Schools and School Districts* (pp. 47–75). New York: Praeger.

Rowan, B. (1982). Organizational Structure and the Institutional Environment: The Case of Public Schools. *Administrative Science Quarterly, 27,* 259–79.

Rowan, B. (1990). Commitment and Control: Alternative Strategies for the Organizational Design of School. *Review of Research in Education, 16,* 353–89.

Rowan, B. (1993). Institutional Studies of Organization: Lines of Analysis and Data Requirements. Annual Meeting of the American Educational Research Association, Atlanta, GA.

Rowan, B. (1998). The Task Characteristics of Teaching: Implications for the Organizational Design of Schools. In R. Bernhardt, C. Hedley, G. Cattari, and V. Svolopoulos (Eds.), *Curriculum Leadership: Rethinking Schools for the 21st Century* (pp. 37–54). Creskill, NJ: Hampton Press.

Rowan, B., Bossert, S. T., and Dwyer, D. C. (1983). Research on Effective Schools: A Cautionary Note. *Educational Researcher, 12,* 24–31.

Rowan, B., and Miskel, C. (1999). Institutional Theory and the Study of Educational Organizations. In J. Murphy and K. S. Louis (Eds.), *Handbook of Research on Educational Administration* (2nd ed., pp. 359–83). San Francisco: Jossey-Bass.

Rowan, B., Raudenbush, S. W., and Cheong, Y. F. (1993). Teaching as a Nonroutine Task: Implications for the Management of Schools. *Educational Administration Quarterly, 29,* 479–99.

Rumelhart, D., and Ortony, A. (1977). *The Representation of Knowledge in Memory.* In R. Anderson, R. Spiro, and W. Montague (Eds.), Schooling and The Acquisition of Knowledge. Hillsdale, NJ: Erlbaum.

Russ, G. S., Daft, R. L., and Lengel, R. H. (1990). Media Selection and Managerial Characteristics in Organizational Communication. *Management Communication Quarterly, 4,* 151–75.

Russell, R. D., and Russell, C. J. (1992). An Examination of the Effects of Organizational Norms, Organizational Structure, and Environmental Uncertainty on Entrepreneurial Strategy. *Journal of Management, 18*(4), 639–56.

Rutter, M., Maugham, B., Mortimore, P., Ousten, J., and Smith, A. (1979). *Fifteen Thousand Hours: Secondary Schools and Their Effects on Children.* London: Open Books.

Ryan, R. M., and Grolnick, W. S. (1986). Origins and Pawns in the Classroom: Self-Report and

Projective Assessments of Individual Differences in the Children's Perceptions. *Journal of Personality and Social Psychology, 50,* 550–58.

Sackney, L. E. (1976). The relationship between organizational structure and behavior in secondary schools. Doctoral diss., University of Alberta, Edmonton.

Salancik, G. R., and Pfeffer, J. (1977). Constraints on Administrative Discretion: The Limited Influence of Mayors on City Budgets. *Urban Affairs Quarterly, 12,* 475–98.

Sanchez, P. (1999). How to Craft Successful Employee Communication in the Information Age. *Communication World, 16*(7), 9–15.

Sashkin, M., and Burke, W. W. (1990). Understanding and Assessing Organizational Leadership. In K. E. Clark and M. B. Clark (Eds.), *Measures of Leadership* (pp. 297–325). West Orange, NJ: Leadership Library of America.

Sayles, L. R., and Strauss, G. (1966). *Human Behavior in Organizations.* Englewood Cliffs, NJ: Prentice Hall.

Scheerens, J., and Bosker, R. (1997). *The Foundations of Educational Effectiveness.* Oxford: Permagon.

Schein, E. H. (1985). *Organizational Culture and Leadership.* San Francisco: Jossey-Bass.

Schein, E. H. (1990). Organizational Culture. *American Psychologist, 45*(2), 109–19.

Schein, E. H. (1992). *Organizational Culture and Leadership* (2nd ed.). San Francisco: Jossey-Bass.

Schein, E. H. (1999). *The Corporate Culture.* San Francisco: Jossey-Bass.

Scherkenbach, W. (1991). *Deming's Road to Continual Improvement.* Knoxville, TN: SPC Press.

Scherkenbach, W. (1992). *The Deming Route to Quality and Production.* Washington, DC: CEEPress.

Schermerhorn, J. R., Hunt, J. G., and Osborn, R. N. (1994). *Managing Organizational Behavior.* New York: Wiley.

Schmidt, F. L., and Hunter, J. E. (1992). Development of a Causal Model of Processes Determining Job Performance. *Current Directions in Psychological Science, 1*(3), 89–92.

Schmitz, J., and Fulk, J. (1991). Organizational Colleagues, Media Richness, and Electronic Mail. *Communication Research, 18*(4), 487–523.

Schmuck, R. A., and Runkel, P. J. (1985). *The Handbook of Organization Development in Schools* (3rd ed.). Prospect Heights, IL: Waveland Press.

Schraw, G., and Moshman, D. (1995). Metacognitive Theories. *Educational Psychology Review, 7,* 351–71.

Schunk, D. (1991). Self-Efficacy and Academic Motivation. *Educational Psychologist, 26,* 207–31.

Schunk, D. H. (1996a). *Learning Theories: An Educational Perspective* (2nd ed.). Columbus, OH: Merrill.

Schunk, D. H. (1996b). Goal and Self-Evaluative Influences During Children's Cognitive Skill Learning. *American Educational Research Journal, 33,* 359–82.

Schwartz, B., and Reisberg, D. (1991). *Learning and Memory.* New York: Norton.

Scott, W. R. (1977). Effectiveness of Organizational Effectiveness Studies. In P. S. Goodman and J. M. Pennings (Eds.), *New Perspectives on Organizational Effectiveness* (pp. 63–95). San Francisco: Jossey-Bass.

Scott, W. R. (1981). *Organizations: Rational, Natural, and Open System.* Englewood Cliffs, NJ: Prentice Hall.

Scott, W. R. (1983). Introduction: From Technology to Environment. In J. W. Meyer and W. R. Scott (Eds.), *Organizational Environments: Ritual and Rationality* (pp. 13–17). Beverly Hills, CA: Sage.

Scott, W. R. (1987a). The Adolescence of Institutional Theory. *Administrative Science Quarterly, 32,* 493–511.

Scott, W. R. (1987b). *Organizations: Rational, Natural, and Open System* (2nd ed.). Englewood Cliffs, NJ: Prentice Hall.

Scott, W. R. (1991). Unpacking Institutional Arguments. In W. W. Powell and P. J. DiMaggio (Eds.), *The New Institutionalism in Organizational Analysis* (pp. 164–82). Chicago: University of Chicago Press.

Scott, W. R. (1992). *Organizations: Rational, Natural, and Open Systems* (3rd. ed.). Englewood Cliffs, NJ: Prentice Hall.

Scott, W. R. (1995). *Institutions and Organizations.* Thousand Oaks, CA: Sage.

Scott, W. R. (1998). *Organizations: Rational, Natural, and Open Systems* (4th. ed.). Englewood Cliffs, NJ: Prentice Hall.

Scott, W. R., and Meyer, J. W. (1991). The Organization of Societal Sectors: Propositions and Early Evidence. In W. W. Powell and P. J. DiMaggio (Eds.), *The New Institutionalism in Organizational Analysis* (pp. 108–140). Chicago: University of Chicago Press.

Selznick, P. (1949). *TVA and the Grass Roots.* Berkeley: University of California Press.

Selznick, P. (1957). *Leadership in Administration.* New York: Harper & Row.

Selznick, P. (1992). *The Moral Commonwealth.* Berkeley: University of California Press.

Semb, G. B., and Ellis, J. A. (1994). Knowledge Taught in School: What Is Remembered? *Review of Educational Research, 64,* 253–86.

Senatra, P. T. (1980). Role Conflict, Role Ambiguity, and Organizational Climate in a Public Accounting Firm. *Accounting Review, 55,* 594–603.

Senge, P. M. (1990). *The Fifth Discipline: The Art and Practice of the Learning Organization.* New York: Doubleday.

Sergiovanni, T. J. (1992). *Moral Leadership: Getting to the Heart of School Improvement.* San Francisco: Jossey-Bass.

Sergiovanni, T. J. (1994). *Building Community in Schools.* San Francisco: Jossey-Bass.

Shakeshaft, C. (1986). *Women in Educational Administration.* Newbury Park, CA: Sage.

Shamir, B., and Howell, J. M. (1999). Organizational and Contextual Influences on the Emergence and Effectiveness of Charismatic Leadership. *Leadership Quarterly, 10*(2), 257–83.

Shamir, B., House, R. J., and Arthur, M. B. (1993). The Motivational Effects of Charismatic Leadership: A Self-Concept Based Theory. *Organization Science, 4*(4), 577–94.

Shamir, B., Zokay, E., Breinin, E., and Popper, M. (1998). Correlates of Charismatic Leader Behavior in Military Units. *Academy of Management Journal, 41*(4), 387–409.

Shanker, A. (1989, May 14). Does Money Make a Difference? A Difference over Answers. *New York Times.*

Sharma, C. L. (1955). Who Should Make What Decisions? *Administrator's Notebook, 3,* 1–4.

Shelby, A. N. (1986). The Theoretical Bases of Persuasion: A Critical Introduction. *Journal of Business Communication, 23,* 5–29.

Shuell, T. (1996). Teaching and Learning in a Classroom Context. In D.Berliner and R. Calfee (eds.), *Handbook of Educational Psychology* (pp. 726–64). New York: Macmillan.

Shuell, T. J. (1986). Cognitive Conceptions of Learning. *Review of Educational Research, 56,* 411–36.

Sickler, J. L. (1988). Teachers in Charge: Empowering the Professionals. *Phi Delta Kappan, 69,* 354–56.

Silins, H. C. (1992). Effective Leadership for School Reform. *Alberta Journal of Educational Research, 38,* 317–34.

Silver, P. (1983). *Educational Administration: Theoretical Perspectives in Practice and Research.* New York: Harper & Row.

Simon, H. A. (1947). *Administrative Behavior.* New York: Macmillan.

Simon, H. A. (1957a). *Administrative Behavior* (2nd ed.). New York: Macmillan.

Simon, H. A. (1957b). *Models of Man.* New York: Wiley.

Simon, H. A. (1968). Administrative Behavior. In D. Suls (Ed.), *International Encyclopedia of the Social Sciences* (pp. 74–79). New York: Macmillan.

Simon, H. A. (1987). Making Management Decisions: The Role of Intuition and Emotion. *Academy of Management Executive, 1,* 57–64.

Simon, H. A. (1991). Keynote Address. UCEA Conference, Baltimore, MD.

Simon, H. A. (1993). Decision-Making: Rational, Nonrational, and Irrational. *Educational Administration Quarterly, 29*(3), 392–411.

Sirotnik, K. A., and Clark, R. (1988). School-Centered Decision Making and Renewal. *Phi Delta Kappan, 69,* 660–64.

Skinner, B. F. (1950). Are Theories of Learning Necessary? *Psychological Review, 57,* 193–216.

Slater, R. O., and Boyd, W. B. (1999). *Schools as Polities.* In J. Murphy and K. S. Louis, (Eds.), *Handbook on Research of Educational Administration* (pp. 297–322). San Francisco: Jossey-Bass.

Slavin, R. E. (1995). *Cooperative Learning* (2nd ed.). Boston: Allyn and Bacon.

Smith, F. (1975). *Comprehension and Learning: A Conceptual Framework for Teachers.* New York: Holt, Rinehart & Winston.

Smith, J. F., and Kida, T. (1991). Heuristics and Biases: Expertise and Task Realism in Auditing. *Psychological Bulletin, 109,* 472–89.

Smith, L. (1993). *Necessary Knowledge: Piagetian Perspectives on Constructivism.* Hillsdale, NJ: Erlbaum.

Smith, M. S., and O'Day, J. A. (1990). Systemic School Reform. In S. H. Fuhrman and B. Malen (Eds.), *The Politics of Curriculum and Testing* (pp. 233–67). London: Falmer.

Smylie, M. A. (1988). The Enhancement Function of Staff Development: Organization and Psychological Antecedents to Individual

Teacher Change. *American Educational Research Journal, 25,* 1–30.

Smylie, M. A. (1994). Redesigning Teachers' Work: Connections to the Classroom. *Review of Research in Education, 20,* 129–77.

Smylie, M. A., and Brownlee-Conyers, J. (1992). Teacher Leaders and Their Principals: Exploring the Development of New Working Relationships. *Educational Administration Quarterly, 28*(2), 150–84.

Smylie, M. A., and Hart, A. W. (1999). School Leadership for Teacher Learning and Change: A Human and Social Capital Development Perspective. In J. Murphy and K. S. Louis (Eds.), *Handbook of Research on Educational Administration* (pp. 421–41). San Francisco, CA: Jossey-Bass.

Smylie, M. A., and Smart, J. C. (1990). Teacher Support for Career Enhancement Initiatives: Program Characteristics and Effects on Work. *Educational Evaluation and Policy Analysis, 12*(2), 139–55.

Snowman, J. (1984). Learning Tactics and Strategies. In G. Phye and T. Andre (Eds.), *Cognitive Instructional Psychology.* Orlando, FL: Academic Press.

Sousa, D. A., and Hoy, W. K. (1981). Bureaucratic Structure in Schools: A Refinement and Synthesis in Measurement. *Educational Administration Quarterly, 17,* 21–40.

Spector, P. E. (1997). *Job Satisfaction: Application, Assessment, Cause, and Consequence.* Thousand Oaks, CA: Sage.

Spencer, B. A. (1994). Models of Organization and Total Quality Management. *Academy of Management Review, 19*(3), 446–71.

Spenner, K. I. (1988). Social Stratification, Work, and Personality. *Annual Review of Sociology, 14,* 69–97.

Spillane, J. P., and Jennings, N. E. (1997). Aligned Instructional Policies and Ambitious Pedagogy: Exploring Instructional Reform from the Classroom Perspective. *Teachers College Record, 98,* 449–81.

Spiro, R. J., Feltovich, P. J., Jacobson, M. L., and Coulson, R. L. (1991). Cognitive Flexibility, Constructivism, and Hypertext: Random Access Instruction for Advanced Knowledge Acquisition in Ill-structured Domains. *Educational Technology, 31*(5), 24–33.

Sproull, L. (1981). Managing Educational Programs: A Microbehavioral Analysis. *Human Organization, 40,* 113–122.

Sproull, L., Weiner, S., and Wolf, D. (1978). *Organizing an Anarchy: Beliefs, Bureaucracy, and Politics in the National Institute of Education.* Chicago: University of Illinois.

Starkie, D. (1984). Policy Changes, Configurations, and Catastrophes. *Policy and Politics, 12,* 71–84.

Staw, B. M. (1984). Organizational Behavior: A Review and Reformulation of the Field's Outcome Variables. *Annual Review of Psychology, 35,* 627–666.

Stearns, T. M., Hoffman, A. N., and Heide, J. B. (1987). Performance of Commercial Television Stations as an Outcome of Interorganizational Linkages and Environmental Conditions. *Academy of Management Journal, 30,* 71–90.

Stedman, L. C. (1987). It's Time We Changed the Effective Schools Formula. *Phi Delta Kappan, 69,* 214–24.

Steers, R. M. (1975). Problems in the Measurement of Organizational Effectiveness. *Administrative Science Quarterly, 20,* 546–58.

Steers, R. M. (1977). *Organizational Effectiveness: A Behavioral View.* Santa Monica, CA: Goodyear.

Steers, R. M., and Porter, L. W. (Eds.). (1983). *Motivation and Work Behavior* (3rd ed.). New York: McGraw-Hill.

Steers, R. M., and Porter, L. W. (Eds.) (1991). *Motivation and Work Behavior* (5th ed.). New York: McGraw-Hill.

Steinfield, C. W., and Fulk, J. (1986). Task Demands and Managers' Use of Communication Media: An Information Processing View. Meeting of the Academy of Management, Chicago.

Stevenson, H., and Stigler, J. W. (1992). *The Learning Gap.* New York: Summit Books.

Stinchcombe, A. L. (1959). Bureaucratic and Craft Administration of Production. *Administrative Science Quarterly, 4,* 168–87.

Stipek, D. J. (1993). *Motivation to Learn* (2nd ed.). Boston: Allyn and Bacon.

Stogdill, R. M. (1948). Personal Factors Associated with Leadership: A Survey of the Literature. *Journal of Psychology, 25,* 35–71.

Stogdill, R. M. (1981). Traits of Leadership: A Follow-Up to 1970. In B. M. Bass (Ed.), *Stogdill's Handbook of Leadership* (pp. 73–97). New York: Free Press.

Stohl, C. (1995). *Organizational Communication.* Thousand Oaks, CA: Sage.

Strang, D. (1987). The Administrative Transformation of American Education: School

District Consolidation. *Administrative Science Quarterly, 32,* 352–66.
Strauss, G. (1964). Workflow Frictions, Interfunctional Rivalry, and Professionalism. *Human Organization, 23,* 137–49.
Strube, M. J., and Garcia, J. E. (1981). A Meta-Analytic Investigation of Fiedler's Contingency Model of Leadership Effectiveness. *Psychological Bulletin, 90,* 307–21.
Sutcliffe, K. M. (1994). What Executives Notice: Accurate Perceptions in Top Management Teams. *Academy of Management Journal, 37*(5), 1360–78.
Sutton, R. I., and Staw, B. M. (1995). What Theory Is Not. *Administrative Science Quarterly, 40,* 371–84.
Swanson, H. L. (1990). The Influence of Metacognitive Knowledge and Aptitude on Problem Solving. *Journal of Educational Psychology, 82,* 306–14.
Sweetland, S. R., and Hoy, W. K. (2000a). School characteristics and educational outcomes: Toward an organizational model of student achievement. Unpublished research paper, The Ohio State University, College of Education.
Sweetland, S. R., and Hoy, W. K. (2000b). Varnishing the truth in schools: Principals and teachers spinning reality. Unpublished research paper, The Ohio State University, College of Education.
Tagiuri, R. (1968). The Concept of Organizational Climate. In R. Tagiuri and G. H. Litwin (Eds.), *Organizational Climate* (pp. 11–32). Boston: Harvard Graduate School of Business Administration.
Tannen, D. (1990). *You Just Don't Understand: Women and Men in Conversation.* New York: Ballantine.
Tarter, C. J., and Hoy, W. K. (1988). The Context of Trust: Teachers and the Principal. *High School Journal, 72,* 17–24.
Tarter, C. J., and Hoy, W. K. (1998). Toward a Contingency Theory of Decision Making. *Journal of Educational Administration, 36,* 212–28.
Tarter, C. J., Hoy, W. K., and Bliss, J. R. (1989). Principal Leadership and Organizational Commitment: The Principal Must Deliver. *Planning and Changing, 20,* 139–40.
Tarter, C. J., Hoy, W. K., and Kottkamp, R. (1990). School Health and Organizational Commitment. *Journal of Research and Development in Education, 23,* 236–43.
Taylor, F. W. (1947). *Scientific Management.* New York: Harper.
Teddlie, C., and Reynolds, D. (Eds.). (2000). *The International Handbook on School Effectiveness Research.* New York: Falmer.
Terreberry, S. (1968). The Evolution of Organizational Environments. *Administrative Science Quarterly, 12,* 590–613.
Thomas, A. R., and Slater, R. C. (1972). The OCDQ: A Four Factor Solution for Australian Schools? *Journal of Educational Administration, 12,* 197–208.
Thomas, H. (1984). Mapping Strategic Management Research. *Journal of General Management, 9,* 55–72.
Thomas, K. (1976). Conflict and Conflict Management. In M. D. Dunnette (Ed.), *Handbook of Industrial and Organizational Psychology* (pp. 889–936). Chicago: Rand McNally.
Thomas, K. (1977). Toward Multi-Dimensional Values in Teaching: The Example of Conflict Behaviors. *Academy of Management Review, 20,* 486–90.
Thompson, D. P., McNamara, J. F., and Hoyle, J. R. (1997). Job Satisfaction in Educational Organizations: A Synthesis of Research Findings. *Educational Administration Quarterly, 33*(1), 7–37.
Thompson, J. D. (1967). *Organizations in Action.* New York: McGraw-Hill.
Tichy, N. M., and Devanna, M. A. (1986). *The Transformational Leader.* New York: Wiley.
Tiegs, R. B., Tetrick, L. E., and Fried, Y. (1992). Growth Need Strength and Context Satisfactions as Moderators of the Relations of the Job Characteristics Model. *Journal of Management, 18*(3), 575–93.
Tobias, S., and Duchastel, P. (1974). Behavioral Objectives, Sequence, and Anxiety in CAI. *Instructional Science, 3,* 232–42.
Trentham, L., Silvern, S., and Brogdon, R. (1985). Teacher Efficacy and Teacher Competency Ratings. *Psychology in Schools, 22,* 343–52.
Trevino, L. K., Lengel, R. H., and Daft, R. L. (1987). Media Symbolism, Media Richness, and Media Choice in Organizations: A Symbolic Interactionist Perspective. *Communication Research, 14,* 553–74.
Trice, H. M., and Beyer, J. M. (1993). *The Culture of Work Organizations.* Englewood Cliffs, NJ: Prentice Hall.
Trusty, F. M., and Sergiovanni, T. J. (1966). Perceived Need Deficiencies of Teachers and Administrators: A Proposal for Restructuring Teacher Roles. *Educational Administration Quarterly, 2,* 168–80.

Tschannen-Moran, M., Woolfolk Hoy, A., and Hoy, W. K. (1998). Teacher Efficacy: Its Meaning and Measure. *Review of Educational Research, 68,* 202–48.

Tsui, A. S. (1990). A Multiple-Constituency Model of Effectiveness: An Empirical Examination at the Human Resource Subunit Level. *Administrative Science Quarterly, 35,* 458–83.

Tubbs, M. E., Boehne, D., and Dahl, J. G. (1993). Expectancy, Balance, and Motivational Force Functions in Goal-Setting Research: An Empirical Test. *Journal of Applied Psychology, 78,* 361–73.

Turban, D. B., and Keon, T. L. (1993). Organizational Attractiveness. An Interactionist Perspective. *Journal of Applied Psychology, 78*(2), 184–93.

Tversky, A. (1969). Intransitivity of Preferences. *Psychological Review, 76,* 31–84.

Tversky, A., and Kahneman, D. (1973). Availability: Heuristic for Judging Frequency and Probability. *Cognitive Psychology, 5,* 207–32.

Tversky, A., and Kahneman, D. (1974). Judgment under Uncertainty: Heuristics and Biases. *Science, 185,* 1124–31.

Tversky, A., and Kahneman, D. (1981). The Framing of Decisions and the Psychology of Choice. *Science, 21,* 453–58.

Tyler, T. R. (1994). Psychological Models of the Justice Motive: Antecedents of Distributive and Procedural Justice. *Journal of Personality and Social Psychology, 67,* 850–63.

Udy, S. H. (1959). "Bureaucracy" and "Rationality" in Weber's Organization Theory. *American Sociological Review, 24,* 791–95.

Uline, C. L., Miller, D. M., and Tschannen-Moran, M. (1998). School Effectiveness: The Underlying Dimensions. *Educational Administration Quarterly, 34*(4), 462–83.

U. S. Department of Health, Education and Welfare (1973). *Work in America, Report of a Special Task Force.* Cambridge: MIT Press.

Urwick, L. F. (1937). Organization as a Technical Problem. In L. Gulick and L. F. Urwick (Eds.), *Papers on the Science of Administration* (pp. 47–88). New York: Institute of Public Administration, Columbia University.

Vance, V. S., and Schlechty, P. C. (1981). Do Academically Able Teachers Leave Education: The North Carolina Case. *Phi Delta Kappan, 63,* 106–12.

Vance, V. S., and Schlechty, P. C. (1982). The Distribution of Academic Ability in the Teaching Force: Policy Implications. *Phi Delta Kappan, 64,* 22–27.

Van de Ven, A. H., and Ferry, D. L. (1980). *Measuring and Assessing Organization.* New York: Wiley.

Van Erede, W. and Thierry, H. (1996). Vroom's Expectancy Models and Work Related Criteria: A Meta-Analysis. *Journal of Applied Psychology,* 81, 575–86.

Van Meter, P., Yokoi, L., and Pressley, M. (1994). College Students' Theory of Note-Taking Derived from Their Perceptions of Note-Taking. *Journal of Educational Psychology, 86,* 323–38.

Vecchio, R. P. (1977). An Empirical Examination of the Validity of Fiedler's Model of Leadership Effectiveness. *Organizational Behavior and Human Performance, 19,* 180–206.

Vecchio, R. P. (1988). *Organizational Behavior.* Chicago: Dryden Press.

Vecchio, R. P. (1993). The Impact of Differences in Subordinate and Supervisor Age on Attitudes and Performance. *Psychology and Aging, 8*(1), 112–19.

Verdugo, R. R., Greenberg, N. M., Henderson, R. D., Uribe, O. Jr., and Schneider, J. M. (1997). School Governance Regimes and Teachers' Job Satisfaction: Bureaucracy, Legitimacy, and Community. *Educational Administration Quarterly, 33*(1), 38–66.

Vroom, V. H. (1960). *Some Personality Determinants of the Effects of Participation.* Englewood Cliffs, NJ: Prentice Hall.

Vroom, V. H. (1964). *Work and Motivation.* New York: Wiley.

Vroom, V. H. (1976). Leadership. In M. D. Dunnette (Ed.), *Handbook of Industrial and Organizational Psychology* (pp. 1527–51). Chicago: Rand McNally.

Vroom, V. H., and Jago, A. G. (1988). On the Validity of the Vroom-Yetton Model. *Journal of Applied Psychology, 63,* 151–62.

Vroom, V. H., and Yetton, P. W. (1973). *Leadership and Decision Making.* Pittsburgh: University of Pittsburgh Press.

Waller, W. (1932). *The Sociology of Teaching.* New York: Wiley.

Watkins, K. E., and Marsick, V. J. (1993). *Sculpting the Learning Organization.* San Francisco, Jossey- Bass.

Webb, N., and Palincsar, A. (1996). Group Processes in the Classroom. In D. C. Berliner and R. C. Calfee (Eds.), *Handbook of Educational Psychology* (pp. 841–76). New York: Macmillan.

Weber, M. (1947). *The Theory of Social and Economic Organizations.* In T. Parsons (Ed.), A. M. Henderson and T. Parsons (Trans.). New York: Free Press.
Weick, K. E. (1976). Educational Organizations as Loosely Coupled Systems. *Administrative Science Quarterly, 21,* 1–19.
Weick, K. (1995). What Theory Is Not, Theorizing Is. *Administrative Science Quarterly, 40,* 385–90.
Weick, K. (1999). Theory Construction as Disciplined Reflexivity: Tradeoffs in the 90s. *The Academy of Management Review, 24,* 797–808.
Weick, K., and Westley, F. (1996). Organizational Learning: Affirming the Oxymoron. In S. Clegg, C. Hardy, and W. Nord (Eds.), *Handbook of Organization Studies* (pp. 440–58). Thousand Oaks, CA: Sage.
Weiner, B. (1972). *Theories of Motivation: From Mechanism to Cognition.* Chicago: Academic Press.
Weiner, B. (1985). An Attributional Theory of Achievement Motivation and Emotion. *Psychological Review, 92,* 548–73.
Weiner, B. (1986). *An Attributional Theory of Motivation and Emotion.* New York: Springer-Verlag.
Weiner, B. (1990). History of Motivational Research in Education. *Journal of Educational Psychology, 82,* 616–22.
Weiner, B. (1992). *Human Motivation: Metaphors, Theories, and Research.* Newbury Park, CA: Sage.
Weiner, B. (1994a). Ability versus Effort Revisited: The Moral Determinants of Achievement Evaluation an Achievement as a Moral System. *Educational Psychologist, 29,* 163–72.
Weiner, B. (1994b). Integrating Social and Persons Theories of Achievement Striving. *Review of Educational Research, 64,* 557–75.
Weinert, F. E., and Helmke, A. (1995). Learning from Wise Mother Nature or Big Brother Instructor: The Wrong Choice as Seen from an Educational Perspective. *Educational Psychologist, 30,* 135–43.
Wendel, F. C., Kelley, E. A., Kluender, M., and Palmere, M. (1983). *Use of Assessment Center Processes: A Literature Review.* Lincoln, NB: Teachers College, University of Nebraska.
Westphal, J. D., Gulati, R., and Shortell, S. M. (1997). Customization or Conformity? An Institutional Network Perspective on the Content and Consequence of TQM Adoption. *Administrative Science Quarterly,* 42(2), 366–94.
Whitehead, A. N. (1925). *Science and the Modern World.* New York: Macmillan.
Wietz, S. (1974). *Non-Verbal Communication.* New York: Oxford.
Wilensky, H. (1964). Professionalization of Everyone? *American Journal of Sociology, 70,* 137–58.
Wilkins,A., and Patterson, K. (1985). You Can't Get There From Here: What Will Make Culture-Change Projects Fail. In R. H. Kilmann, M. J. Saxton, and R. Serpa (Eds.), *Gaining Control of the Corporate Culture* (pp. 262–91). San Francisco: Jossey-Bass.
Wilkins, B. M., and Andersen, P. A. (1991). Gender Differences and Similarities in Management Communication: A Meta-Analysis. *Management Communication Quarterly,* 5(1), 6–35.
Williams, L. B., and Hoy, W. K. (1973). Principal-Staff Relations: Situational Mediator of Effectiveness. *Journal of Educational Administration, 9,* 66–73.
Willis, Q. (1980). The Work Activity of School Principals: An Observational Study. *Journal of Educational Administration, 18,* 27–54.
Willower, D. J. (1963). The Form of Knowledge and the Theory-Practice Relationship. *Educational Theory, 13,* 47–52.
Willower, D. J. (1975). Theory in Educational Administration. *Journal of Educational Administration, 13,* 77–91.
Willower, D. J. (1979). Some Issues in Research on School Organization. In G. L. Immegart and W. Boyd (Eds.), *Currents in Administrative Research: Problem Finding in Education* (pp. 63–86). Lexington, MA: Heath.
Willower, D. J. (1987). Inquiry into Educational Administration: The Last Twenty-Five Years and the Next. *Journal of Educational Administration, 24,* 12–29.
Willower, D. J. (1991). Values, Valuation and Explanation in School Organizations. *Journal of School Leadership,* 4, 446–83.
Willower, D. J. (1993). Explaining and Improving Educational Administration. *Educational Management and Administration, 21,* 153–60.
Willower, D. J. (1994). Values, Valuation, and Explanation in School Organizations. *Journal of School Leadership,* 4(5), 466–83.
Willower, D. J. (1996). Inquiry in Educational Administration and the Spirit of the Times. *Educational Administration Quarterly, 32,* 341–65.

Willower, D. J. (1998). Fighting the Fog: A Criticism of Postmodernism. *Journal of School Leadership, 8,* 448–63.

Willower, D. J., Eidell, T. L., and Hoy, W. K. (1967). *The School and Pupil Control Ideology.* Monograph No. 24. University Park: Pennsylvania State University.

Willower, D. J., and Forsyth, P. B. (1999). A Brief History of Scholarship on Educational Administration. In J. Murphy and K. S. Louis (Eds.), *Handbook of Research on Educational Administration* (2nd ed.). San Francisco: Jossey-Bass.

Willower, D. J., and Jones, R. G. (1967). Control in an Educational Organization. In J. D. Raths, J. R. Pancella, and J. S. V. Ness (Eds.), *Studying Teaching* (pp. 424–28). Englewood Cliffs, NJ: Prentice Hall.

Willower, D. J. and Licata, J. W. (1997). *Values and Valuation in the Practice of Educational Administration.* Thousand Oaks, CA: Corwin Press.

Wilson, T. D., Houston, C. E., Etling, K. M., and Brekke, N. (1996). A New Look at Anchoring Effects: Basic Anchoring and Its Antecedents. *Journal of Experimental Psychology: General, 125* (4), 382–407.

Wimpelberg, R. K., Teddlie, C., and Stringfield, S. (1989). Sensitivity to Context: The Past and Future of Effective Schools Research. *Educational Administration Quarterly, 25,* 82–107.

Wise, A. (1988). The Two Conflicting Trends in School Reform: Legislated Learning Revisited. *Phi Delta Kappan, 69,* 328–32.

Wiseman, C. (1979a). Selection of Major Planning Issues. *Policy Sciences, 12,* 71–86.

Wiseman, C. (1979b). Strategic Planning in the Scottish Health Service—A Mixed Scanning Approach. *Long Range Planning, 12,* 103–13.

Wittrock, M. C. (1992). An Empowering Conception of Educational Psychology. *Educational Psychologist, 27,* 129–42.

Wolin, S. S. (1960). *Politics and Vision: Continuity and Innovation in Western Political Thought.* Boston: Little, Brown.

Wood, D. J., and Gray, B. (1991). Toward a Comprehensive Theory of Collaboration. *Journal of Applied Behavioral Science, 27*(2), 139–62.

Wood, R., and Bandura, A. (1989). Social Cognitive Theory of Organizational Management. *Academy of Management Review, 14,* 361–84.

Wood, S. E., and Wood, E. G. (1999). *The World of Psychology.* Boston: Allyn and Bacon.

Woolfolk, A. E. (1998). *Educational Psychology.* Boston: Allyn and Bacon.

Woolfolk, A. E. (2000). *Educational Psychology* (8th ed.). Boston: Allyn and Bacon.

Woolfolk, A. E., and Hoy, W. K. (1990). Prospective Teachers' Sense of Efficacy and Beliefs about Control. *Journal of Educational Psychology, 82,* 81–91.

Woolfolk, A. E., Rosoff, B., and Hoy, W. K. (1990). Teachers' Sense of Efficacy and Their Beliefs about Managing Students. *Teaching and Teacher Education, 6* (2), 137–48.

Worthy, J. C. (1950). Factors Influencing Employee Morale. *Harvard Business Review, 28,* 61–73.

Wright, P. M., O'Leary-Kelly, A. M., Cortinak, J. M., Klein, H. J., and Hollenbeck, J. R. (1994). On the Meaning and Measurement of Goal Commitment. *Journal of Applied Psychology, 79,* 795–803.

Wright, R. (1985). Motivating Teacher Involvement in Professional Growth Activities. *Canadian Administrator, 24,* 1–6.

Yamagishi, T., Gillmore, M. R., and Cook, K. S. (1988). Network Connections and the Distribution of Power in Exchange Networks. *American Journal of Sociology, 93,* 833–51.

Yekovich, F. R. (1993). A Theoretical View of the Development of Expertise in Credit Administration. In P. Hallinger, K. Leithwood, and J. Murphy (Eds.), *Cognitive Perspectives on Educational Leadership* (pp. 146–66). New York: Teachers College.

Yuchtman, E., and Seashore, S. E. (1967). A System Resource Approach to Organizational Effectiveness. *American Sociological Review, 32,* 891–903.

Yukl, G. A. (1971). Toward a Behavioral Theory of Leadership. *Organizational Behavior and Human Performance, 6,* 414–40.

Yukl, G. A. (1981). *Leadership in Organizations.* Englewood Cliffs, NJ: Prentice Hall.

Yukl, G. A. (1989). *Leadership in Organizations* (2nd ed.). Englewood Cliffs, NJ: Prentice Hall.

Yukl, G. A. (1994). *Leadership in Organizations* (3rd ed.). Englewood Cliffs, NJ: Prentice Hall.

Yukl, G. A. (1998). *Leadership in Organizations* (4th ed.). Upper Saddle River, NJ: Prentice Hall.

Yukl, G. A. (1999). An Evaluation of Conceptual Weaknesses in Transformational and

Charismatic Leadership Theories. *Leadership Quarterly, 10*(2), 285–305.
Zahn, C. L. (1991). Face-to-Face Communication in an Office Setting. *Communication Research, 18*(6), 737–54.
Zald, M. M., and Berger, M. A. (1978). Social Movements in Organizations: Coup d'Etat, Insurgency, and Mass Movements. *American Journal of Sociology, 42,* 823–61.
Zammuto, R. F. (1982). *Assessing Organizational Effectiveness.* Albany: State University of New York Press.
Zbaracki, M. J. (1998). The Rhetoric and Reality of Total Quality Management. *Administrative Science Quarterly, 43*(3), 602–36.
Zenger, T. R., and Lawrence, B. S. (1989). Organizational Demography: The Differential Effects of Age and Tenure Distributions on Technical Communication. *Academy of Management Journal, 32,* 353–76.
Zey, M. (1992). *Decision Making: Alternatives to Rational Choice.* Newbury Park, CA: Sage.
Zielinski, A. E., and Hoy, W. K. (1983). Isolation and Alienation in Elementary Schools. *Educational Administration Quarterly, 19,* 27–45.
Zucker, L. (1987). Institutional Theories of Organization. *Annual Review of Sociology, 13,* 443–64.

Name Index

Subject Index

Page numbers with *f* or *t* indicate figures or illustrations.